HANDBOOK ON PUBLIC POLICY AND ARTIFICIAL INTELLIGENCE

HANDBOOKS OF RESEARCH ON PUBLIC POLICY

Series Editor: Frank Fischer, *Rutgers University, New Jersey, USA*

The objective of this series is to publish *Handbooks* that offer comprehensive overviews of the very latest research within the key areas in the field of public policy. Under the guidance of the Series Editor, Frank Fischer, the aim is to produce prestigious high-quality works of lasting significance. Each *Handbook* will consist of original, peer-reviewed contributions by leading authorities, selected by an editor who is a recognized leader in the field. The emphasis is on the most important concepts and research as well as expanding debate and indicating the likely research agenda for the future. The *Handbooks* will aim to give a comprehensive overview of the debates and research positions in each key area of focus.

For a full list of Edward Elgar published titles, including the titles in this series, visit our website at www.e-elgar.com.

Handbook on Public Policy and Artificial Intelligence

Edited by

Regine Paul

Professor in Political Science, Department of Government, University of Bergen, Norway

Emma Carmel

Professor of Governance and Public Policy, Department of Social and Policy Sciences, University of Bath, UK

Jennifer Cobbe

Assistant Professor in Law and Technology, Faculty of Law, University of Cambridge, UK

HANDBOOKS OF RESEARCH ON PUBLIC POLICY

Edward Elgar
PUBLISHING

Cheltenham, UK • Northampton, MA, USA

Cover image: "People and Ivory Tower AI" by Jamillah Knowles & We and AI/Better Images of AI/CC-BY 4.0.

Published by
Edward Elgar Publishing Limited
The Lypiatts
15 Lansdown Road
Cheltenham
Glos GL50 2JA
UK

Edward Elgar Publishing, Inc.
William Pratt House
9 Dewey Court
Northampton
Massachusetts 01060
USA

A catalogue record for this book
is available from the British Library

Library of Congress Control Number: 2024934169

This book is available electronically in the **Elgar**online
Political Science and Public Policy subject collection
http://dx.doi.org/10.4337/9781803922171

ISBN 978 1 80392 216 4 (cased)
ISBN 978 1 80392 217 1 (eBook)

Printed and bound by CPI Group (UK) Ltd, Croydon, CR0 4YY

Contents

Contributors

Frans af Malmborg is a PhD candidate in the Department of Political Science and Management, University of Agder, Norway. His PhD project centres on the development of AI policy within the European Union and the Nordic countries.

Ilia Antenucci is a Research Associate at the Center for Digital Cultures (CDC), Leuphana University of Lüneburg, Germany, and part of the "Automating the Logistical City" research project. Her work focuses on the impact of digital technologies on urban environments and politics.

Ville Aula is a PhD Researcher in Data, Networks, and Society at the London School of Economics and Politics Science, UK. His research interests include public policy, data and expertise in policymaking, and science and technology studies.

Subhajit Basu is a Professor of Law and Technology in the School of Law at the University of Leeds, UK. He actively contributes to critical policy dialogues encompassing AI, Big Data, health data, autonomous systems (such as autonomous and connected vehicles), robotics, and associated concerns such as privacy, accountability and liability. He is the Editor-in-Chief of *International Review of Law Computers and Technology*.

David M. Berry is Professor of Digital Humanities at the University of Sussex, UK. David writes widely on philosophy and technology, particularly in terms of computation, software and algorithms. His most recent book is *Digital Humanities: Knowledge and Critique in a Digital Age*. His more recent work has looked at explainability, human understanding and the history of the university.

Ingvild Bode is Professor in the Center for War Studies at the University of Southern Denmark. Her research focuses on understanding processes of normative change, especially through studying practices in relation to the use of force, military AI, and associated governance demands. She is the Principal Investigator of the European Research Council-funded "AutoNorms" project.

Sally Brooks is an Honorary Fellow in the School for Business and Society and member of the Interdisciplinary Global Development Centre at the University of York, UK. Her research focuses on the political economy of global development, technology and agrarian change, and the role of philanthropic foundations.

Peter André Busch is an Associate Professor at the University of Agder, Norway. His main research interests are street-level bureaucracy and digital government, dark sides of technology, and implications of artificial intelligence.

Vanja Carlsson is a Senior Lecturer in Public Administration at the University of Gothenburg, Sweden. Her research interests concern public policy in general and the introduction of AI and digitalization in the public sector, gender equality policy and research policy in particular.

Emma Carmel is Professor of Governance and Public Policy at the University of Bath, UK. She is an interdisciplinary scholar with a background in political sociology, whose work investigates how we organize, sustain and contest social and political order in different contexts. Her current work examines the role of AI technologies in shaping automation, autonomy and the idea of public decision-making.

Jennifer Cobbe is an Assistant Professor in Law and Technology in the Faculty of Law at the University of Cambridge, UK. She is generally interested in critical, interdisciplinary work on questions of power, political economy, and the law around internet platforms and informational capitalism, technological supply chains and infrastructures, and AI and automated decision-making.

Cary Coglianese is the Edward B. Shils Professor of Law and Professor of Political Science at the University of Pennsylvania, USA, and founding director of the Penn Program on Regulation. He specializes in the study of administrative law and regulatory processes and has served as a consultant to the Administrative Conference of the United States on agency use of artificial intelligence.

Robert Donoghue is Lecturer of Management at the University of Essex Business School, UK.

Ekkehard Ernst is Chief Macroeconomist at the International Labour Organization in Geneva, Switzerland.

Tero Erkkilä is a Professor of Political Science at the University of Helsinki, Finland. His research interests include global governance and policy, public institutions, and collective identities.

Rory Gillis is a Research Assistant on the Trustworthiness Auditing for AI project and the Governance of Emerging Technologies research programme at the Oxford Internet Institute, UK.

Catriona Gray is a PhD candidate at the University of Bath, UK. Her research applies sociological thinking to questions of AI regulatory policy.

Juan David Gutiérrez is an Associate Professor in the School of Government of Universidad de los Andes, Colombia. He teaches and investigates on public policy, public management, and artificial intelligence. He is a member of the Group of Experts of the Global Partnership on Artificial Intelligence (GPAI) where he co-leads projects of the Responsible AI working group.

Kate Hamblin is Professor in the Centre for International Research on Care, Labour and Equalities at the University of Sheffield, UK. She leads the ESRC Centre for Care's Digital Care research theme and is a member of the ESRC and Health Foundation-funded Improving Adult Care Together (IMPACT) Implementation Centre's Leadership Team.

Roy L. Heidelberg is Associate Professor and Chair of the Department of Public Administration at Louisiana State University, USA. He teaches political and administrative theory and writes about bureaucracy, accountability and public participation.

Helle Zinner Henriksen is Professor at Copenhagen Business School, Denmark. Her research focuses on IT in the public sector, with particular focus on digitalization which is enforced by law.

Sun-ha Hong examines forms of uncertainty, doubt and belief around surveillance, smart machines and AI. He is Assistant Professor in Communication at Simon Fraser University, Canada, and was previously Mellon Postdoctoral Fellow in the Humanities at MIT. Sun-ha is the author of *Technologies of Speculation: The Limits of Knowledge in a Data-Driven Society* (2020), and is working on his next book, *Predictions without Futures*.

Luo Huanxin is a PhD candidate in the Social Law Center and Law and Technology Institute at Renmin University of China.

Mareile Kaufmann is a Professor in the Department of Criminology and Sociology of Law at the University of Oslo, Norway. Her works focus on surveillance and data practices. Mareile wrote the book *Making Information Matter* and co-edited *The Handbook of Digital Criminology*. She serves on several editorial boards and has consulted the Norwegian Data Protection Commission as well as the Norwegian Biotechnology Advisory Board.

Jenny Krutzinna is Senior Researcher in the Department of Media and Communication at the University of Oslo, Norway. Her research focuses on injustices caused by systemic inequalities and power imbalances that affect people's well-being in an increasingly digitized world, with a special focus on giving voice to marginalized groups.

Johann Laux is a British Academy Postdoctoral Fellow at the Oxford Internet Institute, UK. He studies the legal, social and governmental implications of emerging technologies such as AI and Big Data.

Matthias Leese is Assistant Professor for Technology and Governance in the Department of Humanities, Social and Political Sciences at ETH Zurich, Switzerland. His research is interested in the effects of digital technologies on social order, with specific attention to security organizations and their rationales and practices.

Federica Lucivero is a Senior Researcher in Ethics and Data in the Ethox Center at the Big Data Institute of the University of Oxford, UK. She researches the ethical and social aspects of the increasing introduction of digital and data-driven technologies in care pathways, individual health practices, and biomedical research. She co-directs SHADE, a research hub at the intersection of Sustainability, Health, AI, Digital technologies and the Environment.

David Mark is a doctoral scholar at Queen's University Belfast (QUB), UK, enrolled in the Leverhulme Interdisciplinary Network on Algorithmic Solutions (LINAS) programme where he operates at the intersection of law and computer science to explore the intricacies of safety, security and legal compliance in AI decision-making systems. Prior to delving into academia, David was called to the Bar of Northern Ireland and practised as a Barrister at the Bar Library in Belfast.

Tomás McInerney is a postdoctoral researcher in University College London, UK. He was previously a researcher within the Leverhulme Interdisciplinary Network on Cybersecurity and Society based in the School of Law at Queen's University Belfast, where he worked on the PhD project: "When should a computer decide? Judicial decision-making in the age of automation, algorithms and generative artificial intelligence".

Fran Meissner is Assistant Professor of Critical Geodata Studies and Geodata Ethics at the University of Twente, the Netherlands. Her work explores how the global economy of geodata manifests itself in cities and how we might be able to better theorize social phenomena in times of information infrastructures that entail an intimate and ordinary linking of the orbital with the urban.

Brent Mittelstadt is Associate Professor and Director of Research at the Oxford Internet Institute, University of Oxford, UK. He leads the Governance of Emerging Technologies research programme which works across ethics, law and emerging information technologies.

Petra Molnar is a Faculty Associate at Harvard's Berkman Klein Center for Internet and Society, USA and the Associate Director of the Refugee Law Lab, York University, Canada. Her research combines legal analysis with ethnography to highlight the impacts of border surveillance on people-on-the-move. Her first book, the *Walls Have Eyes: Surviving Migration in the Age of Artificial Intelligence* (The New Press) is coming out in early 2024.

Phoebe Moore is Professor of Management and the Futures of Work at the University of Essex Business School, UK and Senior Fellow at the International Labour Organization in Geneva, Switzerland. She writes about digitalization and workers' struggle against surveillance and control. She is prominently involved in policy discourses within the European Union and the United Nations on worker monitoring, algorithmic management, artificial intelligence and affective computing.

John Morison is Professor of Jurisprudence in the School of Law at Queen's University Belfast, UK. He writes in the area of constitutional law and theory as well as new technology, with a particular interest in automated decision-making in the legal system. He is the Coordinator of the Leverhulme Interdisciplinary Network on Algorithmic Solutions (LINAS) exploring the implications of massive-scale data processing, artificial intelligence (AI) and machine learning (ML) including for public decision-making.

Daniel Mügge is Professor of Political Arithmetic at the University of Amsterdam, the Netherlands. There he leads the RegulAite project, which investigates EU AI regulation in the global economic and geopolitical context.

Andreas Öjehag-Pettersson is an Associate Professor in Political Science at Karlstad University, Sweden, with an interest in political theory, methods and philosophy of science. Andreas's research has published widely on questions of power, governing and how rule is accomplished in societies marked by neoliberal rationalities and technologies.

Adekemi Omotubora is a Senior Lecturer in the Department of Commercial and Industrial Law at the University of Lagos, Nigeria. Her research focuses on the intersections of law and technology and the regulation, decolonial and gender aspects of AI. She has been (co-)leading several research projects investigating the regulation and rights implications of AI across use cases in Africa.

Michaela Padden is a PhD candidate in political science at Karlstad University, Sweden. Her research concerns data protection regulation and its relationship to surveillance technologies tied to platform capitalism, and their impact on democratic political systems. She has previously worked as a Principal Policy Analyst in the New South Wales Government in Sydney, Australia.

Regine Paul is Professor in Political Science in the Department of Government at the University of Bergen, Norway. Her research focuses on migration governance, the role of analytical tools in public decision-making, and the politics of risk regulation from a critical political economy and critical policy analysis lens. Regine is also an editor of *Critical Policy Studies*.

Mirjam Pot is a PhD candidate in political science at the University of Vienna, Austria and a researcher at the European Centre for Social Welfare Policy and Research. Her work focuses on policies and practices in primary care, public health and informal care.

Barbara Prainsack is Professor of Comparative Policy Analysis at the University of Vienna, Austria and Director of the Centre for the Studies of Contemporary Solidarity (CeSCoS) and the interdisciplinary research platform "Governance of Digital Practice". Barbara is also the Chair of the European Group on Ethics in Science and New Technologies (EGE), which advises the European Commission.

Guangyu Qiao-Franco is Assistant Professor of International Relations at Radboud University, the Netherlands and Senior Researcher of the ERC-funded AutoNorms Project at the University of Southern Denmark. Her research interests span AI ethics, military AI related arms control, ASEAN regional governance and Chinese foreign policy.

Joanna Redden is an Associate Professor in the Faculty of Information and Media Studies at Western University, Canada. She researches the social justice implications of government uses of data systems, as well as data harms and ways to redress and prevent them. Her most recent book is the co-authored *Data Justice* (Sage, 2022).

Malin Rönnblom is a Professor in Political Science at Karlstad University, Sweden. She has long-standing research experience in critical policy analysis and a strong interest in feminist and political theory. Her more recent research focuses on the marketization and restructuring of the public sector, with an emphasis on the effects on democracy.

Jatinder Singh is based in the Department of Computer Science and Technology (Computer Laboratory), University of Cambridge, UK, where he leads the multidisciplinary Compliant and Accountable Systems research group that works at the intersection of computer science and law. He is also Fellow of the Alan Turing Institute.

Lyndal Sleep is a Senior Lecturer in the Queensland Centre for Domestic and Family Violence Research (QCDFVR) at Central Queensland University, Australia. Lyndal researches intersectional experiences of automated social services delivery among service users with a special focus on those exposed to domestic and gendered violence.

Jarle Trondal is Professor in Political Science in the Department of Political Science and Management at the University of Agder, Norway, a Professor at the ARENA Centre for European Studies at the University of Oslo, Norway and a Senior Fellow in the Institute of European Studies at the University of California, Berkeley, USA.

Lena Ulbricht is research group leader at the Weizenbaum Institute for the Networked Society and at the WZB Berlin Social Science Center, Germany. Her research focuses on platform governance and public sector AI. She co-hosts the intersectional feminist podcast Purple Code and is editor of the *Weizenbaum Journal of the Digital Society*.

Grace Whitfield is a Research Associate working in the Centre for Care at the University of Sheffield, UK, with an interest in digital technologies working conditions, and unionization.

James Wright is Visiting Lecturer in the Digital Environment Research Institute at Queen Mary University of London, UK.

Preface

When we embarked on the process of recruiting themes and authors for a *Handbook on Public Policy and Artificial Intelligence* (AI), back in autumn 2021, the topic was certainly up-and-coming but also still rather "niche". Of course, social science scholarship and some key lines of argument on platform capitalism, AI and democratic societies, AI and the future of work, and normative principles for AI governance were becoming established in 2021 – with the works of scholars such as Ruha Benjamin, Mark Coeckelbergh, Kate Crawford, Virginia Eubanks, Safia Noble, Frank Pasquale or Shoshana Zuboff out and widely discussed. And yet, scholars of public policy and public administration were much less visible in these emerging discussions about the societal and political implications of AI technology diffusion. Many of the early social sciences publications on AI were peculiarly apolitical and devoid of key concepts and lines of inquiry in our disciplines (as highlighted by the systematic review work conducted by Öjehag-Pettersson, Carlsson and Rönnblom, Chapter 2 in this volume).

What a treat to be able to tackle this void head-on through our *Handbook* project. Our first big thanks go to Frank Fischer, Series Editor and Honorary Editor of *Critical Policy Studies*, and to Alex Pettifer and Harry Fabian, our publishers at Edward Elgar Publishing, for trusting us with carving out and consolidating critically minded research at the intersection of public policy and AI. The crafting involved hard editorial work, of course, but was truly enjoyable and rewarding, and we might not have endeavored this project without your kind encouragement.

Our second round of thanks go to the contributors to the *Handbook*. Needless to say that without you the volume would not have been possible. But our gratitude extends to celebrate the enthusiastic answers we received from many of you when we reached out about this project first. Though "niche" to start with, there was a strong sense among many of those we contacted that a project like this was urgently needed to counter the techno-solutionist, apolitical, often positivist and rational choice orientations in much of the research on AI, policy, governance and regulation. The final identity of the *Handbook* took shape through such collegial commitment to a joint cause. Thank you!

We are also grateful for financial and institutional support to run a research event on "Putting Public Policy and AI into Critical Dialogue", 10–13 January 2022 at the University of Bath. This was kindly co-funded by the UKRI-funded ART-AI Doctoral Training Centre at the University of Bath and a Momentum Grant for future research leaders at the University of Bergen. Thanks to these funds, more than a dozen of the contributors to this volume were able to get together to discuss draft versions of chapters and to explore options for future collaboration through funding for networks and research consortia. We already founded a listserv (critpolai) to help integrate and consolidate a community of scholars. Starting from our collaboration for this *Handbook*, we are working on building a research network of critically minded scholars, regulators, civil society members and other practitioners to explore the policy-AI-complex in relation to questions of democracy, power relations and (global) inequalities beyond narrow technical and profit-making concerns.

We further acknowledge the valuable support in producing the final manuscript by several people. Katharina John Nordbø at Bergen's Department of Government performed a meticulous job formatting chapters, checking style sheets and reference lists, and spotting even the smallest inconsistency. We are grateful for the effective support we received during production of this manuscript from Nina Booth at Elgar.

Last but not least, we especially send words of acknowledgment and admiration to betterimagesofai.org, a collaborative research and arts project. Its mission – as stated on their webpage – is to counter "abstract, futuristic or science-fiction-inspired images of AI" which "set unrealistic expectations and misstate the capabilities of AI". Their "images of AI library" was a natural visual ally for a scholarly project seeking to expose how clichés and hyped narratives of AI in the policy world gloss over AI technology's failures in the public sector, power differentials and hard-wired economic interests, and the detrimental societal implications of tech uses in the public sector. The cover image is titled "People and Ivory Tower AI" and was designed by Jamillah Knowles & We and AI. To us, the neural network above people's heads, as it beams out of an anonymous ivory tower, nicely captures core concepts of power, hierarchical control and lack of democratic scrutiny. And as a few people resist and pull the net down, the designers seem to agree with us that critical investigation and political contestation of AI tech development, uses and narratives remain essential.

Regine Paul, Emma Carmel and Jennifer Cobbe
Bergen, Bath and Cambridge, October 2023

1. Introduction to the *Handbook on Public Policy and Artificial Intelligence*: vantage points for critical inquiry

Regine Paul, Emma Carmel and Jennifer Cobbe

INTRODUCTION

In 2015, the US Citizenship and Immigration Services (USCIS) launched a chatbot named Emma. As USCIS explains, Emma is "a computer-generated virtual assistant who can answer your questions and even take you to the right spot on our website" both in English and Spanish (US Citizenship and Immigration Services 2018). Emma is one example of how so-called artificial intelligence technologies (AITs) have entered the public sector (and, of course, beyond). The use of AIT in software and hardware is often much more mundane, and also less visible than Emma, which "simulates" a specific human cognitive capacity relatively holistically based on computer-processed code (here: natural language processing, search for and filtering of suitable answers to a customer query). Emma presents potential and actual immigrants to the US with a friendly tone and being here to help, using the familiar visual grammar of "speech bubbles" and service-oriented structured interaction. Emma feels "easy to use" because such chatbots are so commonplace; they have become an unremarkable feature of everyday digital life, whether paying a utility bill, ordering food, or buying clothes online.

But Emma is not a chatbot of everyday life; it does not facilitate a customer relationship or help someone buy a product. Emma is the bright and shiny fascia of a repressive, opaque and violent infrastructure of the US state – its border regime. As such, it is a key gatekeeper to access information about entering, or staying in, the US. The friendly chatbot projection also glosses over – at least implicitly – both the strong push by corporate actors for designing, testing and deploying AITs in the public sector, and the existence of highly contested AIT applications in immigration and border control in the US from aggressive robot guard dogs and underground fiber optic sensors at the highly policed border with Mexico (Fussell 2022) to the (unsolicited) scanning of social media accounts to enforce "data-driven deportation" of residents without a valid permit (Bedoya 2020).

So what is the policy, political, legal and administrative work actually done by Emma, and other AIT applications in public policy contexts, both visible and hidden? How is the relationship between these diverse technologies, public policy and the state, unfolding, and with what effects: to facilitate or obstruct public policy design and delivery; to improve, disrupt, advance, corrupt the role of the state, government and public sector; to change what states do and how they do it; to transform how states, corporations and citizens relate to each other, where power is located and how it is exercised? This *Handbook* sets out to address these issues across a wide array of geographical, socio-economic, technical, political and policy contexts. It thus contributes distinct public policy and governance expertise to a growing field of critical AI studies (e.g., Lindgren 2023), setting a democratically oriented counterpoint to the high pace and latent unpredictability of AI diffusion in the public sector, but also to the concentrated politico-economic interests, techno-solutionist framings and high-flying promises for a future-oriented public sector that underpin it.

Tensions and Controversies in AI and Public Policy in a Nutshell

Characteristic of wider arguments in favour of introducing AITs in the public sector, chatbot Emma was designed to manage the high volume of "customer" queries (reportedly over 14 million calls on immigration issues each year); reduce the workload for (expensive) human agents; and offer targeted help for people searching the webpage. This promise of AI-driven optimization and rationalization aligns well with wider hegemonic visions of what government, public sector and state are for, and how they should be organized.

In the last fifty years, Western-dominated global narratives about how to improve public policy have centred on a perceived need for cost-effectiveness, value for money and improved "customer" (citizen) experience. These originated in agendas for reform that were promoted by management consultancies and academic economists in the Global North (and imposed by international financial institutions such as the International Monetary Fund) under the global brand of "new public management". Reforms varied widely in practice in their extent, form and outcomes. Nonetheless, overall, they challenged conventional ideas of bureaucratic and rule-based efficiency through which states exercised collective rule, and promoted market-based thinking, in which public sector organizations should be managed through performance indicators and budgetary responsibility, while responding to citizens as customers (seminal overview in: Hood 1991).

These reform agendas went hand in hand with the development of digital technologies, from e-Government to mobile technologies, closely aligned with the presumption that the citizen is a consumer: at first, offering information, and eventually, for those with digital resources, enabling citizens to access information, complete forms or apply for licences, anytime, anywhere. At the same time, facilitating the push for "value for money", monitoring procurement contracts and meeting performance indicators, digital technologies facilitated the collection and analysis of budget data points, operational efficiencies and outputs. Privileging the contribution of digital technologies to "better" policymaking led to techniques of "agile policymaking", which originated in digital product development, being adopted as innovative policymaking methods. Also promoted by management consultancies and international organizations such as the OECD, these sit uncomfortably alongside ever more detailed monitoring of performance and activities of operational and "front-line" staff.

In this context, digital technologies have been offered as the necessary technical solution to the political, policy and operational problems of governing much before the advent of AI. They have been fundamental to the refashioning of citizens as consumers and the state as cost-effective service-provider, but also contributed to the retrenchment of public sector capacities and the development of surveillance technologies able to control public sector workers as well as the wider population (Collington 2022; Fourcade and Gordon 2020; Yeung 2023). Over the last decade, public officials started discovering AITs as a way of radically enhancing their already-existing "technological solutionist" agenda with promises of accuracy, speed and automation in delivering citizen-facing services, providing security and through back-office efficiencies (Veale and Brass 2019; see overview in: Paul 2022). The European Commission, for instance, argues that "AI-enabled solutions in the *public sector* can deliver shorter and richer feedback loops for all levels of governance, providing an opportunity to speed up, improve the efficiency and effectiveness of service delivery" (European Commission 2018b: 19, highlight added). This appears to offer the possibility of improving the quality and consistency of public services, help fine-tune the design and implementation of policy measures, render interventions more efficient and targeted, and enhance the cost-effectiveness of public procurement.

However, we already know that (as yet) many of these claims are overblown or simply untrue (on the AI functionality fallacy see: Raji et al. 2022). This is the case already at a technical level. Exploring our opening example a bit further, Emma's designers have programmed the possibility of "machine failure" into the chatbot: Emma leads users on to human agents when it cannot find the right information, or when visitors (re-)code Emma's answers as not having addressed their queries (a familiar experience for most of us using these relatively unsophisticated chatbots). This anticipation of inevitable "machine failure" speaks to a wider discussion in computer sciences, the humanities, jurisprudence and the social sciences: how autonomous, intelligent and reliable are AITs really, how should, and can, we control AIT systems, and are technical fixes enough, possible or even desirable in public sector use contexts where people's fundamental rights and democratic values are at stake?

These questions are pertinent, because in many cases the consequences of "failure" of an AIT system are much more severe than with Emma the chatbot (i.e., not finding the correct information on immigration procedures in the US). Indeed, the techno-solutionist promise of AIT in public policy is repeatedly jeopardized by individual national scandals. AI-driven automated decision systems have produced illegal effects, for example, in Australia ("robodebt" scandal), the Netherlands (child benefits), Sweden or Britain (education), the US (staff performance assessment) (Henriques-Gomes 2021; Peeters and Widlak 2023; Satariano 2020) – and several chapters of the *Handbook* dive into such cases in more depth. Indeed, the first fine ever to be paid under the EU's General Data Protection Regulation (GDPR) was in 2019 by a Northern Swedish municipality (20,000 euros) which had trialled facial recognition technology to monitor students' school attendance and to relieve teachers from the time-consuming work of keeping handwritten records (European Data Protection Board 2019). A number of these systems were withdrawn after legal or political constestation over bias, data protection violations or incorrect outputs. Importantly, however, a common threat in their scandalization has been around more fundamental questions of how algorithms, AITs and automated decision systems transform the relationship of state and citizens. These scandals also sit alongside political and civil campaigns opposing AI deployments on the grounds of the wider public good. When two dozen cities and states in the US started banning facial recognition technologies from 2019 onwards, or citizen protest halted a "smart city" proposal in Toronto, Canada, campaigners had not only worried about individual rights (such as data protection or privacy) but also about undemocratic corporate and state control of the public space (Berger 2020; Simonite 2021).

Apprehensions of the potentially detrimental societal consequences of AI design and use also feature in education, care, health care and policing. For example, the UN special rapporteur on disability has raised pointed worries about state applications of AITs and the discriminatory effects on vulnerable populations (United Nations 2022); Human Rights Watch (2019) has documented profound concerns over the potentially life-threatening effects for people in extreme poverty of AI-fuelled identification and fraud detection in welfare programmes across the globe from the Indian Aadhaar project to Michigan's MiDAS; and UNICEF (2021) has published a comprehensive description of risks and policy guidelines for AI and children. Allegations in these areas often rest on the conviction that technical fixes just won't do when a technology internalizes and amplifies societal biases and automates patterns of exclusion in public policies and public services (Benjamin 2019; Eubanks 2018; Singh and Jackson 2021).

Techno-solutionist representations of AITs in policymaking also disguise how the design, development and use of these technologies is driven by corporate interests, and that the use of AITs *in* public policy is also structured by the development of public policies *for* AITs. There are numerous reasons why governments are developing public policies to promote the research design development and use of AITs more widely. These include national projects of technological specialization, developing and maintaining high-value economic activity in design and manufacturing, and the protection of key capabilities, especially in defence and security (Bellanova et al. 2022; Calderaro and Blumfelde 2022; Mügge 2023; Paul 2023; Smuha 2021b). Indeed, the design and development of these technologies raise numerous challenges for public policies, both within and between countries/regions, which reach beyond fundamental rights and undemocratic surveillance of citizens: the security and safety of national infrastructures; the global regulation of precarious labour conditions in the production and maintenance of AIT systems from data to minerals (Crawford 2021; Wood et al. 2019); and perhaps most importantly, the contribution of AITs to combatting or worsening the climate crisis: including energy consumption for large data-dependent AITs, biodiversity and environmental degradation from undersea cable-laying and open-cast and artisanal mining of precious metals, and the disposal of components and electronic waste (Dauvergne 2020; Tamburrini 2022; van Wynsberghe 2021). This means that any high-flying positive assumptions as to the 'cost-effectiveness' contributions of AITs – including the evaluation of chatbot Emma's ability to save Federal resources – rely on naïve or wilful blindness to, and wholesale externalization of, the vast environmental, energy and social costs of producing, recycling and disusing AITs.

Three Vantage Points for Critical Inquiry of AI and Public Policy

Overall then, there are significant unresolved (and perhaps unresolvable) tensions in – and controversies about – the relationship of public policy, governance and AITs. In this opening chapter to the *Handbook*, we develop a conceptual-analytical framework for examining "public policy and AI" against this broad backdrop. Our aim is to open discussions and scholarly evaluation beyond narrow technical and positivistic understandings of both AITs and policy. We propose three key vantage points for critical inquiry that are further elaborated and nuanced in the thirty subsequent chapters of this *Handbook*:

- *the politics of conceptualizing AI*, of defining its role and workings in the policy world, including through the normalization of contestable normative precepts for democratic AI governance such as "ethics", "transparency" or "trustworthiness";
- the contingent practices of *AIT design, development, use and regulation* in public policy contexts, understood as highly variable socio-technical assemblages which pull together specific sets of meanings, strategic actions, technological affordances, forms of materialization and their effects;
- the situatedness of AI/policy interactions and their effects *in a highly uneven global political economy of AIT production and regulation*.

The remainder of this introduction carves out these three conceptual-analytical vantage points, and their respective elements, in more detail and ends with a short presentation of the *Handbook*'s structure and contributions.

VANTAGE POINT 1: CONTESTED EPISTEMOLOGIES OF PUBLIC POLICY AND AI TECHNOLOGIES

How we conceptualize and discuss the interaction of AITs and policies, and how we frame risks, challenges and opportunities of AITs, depends a great deal on our understandings of what AI *is*. And this is where the struggles begin. This is not because it is per se harder to define AI than to define democracy, poverty or sustainability. Rather, it is that each definition relies on, and reproduces, particular assumptions, both ontological (what is AI) and epistemological (how can we know what AI is and does). And these assumptions are situated in specific value systems and political struggles, which can be implicit, explicit or completely hidden, in the way AI is understood, discussed, used and regulated.

Critical social scientists suggest that AI (and "algorithms") are "ambiguous concept(s) which some see as a technology, some as a decision tool, others as an epistemology or as a socio-technical process of ordering" (Barocas et al. 2013: 2). We need to explore that ambiguity first, to explain and critically evaluate the politics of defining AI. Although our intention is not to define AI "once and for all", it is necessary to state this volume treats it primarily as a cluster of *technologies*, rather than as scientific discipline or epistemology. We propose that AI in policymaking can only be understood in its specific material expressions as a particular *AIT*, because AI "always relies on other technologies and is embedded in broader scientific and technological practices and procedures" including both software and hardware (Coeckelbergh 2020: 80). This embedding in other practices includes the conceptualizing of AITs through their material production and functioning, and through the discourse, mythologies and politics of technologies in general. In this section, we illuminate the contested business of conceptualizing AI – of delimiting what AI is and is not – to show how such definition work *matters* for how and why AITs are inserted in policymaking and how they get regulated. Since concepts of AI, and concepts with which AI is regulated, are themselves part of the politics of using AI in the public sector, this is where critical understanding begins.

Techno-functional Conceptualizations of AI

It seems quite straightforward to conceptualize AITs through their functions and technical characteristics; through "a system's ability to interpret external data correctly, to learn from such data, and to use those learnings to achieve specific goals and tasks through flexible adaptation" (Kaplan and Haenlein 2019: 15). Such definitions highlight the technical capacities of AITs in reflexive data processing and adaptation – understood as "learning" – and a view of these capacities serving a specified function or set of functions. This historically might have been through the AIT being programmed to achieve specific goals and tasks, whereas contemporary AITs involve semi-autonomous goal identification and adaptation.

Techno-functional definitions of AI span technical and policy worlds. They reference concepts, components and types in a cluster of diverse technologies, with empirical and methodological descriptors of varying generality. These include algorithm, machine learning, neural networks, deep learning, natural language processing, image recognition and automation/automated decision-making (ADM). A simple definition of AI systems in a recent regulation proposal, for example, treats it as "a collection of technologies that combine data, algorithms and computing power" (European Commission 2020: 3). Another recent Communication by the European Commission (2018a: 2) defines AI systems as "systems that display intelligent behaviour by analysing their environment and taking actions – with some degree of autonomy – to achieve specific goals". AI ethicist Marc Coeckelbergh (2020: 64) relates AI to algorithmic calculations, suggesting that "AI can be defined as intelligence displayed or simulated by code (algorithms)".

There is an ambivalence in these "techno-functional" definitions. On the one hand, they short-cut a long-standing debate within AI, in which what it means to "simulate" intelligence, as well as what constitutes "intelligence", is highly contested. Indeed, understandings of AI date to the original coinage of the term "artificial intelligence" in 1956 by John McCarthy (a computer scientist at Stanford), who organized a two-month research series on Artificial Intelligence at Dartmouth College, New Hampshire. The goal was to create a field of research for "building machines able to simulate human intelligence" (Haenlein and Kaplan 2019: 7). The idea of "simulation" speaks directly to Alan Turing's seminal work on "Computing Machinery and Intelligence" on the design of intelligent machines and ways of testing how well they simulate human intelligence. While Turing did not use the term AI yet, for many Turing's famous reflections serve as a litmus test today: "if a human is interacting with another human and a machine and unable to distinguish the machine from the human, then the machine is said to be intelligent" (Haenlein and Kaplan 2019: 6).

On the other hand – and somewhat contradictory to the anthromorphization of capacities and agency ascribed to AITs – policymakers, regulators and more positivist scholars define AI primarily in terms of its technological characteristics. The common use of analogies to human experiences (learning, adaptation, intelligence) generates an anthropomorphic ontology for AI. The machine (or technological system) is presented as possessing qualities that are external, but similar, to humans. The implication is that machines are inserted as ontologically distinct entities into human activities, institutions and decision-making processes. This has become even more pertinent since the introduction of Generative Pre-trained Transformers (GPT) language models qualitatively shifted AI capabilities and scale, with a potential to power a wider set of applications across the policy world in open or hidden ways and to fathom even stronger notions of AI agency (one of our contributions maps the burgeoning but problematic uses of ChatGPT in judicial decision-making). For this *Handbook*'s purposes, these definitions signal that the AITs have independent agency in the process of making and delivering policy (hence also the fears of bureaucrats losing discretion to machines in parts of the literature).

More critical AI scholars – including computer scientists – have contested the usefulness of the Turing test as well as the implied notions of "intelligence" in the context of AI (Broussard 2018; Chrisley and Begeer 2000; Christian 2020). They warn us that treating a technology meant to simulate human capacities (speech, visualization, image recognition, etc.) based on stochastics and mathematical probabilities as "intelligent" obscures how the technologies actually function. In doing so, it hides not only their inherent technical limits, but also how they interact with socio-political processes. This makes it more difficult to clearly identify, or challenge, the political and economic agendas of boosting their sales and use despite such problems (see foundational paper on "the dangers of stochastic parrots": Bender et al. 2021).

What holds the techno-functional definitions coherent – and permits the slippage between narrow techno-functionalist definitions into anthromorphizing the machine – is the underlying conceptualization of independence of the machine from the conditions of its production, the unfolding of its functioning or the effects of its outputs. As our contributors discuss, these conceptualizations lead to blind spots in understanding the political role of AITs in public policy, their strong politico-economic underpinnings, and the possibility and practice of their regulation.

Socio-technical Conceptualizations of AI

In contrast to techno-functional definitions, many social sciences and humanities scholars refute the ontological independence of algorithms, AI and AITs, arguing that, instead, they only exist and can be understood as existing in wider social relations (e.g., Barocas et al. 2013; Coeckelbergh 2020; Katzenbach and Ulbricht 2019; Ziewitz 2016). Furthermore, from a political lens, to consider AI as comprising cognition, reasoning and decision-making that is independent from social interactions is simply utterly misleading. AITs are socio-technical assemblages which – due to their technical functionalities – may represent a specific cognitive and material form of collating and processing data; but this is necessarily always embedded in, and co-produced with, social processes (for the wider argument about socio-technical assemblages, see: Åm 2015; Jasanoff and Kim 2013). Critical sociologists demand that our analyses look beyond the figure of the algorithm in any essentializing way and attend, instead, to "how multiple spaces for agency, opacity, and power open and close in different parts of algorithmic assemblages. The crux of the matter is that actors experience different degrees of agency and opacity in different parts of any algorithmic assemblage" (Lee 2021: 65). As Jasanoff (2016) puts it succinctly, "technological objects are thoroughly enmeshed in society, as integral components of social order". And as such, AITs are "artifacts [that] have politics" (Winner 1980), directly and profoundly relevant to public policy and governance. AITs are not only facilitated by political action or used in political institutions to achieve particular goals. They are also materializations of, and themselves facilitate, relations of inequality, domination, possession and extraction through their design, development, use and disposal (Benjamin 2019; Couldry and Mejias 2019; 2021; Gray 2023; Kwet 2019).

Contributions in the *Handbook* therefore explore the role of AITs, algorithms and data-driven decision-making as part of socio-political ordering processes, including "the economic, cultural, and political contexts that both shape the design of algorithms as well as accommodate their operation" (Katzenbach and Ulbricht 2019: 3; cf., Burrell and Fourcade 2021). For example, an already large literature on critical data studies highlights that AITs (and algorithmic calculations more generally) rely on socially constructed and *always already* pre-interpreted data. Data is never "raw" but emerges from highly contingent ways of categorizing and labelling the social world (Gitelman 2013), and from the unequal distribution of "symbolic power" (the power to name and label things in dominant ways) (Bourdieu 1991). Data and data-based technologies for sorting and classifying people – key uses of AITs – have a "looping effect" (Bowker and Starr 2000; Hacking 1995; Law and Ruppert 2016), coming to shape people and their understandings of themselves over time, and in turn being reshaped by the actions and reactions of those people.

The contrast between techno-functionalist views of AITs (as neutral and rational decision-aids) vs. socio-technical understanding (as integrated in socially constructed governance tools in socio-political ordering processes) echoes longer-standing debates about quantification, analytical models and technical expertise in policy studies. More positivist accounts highlight the role of technical tools, visualizations, numerical analysis and predictive models as neutral informants of rational problem-solving in the policy world (e.g., Majone 2010; Posner 2001; Sunstein 2002), while more constructivist analyses of public policy and governance highlight the inescapable connectedness of these tools, analyses and models to processes (and contestations) of socio-political ordering (e.g., Desrosières 2002; Paul 2021; Porter 1995; Stone 2020).

This chasm also speaks to a wider controversy in policy studies about the epistemological features of policy itself, which predates the arrival of "analytical turns", let alone AITs, in public decision-making. Indeed, Harold D. Lasswell's influential concept of "policy science" ascribes a *neutral* and *rationalizing* role to policy analysts whose expertise informs the search for optimal solutions to politically predefined problems, assisting "the realization of the value goals" (Lasswell 1970: 5). Even though Lasswell acknowledged that the use of policy knowledge was always "contextual" because it will move through differently structured polities and political interactions, in his work, policy expertise itself retains its realist epistemology. As one of us argues elsewhere, many policy scholars conceptualize the more recent rediscovery of analytical tools in policymaking – from risk analysis to cost–benefit analysis – as a Lasswellian move of rationalizing policymaking (Paul 2021). This view clashes with *critical policy studies* which see policymaking as a much more complex, ambiguous and contested process of vesting meanings, normative judgements and selective representations of social reality in a "policy" at the discursive, epistemological, legal as well as practice level (Carmel 2019a; Fischer et al. 2015; Stone 2012; Yanow and Schwartz-Shea 2006). Scholars in this camp treat knowledge claims and their materialization in specific tools, models and institutions as an intrinsic part of the politics of policymaking. This is perhaps doubly important to acknowledge when considering AITs, as they are so reliant on datafication for their technical functioning all while their processes of modelling reduce the expression of contestation, ambiguity and complexity to categorizations and labelling of huge numbers of seemingly unambiguous and neutral data points. It is, in this case, not just that the AI-powered tools themselves present the idea of a rational, truthful and objective analysis (e.g., the identification of a medical risk score for prioritizing patient treatment), but that their entire functioning rests on assumptions that the data points they processed for such analysis are expressions of reality onto which a notionally rational analysis can simply be imposed.

The Role of Law and Regulation in Shaping AI Public Policy Interactions

This wider critique, or orientation, also brings us to consider the role of public policy and law that we can see in burgeoning efforts to regulate the effects of AITs across all scales and diverse contexts and applications. To assess this development, we also adopt a socio-political account of law and technology. Law is constitutive of social relations and political economy and plays an important role in spurring, shaping, and … technological developments. Legal definitions of AI – though primarily techno-functionalist – do not form apolitically as merely a neutral description of a particular technology or activity. Choices about how to define certain terms in law – what to include or exclude, how to include or exclude – are necessarily *political* choices. They are the product of calculations, rationalizations, problematizations and are tied to political and ideological views and assumptions as well as policy considerations and goals.

Indeed, though a common view is that law "falls behind" technology or that law must simply *respond* to how technologies are being used, the relationship between law and technology is a cyclical, symbiotic, *coevolutionary* one. The work going into defining the issues to be regulated by law – AI, "bias", "privacy", "transparency" and so on in our case – generates the framework for which issues in which cases will be ruled by certain legal principles, rules and sanctions.

While this is highly political – and often contested – work in the first instance, legal definitions tend to become sticky and neutralized over time in ways that are no longer visible or debated. The law involves selecting specific permitted relations, actions and processes in society from a much wider set of possibilities. It normalizes and generalizes particular political choices by inscribing them into law and regulation (cf. Paul 2022). In doing so, it also organizes, or makes less visible, the struggle and contestation over those choices. The by now abundant insights from ethical and socio-legal research on AITs' effects on fundamental human rights, rule of law procedures in public decision contexts and other normative baselines for democratic governance (e.g., Ananny 2016; Cobbe and Singh 2020; Coeckelbergh 2020; Dubber et al. 2020; Pasquale 2015; Smuha 2021a; Yeung 2019) highlight that such technology-aided categorizations have profound effects on people's lives. Critical analysis of AITs and public policy must discuss the discriminatory and marginalizing effects of AIT uses. This is especially relevant where official policy or regulatory rhetoric silences or marginalizes them as matters of *individual* rights, even where discriminatory patterns are in fact much more structural in character and would require a wider focus on social justice and equity (cf. on the disregarded "collective dimension" of individual data protection regulation: Mantelero 2016).

A Heuristic for Exploring Public Policy and AI Technologies

For this *Handbook* to unpack the contested ontology of AI, its overlaps with equally contested policy epistemologies, and the relationship between using AITs in the public realm and regulating them we propose a novel heuristic (Table 1.1). This provides a first rough compass for critically situating existing research and policy proposals in a two-dimensional conceptual space of interactions between public policy and AITs. The heuristic provides us with a device to systematically map state-of-the-art research on AI and public policy, for analysing empirical phenomena and policy debates, and for launching informed critique about blind spots of existing research and policy debates. It enables contributors in this *Handbook* – and hopefully other researchers and critical policy analysts after us – to expose what remains hidden from view or is deliberately marginalized through techno-functional interpretations of AI's ontology in policy and regulation.

VANTAGE POINT 2: MEANING-MAKING, POLITICAL ACTION AND MATERIALITY IN AI POLICY PRACTICES

Next to mapping the relative weight of techno-functional AI ontologies in our field of studies and in the policy world, the *Handbook* also aims to examine the implications of socio-technical understandings of how AIT and public policy intersect. In particular, we suggest that a "practice"-oriented approach to public policy and governance can illuminate how actors justify and enact the role of AITs in public policy in different settings "on the ground". We do this with

Table 1.1   *Heuristic for exploring public policy and artificial intelligence technologies*

		Perceived ontology of AIT/policy	
		Techno-functional	*Socio-technical/political*
Relationship between AIT and policy	*AIT as tool in policymaking*	AITs as techno-solutionist decision aids (implicit: policymaking as rational problem-solving)	AITs as governance tools in socio-political ordering processes (implicit: policymaking as political)
	AIT as regulatory issue	Narrow AIT regulation, (implicit: e.g., risk-based regulation as rational problem-solving)	Broad AIT regulation, (implicit: regulation as struggle over wider power relations, capitalist accumulation patterns etc.)

a view to exploring how and why different contexts generate different relationships of AIT and public policy through a three-fold focus:

● actors' meaning-making about AI and its role on policy as constituted in a specific context;
● policymakers' strategic but unpredictable interactions with specific technologies;
● forms of materialization which normalize specific socio-technical imaginaries and actions and thus structure future policy and practice regarding AITs.

Public Policy as Practice

A practice-oriented approach enables us to access three important aspects of policymaking: meaning-making, action and materiality. Critical policy analysts understand policymaking as mediated by "communicative practices" which are mobilized or silenced in specific empirical settings in contingent ways (Fischer et al. 2015: 5; Dubois 2009). This orientation requires exploration of AIT/policy interactions beyond the level of formal policy or regulatory programmes on paper. We need to examine in context, how high-flying promises of accurate, cost-effective and speedy decision-making with AITs come into being, are realized, or not, how they are contested, mediated or appropriated by all involved policy actors, each facing diverse constraints and drivers to action. "Socio-technical imaginaries" shape how individuals, institutions and cultures consider the range of possibilities, threats and proper uses of technologies, and these are themselves saturated in relations of power to define what technologies are and who are their owners, users or objects in use cases (Jasanoff and Kim 2013; also Lewis et al. 2020). But while the politics of "talking AI into being" through specific policy frames has already received increasing attention in research (cf. af Malmborg 2023; Bareis and Katzenbach 2022; Paul 2023), it is in specific use cases on the ground that preliminary normative calls for (or against) using and regulating AITs in policymaking and public service provision, political struggles over these uses, as well as patterns of domination in whose judgement matters, can be revealed.

But practices are not just about "meaning-making". As political actors engage in policymaking, they act: forge alliances, distribute resources, give privileged (or deny) access to other actors. In acting, actors' contingently synthesize ethics, knowledge, normative understandings, interests, strategies and goals for action: whether collectively or as individuals (Shore et al. 2011; Shore and Wright 1997; Wagenaar and Cook 2003). Practices have a concretization function for public policy: they bring policy "into being" on the ground beyond formal declarations of policy goals. But in that grounding, practices also expose tensions between conflicting goals, norms, interests, understandings and so on; and they require actors on the ground to work with, around or against any ambivalences, ambiguities or outright contradictions. Contributions in the *Handbook*, especially in Part IV, illustrate what such a practice lens can reveal about the AI/public policy complex.

In our particular case of public policy's technology orientation, practices involve interactions between human and non-human actors on the ground which are strategic from the side of policymakers but have unpredictable effects. As Henk Wagenaar (2012) stresses, in his definition of what makes policy "actionable", "*practice* is a move or thrust into an only partly known and knowable world. By acting, by intervening, we extend our intentions and understandings into this indeterminate world without being able to predict how its agency will effectuate itself and impact us".

This view on policy, as a practice where policy actors enact their intentions and meanings but still throw themselves into the partly unknown, also concurs with more recent discussions of "technological agency" as an "*iterative process*, ... in which humans construct technologies that impact their users and designers through unforeseen uses and effects" (Campbell-Verduyn and Hütten 2023). Despite its unpredictability then, the contingent and mutually constitutive iteration between policy goals, interests, intentions and meanings vs. technological affordances and their effects in AI-related policy practices is not neutral, accidental or chaotic. We suggest that policymakers act purposefully and strategically in relation to AI – and their actions are structured by inequalities in power, knowledge and resource, and by the meanings they vest in their specific action (Carmel 2019b; from the perspective of Sum and Jessop's cultural political economy: Paul 2023).

From the combination of meaning-making, structuration and action, then we come to a third important aspect of practices, that they "involve the *materialization of* meanings, knowledge and ideas in concrete objects, institutions, and the relations between [them]" (Carmel 2019b: 37, emphasis added). This focus on policy as a continuous, complex and contradictory process of materialization, enables us to explore how the material objects and infrastructures; the component parts of AITs, intersect with the socio-technical imaginaries of what we think such technologies might do or be. In our case, this materialization might be seen in the use, location and networking of data centres; the design of public procurement platforms; the age and structure of existing computer networks; the institutional organization of budget-holders and reporting; datasheets and audit protocols; or the design of user interfaces used by decision-makers. Each of these component parts and processes intersects with what different policy actors think about what is possible or right to do when using AITs – from the national strategy team, to data engineers working on the technology, to social workers and border guards trying to use (or seeking to evade) it.

At the same time, our attention to the materiality of policy's interactions with technologies does not ontologize the material world as external to social production processes. A recent upsurge of critical infrastructure studies (Bellanova and de Goede 2020; Bernards and Campbell-Verduyn 2019; The Critical Infrastructure Collective 2022) shows how the material underpinnings which lend infrastructures – roads, the internet, currencies or the cloud – their sense of durability and material existence, have been socially created and are being constantly reinterpreted and struggled over in everyday practices. Our conceptualization of policy as practice thus also exposes the politics of creating, maintaining and normalizing material structures as a crucial part of existing AI/policy interactions.

Co-production of Technologies and Social Order

Our view on AI policy practice speaks to the older science and technology (STS) assumption that the development, uses and regulation of technology cannot be explored in the abstract: we agree that these processes are inexorably linked and *situated* in specific socio-technical contexts in which technology is *co-produced* with societal knowledge, institutions and power (Jasanoff 2016; Jasanoff and Kim 2013). Rather than focusing on AIT uses in narrow cases, contributions in this *Handbook* provide a contextualized understanding of socio-technical systems as "contingent on social, political, and economic forces and can take different shapes" (on "algorithmic governance": Katzenbach and Ulbricht 2019: 7). While proponents of "trust-worthy AI" or "proportionate" regulation of ADM systems acknowledge that context matters for assessing AI-related risks and benefits (Chatila et al. 2021; Krafft et al. 2022), we are yet to consolidate critical policy-analytical insights on how the public sector *actually adopts and incorporates* AITs. In particular: how are these technologies being mapped onto or disrupt existing institutional practices, how are such diffusion processes shaped by sector-specific norms, and how do actors in different contexts enact and contest abstract regulatory safeguards such as "accountability", or protection against "bias" on the ground?

A comprehensive review of public sector uses of AI in the US includes the 142 most significant Federal Agencies and Departments (Engstrom et al. 2020). This concludes that while 45 per cent of these have experimented with machine learning, there is a grave lack of technical capacity and knowledge within the administration that defies reflexive use and careful inspection of AI-based decision recommendations. And there is more than one in which appropriation of technologies can unfold. For the British police (Sandhu and Fussey 2021: 79) highlight "a range of fissures" occurring as police officers find the smart technologies they are expected to use flawed, and resist AI's intrusion of their discretion. This also reflects studies in the Canadian border force, although Côté-Boucher (2020) found variation in how officers endorsed or resisted the AIT recommendations. In a rather different context of technological appropriation, Koulish and Evans (2021) show that in the US border force, officers overrode an original automated decision recommendation system so that it better conformed to their norms/preferences. Several system redesigns tried to better match the AI system to the officers' decisions, eventually resulting in the automation of their discriminatory decision-making. Another study on police uses in the Netherlands shows that officers only adopted AI-recommended decisions when they matched their own intuition (Selten et al. 2023). These contrasting cases imply diverse relationships between different policy actors, institutions, norms, expectations and how the technologies function over time, in which we have yet to have a systematic explanation of these variations. A practices perspective that examines meanings, action and materiality is critical to understanding individual cases and to explaining varieties of AIT/public policy relations in different contexts.

Importantly, these cases also bely references to the generic "human" of classic AI ethics literature, and highlight specific contributions of comparative law and regulation in examining what "human control" might mean, and how it is enacted in highly variable and contingent ways, across policy sectors and jurisdictions (Elish 2019). These discussions also highlight how institutional norms, material limits of technologies and our ideas about what technology is, profoundly shape the regulatory meaning of "control", "accountability" or "liability" (Firlej and Taeihagh 2021).

We propose that empirical analyses of policy and regulatory practice must address the highly contingent sociotechnological articulation of AITs and human actions in policy, and explore the intricacies of complexly interwoven meaning- and decision-making processes beyond the widespread man/machine dichotomy. In that context, the widespread parlance in AIT regulation of keeping "the human in the loop" (e.g., Firlej and Taeihagh 2021) is utterly counterproductive. It assumes a neat distinction of human/machine decisions in AI-powered policymaking, with humans ready to interfere when – and just when – the machine fails. Such dichotomy is not only *conceptually flawed* (useful discussion of such flaws also in: Jones 2015); it is also *democratically problematic* in public sector applications, for at least three reasons:

- focus on the AIT as a machine actor releases publicly accountable actors from liability for choices on procuring and designing an AI, selecting data, initial coding and programming, or how to incorporate the AI into hardware and how to use it in decision-making; choices which co-shape how AI works in practice and how it affects citizens;
- the "human-in-the-loop" model also turns policy experts and bureaucrats into "moral crumple zones" who soak up liability for machine failure but have little discretion for professional, moral or empathy-based judgement otherwise, and are being increasingly de-qualified in taking decisions in the first place (Elish 2019; cf. Yeung 2019). There is a risk that humans are degraded to mere correctors of machine decisions but cannot and ought not improvise to deal with contingency (Green 2022);
- while actual oversight of systems is therefore currently difficult or impossible to secure, claiming to have this oversight also releases the institution procuring and using such systems from responsibility (Green 2022). Beyond the individual system user who bears a responsibility they cannot exercise, then, the wider accountability of public bodies for any individual or collective harms from the functioning of these systems is also displaced by this "human-in-the-loop" framing.

In conclusion, the empirical exploration of AI/policy interactions necessitates moving beyond dichotomous understandings of human–machine autonomy, decisions, cognition or knowledge. Practice-oriented policy research on AITs needs to tease out the politics of perceiving, enacting and contesting the fluid boundaries and interactions between humans and machine – and the overriding role of encoded norms, values and inequities – in concrete cases. Our socio-technical examination of AI's ontology in policymaking (the first vantage point for critical inquiry) then aligns with STS-inspired examinations of technology *affordances* in policymaking not as neutral tools at the disposal of the rational human actors pursuing their policy goals, but as integral but also rather unruly parts of the social production of order and power.

VANTAGE POINT 3: (GLOBAL) POLITICAL ECONOMIES OF TECHNOLOGY, LABOUR AND NATURE

A focus on meanings and practices, however, can still not fully expose the "political" in the AI/public policy complex. From our *critical* perspective, we need to situate these assemblages in the wider structures of AI production, development and use. To us, this particularly concerns the ways in which AITs and their production depend on and reproduce global, but also more local, power inequalities and injustices, and the ways in which public policy measures in the

AI domain contribute to specific production patterns and their unequal effects (also see de Freitas Boullosa et al. 2023). Such critique falls into three categories:

- the socio-economic injustices of informational capitalism and its inherent data production processes;
- the environmental injustices created by AIT systems' hardware and energy demands; and
- the larger scale corporate transformation of the state.

Socio-economic Injustices in AI's Production Processes

In efforts to expose the socio-economic injustices of specific AI-fuelled governance projects, policy scholars have already taken pains to specify generic concerns over bias and equity, and contextualized their analyses of distinct AIT use cases in wider societal structures. For example, analysts of "smart" border control policies highlight the risk of state authorities violating migrants' fundamental rights (such as non-discrimination or fair treatment) without noticing these violations, being able to account for their occurrence or correcting them in due course (Amoore and Raley 2017; Leese 2014; Molnar and Gill 2018). Scholars of predictive policing point to similar dynamics and discuss the self-fulfilling prophecies of algorithmic racial profiling, targeted interventions in "Black" neighbourhoods, "finding" crime and feeding this "information" back into an algorithm that has been trained with data that is *always already* racially biased (Ferguson 2017; Kaufmann et al. 2019). Social policy analysts equally worry about automated forms of discrimination which could deepen structural inequalities in access to social benefits and services (Dencik and Kaun 2020; Eubanks 2018; Redden et al. 2020).

Such focus on the societal injustices stemming from, and/or perpetuated through, uses of AIT systems in the public sector remains crucial also for contributions in this *Handbook*. However, if we more closely consider AI production at the level of data, additional socio-economic injustices come into view. We suggest that the political economy of AIT, and its interactions with public policy, emerges from the wider systems and structures of informational capitalism, in which data – its collation, curation, labelling and "refining" (Cohen 2018), parsing, aggregation, reconstitution and use – is central. For Cohen, informational capitalism depends on the imagining and constitution of what she calls a "biopolitical public domain": a "construct that enables both the marshalling of informational resources and the exercise of biopower over subject populations" (Cohen 2018: 215). Technological systems (cookies), legal precepts (consent, privacy, intellectual property) and the interest in selling products (targeting potential buyers) combine to facilitate a drive to appropriate the resources of this public domain. Platform economy companies such as Google, Amazon, Meta or Apple drive the mass generation, extraction and processing of user data at the heart of their business models. It is not data per se that is the asset to be traded and capitalized, as Zuboff (2019) argues, but the "behavioural surplus" generated through the algorithmic structuration of data into patterns that enable customers – such as advertisement companies – to predict individual behaviour and preferences and micro-target interventions. Monopoly endeavours of these companies as part of the business model of "data rentiership" (Birch et al. 2020; cf. Petit 2020).

Importantly, this data-generation is also produced and curated by workers. Thousands of data-workers, employed through less well-known firms and their chains of sub-contractors, spend all day every day coding and (re-) labelling data on which AITs depend. These are often workers who sit in unexpected relations to the forces and flows that mark global capitalism. They are often well educated but also marginalized and low-paid, based in the Global South but in key, digitally connected and well-serviced hotspots (e.g., migrant workers and women in Venezuela, Kenya, Philippines and Bulgaria (Posada 2022; Miceli et al. 2020), as well as prisoners in countries across the globe, from Finland to China (Hao 2019)).

"Generative AI" is a particularly pertinent example of these systems of production (see Hao and Seetharanam 2023). The proprietary "ChatGPT" produced by the innocuous-sounding company "OpenAI" (in reality, Microsoft) was released in early versions for use without a fee (the so-called "freemium" model), so suggesting the idea of something automatic and cost-free, just sitting there, as an interface on the web, for fun or as a convenience. Yet, the production of this tool not only extracted and used the creative work of humans without attribution or payment (e.g., works of literature); and the freely donated and enthusiastic interactions of millions of users to adapt and improve the tool for later sale as proprietary product. It also required millions of US dollars to produce, process and label the data that underpins it. In that context, it is not sufficient to discuss racial and other forms of "bias" and discrimination in AIT design and practice (Benjamin 2019; Eubanks 2018); but there is wider political economy of data-dependent AITs in which discriminatory effects are somewhat cynically produced by a highly unequal global labour infrastructure which supports the technological wonders of AI (Casili and Posada 2019; Irani 2015).

The intersection of AITs and public policy thus raises long-standing questions of labour rights and social justice, corporate power, and the role of the public policy in regulating these, not only over the use of AI to govern work and workers (e.g., Amazon in the US), but also in the use of gig forms of work to produce AITs in the first place. This has led to legal contestation (against Meta in Kenya, for example); calls for data justice and new forms of regulation; and to calls for participatory data work. Yet these approaches still leave the solution "in place" – where this data work is undertaken. The real challenge for the relationship between AI and public policy is to make more visible, and to act on, the connection between the production of AITs, and their consumption (for a comprehensive and insightful review, see Dencik et al. 2022).

Socio-ecological Injustices of AI Production

Secondly, the structural injustices of this political economy are intensified by the socio-ecological injustices of AI production – again not usually central to existing regulation and policy studies in the AI domain. As Dauvergne (2022) argues, while there are efficiency gains from the use of AI, in energy management and use of renewables, in transport, for geological surveys and for supply chain management (pp. 702–705), but these savings tend to "accelerate extraction" (p. 705), especially at the point of system structure (e.g., hardware and infrastructure production). The marginal efficiency gains are used to extract profit and intensify production; the efficiency gains of AI at the micro-level outweigh the costs at macro-level. This is especially so since such costs are usually "externalized"; i.e., neither borne by corporate producers nor key users of AIT systems (see below and cf. discussion of the "responsibility gap" for environmental costs of AI diffusion by Lucivero, Chapter 12 in this volume).

Transnational corporations are, at the point of extraction, doing "everything in their power to spur inefficient consumption of natural resources, reengineering cultures toward hyper-consumerism, and designing products for disposability, rapid obsolescence, and fast turnover" (Dauvergne 2022: 711). Such hyper-consumerism of AIT products and services is already taking hold in the public sector, too – not least because dominant techno-solutionist narratives of AI boosting cost-effectiveness and rational problem-solving in public service delivery may unfold isomorphic pressure among policymakers and public sector organizations across the globe. The emulation of AIT practices based on states' wish to seem future-oriented is likely to continue without due attention to whether specific applications' purposes and public value are worth their carbon emissions, energy consumption levels and labour costs.

The intensification of environmental degradation produced by mining and petro-chemical processing for plastics required for AIT production is evident in places on every populated continent. And, as Crawford (2021) argues, such intensification is integral to what AITs are, what they promise and how they work. The toxic consequences of "cheap" global production of the hardware of AITs are borne very often by rural communities faced with unsafe, unprotected working conditions and the destruction of landscapes and ecosystems. And they are a feature not only of production, but also AIT disposal, as the global tonnage of e-waste is estimated at 61 million tonnes, predicted to rise to 74 million tonnes by 2030: and less than 20 per cent estimated to be recycled (Statista 2023), with the deleterious ecological effects concentrated in impoverished communities.

Wilful blindness to these costs, and the related injustices, intensifies colonial forms of domination and oppression in the global political economy (Bhambra 2021). Extraction costs in areas settled by formerly colonized and indigenous populations (including the so-called "Global North") are glossed over, disguised or notionally ameliorated. At the same time, technological "benefits" and economic profits are extracted and secured by a relatively small range of companies – many directly colonial or settler-colonial in origin – and their host states in the Global North.[1] All told, this structural condition of AIT production raises profound questions about the "high-tech future(s)" they promise, and whether they are yet – or even can be – compatible with climate goals. For our contributors, such questions require critically discussing whether and how policymakers and regulators address global socio-ecological injustices related to AIT production and how any failure to do so jeopardizes their climate action, (formal) commitment to sustainable development and decolonial agendas (Carmel and Paul 2022).

Transformations of States in the Global Political Economy of AI

Thirdly, and drawing on the previous two points, the state is positioned ambivalently in relation to AI and its production. On the one hand, corporate logics in informational capitalism seem to change how states think about and do policy and governance. With pushes to "mint" data and governing what is measurable, states become an "open data portal" also for private firms and a "provider of digital services", and which thereby "opens itself up to competition from private alternatives that may command equal or greater legitimacy on these terms" (Fourcade and Gordon 2020: 95). Several commentators warn that the diffusion of AI-driven systems will bring a corporate and neoliberal remaking of states, unless data and models are brought into collective public ownership and/or created in more participatory ways (Boyer 2022; Dencik et al. 2019; Pasquale 2016; Pistor 2020) and unless technologies are used for the common good rather than for punishment and control (Bondi et al. 2021; Floridi et al. 2021; Rider 2021).

Pessimistic accounts even suggest that the digital age will eventually obliterate territorial forms of state organization as a provider for public services and welfare altogether, as informational capitalism enables corporate "data controllers" both to monetarize data/patterns *and* to increasingly determine access to private and public services (Pistor 2020). In addition, the pursuit of an imagined "disruptive innovation" and interstate or interregional competition might lead regulators like the EU to eagerly "[privilege] economic growth over individual rights" in their regulatory proposals (Padden and Öjehag-Pettersson 2021) that further cement the corporate appropriation and valuation of public data. From this then emerges competition among the largest corporations to shape and determine the role of international standards and global regulatory measures in AI to help generate or consolidate global market power, thus reifying and intensifying existing economic and political hierarchies.

On the other hand, claims to state losses of control and capture by tech-corporate power are rather reductionist, and might be unhelpful for thinking through states' complex relationship with data, surveillance and rule in specific applications of AITs (Işın and Ruppert 2019; Tréguer 2019). For example, critical political economy accounts suggest that data appropriation strategies and the push to widely deploy AITs in the public sector might not be a one-sided process of corporate imperialism. Instead, these processes are proactively supported by "AI competition states" (Paul, Chapter 20 in this volume) which think of investment and market enhancing regulation as tools for boosting their national/regional economies' competitiveness in the "race to AI" (cf. Smuha 2021b). As we discuss elsewhere (Paul 2023), the regulatory fabrication of "trustworthy" and "human-centric" AI in the EU's proposed AI regulation can be understood as a tool for "regulating into being" a trademark of ethically superior AI meant to boost the EU's AI competitiveness against the US and China.

AITs did not emerge from a uniquely creative, risk-taking or innovative culture, expressed in the idea of "tech-bros" of Silicon Valley. Computing technologies, including AI, developed from an organized and well-funded "military-industrial-compute complex", to paraphrase C. Wright Mills. Huge-scale public funding of security and defence (in the US notably through DARPA), as well as public university funding, subsidized major technological advancements that underpin contemporary uses of AITs, and continue to provide a steady supply of highly qualified researchers to work (e.g., for Canada: Brandusescu 2021). And local computer networks built around pioneering public schools and libraries were later incorporated by major telecommunication companies for the digital infrastructure that later became the internet (Rankin 2018). Importantly, however, this entanglement of state/public and corporate/private knowledge production is now intensified in the reverse process of appropriating AI research through technology company funding of projects, research programmes, Chairs, university centres and sponsorship of discipline research events (Young et al. 2022). This is critical in shaping how select AI "problems" are prioritized, investigated or addressed, while being liberated from the requirements to contribute to the wider domain of public goods through excessively low and arbitraged taxation. These developments are exacerbated by the material demands of AIT development. They also privilege large technology companies due to the huge resource requirements (energy, computer power, data volumes), in which universities in the Global South, and increasingly in the Global North, are not able to access, without the cash and infrastructure offered by the largest global corporations (see Strubell et al. 2020).

Last, not least, the emerging state-corporate complexes in how AITs are being produced, fuelled with data and research, and used also risk perpetuating as well as creating new forms of colonial domination, extraction and exploitation. The decolonial turn in data and technology studies highlights, for example, how processes of data extraction, value generation, the design of applications and the use of AITs in Global South contexts privileges the interests of a few states and corporations in the Global North – increasingly including China – while severely curbing the room for locally owned and independent policy and socio-economic development (Birhane 2020; Couldry and Mejias 2021; Gray 2023; Kwet 2019; Mann 2018). Several of our contributors draw attention to such global power asymmetries by discussing the concept of colonialism explicitly in their work.

ORGANIZATION OF THE HANDBOOK

Keeping with the objective of unpacking the conflictual and ambivalent relationship between AI and public policy, beyond techno-solutionist claims and positivist methodologies, the *Handbook* is structured in four parts which reflect our vantage points for critical inquiry.

Part I, titled "AI and Public Policy: Challenges to Key Concepts", addresses the conceptual foundations for capturing the relationship between AI and policy. How does AI challenge key notions on public administration and policymaking such as power, bureaucratic decision-making or discretion? How do we need to extend these concepts to account for the relationship beyond simplistic man/machine dichotomies and without depoliticizing public policy? How can critical social science contribute to grounding such conceptual discussions? The part starts with a systematic literature review by Andreas Öjehag-Pettersson, Vanja Carlsson and Malin Rönnblom of concepts of "politics", highlighting a surprising lack of engagement with the political nature of AI in social science research. Lena Ulbricht's chapter brings the political centre stage by discussing different concepts of power in AI and public policy, while Roy L. Heidelberg shows that AI in the public sector may be the fulfilment of an ultimately rational bureaucracy which even Herbert Simon and Max Weber might not have believed possible, and which might already have spiralled itself beyond democratic control. The chapter by Frans af Malmborg and Jarle Trondal reflects upon how AITs transform or clash with existing logics of public sector organizations. The part closes with Peter André Busch and Helle Zinner Henriksen examining how AITs reconfigure discretion in street-level bureaucracy and why such transformation is problematic for democracies and the rule of law.

Part II is concerned with "AI and the Politics of Governance: Deconstructing Normative Precepts". Chapters in this part unpack the political work done by guiding principles for AI regulation and governance in different contexts. Authors critically review the following debates in research and policy in alphabetical order: accountability (Jennifer Cobbe and Jatinder Singh), bias (Sun-ha Hong), ethics (Malin Rönnblom, Vanja Carlsson and Michaela Padden), explainability and interpretability (David M. Berry), interoperability (Matthias Leese), sustainability and "digital pollution" (Federica Lucivero), transparency (Ville Aula and Tero Erkkilä) and trust/trustworthiness (Rory Gillis, Johann Laux and Brent Mittelstadt). Taken together, these chapters map the history of related debates and regulatory foci, identify key shifts and struggles over how researchers and policymakers think about these norms, and critically examine the implications of what remains out of scope in research and public discourse on, and the regulation of, AITs.

Part III examines "AI and the Political Economy of Public Policy and Regulation", thus setting the *Handbook*'s contributions in the wider context of AIT production and its implications for global justice. The chapter by Catriona Gray reviews decolonial critiques of

AI and discusses implications for how we study and develop policy and regulation. Sally Brooks takes on the detrimental socio-economic and political effects of deploying AITs and other data-driven systems, including increases in corporate power in the Global North, in development policy contexts. Adekemi Omotubora and Subhajit Basu discuss colonial path dependence and copycat dynamics in AI legislation and governance frameworks in the Global South and highlight how these marginalize local interpretations of AI risks and harm. Cary Coglianese's chapter examines the two-fold implications of AI for public procurement: challenging how AI systems may be used in public procurement, and the extent to which public procurement may have potential as de facto regulation of AI systems in public decision-making. In his discussion of regulatory interdependence, Daniel Mügge systematizes discussions of global AI governance by reflecting critically upon the extent to which different national jurisdictions can control uses and effects of AITs. Finally, Regine Paul's chapter develops the concept of "AI competition states" to explore states' strategic role in regulating AITs in line with visions of their future techno-economic competitiveness.

Part IV turns to critical examinations of "AI and Public Policy on the Ground: Practices and Contestations". We have curated an insightful collection of chapters across ten selected policy domains to offer readers intimate insights into the wide and growing range of different technologies used, the various public purposes and goals inscribed into deploying AI systems, diversity of practices within the same policy domain across time and space, and dominant struggles over AIT uses in different policy domains. The part includes both widely discussed AIT applications, such as in predictive policing or welfare fraud detection, and a range of less researched but nonetheless highly impactful ones. Chapters cover military uses of AI in warfare (Ingvild Bode and Guangyu Qiao-Franco), policing and law enforcement (Mareile Kaufmann), migration and border control (Petra Molnar), judicial decision-making (Juan David Gutiérrez as well as David Mark, Tomás McInerney and John Morison), labour and employment (Robert Donoghue, Huanxin Luo, Phoebe Moore and Ekkehard Ernst), welfare services (Lyndal Sleep and Joanna Redden), social care (Grace Whitfield, James Wright and Kate Hamblin), child protection (Jenny Krutzinna), health care (Mirjam Pot and Barbara Prainsack) and urban governance (Ilia Antenucci and Fran Meissner).

NOTE

1. Of course, in the end, the consequences of the climate emergency, biodiversity loss, landscape degradation and poisoning of life from such activities, will be felt by all. But, as with the discussion on informational capitalism, the loss is first and mostly felt by those people and places who were the first objects of such appropriations and extractions.

REFERENCES

af Malmborg, F. (2023), 'Narrative dynamics in European Commission AI policy: Sensemaking, agency construction, and anchoring', *Review of Policy Research*, **40** (5), 757–80.

Åm, H. (2015), 'Co-production and public policy: Evidence, uncertainty and socio-materiality', in F. Fischer, D. Torgerson, A. Durnová and M. Orsini (eds), *Handbook of Critical Policy Studies*, Cheltenham, UK and Northampton, MA, USA: Edward Elgar Publishing, pp. 297–316, accessed 29 November 2021 at https://www.elgaronline.com/view/edcoll/9781783472345/9781783472345.00024 .xml.

Amoore, L. and R. Raley (2017), 'Securing with algorithms: Knowledge, decision, sovereignty', *Security Dialogue*, **48** (1), 3–10.

Ananny, M. (2016), 'Toward an ethics of algorithms: Convening, observation, probability, and timeliness', *Science, Technology, & Human Values*, **41** (1), 93–117.

Bareis, J. and C. Katzenbach (2022), 'Talking AI into being: The narratives and imaginaries of national AI strategies and their performative politics', *Science, Technology, & Human Values*, **47** (5), 855–81.

Barocas, S., S. Hood and M. Ziewitz (2013), *Governing Algorithms: A Provocation Piece*, SSRN Scholarly Paper ID 2245322, Rochester, NY: Social Science Research Network, 29 March, accessed at https://doi.org/10.2139/ssrn.2245322.

Bedoya, A. M. (2020), 'The cruel new era of data-driven deportation', *Slate*, 22 September, accessed 28 March 2022 at https://slate.com/technology/2020/09/palantir-ice-deportation-immigrant-surveillance-big-data.html.

Bellanova, R. and M. de Goede (2020), 'The algorithmic regulation of security: An infrastructural perspective', *Regulation & Governance*, **16** (1), 102–18, accessed at https://doi.org/10.1111/rego.12338.

Bellanova, R., H. Carrapico and D. Duez (2022), 'Digital/sovereignty and European security integration: An introduction', *European Security*, **31** (3), 337–55.

Bender, E. M., T. Gebru, A. McMillan-Major and S. Shmitchell (2021), 'On the dangers of stochastic parrots: Can language models be too big?', in *Proceedings of the 2021 ACM Conference on Fairness, Accountability, and Transparency*, New York: Association for Computing Machinery, pp. 610–23.

Benjamin, R. (2019), *Race After Technology: Abolitionist Tools for the New Jim Code*, 1st edn, Medford, MA: Polity.

Berger, B. (2020), 'Sidewalk labs' failure and the future of smart cities', *Triple Pundit*, 16 June, accessed at https://www.triplepundit.com/story/2020/sidewalk-labs-failure-smart-cities/120616.

Bernards, N. and M. Campbell-Verduyn (2019), 'Understanding technological change in global finance through infrastructures', *Review of International Political Economy*, **26** (5), 773–89.

Bhambra, G. K. (2021), 'Colonial global economy: Towards a theoretical reorientation of political economy', *Review of International Political Economy*, **28** (2), 307–22.

Birch, K., M. Chiappetta and A. Artyushina (2020), 'The problem of innovation in technoscientific capitalism: Data rentiership and the policy implications of turning personal digital data into a private asset', *Policy Studies*, **41** (5), 468–87.

Birhane, A. (2020), 'Algorithmic colonisation of Africa', accessed 13 September 2023 at https://www.theelephant.info/long-reads/2020/08/21/algorithmic-colonisation-of-africa/.

Bondi, E., L. Xu, D. Acosta-Navas and J. A. Killian (2021), 'Envisioning communities: A participatory approach towards AI for social good', in *Proceedings of the 2021 AAAI/ACM Conference on AI, Ethics, and Society*, New York: Association for Computing Machinery, pp. 425–36.

Bourdieu, P. (1991), *Language and Symbolic Power*, Cambridge: Polity Press.

Bowker, G. C. and S. L. Starr (2000), *Sorting Things Out: Classification and its Consequences*, Cambridge, MA: MIT Press.

Boyer, R. (2022), 'Platform capitalism: A socio-economic analysis', *Socio-Economic Review*, **20** (4), 1857–79.

Brandusescu, A. (2021), 'Artificial intelligence policy and funding in Canada: Public investments, private interests', http://dx.doi.org/10.2139/ssrn.4089932.

Broussard, M. (2018), *Artificial Unintelligence: How Computers Misunderstand the World*, Cambridge, MA: MIT Press.

Burrell, J. and M. Fourcade (2021), 'The society of algorithms', *Annual Review of Sociology*, **47**, 213–37.

Calderaro, A. and S. Blumfelde (2022), 'Artificial intelligence and EU security: The false promise of digital sovereignty?', *European Security*, **31** (3), 415–34.

Campbell-Verduyn, M. and M. Hütten (2023), 'Locating infrastructural agency: Computer protocols at the finance/security nexus', *Security Dialogue*, **54** (5), 455–74.

Carmel, E. (ed.) (2019a), *Governance Analysis: Critical Enquiry at the Intersection of Politics, Policy and Society*, Cheltenham, UK and Northampton, MA, USA: Edward Elgar Publishing.

Carmel, E. (2019b), 'Regimes of governing practices, socio-political order and contestation', in E. Carmel (ed.), *Governance Analysis: Critical Enquiry at the Intersection of Politics, Policy and Society*, Cheltenham, UK and Northampton, MA, USA: Edward Elgar Publishing, pp. 24–46.

Carmel, E. and R. Paul (2022), 'Peace and prosperity for the digital age? The colonial political economy of European AI governance', *IEEE Technology and Society Magazine*, **41** (2), 94–104, accessed at https://doi.org/10.1109/MTS.2022.3173340.

Casilli, A. and J. Posada (2019), 'The platformization of labor and society', in M. Graham and W. Dutton (eds), *Society and the Internet: How Networks of Information and Communication Are Changing our Lives*, 2nd edn, Oxford: Oxford University Press, pp. 293–306.

Chatila, R., V. Dignum, M. Fisher, F. Giannotti, K. Morik, S. Russell and K. Yeung (2021), 'Trustworthy AI', in B. Braunschweig and M. Ghallab (eds), *Reflections on Artificial Intelligence for Humanity*, Cham: Springer International Publishing, pp. 13–39.

Chrisley, R. and S. Begeer (2000), *Artificial Intelligence: Critical Concepts*, London: Routledge.

Christian, B. (2020), *The Alignment Problem: Machine Learning and Human Values*, 1st edn, New York: W. W. Norton & Company.

Cobbe, J. and J. Singh (2020), 'Reviewable automated decision-making', *Computer Law & Security Review*, **39**, 105475.

Coeckelbergh, M. (2020), *AI Ethics*, Cambridge, MA: MIT Press.

Cohen, J. E. (2018), 'The biopolitical public domain: The legal construction of the surveillance economy', *Philosophy & Technology*, **31** (2), 213–33.

Collington, R. (2022), 'Disrupting the welfare state? Digitalisation and the retrenchment of public sector capacity', *New Political Economy*, **27** (2), 312–28.

Côté-Boucher, K., (2020), *Border Frictions: Gender, Generation and Technology on the Frontline*. London: Routledge.

Couldry, N. and U. A. Mejias (2019), *The Costs of Connection: How Data Is Colonizing Human Life and Appropriating It for Capitalism*, Stanford, CA: Stanford University Press.

Couldry, N. and U. A. Mejias (2021), 'The decolonial turn in data and technology research: What is at stake and where is it heading?', *Information, Communication & Society*, FirstOnline.

Crawford, K. (2021), *Atlas of AI: The Real Worlds of Artificial Intelligence*, New Haven, CT: Yale University Press.

Dauvergne, P. (2020), *AI in the Wild: Sustainability in the Age of Artificial Intelligence*. Cambridge, MA: MIT Press.

Dauvergne, P. (2022), 'Is artificial intelligence greening global supply chains? Exposing the political economy of environmental costs', *Review of International Political Economy*, **29** (3), 696–718.

de Freitas Boullosa, R., R. Paul and T. Smith-Carrier (2023), 'Democratizing science is an urgent, collective, and continuous project: Expanding the boundaries of critical policy studies', *Critical Policy Studies*, **17** (1), 1–3.

Dencik, L., A. Hintz, J. Redden and E. Treré (2019), 'Exploring data justice: Conceptions, applications and directions', *Information, Communication & Society*, **22** (7), 873–81.

Dencik, L. and A. Kaun (2020), 'Datafication and the Welfare State', *Global Perspectives*, **1** (1), 12912, accessed at https://doi.org/10.1525/gp.2020.12912.

Dencik, L., A. Hintz, J. Redden and E. Treré (2022), *Data Justice*. London: Sage.

Desrosières, A. (2002), *The Politics of Large Numbers – A History of Statistical Reasoning*, Cambridge, MA: Harvard University Press.

Dubber, M. D., F. Pasquale and S. Das (eds) (2020), *The Oxford Handbook of Ethics of AI*, Oxford and New York: Oxford University Press.

Dubois, V. (2009), 'Towards a critical policy ethnography: lessons from fieldwork on welfare control in France', *Critical Policy Studies*, **3** (2), 221–39.

Elish, M. C. (2019), 'Moral crumple zones: Cautionary tales in human-robot interaction' (pre-print), *SSRN Research Papers*, accessed at https://doi.org/10.2139/ssrn.2757236.

Engstrom, D. F., D. E. Ho, C. M. Sharkey and M.-F. Cuéllar (2020), *Government by Algorithm: Artificial Intelligence in Federal Administrative Agencies*, Stanford, CA: Administrative Conference of the United States, accessed 18 May 2021 at https://www-cdn.law.stanford.edu/wp-content/uploads/2020/02/ACUS-AI-Report.pdf.

Eubanks, V. (2018), *Automating Inequality: How High-Tech Tools Profile, Police, and Punish the Poor*, New York: St. Martin's Press.

European Commission (2018a), *Communication on Artificial Intelligence for Europe*, COM(2018) 237 final, accessed at https://eur-lex.europa.eu/legal-content/EN/TXT/PDF/?uri=CELEX:52018DC0237 &from=EN.

European Commission (2018b), *Coordinated Plan on Artificial Intelligence*, COM(2018) 795 final, accessed at https://ec.europa.eu/info/sites/info/files/5._h2020_ethics_and_data_protection.pdf.

European Commission (2020), *White Paper on Artificial Intelligence – A European Approach to Excellence and Trust*, COM(2020) 65 final, accessed at https://op.europa.eu/o/opportal-service/ download-handler?identifier=ac957f13-53c6-11ea-aece-01aa75ed71a1&format=pdf&language=en& productionSystem=cellar&part=.

European Data Protection Board (2019), *Facial Recognition in School Renders Sweden's First GDPR Fine*, accessed 24 October 2023 at https://edpb.europa.eu/news/national-news/2019/facial-recognition -school-renders-swedens-first-gdpr-fine_sv.

Ferguson, A. G. (2017), *The Rise of Big Data Policing: Surveillance, Race, and the Future of Law Enforcement*, New York: NYU Press.

Firlej, M. and A. Taeihagh (2021), 'Regulating human control over autonomous systems', *Regulation & Governance*, **15** (4), 1071–91, accessed at https://doi.org/10.1111/rego.12344.

Fischer, F., D. Torgerson, A. Durnová and M. Orsini (2015), 'Introduction to critical policy studies', *Handbook of Critical Policy Studies*, Cheltenham, UK and Northampton, MA, USA: Edward Elgar Publishing, pp. 1–24, accessed 29 November 2021 at https://www.elgaronline.com/view/edcoll/ 9781783472345/9781783472345.00005.xml.

Floridi, L., J. Cowls, T. C. King and M. Taddeo (2021), 'How to design AI for social good: Seven essential factors', in L. Floridi (ed.), *Ethics, Governance, and Policies in Artificial Intelligence*, Cham, Switzerland: Springer International Publishing, pp. 125–51.

Fourcade, M. and J. Gordon (2020), 'Learning like a state: Statecraft in the digital age', *Journal of Law and Political Economy*, **1** (1), 78–108.

Fussell, S. (2022), 'Dystopian robot dogs are the latest in a long history of US-Mexico border surveillance', *The Guardian*, 16 February, accessed 28 March 2022 at https://www.theguardian.com/us -news/2022/feb/16/robot-dogs-us-mexico-border-surveillance-technology.

Gitelman, L. (ed.) (2013), *'Raw Data' is an Oxymoron*, Cambridge, MA: MIT Press.

Gray, C. (2023), 'More than extraction: Rethinking data's colonial political economy', *International Political Sociology*, **17** (2), olad007.

Green, B., (2022), 'The flaws of policies requiring human oversight of government algorithms', *Computer Law & Security Review*, **45**, 105681.

Haenlein, M. and A. Kaplan (2019), 'A brief history of artificial intelligence: On the past, present, and future of artificial intelligence', *California Management Review*, **61** (4), 5–14.

Hacking, I. 1995. 'The looping effects of humankinds', in D. Sperber, D. Premack and A. Premack (eds), *Causal Cognition: A Multidisciplinary Debate*. Symposia of the Fyssen Foundation. Oxford: Clarendon Press, pp. 351–83.

Hao, K. (2019), 'An AI start-up has found a new source of cheap labour for training algorithms', *MIT Technology Review*, 29 March. https://www.technologyreview.com/2019/03/29/136262/an-ai-startup -has-found-a-new-source-of-cheap-labor-for-training-algorithms/. Last accessed 2 November 2023.

Hao, K. and D. Seetharanam (2023), Cleaning up ChatGPT takes heavy toll on human workers', *Wall Street Journal*, 24 July. https://www.wsj.com/articles/chatgpt-openai-content-abusive-sexually -explicit-harassment-kenya-workers-on-human-workers-cf191483. Last accessed 2 November 2023.

Henriques-Gomes, L. (2021), 'Robodebt: Court approves $1.8bn settlement for victims of government's "shameful" failure', *The Guardian*, 11 June, accessed 14 March 2022 at https://www .theguardian.com/australia-news/2021/jun/11/robodebt-court-approves-18bn-settlement-for-victims -of-governments-shameful-failure.

Hood, C. (1991), 'A public management for all seasons?', *Public Administration*, **69** (1), 3–19.

Human Rights Watch (2019), *Submission to the UN Special Rapporteur on Extreme Poverty & Human Rights Regarding His Thematic Report on Digital Technology, Social Protection & Human Rights|Human Rights Watch*, accessed 24 October 2023 at https://www.hrw.org/news/2019/05/21/ submission-un-special-rapporteur-extreme-poverty-human-rights-regarding-his.

Irani, L. (2015), 'Difference and dependence among digital workers: The case of Amazon Mechanical Turk', *South Atlantic Quarterly*, **114** (1), 225–34.

Işın, E. and Ruppert, E. (2019), 'Data's empire: Postcolonial data politics', in D. Bigo, E. Işın, and E. Ruppert (eds), *Data Politics: Worlds, Subjects, Rights*, Abingdon, UK and New York: Routledge, pp. 207–28.

Jasanoff, S. (2016), *The Ethics of Invention: Technology and the Human Future*, New York: W. W. Norton & Co.

Jasanoff, S. and S.-H. Kim (2013), 'Sociotechnical imaginaries and national energy policies', *Science as Culture*, **22** (2), 189–96.

Jones, M. L. (2015), 'The ironies of automation law: Tying policy knots with fair automation practices principles', SSRN Scholarly Paper ID 2549285, Rochester, NY: Social Science Research Network, pp. 1–46, 13 January.

Kaplan, A. and M. Haenlein (2019), 'Siri, Siri, in my hand: Who's the fairest in the land? On the interpretations, illustrations, and implications of artificial intelligence', *Business Horizons*, **62** (1), 15–25, accessed at https://doi.org/10.1016/J.BUSHOR.2018.08.004.

Katzenbach, C. and L. Ulbricht (2019), 'Algorithmic governance', *Internet Policy Review*, **8** (4), accessed 10 November 2020 at https://policyreview.info/concepts/algorithmic-governance.

Kaufmann, M., S. Egbert and M. Leese (2019), 'Predictive policing and the politics of patterns', *The British Journal of Criminology*, **59** (3), 674–92.

Koulish, R. and K. Evans, (2021), Punishing with impunity: The legacy of risk classification assessment in immigration detention, *Georgetown Immigration Law Journal*, **36** (1), 1–178.

Krafft, T. D., K. A. Zweig and P. D. Koenig (2022), 'How to regulate algorithmic decision-making: A framework of regulatory requirements for different applications', *Regulation & Governance*, **16** (1), 119–36.

Kwet, M. (2019), 'Digital colonialism: US empire and the new imperialism in the Global South', *Race & Class*, **60** (4), 3–26.

Lasswell, H. D. (1970), 'The emerging conception of the policy sciences', *Policy Sciences*, **1** (1970), 3–14.

Law, J. and E. Ruppert (eds) (2016), *Modes of Knowing: Resources from the Baroque*. Manchester: Mattering Press.

Lee, F. (2021), 'Enacting the pandemic: Analyzing agency, opacity, and power in algorithmic assemblages', *Science & Technology Studies*, **34** (1), 65–90.

Leese, M. (2014), 'The new profiling: Algorithms, black boxes, and the failure of anti-discriminatory safeguards in the European Union', *Security Dialogue*, **45** (5), 494–511.

Lewis, P., S. March and J. Pitt (2021), 'AI vs "AI": Synthetic minds or speech acts', *IEEE Technology and Society Magazine*, June, accessed at https://ieeexplore.ieee.org/stamp/stamp.jsp?tp=&arnumber=9445758.

Lindgren, S. (ed.) (2023), *Handbook of Critical Studies of Artificial Intelligence*, Cheltenham, UK and Northampton, MA, USA: Edward Elgar Publishing.

Majone, G. (2010), 'Strategic issues in risk regulation and risk management', in *OECD Reviews of Regulatory Reform*, Organisation for Economic Co-operation and Development, pp. 93–128.

Mann, L. (2018), 'Left to other peoples' devices? A political economy perspective on the big data revolution in development', *Development and Change*, **49** (1), 3–36.

Mantelero, A. (2016), 'Personal data for decisional purposes in the age of analytics: From an individual to a collective dimension of data protection', *Computer Law & Security Review*, **32** (2), 238–55.

Miceli, M., M. Schuessler and Yang, T. (2020), Between subjectivity and imposition: Power dynamics in data annotation for computer vision. *Proceedings of the ACM on Human-Computer Interaction*, **4** (CSCW2), pp. 1–25

Molnar, P. and L. Gill (2018), *Bots at the Gate. A Human Rights Analysis of Automated Decision-Making in Canada's Immigration and Refugee System*, University of Toronto, accessed at https://citizenlab.ca/wp-content/uploads/2018/09/IHRP-Automated-Systems-Report-Web-V2.pdf.

Mügge, D. (2023), 'The securitization of the EU's digital tech regulation', *Journal of European Public Policy*, **30** (7), 1431–46.

Padden, M. and A. Öjehag-Pettersson (2021), 'Protected how? Problem representations of risk in the General Data Protection Regulation (GDPR)', *Critical Policy Studies*, **15** (4), 486–503.

Pasquale, F. (2015), *The Black Box Society: The Secret Algorithms that Control Money and Information*, Cambridge, MA: Harvard University Press.

Pasquale, F. (2016), 'Two narratives of platform capitalism', *Yale Law and Policy Review*, **35**, 309–19.

Paul, R. (2021), *Varieties of Risk Analysis in Public Administrations*, London: Routledge.

Paul, R. (2022), 'Can critical policy studies outsmart AI? Research agenda on artificial intelligence technologies and public policy', *Critical Policy Studies*, **16** (4), 497–509.

Paul, R. (2023), 'European AI "trusted throughout the world": How risk-based regulation fashions a competitive common market for artificial intelligence', *Regulation & Governance*, First online, https://doi.org/10.1111/REGO.12563.

Peeters, R. and A. C. Widlak (2023), 'Administrative exclusion in the infrastructure-level bureaucracy: The case of the Dutch daycare benefit scandal', *Public Administration Review*, **83** (4), 863–77, accessed at https://doi.org/10.1111/puar.13615.

Petit, N. (2020), *Big Tech and the Digital Economy: The Moligopoly Scenario*, Oxford: Oxford University Press.

Pistor, K. (2020), 'Statehood in the digital age', *Constellations*, **27** (1), 3–18.

Porter, T. M. (1995), *Trust in Numbers. The Pursuit of Objectivity in Science and Public Life*, Princeton, NJ: Princeton University Press.

Posada, J. (2022), 'Embedded reproduction in platform data work', *Information, Communication & Society*, **25** (6), 816–34.

Posner, E. A. (2001), 'Controlling agencies with cost-benefit analysis: A positive political theory perspective', *University of Chicago Law Review*, **68**, 1137–200.

Raji, I. D., I. E. Kumar, A. Horowitz and A. Selbst (2022), 'The fallacy of AI functionality', in *Proceedings of the 2022 ACM Conference on Fairness, Accountability, and Transparency*, New York: Association for Computing Machinery, pp. 959–72.

Rankin, J. L. (2018), *A People's History of Computing in the United States*, illustrated edition, Cambridge, MA: Harvard University Press.

Redden, J., L. Dencik and H. Warne (2020), 'Datafied child welfare services: Unpacking politics, economics and power', *Policy Studies*, **41** (5), 507–26.

Rider, K. A. (2021), 'Volunteering the Valley: Designing technology for the common good in the San Francisco Bay Area', PhD, Canada: Queen's University (Canada), accessed 11 April 2022 at https://www.proquest.com/docview/2600709833/abstract/A6DAB24997E84564PQ/1.

Sandhu, A. and P. Fussey (2021), 'The "uberization of policing"? How police negotiate and operationalise predictive policing technology', *Policing and Society*, **31** (1), 66–81.

Satariano, A. (2020), 'British grading debacle shows pitfalls of automating government', *The New York Times*, 20 August, accessed 4 March 2022 at https://www.nytimes.com/2020/08/20/world/europe/uk-england-grading-algorithm.html.

Selten, F., M. Robeer and S. Grimmelikhuijsen (2023), '"Just like I thought": Street-level bureaucrats trust AI recommendations if they confirm their professional judgment', *Public Administration Review*, **83** (2), 263–78.

Shore, C. and S. Wright (eds) (1997), *Anthropology of Policy: Perspectives on Governance and Power*, London: Routledge.

Shore, C., S. Wright and D. Però (2011), *Policy Worlds: Anthropology and the Analysis of Contemporary Power*, New York: Berghahn Books.

Simonite, T. (2021), 'Face recognition is being banned – but it's still everywhere', *Wired*, 22 December, accessed 24 October 2023 at https://www.wired.com/story/face-recognition-banned-but-everywhere/.

Singh, R. and S. Jackson (2021), 'Seeing like an infrastructure: Low-resolution citizens and the Aadhaar Identification Project', *Proceedings of the ACM on Human-Computer Interaction*, **5** (CSCW2), 315:1–315:26.

Smuha, N. A. (2021a), 'Beyond the individual: Governing AI's societal harm', *Internet Policy Review*, **10** (3), accessed 14 May 2023 at https://policyreview.info/articles/analysis/beyond-individual-governing-ais-societal-harm.

Smuha, N. A. (2021b), 'From a "race to AI" to a "race to AI regulation": Regulatory competition for artificial intelligence', *Law, Innovation and Technology*, **13** (1), 1–28.

Statista (2023), 'Projected electronic waste generation worldwide from 2019 to 2030', at https://www.statista.com/statistics/1067081/generation-electronic-waste-globally-forecast/. Last accessed 2 November 2023.

Stone, D. (2012), *Policy Paradox: The Art of Political Decision Making*, New York: W. W. Norton & Co.

Stone, D. (2020), *Counting: How We Use Numbers to Decide What Matters*, New York: Norton.

Strubell, E., A. Ganesh and A. McCallum (2020), 'Energy and policy considerations for modern deep learning research', *Proceedings of the AAAI Conference on Artificial Intelligence*, **34** (9), 13693–96.

Sunstein, C. R. (2002), *Risk and Reason: Safety, Law, and the Environment*, Cambridge: Cambridge University Press.

Tamburrini, G. (2022), 'The AI carbon footprint and responsibilities of AI scientists', *Philosophies*, **7** (1), 4.

The Critical Infrastructure Collective (2022), 'Infrastructures, processes of insertion and the everyday: Towards a new dialogue in critical policy studies', *Critical Policy Studies*, **16** (1), 121–30.

Tréguer, F. (2019), 'Seeing like big tech: Security assemblages, technology, and the future of state bureaucracy', in D. Bigo, E. Işın, and E. Ruppert (eds), *Data Politics: Worlds, Subjects, Rights*, Abingdon, UK and New York: Routledge, pp. 145–64.

UNICEF (2021), *Policy Guidance on AI for Children*, accessed at https://www.unicef.org/globalinsight/media/2356/file/UNICEF-Global-Insight-policy-guidance-AI-children-2.0-2021.pdf.

United Nations (2022), *Report of the Special Rapporteur on the Rights of Persons with Disabilities on Artificial Intelligence and the Rights of Persons with Disabilities*, New York: UN, accessed at https://www.ohchr.org/en/calls-for-input/2021/report-special-rapporteur-rights-persons-disabilities-artificial-intelligence.

US Citizenship and Immigration Services (2018), *Meet Emma, Our Virtual Assistant*, accessed 23 March 2022 at https://www.uscis.gov/tools/meet-emma-our-virtual-assistant.

van Wynsberghe, A. (2021), 'Sustainable AI: AI for sustainability and the sustainability of AI', *AI and Ethics*, **1** (3), 213–18.

Veale, M. and I. Brass (2019), 'Administration by algorithm? Public management meets public sector machine learning', in K. Yeung and M. Lodge (eds), *Algorithmic Regulation*, Oxford and New York: Oxford University Press, pp. 121–49.

Wagenaar, H. (2012), 'Dwellers on the threshold of practice: The interpretivism of Bevir and Rhodes', *Critical Policy Studies*, **6** (1), 85–99.

Wagenaar, H. and S. D. N. Cook (2003), 'Understanding policy practices: Action, dialectic and deliberation in policy analysis', in M. A. Hajer and H. Wagenaar (eds), *Deliberative Policy Analysis: Understanding Governance in the Network Society*, Cambridge: Cambridge University Press, pp. 139–71.

Winner, L. (1980), 'Do artifacts have politics?', *Daedalus*, **109** (1), 121–36.

Wood, A. J., M. Graham, V. Lehdonvirta and I. Hjorth (2019), 'Good gig, bad gig: Autonomy and algorithmic control in the global gig economy', *Work, Employment and Society*, **33** (1), 56–75.

Yanow, D. and P. Schwartz-Shea (eds) (2006), *Interpretation and Method. Empirical Research Methods and the Interpretive Turn*, New York: M.E. Sharpe.

Yeung, K. (2019), 'Why worry about decision-making by machine?', in K. Yeung and M. Lodge (eds), *Algorithmic Regulation*, Oxford and New York: Oxford University Press, pp. 21–48.

Yeung, K. (2023), 'The new public analytics as an emerging paradigm in public sector administration', *Tilburg Law Review*, **27** (2), 1–32.

Young, M., M. Katell and P. M. Krafft (2022), 'Confronting power and corporate capture at the FAccT Conference', *Proceedings of the 2022 ACM Conference on Fairness, Accountability, and Transparency*, pp. 1375–86. https://dl.acm.org/doi/abs/10.1145/3491102.3517672.

Ziewitz, M. (2016), 'Governing algorithms: Myth, mess, and methods', *Science, Technology, & Human Values*, **41** (1), 3–16.

Zuboff, S. (2019), *The Age of Surveillance Capitalism: The Fight for a Human Future at the New Frontier of Power*, 1st edn, New York: PublicAffairs.

PART I

AI AND PUBLIC POLICY: CHALLENGES TO KEY CONCEPTS

2. Researching the politics of automated systems of governing: a thematic review

Andreas Öjehag-Pettersson, Vanja Carlsson and Malin Rönnblom

INTRODUCTION

In this chapter we present a broad overview of research on what we call the politics of *automated systems of governing* (ASG). As pointed out in the Introduction to this *Handbook*, how we approach and conceptualize the presence of various new forms of information technology in the public sector is not an innocent endeavour. Rather, such conceptualization is important in setting up a vantage point for critical inquiry, since how we make sense of the ontological and epistemological qualities of these new technologies shapes the questions we find most important to raise.

In our case then, we define ASG as the enlisting of algorithms, artificial intelligence (AI), machine learning (ML) and various utilizations of so-called "big data" with the purpose of controlling, directing, steering or guiding something or someone. In other words, ASG are instruments that govern through recent developments in computer technology. Moreover, for us, ASG cannot be understood as neutral instruments that simply "solve" objective problems in the public sector. Instead, in line with what is labelled "socio-technical understandings" (see Paul, Carmel and Cobbe, in the Introduction to this volume), we view them as governmental technologies, which are simultaneously produced by and (re)produce certain political rationalities, not least, prevailing modes of neoliberal governing. Indeed, we argue that treating ASG as non-political is itself a political position.

Nevertheless, while research that recognizes ASG as political instruments is starting to take off, our studies show that the field in general is dominated by works that take a techno-functionalist approach to understanding these systems (Öjehag-Pettersson et al. 2023). Even when we explicitly search for political studies of ASG, by far the most common approach is to view them as part of rational problem-solving and as solutionist decision aids (on apolitical discussions of AIT regulation, see also Mark, McInerney and Morison, Chapter 25 and Paul, Chapter 20 in this volume). Therefore, given how we understand ASG, we argue that it is important to sift through the exponentially growing literature in order to take stock of how scholars actually approach them as political instruments. We are not aware of any larger, systematic takes on the context of such studies in terms of empirical and theoretical themes and topics. Moreover, while it is one thing to recognize ASG as political, there is of course a wide variety of understandings of what "political" actually means among critical scholars as well.

With these points in mind, the purpose of this chapter is twofold. On the one hand we wish to take stock of the literature that treats ASG as political phenomena. We seek to illustrate its context in terms of themes and topics and investigate it in terms of its possible concentration or diversity. On the other hand, we also aim to discuss theoretically the different ways in which this literature treats ASG as political. To this end, we discuss selected parts of a larger study in which we analyzed 1,667 peer-reviewed articles dealing with "politics" in relation to AI, big data and algorithms. We begin with a short description of the analytical process before we move to present seven major themes in this body of research. Finally, we conclude by drawing on the illustrations of research as distributed over the seven themes in order to theorize how politics is articulated by researchers in this context as a dimension relating to ontology, epistemology and ideology.

ANALYTICAL PROCESS: SELECTING, INTERPRETING AND SUMMARIZING RESEARCH ON ASG

The starting point for what we present here is a large corpus of scholarly work that we constructed with the help of specific search strings in the Scopus database. These were originally designed to find all published books, book chapters and articles that included "algorithms", "big data" or "artificial intelligence" in combination with different stems of "politics" in the titles, keywords or abstracts of works listed in the database. Later, we also performed searches with additional keywords in order to capture terms that have become relatively established in different fields and social science disciplines when studying the political effects of ASG. These include, but are not limited to: "automated decision making" (ADM), "robotic process automation" (RPA) "data-driven governance" and "autonomous weapons". Adding such terms made very little difference to the end search result and we felt confident that our search strings managed to capture most of the works we aimed to find.

Our searches were limited to the social sciences as defined by Scopus, and the results include publications from as far back as 1941 up to 2021. That being said, out of the 1,667 texts that formed our corpus, only a few scattered ones were published before 2011, indicating how research on ASG is a new and emerging field. From this point we started a selection process. We read all 1,667 abstracts and made quick scans of the articles in order to ensure that politics or "the political" were used as analytical concepts with respect to ASG. Specifically, this meant that the authors would have to articulate the political dimensions of ASG rather than apply or draw on algorithms, AI or big data as methodological tools for analyzing political phenomena, which turned out to be a frequently used approach. In the end, only about 16 per cent, or 267 articles could be said to analyze ASG as political phenomena, a finding that we argue indicates that techno-functionalist approaches to ASG often found in policy also dominates research.

We then moved on with these 267 texts and started a more fine-tuned analytical work. Based on the abstracts and additional broad-brush coding of the texts, we performed a qualitative content analysis. As part of this, we approached the texts with a number of codes that we expected to be important for understanding the development of the field such as "approach", "methods" and "theories". The major work, however, was an inductive coding through which we assigned any number of what we call "topics" for each text. Such topics were simple labels for what the article was about empirically as well as theoretically. After coding the 267 articles this way, we used the topics to build themes and sub-themes that represent salient groupings of research which engages with ASG as political phenomena.

We argue that this process allows us to take stock of the literature and discuss the different contexts of ASG with respect to themes and topics, which we have articulated as our first purpose of this text. In order to be able to further address our second aim, we also selected a set of articles for each theme that we used as a basis for a thorough and nuanced reading that would allow for a more precise understanding of how scholars understand ASG as political. Those texts were strategically selected as "influential", based on the number of citations and publication year. This is certainly not a perfect way of defining influence, yet it was nevertheless the most readily available means of selecting articles, so we chose to proceed with it. Additionally, however, we included a number of more recent texts to account for possible emerging new discussions and ways of working with politics and ASG.

Before moving on to the next section a caveat is necessary. We conducted the analysis almost solely using academic peer-reviewed articles in our corpus. While a few book chapters were easily accessible and were retained, several were not available to us as electronic copies. Likewise, monographs were even harder to access as electronic versions and, in the end, we decided not to include them. We recognize that some of the most influential publications on the politics of ASG have been made in book form and the fact that they are missing here is something that should be kept in mind.

RESEARCH ON THE POLITICS OF AUTOMATED SYSTEMS OF GOVERNING

In this section we present our analysis of the research articles that treat ASG as *political* instruments. The main focus here is to illustrate the topics and themes through which this research makes sense of ASG. Later, in the concluding section we provide a further elaboration of how the concept of politics is articulated across themes and topics. To start with, Table 2.1 below summarizes the seven major themes that we reconstructed from our reading of the research.

As can be seen from the overview in Table 2.1, the seven themes vary in terms of how many articles have been coded to them. However, they are not primarily reconstructed on that basis, but rather we determined their saliency using qualitative interpretation of, among other things, their intensity of expression, their consistency across the corpus as well as reflexive discussion and consideration among the three of us. Furthermore, the themes are not mutually exclusive. Many articles have been coded under more than one theme and in particular theme 7, *The digital and technological development*, stands out. On the one hand we argue that there is a distinct stream of research that focuses precisely on technological development, evolution and innovation that theorizes technology as a social phenomenon in relation to ASG; however, at the same time, given the searches we made, most articles even with a different primary focus, also concern this theme secondarily. Thus, there is a significant overlap between this and other themes.

In Table 2.2 we cross tabulate the themes with our coding for how researchers *approach* the study of ASG as political. The different approaches account for about a third of the research each, however, there are differences among the themes. Some of the explanation for these different distributions are rather straightforward. For example, it is not surprising that the theme of analytical categories, concepts and theories is leaning towards theoretical articles. At the same time, we can nevertheless speak of some areas as more empirically oriented than others, and perhaps it would be a good idea for scholars to look for inspiring examples in themes that they usually do not work within. Indeed, the call for more empirical studies is also a common reference point for many researchers who argue that empirical studies of algorithms, AI or ML

Table 2.1   Themes, sub-themes and topics in the corpus

	Theme	Sub-theme	Topic examples	Articles
1.	Analytical categories, concepts and theories	1a. Methods 1b. Philosophical concepts 1c. Social concepts	Epistemology, ontology, methodology, ethics, aesthetics, affect, self, citizenship, feminism, the political, race and racism	95
2.	Capitalism, labour and industry	2a. Economy and finance 2b. System of production	Bitcoin, High Frequency Trading (HFT), financial markets, political economy, gig-economy, capitalism	42
3.	Governance, political organization and democracy	Not applicable	Democracy, policy, governance, public administration, smart cities, urban and regional development, marketization, legal frameworks, IR, decision-making	87
4.	Health, education and culture	Not applicable	Children, education, food, health, farming, science fiction, medicine, psychology	26
5.	Internet and online activities	Not applicable	Platforms, Google, Fake news, digital media, social media, news selection, filter bubble, deepfake	55
6.	Security and surveillance	Not applicable	Crime and police, hacking, security, terrorism, autonomous weapons, war, social control, surveillance, harassment	44
7.	The digital and technological development	7a. Technology as a social phenomenon 7b. Technological tools	Big data, calculation, data mining, prediction, algorithms, AI, robots, automation, bots, digital archives, dataveillance,	179
	TOTAL			528

Note: Each article can be coded to more than one theme, thus the total number of tallies is larger than the total number of articles (n = 254).

really require methodological development and ways to move past certain hurdles (particularly access to and understanding of code). This interpretation is also supported by the prevalence of the category *discussion* in our corpus. These were texts where researchers did use some empirical grounding in the form of well-known examples or secondary data, however, they did not use data originally generated for the purpose of their own research. Moving forward, we now turn to a more detailed description of each of the seven themes based on our qualitative analysis of the articles in our corpus.

Theme 1: Analytical Categories, Concepts and Theories

This theme represents a strand of the literature that primarily revolves around conceptualizing what ASG "really are", how they can be understood and why they are important to study in the first place. To this end, scholars in this theme mobilize and develop analytical categories and theories that can help us "deal with the ambiguity of algorithms as analytical objects" (Ziewitz 2016, p. 11). In our analysis we reconstructed this theme by starting out with what later became three sub-themes. First, we recognized how researchers were drawing on what we label philosophical concepts (i.e., relating to being, becoming or ethical frameworks) to discuss the nature of ASG; second, how other articles focused on social concepts in relation to ASG (i.e., relating to power, ideology or governance); and third, how some scholars discussed methodological concerns with respect to how we may approach ASG in empirical studies (cf. Crawford 2016; Introna & Wood 2004; Kitchin 2017).

Table 2.2   *Themes and approach*

Theme	Approach			Total
	Discussion	Empirical	Theoretical	
Analytical categories, concepts	29	27	39	95
and theories	(0.31)	(0.28)	(0.41)	(1.00)
Capitalism, labor and industry	9	18	15	42
	(0.21)	(0.43)	(0.36)	(1.00)
Governance, political	32	34	20	86
organization and democracy	(0.37)	(0.40)	(0.23)	(1.00)
Health, education and culture	11	10	5	26
	(0.42)	(0.38)	(0.19)	(0.99)
Internet and online activities	17	23	15	55
	(0.31)	(0.42)	(0.27)	(1.00)
Security and surveillance	11	21	12	44
	(0.25)	(0.48)	(0.27)	(1.00)
The digital and technological	57	59	63	179
development	(0.32)	(0.33)	(0.35)	(1.00)
TOTAL	166	192	169	527
	(0.31)	(0.36)	(0.32)	(0.99)

Note: Figures represent the total number of articles coded to combinations of theme and approach. Each article can be coded to more than one theme, thus the total number of tallies is larger than the total number of articles (n = 254).

For instance, in her work with the social platform and community site Reddit, Adrienne Massanari (2015) showed how feminist analysis and concepts can help understand how ASG intertwine with what she labels "toxic technocultures". This particular expression of "geek culture" and "geek masculinity" is intimately related to the sorting algorithms that govern the popular site, and thus, among other things, Massanari's study shows how social concepts with their roots in feminist theory can be vital for understanding how ASG work in practice. Similarly, Introna (2016) draws on feminist concepts, governmentality and STS-reasoning as he investigates the algorithmic system *Turnitin* which is designed to uncover plagiarism among student essays and academic research papers. His analysis, showing how this system introduced a range of governing effects such as new subjectivities for students and teachers, is another example of how social and political concepts can be used to unearth insights about the politics of ASG.

   In Kate Crawford's (2016) work, philosophical notions and political theory occupy centre stage as she investigates if and how algorithms can be agonistic, drawing on political theorist Chantal Mouffe (e.g., 2013). For Crawford (2016, p. 78), and many other papers that we coded under this theme, the explicit focus and interest concerns to what extent, and how, we can "speak of a politics of algorithms". By working through ten different "scenes" that show contemporary, everyday instances of algorithms at work in society in spectacular as well as mundane ways, Crawford (2016) illustrates how social, philosophical and methodological concepts are crucial for understanding how ASG function as political devices in practice.

Theme 2: Capitalism, Labour and Industry

Here we identified a set of articles that share specific commonalities in that they primarily seek to understand how the emergence of ASG is linked to the capitalist system with its distinct ways of framing labour, industrial development and innovation. We reconstructed this theme by combining what were originally two separate sub-themes in our qualitative analysis. The first centres on economy and finance where scholars theorize the role and impact of ASG with respect to for instance the stock market, various trading practices as well as cryptocurrencies and payment technologies relying on so-called blockchains for security (cf. MacKenzie 2017). The second sub-theme revolves around aspects of working life, labour politics and the future horizons of industrial development such as the frequently mentioned fourth industrial revolution (4IR).

A prominent example of the types of questions that are being asked in papers under this theme is the work of Astrid Mager (2012) on search engines. In this oft-cited paper, she connects the functions of what is now an everyday practice for most humans – the Google search – with capitalist ideology by focusing on understanding how the search engine facilitates the more important business of extracting data, aligning advertisement and understanding user behaviour. Her empirical study draws on interviews with 17 engineers, software developers, programmers and other people working closely with the production of search engines. Based on this she argues that what makes Google a good example of the "new spirit of capitalism" is that it showcases how "techno-fundamentalist ideology gets aligned with capitalist ideology and the exploitation schemes of the 'connexionist' world" (Mager 2012, p. 782). By ideology Mager (2012) draws on what resembles neo-Marxist accounts. Thus, the capitalist ideology that frames and gives meaning to ASG such as the search engine is "a set of shared beliefs, inscribed in institutions, bound up with actions, and hence anchored in reality" (Mager 2012, p. 773). Therefore, she argues, to understand how ASG enables new forms of exploitation and affects power relations, it is important to study the social practices that tie different groups and discourses together and fuse them with seemingly benign algorithms.

In addition to analyzing such ideological entanglement in ASG, the papers under this theme also stress how critical scholars should pay more attention to exactly what kind of instruments ASG are and how they run on "data". Indeed, following Pasquinelli (2014, p. 63) ASG can be understood as "machines of the information age", or in other words "a machine for the control, accumulation, circulation and augmentation of surplus value". There are also echoes of such descriptions in more detailed empirical case studies such as the analysis in Veen, Barrat and Goods (2020) of the ASG and platforms in the new gig economy.

Similarly, Thatcher, O'Sullivan and Mahmoudi (2016) argue that we may view the current era as one marked by a new primitive accumulation. In short, capital is currently able to extract value at extremely low costs, similar to other eras of accumulation by dispossession such as in colonialist times. Moreover, to understand ASG that runs on such data can also require a shift in terms of analyzing how this data is being used. As argued by Sadowski (2019), a common approach is to understand data as a commodity. If we instead analyze and understand its part of ASG and capitalist ideology as capital, one consequence would be that "data collection is thus driven by the perpetual cycle of capital accumulation" (Sadowski 2019, p. 8). Like other forms of capital, the accumulation of data needs no purpose beyond itself. Thus, extracting data can very much be seen as the main purpose of various ASG, again illustrating the overarching concerns of articles coded under this theme, namely how capitalist ideology and mode of production are intertwined with how AI, ML and algorithms are put to work, and therefore vital for understanding their political origins and consequences.

Theme 3: Governance, Political Organization and Democracy

The topics within the theme of governance are many and diverse, including organization, learning, higher education and more. Several scholars are interested in smart cities and urbanism (e.g., Krivý 2018), and there is a focus on the use of digital and algorithmic technology in the organization and coordination of individuals, actors and interests. In addition, research under the theme of governance centres on how algorithmic systems will transform expertise and what is perceived as expertise in an organizational setting. In this sense, Faraj et al. (2018) argue that algorithmic technology is performative and likely to change people's shared conceptions of the social reality and Williamson (2018a) stresses that technological development creates new utopian ideals and imaginaries of "smartness". In a similar vein, issues of control of data and the uneven distribution of knowledge and of technological influence is addressed. This is illustrated by Kemper and Kolkman who state that "[t]here is a significant lack of people who know how to effectively formulate algorithms" (Kemper & Kolkman 2019, p. 2090). This general and widespread lack of knowledge will pave the way for technological experts and data infrastructure owners to gain control at the expense of democratic processes in technological development (e.g., Williamson 2018a). From a public policy perspective, scholars within this theme urge us to critically discuss the effects of digital technology on citizenship, trust and processes of public organizations (e.g., Rabari & Stroper 2015).

The overall governance perspective within the theme comprises two sub-perspectives. One where the focus is on the coordination and governance of actors and organizations, specifically in terms of socio-technical networks, aiming to enforce the marketization of the public sector in the light of technological development. For instance, Williamson (2018b) describes how the building of data infrastructure often requires an entanglement of public and private actors, particularly in the form of consultants and expertise that firmly pushes marketizing practices along with ASG.

Within the other sub-perspective, the relationship between digital technology and the political subject is centre stage, and here, two additional categories emerge; one category focusing on how individuals act, or should act, in order to govern and take control of the technology and technological development, and one focusing on how the technology itself governs and controls the subject and in this sense has significant subjectivizing effects. The latter category is often informed by a Foucauldian and/or Latourian perspective emphasizing how "governing from a distance" shapes the possibilities and limits of actions of individuals and how assemblages of governance practices across state and non-state, public and private spheres are mediated through digital technological systems (Bulkeley et al. 2016).

In other words, the works coded under this theme repeatedly illustrate how marketization, fluid and hybrid public–private governance collaborations as well as socio-technical assemblages are all important dimensions of how ASG operate as political instruments.

Theme 4: Health, Education and Culture

In this theme we gathered a number of distinct and salient topics that revolved around children, education, health, medicine, psychology, agriculture and culture. For instance, there is an influential and ongoing discussion among scholars who analyze science fiction in films, books, games and other media in order to connect such imaginations of ASG in popular culture with the imaginaries that now guide trajectories for actually emerging systems. Along these lines, Rieder and Voelker (2020) engage with popular works of what they label "speculative fiction". They do so in order to analyze how ASG figure as important tropes of surveillance, social sorting, prediction, advertising and corporate power as well as in relation to hubris, breakdown and the end of big data across these works. This kind of analysis, they argue, should not be overlooked in a wider ASG context as "works of fiction can serve as a valuable tool for supporting critical thinking across educational, democratic, and innovation settings – a way to draw people in and stimulate public debate" (Rieder & Voelker 2020, p. 16).

Moreover, works of fiction and cultural artifacts relating to ASG can also be used as points of departure for understanding the encoding of present power orders into works of art, and back. In this way, Sutko (2020) draws on feminist theories to analyze movies where feminized AI personalities are at the centre of the story. He then connects this to the range of actually existing female AI assistants such as Siri, Cortana and Alexa and is able to show how this feminization of AI is a representation of a docile, domesticated woman who can help and nurture, while still being in need of constant attention, care and even updating.

In terms of health, medicine and psychology, the works included in our review focus on, for example: the connection between surveillance and public health in the light of COVID-19 (Couch et al. 2020); the development of psychometrics and the production of a new scalable subject with the help of ASG and social media platforms (Stark 2018); as well as charting discourses of how big data is represented and understood to make epistemological claims in health care (Stevens et al. 2018) (for a deeper discussion of AITs in health care and medicine, see Pot and Prainsack, Chapter 30 in this volume).

For Williamson (2015; 2019) and others the main context is education, particularly higher education. Thus, as part of this theme, researchers highlight how ASG are becoming more common and influential around the globe both for practising higher learning and for envisioning its future. In this regard, ASG can be understood as extensions of already existing infrastructures constituted by "a complex of relations between technical systems, social actors, policies, politics and values" (Williamson 2019, p. 2797). Indeed, in the works analyzed for this review, scholars seem to be in agreement that ASG within the educational sector are particularly entangled with private interests and that, as such, they are important vehicles for the realization of neoliberal modes of governing, even in China (Knox 2020). In sum, while being something of a heterogenous theme, we argue that together the articles we coded here often work with tropes of ASG as the next big thing. In doing so, the studies of science fiction as well as of new developments in medicine and education allow researchers to show how such imaginaries are based on political, rather than neutral, visions of the future.

Theme 5: Internet and Online Activities

The underlying connections between works categorized in this theme concern how algorithms, AI and big data are shaping what we generally refer to as "the internet" and the online practices we carry out there. Thus, we reconstructed the theme from a range of articles dealing with the particular functions of the internet and online activities that are increasingly nested with ASG such as filter bubbles, news selection, platforms, social media and the rise of so called "deepfake" technologies.

Importantly, the way ASG help shape how we interact with the internet, and indeed, how "the web" appears to us in our daily lives involve far-reaching political dimensions. For example, as Jayson Harsin (2015) argues in a theoretically driven and highly cited commentary to this development, the current expressions of our online environments and platforms, in conjunction with the widespread use of ASG in general, help produce regimes of "posttruth" and "postpolitics". Among the scholars in our corpus, this link between new online possibilities, powered by ASG, and a profound shift in terms of how notions of truth and facts can be negotiated is a salient and recurring topic.

In our corpus, scholars are trying to make sense of this transition in various ways, however, many of the texts overlap in their interest in what may broadly be labelled "content moderation" (Gorwa et al. 2020). While ways of moderating how, and under what circumstances, different content should be accessible for users of the internet has been around since its inception, its rapid expansion to billions of sites, repositories and platforms produced a scale of information where automation became needed. Therefore, the current landscape involves sophisticated ASG that help filter, restrict and match the vast terrain that is the internet with respect to individual users in different contexts. In everything from basic Google searches (Gillespie 2017) to selection and sorting of news content (Bucher 2017), in posting and interacting with the most popular social media platforms, as well as on large discussion forums, ASG are actively at work. Many of them are also nested in commercial interests so that the content users encounter has often been made visible through a range of marketing and advertising techniques. According to Gorwa et al. (2020), the three main areas where ASG are hard at work moderating the content of the internet are copyright issues, terrorism and hate speech.

In sum then, the research sorted under this theme points to how the ongoing content moderation, and more generally the production of a segmented and individualized experience of the internet through ASG, involves a number of political dimensions. Not least, these include issues of transparency, justice and, in particular, the depoliticizing practices that render the entire process of *how* we are able to access the internet in the first place as merely a technical issue safe in the hands of experts (cf. Gillespie 2017; Gorwa et al. 2020).

Theme 6: Security and Surveillance

A distinct group of articles among those included in our analysis investigates how ASG have come to be expressed in relation to topics such as crime, policing, terrorism, war, security, hacking and more general forms of surveillance (cf. Bode and Qiao-Franco, Chapter 21, Kaufman, Chapter 22 and Molnar, Chapter 23 all in this volume). These commonalities helped us reconstruct a theme we label as concerning security and surveillance. Scholars articulate the political in slightly different ways in this context, however, they generally refer to a supposedly new situation where the relationship between humans, societies and machines may produce new forms of social control (Amicelle et al. 2015). Along these lines then, researchers who are trying to make sense of politics, surveillance and new technological developments such as big data, AI and algorithmic operations often highlight the performative aspects of the new machines. In doing so, they seek to conceptualize a new reality where surveillance practices are marked by the intertwined agency of humans and ASG. One example of this is Amicelle et al. (2015, p. 298) and their conceptual refashioning of what a device is, or more specifically how "security devices are performative in that they not only enact or alter particular realities and categories depending on the successful stabilization of complex socio-technical configurations, but also draw legal, gender, race or class boundaries and lines of exclusion".

Interestingly, some of the most highly cited works under this theme have in common that they are relatively old. Indeed, while the theme has by no means stopped being relevant in present times, the prevalence of texts from 2011–2015 is high compared to the other themes in our corpus. Thus, it makes sense to view security and surveillance as one of the first themes where scholars started to analyze the political dimensions of ASG. One important reason for this seems to be the so-called war on terror that manifested as a powerful discourse and practice in the aftermath of 9/11 in the first decade of the new millennium.

For example, twenty years before today's rapidly expanding literature, Introna and Wood (2004) made pioneering connections in their Foucauldian and Actor-Network Theory-based study of facial recognition systems and their algorithms. In certain ways they can be said to have paved the way for a range of works to come that explicitly try to connect the field of surveillance studies with the politics of technology and new developments in computers and information systems. Similarly, Louise Amoore's (2009a; 2009b) early work in this context drew on the war on terror to investigate how new security regimes and the wide range of data they build on fashion new visual fields and pre-emptive lines of sight with the aim of visualizing unknown futures. She makes the point that the algorithmic calculations put in motion within these new forms of security regimes bring some of the "warlike architecture" to bare on everyday life. This is not only in the sense that new surveillance technologies are now present throughout airports and similar security checkpoints, but also because they install a certain antagonism in society, "a drawing of the lines between self/other; us/them; safe/risky; inside/outside, that makes going to war possible" (Amoore 2009a, p. 51).

Early insights notwithstanding, research dealing with security and surveillance in relation to ASG has expanded in line with the interest of AI, algorithms and big data in general. Not only has it started to move beyond traditional western contexts as empirical sites (cf. Lim 2017), it has also engaged with critically examining the underlying assumptions among scholars around what data is, how algorithms work and what kind of discourses guide security professionals in their increasingly important roles (Aradau & Blanke 2015).

Theme 7: The Digital and Technological Development

The works that we coded under this theme often draw on examples, including surveillance techniques and social media, as they relate to what we treat as two distinct sub-themes. The first theme included articles that primarily focus on how to understand technology in general, and ASG in particular, as social phenomena. The second is comprised of works that focus on specific tools and instruments that are important in this context, such as bots or digital archives. With respect to these sub-themes scholars are often concerned with a form of demystification of technology and technological development.

For instance, many approaches revolve around the ontological dimension of technology. This means that analytical questions about what technology is and how it should best be understood, conceptualized and named is central to theoretical discussions. In order to demystify the technology, scholars often start by zooming in, identifying and framing the technique itself and then discuss the interrelation between technology and society from a socio-technical perspective. This approach is illustrated by Kitchin who states that algorithms "are best understood as being contingent, ontogenetic and performative in nature, and embedded in wider socio-technical assemblages" (Kitchin 2017, p. 14).

This demystification of the technology also brings researchers to unveil processes in which data is dependent on and intertwined with its social, economic and political context (e.g., Kitchin 2014). As Couldry and Mejias argue, this focus and standpoint "rejects the idea that the continuous collection of data from human beings is natural, let alone rational" rather it is "a commercially motivated form of extraction that advances particular economic and/or governance interests" (Couldry & Mejias 2019, p. 346). Thus, taken together, a common reference point in our corpus is the significance of digital and technological development, evolution and innovation and how scholars need to stay open to the analytical question of what the digital technology is, how it is developed and with what consequences for social life, knowledge production, truth claims and discrimination (boyd & Crawford 2012).

CONCLUDING DISCUSSION: THE POLITICS OF ASG

As we have illustrated, politics in relation to ASG can mean a number of things. However, based on the examples we have used throughout the seven themes, we argue that three main notions of the concept are at work as researchers critically examine ASG. While some of the seven themes can be said to be more or less dominated by one of these three ways of conceiving the political nature of ASG, the different notions cut across the themes and sometimes also sit side by side in the same articles. Thus, the following discussion is more a heuristic device than an attempt to sort all articles into perfect, mutually exclusive categories.

The first way politics figures in the works we have analyzed is in relation to *ontology*. As illustrated, a common denominator for a number of articles is how they try to make sense of what ASG really are. As part of this, they often work with post-structural notions of "the political" (e.g., Mouffe 2013). The political, rather than politics, is then conceived of as a constitutive category of reality. It is the dimension of antagonism that arises in all social formations on account of an indeterminacy of the world and the corresponding attempts of any social order to produce meaning and close the openness of such a world. In relation to ASG, it means that there is no possible way to position them beyond "the political". What they are and how they are currently being installed throughout human societies is the result of different political projects that determine their contingent meaning.

The second way scholars work with politics in relation to ASG is with respect to questions of *epistemology*, or ways of knowing the effects of such systems. To elaborate, many scholars and articles are primarily interested in pointing out various biases, injustices or other effects of power that arise in relation to the increasing presence of ASG in our lives. Therefore, they take as one of their most important tasks the fashioning of theories or methodological tools which allow us to grasp more precisely how, and in what circumstances, ASG may turn out to produce political effects in terms of, for instance, equality and justice. This notion of politics in relation to ASG also has an additional aspect in the sense that, in some instances, the main question is more directly geared towards "knowing the world" through ASG, or in other words what it may mean politically as new systems of governing produce new realities.

The third, and final, notion of the political that we find among scholars working with ASG can be said to relate to ideology and, in particular, capitalist ideology or perhaps the political economy of the new systems. In essence, this notion positions the political as part of the dynamics of the development of capitalism as it moves into what is often understood as a new phase of this global system of production. As in the examples of theme 2 above, scholars who articulate the political along these lines often work with neo-Marxist accounts of ideology in the vein of Gramsci or Althusser.

In sum then, we argue that the burgeoning scholarly works that investigates ASG as political instruments show a wide variety of themes and topics. In terms of how they treat politics, from our perspective, we find what we take to be a productive and varied register of understandings. While there may be clashes between various notions of the politics of ASG, the many possible connections between politics as ontology, epistemology and ideology in this case is a strong argument for critical scholars to look for common grounds as well as to continue working with distinct takes on the political. Moreover, the different ways of articulating the political dimensions of ASG are very much united in their rejection of techno-solutionist claims and ideas. We find this to be important, not only in relation to policy, but also among researchers.

REFERENCES

Amicelle, A., Aradau, C., & Jeandesboz, J., 2015. Questioning security devices: Performativity, resistance, politics. *Security Dialogue* 46, 293–306.

Amoore, L., 2009a. Algorithmic war: Everyday geographies of the war on terror. *Antipode* 41, 49–69.

Amoore, L., 2009b. Lines of sight: On the visualization of unknown futures. *Citizenship Studies* 13, 17–30.

Aradau, C. & Blanke, T., 2015. The (big) data-security assemblage: Knowledge and critique. *Big Data & Society* 2, https://doi.org/10.1177/2053951715609066.

boyd, danah & Crawford, K., 2012. Critical questions for big data. *Information, Communication & Society* 15(5), 662–79.

Bucher, T., 2017. 'Machines don't have instincts': Articulating the computational in journalism. *New Media & Society* 19, 918–33.

Bulkeley, H., McGuirk, P. M., & Dowling, R., 2016. Making a smart city for the smart grid? The urban material politics of actualising smart electricity networks. *Environ Plan A* 48, 1709–26.

Couch, D. L., Robinson, P., & Komesaroff, P. A., 2020. COVID-19 – Extending surveillance and the panopticon. *Bioethical Inquiry* 17, 809–14.

Couldry, N. & Mejias, U. A., 2019. Data colonialism: Rethinking big data's relation to the contemporary subject. *Television & New Media* 20, 336–49.

Crawford, K., 2016. Can an algorithm be agonistic? Ten scenes from life in calculated publics. *Science, Technology, & Human Values* 41, 77–92.

Faraj, S., Pachidi, S., & Sayegh, K., 2018. Working and organizing in the age of the learning algorithm. *Information and Organization* 28, 62–70.

Gillespie, T., 2017. Algorithmically recognizable: Santorum's Google problem, and Google's Santorum problem. *Information, Communication & Society* 20, 63–80.

Gorwa, R., Binns, R., & Katzenbach, C., 2020. Algorithmic content moderation: Technical and political challenges in the automation of platform governance. *Big Data & Society* 7, https://doi.org/10.1177/2053951719897945.

Harsin, J., 2015. Regimes of posttruth, postpolitics, and attention economies. *Communication, Culture & Critique* 8, 327–33.

Introna, L. D., 2016. Algorithms, governance, and governmentality: On governing academic writing. *Science, Technology, & Human Values* 41, 17–49.

Introna, L. D. & Wood, D., 2002. Picturing algorithmic surveillance: The politics of facial recognition systems. *Surveillance & Society* 2, https://doi.org/10.24908/ss.v2i2/3.3373.

Kemper, J. & Kolkman, D., 2019. Transparent to whom? No algorithmic accountability without a critical audience. *Information, Communication & Society* 22, 2081–96.

Kitchin, R., 2014. The real-time city? Big data and smart urbanism. *GeoJournal* 79, 1–14.

Kitchin, R., 2017. Thinking critically about and researching algorithms. *Information, Communication & Society* 20, 14–29.

Knox, J., 2020. Artificial intelligence and education in China. *Learning, Media and Technology* 45, 298–311.

Krivý, M., 2018. Towards a critique of cybernetic urbanism: The smart city and the society of control. *Planning Theory* 17, 8–30.

Lim, M., 2017. Freedom to hate: Social media, algorithmic enclaves, and the rise of tribal nationalism in Indonesia. *Critical Asian Studies* 49, 411–27.

MacKenzie, D., 2017. A material political economy: Automated trading desk and price prediction in high-frequency trading. *Social Studies of Science* 47, 172–94.

Mager, A., 2012. Algorithmic ideology: How capitalist society shapes search engines. *Information, Communication & Society* 15, 769–87.

Massanari, A., 2017. #Gamergate and The Fappening: How Reddit's algorithm, governance, and culture support toxic technocultures. *New Media & Society* 19, 329–46.

Mouffe, C. (2013). *Agonistics: Thinking the World Politically*. London: Verso.

Öjehag-Pettersson, A., Carlssson, V. & Rönnblom, M., 2023. Political studies of automated governing: A bird's eye (re)view. *Regulation & Governance*, 1–16. doi:10.1111/rego.12569.

Pasquinelli, M., 2014. Italian Operaismo and the information machine. *Theory, Culture & Society* 32, 49–68.

Rabari, C. & Storper, M., 2015. The digital skin of cities: Urban theory and research in the age of the sensored and metered city, ubiquitous computing and big data. *Cambridge Journal of Regions, Economy and Society* 8, 27–42.

Rieder, G. & Voelker, T., 2020. Datafictions: Or how measurements and predictive analytics rule imagined future worlds. *Journal of Science Communication* 19, A02.

Sadowski, J., 2019. When data is capital: Datafication, accumulation, and extraction. *Big Data & Society* 6, https://doi.org/10.1177/2053951718820549.

Stark, L., 2018. Algorithmic psychometrics and the scalable subject. *Social Studies of Science* 48, 204–31.

Stevens, M., Wehrens, R., & de Bont, A., 2018. Conceptualizations of big data and their epistemological claims in healthcare: A discourse analysis. *Big Data & Society* 5, https://doi.org/10.1177/2053951718816727.

Sutko, D. M., 2020. Theorizing femininity in artificial intelligence: A framework for undoing technology's gender troubles. *Cultural Studies* 34, 567–92.

Thatcher, J., O'Sullivan, D., & Mahmoudi, D., 2016. Data colonialism through accumulation by dispossession: New metaphors for daily data. *Environment and Planning D* 34, 990–1006.

Veen, A., Barratt, T., & Goods, C., 2020. Platform-capital's 'App-etite' for control: A labour process analysis of food-delivery work in Australia. *Work, Employment and Society* 34, 388–406.

Williamson, B., 2015. Governing software: Networks, databases and algorithmic power in the digital governance of public education. *Learning, Media and Technology* 40, 83–105.

Williamson, B., 2018a. Silicon startup schools: technocracy, algorithmic imaginaries and venture philanthropy in corporate education reform. *Critical Studies in Education* 59(2), 218–36.

Williamson, B., 2018b. The hidden architecture of higher education: building a big data infrastructure for the 'smarter university'. *International Journal of Educational Technology in Higher Education* 15(1), 1–26.

Williamson, B., 2019. Policy networks, performance metrics and platform markets: Charting the expanding data infrastructure of higher education. *British Journal of Educational Technology* 50, 2794–809.

Ziewitz, M., 2016. Governing algorithms: Myth, mess, and methods. *Science, Technology, & Human Values* 41, 3–16.

3.   Power in AI and public policy
Lena Ulbricht

INTRODUCTION

Recent discourses about AI have stressed that it has the potential to shift power relations considerably and might even become a power in its own right and get out of control. Critics of AI warn that it is opening the door to massive discrimination against vulnerable populations and increased citizen oppression by governments, especially where it is used for public sector functions, for example public service provision, regulation and oversight, public health, security and welfare or infrastructure development. Public sector AI often involves the private sector, for example as provider of infrastructure, technology and services. The technologies are therefore often similar or identical to those deployed in the private sector, but become effective in the asymmetrical relationship between governments and populations. Critics of public sector AI stress that AI as a resource is unequally distributed and that it does not benefit all social groups in the same way. Others denounce AI as a tool of domination: "We specifically recognise that AI systems exacerbate structural imbalances of power, with harms often falling on the most marginalized in society" (Collective statement of 114 civil society organizations towards AIA 2021). In her *Atlas of AI* Kate Crawford points out how technical systems, that are often described as neutral, reinforce power structures and enable many forms of exploitation and abuse, including inhumane working conditions and environmental destruction (Crawford 2021). Advocates of public sector AI, on the contrary, expect better insights and steering capacity with regard to complex social problems and an improved societal self-determination, as Google's AI team puts it: "We believe that AI is a foundational and transformational technology that will provide compelling and helpful benefits to people and society through its capacity to assist, complement, empower, and inspire people in almost every field of human endeavor" (Manyika et al. 2023).

For many observers, AI is a tool which can increase the power of any social actor who can dispose of it, as former President of the European Research Council Helga Nowotny points out in a recent book about AI: "prediction is not primarily a technological means for knowing future outcomes, but a social model for extracting and concentrating discretionary power" (Nowotny 2021). Others argue that AI is no longer a tool for human use, but on the verge of getting out of hand and becoming a power in its own right. In May 2023, industry leaders signed a public statement stressing the risk of extinction from AI, which ignited heavy public debate (Roose 2023). MIT physics professor May Tegmark warns of the existential threat of what he calls "unaligned superintelligence": "We may soon have to share our planet with more intelligent 'minds' that care less about us than we cared about mammoths" (Tegmark 2023). Many more authors see AI as a potential threat to civilization (Freedland 2023). This "tool versus creature" debate about AI highlights opposed conceptions of power: if AI is a tool to achieve an end defined by a human or a collective of humans – how can it possibly be a power in its own right and extinguish civilization?

As these examples from recent public debates illustrate, contemporary societies are only starting to untangle the many facets of the power of AI and the relevant power struggles. This chapter therefore asks: *What is AI and how is it related to power relations? And what can those of us who study power contribute to the debate about public sector AI?* The chapter starts by developing a systematization of different conceptions of power that encompasses various ontological and dimensional distinctions of power. The next section scrutinizes how these conceptions of power relate to dominant discourses about the power of AI in public policy: the use of AI in public policy, recent initiatives to regulate AI, and AI-triggered systemic criticism and propositions for new social orders and utopias. The final section discusses the implications of the insights for our understanding of power and public sector AI.

WHAT IS POWER?

Decades of social science research have outlined that power is formed, justified and executed in many ways, for example through violence, legitimacy, discourse, institutions, epistemology, subjectivation and hegemony. This section outlines a typology of power ontologies and dimensions which facilitate the analysis of public controversies about public sector AI.

Power Ontologies

Power is traditionally understood as the capacity of an actor to impose its will upon another, if necessary against resistance (Weber 2012). However, power is more than domination. A common distinction is the one between *relational power* ("power over"); and social *constitutional power* ("power to"). Relational power stresses relations of subordination between individuals and/or groups (Bourdieu 2010; Weber 2012). Social constitutional power has a focus on how social interaction enables actions or positions of individuals or groups (Arendt 1998). This ontological differentiation centres on *capability*, as it is concerned with the question of whether power increases or reduces capabilities. Combining both ontologies, Barnett and Duvall define power as "the production, in and through social relations, of effects that shape the capacities of actors to determine their circumstances and fate" (Barnett and Duvall 2005).

Another important ontological distinction is that, other than in common sense, it is not only and not always an instrument to attain one's aim. Power can be a *resource*, but it can also be seen as an *effect*: power is seen as a resource to realize one's will, as a tool that serves an aim (Bourdieu 2010; Schmitt 2008; Weber 2012).[1] From a different perspective, power is something that cannot be owned, but rather an effect: the manifestation of social (or sociotechnical) relations (Schäfer 2016) that are often unequal. Foucault stresses that, while power is often intangible and invisible, practices and effects are observable and thus revealing about power structures in a given field (Foucault 1995). This perspective does not neglect the fact that resources might play a role in determining power relations. However, the analytic focus lies on how power plays out in specific *practices* and less on power *structures* (Castells 2016). I call this *ontological* differentiation *utilitarian*, because it focuses on the question of whether power is a utility (or not). A resource and an effect-centred definition of power are not mutually exclusive – they rather indicate a specific focus of the analysis. Effect-based definitions are strong when it comes to analyzing situations where relevant resources are not observable,

Table 3.1   Ontologies of power (what is the nature of power?)

Power ontology	Analytic focus	Analytic strength
Ontology of capability: subordination vs constitution:		
Relational power, 'power over'	Focus on relations of subordination between individuals and/or groups	Understanding the acting and thinking autonomy of specific actors (or acting agents)
Social constitutional power, 'power to'	Focus on how social interaction enables actions or positions of individuals or groups	Understanding why some actions or ideas are possible and others are not
Utilitarian ontology (is power a utility or not): resource vs effect		
Power as a resource	Resource to realize one's will; tool that serves an aim	Strong in analyzing situations within which the structures and resources that determine power are observable and relatively stable
Power as an effect	Manifestation of unequal social or sociotechnical relations; observable mainly in practices (and less in structures)	Strong when power structures and conditions are not observable and when power seems to constantly shift and change its shape

when it is not clear which resources (or other influencing factors) determine power relations, who are the relevant agents (Hayward and Lukes 2008), or when power seems to constantly shift and change its shape. In addition, an effect-based power definition is less interested in the ultimate aim to which power contributes – it is open towards situations in which there is no clear aim or in which unintended or unexpected effects emerge (Foucault 1982). For a summary of different power ontologies, their analytic foci and strengths, see Table 3.1.

To acknowledge that power can be seen as an effect rather than a tool is crucial to understanding the narratives that see AI as a power in its own right, as a creature. From a resource-based perspective it is difficult to conceive of an AI system that grows until it escapes the control of those who have created and used it. If AI is a human-made tool, it is difficult to adhere to the idea that the tool might one day dominate its creators. Such a vision can only be sustained when assigning human attributes to digital technologies, a vision that many technological experts reject (Weizenbaum 1976). In order to understand why puppet-to-master narratives are so predominant, also in current AI debates, the effect-based conception of power is very illuminating: if AI is not (only) a tool to obtain power, but a set of structures and practices that lead to observable effects on the capacities and limitations of agents, AI can indeed outgrow the functions that were intended at the moment of its creation. For example, AI could in principle become the main epistemic and coordination mechanism in ever more social contexts (social welfare, adjudication, domestic security, education, etc.). Here, an effect-based power perspective allows us to conceive of a possible quasi-hegemony of AI, without reverting to anthropomorphism and without having to prove that such a development has been intended by its developers.

Dimensions of Power

If we want to have a comprehensive view of the power implications of AI, it is important to acknowledge that power manifests itself in many different ways and therefore has various dimensions. The subsequent systematization of power distinguishes between six *dimensions* of power.[2] All are connected to specific forms of power struggle and social conflict.

Material power designates how the distribution of material resources affects the capabilities of actors – be it countries, organizations or individuals. Material power struggles are a competition about scarce material resources, such as raw materials, territory, people, allies, artefacts, infrastructures, etc. Material perspectives on power have been dominant in international relations (Cowhey 1978), but also in the sociology of inequality of Bourdieu who differentiates between material power and cultural and social power (Bourdieu 2010).

Communicative or *discursive power* consists in language, expression, narratives and symbols that shape societal worldviews, meaning, perceptions, assessments and evaluations. Discursive power defines whose or which statements find acceptance and support; relevant struggles are about competing public frames and (e)valuations (Carstensen and Schmidt 2016). Foucault and Butler have for instance analyzed the many ways in which discourses become dominant and establish norms, values and ideologies that shape individual and collective identities and opportunities (see also subjectivational power below) (Butler 2006; Foucault 1982).

Epistemic power is concerned with what is considered as true, which methods of inquiry are accepted, and who is considered as legitimate epistemic authority. Epistemic power is especially important in feminist and decolonial thinking: Fanon sheds light on how colonial ideologies and knowledge structures are used to justify and perpetuate the exploitation and marginalization of colonized populations who internalize these dominant epistemologies and suffer a loss of self-confidence and identity (Fanon 2008). Struggles about epistemic power challenge dominant sources, forms and authorities of knowledge. Fanon called for counter-knowledges that challenge colonial representations and assert the agency and dignity of the colonized.

Subjectivational or identitarian power is centred on the process of individuals and social groups who, in response to discourses, norms, knowledge and practices, form identities and subjectivities that place them in specific social roles, power relations and power constellations. Foucault famously carved out how social institutions such as hospitals, schools and prisons contribute to the formation of subjectivities and identities that uphold the existing power order (Foucault 1995). Butler explains how gender subjectivities and identities cement or challenge the patriarchal social order (Butler 2006). Struggles about subjectivational and identitarian power centre on who belongs to a community, what determines an identity, and struggles between competing communities and identities.

Institutional power is power that is related to institutions, which can be formal or informal; material or symbolic. As Max Weber explains with regard to the authority of legal norms and procedures (Weber 2019), power relations are often implemented in and stabilized through institutional norms and practices, for example within schools and hospitals, in elections and welfare applications. Struggles arise when there is competition about institutional power positions or competition about institutional design.

Hegemonic power describes an entire system of ideology, practices and structures, that exert domination by one ruling class over another – for Gramsci the bourgeoisie (Gramsci et al. 2011); for Laclau and Mouffe neoliberal capitalism (1985). Hegemony is a state of power that reaches beyond punctual and unidimensional domination, but is relatively durable and based on a broad range of powers, including institutional, cultural and moral power, in a way that benefits from the consent of the dominated class. Struggles consist in competitions about hegemony and about the stabilization and destabilization of power structures, where counter-hegemonic efforts can try to challenge the existing order.

For an overview of the dimensions of power and related power struggles see Table 3.2.

Table 3.2   Dimensions of power and power struggles

Power dimension	Relevant questions	Power struggles
Material power	How are material resources distributed?	Competition about scarce material resources, such as raw materials, territory, people, artefacts, infrastructures etc.
Communicative/discursive power	Whose statements find acceptance and support?	Competing public frames, (e)valuations
Epistemic power	What is considered to be true?	Competing forms and sources of knowledge
Subjectivational/identitarian power	Who is part of a community? What determines an identity?	Competing identities and communities
Institutional power	How are power relations implemented in institutional norms and practices?	Competition about institutional power positions; competition about institutional design
Hegemonic power	How wide is the reach of power structures and how stable are they?	Competition about the stabilization and destabilization of power structures and relations and about the boundaries of power

Depending on what we analyze, power takes on different forms. Yet, power concepts are not rivals; they can co-exist, but direct our gaze towards different aspects. As a consequence, many stories about the power of AI can be written, and it is time to systematically scrutinize current debates about the power in AI and public policy. It will help us understand the dominant foci and the blind spots and understand how meta-knowledge about the power implications of AI stabilizes or challenges the status quo. With this foundation, we can zoom in on the power implications of public sector AI.

PUBLIC SECTOR AI AND POWER

There are many spaces where AI-related power is disputed, for example with regard to geo-political power distributions, struggles around economic power and political competition. The following section will focus on the power implications of public sector AI: how public sector AI plays out in state–citizen relations and manifests as material, communicative, epistemic and subjectivational power; how regulation aims at balancing the power between those who deploy technologies and those who are subject to them, targeting institutional forms of power; and how AI can become the centre of systemic power critique and alternative utopias though a perspective of hegemonic power.

Unequal Power: Public Sector AI as Technocratic Domination

Drawing from the various forms of power introduced above, this section explains how public sector AI often promises to increase public service efficiency and effectiveness and potentially render public policy more democratic (Ulbricht 2020b). Governments all over the world express their hopes in AI as a tool of government that should serve citizens: "These disruptive technologies are spawning a myriad of services to citizens and therefore positively impact their daily lives by changing the way they take care of themselves, feed themselves and even the way of communication" (African Union 2020: 42–3). At the same time, AI has often been criticized for various forms of abuse and oppression, as epitomized in various power critiques.

The literature about AI and power covers all six outlined dimensions of power: a very common approach to the power implications of AI is to see it as a range of material resources and forms of value extraction and creation that determine the capacities and social position of those who have access to them and that are unevenly distributed between those who develop the systems and those who are subject to them (Flensburg and Lai 2023), but also between regions and nations; much in line with our definition of *material power*. Public sector AI seems to lead to novel forms of discrimination, exploitation and manipulation of users and citizen, etc. (European Commission 2021). Zuboff denounces the large-scale extraction of data, work and capital from users by their companies and governments in a system that she names surveillance capitalism (Zuboff 2019). Scholars who study the use of AI and algorithms in public services, have shown that these "new public analytics" (Yeung 2023) are often fuelled by a new public management ideology and result in the rationalization of public welfare and increased responsibilization and pressure on the most vulnerable populations (Dencik et al. 2018; Eubanks 2018, cf. af Malmborg and Trondal, Chapter 5 in this volume; Heidelberg, Chapter 4 in this volume; Sleep and Redden, Chapter 27 in this volume), known as "surveillance of the poor" and "social sorting" (Fourcade and Gordon 2020; Lyon 2014). As the initiative Coding Rights denounces:

> we're critical of the idea of AI systems being conceived to manage the poor or any marginalized communities. These systems tend to be designed by privileged demographics, against the free will and without the opinion or participation from scratch of those who are likely to be targeted or 'helped,' resulting in automated oppression and discrimination from the Digital Welfare States that use Math as an excuse to skip any political responsibility. (Coding Rights 2021)

The importance of AI as an element of *discursive power* is also often mentioned: AI is seen as a vehicle of societal self-assessment, reflection and evaluation, and the origin of imaginaries about possible futures (Bareis and Katzenbach 2022). For instance, a recent study about public AI discourses highlights how the German government strategically uses its AI future vision to uphold a power constellation characterized by a close unity of politics and industry. This public AI discourse is supported by German media who largely ignore alternative AI narratives (Köstler and Ossewaarde 2022). Another analysis emphasizes how the discourse relating to the technical sophistication of AI systems shields the creators of the systems from public scrutiny and social accountability (Campolo and Crawford 2020).

The *epistemic power* of AI has been addressed by the abundant field of critical data and algorithm studies, revealing how data and models structure decisions and perpetuate social injustices. Similarly, feminist approaches strongly focus on the epistemic reproduction of power structures: "Traditional criticisms of AI converge on the possibility of creating true artificial intelligence, whereas a feminist argument looks instead to the cultural setting of AI – whose knowledge and what type of knowledge is to be represented" (Adam 1995). The growing and interdisciplinary research and public debates about fairness, accountability, transparency and ethics explore ways to critique data voracity, intrusive surveillance and the abusive use of AI (cf. Cobbe and Singh, Chapter 7; Aula and Erkkilä, Chapter 13; Rönnblom, Carlsson and Padden, Chapter 9 all in this volume). However, only those who have a deep understanding of the power structures of the societies within which AI plays out, acknowledge that deep social problems such as racist or sexist discrimination cannot be solved on the level of data sets and modelling, but need a profound critique of the broader epistemic context of AI production, use and regulation (Barabas et al. 2020; Miceli et al. 2022; Wachter et al. 2021; cf.

Hong, Chapter 8 in this volume). As Miceli et al. acutely ask: "Why Talk About Bias When We Mean Power?" (2022). And the Coding Rights initiative claims: "We don't believe in a fair, ethical and/or inclusive AI if automated decision systems don't acknowledge structural inequalities and injustices that affect people whose lives are targeted to be managed by these systems. Transparency is not enough if power imbalances are not taken into account" (Coding Rights 2021). Indeed, AI systems evolve within other sociotechnical trends such as poverty, war, political polarization, democratic erosion, securitization, ecocide, neocolonial exploitation, etc. It is therefore clear that fairness and justice are too complex to be easily automated.

Finally, the *subjectivational* or *identitarian power* of AI is present in the accounts of how AI shapes user and citizen subjectivities and identities, creates and dissolves communities, and thereby opens and closes opportunities for thought and action: "Algorithms shape human behavior on various levels: they influence not only the aesthetic reception of the world but also the well-being and social interaction of their users" (Quadflieg et al. 2022). Relevant studies show how public sector AI can force identities onto individuals and groups, as in border technologies (Metcalfe and Dencik 2019) or data mining for population management (Johns 2017), but also how users actively engage with technologies and develop their subjectivities and identities, as in "quantified self"-movements (Lupton 2016), open source movements (Zhang and Carpano 2023) and as digital citizens (Ohme 2019). To acknowledge the subjectivational and identitarian power of AI also requires a public reflection upon the expertise and ethical norms of those who use AI, including public servants (cf. Busch and Henriksen, Chapter 6; Kaufmann, Chapter 22; and Krutzinna, Chapter 29, all in this volume).

Summing up, the first four dimensions of power (material, discursive, epistemic and subjectivational) are present in the debate about public sector AI. With regard to the different power ontologies, not surprisingly, the proponents of AI often deploy a social constitutional power concept and zoom in on the new opportunities offered by AI; while the AI critics stress the relational power of AI and emphasize the risk of oppression and the need for safeguards and defence against oppression. With regard to the tool-versus-creature duality, AI is pictured both as a tool and as an effect. AI as an effect of power is a perspective that is especially relevant in the debate about algorithmic discrimination and manipulation, where differential effects of algorithms between social groups can be observed, but where the power-related intentions of AI developers and users is often not clear.

While the present section focused on carving out the first four dimensions of power in the discourse about public sector AI, the next two sections will emphasize the other two dimensions of power: *institutional* power is often connected to regulatory debates; *hegemony-related* power conceptions nurture more systemic critique.

Balancing Power: Current Attempts to Regulate AI

In the face of many criticisms, regulatory initiatives have emerged to better distribute power in and through public sector AI: "Without proper regulation, AI systems will exacerbate existing societal harms of mass surveillance, structural discrimination, centralized power of large technology companies, the unaccountable public decision-making and environmental extraction" (Collective statement regarding EU AI Act, signed by 123 civil society organizations 2023).

Regulation, in its narrow sense as state control of companies and other market actors, for example consumers and public agencies who use AI (Baldwin et al. 2011), encompasses many ways in which power is institutionally entrenched. After decades of low regulatory activity, this has changed in recent years. Some of the recent AI regulation aims at limiting the power of companies and citizens vis-a-vis users/citizens, for example by securing privacy rights (Bennett and Raab 2006), freedom of expression (Coche 2018), protection from online harm (Price 2022) and consumer protection (European Data Protection Supervisor 2014), to name a few. Other attempts try to strengthen the power of citizens and users in controlling and using digital technologies, as in public consultations (Rottinghaus and Escher 2020), civic tech (Gordon and Lopez 2019) and open government initiatives (Attard et al. 2015). While this chapter cannot delve into the important differences between AI regulation in the EU, China, the US and other jurisdictions (cf. Mügge, Chapter 19; Paul, Chapter 20; and Omotubora and Basu, Chapter 17, all in this volume), the overall outlook is rather dire: regulation mainly aims at preventing "social risk" through mostly liberal regulatory approaches which overburden individual users and citizens (Laux et al. 2022). And civic tech, instead of shifting the power balance towards citizens and civil society, often follows a technocratic paradigm (Kelty 2017; Ulbricht 2020b). Instead of achieving empowerment, they rather manage void procedures of participation and transparency.

AI as Object of Systemic Critique and Alternative Utopias

The disputes around AI are not only struggles around the distribution of a scarce resource or control of the existing technologies, but a critique of stable structures of domination, and the bone of content in larger ideological struggles that imply profound redistributions of power. To some observers, AI is a product of a capitalist, neoliberal or neocolonial *hegemony*: capitalism-critical approaches challenge for instance the socio-economic foundations of contemporary AI and denounce the extractivist and dehumanizing effects of AI (Crawford 2021; Dauvergne 2020):

> A.I. is dangerous inasmuch as it increases the power of capitalism. The doomsday scenario is not a manufacturing A.I. transforming the entire planet into paper clips, as one famous thought experiment has imagined. It's A.I.-supercharged corporations destroying the environment and the working class in their pursuit of shareholder value. Capitalism is the machine that will do whatever it takes to prevent us from turning it off, and the most successful weapon in its arsenal has been its campaign to prevent us from considering any alternatives. (Chiang 2023)

Here, AI is seen as the element that achieves the legitimacy and stability of a stable structure of domination and is therefore foundational to hegemony.

Critique of hegemony opens up new ways of imagining the social order and power relations around AI: alternative social utopias for AI are, for example, communitarian approaches that promote collective creation and responsibility of technologies (Staab and Piétron 2021), as in commons-based, socialist, corporatist or cooperative structures.

Decolonial approaches emphasize the colonial legacy of the above-mentioned capitalist, extractivist, inhumane and patriarchal foundations upon which AI currently strives (Couldry and Mejias 2023; Ricaurte 2019, cf. Gray, Chapter 15 in this volume; Omotubora and Basu, Chapter 17 in this volume). They refer to the exploitation of primary resources, digital waste, inhumane labour conditions of data and crowd workers, and the unlawful collection of user data in the Global South and of vulnerable populations in humanitarian contexts. They also criticize the unequal business relations between the world-leading technology companies based mainly in the Global North, and Global South companies and governments, as well as the economic and political expansionism of Global North governments in the Global South, which are often pressured to adopt their regulation to Northern standards, and to open their markets to Northern companies (Tait et al. 2022). They also stress how AI epistemically reinforces global injustice: Katz describes the ideology embedded in the concept of AI as one of supremacy and AI as based on "models of knowledge that assume white male superiority and an imperialist worldview" (Katz 2020). Decolonial counter-propositions stress human and environmental rights and dignity, regional and historical fairness, especially with regard to epistemic justice, and a diversification and decentralization of technology development, use and control: "We reject the premise that only wealthy white men get to decide what constitutes an existential threat to society ... For people of color, women, LGBTQIA+ people, religious and caste minorities, indigenous people, migrants and other marginalized communities, technology has always posed an existential threat, it has repeatedly been harnessed to ensure our inferiority in societal power structures ... We urge you to actively engage our deep expertise" (Tech experts from the Global Majority 2023) (e.g., on AIT uses for migration and border control see Molnar, Chapter 23 in this volume).

Feminist systemic critique of AI focuses on the effects of gender stereotypes and patriarchal social order on AI and its societal implications (Haraway 1991); pointing out the intersections of gender with other structures of oppression, such as class and race (Toupin 2023). Finally, feminist utopias often envision epistemic justice, diversity and decentralized and experimental forms of technology creation and control.

CONCLUSION

The main bonus of returning to power theory is to understand that there is a rich legacy of social science research about power and domination which has yielded many different concepts of power. Another important insight is that each power concept has a different focus, history and analytic strength. Adopting a narrow power concept means to miss important aspects of the phenomena in which we are interested and not to explore the potential of power critique. From here, we can write genealogies of power in AI, anatomies of sociotechnical systems and scrutinize with precision how power is created, challenged, defended, transformed and so on.

In the debates about power in AI and public policy we find a variety of views regarding the *ontology of capability*: there is no opposition between relational (subordination) power and constitutional power, but rather a functional differentiation, where the proponents of public sector AI stress the opportunities of social constitutional power whereas its critics fear the adverse effects of relational power. In addition, fears of relational power seem to fuel new propositions for harnessing the constitutional power of AI. As to the *utilitarian ontology*, AI is seen as both resource and effect. It is clear that often, the precise responsibilities, effects and mechanisms are not yet clearly observable and defined. The current difficulty of assessing who is responsible for AI and what intentions are associated with it (if there are any), has directed the focus of critical AI researchers towards its observable societal effects, for example discrimination. We do not know in detail how ChatGPT or face-recognition software systems work, who uses them and with what intentions, but we can assess their effects on, for instance, policing, education or political communication. As a consequence, while in other domains, power is commonly rather seen as a tool than an effect, in the case of AI, the power-as-an-effect aspect has grown in importance and can certainly inspire other fields of analysis in which to societies it is not (yet) clear where the centre of power is located, where the line of conflict lies and what the broader social consequences are – as for example with regard to climate change. The insights relating to power in AI in its various dimensions, material, discursive, epistemic and subjectivational, highlight that we have left behind the times when AI was seen mainly as a technical object which could only be evaluated by technical experts. Major public debates, such as the one recently generated by ChatGPT, have called many societal actors to contribute to how they view AI and its power implications and therefore broadened the public perspective on it. Thus, the times when technical experts took most of the important decisions about AI, far removed from public scrutiny, are gone. However, as the public letter of experts from the Global South show, not all voices have the same weight. In addition, it is still an open question how the variety of power conceptions in AI translates into politics. A wide range of perspectives might never be represented in important decisions about AI.

A theory-based systematization of power in AI also allows us to dismiss the AI-out-of-control narrative as a red herring, to distract us from the less bombastic, subtle, but important consequences of AI becoming an increasingly pervasive mode of coordination. These consequences are less visible, but just as influential in the long run, and rely upon many large and small decisions that are being taken *today* and that need critical observation. To stay metaphorical: AI cannot become a creature, but it can become a single set of rules for each and every game that we play.

In the end, AI has the potential to do both: to obfuscate and to disclose power and oppression. Much has been written about the systemic and systematic opacity surrounding AI systems (Ananny and Crawford 2017; Burrell 2016). In this sense, AI has an immense potential to make violence invisible and to claim that domination is legitimate where it is not. At the same time, this opacity is increasingly challenged (Ulbricht 2020a), by public accountability claims, by new regulation, stricter adjudication, research investments in explainable and accountable AI, in systemic critique and in alternative technological utopias, creation, use.

NOTES

1. Through such a perspective AI can be seen as a tool to obtain something, for example military and economic supremacy or individual wealth, but also administrative efficiency, democratic legitimacy and individual autonomy.
2. The categories were chosen by the author with the aim of showing that there are various dimensions of power, drawing from influential power theories. The list of dimensions is not complete, however; there are more, especially when choosing fine-grained categories.

REFERENCES

Adam, A. (1995), 'Artificial intelligence and women's knowledge', *Women's Studies International Forum*, **18** (4), 407–15.

African Union (2020), *The Digital Transformation Strategy for Africa (2020–2030)*, 18 May, accessed 26 July 2023 at https://au.int/sites/default/files/documents/38507-doc-dts-english.pdf.

Ananny, M. and K. Crawford (2017), 'Seeing without knowing: Limitations of the transparency ideal and its application to algorithmic accountability', *New Media & Society*, **33** (4), 1–17.

Arendt, H. (1998), *The Human Condition*, 2nd ed., Chicago: University of Chicago Press.

Attard, J., F. Orlandi, S. Scerri and S. Auer (2015), 'A systematic review of open government data initiatives', *Government Information Quarterly*, **32** (4), 399–418.

Baldwin, R., M. Cave and M. Lodge (2011), *Understanding Regulation: Theory, Strategy, and Practice*, 2nd ed., Oxford and New York: Oxford University Press.

Barabas, C., C. Doyle, J. Rubinovitz and K. Dinakar (2020), 'Studying up: Reorienting the study of algorithmic fairness around issues of power', in *Proceedings of the 2020 Conference on Fairness, Accountability, and Transparency*, Barcelona, Spain: ACM, pp. 167–76.

Bareis, J. and C. Katzenbach (2022), 'Talking AI into being: The narratives and imaginaries of national AI strategies and their performative politics', *Science, Technology, & Human Values*, **47** (5), 855–81.

Barnett, M. and R. Duvall (2005), 'Power in international politics', *International Organization*, **59** (1), 39–75.

Bennett, C. J. and C. D. Raab (2006), *The Governance of Privacy: Policy Instruments in Global Perspective*, 2nd ed., Cambridge, MA: MIT Press.

Bourdieu, P. (2010), *Distinction: A Social Critique of the Judgement of Taste*, London: Routledge.

Burrell, J. (2016), 'How the machine "thinks": Understanding opacity in machine learning algorithms', *Big Data & Society*, **3** (1), 1–12.

Butler, J. (2006), *Gender Trouble: Feminism and the Subversion of Identity*, New York: Routledge.

Campolo, A. and K. Crawford (2020), 'Enchanted determinism: Power without responsibility in artificial intelligence', *Engaging Science, Technology, and Society*, **6**, 1–19.

Carstensen, M. B. and V. A. Schmidt (2016), 'Power through, over and in ideas: Conceptualizing ideational power in discursive institutionalism', *Journal of European Public Policy*, **23** (3), 318–37.

Castells, M. (2016), 'A sociology of power: My intellectual journey', *Annual Review of Sociology*, **42** (1), 1–19.

Chiang, T. (2023), 'Will A.I. become the new McKinsey?', *The New Yorker* (4 May). Available at: https://www.newyorker.com/science/annals-of-artificial-intelligence/will-ai-become-the-new-mckinsey.

Coche, E. (2018), 'Privatised enforcement and the right to freedom of expression in a world confronted with terrorism propaganda online', *Internet Policy Review*, **7** (4), accessed at https://doi.org/10.14763/2018.4.1382.

Coding Rights (2021), *Why is A.I. a Feminist Issue?*, accessed 26 July 2023 at https://notmy.ai/about/.

Collective statement of 114 civil society organisations towards AIA (2021), *An EU Artificial Intelligence Act for Fundamental Rights. A Civil Society Statement*, accessed 26 July 2023 at https://edri.org/wp-content/uploads/2021/12/Political-statement-on-AI-Act.pdf.

Collective statement regarding EU AI Act, signed by 123 civil society organizations (2023), 'European Parliament: Make sure the AI act protects peoples' rights!', accessed 26 July 2023 at https://www.amnesty.eu/news/european-parliament-make-sure-the-ai-act-protects-peoples-rights/.

Couldry, N. and U. A. Mejias (2023), 'The decolonial turn in data and technology research: What is at stake and where is it heading?', *Information, Communication & Society*, **26** (4), 786–802.

Cowhey, P. F. (1978), '*Power and Interdependence: World Politics in Transition*, by Robert O. Keohane and Joseph S. Nye, Jr.', *Political Science Quarterly*, **93** (1), 132–34.

Crawford, K. (2021), *The Atlas of AI: Power, Politics, and the Planetary Costs of Artificial Intelligence*, New Haven, CT: Yale University Press.

Dauvergne, P. (2020), *AI in the Wild: Sustainability in the Age of Artificial Intelligence*, Cambridge, MA: MIT Press.

Dencik, L., A. Hintz, J. Redden and H. Warne (2018), *Data Scores as Governance: Investigating Uses of Citizen Scoring in Public Services [Project Report]*, Open Society Foundations, Cardiff University, accessed at http://orca.cf.ac.uk/117517/.

Eubanks, V. (2018), *Automating Inequality: How High-Tech Tools Profile, Police, and Punish the Poor*, New York: St. Martin's Press.

European Commission (2021), *Algorithmic Discrimination in Europe: Challenges and Opportunities for Gender Equality and Non Discrimination Law*, Brussels: Publications Office of the European Union.

European Data Protection Supervisor (2014), *Privacy and Competitiveness in the Age of Big Data: The Interplay between Data Protection, Competition Law and Consumer Protection in the Digital Economy*, Brussels, March, accessed 26 July 2023 at https://edps.europa.eu/sites/default/files/publication/14-03-26_competitition_law_big_data_en.pdf.

Fanon, F. (2008), *Black Skin, White Masks*, 1st ed., new ed., New York: Grove Press.

Flensburg, S. and S. S. Lai (2023), 'Follow the data! A strategy for tracing infrastructural power', *Media and Communication*, **11** (2), 319–29.

Foucault, M. (1982), 'The subject and power', *Critical Inquiry*, **8** (4), 777–95.

Foucault, M. (1995), *Discipline and Punish: The Birth of the Prison*, 2nd ed., New York: Vintage Books.

Fourcade, M. and J. Gordon (2020), 'Learning like a state: Statecraft in the digital age', *Journal of Law and Political Economy*, **1** (1), 78–108.

Freedland, J. (2023), 'The future of AI is chilling – humans have to act together to overcome this threat to civilization', *The Guardian*, 26 May, accessed 26 July 2023 at https://www.theguardian.com/commentisfree/2023/may/26/future-ai-chilling-humans-threat-civilisation.

Gordon, E. and R. A. Lopez (2019), 'The practice of civic tech: Tensions in the adoption and use of new technologies in community based organizations', *Media and Communication*, **7** (3), 57–68.

Gramsci, A., J. A. Buttigieg and A. Callari (2011), *Prison Notebooks. Vol. 1*, Paperback ed., New York: Columbia University Press.

Haraway, D. J. (1991), *Simians, Cyborgs, and Women: The Reinvention of Nature*, New York: Routledge.

Hayward, C. and S. Lukes (2008), 'Nobody to shoot? Power, structure, and agency: A dialogue', *Journal of Power*, **1** (1), 5–20.

Johns, F. E. (2017), 'Data mining as global governance', in R. Brownsword, E. Scotford, and K. Yeung (eds), *Oxford Handbook on the Law and Regulation of Technology*, Oxford: Oxford University Press, pp. 776–98.

Katz, Y. (2020), *Artificial Whiteness: Politics and Ideology in Artificial Intelligence*, New York: Columbia University Press.

Kelty, C. M. (2017), 'Too much democracy in all the wrong places: Toward a grammar of participation', *Current Anthropology*, **58** (S15), 77–90.

Köstler, L. and R. Ossewaarde (2022), 'The making of AI society: AI futures frames in German political and media discourses', *AI & Society*, **37** (1), 249–63.

Laclau, E. and C. Mouffe (1985), *Hegemony and Socialist Strategy: Towards a Radical Democratic Politics*, London: Verso.

Laux, J., S. Wachter and B. Mittelstadt (2022), 'Trustworthy artificial intelligence and the European Union AI act: On the conflation of trustworthiness and the acceptability of risk', *SSRN Electronic Journal*, accessed at https://doi.org/10.2139/ssrn.4230294.

Lupton, D. (2016), *The Quantified Self: A Sociology of Self-Tracking*, Cambridge, MA: Polity.

Lyon, D. (2014), 'Surveillance, Snowden, and big data: Capacities, consequences, critique', *Big Data & Society* (July–December), 1–13.

Manyika, J., J. Dean, D. Hassabis, M. Croak and S. Pichai (2023), *Why We Focus on AI (and to What End)*, accessed 26 July 2023 at https://ai.google/why-ai/.

Metcalfe, P. and L. Dencik (2019), 'The politics of big borders: Data (in)justice and the governance of refugees', *First Monday*, **24** (4), accessed at https://doi.org/10.5210/fm.v24i4.9934.

Miceli, M., J. Posada and T. Yang (2022), 'Studying up machine learning data: Why talk about bias when we mean power?', *Proceedings of the ACM on Human-Computer Interaction*, **6** (GROUP), 1–14.

Nowotny, H. (2021), *In AI We Trust: Power, Illusion and Control of Predictive Algorithms*, Medford, MA: Polity Press.

Ohme, J. (2019), 'Updating citizenship? The effects of digital media use on citizenship understanding and political participation', *Information, Communication & Society*, **22** (13), 1903–28.

Price, L. (2022), 'Platform responsibility for online harms: Towards a duty of care for online hazards', *Journal of Media Law*, 2022 (Online First), accessed at https://doi.org/10.1080/17577632.2021.2022331.

Quadflieg, S., K. Neuburg and S. Nestler (eds) (2022), *(Dis)Obedience in Digital Societies: Perspectives on the Power of Algorithms and Data*, Edinburgh: Edinburgh University Press.

Ricaurte, P. (2019), 'Data epistemologies, the coloniality of power, and resistance', *Television & New Media*, **20** (4), 350–65.

Roose, K. (2023), 'A.I. Poses "Risk of Extinction," Industry Leaders Warn', *The New York Times*, 30 May, accessed 26 July 2023 at https://www.nytimes.com/2023/05/30/technology/ai-threat-warning.html.

Rottinghaus, B. and T. Escher (2020), 'Mechanisms for inclusion and exclusion through digital political participation: Evidence from a comparative study of online consultations in three German cities', *Zeitschrift Für Politikwissenschaft*, **30** (2), 261–98.

Schäfer, H. (2016), *Praxistheorie: Ein Soziologisches Forschungsprogramm*, Bielefeld: transcript.

Schmitt, C. (2008), *Concept of the Political: Expanded Edition*, Chicago: University of Chicago Press.
Staab, P. and D. Piétron (2021), 'Würde. Gemeinwohlorientierte Plattformen als Grundlage sozialer Freiheit', in C. Piallat (ed.), *Der Wert der Digitalisierung: Gemeinwohl in der digitalen Welt*, Bielefeld: transcript, pp. 187–206.
Tait, M. M., A. E. dos Reis Peron and M. Suárez (2022), 'Terrestrial politics and body-territory: Two concepts to make sense of digital colonialism in Latin America', *Tapuya: Latin American Science, Technology and Society*, **5** (1), 2090485.
Tech experts from the Global Majority (2023), 'Digital-justice and human-rights experts from around the globe raise concerns about the white-male-dominated AI debate*', accessed 26 July 2023 at https://codingrights.org/en/library-item/open-letter-to-news-media-and-policy-makers-tech-experts-from-the-global-majority/.
Tegmark, M. (2023), 'The "don't look up" thinking that could doom us with AI', *Time*, 25 April, accessed 26 July 2023 at https://time.com/6273743/thinking-that-could-doom-us-with-ai/.
Toupin, S. (2023), 'Shaping feminist artificial intelligence', *New Media & Society*, **26**, https://doi.org/10.1177/14614448221150776.
Ulbricht, L. (2020a), 'Algorithmen und politisierung', *Leviathan, Sonderband 35/2020 (Ent-)Politisierung? Die Demokratische Gesellschaft Im 21. Jahrhundert*, 253–78.
Ulbricht, L. (2020b), 'Scraping the demos. Digitalization, web scraping and the democratic project', *Democratization, Special Issue Democratization beyond the Post-Democratic Turn. Political Participation between Empowerment and Abuse*, **27** (3), 426–42.
Wachter, S., B. Mittelstadt and C. Russell (2021), 'Why fairness cannot be automated: Bridging the gap between EU non-discrimination law and AI', *Computer Law & Security Review*, **41**, 105567.
Weber, M. (2012), *Max Weber: The Theory of Social and Economic Organization*, Mansfield Centre, CT: Martino Publishing.
Weber, M. (2019), *Economy and Society*, Cambridge, MA: Harvard University Press.
Weizenbaum, J. (1976), *Computer Power and Human Reason: From Judgment to Calculation*, San Francisco: Freeman.
Yeung, K. (2023), 'The new public analytics as an emerging paradigm in public sector administration', *Tilburg Law Review*, **27** (2), 1–32.
Zhang, B. and D. Carpano (2023), 'Chromium as a tool of logistical power: A material political economy of open-source', *Big Data & Society*, **10** (1), 1–12.
Zuboff, S. (2019), *The Age of Surveillance Capitalism: The Fight for a Human Future at the New Frontier of Power*, New York: PublicAffairs.

4.   What's old is new: AI and bureaucracy

Roy L. Heidelberg

INTRODUCTION

There is not much debate as to whether artificial intelligence (AI) technology ought to be regulated. The consensus that it should is unusual in the political theatre of our time. The question is *how*. There have been many essays and reports that call for the development of governance systems in response to the emergence of AI. These calls typically express some form of policy response that can be categorized as either regulation, or democratization, or a combination of the two. In this chapter I explore these aspirations by situating AI in the intellectual foundations of bureaucratic theory, specifically by attempting to understand AI as something more than a tool, as a social and political phenomenon. I propose that we can understand AI through Weberian bureaucratic theory and as a design choice made as part of the intellectual system supporting contemporary public administration by advancing bureaucracy and management. This perspective makes calls for regulation and democratization hard to accept as a practical response to perceived problems of the technology because AI is inseparable from the process needed to regulate it. I explain AI as a perfection of bureaucracy, and in doing so I challenge the position that AI ought to be regulated by questioning if it *can* be regulated. The simple thesis that I will explore is that regulating AI is not feasible without AI, so the practical implications of these hopeful calls for regulating this technology are empty. It raises the perennial question of *Quis custodiet ipsos custodes*, who will watch the watchmen, at a level never before experienced.

While the functionality of AI is relatively new, the idea of it is not. Within this chapter, I will explore how AI is connected to political and social theories of the early- and mid-twentieth century. Specifically, AI is an explicit component of management theory and an implicit component of modern bureaucracy. Early expressions of AI were motivated by hopes for optimizing management (explored through the ideas of Herbert Simon in the first section). And before that, the hopes for mass democracy produced a need for an authority that was impersonal (explored through Weberian bureaucracy in the second section). AI combines these social drives for optimizing decision making (operations research) and the modality for achieving social action in an impersonal way (bureaucracy). These generally sanguine endeavours – for optimized leadership and a democratic society – help us to understand why there is little to be done about AI despite the unusual consensus that it must be regulated. AI cannot be regulated without AI. I will consider this aporia of regulating AI in the third section. In doing so, I take regulation to imply an independent control over AI, something more than guidelines and principles of good practice as typically results from summits and meetings to discuss AI. Regulation implies agency capable of understanding and directly influencing in order to enforce the rules that structure the regulatory regime itself. As discussed in this chapter, that capability is itself the function of AI by design.

The political capacity to confront AI is prefigured by bureaucracy and, indeed, bureaucracy is a prefiguration of AI itself. The tool is different, but the technology is not. Most troublesomely, the political conditions presently shaping AI are positioned to reinforce AI. It seems as if we have relinquished the creative capacities and political imagination that are necessary to see and confront AI in a political way. I offer these remarks primarily as a kind of confession upon which this chapter depends, because I do not know where these human contrivances and cunning instruments that we call AI will go or will take us in the next decade. But within my ignorance dwells a tingling scepticism that there is not much that we modern humans can do because our doing is a central source of the problem.

AI AND MANAGEMENT

In 1958 Herbert Simon and Allen Newell published a short piece in *Operations Research* that defined the field of operations research and the nascent ideas behind AI:

> Our professional activity, the application of intelligence in a systematic way to administration, has a history that extends much farther into the past. One of its obvious antecedents is the scientific management movement fathered by Frederick W. Taylor... an appropriate patron saint for our profession [is] Charles Babbage. (Simon & Newell, 1958, p. 1)

Herbert Simon's role in this essay is especially notable. He was a pioneer of decision theory and of the study of administration and leadership. His ideas about AI stemmed directly from his observations that human decision making was limited in important ways. He introduced the word "satisfice" to mean that people will make decisions that are just enough rather than optimal, something we do because as individuals we are limited in our rational capacities (which he called bounded rationality). To work around these limitations required, according to Simon, organization, which could be designed for optimization and rationality.

The essay from which the above quotation is taken is a type of intellectual appeal based on the ambition to optimize management to the point that common sense and human cleverness are no longer requisite of management decisions. Simon and Newell distinguished between well-structured and ill-structured problems. For the professional activity of operations research to succeed, problems needed to be rendered as calculation; this is what made them "well-structured". In the mid-twentieth century, there were technical limits to how far this calculable rendering could extend, which meant that well-structured problems were limited to matters of middle management (presumably where orders were implemented and discretion was limited). Top-level management problems, meanwhile, lacked the structure of formal techniques, "hardly touched by operations research or the advances of management science" (Simon and Newell, 1958, p. 4). As the essay made clear, an operations researcher performed best where the problems were well structured, formulated clearly and in a quantitative way, but when the problems were ill structured, an operations researcher became a *management consultant*. In that case, they performed according to judgement and guesswork, and it was Simon's contention that "most of us look forward to the day when our science [the rational and calculable approach of operations research] will enable us to handle with appropriate analytic tools those problems that we now tackle with judgment and guess" (Simon and Newell, 1958, p. 6). Top do so meant rendering those problems of judgement and guess in the calculable terms of well-structured problems. This rendering is one way to understand algorithms, though Simon preferred to speak of "heuristics".

Simon and Newell did not use the phrase "artificial intelligence" in the essay, though the sensibility behind it was evident throughout. Instead, they referred to "the intelligence of machines", focusing primarily on the promise that the development of such intelligence offered the improvement of management and of the social ability to address problems, both well- and ill-structured types. The promise in Simon's and Newell's organized intelligence of machines was described in extraordinary terms: "to take the place of humans in solving ill-structured problems; ... to tackle ill-structured problems of such magnitude and difficulty that humans have not been able to solve them ... [and] with the aid of heuristic programs, we will help man obey the ancient injunction: Know thyself" (Simon and Newell, 1958, p. 8). Simon distinguished between heuristics and algorithms in order to clarify the necessary advancements for optimizing management. Computers and machines were being developed with the ability to operate through heuristic reasoning, employing "intuition, insight and learning [, which] are no longer exclusive possessions of humans" (Simon and Newell, 1958, p. 6), and not limited to what Simon called algorithmic problem solving, which is suitable to well-structured problems. Dreyfus and Dreyfus referred to this model of AI as making a mind, which they contrasted with the other approach to AI of making a brain (1988). In the case of Simon (and Newell), the progress of AI depended upon the development of how symbols operate in intelligence. The idea was not to model how the brain works but how people use symbols and what symbols were. In the Turing Lecture from 1975, Newell and Simon (1976) explained that one condition of intelligence is an "ability to store and manipulate symbols". This insight was critical to the development of AI in the field of operations research. Simon explained that "our science (operations research) is to be coextensive with the field of management, [so] we must have the tools and techniques that will extend its range to that whole field" (Simon and Newell, 1958, p. 6). This meant that the intelligence of machines must be applicable to the operations of top-level management, where decisions tend to be ill-structured and thus subject to judgement and guesswork. The development of a symbol-based empirical science of management (which is what Newell and Simon (1976) saw computer science to be), transformed the idea of a heuristic into the modern equivalent of an algorithm.[1] In other words, AI was designed to overcome the shortcomings of human decision making and judgement and rendered higher-level reasoning in an impersonal and calculable way specifically to remove human fallibility from top-level decision making. In effect, the power of calculation became so great through computation that what Simon called a heuristic was eventually coextensive with an algorithm.

AI was not intended to be human natural intelligence but was intended as an advanced form of information processing, as *artificial* intelligence. As Simon made clear, in applying computer technology to management, a primary objective was to process information more rapidly, more efficiently, and better than a human. The purpose was decision making within boundaries, not creativity. While it was not outside of the scope of ambition that AI and computer science might illuminate our understanding of the human mind and the human brain (though arguably neuroscience is a better arena for the latter), it was patently clear from Herbert Simon that a central objective is to augment humans in management operations to the edge of replacement. This should come as little surprise to those who know Simon for his contributions to administrative theory, which partly consisted of recognizing the inherent limits in human reasoning that he labelled bounded rationality and in coining the portmanteau "satisfice" to explain how humans make decisions (Simon, 1957). The path for optimization was through organization, specifically the organization of intelligence itself. These observations were not simply theoretical. They were challenges to rationality, challenges that Simon would later claim could be addressed by optimization and design (see, especially, his *Sciences of the Artificial*, 1969). Simon connected management science based on calculable reason with computerization as the mechanism for optimizing decision making. In this ambition, Simon carried the torch of bureaucracy, though it is doubtful that he would have seen it that way. And through this connection between AI and bureaucracy, we can more clearly grasp the potential, or the limited feasibility, for confronting AI through our current political categories, concepts, and imagination.

BUREAUCRACY AND AI

There does seem to be some confusion about the relationship between AI and bureaucracy. Often, bureaucracy is viewed or described through an overstatement of its features: it tends toward increasing costs, functions on the basis of rules that are designed for precision and inflexibility, and operates according to the principle that the functional elements ("bureaucrats") make decisions according to objective, written rules and not on a case-by-case basis. Meanwhile, it is often proposed that AI will address the cumbersome, "red-tape" infected bureaucracies through efficient processing. In this chapter I will use bureaucracy not in the popular sense that is associated with cumbersome stupidity (though it is also not dissociated with that sense), but as a term of art introduced by Max Weber. Seen in this technical way, bureaucracy is the organizational condition of modern society that helps to explain the rise of AI, an operation-based processing technology dependent on impersonal execution of rules. Our contemporary politics have been primed for the rise of AI by bureaucracy, a point I will make through two facets of bureaucratic theory: objectivity of decision and democratization.

The Objectivity of Decision

Many of the hopeful scenarios associated with AI are based on the sense that the technology will address the problems associated with decision making at or near the executive level, meaning that decisions will be based primarily, perhaps exclusively, upon the procedures and structures built into AI. In a phrase, the dawning of AI is a development in the perfection of bureaucracy. What connects the motivations behind the development of the science of operations research with bureaucracy as the modern organizational form is a completion of the *objective decision*. Weber viewed bureaucracy as a sociological concept because it replaced traditional forms and practices of authority – those ordered by social structures premised on personal sympathy, favour, grace, and gratitude – with an impersonal authority. Bureaucracy proceeds on the principle of *sine ira et studio*, a phrase that Weber likely borrowed from Tacitus to express the principle of objectivity in contrast to personal or subjective understanding. Weber thus claimed that "bureaucracy develops the more perfectly, the more it is 'dehumanized,' the more completely it succeeds in eliminating from official business love, hatred, and all purely personal, irrational, and emotional elements which escape calculation" (Weber, 2013, see XI.6). He would go on to claim this quality of bureaucracy to be its "special virtue". Calculability and the discharge of business "without regard for persons" are the central features of objective decisions. Bureaucracy ushered a form of organization for the discharge of official business in the state to replace the traditional administration of notables that shaped collegiate or honorific forms of administration where personal connections prevailed.

The idea of objectivity in bureaucracy was not about truth but about fact. Facts are the basis for rules and are complemented to a limited extent by norms (discussed below). Within bureaucracy, there is some tension between the comprehensiveness of rules and the retention of space for discretion and judgement about the rules. At the dawning of modern bureaucracy, as Weber put it, "the idea of a 'law without gaps' is, of course, under vigorous attack", a reference to the repeated social resistance to a set of rules that would fully preclude judgement. He carried on the point by noting that

> The conception of the modern judge as an automaton into which legal documents and fees are stuffed at the top in order that it may spill forth the verdict at the bottom along with the reasons, read mechanically from codified paragraphs – this conception is angrily rejected, perhaps because a certain approximation to this type *would precisely be implied by a consistent bureaucratization of justice*. (Weber, 2013, XI.6.B, emphasis added)

The "law without gaps" also expresses the algorithmic reasoning inherent to AI and to the kind of intelligence that Simon and Newell celebrated as dawning alongside the advancements in computing technology. Calculability was a central piece of making problems soluble for operations research, and bureaucracy is an organizational form that operates through calculation. As Weber described it, bureaucracy elevates the intelligence of formal rationality into the organizational ideal type. Bureaucracy was revolutionary insofar as it destroyed traditional structures of domination that were not based on rules, means–ends calculation, and matter-of-factness or, as Weber put it in his technical language, the "march of bureaucracy destroyed structures of domination which were not rational" (Weber, 2013, XI.14). But it was also a social revolution that concluded the possibility of future revolutions. Its technical superiority made it possible that future organizational types would be shaped by the form of bureaucracy, so long as complex social action was pursued. A consistent bureaucratization of justice, as mentioned in the above quotation, would bring under its authority decisions at the highest feasible level to be made not on the basis of personal or traditional considerations, but on a rational, that is to say calculable and rule-based, manner. This would be the application of intelligence in a systematic way to administration that Simon celebrated, a perfection of bureaucracy such that its "rational character", as Weber put it, extended to the highest levels of decision making.

While the operations research goal was to merge higher-level machine reasoning with executive-level decision making, nevertheless a resistance to such a development was present at the nascence of bureaucracy. Much of the opposition concerned the consequences of a prescriptive reasoning on judgement and the particulars through which judgement as a form of reasoning proceeded. Bureaucracy precluded judgement to the extent that the decision was made according to rationally derived reasons (and thus rationally debated), meaning the actions of bureaucracy were always subsumed under explicit norms or determined by means–end calculation. Weber acknowledged that this perfection, potentially realized in the "consistent bureaucratization of justice", was not accepted widely. There remained a sense of the need for some "individualizing" of justice. Nevertheless, the description from the early twentieth century of an automaton into which legal documents and fees are stuffed at the top in order that it may spill forth the verdict at the bottom anticipated the algorithmic array of large language models (LLMs), stuffed with human artefacts and spilling forth calculated responses to queries and requests. The design of an impersonal authority, an inherent component of bureaucracy, was a foundational development for the emergence of AI as citizens sought more objectivity in the decisions of authority. The resistance or angry rejections that Weber postulated were muted by the growing demand for impersonal and unbiased conduct of authority.

The muted anger is likely correlated with the idea developed in the latter half of the twentieth century that high-level decision making is essentially programmable as algorithms. The limit to algorithms and AI systems has theoretically been the judgement of norms, but this limit was itself revealed to be nothing of the sort by the middle of the twentieth century when AI systems were being conceived and early programmes were being developed. The implementation of norms through objective decision making, which would under the scope of judgement be addressed on a case-by-case basis, became what is called the Alignment Problem in AI. The framing of this problem, historically attributed to Norbert Wiener, a pioneering mathematician and cybernetician, described the problem frequently raised about AI concerning assurances that the basis of its decision making is "right". Wiener put the matter in terms of moral and technical concerns with the speed with which artificial systems are able to automate processes. He explained,

> If we use, to achieve our purposes, a mechanical agency with whose operation we cannot efficiently interfere once we have started it, because the action is so fast and irrevocable that we have not the data to intervene before the action is complete, then we had better be quite sure that the purpose put into the machine is the purpose which we really desire and not merely a colorful imitation of it. (Wiener, 1960)

The Alignment Problem is in many respects at the heart of contemporary calls for regulating AI, but what it describes is a problem that assumes certain superiorities of the machine or AI. The solution to the Alignment Problem is an objectification of norms, a need to articulate to the machine what norms must guide it, similar to how guardrails are placed on a bureaucracy, but different insofar as "the action is so fast and irrevocable that we have not the data to intervene before the action is complete". There is little room for error, and the human capacity for interference is limited. So, an objective expression of what we deem the purpose to be is necessary (we had better "get it right" before we turn it on) because our capacity for control is conceptually impossible. Every act of bureaucratic administration is guided by either a weighing of means–ends or the subsumption under norms (see Weber on the technical superiority of bureaucracy, 2013, XI.6). The weighing of means–ends is rational in the calculable sense and thus objective. The subsumption under norms requires an objective expression of judgement so that the actions are fulfilled according to prescribed rules expressing norm behaviour and not on a case-by-case basis, which is in principle contrary to bureaucracy. The latter is, in its essence, the expression of the Alignment Problem in AI, which is solved to the extent that norms can be expressed in the language of AI and applied objectively.

Authority and Democratization

An important lingering political issue behind the rise of AI, beyond questions of alignment and technical superiority, is the question of legitimacy in social action. In order to understand how AI can perform as a legitimate operation in society, it is helpful to understand the formal legitimacy that supports bureaucracy and, thus, the potential to make AI "more democratic". Why do we follow the commands or orders of bureaucracy in a democracy? This question concerns the legitimacy of a specifically modern type of authority upon which bureaucracy depends. Weber postulated an essentially new form of authority in bureaucracy that eschewed personal legitimacy altogether, what he labelled legal-rational authority (sometimes shortened to legal authority), which in its purest form exercises authority through a dehumanized bureaucratic administrative staff. The rationality of this authority derives from the fact that what Weber (2013) called domination (defined as the probability that a command will be obeyed) is realized through knowledge (see 2013, III.ii.5). This is part of the basis of the claims to legitimacy under legal authority, which begins with gaining the right to give orders through enacted rules and proceeds to a higher level of domination (likelihood that the order will be obeyed) by virtue of knowledge. Obedience, then, is owed not to any person by virtue of tradition or charisma but rather to the impersonal order established by legal structures. The highest level of authority in what Weber called the "specifically modern type of administration" is the impersonal law:

> ... the typical person in authority, the "superior," is himself subject to an impersonal order by orienting his actions to it in his own dispositions and commands. (This is true not only for persons exercising legal authority who are in the usual sense "officials," but, for instance, for the elected president of a state).

The law expresses knowledge for the sake of social action such that the action can be objective and impersonal.

As Weber observed, though, this rule of no one in particular was and is an inevitable byproduct of the democratization of society in its totality. Modern mass democracy produced bureaucracy because it was a system to hold authority in an impersonal way. As Weber put it,

> The democratization of society in its totality, and in the modern sense of the term, whether actual or perhaps merely formal, is an especially favorable basis of bureaucratization ... We must remember the fact which we have encountered several times and which we shall have to discuss repeatedly: that "democracy" as such is opposed to the "rule" of bureaucracy, *in spite and perhaps because of its unavoidable yet unintended promotion of bureaucratization.* (2013, XI.11.A, emphasis added)

And earlier in the same essay,

> Bureaucracy inevitably accompanies modern *mass democracy*, in contrast to the democratic self-government of small homogeneous units. This results from [bureaucracy's] characteristic principle: the abstract regularity of the exercise of authority, which is a result of the demand for "equality before the law" in the personal and functional sense – hence, of the horror of "privilege," and the principled rejection of doing business "from case to case." (2013, XI.8.A)

Democratization "in the modern sense of the term" demanded impersonal authority because it eschewed privilege, but in this demand was the creation of a form of rule that is impersonal to the extent that it cannot be questioned and at the same time essential to satisfying the demands of democratization. This persistent tension operates by and through bureaucracy itself, and although Weber wrote his observations of this specifically modern form of organization and officialdom more than a century ago, a contemporary in the twenty-first century must readily observe the fact that bureaucracy is the dominating process of modern politics, not democracy. The legitimate domination of modern society, authority, may seem to have vanished, as Arendt claimed, but its disappearance is only an illusion of our commitment to the legal rationality built upon knowledge itself, a sense of knowing comprehensive enough to correct for any errors produced through a democratic process. What Weber recognized was that modern society was more complicated and more specialized partly, perhaps largely, due to mass democracy, and "the more complicated and specialized modern culture becomes, the more its external supporting apparatus demands the personally detached and strictly objective expert" as opposed to the traditional structures that were more likely to be moved by personal sympathy (Weber, 2013, XI.6). Objectivity is achieved through impersonality above all else, and this is what the complications wrought by mass democracy require.[2] By the middle of the twentieth century, concerns had turned away from the structure of bureaucracy and toward the decision making of these newly minted experts of the modern state, a problem taken up by Simon and his peers who sought to organize intelligence to minimize judgement and guesswork, the hallmarks of personal decision making. Solving that problem was the next step in democratization, leading to the development of an AI to possess the knowledge required for impersonal authority, which is the central project of operations research.

WHY AI CANNOT BE REGULATED

The previous two sections have expressed an idea of AI as an extension of modern bureaucracy and optimized management. This section considers how the fulfillment of AI fits ambitions of perfect decision and bureaucracy and what this means for confronting it through policy tools. Significantly for aspirations of control, AI fulfills the ambitions of ultimate rationality that are themselves essential to the success of impersonal systems of control and regulation, meaning it is the more perfect form of the regulatory capacity itself. Nevertheless, the answer to what must be done about AI is typically some variation on a combined counter process of regulation or democratization. Even those who are central to the development of AI (perhaps because of their centrality to the technology) openly call for its regulation. The CEO of OpenAI declared (via Twitter) that AI is simply a precursor to artificial general intelligence (AGI), a capacity for thinking that people would find impossible to grasp. He said that there were three conditions to a "good AGI future": (1) a technical ability to align the intelligence; (2) coordination among the leading efforts to generate AGI; and (3) an effective global regulatory framework including democratic governance.[3] In other words, for the sake of the future, there must be coordination between those who can build AI (technical ability) and those who can protect us from its misuse (global regulatory framework and democratic governance).

There is some scepticism, but even the sceptical still place their hopes in the very structures that AI optimizes. In March 2023 a letter was circulated widely calling on a "pause" of AI development, signed by around 1,000 AI experts and engineers. The signatories expressed a need for government intervention in collaboration with AI companies:

> In parallel, AI developers must work with policymakers to dramatically accelerate development of robust AI governance systems. These should at a minimum include: new and capable regulatory authorities dedicated to AI; oversight and tracking of highly capable AI systems and large pools of computational capability; provenance and watermarking systems to help distinguish real from synthetic and to track model leaks; a robust auditing and certification ecosystem; liability for AI-caused harm; robust public funding for technical AI safety research; and well-resourced institutions for coping with the dramatic economic and political disruptions (especially to democracy) that AI will cause.[4]

The efforts around the governance and potential regulation of AI are an ongoing concern (cf. Mügge, Chapter 19; Omotubora and Basu, Chapter 17; Paul, Chapter 20 all in this volume), so any attempt to express the current state will likely be dated in short order. Nevertheless, the convergence of academic and practitioner concerns around the governance of AI is clear and is an event in itself. There is so much eagerness in the call for regulation of AI by some of the largest and most prominent companies, such as OpenAI or Anthropic, that some are warning of regulatory capture. In May 2023, OpenAI issued an article authored by CEO Sam Altman and two co-founders of OpenAI, Greg Brockman and Ilya Sutskever. The article is short, fewer than a thousand words, and it reads almost like a manifesto for what they call "responsible AI".[5] They offer three sensible and appealing ways to address a future superintelligence that will "exceed expert skill level in most domains" within ten years: first, coordination among the leading AI efforts; second, an international regulatory body such as the IAEA; third, technical capability to make superintelligence safe. The appeal and sensibility of these suggestions comes primarily from their conventional quality. The suggestion is simply a coordinated acceptance of limits to production or creation, an independent body to monitor those limits, and the technical capacity of that independent body to monitor. This is a basic expression of regulation, and the question then is how?

Regulation without AI?

The question of regulating AI typically ignores that last provision expressed by the OpenAI leadership, namely, the technical capability. This is because to regulate AI requires AI: artificial intelligence is the advancement of the principle of regulation itself. Human intelligence promotes and enables functional regulation, and the organization of that intelligence is realized through the rule-based structure that we call bureaucracy. The superiority of collective intelligence (which is implied in the political expression of democracy) allows for the discovery of rules and the invention of rules through which some organized entity can exert control over another entity. Certainly, this also involves political questions of legitimacy, but as Weber made plain in his analysis of modern society, when legitimacy was decoupled from tradition, its basis was found in the impersonal, objective *rule*. We might add to Weber's observation also the practical application of the rule, as expressed in the pragmatist expression of truth as that which works, and the elevation of the "one best way" that is the driving force of technology (or, as Ellul expressed it, *technique*). Bureaucracy is legitimate because it works (Weber referred to this as its technical superiority) and is impersonal. The limit has always involved the extent of discretion permitted to officials, and the design and functionality of bureaucracy as management, motivated as it has long been toward the "one best way" (the mantra of scientific management that Simon acknowledged as antecedent to operations research), has tended toward the achievement of superior intelligence in the highest levels of management available. Bringing AI into the social and political arena is the completion of, the perfection of, bureaucracy itself. A key to perfecting bureaucracy is the elimination of bias, or in the words of Weber, dehumanization (which he noted to be the special virtue of bureaucracy), which is realized in AI by design. Eliminating bias is a design problem for the social alignment of values, especially since some bias is inevitable in decision making. This elimination of bias is ultimately the Alignment Problem discussed by Wiener.

Regulation means rule and control, so a call for regulation implies an agent's ability to control that which is being regulated. In the case of AI (setting aside for now questions of AGI and superior intelligence) regulating AI is partly about bringing forth objectivity in the name of fairness and equity, and objectivity is determined by the extent to which bias is eliminated. It is, of course, this feature of being without emotion or feeling, or as Weber put it *sine ira et studio*, that aligns AI so closely with bureaucracy. What AI promises is not a replacement of thinking, but a system that makes thinking less relevant to social action, similar to bureaucracy. Issues and problems identified in AI, including bias, are not detrimental to the programme but actually feed its improvement. Much like bureaucracy, AI is built on a framework through which problems are subsumed under it, including intrinsic problems. Problems and issues can be addressed through better specification and design, as any programmer is aware; or, as anyone who studies bureaucracy and organizations is aware, problems in organizations or bureaucracy are simply design problems that we use bureaucracy to address. This feature is evident in how the CEO of OpenAI, the company that developed ChatGPT, discussed improving it. He acknowledged that ChatGPT is "incredibly limited" and serves primarily as a preview of what is to come. But to bring about what is to come, it is imperative that people *use* ChatGPT and help to improve it. The point could not be clearer: AI is made by humans and refined by humans, and it carries all the problems that humans bear, but unlike humans, AI can be designed and refined to mitigate those problems, possibly even eliminate some of them, but to get there, we must endure problems. Using the AI will improve the artificial intelligence. In the parlance of large language models, this is called reinforced learning through human feedback, or RLHF.

Operationally, AI optimizes the very faculty that is necessary for humans to have any control over and, thus, to regulate it. Human use of AI is a design feature to improve it insofar as that use exposes potential or real problems that can be solved through improved design. The inherent logic of large-scale regulation, premised on the impartial execution of objective values, is the very logic through which AI operates and optimizes decisions.

Democratizing AI? The Iatrogenic Problem

One of the ways that proponents of AI regulation hope to prevent disaster is by incorporating humans into the process of fine-tuning the AI. In the case of an LLM, the process begins on a relatively small scale with "crowdworkers" providing feedback on the responses generated by the AI after it is pretrained using a massive corpus of text. The programme is then fine-tuned on features of quality (defined as sensibleness, specificity, and interestingness), safety, and groundedness (Thoppilan et al., 2022).

The incorporation of humans into the fine-tuning of AI is unsurprising from the standpoint that AI is a social tool like bureaucracy. Efforts to improve bureaucracy have consistently incorporated a "participatory" element to ensure that bureaucratic operations do not violate common customs and moral guidelines, reflecting the inherent tension between democracy and bureaucracy. The literature on bureaucracy and participation is extensive, but the essential idea is that providing a platform for people at least to comment on the operations of administration (bureaucracy) will improve it. Bureaucracy will be more responsive and less biased and will better serve the public.

This same sensibility is behind the attempts to improve AI through human intervention or "democratization". Calls for the democratization of AI are similar in tone and objective to the participatory moves made toward bureaucracy, moves that ultimately reinforced the bureaucratic system itself, as Weber predicted, because democratization is not necessarily democracy.

In the case of AI, the scope and scale of what is required to democratize reinforces the concept of bureaucracy that accompanies mass democracy rather than democracy as self-government. The social preconditions of a "democratized" AI are procedures, processes, and institutions of regularity primed by the development of bureaucracy itself as an objectivity of norms. These calls for democratization are more for the sake of AI than for democracy, and this point, too, can be made through an understanding of bureaucracy. To put the matter simply, democratization is bureaucratization, or the product of democratization is bureaucracy, not democracy. Democratization is a process of levelling, specifically of social and economic differences, and as Weber said, "Bureaucracy inevitably accompanies modern *mass democracy*, in contrast to the democratic self-government of small homogeneous units" (Weber, 2013, XI.8.A, emphasis original). Bureaucracy is produced by democratization, where the levelling through objectivity is designed to approach the impersonal universal. The exercise of authority falls to *nobody,* an intentional result of democratization. Ensuring that this nobody acts in accordance with prevailing norms and standards is essentially what is meant by the call for democratizing AI. Such a call has a legacy in the field, going back to Norbert Wiener's work in cybernetics and the idea of alignment. As already noted, Wiener framed the problem based on the speed and efficiency of the new controlling systems he expected to be developed, noting pessimistically the ability of humans to react if the purposes of the impersonal authority contravened norms or expectations, so it was and is imperative for the purposes and norms to be included at the start. The primary mode of alignment in programmes like ChatGPT is RLHF, and as such another way of viewing RLHF is as a legitimacy process. It is an elaborate scheme to learn from human responses to artificial responses what kinds of artificial responses will spur the least resistance or concern. This is the notion of democratization inherent in AI development, a democratization that strengthens not democracy but bureaucracy insofar as it strengthens the impersonal authority.

Society has been primed for the emergence of AI by bureaucracy. What we are currently witnessing in the development of AI is a step in the perfection of bureaucracy, contrary to the commonplace that AI will serve as a remedy to bureaucracy. For over a century the impetus of our politics has been to depoliticize, to remove the contentious qualities of politics in favour of a data-driven, technocratic system that features dehumanization in a favoured way. The point of AI is not to be human but to rectify the issues in our politics that being human causes. Implicit in criticisms of AI, from concern of its biases to its "hallucinations" and errors, is the challenge to make the technology better not by making it more human, but by rectifying the human-like errors. Efforts to democratize AI by incorporating human feedback strengthen the programme by reinforcing its status as *greater than* human in the sense that humans are limited in their rational capacities (or, to paraphrase Herbert Simon, humans are boundedly rational). The human is *useful to the AI* insofar as the human provides information that improves the AI. The human is important to the extent of complementing or improving the impersonal authority undergirding the AI.

This is the reinforcement loop of democratization, a process of affirming bureaucracy and impersonal authority in the name of democracy. To adopt a medical metaphor, this solution of democratization is like an iatrogenic disease, one that is prompted by a physician's treatment and then requires more physician treatment. The advancement of bureaucracy through AI requires democratization to ensure that the impersonal authority aligns with norms and expectations, that its purpose is what we really desire, as Wiener put it. But it was democratization itself that spurred the bureaucratic culture and society that primed us for the rise of

AI, as is evident in the development of operations research from leading thinkers like Simon and Newell. The conception of democratization behind the treatment of AI is not a process of strengthening democracy but, on the contrary, of treating the disease that continues to afflict democracy, the disease of impersonal authority, bureaucracy, and convenience, using the same treatment to address the disease of bias and limited human cognitive capacity that brought on the affliction.

CONCLUSION

The question of what is to be done, raised in the last section, tends to be answered in the terms of bureaucracy. Weber's warning that democracy can oppose the "rule" of bureaucracy but inevitably promotes it anyway might be the injunction needed to question the rise of AI and the concomitant solutions to its rising threat: talk of regulating or democratizing AI is simply obfuscation masking an emerging impersonal authority of superintelligence. It is the height of Kafkaesque absurdity to believe that there will be any control over a system designed for optimal impersonal control. We have built and continue to build a world in which AI is an operative necessity. AI will not liberate society from bureaucracy. It will liberate bureaucracy from humans.

Attempting to solve a problem with the same system that created it has a low level of potential success. To grasp the context of AI, one must ask what problem it solves? The answer is that it does not solve any particular problem of an engineering concern. The problem it aims to solve is the problem of the human, the human problem, the slow, bumbling sensibility of human thinking that slows down processes but allows for creativity. Simon's breakthrough idea of bounded rationality was ultimately an observation of a problem to be solved. Satisficing is a shortcut, a heuristic that can be mitigated against through organization and the artificial. Simon observed in the sciences of the artificial the ability to design systems of optimization to mitigate against the human limits of cognition and reasoning. AI is, like bureaucracy, a solution to a problem of human collectivity, the problem of mass democracy, a problem that is both expressed through and solved through the simple expression of "organization" – it is not a thing but a process. You cannot regulate AI in the sense of exerting control over it because it is the process by which such potential control is exerted.

The concern is not about regulating AI, which admits a process of improving it, but of creating spaces and practices that reject it. That means rethinking our institutions that demand the kind of logic that demands AI, down to the practices. It is difficult to see how any form of AI is not an admission of a new master, of a superintelligence, and this is before the emergence of AGI, which the progenitors of AI see as inevitable at this point.

There is a line in the 32nd chapter of the *Daodejing* that reads "when unhewn wood is carved then there are names. Now that there are names, know enough to stop. To know when to stop is how to stay out of danger" (Ivanhoe, 2003). This notion of knowing when to stop to avoid danger is repeated in chapter 44. Unhewn wood represents the world left alone, but it cannot always be left alone. The human ability to shape the world in accordance with our desires is a distinctive trait of being human, for better or worse. The potential within that ability is a primary source of our compulsion toward organization. Carving wood represents manipulation and artifice, and doing it creates the artificial order through which we prosper, beginning with names and concepts. Knowing when to stop requires knowing, following the

Daodejing, non-action (wu wei) against action, the theoretical against the practical. As is evident from the earliest expressions of AI, as I noted here using operations research and the legacy of Herbert Simon, AI is not simply a product, a carved wood, but is the carving out of the capacity to carve wood, it is the manipulation of the ability to manipulate. AI is process, and it directly infringes upon our executive capacity of knowing when to stop since it is only with its aid that we can observe the limits of it and of our use of and subjection to it.

NOTES

1. To avoid misunderstanding, I am noting one of the paths of execution that AI has taken and takes by way of operations research and the connection to the political and institutional developments associated with it and with the modern state. That is not to say that the development of AI is exclusive to this way of thinking. Obviously there are developments of AI in visual graphics, coding, private corporate operations, "white collar" jobs, education, and other areas. But the question I am posing antecedes these types of developments to the extent that the governance system aspires to exert some kind of control over AI in its myriad functions and forms.
2. Mass democracy is one of the important impetuses behind the development of modern bureaucracy. Another, which I do not address here for the sake of space, is capitalism. Weber provided detailed connections between capitalism and bureaucracy, but the important aspect upon which I am focused here are political concerns leading to a demand for "right decisions", which is why I attend more to the issue of mass democracy.
3. Sam Altman @sama, 29 March 2023 https://twitter.com/sama/status/1641229941131051008.
4. "Pause Giant AI Experiments: An Open Letter", available through the Future of Life Institute at https://futureoflife.org/open-letter/pause-giant-ai-experiments/ (accessed 15 May 2023). At the time of writing, over 27,000 people had offered their signature to this letter.
5. "Governance of Superintelligence." 2023. Sam Altman, Greg Brockman, and Ilya Sutskever. Available at https://openai.com/blog/governance-of-superintelligence (accessed 30 May 2023).

REFERENCES

Ivanhoe, P. J. (2003). *The Daodejing of Laozi.* Indianapolis, IN: Hackett.

Newell, A., & Simon, H. A. (1976). Computer science as empirical inquiry: Symbols and search. *Communications of the ACM,* **19** (3), 113–26.

Simon, H. A. (1957). *Administrative Behavior* (2nd ed.). New York: The Free Press.

Simon, H. A. (1969). *The Sciences of the Artificial.* Cambridge, MA: MIT Press.

Simon, H. A., & Newell, A. (1958). Heuristic problem solving: The next advance in operations research. *Operations Research,* **6** (1), 1–10. Retrieved from http://www.jstor.org/stable/167397.

Thoppilan, R., De Freitas, D., Hall, J., Shazeer, N., Kulshreshtha, A., Cheng, H.-T., …, & Le, Q. (2022). LaMDA: Language Models for Dialog Applications. *arXiv.* Retrieved from https://arxiv.org/abs/2201.08239.

Weber, M. (2013). *Economy and Society: An Outline of Interpretive Sociology* (edited by G. Roth & C. Wittich). Los Angeles, CA: University of California Press.

Wiener, N. (1960). Some moral and technical consequences of automation. *Science,* **131** (3410), 1355–58. Retrieved from http://www.jstor.org.libezp.lib.lsu.edu/stable/1705998.

5.   AI and the logics of public sector organizations
Frans af Malmborg and Jarle Trondal

INTRODUCTION

> The economic value of a complete introduction of AI (current AI technology) in Swedish public administration is significant. The potential is estimated to amount to approximately SEK 140 billion annually, corresponding to approximately 6 per cent of today's total public expenditure. (Swedish Agency for Digital Government (DIGG), 2020: 2)

In the quote above, the Swedish Agency for Digital Government suggests how the Swedish public administration could benefit from using Artificial Intelligence Technologies (AITs) to automate and digitalize decision-making processes. For public sector organizations (PSOs), a lot of the hype around AITs has been centred on the idea that it could cut costs, make the public sector more efficient and free up the time of public servants. Arguments, such as the one above, are underpinned by assumptions about how technologies can be "inserted" into pre-existing organizational structures, yielding relatively foreseeable results. This however does not consider the complexities of organizations (Fountain, 2001). Writing from an explicitly organizational-institutional perspective, this chapter nuances such conceptions arguing that implementing novel technologies are not just a matter of "inserting" – like downloading the latest upgrade for one's laptop. Instead, we argue that PSOs are highly complex normative orders, having a life of their own. This entails that the concept of PSO also means that we must understand the ways in which AITs interact with these complex normative orders.

The chapter is aimed towards organization scholars, public administrators and policymakers, as well as those who have an above average interest in the subject matter. We argue that there are some excellent conceptual tools provided by organization theory and institutionalist scholarship which can help to illuminate the mechanisms by which AITs proliferate within PSOs. We argue that these conceptual tools can be used both by practitioners to critically problematize the "promises" of AITs as well as for students and researchers who wish to further disentangle these issues. The chapter pulls out several classic organization theory concepts such as diffusion, decoupling, symbolic action, appropriateness and organizational capacities and illustrates them with empirical examples. We think that scholars of PSOs have a huge task ahead to unpack the intricacies of the alleged AI transformation and suggest some ways forward to approach this issue with equal amounts of prudence and curiosity.

STATE OF THE ART: AI IN THE PUBLIC SECTOR

Even though AI proliferation in the public sector is at a nascent stage and a lot more research is needed, there has been a recent upsurge of research over the past few years which outlines AITs challenges and opportunities for the public sector more generally (Dwivedi et al., 2021). AITs are widely seen as a game-changer even for those who are typically sceptical about the transformative impact of technologies (Yeung & Lodge, 2019). When it comes to challenges, the most obvious examples are algorithmic bias and algorithmic opacity. As research has shown, algorithms which build on already biased data can make unjust and unlawful decisions towards citizens no matter the public service (Buolamwini & Gebru, 2018; Eubanks, 2018). Algorithmic opacity concerns the way in which increasingly complex algorithms may be hard to look into, which risks creating a "black box society" (Pasquale, 2015). Since PSOs are governed by strict laws of transparency in most cases, this poses an issue for public sector accountability and auditability (Power, 1997).

The opportunities with AI in the public sector on the other hand seem open-ended. They reach from freeing up workers' time (Eggers et al., 2017), making public services more efficient and doing more with less (Veale & Brass, 2019) to increasing the performance in data processing and analysis, making public services more adapted towards its citizens (Wirtz & Müller, 2019). The OECD, for example, states that:

> Artificial Intelligence (AI) is an area of research and technology application that can have a significant impact on public policies and services in many ways. In just a few years, it is expected that the potential will exist to free up nearly one-third of public servants' time, allowing them to shift from mundane tasks to high-value work. (OECD, 2019: 3)

Similar to the quote in the introduction, the OECD here pictures AI as a cost-saving efficiency booster for public administration (see Heidelberg, Chapter 4 in this volume, on the rationalist project of AI as the ultimate form of bureaucracy). This reasoning is illustrated in Figure 5.1, which also outlines how technologies are often seen as independent variables while institutions are seen as dependent variables.

| information technology | ➡ | Predictable institutional change |

Note: Figure building on theorization in Fountain (2001).

Figure 5.1   *A common-sense view of technology implementation in institutions*

While the majority of public administration scholars suggests both challenges and opportunities in relation to AITs (Coglianese & Lai, 2022; Gupta & Kumari, 2017; Sun & Medaglia, 2019; Wirtz et al., 2019), there still seems to be an instrumentalist and solutionist tendency in the overarching AI *policy discourse* on AITs, which frequently promotes universalistic solutions. In the face of alleged uncertainties and challenges, the proposed solutions include better data, more advanced algorithms and a stronger digital infrastructure, leading scholars to critique AI policy for promoting "technological solutionism" – a highly instrumentally reductionist view of political problems (Morozov, 2013; Ossewaarde & Gulenc, 2020; Paul, 2022; Paul, Carmel and Cobbe, Chapter 1 in this volume). AIT implementation is thus often imbued with strong normative justifications for solving societal challenges and promoting leadership (Bareis & Katzenbach, 2022). We argue that AITs are better understood as a part of the establishment of idealized organizational images. Such an approach goes beyond the mere technical and functionalist definitions and allows scholars to engage with AITs narrative and imaginative value – how they may form a spine in narrating the modern, innovative and legitimate organization (Beckert & Bronk, 2018; Jasanoff & Kim, 2015).

PUBLIC SECTOR ORGANIZATIONS AND AITS: AN INSTITUTIONAL PERSPECTIVE

"Organizations matter" is a widely used expression in organization studies – a rallying cry bringing together various scholars engaged in studying organizations. A simple answer to why organizations matter is presented by March and Simon (1958); since people spend so much time in them they become ubiquitous arenas for social life. Organizations are hereby seen as relatively stable normative orders, wielding prescribed rules and cues for values, heuristic frames and appropriate behaviour (Egeberg & Trondal, 2018; Scott, 2014; March & Olsen, 1996; 1998). Norms are defined as reciprocal typifications of habitualized actions and institutionalization occurs when these actions become infused with value beyond the task at hand (Berger & Luckmann, 1967; Selznick, 1996). This means that organizations exist beyond their material structure and instrumental goal – they are "packages" of normative, ideational, cognitive, discursive and material/visual elements that are co-constitutive of each other (Meyer et al., 2021).

Institutional theory starts from the assumption that institutional structures mobilize biases because they supply cognitive and normative shortcuts and categories that simplify and guide actors' search for problems, solutions and their consequences (Schattschneider, 1975; Simon, 1965). Institutional theory assumes that organizations possess capacities to shape institutional dynamics quite independently of societal influence. Concepts such as "historical inefficiency" and "path dependence" suggest that the match between environments, organizational structures and decision-making behaviour is not automatic and precise (Olsen, 2010). Mechanisms such as socialization, disciplining and control ensure that organizations perform their tasks relatively independently from outside influences. But they do so within the boundaries set by the legal authority and the political leadership they serve, which thus creates a semi-permeable shield for disruptive changes. Causal emphasis is thus placed on the architecture of organizations and how this may contribute to mobilizing bias in organizational dynamics. Institutional theory thus provides a picture of organizations as creators of the "organizational man" (Simon 1965) and as a stabilizing element in politics more broadly (Olsen 2010). Public organizations may hereby develop their own endogenous nuts and bolts quite independently of the societies to which they belong, thus providing elements of robustness to politics. Organizational dynamics and decision-making behaviour are assumed to be shaped by "in-house" organizational structures of the unit in question (Radin, 2012: 17).

Differing from private sector organizations, PSOs are situated within political systems and thus operate within constitutionally and institutionally confined contexts that are politically constituted. PSOs' raison d'etre therefore derives from a "relatively stable" political-normative consensus. In consequence, how PSOs should be structured and governed is subject to debate and contestation (Olsen, 2007). PSOs also need to adhere to high normative standards for good governance. In relatively stable liberal democracies, checks and balances are set in place to control for efficient use of government funds, as well as trying to ensure that governing processes are sufficiently transparent, accountable and non-discriminatory (Dahlström et al., 2017). On a very general level, the adherence to these standards is one of the reasons why novel technologies such as AI may be more complicated to implement within PSOs in comparison to private organizations.

Despite the fact that much contemporary organizational research has left rational choice theories behind in favour of institutionalist approaches (Eriksson-Zetterquist, 2015), old habits die hard. Policymakers' obsession with efficiency and cost saving is conceptually similar to the "classical" organization theory of Fordism and scientific management, where the goal of organization theory was to achieve the optimal division of labour given a general organizational purpose (Fayol, 1930; Gulick & Urwick, 1937; Heidelberg, Chapter 4 in this volume). This conceptually flawed position, however, does not consider the post-rational choice theory literature on organizations and their contexts, and offers a highly stylized, reductionist and uniform view of organizational dynamics.

On the contrary, an institutional perspective highlights the contingent processes of how actors within organizations shape and are being reshaped by the normative orders that organizations provide (Hall & Taylor, 1996). Such structures are thus likely to shape how organizations adopt, understand, frame and use new technologies. New technologies also co-exist with old ones which might yield organizational superstructures, decoupling and a complex web of differentiated goals (Hall, 2012). Based on institutionalist literature, we outline four mechanisms which help to better understand the field of AITs within the public sector, along with some illustrative examples of contemporary AIT implementation.

Organizational Filtering

A hugely influential figure in modern organization theory, Herbert Simon was one of the founders of the academic field of AI, participating in the by now famous Dartmouth workshop in 1956.[1] In their ground-breaking work *Organizations: Cognitive Limits on Rationality* James G. March and Herbert Simon laid out much of the groundwork that has guided post-rational choice schools of thought within the study of organizations from the late 1950s onwards. One of their core assumptions was that organizations "filter" information through organizational specialization – an inherent feature which allows for organizations to internally decouple problems and solutions into distinct components. By filtering, organizations provide members with "bounded" choice situations through which organizational members go about their day-to-day routines. Organizational filtering is thus a way for organizations to reduce complexity and uncertainty regarding problems, solutions and their consequences. March & Olsen (2004) later also outlined how organizational actors (private and public) adhere to an identity-driven logic of appropriateness and not only to a utility-driven consequential logic of social action. Given that AITs begin to permeate PSOs, we can assume that AITs – similar to organizational structures – may "filter" the perception of public servants and have an impact on public servant's heuristic models and ultimately their choices and decisions.

One example of this is the Spanish automated decision-making system VioGén – an algorithm which assesses the risk of females being subject to gender violence. Described as one of the most complex of its sort, introduced in 2007, the system had assessed 600,000 cases by January 2020, gathering data from reporting victims through a 39-point list which assesses the likelihood that the aggressor will repeat violent behaviour. Depending on the level of risk, follow-up meetings for data-gathering are conducted, keeping the score of the threat of women at risk as a decision-support technology for looking into what cases to pursue (Chiusi et al., 2020). However, since its inception, several low-risk cases have ended up in homicide.

Officers can manually increase the risk-score, but a study found that 95 per cent of officers adhere to the algorithmically suggested score (ibid., 2020). Hence, in a data-driven public sector AITs may increasingly filter public servants' choice situations through automated classifications. Without going into detail on the complex interaction between street-level bureaucrats and AI (Busch and Henriksen, Chapter 6 in this volume), some research suggest that street-level bureaucrats use technologies selectively to retain their discretion (Busch, 2019), but at the same time see a systematic decline in discretion (see for example Busch & Henriksen, 2018). However, if AITs become institutionalized, they are seen as an inherent part of the organizational normative structure. Since the VioGén algorithm was introduced in 2007, we might expect that the sheer length of time it has been part of the organization means that it has been integrated into the organizational fabric and thus is no longer seen as external or exceptional to established decision-making routines – and is thus not questioned to the extent a "novel" form of technology would have been.

As an increasingly ubiquitous part of organizations, AITs can filter organizational perception in many ways including, but not limited to, scoring, classification and risk assessments, becoming an inherent part of the appropriate norms for public servants. As AITs continue to develop across PSOs, it becomes increasingly relevant to study the many contexts of how this filtering unfolds. One suggestion for novel scholarship in this direction is the study of "thinking infrastructures". Bowker et al. (2019) argues that the beginning of the twenty-first century is marked by the significant development of digital thinking infrastructures. Such infrastructures are valuation regimes which constitute orders of worth (Boltanski et al., 2006), having consequences for sorting (Bowker & Star, 1999), governing (Lessig, 1999), tracing and data-gathering (Bowker et al., 2019). Thus, more research is needed to outline empirically and conceptually how AITs serve as filtering devices within the institutionalized settings of PSOs.

Organizational Capacities

Organizational capacities are a second variable that may be used to study how public organizations may implement AITs. Organizational capacity refers to the resources available in organizations to solve problems, coordinate, learn and so on (Joaquin & Greitens, 2021). In extant literature it often refers to the existence of departments, units or positions devoted to a particular policy area. The idea is that in an information-rich world systematic interest articulation, problem attention and problem solving are dependent on the degree to which such activities are underpinned by organizational resources (Egeberg & Trondal, 2018). Organizational capacities focus and mobilize attention and action capacity around certain problems and solutions while ignoring others (Simon, 1990). On a grand scale, democracies may be seen as an organizational capacity that routinizes attention by systematically organizing partisan opposition and policy contestation into parliaments and governments.

Studies suggest that the European Commission and EU-level agencies serve as organizational capacities at a supranational level of governance that may control how member-state public authorities implement and practise EU legislation. EU agencies also serve as hubs of transnational agency networks (Egeberg & Trondal, 2017). This capacity serves to mobilize national bureaucrats and external stakeholder groups. Through horizontal specialization of organizations, certain interests and concerns become routinely supported by organizational capacity while others are ignored. A study of the transfer of the European Commission's pharmaceutical unit from DG Enterprise and Industry to DG Health and Consumers showed that the unit's policy focus changed from being biased towards business interests to becoming more attentive to patient and public health concerns. The unit's external environment also changed from being dominated by industry organizations towards being more populated by patient and consumer groups (Vestlund, 2015). Studies also indicate that a loss of political control by the political leadership of a government that hived off agencies at arm's-length distance, can be partly compensated for by creating organizational capacity in the form of a unit in the ministerial department that duplicates work being done in the agency (Egeberg & Trondal, 2009; Verhoest et al., 2010).

In crisis literature, it is similarly argued that since surprises are difficult to predict, and hence, to prepare for, organizations sometimes build resilience by creating the capacities to adapt to surprises. Timeus & Gascó (2018) show how organizations mobilize innovation capacity by establishing permanent attention to it through innovation "labs". Such labs serve as a permanent organizational capacity to initiate and implement reforms. They illustrate the argument by how the city government of Barcelona strengthened its innovation capacity through such labs. Routinizing innovation through permanent structures made it easier to initiate innovation, but not to implement it.

AITs are often framed as having the potential to magnify existing organizational capacities by expanding their technical capacities, through increased accuracy, speed, automating services and capacity for data management (Veale & Brass, 2019). At the same time, pre-existing organizational capacities may also impede the implementation of AITs. We argue that organizational capacities may function as a mediating variable in the spread of AI policy. Comparing the Nordic countries' AI strategies in relation to each other and the EU has shown that Finland stands out in assembling robust AI policy through the involvement of a variety of stakeholders and the production of several policy documents. In contrast, other Nordic countries had weaker administrative capacities installed to craft policy documents and involving stakeholder groups (af Malmborg & Trondal, 2021). While the sheer amount of government expertise dedicated to the formulation of a national AI agenda does not safeguard a smooth implementation, it does however suggest that some governments have dedicated more organizational capacities to thinking about AI than others. The literature on organizational capacities put this rather simply; there is no such thing as a free lunch. The implementation of AITs is dependent on pre-existing organizational capacity and does not automatically translate into enhanced organizational capacity.

And yet AITs are frequently "sold" as *capacity-enhancing* technologies for PSOs. Over the period 2016–2019 iBorderCtrl – an automation system with AI-powered interview software was tested by the EU across the borders of Hungary, Latvia and Greece. The project, funded by Horizon 2020, promised a web camera based face expression lie-detector which would decrease subjective control and the workload of human agents and increase objective control by automated means (iBorderCtrl.eu, 2023). Migrants coming to the EU were tasked to upload documentation online and then conduct a prescreening online automated interview with a built-in "lie detector software". Assessing iBorderCtrls decision-making structure and underpinning assumptions, Sánchez-Monedero & Dencik (2022) argue that it is highly unlikely that such form of deception detection based on facial expressions via webcams would work in practice. The project subsequently attracted a lot of criticism and was discontinued in 2019, even facing court scrutiny due to transparency issues (Bacchi, 2021; Sánchez-Monedero & Dencik, 2022). So, while AITs can be promoted as capacity-enhancing mechanisms within PSOs, this case shows why it is of paramount importance to remain vigilant towards such promises. It is worth remaining especially sceptical of promises of "increased objectivity" in decision-making processes, since they do not chime well with much existing AI research on bias, discrimination and legal uncertainty. This case begs repeating our initial question in the chapter: can AITs be inserted into existing organizations yielding predictable results? In this case they did not. This is why further research is needed to study the extent to which organizational capacities structure the implementation of AITs as well as how AITs are framed as capacity-enhancing technologies. In the next section we will dive deeper into the "policy to practice" issue and the relations between overarching plans and what might really happen "on the ground".

Decoupling and Symbolic Action

A third variable that may be used to study how public organizations may implement AITs is organizational decoupling and symbolic action. Going back to classic institutional theory, Meyer and Rowan (1977: 341), argue that "the formal structures of many organizations in postindustrial society … dramatically reflect the myths of their institutional environments instead of the demands of their work activities". Instead of focusing on core tasks, they argued that organizations tend to respond symbolically to different types of normative pressures in their environment. This "ceremonial" work done by managers has been described by Fisher (2009) as "market Stalinism" – the valuing of symbols of achievement over actual achievement to keep appearances and "good faith" (cf. Meyer and Rowan, 1977). This paradigmatic shift in studying modern organizations allowed scholars to start uncovering processes of institutional adaptation and decoupling. Decoupling refers to processes in which organizations disconnect and to some extent also disintegrate demands derived from institutional environments and organizational responses, as well as internal disconnects between *talk*, *decisions* and *actions* of the organization (Brunsson, 2019). Even organizational structures may be subsequently decomposed and specialized, which may lead to the creation of organizational clusters and sub-groups. Parts of these structures may serve as myth and ceremony vis-à-vis external audiences, whereas other structures might serve to guide decision-making processes within the organization. For Meyer and Rowan (1977) "myth and ceremony" meant that organizations could respond to institutional pressures, remain legitimate and survive because they enacted "superficial" myths and ceremonies. Such a perspective is at odds with the notion of organizational rationality as goal oriented and based on optimizing utility.

Decoupling remains an illuminating field within organization studies generally and provides specific insight to the development of AITs within PSOs, focusing on the discrepancies (the relative "distance") between formal representations of AITs and their implementation. It is here important for public servants to remain vigilant towards narratives used to promote AITs. At a macro level, a highly vibrant field of study is the (i) flurry of AI policy which has diffused across governments, the private sector and non-governmental organizations, and (ii) to what extent such policies achieve or decouple talk, decision and action. If organizational capacities define the capability of organizations to launch AIT initiatives, the reason for them to do so is better explained by the mechanisms through which technological ideals fluctuate within institutional fields. A symbolic perspective hypothesizes that organizations adopt technologies and policies for their symbolic value – so they are seen as legitimate, modern, rational and future oriented. In addition, many scholars argue that novel technologies themselves often are imbued with hopes, fears, myths and visions (Bareis & Katzenbach, 2022; Bory, 2019; Campolo &

Crawford, 2020; Natale & Ballatore, 2020; Ossewaarde & Gulenc, 2020), implying that the (at least superficial or symbolic) adoption of such technologies can be seen as a way to incorporate such idealized myths into an organizational identity. Symbolic adoption of AITs may therefore manifest itself in the form of "talk" – as described by Robinson (2020: 1) "Countries around the world are jockeying to come out ahead (or at least get a piece) of the AI buzz, and, in doing so, are trying to position themselves as business-driven or trustworthy stakeholders in AI". The fact that all Nordic countries (af Malmborg and Trondal, 2021), the EU (Larsson et al., 2020), China, the United States, France and Germany (Bareis & Katzenbach, 2022) all state that they will be world leaders of AI in their AI strategies points towards a global trend of embodying the myths of leadership and innovation.

Symbolic institutionalism thus holds that PSOs do not reside in a vacuum, but their survival prospects are contingent on their (at least superficial or symbolic) adherence to pre-existing and dominant norms and myths in their institutional environments (DiMaggio & Powell, 1983). However, research has yet to empirically examine these from macro-ideologically sustained hypotheses to simply meso- and micro-level propositions (Greenwood et al., 2017; Powell & DiMaggio, 1991). One timely contribution to this literature is the doctoral thesis by Lisa Reutter (2023) studying datafication in Norwegian public administration "from policy to practice". Reutter (2023) concludes that the "data-driven public sector" remains a future vision and that there are obstacles such as legal assessments, data quality, data access and a lack of financing as well as a great rift between how things are understood from a policymaker and a practitioner perspective (Reutter, 2023). Instead of the realization of overarching political goals of digitalization, Reutter shows how structural and institutional constraints hamper such processes (Reutter, 2022). These findings substantiate our overall critique of the commonly held view of technology implementation.

Sociotechnical Perspectives

A fourth mechanism that may be used to study how public organizations may implement AITs is offered by sociotechnical perspectives. In an influential piece from 1986, Stephen Barley studied the introduction of CT scanners at radiology departments in hospitals. Barley found that despite the exact same technology having been introduced, it produced widely different forms of social structuring and organizing in different hospitals (Barley, 1986). Arguing that technology can be seen as an occasion for social structuring, Barley puts his finger on the ambiguity of technology implementation and suggests understanding technology as a social object whose intended and unintended consequences may follow a contextual logic (p. 107). Sociotechnical perspectives thus theorize technology as social objects which are imbued with certain norms, values and ways of organizing. Many scholars have argued for the need to more properly theorize this interrelation (Fountain, 2001; Leonardi & Barley, 2008; Orlikowski, 2007) but often conclude that accurate theorization remains elusive. In our view, organization scholars need to be open to both variation and standardization when studying AITs within PSOs.

Langdon Winner (1980) notes that the relation between technology and political organization goes as far back as Plato, who argued that certain technologies demand certain forms of social and political organization and control. Winner refers to an example made by Plato when he argues that a ship at sea cannot be run by a democracy, but by an authoritative captain and an obedient crew; certain technologies are imbued with implicit ways of thinking about society and social relations. On the other hand, Barley (1986) concluded that the same technology prompted two completely *different* forms of social organizing in two different contexts. The caveat though is that the way in which technologies translate into different forms of organizing cannot be determined *ex ante*: the context they are a part of structures how technologies such as AITs constrain and enable action. If we were to study it more closely, we might find variation among crews and ships – some tending towards authority-rule and some towards more flexible arrangements.

Sociotechnical perspectives remain attentive towards contextual differences, but should also account for standardization (Leonardi & Barley, 2008). Research questions for AITs within PSOs should therefore both encompass how relatively similar organizations implementing relatively similar AITs may yield different results. But also the reverse: how may relatively similar organizations which implement relatively similar AITs yield similar results? Organization theory is well positioned to study such variation. Thus, a robust research agenda for the impact of AITs on PSOs should account both for examples of variation as well as homogenization within PSOs. The introduction of novel technologies may for example yield new administrative burdens (Heggertveit et al., 2022). Core personnel may be substituted by technology specialists, shift focus from core organizational tasks to peripheral tasks and create administrative superstructures of managers and controllers (Hall, 2012). In some cases the introduction of new AITs may yield blunt "exits" (Hirschman, 1970) by professionals who may feel alienated by the introduction of new technologies. As we have argued earlier, PSOs are institutionalized organizations and not merely utility structures. They encompass norms and duties on professionalism, neutrality and loyalty as well as overarching values on what broader contribution the organization has in society.

One empirical example from Sweden illustrates this. In 2014, the Trelleborg municipality in Sweden initiated the implementation of a Robotic Process Automation (RPA) system within the area of economic aid within the social services, an area of social work with a high level of repetitive tasks. The goal was to free up time for caseworkers to conduct more pre-emptive work by digitalizing and automating the monthly application procedures and shortening waiting times (Lindgren et al., 2019, 2022). Implementation of the RPA in Trelleborg was initially met with some resistance, but with organizational anchoring as well as firm and transparent leadership and political support the reform could be pushed through. Social workers who felt that this reform was at odds with their professional identities left the organization and the reform was later described it as a success story (Höglund Rydén, 2019). By 2016 the municipality received a grant from the Swedish Innovation Agency (Vinnova) to spread this methodology to other enthusiastic municipalities (Vinnova, 2017). Ranerup and Svensson (2022) studied five of these municipalities and argue that such technologies need to be considered actors in their own right with the potential to reframe work entirely within PSOs. In one of the municipalities outside their field of study, 12 out of 16 social workers left office in protest due to changed working environment and job contents. This resulted in a costly reorganization of the social services (Grönlund, 2018).

The above case illustrates many relevant issues for AIT development within PSOs. It illustrates how different organizational capacities constrain and enable technology adoption. It also shows that the "new" and modern organization did not have room for those who were not on board with the reform – leading to "exits". It shows that a "best practice" may not be experienced as a "best practice" on the ground and may travel across time and space and become instantiated in a different context and yield widely different organizational processes. It shows how AITs are socio-institutional artefacts which are at odds with overarching efficiency rationale pertaining to large-scale implementation of AIT within PSOs. Therefore, we see the need for future research from a sociotechnical perspective which could highlight the context specific dynamics within different cases of AIT implementation within PSOs.

CONCLUSIONS

This chapter has outlined a research agenda for AITs and PSOs. We suggested and illustrated the analytical use of institutional mechanisms in our endeavours to critically examine how AITs proliferate within the public sector more generally. Research questions can include, but are not limited to:

- How AITs spread between PSOs as ritualistic symbols of modernity and rationality.
- How organizations may superficially adopt AITs and subsequently decouple talk from decision, and decision from action, to gain legitimacy within institutional environments.
- How AITs can be understood as inherently social objects which may cause a variety of different forms of organizing but also disruptions and exits within different institutional contexts.
- How AITs can contribute to filtering the perception of public servants through processes of classification, counting, grading, valuing and risk management.
- How AITs may both expand organizational capacities but also how the implementation of AITs may weigh heavily on pre-existing organizational capacities which in short supply may delimit potential impact.

As already outlined, an institutional-organizational approach holds that "organizations matter" and this chapter has provided some arguments for why that is the case. We suggest studying institutions as relatively stable sociotechnical normative ecosystems where different and sometimes contradictory rationalities may exist even before the eventual introduction of new technology. Organizations provide a stabilizing element to politics more broadly, but as AITs come to inhabit a more prominent role within them, organizations also change, however incrementally. One thing remains clear: the ways and extent to which AITs interact with such ecosystems evolve in real time and need to be studied more widely and critically as an ever-emergent organizational condition. This chapter argues that institutional theories are well positioned for doing some of this heavy lifting beyond universally optimistic and pessimistic premonitions of AIT development in the public sector.

NOTE

1. The Dartmouth Conference of 1956 at Dartmouth College marks the beginning of Artificial Intelligence as a research field and included organizational theorist Herbert Simon (see *Artificial Intelligence: A Modern Approach* by Russell, Norvig and Davis (2010).

REFERENCES

af Malmborg, F., & Trondal, J. (2021). Discursive framing and organizational venues: Mechanisms of artificial intelligence policy adoption. *International Review of Administrative Sciences*, **89** (1), 39–58. https://doi.org/10.1177/00208523211007533.

Bacchi, U. (2021, February 5). EU's lie-detecting virtual border guards face court scrutiny. *Reuters*. https://www.reuters.com/article/europe-tech-court-idUKL8N2KB2GT.

Bareis, J., & Katzenbach, C. (2022). Talking AI into being: The narratives and imaginaries of national AI strategies and their performative politics. *Science, Technology, & Human Values*, **47** (5), 855–881. https://doi.org/10.1177/01622439211030007.

Barley, S. R. (1986). Technology as an occasion for structuring: Evidence from observations of CT scanners and the social order of radiology departments. *Administrative Science Quarterly*, **31** (1), 78–108.

Beckert, J., & Bronk, R. (eds). (2018). *Uncertain Futures: Imaginaries, Narratives, and Calculation in the Economy* (1st edition). Oxford: Oxford University Press.

Berger, P. L., & Luckmann, T. (1967). *The Social Construction of Reality*. Penguin Books.

Boltanski, L., Thévenot, L., & Porter, C. (2006). *On Justification: Economies of Worth*. Princeton, NJ: Princeton University Press.

Bory, P. (2019). Deep new: The shifting narratives of artificial intelligence from Deep Blue to AlphaGo. *Convergence: The International Journal of Research into New Media Technologies*, **25** (4), 627–642. https://doi.org/10.1177/1354856519829679.

Bowker, G. C., Elyachar, J., Kornberger, M., Mennicken, A., Miller, P., Nucho, J. R., & Pollock, N. (2019). Introduction to thinking infrastructures. In M. Kornberger, G. C. Bowker, J. Elyachar, A. Mennicken, P. Miller, J. R. Nucho, & N. Pollock (eds), *Research in the Sociology of Organizations* (pp. 1–13). Leeds: Emerald Publishing Limited. https://doi.org/10.1108/S0733-558X20190000062001.

Bowker, G. C., & Star, S. L. (1999). *Sorting Things Out: Classification and its Consequences*. Cambridge, MA: MIT Press.

Brunsson, N. (2019). *The Organization of Hypocrisy: Talk, Decisions and Actions in Organizations*. Copenhagen: Copenhagen Business School Press.

Buolamwini, J., & Gebru, T. (2018). Gender shades: Intersectional accuracy disparities in commercial gender classification. *Conference on Fairness, Accountability and Transparency*, 77–91.

Busch, P. A. (2019). *Digital Discretion Acceptance and Impact in Street-Level Bureaucracy*. Doctoral dissertation. Agder University.

Busch, P. A., & Henriksen, H. Z. (2018). Digital discretion: A systematic literature review of ICT and street-level discretion. *Information Polity*, **23** (1), 3–28. https://doi.org/10.3233/IP-170050.

Campolo, A., & Crawford, K. (2020). Enchanted determinism: Power without responsibility in artificial intelligence. *Engaging Science, Technology, and Society*, **6**, 1–19. https://doi.org/10.17351/ests2020.277.

Chiusi, F., Fischer, S., Kayser-Bril, N., Spielkamp, M., & Penner, K. (2020). *Automating Society 2020*. Algorithmwatch. https://automatingsociety.algorithmwatch.org/wp-content/uploads/2020/12/Automating-Society-Report-2020.pdf.

Coglianese, C., & Lai, A. (2022). Algorithm vs. Algorithm. *Duke Law Journal*, **72**, 1281.

Dahlström, C., Lapuente, V., & Gine, V. L. (2017). *Organizing Leviathan*. Cambridge: Cambridge University Press.

DiMaggio, P. J., & Powell, W. W. (1983). The iron cage revisited: Institutional isomorphism and collective rationality in organizational fields. *American Sociological Review*, **48** (2), 147. https://doi.org/10.2307/2095101.

Dwivedi, Y. K., Hughes, L., Ismagilova, E., Aarts, G., Coombs, C., Crick, T., Duan, Y., Dwivedi, R., Edwards, J., Eirug, A., Galanos, V., Ilavarasan, P. V., Janssen, M., Jones, P., Kar, A. K., Kizgin, H., Kronemann, B., Lal, B., Lucini, B., …, & Williams, M. D. (2021). Artificial intelligence (AI): Multidisciplinary perspectives on emerging challenges, opportunities, and agenda for research, practice and policy. *International Journal of Information Management*, **57**, 101994. https://doi.org/10.1016/j.ijinfomgt.2019.08.002.

Egeberg, M., & Trondal, J. (2009). Political leadership and bureaucratic autonomy: Effects of agencification. *Governance*, **22** (4), 673–688. https://doi.org/10.1111/j.1468-0491.2009.01458.x.

Egeberg, M., & Trondal, J. (2017). Researching European Union agencies: What have we learnt (and where do we go from here)? European Union agencies. *JCMS: Journal of Common Market Studies*, **55** (4), 675–690. https://doi.org/10.1111/jcms.12525.

Egeberg, M., & Trondal, J. (2018). *An Organizational Approach to Public Governance: Understanding and Design*. Oxford: Oxford University Press.

Eggers, W. D., Schatsky, D., & Viechnicki, P. (2017, April 26). AI-augmented government: Using cognitive technologies to redesign public sector work. *Deloitte Insights*. https://www2.deloitte.com/us/en/insights/focus/cognitive-technologies/artificial-intelligence-government.html.

Eriksson-Zetterquist, U. (2015). *Organization och organisering* (4th edition). Malmö: Liber.

Eubanks, V. (2018). *Automating Inequality: How High-Tech Tools Profile, Police, and Punish the Poor*. New York: St. Martin's Publishing Group.

Fayol, H. (1930). *Industrial and General Administration*. Berkeley, CA: Sir I. Pitman & Sons, Limited.

Fisher, M. (2009). *Capitalist Realism: Is There No Alternative?* Winchester, UK: Zero Books.

Fountain, J. E. (2001). *Building the Virtual State: Information Technology and Institutional Change*. Washington, DC: Brookings Institution Press.

Greenwood, R., Oliver, C., Lawrence, T. B., & Meyer, R. E. (2017). *The Sage Handbook of Organizational Institutionalism* (2nd edition). Los Angeles: SAGE Publications.

Grönlund, M. (2018). *Omorganization kostade Kungsbacka sex miljoner*. Sveriges Radio. Available at: https://sverigesradio.se/artikel/7097736 (accessed 13 June 2023).

Gulick, L., & Urwick, L. (eds). (1937). *Papers on the Science of Administration*. New York: Columbia University Press.

Gupta, R. K., & Kumari, R. (2017). Artificial intelligence in public health: Opportunities and challenges. *JK Science*, **19** (4), 191–192.

Hall, P. (2012) *Managementbyråkrati – organizationspolitisk makt i offentlig förvaltning*. Malmö: Liber.

Hall, P. A., & Taylor, R. C. R. (1996). Political science and the three new institutionalisms. *Political Studies*, **44** (5), 936–957. https://doi.org/10.1111/j.1467-9248.1996.tb00343.x.

Heggertveit, I., Lindgren, I., Madsen, C. Ø., & Hofmann, S. (2022). Administrative burden in digital self-service: An empirical study about citizens in need of financial assistance. In R. Krimmer, M. Rohde Johannessen, T. Lampoltshammer, I. Lindgren, P. Parycek, G. Schwabe, & J. Ubacht (eds), *Electronic Participation* (Vol. 13392, pp. 173–187). Springer Nature Switzerland. https://doi.org/10.1007/978-3-031-23213-8_11.

Höglund Rydén, H. (2019). *Trelleborgsmodellen – Conditions, Opportunities and Challenges for Digitalization in Public Administration*. Master thesis in public administration, School of Public Administration, Gothenburg University.

Hirschman, A. O. (1970). *Exit, Voice, and Loyalty: Responses to Decline in Firms, Organizations, and States*. Cambridge, MA: Harvard University Press.

iborderCtrl.eu (2023). iborderCtrl – Frequently asked questions. Available at: https://www.iborderctrl.eu/Frequently-Asked-Questions/ (accessed 13 June 2023).

Jasanoff, S., & Kim, S. H. (2015). *Dreamscapes of Modernity: Sociotechnical Imaginaries and the Fabrication of Power*. Chicago: University of Chicago Press.

Joaquin, M. E., & Greitens, T. J. (2021). *American Administrative Capacity: Decline, Decay, and Resilience*. Cham, Switzerland: Springer.

Larsson, E. S., Bogusz, C. I., & Schwarz, J. A. (2020). *Human Centered AI in the EU – Trustworthiness as a Strategic Priority in the European Member States*. Brussels: European Liberal Forum.

Leonardi, P. M. (2008). Indeterminacy and the discourse of inevitability in international technology management. *Academy of Management Review*, **33** (4), 975–984. https://doi.org/10.5465/amr.2008.34422017.

Leonardi, P. M., & Barley, S. R. (2008). Materiality and change: Challenges to building better theory about technology and organizing. *Information and Organization*, **18** (3), 159–176. https://doi.org/10.1016/j.infoandorg.2008.03.001.

Lessig, L. (1999). *Code and Other Laws of Cyberspace*. New York: Basic Books Inc.

Lindgren, I., Madsen, C. Ø., Hofmann, S., & Melin, U. (2019). Close encounters of the digital kind: A research agenda for the digitalization of public services. *Government Information Quarterly*, **36** (3), 427–436. https://doi.org/10.1016/j.giq.2019.03.002.

Lindgren, I., Madsen, C. Ø., Höglund Rydén, H., & Heggertveit, I. (2022). Exploring citizens' channel behavior in benefit application: Empirical examples from Norwegian welfare services. *15th International Conference on Theory and Practice of Electronic Governance*, 416–423. https://doi.org/10.1145/3560107.3560312.

March, J. G., & Olsen, J. P. (1996). Institutional perspectives on political institutions. *Governance*, 9 (3), 247–264. https://doi.org/10.1111/j.1468-0491.1996.tb00242.x.

March, J. G., & Olsen, J. P. (1998). The institutional dynamics of international political orders. *International Organization*, 52 (4), 943–969. https://doi.org/10.1162/002081898550699.

March, J. G., & Olsen, J. P. (2004). The logic of appropriateness. ARENA Working papers WP 04/09. University of Oslo.

March, J. G. & Simon, H. (1958). *Organizations: Cognitive Limits on Rationality*. Cambridge: Blackwell Publishing.

Meyer, R., Jancsary, D., & Höllerer, M. A. (2021). Zones of meaning, Leitideen, institutional logics – and practices: A phenomenological institutional perspective on shared meaning structures. In M. Lounsbury, D. A. Anderson, & P. Spee (eds), *On Practice and Institution: Theorizing the Interface* (pp. 161–186), Leeds: Emerald Publishing Limited. https://doi.org/10.1108/S0733-558X20200000070005.

Meyer, J. W., & Rowan, B. (1977). Institutionalized organizations: formal structure as myth and ceremony. *American Journal of Sociology*, 83 (2), 340–363. http://www.jstor.org/stable/2778293.

Morozov, E. (2013). *To Save Everything, Click Here: The Folly of Technological Solutionism*. New York: Public Affairs.

Natale, S., & Ballatore, A. (2020). Imagining the thinking machine: Technological myths and the rise of artificial intelligence. *Convergence: The International Journal of Research into New Media Technologies*, 26 (1), 3–18. https://doi.org/10.1177/1354856517715164.

OECD (2019). *Hello, World: Artificial Intelligence and its Use in the Public Sector*. OECD Working Papers on Public Governance, 36. https://doi.org/10.1787/726fd39d-en.

Olsen, J. P. (2007). The institutional dynamics of the European university. In J. P. Olsen & P. Maassen (eds), *University Dynamics and European Integration* (pp. 25–54), Dordrecht: Springer.

Olsen, J. P. (2010). *Governing through Institution Building: Institutional Theory and Recent European Experiments in Democratic Organization*. Oxford: Oxford University Press.

Orlikowski, W. J. (2007). Sociomaterial practices: exploring technology at work. *Organization Studies*, 28 (9), 1435–1448. https://doi.org/10.1177/0170840607081138.

Ossewaarde, M., & Gulenc, E. (2020). National varieties of artificial intelligence discourses: Myth, utopianism, and solutionism in West European policy expectations. *Computer*, 53 (11), 53–61. https://doi.org/10.1109/MC.2020.2992290.

Pasquale, F. (2015). *The Black Box Society: The Secret Algorithms that Control Money and Information*. Cambridge, MA: Harvard University Press.

Paul, R. (2022). Can *critical policy studies* outsmart AI? Research agenda on artificial intelligence technologies and public policy. *Critical Policy Studies*, 16 (4), 497–509. https://doi.org/10.1080/19460171.2022.2123018.

Powell, W. W., & DiMaggio, P. J. (eds). (1991). *The New Institutionalism in Organizational Analysis*. Chicago: University of Chicago Press.

Power, M. (1997). *The Audit Society: Rituals of Verification*. Oxford: Oxford University Press.

Radin, B. A. (2012). *Federal Management Reform in a World of Contradictions*. Washington, DC: Georgetown University Press.

Ranerup, A., & Svensson, L. (2022). *Service Automation in the Public Sector: Concepts, Empirical Examples and Challenges* (G. Juell-Skielse, I. Lindgren, & M. Åkesson, eds). Springer International Publishing. https://doi.org/10.1007/978-3-030-92644-1.

Reutter, L. (2022). Constraining context: Situating datafication in public administration. *New Media & Society*, 24 (4), 903–921. https://doi.org/10.1177/14614448221079029.

Reutter, L. (2023). *Datafication of Public Administration*. Doctoral dissertation. Norwegian University of Science and Technology.

Robinson, S. C. (2020). Trust, transparency, and openness: How inclusion of cultural values shapes Nordic national public policy strategies for artificial intelligence (AI). *Technology in Society*, 63, 101421. https://doi.org/10.1016/j.techsoc.2020.101421.

Russell, S. J., Norvig, P., & Davis, E. (2010). *Artificial Intelligence: A Modern Approach.* (3rd edition). Harlow and Upper Saddle River, NJ: Prentice Hall.

Sánchez-Monedero, J., & Dencik, L. (2022). The politics of deceptive borders: 'Biomarkers of deceit' and the case of iBorderCtrl. *Information, Communication & Society,* **25** (3), 413–430. https://doi.org/10.1080/1369118X.2020.1792530.

Schattschneider, E. E. (1975). *The Semisovereign People: A Realist's View of Democracy in America.* New York: Holt, Rinehart and Winston.

Scott, W. R. (2014). *Institutions and Organizations: Ideas, Interests, and Identities* (4th edition). Los Angeles: SAGE.

Selznick, P. (1996). Institutionalism 'old' and 'new'. *Administrative Science Quarterly,* **41** (2), 270. https://doi.org/10.2307/2393719.

Simon, H. (1990). *Reason in Human Affairs.* Stanford, CA: Stanford University Press.

Simon, H. (1965). Administrative decision making. *Public Administration Review,* **25** (1), 31–37. https://doi.org/10.2307/974005.

Sun, T. Q., & Medaglia, R. (2019). Mapping the challenges of Artificial Intelligence in the public sector: Evidence from public healthcare. *Government Information Quarterly,* **36** (2), 368–383. https://doi.org/10.1016/j.giq.2018.09.008.

Swedish Agency for Digital Government (DIGG) (2020). *Främja den offentliga förvaltningens förmåga att använda AI.* Available at: https://www.digg.se/analys-och-uppfoljning/publikationer/publikationer/2023-01-23-slutrapport-uppdrag-att-framja-offentlig-forvaltnings-formaga-att-anvanda-artificiell-intelligens (accessed: 23 March 2023).

Timeus, K., & Gascó, M. (2018). Increasing innovation capacity in city governments: Do innovation labs make a difference? *Journal of Urban Affairs,* **40** (7), 992–1008.

Veale, M., & Brass, I. (2019). Administration by algorithm? In Yeung, K. & M. Lodge (eds), *Algorithmic Regulation* (pp. 121–149), Oxford: Oxford University Press.

Verhoest, K., Roness, P., Verschuere, B., Rubecksen, K., & MacCarthaigh, M. (2010). *Autonomy and Control of State Agencies: Comparing States and Agencies.* London: Springer.

Vestlund, N. M. (2015). *Between Centralization and Decentralization.* ARENA Report No. 4/15, University of Oslo.

Vinnova (2017). *Implementering av Trelleborgsmodellen.* The Swedish Innovation Agency. Available at: https://www.vinnova.se/p/implementering-av-trelleborgsmodellen/ (accessed 13 June 2023).

Winner, L. (1980). Do artifacts have politics? *Daedalus,* **109** (1), 121–136. https://www.jstor.org/stable/20024652.

Wirtz, B. W., & Müller, W. M. (2019). An integrated artificial intelligence framework for public management. *Public Management Review,* **21** (7), 1076–1100. https://doi.org/10.1080/14719037.2018.1549268.

Wirtz, B. W., Weyerer, J. C., & Geyer, C. (2019). Artificial intelligence and the public sector: Applications and challenges. *International Journal of Public Administration,* **42** (7), 596–615. https://doi.org/10.1080/01900692.2018.1498103.

Yeung, K., & M. Lodge (eds). (2019). *Algorithmic Regulation* (1st edition). Oxford: Oxford University Press.

6. AI technologies and the reconfiguration of discretion in street-level bureaucracy

Peter André Busch and Helle Zinner Henriksen

INTRODUCTION

Since the turn of the millennium, there has been an increased interest in, and focus on, using information and communications technologies (ICTs) in public administration, often termed e-government or digital government. More recently AI technology has become part of public administration too (Henman 2020; Selten et al. 2023). AI technology is premised on the use of algorithms in a variety of governmental tasks such as calculating financial benefits, identifying potential tax fraud, regulating traffic flows, and improving decision-making (Janssen & Kuk 2016; Part IV of this *Handbook*). For example, Latvia introduced UNA (a chatbot), assisting entrepreneurs with inquiries, and shifting civil servants from routine tasks. Since its 2018 launch, UNA has tackled over 22,000 questions from nearly 4,000 users and is eyed as a training model across the public sector (Berryhill et al. 2019). Another application in Trelleborg, Sweden, uses robotic process automation for citizens to justify that they are eligible for social services by demonstrating an inability to work, and decision-support in the further process (Ranerup & Henriksen 2022).

This development has been influenced by global benchmarks from entities like the European Union (EU) (Yeung 2023) and the United Nations (UN). Over the past two decades for example, the UN has published its e-government survey aiming at mapping countries' "efforts to provide effective, accountable and inclusive digital services to all and to bridge the digital divides" (United Nations 2020) along with ambitions to modernize public administration with the latest technologies. These efforts sometimes turn into national competitions, echoing a digital beauty contest, and realizing political aspirations for digitization (Ngwenyama et al. 2023).

So far, digital government literature often focuses on front-office processes and strategies, such as the implementation and use of digital self-services, streamlining interactions with citizens (cf., MacLean & Titah 2022). How back-office processes transform (or not) with the advent of AI and digital technologies has received less attention in research (cf., Selten et al. 2023). This relative scholarly oversight is problematic. Back-office operations often concern how street-level bureaucrats use their judgement to decide in specific cases (Lipsky 2010). With ICTs' growing influence, street-level work has seen changes in citizen interactions and discretion, presenting both challenges and opportunities (Busch & Henriksen 2018). For example, in Norway, tax reporting is no longer handled locally by street-level bureaucrats, but instead nationally and assisted through technology. Busch et al. (2018) found that street-level bureaucrats perceive this impact differently based on profession.

The public sector manages high caseloads and is governed by clear rules, often resulting in impactful decisions for the affected individuals (Lipsky 2010). Therefore, expertise among workers is paramount. Moreover, the legislation mandates equal treatment, transparency, and accountability in the sector (Yeung 2023). What is at stake in public sector AI applications is very different than recommendations of Netflix movies (Pajkovic 2022) or targeted product offers (Bradlow et al. 2017). Research on the role of AI technologies in areas like social benefits (Ranerup & Henriksen 2019; 2022; cf. Sleep and Redden, Chapter 27 in this volume), welfare services (Løberg 2021; cf. Krutzinna, Chapter 29 in this volume; Whitfield, Wright, and Hamblin, Chapter 28 in this volume), unemployment (Ammitzbøll Flügge et al. 2021; Breit et al. 2021), housing (McCall et al. 2021), and immigration (Evans & Koulish 2020; cf. Molnar, Chapter 23 in this volume) involve intricate cases, often concerning vulnerable individuals, with multifaceted challenges; a cocktail that requires trained professionals with cognitive, affective, and moral capabilities (Susskind & Susskind 2015). The AI technologies' self-learning capabilities and extensive data use raise concerns in public administration about bias, fairness, transparency and explainability, autonomy, accountability, and ethical implications of their impact on human lives (Henman 2017; also see on accountability: Cobbe and Singh, Chapter 7 in this volume; on bias: Hong, Chapter 8 in this volume; on explainability: Berry, Chapter 10 in this volume; on transparency: Aula and Erkkilä, Chapter 13 in this volume).

In prior work, we introduced the term "digital discretion" to discuss the intersection of street-level discretion and digitalization, emphasizing the relationship between public values and technology (Busch & Henriksen 2018). This chapter discusses how AI technologies can impact discretionary practices. We use the term "algorithmic discretion" to describe this influence, understood as the scope of choices an algorithm might make, given its design and the data it has been trained on. We highlight three major trends arising from AI's integration into public administration: (1) the de-skilling of street-level bureaucrats; (2) automated inequality; and (3) the challenges related to transparent, explainable algorithms where street-level bureaucrats have to explain AI-driven decisions which may be hard to understand for humans (including themselves, of course).

The chapter unfolds as follows: we first delve into the street-level bureaucracy perspective, highlighting its main features. Drawing from recent research, we continue with an examination of both techno-optimism and techno-pessimism views on AI technologies' impact on public administration. These insights set the stage for our discussion on global trends in AI technology adoption in public administration and its potential to reconfigure street-level discretion. We conclude with thoughts on future research directions in AI technologies and street-level discretion.

STREET-LEVEL DISCRETION AND PUBLIC IDEALS

Street-level bureaucracy constitutes a substantial part of government. It refers to a subset of government where civil servants such as police officers, teachers, and social workers, coined street-level bureaucrats, have direct interactions with the public and interpret and decide on policy applications in real-time scenarios (Lipsky 1980; 2010). Despite varied responsibilities, they often face large workloads, must deal with policy ambiguities, and have considerable decision-making autonomy. For example, a police officer deciding how to handle a minor offence, a teacher assisting a struggling student, or a social worker evaluating a family's needs. Street-level work is characterized by considerable inequities in terms of power, professional expertise, and administrative knowledge in favour of street-level bureaucrats (Lipsky 2010).

Citizens, on the other hand, may be unaware of and unable to claim their rights, as well as being at the mercy of street-level bureaucrats who actually make decisions about their matters.

Discretion is central to the role of street-level bureaucrats. To make decisions, street-level bureaucrats exercise discretion based on their experience and understanding of policies and protocols. Discretion can be understood as the ability to judge, decide, and act within a certain scope during policy execution (Molander & Grimen 2010). The term 'street-level bureaucracy' has two implications. Firstly, the 'bureaucracy' aspect alludes to the rule-bound nature of these roles where specific situations and associated decisions fall within legal guidelines, emphasizing transparency and legitimacy (March 1994). Traditional bureaucracy, as envisioned by Max Weber, minimizes discretion (cf. Heidelberg, Chapter 4 in this volume, on Weberian bureaucracy and AI). Instead, more recent views, including those of Lipsky (2010), recognize that discretion is inevitable because legal directives can be ambiguous, and the intricate nature of societal issues does not always fit neatly into static rules. These rules, while guiding decisions, also provide transparency and legitimacy. Secondly, the "street-level" facet emphasizes the practical interpretation of these rules, allowing for flexibility in decision-making. Through training and experience, bureaucrats develop practical expertise in their respective fields. Their primary goal is to fulfil the objectives of policies set by democratically elected officials (Hupe 2013), ensuring the policy's core intentions are upheld (May & Winter 2009). Circumstances often demand discretion to be able to fulfil policy intentions, whether due to the complexity of a situation, the uniqueness of a case, or the need for on-the-spot decisions.

The concept of public values is often used to express underlying purposes and motivations, which guide street-level bureaucrats during policy implementation. We review them here briefly because they are also important standards against which potential transformations of discretionary decision-making under the rise of AI technologies ought to be measured to maintain a trustworthy public administration (for a similar discussion of the professional ethics guiding frontline administrators see Krutzinna, Chapter 29 in this volume). Public values refer to enduring beliefs, norms, principles, and standards that are widely held or shared within a community, society, or country, which is important in the public sector where the success or failure of ICT is associated with a multiplicity of stakeholder objectives that need to be addressed (Almarabeh & AbuAli 2010). These public values are broader than objectives expressed in single ICT projects and can thus be used for the evaluation of public activities, including street-level work. In our previous work, we used the concept of public service values, suggesting that the increased impact of ICT on discretion can strengthen ethical and democratic values but weaken professional and relational values (Busch & Henriksen 2018).

Key values steering street-level work include accountability, transparency, justice, and fairness. Accountability is understood as the obligation for street-level bureaucracies to explain to a legitimate authority their actions, accept responsibility for them, and transparently disclose the results (Bovens 2007; Gregory 2017; Mulgan 2019). Accountability often pertains to both the responsibilities of street-level bureaucrats and their associated entities and the rights of those affected by their actions. To ensure accountability, mechanisms exist both internally ("vertical" – answering to superiors) and externally ("horizontal" – answering to entities like the media, ombudsmen, and courts) (Mulgan 2019; cf. Cobbe and Singh, Chapter 7 in this volume for a wider discussion of accountability narratives and regulations for AI). Transparency, closely linked to accountability, refers to the quality of being easily seen through or understood, often relating to processes, decisions, or activities. Transparency involves sharing information openly so that the logic or rationale behind decisions is clear to those who are influenced by them. Transparency is under pressure when applying AI technologies due to its complexity. This openness aims at building trust and enabling stakeholders to understand, validate, or critique processes and outcomes, crucial for informed participation by stakeholders (for a longer discussion of transparency and AI, see Aula and Erkkilä, Chapter 13 in this volume). One of the immediate threats to key values of accountability and transparency, which is directly driven by AI technologies, is information asymmetry (Lepri et al. 2018). Lepri and colleagues highlight different dimensions of information asymmetry leading to opacity: intentional, illiterate, or intrinsic opacity which challenges the perception of fairness. The importance of fairness concerns procedural justice. That is, in the public sector, citizens should expect impartial treatment or behaviour without favouritism or discrimination. Fairness pertains to decisions and processes that are consistent, unbiased, and equitably applied.

The extent and manner of discretion can vary based on multiple factors, such as bureaucratic knowledge, digital tools at the disposal of the street-level bureaucrats, and enduring public values underlying street-level work required to make sense of a multiplicity of stakeholder objectives (Almarabeh & AbuAli 2010).

THE RISE OF AI TECHNOLOGIES IN STREET-LEVEL BUREAUCRACY

Public digitalization strategy documents typically emphasize the significance of transforming street-level work through digital means to enhance efficiency, transparency, and the quality of public services (Ngwenyama et al. 2023; cf. discussions of the ultimately rational bureaucracy: Heidelberg, Chapter 4 in this volume). In complex street-level tasks, ICT usually acts as a support tool in hybrid multi-agent environments, rarely performing competently as expected by street-level bureaucrats (Bullock & Kim 2020; Busch & Henriksen 2018; Medaglia et al. 2023; Ranerup & Henriksen 2022). Yet, tasks that previously required the discretion of street-level bureaucrats, such as automated tax reporting and financial application processing, are now fully conducted by ICT (Busch & Henriksen 2018). Whereas the influence of ICT on street-level work has been prevalent for a long time, only recently can a heightened interest in AI be traced in the street-level bureaucracy literature (Alshallaqi 2022; Ammitzbøll Flügge et al. 2021; Bullock et al. 2020; Grimmelikhuijsen 2022).

AI's integration into street-level bureaucracy is seemingly driven by similar goals as other ICTs, and the optimism salient in early discussions about ICT in street-level bureaucracy is also characteristic of recent AI technology discussions (e.g., Bracci 2023; Henman 2020; van Noordt and Misuraca 2022). AI, with its ability to quickly process vast amounts of data, offers the allure of speeding up decision-making, reducing human error, and ensuring consistency in the application of rules and policies (cf. Paul 2022; Paul, Carmel and Cobbe, Chapter 1 in this volume). Technology is seen as superior to humans because it is assumed to be based on "objective calculations", rather than subjective assessments by individual employees (Marston 2006; cf. Heidelberg, Chapter 4 in this volume). For example, by providing expert AI-driven recommendations to street-level bureaucrats (Ammitzbøll Flügge et al. 2021), detecting social issues more quickly (van Noordt and Misuraca 2022), and profiling unemployed individuals (Bracci 2023). Those aspects are independent of the specific role of public administration and the tasks undertaken by street-level bureaucrats in their case-handling practices.

Policy goals further reflect a general evolutionary direction of ICT from simple office automation, towards more complex use. For example, The United States Bureau of Labor Statistics analyses numerous surveys on workplace ailments annually, crucial for understanding and future prevention. The manual analysis, involving a complex coding system, consumed 25,000 employee hours yearly. In 2014, the bureau started employing AI to code surveys, now handling half of them. AI achieves in a day what an employee did in a month, and more accurately. The bureau offered training to the employees providing them with information about how AI could augment their work (Berryhill et al. 2019). Similar to this application of AI, the Queensland government in Australia uses machine learning and computer vision to automatically map and classify land use features in satellite imagery. This marks a major change from when street-level bureaucrats hand-digitized features on the screen map; a very resource-demanding task. The method has not only proved to be highly efficient but also very accurate with an accuracy of 97 per cent, way above the required threshold of 80 per cent (Berryhill et al. 2019).

This techno-optimism narrative, reflected in policy documents, suggests that the introduction of AI is quite uncomplicated and only leads to improvements. Potential downsides of AI initiatives are seldom discussed or even mentioned in public policy documents. However, as we will discuss next, this view of AI has been criticized as oversimplistic, raising several caveats about its suitability in street-level bureaucracies and the problematic ways in which discretionary decisions are being transformed/affected.

IS MORE TECHNO-PESSIMISM APT? AI TECHNOLOGIES IN STREET-LEVEL BUREAUCRACY

Whereas policy documents to a large extent present favourable views of AI in the public sector, the research literature has raised several caveats (e.g., Coglianese & Lehr 2017). Susskind and Susskind (2015) argue that the technology-optimistic view of AI is based on what they term the "AI fallacy". They problematize the assumption that the only way that systems can make good decisions is to replicate human behaviour. They further argue that this is a fallacy because the important aspect of case handling is the quality of the outcome, not the process leading to and supporting the outcome. This logic undermines the role of street-level bureaucrats since their role is to exercise discretion adhering to principles of accountability, transparency, and systematic case handling (Lipsky 2010). However, apart from the examples provided by Susskind and Susskind (2015), at present, there is limited empirical research supporting this hypothesis. Administrative processes guided by public values are still the dominant principles for public administration and administrative practices (Busch & Henriksen 2018).

Central to the ethos of street-level work is the granted permission to exercise discretion. AI technologies, especially in their current forms, often rely on preset algorithms and parameters, which may not always allow for nuance (Henman 2017). In fact, AI technologies can be counter-productive to discretionary practices by emphasizing computationally derived commonalities rather than paying attention to individual cases, meaning that administrative uncertainty may be reinforced by technology (Pääkkönen et al. 2020). Thus, there is a risk that reliance on AI technologies could lead to overly standardized and impersonal responses, potentially alienating citizens. A further risk is that the rules that are applied do not fit the case because the AI technologies fail to recognize the situation and apply the correct rule.

For street-level bureaucrats, their professional experience and capabilities play a central role (Susskind & Susskind 2015) in helping citizens understand the rationale behind a decision. Considering that street-level bureaucrats can fail to live up to the ideals of justice, fairness, accountability, and transparency (Alkhatib & Bernstein 2019), the fundamental question is therefore: are AI technologies better aligning with the ideals of public administration than humans?

One of the main concerns raised in the techno-pessimism camp relates to the de-skilling of street-level bureaucrats. Whereas new technologies may be introduced for street-level bureaucrats as tools to improve street-level work, they bear a resemblance to performance management (Møller & Hill 2021; Raso 2017). Street-level bureaucrats navigate ambiguous goals, making it challenging for politicians and officials to set clear objectives without prompting strategic behaviours on the street level (Møller & Hill 2021; Zacka 2017). Measurement results do not necessarily reflect the specific needs of citizens and can be misunderstood by politicians and citizens either due to strategic interests or complexity (Jansen 2008; Moynihan & Hawes 2012).

Therefore, this performance management may lead to an overemphasis on metrics, and street-level work risks becoming what is measurable (De Bruijn 2007), often at the expense of its more qualitative aspects (Green & Chen 2021; Raso 2017). Instead of street-level bureaucrats using their professional experience – exercising discretion – the consequence is routinization or checklist behaviour. Street-level bureaucrats may lean towards a "technocratic" mindset, where the process becomes more important than the outcome (Møller & Hill 2021), leading to a de facto de-skilling of street-level work.

The risk of automated inequality is a second and prominent concern of the techno-pessimism camp. The term received wide attention from the book by Eubanks (2018), as she highlights how automated practices lead to systematic biases that disfavour already vulnerable groups in society. From a policy-maker perspective, the increased digitalization of street-level work often relates to the risk of leaving some groups behind due to their limited technical capabilities. This echoes both the well-known digital divide discussion (Helbig et al. 2009), and its specification as "administrative literacy" where the capacity to obtain, process, and understand basic information and services from public administrations is paramount for getting access to services (Döring & Jilke 2023). However, with AI technologies, examples from recent research suggest that limited digital literacy and access to technology is also a hindrance for vulnerable groups to "feed" the algorithms with the information needed to be considered for benefits and support (Considine et al. 2022; Pors & Schou 2021; Ranerup & Henriksen 2022). Thus, the wrong decisions can be made since AI may make recommendations that are based on non-representative datasets. Pors and Schou (2021) highlight the moral implications for frontline employees who are confronted with the digital shortcomings of citizens.

Transparency and accountability present a third set of challenges. Firstly, AITs used in public decision-making challenge the possibilities for citizens to understand precisely how a decision is made (Ghosh 2019; Newell & Marabelli 2015). Secondly, it becomes difficult for citizens to hold street-level bureaucracies accountable for their actions and decisions. With traditional human-led decision-making, the reasoning behind a decision, even if not always agreed upon, is generally discernible. In contrast, AI algorithms, especially sophisticated ones like deep learning models, can operate as "black boxes". Thus, AI technologies introduce a "wicked problem" in that its outcomes could be unexplainable even to its developers. Whereas decision trees are the easiest to explain to users, AI technologies with high-performing methods (e.g., deep learning) are the least explainable (Gunning et al. 2019). Fundamentally, it adds to the older concerns raised by Bovens and Zouridis (2002) concerning the move from street-level bureaucracy to system-level bureaucracy where the logics of computer scientists and system developers might displace those of street-level bureaucrats with administrative expertise. The lack of algorithmic transparency has the potential to challenge the trustworthiness and accountability of bureaucratic decision-making (Grimmelikhuijsen 2022), and hence its legitimacy.

AI AS A MOTOR FOR RECONFIGURING STREET-LEVEL DISCRETION

In our previous work, we looked at how ICT impacted discretionary practices on the street level of public sector decision-making. We concluded that the impact of ICT on discretion, what we termed "digital discretion", could strengthen ethical and democratic values such as fair and uniform decision-making and empowerment of citizens, and weaken professional and relational values such as decision quality and individualized care in traditional street-level bureaucracies (Busch & Henriksen 2018). In this chapter, we draw on this previous discussion and illustrate how AI technologies hold the potential to influence discretionary practices further, working towards an "algorithmic discretion" model. Adding a critical lens, we have pointed to three megatrends in relation to AI and street-level bureaucracy: public sector workforce de-skilling, automated inequality, and algorithmic opacity.

First, the reliance on algorithmic street-level work may alienate street-level bureaucrats from work previously characterized by strong professionalism and intrinsic motivation. The debate about technology's role in de-skilling has persisted for decades (Zuboff 1988). ICT often results in isolated systems per department, causing street-level bureaucrats to lose a holistic case view (Bannister 2001). The overview of a case and its context can be lost even though each step in the case-handling process lives up to all standards (Bannister 2001). In her original work, Zuboff (1988) referred to the fragmentation of processes as de-skilling, where humans only handle redundant tasks left by machines. For example, electronic health records (EHRs) may diminish a clinician's judgement, pushing a "checkbox mentality" over nuanced patient assessments, and potentially reducing the clinician's critical thinking skills. De-skilling can also take the form of following technological scripts at the expense of professional opinions. Research suggests that street-level bureaucrats are afraid of defying computer screens, which can be perceived as very persuasive (Wihlborg et al. 2016). However, the literature also has examples of street-level bureaucrats who are critical of the adoption of new, persuasive technology, for example, police officers being reluctant to follow predictive prompts, instead arguing for the persistence of intuition-led policing (Sandhu & Fussey 2021). Chapters in this *Handbook*, especially in Part IV, also contain plenty of examples of how public sector workers navigate this new technologically supported (or constrained) space.

A study of the impact of performance management among case handlers suggests that technology led to adherence to law and thus a high level of public values but at the same time also dysfunctional organizational behaviours (Wastell et al. 2010). This development may have a negative impact on job satisfaction, as street-level bureaucrats may feel that they are no longer able to use their skills and expertise to make a difference in the lives of individuals and communities. With AI as an effective new colleague, communities of practice can be lost at the expense of technology leading to "isolation by digitalization" (Håkansta 2022). This is a technology-driven de-skilling of street-level bureaucrats that resonates with our previous findings, putting less emphasis on professional and relational values (Busch & Henriksen 2018; for childcare services, see Krutzinna, Chapter 29 in this volume; for social care work, see Whitfield, Wright and Hamblin, Chapter 28 in this volume). At the moment, research speaks in favour of the techno-optimist re-skilling perspective, where trivial tasks are taken over by AI leaving more inspiring tasks for humans, moving towards "human-algorithm decision systems" (Burton et al. 2020). However, existing control practices may challenge such re-skilling of the citizens (Juell-Skielse & Wohed 2010).

Second, disadvantaged users have historically been those who possess less social and cultural capital as well as relevant training required for effective computer usage (Kvasny & Keil 2006). However, what we may observe with the use of AI, is the emergence of new groups of users who struggle with outcomes generated from AI technologies. Those are citizens who possess the resources to navigate in society, use technological solutions, and furthermore have an inherent drive to understand the rationale behind the decisions affecting their life, the *bonus pater familias*. To satisfy this group of citizens, it becomes imperative to explain algorithmic street-level work. If we fail to do so, it could potentially have consequences for our understanding of citizenship. A stream of literature discusses changes in citizenship through the label of digital citizenship, understood as the evolving rights and responsibilities of citizens in the digital realm (Jæger 2021). In citizen-to-government transactions, there is an underlying expectation that citizens should facilitate their own service needs without any involvement from street-level bureaucrats. Yet, not all citizens are equipped to navigate these digital processes with ease, which is further complicated by the use of AITs due to their opaqueness. Whereas all citizens have equal rights to services (Ranerup & Henriksen 2022), we may observe citizens in need of other digital competencies in the future to be able to access public benefits fully. Breit et al. (2021) refer to "digital coping" where employees who use technologies in their case-handling practices experience technology as a resource that helps manage caseloads, but at the same time experience it to be a demanding resource because of the need to embrace vulnerable citizens who cannot handle digital self-service which is a prerequisite for getting automation to work (Ranerup & Henriksen 2022). A consequence is the risk of technology-driven administrative exclusion (Peeters & Widlak 2018). Pors and Schou (2021) take this observation even further. They highlight the moral and ethical dilemmas frontline workers face in digitized welfare services.

Third, the lack of transparency can have a profound impact on accountability and trust in street-level work. Accountability is becoming increasingly dense through the use of AI technologies. To hold street-level bureaucrats accountable involves providing information about their work, discussing their performance, and enforcing potential measures to improve street-level work (Olsen 2014). However, making judgements about accountability issues when AI technologies are involved would require insights not only into the data that the AI technology is trained by but also the algorithmic logic behind its outcomes (Busuioc 2021). To do so will further require an understanding of how street-level bureaucrats interact with AI technologies (Bullock & Kim 2020), as well as the ability to unpack the algorithmic processes behind the AI system (Alkhatib & Bernstein 2019; for sceptical positions on whether that is even possible: Berry, Chapter 10 in this volume; Heidelberg, Chapter 4 in this volume). With self-learning abilities, AI technologies develop and potentially adjust the parameters used to produce their output. With huge amounts of data and black-boxed algorithmic processes, it would be beyond the interpretation of street-level bureaucrats, citizens, and even the AI designers themselves to identify these parameters. Thus, the very advantage of AI has become its problem (Busuioc 2021; also see Heidelberg, Chapter 4 in this volume).

Some suggest that explainable AI (XAI) can enhance street-level work by providing understandable reasoning behind the AI system's inferences and outcomes (Grimmelikhuijsen 2022). This would help increase trust and accountability in AI systems, especially in high-stakes or sensitive situations. For example, in emergency services, XAI can help first responders understand the reasoning behind an AI-generated disaster response plan, improving the effectiveness of the response. Opening up the black box of AI technology could thus enable street-level bureaucracies to ensure fair and accurate outcomes and correct potential errors. However, the application of XAI is not straightforward. The ability to identify intricate patterns in huge datasets is considered to be better in AI models like deep learning neural networks. These models are inherently complex, and making them interpretable might mean simplifying the models, which can reduce their predictive power. Moreover, the notion of "explainable" is itself highly subjective and contested (also see Berry, Chapter 10 in this volume). We suggest that human oversight remains important to be able to override AI systems, as does the effort to render data used to train AI systems more representative of the population they will serve (on bias see: Hong, Chapter 8 in this volume).

CONCLUSION

To summarize, the use of AI technologies in street-level work raises important questions about power and control in society (see Ulbricht, Chapter 3 in this volume). We suggest that Castells' (1996) perspective, that technology is neither inherently good or bad, nor neutral, is also crucial for AI technologies' role in public administration. Whereas the integration of AI technologies in street-level bureaucracy aims to streamline processes and boost the cost-effectiveness of decisions, they inadvertently also introduce complexities in the forms of potential street-level de-skilling, opacity, and automated inequality; consequences that can be contrary to democratic, ethical, professional, and relational public sector values, and may reduce rather than enhance the quality of public services. Trained on historical data, AI technologies may also reinforce societal biases without displaying how and why this is done in obscure decision-making mechanisms and calculations. Such developments can undermine the potential for social and political change and requires more critical discussion in seemingly technocratic calls for AI-based cost-effectiveness in the public sector.

If AI technologies are promoted without critical exploration, we face the risk that street-level bureaucrats, reluctantly or not, will follow digital scripts rather than use their own discretion and professional expertise. If this doomsday scenario unfolds, we may again question the term street-level bureaucracy as Bovens and Zouridis (2002) already did more than two decades ago, beginning to talk about systems of digital, artificial, or automated bureaucracies, that are truly efficient but less emphatic of individual citizens. As they constitute a substantial part of the public sector, street-level bureaucrats are important for public service delivery and the idea of solving problems together. If citizens feel that public service provision results in decisions they cannot interpret or justify, especially when such decisions have significant impacts on their lives, a problematic erosion of trust and public sector legitimacy may be the consequence.

Some may argue that the negative effects of these megatrends may be outweighed by the benefits of a successful implementation of AI technologies, or perhaps a peaceful co-existence between humans and algorithms. A technological rationality lens would have highlighted other perspectives on the introduction of AI technologies to discretionary practices. Currently, most research on introducing AI technologies, machine learning, and other advanced technologies is driven by technological rationality or techno-optimism. Revisiting our work, and similar to our previous conclusions (Busch & Henriksen 2018), we suggest that AI technologies also can weaken professional and relational values. However, contrary to our conclusions then, we suggest that AI technologies can be harmful to democratic values and ethical principles at large. Therefore, a critical view is required when discussing the potential of AI technologies for the public sector.

REFERENCES

Alkhatib, A. and M. Bernstein (2019), 'Street-level algorithms: A theory at the gaps between policy and decisions', in *Proceedings of the 2019 CHI Conference on Human Factors in Computing Systems*, pp. 1–13.

Almarabeh, T. and A. AbuAli (2010), 'A general framework for e-government: Definition maturity challenges, opportunities, and success', *European Journal of Scientific Research*, **39** (1), 29–42.

Alshallaqi, M. (2022), 'The complexities of digitization and street-level discretion: A socio-materiality perspective', *Public Management Review*, 25–47. https://doi.org/10.1080/14719037.2022.2042726.

Ammitzbøll Flügge, A., T. Hildebrandt and N. H. Møller (2021), 'Street-level algorithms and AI in bureaucratic decision-making: A caseworker perspective', *Proceedings of the ACM on Human-Computer Interaction*, **5** (CSCW1), 1–23.

Bannister, F. (2001), 'Dismantling the silos: Extracting new value from IT investments in public administration', *Information Systems Journal*, **11** (1), 65–84.

Berryhill, J., K. K. Heang, R. Clogher and K. McBride (2019), *Hello, World: Artificial Intelligence and its Use in the Public Sector*, OECD Working Papers on Public Governance No. 36, Paris.

Bovens, M. (2007), 'Analysing and assessing accountability: A conceptual framework', *European Law Journal*, **13** (4), 447–68.

Bovens, M. and S. Zouridis (2002), 'From street-level to system-level bureaucracies: How information and communication technology is transforming administrative discretion and constitutional control', *Public Administration Review*, **62** (2), 174–84.

Bracci, E. (2023), 'The loopholes of algorithmic public services: An "intelligent" accountability research agenda', *Accounting, Auditing & Accountability Journal*, **36** (2), 739–63.

Bradlow, E. T., M. Gangwar, P. Kopalle and S. Voleti (2017), 'The role of big data and predictive analytics in retailing', *Journal of Retailing*, **93** (1), 79–95.

Breit, E., C. Egeland, I. B. Løberg and M. T. Røhnebæk (2021), 'Digital coping: How frontline workers cope with digital service encounters', *Social Policy & Administration*, **55** (5), 833–47.

Bullock, J. and K.-C. Kim (2020), 'Creation of artificial bureaucrats', in *Proceedings of European Conference on the Impact of Artificial Intelligence and Robotics*, accessed at https://doi.org/10.34190/EAIR.20.001.

Bullock, J., M. M. Young and Y.-F. Wang (2020), 'Artificial intelligence, bureaucratic form, and discretion in public service', *Information Polity*, **25** (4), 491–506.

Burton, J. W., M. Stein and T. B. Jensen (2020), 'A systematic review of algorithm aversion in augmented decision making', *Journal of Behavioral Decision Making*, **33** (2), 220–39.

Busch, P. A. and H. Z. Henriksen (2018), 'Digital discretion: A systematic literature review of ICT and street-level discretion', *Information Polity*, **23** (1), 3–28.

Busch, P. A., H. Z. Henriksen and Ø. Sæbø (2018), 'Opportunities and challenges of digitized discretionary practices: A public service worker perspective', *Government Information Quarterly*, **35** (4), 547–56.

Busuioc, M. (2021), 'Accountable artificial intelligence: Holding algorithms to account', *Public Administration Review*, **81** (5), 825–36.

Castells, M. (1996), 'The space of flows', in M. Castells (ed.), *The Rise of the Network Society*, Oxford: Blackwell, pp. 376–482.

Coglianese, C. and D. Lehr (2017), 'Regulating by robot: Administrative decision making in the machine-learning era', *Faculty Scholarship at Penn Carey Law*, (1734), 1147–223.

Considine, M., M. Mcgann, S. Ball and P. Nguyen (2022), 'Can robots understand welfare? Exploring machine bureaucracies in welfare-to-work', *Journal of Social Policy*, **51** (3), 519–34.

De Bruijn, H. (2007), *Managing Performance in the Public Sector*, London: Routledge.

Döring, M. and S. Jilke (2023), 'Cream-skimming at the frontline: The role of administrative literacy', *Public Administration*, **101** (4), 1569–86.

Eubanks, V. (2018), *Automating Inequality: How High-Tech Tools Profile, Police, and Punish the Poor*, New York: St. Martin's Press.

Evans, K. and R. Koulish (2020), 'Manipulating risk: Immigration detention through automation', *Lewis & Clark Law Review*, **24** (3), 789–855.

Ghosh, R. (2019), 'Appetite for imprecision: The role of bureaucracy in implementing a pay-for-performance program', *Annals of the American Association of Geographers*, **109** (4), 1208–25.

Green, B. and Y. Chen (2021), 'Algorithmic risk assessments can alter human decision-making processes in high-stakes government contexts', *Proceedings of the ACM on Human-Computer Interaction*, **5** (CSCW2), 1–33.

Gregory, R. (2017), 'Accountability and responsibility', in *Oxford Research Encyclopedia of Politics*, Oxford: Oxford University Press, accessed at https://doi.org/10.1093/acrefore/9780190228637.013 .525.

Grimmelikhuijsen, S. (2022), 'Explaining why the computer says no: Algorithmic transparency affects the perceived trustworthiness of automated decision-making', *Public Administration Review*, **83** (2), 241–62.

Gunning, D., M. Stefik, J. Choi, T. Miller, S. Stumpf and G.-Z. Yang (2019), 'XAI – Explainable artificial intelligence', *Science Robotics*, **4** (37).

Håkansta, C. (2022), 'Ambulating, digital and isolated: The case of Swedish labour inspectors', *New Technology, Work and Employment*, **37** (1), 24–40.

Helbig, N., J. R. Gil-García and E. Ferro (2009), 'Understanding the complexity of electronic government: Implications from the digital divide literature', *Government Information Quarterly*, **26** (1), 89–97.

Henman, P. (2017), 'The computer says "DEBT": Towards a critical sociology of algorithms and algorithmic governance', in *The Proceedings of Data for Policy*, London.

Henman, P. (2020), 'Improving public services using artificial intelligence: Possibilities, pitfalls, governance', *Asia Pacific Journal of Public Administration*, **42** (4), 209–21.

Hupe, P. (2013), 'Dimensions of discretion: Specifying the object of street-level bureaucracy research', *Dms – Der Moderne Staat – Zeitschrift Für Public Policy, Recht Und Management*, **6** (2), 23–4.

Jæger, B. (2021), 'Digital citizenship – a review of the academic literature/Digital citizenship: eine systematische Literaturanalyse', *Dms – Der moderne Staat: Zeitschrift für Public Policy, Recht und Management*, **14** (1), 5–6.

Jansen, E. P. (2008), 'New public management: Perspectives on performance and the use of performance information', *Financial Accountability & Management*, **24** (2), 169–91.

Janssen, M. and G. Kuk (2016), 'The challenges and limits of big data algorithms in technocratic governance', *Government Information Quarterly*, **33** (3), 371–7.

Juell-Skielse, G. and P. Wohed (2010), 'Design of an open social e-service for assisted living', in *Electronic Government: 9th IFIP WG 8.5 International Conference, EGOV 2010, Lausanne, Switzerland, August 29–September 2, 2010. Proceedings 9*, Springer, pp. 289–300.

Kvasny, L. and M. Keil (2006), 'The challenges of redressing the digital divide: A tale of two US cities', *Information Systems Journal*, **16** (1), 23–53.

Lepri, B., N. Oliver, E. Letouzé, A. Pentland and P. Vinck (2018), 'Fair, transparent, and accountable algorithmic decision-making processes: The premise, the proposed solutions, and the open challenges', *Philosophy & Technology*, **31** (4), 611–27.

Lipsky, M. (1980), 'Street-level bureaucracy: Dilemmas of the individual in public service', New York: Russell Sage Foundation.

Lipsky, M. (2010), *Street-Level Bureaucracy: Dilemmas of the Individual in Public Service*, 2nd ed., New York: Russell Sage Foundation.

Løberg, I. B. (2021), 'Efficiency through digitalization? How electronic communication between frontline workers and clients can spur a demand for services', *Government Information Quarterly*, **38** (2), 101551.

MacLean, D. and R. Titah (2022), 'A systematic literature review of empirical research on the impacts of e-government: A public value perspective', *Public Administration Review*, **82** (1), 23–38.

March, J. G. (1994), *Primer on Decision Making: How Decisions Happen*, New York: The Free Press.

Marston, G. (2006), 'Employment services in an age of e-government', *Information, Community & Society*, **9** (1), 83–103.

May, P. J. and S. C. Winter (2009), 'Politicians, managers, and street-level bureaucrats: Influences on policy implementation', *Journal of Public Administration Research and Theory*, **19** (3), 453–76.

McCall, V., L. Hoyle, S. Gunasinghe and S. O'Connor (2021), 'A new era of social policy integration? Looking at the case of health, social care and housing', *Journal of Social Policy*, **50** (4), 809–27.

Medaglia, R., J. R. Gil-García and T. A. Pardo (2023), 'Artificial intelligence in government: Taking stock and moving forward', *Social Science Computer Review*, **41** (1), 123–40.

Molander, A. and H. Grimen (2010), 'Understanding professional discretion', in L. G. Svensson and J. Evetts (eds), *Sociology of Professions: Continental and Anglo-Saxon Traditions*, Gothenburg: Daidalos, pp. 167–87.

Møller, M. Ø. and M. Hill (2021), 'Performance measurement and professional decision making: A resolvable conflict?', *Human Service Organizations: Management, Leadership & Governance*, **45** (5), 392–409.

Moynihan, D. P. and D. P. Hawes (2012), 'Responsiveness to reform values: The influence of the environment on performance information use', *Public Administration Review*, **72** (s1), S95–105.

Mulgan, R. (2019), 'The extended scope of accountability in public administration', in *Oxford Research Encyclopedia of Politics*, Oxford: Oxford University Press, accessed at https://doi.org/10.1093/acrefore/9780190228637.013.1369.

Newell, S. and M. Marabelli (2015), 'Strategic opportunities (and challenges) of algorithmic decision-making: A call for action on the long-term societal effects of "datification"', *The Journal of Strategic Information Systems*, **24** (1), 3–14.

Ngwenyama, O., H. Z. Henriksen and D. Hardt (2023), 'Public management challenges in the digital risk society: A critical analysis of the public debate on implementation of the Danish NemID', *European Journal of Information Systems*, **32** (2), 108–26.

Olsen, J. P. (2014), 'Accountability and ambiguity', in M. Bovens, R. E. Goodin, and T. Schillemans (eds), *The Oxford Handbook of Public Accountability*, Oxford: Oxford University Press, pp. 106–24.

Pääkkönen, J., M. Nelimarkka, J. Haapoja and A. Lampinen (2020), 'Bureaucracy as a lens for analyzing and designing algorithmic systems', in *Proceedings of the 2020 CHI Conference on Human Factors in Computing Systems*, pp. 1–14.

Pajkovic, N. (2022), 'Algorithms and taste-making: Exposing the Netflix Recommender System's operational logics', *Convergence*, **28** (1), 214–35.

Paul, R. (2022), 'Can critical policy studies outsmart AI? Research agenda on artificial intelligence technologies and public policy', *Critical Policy Studies*, **16** (4), 497–509.

Peeters, R. and A. Widlak (2018), 'The digital cage: Administrative exclusion through information architecture – the case of the Dutch civil registry's master data management system', *Government Information Quarterly*, **35** (2), 175–83.

Pors, A. and J. Schou (2021), 'Street-level morality at the digital frontlines: An ethnographic study of moral mediation in welfare work', *Administrative Theory & Praxis*, **43** (2), 154–71.

Ranerup, A. and H. Z. Henriksen (2019), 'Value positions viewed through the lens of automated decision-making: The case of social services', *Government Information Quarterly*, **36** (4), 101377.

Ranerup, A. and H. Z. Henriksen (2022), 'Digital discretion: Unpacking human and technological agency in automated decision making in Sweden's social services', *Social Science Computer Review*, **40** (2), 445–61.

Raso, J. (2017), 'Displacement as regulation: New regulatory technologies and front-line decision-making in Ontario works', *Canadian Journal of Law and Society/La Revue Canadienne Droit et Société*, **32** (1), 75–95.

Sandhu, A. and P. Fussey (2021), 'The "uberization of policing"? How police negotiate and operational-ise predictive policing technology', *Policing and Society*, **31** (1), 66–81.

Selten, F., M. Robeer and S. Grimmelikhuijsen (2023), '"Just like I thought": Street-level bureaucrats trust AI recommendations if they confirm their professional judgment', *Public Administration Review*, **83** (2), 263–78.

Susskind, R. E. and D. Susskind (2015), *The Future of the Professions: How Technology Will Transform the Work of Human Experts*, Oxford: Oxford University Press.

United Nations (2020), *E-Government Survey 2020: Digital Government in the Decade of Action for Sustainable Development'*, New York: United Nations.

van Noordt, C. and G. Misuraca (2022), 'Artificial intelligence for the public sector: Results of landscap-ing the use of AI in government across the European Union', *Government Information Quarterly*, **39**, 101714.

Wastell, D., S. White, K. Broadhurst, S. Peckover and A. Pithouse (2010), 'Children's services in the iron cage of performance management: Street-level bureaucracy and the spectre of Švejkism', *International Journal of Social Welfare*, **19** (3), 310–20.

Wihlborg, E., H. Larsson and K. Hedström (2016), '"The computer says no!" – a case study on auto-mated decision-making in public authorities', in *2016 49th Hawaii International Conference on System Sciences (HICSS)*, IEEE, pp. 2903–12.

Yeung, K. (2023), 'The new public analytics as an emerging paradigm in public sector administration', *Tilburg Law Review*, **27** (2), 1–32.

Zacka, B. (2017), *When the State Meets the Street: Public Service and Moral Agency*, Cambridge, MA: Harvard University Press.

Zuboff, S. (1988), *In the Age of the Smart Machine: The Future of Work and Power*, New York: Basic Books.

PART II

AI AND THE POLITICS OF GOVERNANCE: DECONSTRUCTING NORMATIVE PRECEPTS

7.   Accounting for context in AI technologies
Jennifer Cobbe and Jatinder Singh

INTRODUCTION

'Accountability' has become a hot topic in legal, regulatory and policy discussions around artificial intelligence technologies (AITs), and in research aimed at empowering and protecting people and societies. This has reflected concerns about a lack of transparency and understanding of these technologies as well as questions around who controls and benefits from them. The idea that AITs (and algorithmic systems more generally) are unknowably complex and opaque 'black boxes' (Pasquale 2015) is widespread. Concern about algorithmic opacity has brought warnings that unaccountable systems may replace humans in and undermine the legitimacy of public decision-making (Danaher 2016a). Opacity in machine learning systems has been widely discussed and various forms identified (Burrell 2016; Danaher 2016b). Opacity can arise through incompatibilities between the AITs' mathematical nature and human reasoning and understanding ('intrinsic' opacity (Burrell 2016; Danaher 2016b)). Moreover, the nature of AITs means technical experts may understand their workings, while they remain largely incomprehensible to others ('illiterate' opacity (Burrell 2016; Danaher 2016b)).

Yet opacity is not simply a technical problem, but often a choice by those responsible for AITs (Burrell 2016; Foryciarz et al. 2020). Organisations may conceal their processes for commercial reasons ('intentional' opacity (Burrell 2016; Danaher 2016b)), relying on intellectual property protections, for instance, or presenting information about systems in deliberately inaccessible ways ('strategic' opacity (Stohl et al. 2016)). Even where intrinsic or illiterate opacity exists, organisations may have chosen more obfuscating architectures instead of easier understood technologies. Alternatively, those responsible for AITs may present information in *unintentionally* inaccessible ways ('inadvertent' opacity (Stohl et al. 2016)), or simply be unaware that various aspects of algorithmic systems are relevant for accountability purposes ('unwitting' opacity (Cobbe et al. 2021)).

Whatever opacity's source, non-transparent AITs are difficult to oversee, review, or contest. Deliberately opaque organisations can avoid scrutiny and legal or other responsibilities, liabilities, or consequences. Even well-intentioned organisations can obscure their systems by giving too much information, or the wrong information, or presenting it in the wrong way. People and communities may thus have little usable information about the technologies which increasingly make or recommend decisions about them, and few avenues to challenge, contest, or resist the AI-enabled forms of power, production, discipline, and control they face. Moreover, in assuming that all AITs are unknowable black boxes, even easier to interrogate systems may escape scrutiny (Foryciarz et al. 2020).

Yet algorithmic accountability's problems go beyond the complex nature of AITs themselves, efforts by organisations to shield themselves from scrutiny, or misguided attempts to provide information which ultimately obfuscates. While 'accountability' is often claimed to empower and protect people, the term itself is slippery – used in different ways, in different times and places, which are not always reconcilable (Williams et al. 2022; Mulgan 2000).

Indeed, the focus of accountability-related discussions around AITs has shifted over time – from narrower work on explanations for models, to broader attempts to understand how AITs are developed and used, and more recently to recognise the challenges brought by cloud-driven AI deployments. As a result, it is not always clear what is meant by 'accountability' in relation to AITs; nor that established approaches to 'algorithmic accountability' can produce the change that some might hope for.

This chapter seeks to bring some clarity to debates around algorithmic accountability. First, by tracing changes in focus of accountability research around AITs, then placing these changes in their context. In particular, developments in algorithmic accountability research can broadly be understood by reference to two distinctions: between a first and second *wave* of research; and between differing *concepts* of accountability. Understanding these distinctions highlights the *contextual* nature of accountability and the need for numerous mechanisms, targeted appropriately at relevant people. Indeed, we argue, for algorithmic accountability to make the difference it is claimed to make, multiple legal, non-legal, institutional, and organisational avenues are needed for affected people and communities to understand how and why AITs are developed and deployed, with what purposes, for whose benefit, and to whose detriment. More importantly, these mechanisms must offer effective avenues for those people and communities to meaningfully effect change where needed.

ALGORITHMIC ACCOUNTABILITY: AN EVOLVING FIELD

Algorithmic accountability research has evolved over time. While the focus in the past was predominantly on information about the capabilities and workings of the models which power AITs, other work has gradually sought information about the processes of developing, deploying, and using algorithmic systems. Recent work considers the broader supply chain context around AITs, and participatory approaches seek to include affected people and communities in producing and deploying AITs.

Model-focused Accountability

Model-focused algorithmic accountability typically seeks to provide technical information – offering explanations for model workings, or making code available – and is aimed at addressing forms of *intrinsic* and *illiterate* opacity. This has been consistently closely tied to notions of transparency that helps humans understand and appropriately trust and manage technical systems (Gunning et al. 2017).

Much of this work was prompted by claims that the EU's General Data Protection Regulation (GDPR) included a 'right to an explanation' for certain kinds of automated decision-making (specifically, affecting a person's legal or similarly important rights and entitlements and undertaken without meaningful human involvement (GDPR, article 22)). The existence, extent, and utility of this right is a matter of debate. While various writers have argued for such a right existing implicitly in the GDPR (Goodman and Flaxman 2016; Selbst and Powles 2017), others have cast some doubt on this claim (Wachter et al. 2017; Malgieri and Comandé 2017), or argued that there *may* be only a limited right for certain narrow kinds of decision (Edwards and Veale 2017). The law clearly includes rights to be informed of an automated decision's existence and logic (GDPR, article 15), and may provide for a right to an explanation of the outcome of any human review of that decision (GDPR, recital 71).

Whatever the actual position, the idea that explanations may be legally mandated spurred academic and other research into explanations for models and for automated decisions and other outputs of AITs. Following GDPR's passage in 2016, a vast number of approaches to 'explainable' AI have been proposed (Barredo Arrieta et al. 2020; Verma et al. 2020). These broadly seek either 'global' or 'local' explanations (Radensky et al. 2022). Global explanations provide information about the model's characteristics and behaviour in general. Local explanations provide information about how models produced specific decisions or outputs.

The complexity of some AITs and the quantities of data involved make producing such explanations difficult. It may also be hard to produce explanations that are comprehensible to the people who want to engage with them (Stohl et al. 2016). There is little point, after all, in giving complex technical information about an AIT's workings to people without the expertise or ability to make sense of it (Stohl et al. 2016; Ananny and Crawford 2018). In seeking to address technical (i.e. *intrinsic* and *illiterate*) forms of opacity, doing so may simply produce other forms of (*strategic, unwitting,* or *inadvertent*) opacity (Edwards and Veale 2017; Cobbe et al. 2021) – the so-called 'transparency paradox' (Stohl et al. 2016).

Wachter et al. propose that *counterfactual explanations* might help people understand why certain outcomes have been reached (Wachter et al. 2018). Counterfactuals explain a decision in terms of what might have happened had some relevant factor been different: if a person was older, or had a higher income, or a better credit rating, for example, then the system would have produced a different outcome. Hundreds of papers proposing methods for counterfactual explanations have followed (for reviews, see: Verma et al. 2020; Guidotti 2022). Some companies have sought to integrate counterfactual explanations into their systems as well as in the cloud AI services they offer.[1]

While counterfactuals have received considerable attention, there are concerns about how useful they might be in different contexts, particularly when used to explain complex decisions to people (Barocas et al. 2020; Warren et al. 2023). Indeed, counterfactuals may suit situations where clearly defined *human* decision-making is automated – explaining a loan refusal, for instance, accounting for age, employment status, income, and home ownership. When employed for more complex decisions, many factors may need to change to get a different result (Barocas et al. 2020; Kasirzadeh and Smart 2021). Even in simpler cases, however, counterfactuals may not help if the key point underpinning a decision is some intrinsic factor beyond the affected person's control (Barocas et al. 2020; Kasirzadeh and Smart 2021). Simply knowing that the outcome would be different if some unchangeable factor were different may not be useful information.

The usefulness of explanations more generally has also been questioned. Edwards and Veale argue that the technical information provided by some explanations probably will not give the kind of accountability that subjects of decisions might look for (Edwards and Veale 2017), while others point out that legal accountability is often not concerned with model workings (Cobbe et al. 2021). Moreover, explanations only get to the capabilities or workings of models in operation (i.e. at *runtime*), rather than broader aspects of algorithmic systems, and local explanations only provide information about specific decisions or outputs. As such, neither global nor local explanations offer avenues to understand how systems are designed, developed, or deployed, nor do they assist in understanding systemic issues that might arise from design, development, or deployment (Singh and Walden 2016; Cobbe et al. 2021).

System-level Accountability

Recognising the limitations of model-focused accountability, increasing attention has been paid to broader, system-level aspects of AITs. This has increasingly emphasised questions about the design, development, deployment, and use of technologies rather than the workings of models. This has broadly sought to understand the contexts of AITs and the fundamentally *human* decisions made in developing and using them as well as the intended and actual capabilities of systems. In doing so, such research has moved away from focusing on 'algorithms' or models themselves, with AITs typically understood as *algorithmic systems* – people and code working together (Seaver 2013) – and recognising that human choices around design, development, and deployment perhaps matter more than anything else (also see Paul, Carmel and Cobbe, this volume's Introduction). Broadly speaking, two approaches to systems-level accountability have arisen: *point-oriented* and *process-oriented.*

Point-oriented system-level accountability seeks to help interested parties understand the capabilities and limitations of AITs and the choices made by developers and others at specific *points* in the algorithmic life cycle. Generally, these are intended to help those who might want to use or engage with AITs at a technical level – and potentially those who might be affected by decisions made using those technologies – to understand how the system has been developed, what it should be used for, what it might be capable of, and where its limitations may lie. Many point-oriented proposals originated with researchers working in industry and are framed in terms of improving transparency.

Perhaps the first such proposal that gained attention was 'datasheets for datasets' (Gebru et al. 2021), from researchers at Microsoft and elsewhere. Drawing from the datasheets used to describe the characteristics of electronic components, datasheets for datasets offer information on the composition and potential uses of datasets used in AI development. 'Model cards' (from researchers at Google) provide benchmarked evaluations of model performance and capabilities (Mitchell et al. 2019). 'System cards' from researchers at Meta offer information on how the various components of complex algorithmic systems interact (Meta 2022). IBM's 'fact sheets' seek to provide consistent methodologies to produce these various forms of documentation (Richards et al. 2021). These often seek to help developers understand the technologies and resources they are dealing with and have seen some uptake in industry. Microsoft provides a template for datasheets.[2] Google provides limited model cards for some aspects of its AI services,[3] while Amazon[4] and HuggingFace[5] have tools for customers of their cloud AI services to produce model cards. TensorFlow offers a Model Card Toolkit.[6] Meta[7] and OpenAI[8] both provide system cards for some of their services.

While these tools work more at a system level than model-focused approaches, and can help understand specific aspects of system development, they do not allow for the system as a whole to be interrogated (nor are they intended to). Moreover, they offer information which may help understand and evidence problems, but few routes for those affected by AITs to challenge systems or seek redress. The industry focus on transparency of specific points in the algorithmic life cycle thus arguably obscures the need for more systematic approaches to accountability which allow for fuller investigations into the production and use of AITs and open up avenues for deeper change (Ananny and Crawford 2018; Cobbe et al. 2021).

Process-oriented approaches, by contrast, are the human and organisational processes and choices in commissioning, designing, developing, deploying, and using AITs. The goal is generally an understanding of the *process* of producing, deploying, using, and the operation of an algorithmic system (Singh and Walden 2016), to support oversight and intervention where needed (Wieringa 2020; Cobbe et al. 2021). Process-oriented approaches may provide conceptual frameworks which integrate narrower interventions (like datasheets or model cards) into a more holistic view across algorithmic systems. Examples include work on applying Mark Bovens' model of accountability to algorithmic systems (Wieringa 2020); research on *auditability* of AITs which proposes socio-technical audits across the system life cycle (Raji et al. 2020; Metaxa et al. 2021; Williams et al. 2022); frameworks intended to facilitate legal and other *review* of the processes of developing, deploying, using, and overseeing AITs (Cobbe et al. 2021); and other work on forms of contestability (Kaminski and Urban 2021; Alfrink et al. 2022), traceability (Kroll 2021), and similar concepts (Ada Lovelace Institute 2020). Other proposals have further developed point-oriented approaches to better assist across the process of AITs being developed and updated iteratively.

In public administration, specifically, administrative law also provides process-oriented accountability. Administrative law is concerned with ensuring that public sector decision-makers act lawfully and in line with legal standards for due process and natural justice. The law's principles and standards are general, applying to public decision-makers whether they use AITs or not. They are common across many jurisdictions and developed organically over centuries through cases involving even the most serious questions of life and death. Importantly, administrative law typically addresses decision-making *processes* rather than the merits of individual decisions as such. Administrative law has therefore been an obvious focus for those concerned with public-sector automated decision-making and AI in various jurisdictions (Coglianese and Lehr 2017; Oswald 2018; Cobbe 2019; Cobbe 2020, Tomlinson 2020; Raso 2021; Williams 2021; Wolswinkel 2022). Moreover, administrative law has explicitly informed some work which takes a process-oriented approach to algorithmic accountability beyond the public sector (Keats Citron and Pasquale 2014; Cobbe et al. 2021).

Process-oriented algorithmic accountability – while broader than point-oriented approaches – typically conceives of algorithmic systems as *discrete* systems. However, AITs are often developed by major cloud providers or rely on their infrastructure; moreover, when deployed in practice, they often interconnect with other systems which give inputs and receive and apply outputs (Gürses and van Hoboken 2017; Singh and Walden 2016; Cobbe et al. 2023; Widder et al. 2023). As such, AITs often form one part of a *system-of-systems* which together produces and gives effect to their outcomes and decisions. While system-level accountability offers greater potential to understand AITs beyond model-focused approaches, even process-oriented frameworks do not generally capture these dynamics.

Supply Chain Accountability

Some research has addressed the changes brought by cloud computing infrastructures and services distribution models. Most model-focused and systems-level research has implicitly assumed that one party will develop and control AITs. In reality, however, developers often integrate modular components produced and offered by others as services which provide functionality. In doing so, they delegate control over core aspects of their applications to other parties who together form the application's *supply chain*. AI services are one example. Providers' offerings range from pretrained models for customers to deploy in their applications, to production environments for customers to build bespoke AITs using (and often tailored to) the provider's cloud infrastructure. This brings legal and regulatory questions around which party is responsible for which aspects of developing, deploying, and using AITs (Gürses and van Hoboken 2017; Cobbe and Singh 2021; Cobbe et al. 2023).

Recognising these changes, research has investigated the contexts of and (technical, political economic, and legal) conditions for producing AITs using cloud infrastructures and supply chain architectures (Gürses and van Hoboken 2017; Cobbe and Singh 2021; Cobbe et al. 2023; Brown 2023; Widder and Wong 2023; Widder et al. 2023). This typically shows increased concern with control of underlying infrastructures by a few companies (Cobbe et al. 2023; Widder et al. 2023), the rights and working conditions of (predominantly) Global South data labellers and others involved in producing these services (Png 2022), the environmental impact of advanced AI services (Lucivero, Chapter 12 in this volume; van Wynsberghe 2021; Dodge et al. 2022; Luccioni et al. 2022), and additional risks brought by general purpose services when deployed in specific customer applications (Lewicki et al. 2023). This has also recognised challenges to accountability brought by supply chains, which may change and evolve rapidly and involve many parties each contributing to AITs with complex distributions of responsibilities between them. Moreover, supply chains are structured by major providers to minimise their accountability, and lack mechanisms for the visibility across different parties needed to properly answer key questions which arise in production and deployment of AITs (the 'accountability horizon' (Cobbe et al. 2023)).

Participatory Accountability

Algorithmic accountability has also increasingly turned to participatory methods for producing and using AITs (Martin Jr et al. 2020; Donia and Shaw 2021; Birhane et al. 2022; Suresh et al. 2022; Organizers of QueerInAI 2023; Groves et al. 2023). This has sought to make processes of production and deployment more accountable to affected people and communities. This has particularly focused on the Global South and on marginalised groups (such as people of colour, LGBT people, and people with disabilities). Participatory approaches to AITs typically reject – explicitly or implicitly – the imposition of AITs on affected people and communities by outside actors who may lack the perspectives or incentives needed to ensure that the technologies work for their benefit and not to their detriment (Birhane et al. 2022). The result is a focus on including affected communities throughout the process of designing, deploying, and using AITs, and building in accountability mechanisms across that process to ensure they have a strong voice where decisions about system specification, development, and operation are made.

Participatory approaches may risk 'participation washing', whereby token participation afforded to affected people and communities is used to legitimise and manufacture consent to AITs which work against their interests (Sloane 2020; Sloane et al. 2022). Meaningful participation requires proper representation of a range of stakeholders who have interests in, use, or are otherwise affected (directly or indirectly) by the deployment of AITs (whom those implementing participatory approaches may be unaware of). To avoid participation washing, it is also crucial to ensure that the participation of affected people and communities means more than simply including them or giving them a voice, but actually produces change in line with their contributions. As such, participatory processes must *themselves* be accountable and responsive to the needs of affected people. This may be easier with AITs produced and deployed by one organisation than with systems working through supply chains. In that case, obtaining good faith involvement of the relevant parties who are actually able to realise the participants' demands may be hard.

DISENTANGLING ALGORITHMIC ACCOUNTABILITY

Developments in algorithmic accountability research reflect that accountability is an essentially contested concept, changing over time (Mulgan 2000). Indeed, in the English language 'accountability' is closely related to other terms and concepts which are often used alongside or in its place (Mulgan 2000; Bovens 2010). When used in relation to AITs, accountability is often closely related to or conflated with other terms including transparency, auditability, reviewability, traceability, and contestability (Williams et al. 2022). Moreover, as research has moved from models, then to systems, and to supply chains and participatory methods, the focus of this work, the mechanisms proposed, and the kinds of questions asked have changed. These developments in algorithmic accountability research can broadly be framed by two distinctions: first, between a first and second *wave* of algorithmic accountability; second, between two understandings of what 'accountability' means. We now explore these further.

Two *Waves* of Algorithmic Accountability

Borrowing from the well-known distinctions between different *waves* in feminist thought, activism, and organising, Pasquale has argued that algorithmic accountability research can broadly be understood in two waves (Pasquale 2019). The first wave addresses transparency and questions of fairness and accuracy, focusing broadly on improving the technical performance of AITs. This includes work pursuing explanations (both global and local), as well as some point-oriented system-level mechanisms around specific aspects of system development or operation. First wave proposals often seek forms of inclusion and representation – explaining decisions to individual people; improving the fairness of systems – without necessarily challenging the power dynamics around AITs' development and use. This is perhaps unsurprising given that first wave ideas and approaches generally originated in narrower technical understandings of transparency and accountability or with employees of major technology companies. Yet first wave approaches to algorithmic accountability risk contributing to forms of predatory inclusion (Weinberg 2022), such as improving the accuracy across ethnic groups of facial recognition systems which disproportionately surveil people of colour, without seeking forms of participation which might shape or even prevent production and deployment of those technologies.

The second wave focuses more on questions of power, politics, and political economy (Pasquale 2019; Powles and Nissenbaum 2018). Concerns relate to whether systems should be built or used at all, how AITs' contexts shape their production and use to benefit certain people at others' expense, what kinds of governance and accountability mechanism can help challenge power, and who actually gets to govern. Second wave research generally recognises that AITs are bound up in public and private processes of production, discipline, and control across societies, and that the development, deployment, use, and effects of these technologies are shaped by all sorts of legal, technical, social, and political economic conditions. The second wave has often been more interdisciplinary than the first, drawing extensively from concepts and methods found in law, social sciences, and the humanities. Trends broadly in the second wave include much of the more process-oriented work on system-level accountability (particularly around questions around development and deployment of AITs), as well as work on supply chains (emphasising the political economic context of AITs and the power of major cloud providers) and on participatory approaches to AI (centring affected people and communities beyond inclusion and representation).

These two waves may appear to be in tension, but both have a place and address things which are distinct but potentially complementary. There is certainly a case for banning certain technologies (such as police use of live facial recognition), or restricting them only to socially beneficial uses, or for advancing new forms of social ownership and democratic control of AITs (all second wave concerns). But first wave issues like differences in performance of AITs across genders and ethnic groups, with potential for discrimination and exclusion along historical lines of marginalisation, are important *regardless* of questions around who actually owns or controls those technologies. However, in foregrounding issues of power and political economy, the second wave offers avenues towards more structural, long-term interventions to address the underlying causes of these issues. For first wave interventions to avoid superficial forms of representation and predatory inclusion, second wave interventions are also needed to fundamentally redistribute power and protect people and societies.

Two *Concepts* of Algorithmic Accountability

Different kinds of algorithmic accountability can also be framed by reference to the two concepts of accountability identified by Mark Bovens (2010): accountability understood as a *virtue*, and accountability understood as a *mechanism*. As a virtue – more commonly seen in the US – accountability is viewed as a positive quality which organisations, institutions, systems, and processes can possess. In this sense, accountability is closely related to concepts of fairness, transparency, responsiveness, and equitable treatment, and invoked in many contexts and for many purposes, yet is rarely defined or delineated explicitly (Bovens 2010). When understood as a mechanism – more common in Europe and non-US Anglophone countries – accountability generally involves one person giving some kind of *account* to a second. This typically involves some explanation or justification of the first person's conduct, often to allow the second to understand their actions and intervene if needed (Bovens 2007; Bovens 2010).

As a virtue – a positive quality of 'being accountable' which AITs can have – algorithmic accountability is closely related to concepts of fairness and transparency (Williams et al. 2022). These are sometimes used interchangeably, or accountability referred to incidentally while speaking primarily of transparency. It is a testament to the early domination of algorithmic accountability research by researchers at US-based institutions and technology companies that accountability-as-virtue approaches appeared first and have received the most attention, while only more recently are other approaches gaining traction. There is also – as a result – a correlation with first wave approaches to algorithmic accountability.

While 'algorithmic accountability' has become a touchstone for some concerned with the effects and implications of AITs, the broad and ill-defined nature of accountability-as-a-virtue – and its common conflation with transparency, fairness, and other concepts (also see Aula and Erkkilä, Chapter 13 in this volume) – makes it difficult to establish standards by which accountability may be evaluated or to integrate these proposals into broader attempts at challenging the changing power relations around AITs. While accountability has become a rallying cry, this lack of precision and specificity when treated as a virtue has made it an increasingly unclear one. Moreover, given accountability-as-virtue's correlation with first wave approaches to algorithmic accountability, there is a risk of virtuewashing – emphasising perceived positive qualities which improve the acceptability of particular technologies rather than more meaningful, structural change.

Accountability-as-a-*mechanism*, on the other hand, has been invoked more in support of second wave proposals and interventions. Approaching accountability-as-a-mechanism involving account-giving foregrounds important questions: Accounts from whom? For which things? Given to whom? And for what purpose? Accountability-as-a-mechanism necessarily frames accountability *relationally*, emphasising accountability *for* systems rather than accountability *of* systems. This sidesteps problems around imbuing socio-technical systems like AITs with positive human virtues like 'accountability' (Cobbe et al. 2023). With accountability-as-a-mechanism, it is clear that some person – whether a *natural person* (an individual human being) or a *legal person* (a government, company, or other organisation with *legal personality*) – will be accountable *for* the system, its development, and its operation, and that they will be accountable *to* some other.

Bovens describes accountability-as-a-mechanism as involving an actor (providing accounts), a forum (receiving those accounts, deliberating on them, and, if needed, imposing some kind of consequence on the actor), and a *relationship of accountability* between them (Bovens 2007). This framing has been explicitly taken up in some algorithmic accountability work (Wieringa 2020; Cobbe et al. 2021; Cobbe et al. 2023). A key feature of accountability-as-a-mechanism is therefore account-giving: this requires *some* form of transparency – potentially both at model level (such as explanations for decisions) and at system level (whether of specific points in the algorithmic life cycle or of the broader process). Accountability-as-a-mechanism makes clear, however, that transparency is not itself accountability, nor is it sufficient to achieve accountability (though it can provide useful information). Rather, accountability requires organisational and institutional processes, mechanisms, and arrangements for account-giving, deliberation, and intervention. While accountability-as-a-mechanism inherently frames accountability *relationally*, it thus does so to structure those relations in particular ways to support intervention.

Understood in this way, algorithmic accountability is often framed in process-oriented and supply chain approaches – sometimes explicitly – as a mechanism for challenging power, contesting systems, and bringing legal or other intervention to protect people and communities. Similarly, participatory approaches to algorithmic accountability necessarily draw on accountability-as-a-mechanism – for involving affected communities centrally in decision-making around producing, deploying, and using AITs.

TOWARDS *CONTEXTUAL ACCOUNTABILITY* FOR AITS

If algorithmic accountability is to help challenge, contest, and redistribute power – rather than affording superficial or tokenistic changes and risking predatory inclusion – then several things are needed. First, accountability should be viewed relationally as a *mechanism* for people and communities to understand and contest AIT deployment and use. Second, accountability mechanisms must regard AITs as algorithmic systems, looking not simply at technical components or specific points in the life cycle, but at the broader *process* of commissioning, designing, developing, deploying, and using AI, considering both technical and human and organisational factors. Third, accountability challenges arising from *supply chain* architectures must be accounted for. Fourth, *participatory* approaches to AI are needed with thorough stakeholder identification, careful design of relevant processes, and genuine intent to empower. Through these, key *second wave* questions must be considered: Who gets a say? Who controls technologies which make decisions about people's lives? Who is empowered by these technologies? Who is disempowered? And which technologies should even be built at all? While these questions matter across many contexts and circumstances, they are naturally particularly relevant to public sector use of AITs.

Understanding accountability relationally also makes clear its inherently *contextual* nature. There may be many relevant forums – both internal and external – for an AIT and many coexistent accountability relationships between an actor and many forums (Bovens 2007). These could be *external* forums, such as regulators, customers, and people affected by AI decisions. They may also be *internal* – such as quality assurance or compliance teams within the same organisation. Different forums may have different interests in the system, different levels of technical understanding and capability, and different goals and intentions for the accountability relationship. As such, the information needed for meaningful accounts which support deliberation and intervention will differ between forums – sometimes drastically. Accountability cannot therefore be one-size-fits-all. For accountability mechanisms to empower and protect people, they must provide the right information, from the right actors, to the right forums, with appropriate processes for forums to assess it, decide what should be done, and translate that into meaningful change.

Meaningful accountability thus requires *contextually appropriate information* (Cobbe et al. 2021). For accountability to be a mechanism for people and communities to understand what is happening and intervene where necessary, they need information which is (i) *relevant* to the accountability relationships involved; (ii) *accurate*, being correct, complete, and representative; (iii) *proportionate* to the level of transparency needed; and (iv) *comprehensible* by the people receiving it. The contextual nature of this information in turn shapes which mechanisms are needed to produce records and documentation on relevant parts of the algorithmic process. This requires a systematic consideration of relevant stakeholders to properly tailor mechanisms and information to them according to their differing needs.

This is particularly challenging for AITs developed and deployed through supply chains (Cobbe et al. 2023). In this context, the range of potential forums and accountability relationships (for both providers and customers) is vast. Providers may owe accounts of many kinds to many customers, and may themselves require accounts from 'upstream' actors (such as data labellers or technical infrastructure providers). Providers and customers may both owe accounts to many users, partners, regulators, and others. AI supply chains thus involve *chains of accountability* where any given party may be both an actor and a forum to various other parties at the same time. Information from multiple actors may be needed to provide meaningful accounts to various internal and external forums, who may be several steps removed in the chain from the relevant actors. Moreover, multiple forums might have interests in bringing about changes in processes and systems further up such chains (again with the possibility of being several steps removed from the relevant actors).

Providing appropriate information for each potential forum will be hard, however – not least because accountability relationships often mirror commercial, legal, regulatory, and other relationships and each party in a chain will typically have little insight into which such relationships others are involved in. Moreover, it may be unclear which parties in AI supply chains are relevant for accountability purposes. And the party who might *normatively* be most appropriate or desirable (often a customer who has deployed an AI service in their application, such as a public sector organisation) may not be able to provide meaningful accounts or do anything about the AIT itself (often developed by and running on a provider's hardware, who generally adds layers of intentional and strategic opacity through intellectual property rights and selective disclosure of information).

Contextual mechanisms must therefore account for supply chain and the complex relationships involved. Because accountability relationships often mirror legal, commercial, and technical relationships, mapping supply chains to understand the chains of accountability within is a starting point. This might involve tracing legal and commercial relationships through analysis of contracts, policies, and other documentation (Millard 2021), or tracking data flow between parties to investigate technical relationships (Singh et al. 2019). AI service providers should provide customers with the information they need, presented in the way they need it, to tailor accounts to their forums. This requires a much greater degree of transparency by providers than to date, and legal and regulatory interventions may be needed to address intentional, strategic, and unwitting opacity.

Affected people and communities are important forums in participatory accountability. Given accountability's contextual nature, information about the aims, objectives, and motivations for – and relationships involved in – developing AITs must be provided in a way which is practically useful to them. Yet there are relatively few tools to give information about earlier points in the algorithmic system life cycle – around conceptualisation, specification, and development. Existing point-oriented tools typically instead offer information about datasets, models, or systems *once they are complete*, rather than at preceding stages of production. Contextually appropriate information about these stages is essential for participatory methods to empower relevant forums.

CONCLUSION AND FUTURE DIRECTIONS

Earlier algorithmic accountability research addressed technical aspects of AI technologies, often focusing on interpretability and explanations of model capabilities and workings. Yet researchers have increasingly recognised that technical components are only one part of the picture: human and organisational processes around commissioning, developing, deploying, and using AITs are more relevant for many accountability purposes. Various proposals have suggested ways to address these aspects of AITs, either at specific points in the system's life cycle or aiming at the broader process of producing and deploying systems. More recently, research has considered the contexts of AITs produced and deployed with or through cloud computing infrastructures, as well as participatory approaches to bringing affected people and communities into key decision-making processes.

As we show, these developments in algorithmic accountability research broadly reflect two distinctions: first, between a first and second *wave* of research (the latter addressing questions of power and political economy); second, between differing understandings of accountability (as a *virtue* or as a *mechanism*). These distinctions indicate useful directions for research and emphasise the *contextual* nature of accountability: not just in terms of the relationships involved and the information needed; but which aspects of algorithmic systems are relevant to different relationships, and the range of mechanisms required across them.

Achieving contextual algorithmic accountability is hard, particularly with the supply chain architectures common to AITs in both the public and private sectors. Research is needed on legal, regulatory, and other approaches to contextual accountability, taking a process-oriented approach, integrating participatory methods to empower affected people and communities, and attending to the legal, technical, and political economic contexts in which AITs are produced and deployed. Within that, a range of point-oriented tools across the algorithmic life cycle are needed to systematically and consistently record and provide relevant information (in addition to existing mechanisms like datasheets for datasets and model cards). Moreover, many important questions remain open: What kind of mechanisms are appropriate to what kinds of relationships? What kinds of legal and organisational arrangements can support proper account-giving? How can we reliably identify actors and forums in supply chains, given their lack of visibility and distributions of responsibility? How can chains of accountability work to ensure the right information reaches the right forums? How can those forums bring about changes in the activities of the right actors? Importantly, there is also much work to do on processes for identifying and providing contextually appropriate information to support all of the above.

NOTES

1. Microsoft Azure, 'Counterfactuals analysis and what-if' (2022). Available at https:// learn .microsoft.com/en-us/azure/machine-learning/concept-counterfactual-analysis?view=azureml-api -2 (accessed 3 December 2023); Amazon Web Services, 'Amazon SageMaker Clarify'. Available at: https:// aws .amazon .com/ sagemaker/ clarify (accessed 3 December 2023); Google Research, 'What-If Tool'. Available at: https://pair-code.github.io/what-if-tool (accessed 3 December 2023).
2. Microsoft Research, 'Data documentation'. Available at https://www.microsoft.com/en-us/research/ project/datasheets-for-datasets (accessed 3 December 2023).
3. Google Cloud, 'Model Cards'. Available at: https://modelcards.withgoogle.com/about (accessed 3 December 2023).
4. Amazon Web Services, 'Amazon SageMaker Model Cards'. Available at: https://docs.aws.amazon .com/sagemaker/latest/dg/model-cards.html (accessed 3 December 2023).
5. HuggingFace, 'Model Cards'. Available at: https://huggingface.co/docs/hub/model-cards (accessed 3 December 2023).
6. TensorFlow, 'Model Card Toolkit' (2023). Available at: https://www .tensorflow .org/ responsible _ai/model_card_toolkit/guide (accessed 3 December 2023).
7. Meta, 'Introducing 22 system cards that explain how AI powers experiences on Facebook and Instagram' (2023). Available at: https:// ai .meta .com/ blog/ how -ai -powers -experiences -facebook -instagram-system-cards (accessed 3 December 2023).
8. OpenAI, 'GPT-4 (Vision) System Card' (2023). Available at: https://openai.com/research/gpt-4v -system-card (accessed 3 December 2023).

REFERENCES

Ada Lovelace Institute, *Examining the Black Box: Tools for Assessing Algorithmic Systems* (2020).
Alfrink, Kars et al., 'Contestable AI by design: Towards a framework' (2022) *Minds and Machines*.
Ananny, Mike and Kate Crawford, 'Seeing without knowing: Limitations of the transparency ideal and its application to algorithmic accountability' (2018) **20** *New Media & Society.*
Barredo Arrieta, Alejandro et al., 'Explainable artificial intelligence (XAI): Concepts, taxonomies, opportunities and challenges toward responsible AI' (2020) **58** *Information Fusion*.

Barocas, Solon et al., 'The hidden assumptions behind counterfactual explanations and principal reasons' (2020) *ACM Conference on Fairness, Accountability, and Transparency (ACM FAT* 20).*

Birhane, Adeba et al., 'Power to the people? Opportunities and challenges for participatory AI' *(2022) ACM Conference on Equity and Access in Algorithms, Mechanisms, and Optimization (EAAMO 22).*

Bovens, Mark, 'Analysing and assessing accountability: A conceptual framework' (2006) **13** *European Law Journal.*

Bovens, Mark, 'Two concepts of accountability: Accountability as a virtue and as a mechanism' (2010) **33** *West European Politics.*

Brown, Ian, 'Expert explainer: Allocating accountability in AI supply chains' (2023) *Ada Lovelace Institute.*

Burrell, Jenna, 'How the machine "thinks": Understanding opacity in machine learning algorithms' (2016) **3** *Big Data & Society.*

Cobbe, Jennifer, 'Administrative law and the machines of government: Judicial review of automated public-sector decision-making' (2019) **39** *Legal Studies.*

Cobbe, Jennifer, 'Centring the rule of law in the digital state' (2020) **53** *IEEE Computer.*

Cobbe, Jennifer, et al., 'Reviewable automated decision-making: A framework for accountable algorithmic systems' (2021) *ACM Conference on Fairness, Accountability, and Transparency (ACM FAccT 21).*

Cobbe, Jennifer and Jatinder Singh, 'Artificial intelligence as a service: Legal responsibilities, liabilities, and policy challenges' (2021) **42** *Computer Law & Security Review.*

Cobbe, Jennifer et al., 'Understanding accountability in algorithmic supply chains' (2023) *ACM Conference on Fairness, Accountability, and Transparency (ACM FAccT 23).*

Coglianese, Cary and David Lehr, 'Regulating by robot: Administrative decision making in the machine-learning era' (2017) **105** *Georgetown Law Journal.*

Danaher, John, 'The threat of algocracy: Reality, resistance and accommodation' (2016a) **29** *Philosophy & Technology.*

Danaher, John, 'What's happening inside the black box? Three forms of algorithmic opacity' (2016b) *Philosophical Disquisitions.*

Dodge, Jesse et al., 'Measuring the carbon intensity of AI in cloud instances' (2022) *ACM Conference on Fairness, Accountability, and Transparency (ACM FAccT 22).*

Donia, Joseph and James A. Shaw, 'Co-design and ethical artificial intelligence for health: An agenda for critical research and practice' (2021) **8** *Big Data & Society.*

Edwards, Lilian and Michael Veale, 'Slave to the algorithm? Why a "right to an explanation" is probably not the remedy you are looking for' (2017) **16** *Duke Law & Technology Review.*

Foryciarz, Agata et al., 'Black-boxed politics: Opacity is a choice in AI systems' (2020) *Panoptykon Foundation.*

Gebru, Timnit et al., 'Datasheets for datasets' (2021) **64** *Communications of the ACM.*

Goodman, Bryce and Seth Flaxman, 'European Union regulations on algorithmic decision-making and a "right to explanation"' (2016) *2016 ICML Workshop on Human Interpretability in Machine Learning (WHI 2016).*

Groves, Lara et al., 'Going public: The role of public participation approaches in commercial AI labs' (2023) *ACM Conference on Fairness, Accountability, and Transparency (ACM FAccT 23).*

Guidotti, Riccardo, 'Counterfactual explanations and how to find them: Literature review and benchmarking' (2022) *Data Mining and Knowledge Discovery.*

Gunning, David et al., 'XAI – Explainable artificial intelligence' (2019) **4** *Science Robotics.*

Gürses, Seda and Joris van Hoboken, 'Privacy after the agile turn' in Evan Selinger et al. (eds), *The Cambridge Handbook of Consumer Privacy* (Cambridge University Press 2017).

Kaminski, Margot and Jennifer M. Urban, 'The right to contest AI' (2021) **121** *Columbia Law Review.*

Kasirzadeh, Atoosa and Andrew Smart, 'The use and misuse of counterfactuals in ethical machine learning' (2021) *ACM Conference on Fairness, Accountability, and Transparency (ACM FAccT 21) .*

Keats Citron, Danielle and Frank Pasquale, 'The scored society: Due process for automated predictions' (2014) **89** *Washington Law Review.*

Kroll, Joshua, 'Outlining traceability: A principle for operationalising accountability in computing systems' (2021) *ACM Conference on Fairness, Accountability, and Transparency (ACM FAccT 21).*

Lewicki, Kornel et al., 'Out of context: Investigating the bias and fairness concerns of "artificial intelligence as a service"' (2023) *ACM Conference on Human Factors in Computing Systems (ACM CHI 23)*.

Luccioni, Alexandra Sasha et al., 'Estimating the carbon footprint of BLOOM, a 176B parameter language model' (2022) *arXiv preprint arXiv:2211.02001*.

Malgieri, Gianclaudio and Giovanni Comandé, 'Why a right to legibility of automated decision-making exists in the general data protection regulation' (2017) 7 *International Data Privacy Law*.

Martin Jr, Donald et al., 'Participatory problem formulation for fairer machine learning through community based system dynamics' (2020) *arXiv preprint arXiv:2005.07572*.

Meta, 'System cards, a new resource for understanding how AI systems work' (2022).

Metaxa, Danaë et al., 'Auditing algorithms: Understanding algorithmic systems from the outside in' (2021) **14** *Foundations and Trends in Human – Computer Interaction*.

Millard, Christopher, *Cloud Computing Law* (2nd ed, Oxford University Press 2021).

Mitchell, Margaret, 'Model cards for model reporting' (2019) *ACM Conference on Fairness, Accountability, and Transparency* (ACM FAT* 19).

Mulgan, Richard '"Accountability": An ever-expanding concept?' (2000) **78** *Public Administration*.

Organizers of QueerInAI, 'Queer in AI: A case study in community-led participatory AI' (2023) *ACM Conference on Fairness, Accountability, and Transparency (ACM FAccT 23)*.

Oswald, Marion, 'Algorithm-assisted decision-making in the public sector: Framing the issues using administrative law rules governing discretionary power' (2018) **376** *Philosophical Transactions of the Royal Society A*.

Pasquale, Frank, *The Black Box Society: The Secret Algorithms that Control Money and Information* (Harvard University Press 2015).

Pasquale, Frank, 'The second wave of algorithmic accountability' (2019) *Law & Political Economy Blog*.

Png, Marie-Therese 'At the tensions of South and North: Critical roles of Global South stakeholders in AI governance' (2022) *ACM Conference on Fairness, Accountability, and Transparency (ACM FAccT 22)*.

Powles, Julia and Helen Nissenbaum, 'The seductive diversion of "solving" bias in artificial intelligence' (2018) *OneZero*.

Radensky, Marissa et al., 'Exploring the role of local and global explanations in recommender systems' (2022) *CHI EA '22: Extended Abstracts of the 2022 CHI Conference on Human Factors in Computing Systems*.

Raji, Inioluwa Deborah et al., 'Closing the AI accountability gap: Defining an end-to-end framework for internal algorithmic auditing' (2020) *ACM Conference on Fairness, Accountability, and Transparency (ACM FAT* 20)*.

Raso, Jennifer 'AI and administrative law', in Florian Martin-Bariteau and Teresa Scassa (eds) *Artificial Intelligence and the Law in Canada* (LexisNexis Canada 2021).

Regulation (EU) 2016/679 on the protection of natural persons with regard to the processing of personal data and on the free movement of such data, and repealing Directive 95/46/EC [2016] OJ L119/1 ('GDPR').

Richards, John et al., 'A human-centered methodology for creating AI factsheets' (2021) IEEE *Data Engineering Bulletin*.

Seaver, Nick, 'Knowing algorithms' (2013) *Paper presented at Media in Transition 8*.

Selbst, Andrew D., and Julia Powles, 'Meaningful information and the right to explanation' (2017) 7 *International Data Privacy Law*.

Singh, Jatinder and Ian Walden, 'Responsibility & machine learning: Part of a process' (2016).

Singh, Jatinder et al., 'Decision provenance: Harnessing data flow for accountable systems' (2019) 7 *IEEE Access*.

Sloane, Mona, 'Participation-washing could be the next dangerous fad in machine learning' (2020) *MIT Technology Review*.

Sloane, Mona et al., 'Participation is not a design fix for machine learning' (2022) *ACM Conference on Equity and Access in Algorithms, Mechanisms, and Optimization (EAAMO 22)*.

Stohl, Cynthia et al., 'Managing opacity: Information visibility and the paradox of transparency in the digital age' (2016) **10** *International Journal of Communication*.

Suresh, Harini et al., 'Towards intersectional feminist and participatory ML: A case study in supporting feminicide counterdata collection' (2022) *ACM Conference on Fairness, Accountability, and Transparency (ACM FAccT 22)*.

Tomlinson, Joe, 'Justice in automated administration' (2020) **40** *Oxford Journal of Legal Studies*.

van Wynsberghe, Aimee, 'Sustainable AI: AI for sustainability and the sustainability of AI' (2021) **1** *AI and Ethics*.

Verma, Sahil et al., 'Counterfactual explanations and algorithmic recourses for machine learning: A review' (2020) *arXiv preprint arXiv:2010.10596*.

Wachter, Sandra et al., 'Why a right to explanation of automated decision-making does not exist in the general data protection regulation' (2017) **7** *International Data Privacy Law*.

Wachter, Sandra et al., 'Counterfactual explanations without opening the black box: Automated decisions and the GDPR' (2018) **31** *Harvard Journal of Law & Technology*.

Warren, Greta et al., 'Categorical and continuous features in counterfactual explanations of AI systems' (2023) *28th International Conference on Intelligent User Interfaces (IUI 23)*.

Weinberg, Lindsay, 'Rethinking fairness: An interdisciplinary survey of critiques of hegemonic ML fairness approaches' (2022) **74** *Journal of Artificial Intelligence Research*.

Widder, David Gray and Richmond Wong, 'Thinking upstream: Ethics and policy opportunities in AI supply chains' (2023) *arXiv preprint arXiv:2303.07529*.

Widder, David Gray et al., 'Open (for business): Big tech, concentrated power, and the political economy of open AI' (2023).

Wieringa, Maranke, 'What to account for when accounting for algorithms: A systematic literature review on algorithmic accountability' (2020) *ACM Conference on Fairness, Accountability, and Transparency* (ACM FAT* 2020).

Williams, Rebecca, 'Rethinking administrative law for algorithmic decision-making' (2021) **42** *Oxford Journal of Legal Studies*.

Williams, Rebecca, 'From transparency to accountability of intelligent systems – moving beyond aspirations' (2022) **4** *Data and Policy*.

Wolswinkel, Johan, 'Artificial intelligence and administrative law' (2022) Council of Europe.

8.   AI and bias

Sun-ha Hong

INTRODUCTION

AI ethics – as a field of study, as a space for corporate capture, as a policy talking point – is a fledgling project in need of a reset. At its best, contemporary AI ethics seeks to account for the societal impact of AI and algorithmic systems, and to hold accountable the makers and users of those systems for those impacts (e.g. Coeckelbergh 2020). These are crucial interventions into an industry and culture that remains dominated by familiar myths: of transgressive geniuses who change the world by "breaking things and moving fast", of technological models that are universally scalable across social and cultural differences, and of data as capturing objective reality. Yet AI ethics has also proven vulnerable to co-option, obfuscation and glass ceilings; lofty principles around transparency or privacy are often bereft of the power to enforce, while research agendas are increasingly shaped by the caprice of corporate power and influence.

The notion of *bias* is central to this pattern of breakthrough, blockage and paradigm shift in what it means to hold AI and algorithmic systems accountable. Below, I describe how bias came to be a standard-bearer of ethical critique in the age of machine learning, propelling the harmful consequences of often hastily scaled and scientifically dubious technical systems into public and policy attention. I then discuss the growing limitations of this "bias critique": its capture and co-option by industry, and its narrowing into techno-solutionist fixes. Often contrary to the recommendations of the best scholarly work on the subject, the focus on bias today risks overdetermining the problem space around calculating away discriminatory outputs at the expense of more fundamental issues: can AI and algorithms adequately represent socially and historically shaped phenomena, such as emotion or criminality? How do such data-driven models interact with pre-existing inequalities and power asymmetries when deployed into concrete social situations, like hiring or immigration?

Tara McPherson (2012) once argued that the history of computing is organised by a lenticular logic, referencing the lenses in old 3D postcards. There, you can flick between multiple images, but the lens is constructed such that you can never see the images *together*. Bias – through the emergent play of political economic interests rather than conceptual necessity – has become a funnel, leading critique into an increasingly formulaic sequence of questions and answers. In this form, bias risks becoming something like a "loyal opposition" in parliamentary politics: it diligently raises a familiar set of criticisms against the governing regime, which prove easy enough to acknowledge and dismiss in well-rehearsed ways. In Britain, the term was originally used to praise opposition parties that remained faithful to the baseline of democratic government; here, we may retain the metaphor of a group which occupies the role of opposition, but in doing so, forecloses more radical challenges to the dominant paradigm. Thus, more fundamental kinds of critique are further marginalised from public and policy debate – not through the "fault" of bias critique, per se, but through practices of capture and co-option that seeks to ossify bias and lock in the space for critical conversations around AI.

I further outline emerging ways in which researchers are seeking to move critique beyond bias – that is, beyond the growing pressures to narrow ethics and accountability, rather than a repudiation of earlier, pioneering research on the subject. Frank Pasquale (2019) explains that if the "first wave" of algorithmic accountability had focused on exposing and correcting discriminatory outputs, then a "second wave" must ask what kinds of structural conditions make such outputs likely in the first place. Increasingly, the question is not how AI and algorithms might be biased one way or the other, but the ways in which their modelling of social reality might be harmful, unhelpful and scientifically dubious *in the first place*. Before asking whether the scale is biased, we must question whether it is measuring the wrong thing to begin with.

MAKING BIAS

Every technological breakthrough is eventually bestowed a mythical origin point. The current wave of AI enthusiasm is generally traced back to 2012, when deep learning methods, especially those involving convolutional neural networks (CNNs), demonstrated major performance gains in a range of technical contests. Public perception lagged behind somewhat: 2012 had been largely dedicated to coronating big data, a term whose increasing usage (and increasing lack of clear definition) extended a broader narrative that technology would overwhelm human cognition and labour through sheer computational power. By 2016 or so, AI had seamlessly taken the baton for this symbolic role, aided by a series of high-profile public spectacles, such as AlphaGo's defeat of Lee Sedol in the ancient game of Go that year (for more on this chronology, see Broussard 2018; O'Neill 2016). It is no surprise that these terms prove so interchangeable. Big data has always been a leaky, relative term for practitioners as well, and artificial intelligence has never provided a robust definition of "intelligence" in its lifetime – an ambiguity which the field has exploited to its fullest to capture imagination and funding. The present era of "AI", in other words, continues to recycle longstanding beliefs about technology's ability to measure, optimise and ultimately replace human communication through data, underwritten by the promise that "raw" data supplies an objective basis for such computation (Gitelman and Jackson 2013; Hong 2020).

It is this insistence on the *objectivity* of data that organises so many of the cultural and political battle lines around AI, including the emergence of bias as a primary lens of critique. Throughout modernity, objectivity has been characterised by a perpetual flirtation with the fantasy of perfectly stable knowledge, firmly rooted in some unchanging bedrock of the real against the caprice of human subjectivity – and an equally perennial failure to achieve that stability (e.g. Daston and Galison 2007). Novel technologies for large-scale datafication have tended to be accompanied by grand projects of total archival, from microcards for global dream databases (Lemov 2015) to Dewey decimal systems for universal libraries (Jardine and Drage 2018). In much AI and algorithm discourse today, we find (1) the presumption that data can access and represent empirical reality untainted by human subjectivity, combined with (2) a mystification of the subsequent computational process to produce (3) a powerful and universalising claim to the true and the optimal. Scholars have called it "enchanted determinism" (Campolo and Crawford 2020), or even a "cathedral of computation" – one which succeeds "the cathedral of the Enlightenment's [longstanding] ambitions for a universal system of knowledge" (Finn 2017: 8). Thus the public presentation of much contemporary AI follows the formula: "this machine is so complex that nobody knows exactly how it operates – but that is precisely how it achieves greater objectivity and optimisation".

It is because so much of AI's public legitimacy hinges on this claim to objectivity that, in turn, bias has emerged as the central site for public evaluations of the technology. Bias makes a direct intervention into narratives of technological objectivity by subjecting AI output to independent verification – and demonstrating that output to be, in some socially unacceptable way, *skewed*. In 2016, ProPublica released its analysis of COMPAS, the recidivism prediction software that is widely used in US court proceedings, showing its output to be "remarkably unreliable" at forecasting violent crime, and featuring major racial disparities against black defendants (Angwin et al. 2016). The same year, Joy Buolamwini, then a graduate student at MIT, built a white mask to demonstrate facial recognition technologies' inability to reliably detect darker-skinned faces. This would eventually develop into Gender Shades (Buolamwini and Gebru 2018), a systematic evaluation of leading facial recognition tools demonstrating significant loss of accuracy for female and darker-skinned faces. Books from researchers and journalists compiled an expansive array of concrete cases where algorithmic predictions of social outcomes would lead to a deepening of existing disparities (e.g. Benjamin 2019; Cheney-Lippold 2017; O'Neill 2016; Pasquale 2015). Safiya Umoja Noble's *Algorithms of Oppression* (2018) has been remarkably influential, and its analysis of search engines as a vector for amplifying and naturalising historical racism has passed into a common-sense instance of algorithmic harm. This period saw a "mainstream" understanding of bias critique as testing AI and algorithmic systems against their own quantified definitions of objective accuracy, and identifying two major genres of error: (1) where the model proves inaccurate for its own stated goal, e.g. identifying a human face as a face; (2) where, *accuracy aside*, model output reproduces social disparities, e.g. search engines and sexualised images of young black women.

None of this would have been surprising to critical humanistic and social scientific researchers of datafication, who had long shown that data, old and new, are far from objective, and often serve to entrench imperfect assumptions and longstanding power asymmetries *as if* objective. Historians of science and technology have explored how the quantification of social phenomena, such as human intelligence or emotion, often emerged to support specific political projects rather than pure intellectual inevitability. Karl Pearson's foundational work in correlation was directly developed to support his arguments on eugenics (Chun 2021), for example, while Alphonse Quetelet's enormously consequential work on *l'homme moyen* (the average man) relied on assuming a mathematically dubious constancy in human nature to derive a *moralised* sense of the average person and life (Desrosières 1998). Contemporary AI often reproduces these historical missteps, most obviously in facial recognition, which too often retraces the epistemic assumptions of nineteenth-century physiognomy and phrenology (Stark and Hutson 2022).

But in public and policy spheres, the deep learning "revolution" had arrived to a warm welcome, slotting into a cultural milieu still deeply primed to consider datafication as an objective instrument of inevitable progress. In the early 2010s, Silicon Valley was still basking in mainstream glamour. The idea of nerdy, depoliticised outcasts disrupting a tired society with gee-whiz technical tricks was celebrated largely across the political and media spectrum. In 2010, Mark Zuckerberg was TIME's Person of the Year, marking tech's return to the list for the first time since 1999's Jeff Bezos and the subsequent dot-com crash. It took a wider shift in public sentiment, with the Cambridge Analytica scandal in 2016 a turning point, for longstanding critiques of datafication to obtain a modicum of visibility. In this context, studies like "Gender Shades" and *Algorithms of Oppression* were so consequential partly because they found a way to show, visibly and viscerally, the stark consequences of algorithmic bias. Buolamwini's eerie white mask, or the American Civil Liberties Union's (ACLU's) 2018 demonstration where Amazon's facial recognition misidentified 28 members of US Congress with mugshots (Snow 2018), provided a flexible language for describing "smoking gun" cases of bias that could be acknowledged without necessarily exploring the accompanying analyses of historical and structural harms.

This rapid mainstreaming of bias critiques played a crucial role in coalescing public opinion and policy momentum in the post-2016 period. Facial recognition technology, which was being pushed as the next great technological breakthrough, began to receive greater scrutiny. In 2020, the Association of Computing Machinery (ACM), the largest professional organisation for computing research, called for a general suspension of facial recognition due to a lack of adequate standards – citing "ethnic, racial, gender", and other forms of bias as the foremost risk (ACM 2020). Local governments, like San Francisco in 2019, also moved to specific bans and moratoria on facial recognition, with the European Union now considering a similar move. Pioneering researchers behind these initial breakthroughs would also effectively leverage this impact to form research centres focused on algorithmic harm and social justice – including Joy Buolamwini and Safiya Noble at the Algorithmic Justice League, Alex Hanna and Timnit Gebru at the Distributed AI Research Institute (DAIR) – seeking to build wide-ranging and structural examinations of how AI systems impact actually existing social situations.

One visible, concrete aspect of this critical momentum was the rise of algorithmic audits. By the early 2020s, we find – at least in North America and Europe – a growing cohort of commercial, journalistic and nonprofit/academic auditors, and active conversation around best practices and frameworks (Brown et al. 2021; Costanza-Chock et al. 2022; Raji et al. 2020b). Yet audits also reveal fundamental difficulties around how bias and other critiques might be translated into meaningful forms of accountability. Audits are often retrospective inquiries that navigate inadequate documentation, resistant auditees and other "messy" organisational obstacles (Keyes and Austin 2022). They also risk reproducing some of the problems they are trying to audit against – for example, by helping normalise a fundamentally misguided task, or because dataset audits run into similar privacy issues as the datasets themselves (Raji et al. 2020a). As well as some immediate practical challenges (and benefits), the rise of algorithmic audits points to the broader dangers of instrumentalising bias and ethics into corrective measures.

CAPTURING BIAS

The widespread uptake of the bias critique, in other words, has often been co-opted into a *narrowing* of the horizon of ethical and normative discussion into a simpler matter of detecting and "correcting" certain familiar kinds of bias (e.g. racial). Captured this way, bias becomes a point of critical and ethical *closure*: places where one can be satisfied as having done due diligence, and the overall project of datafication may resume more or less as planned.

Thus, the most common response to bias critiques – other than dismissing their seriousness, which remains widespread – has been to instrumentalise bias into a technical parameter which might be measured and eliminated using the same technical tools that had created the biased models to begin with. This techno-solutionist (Morozov 2013) logic argues that if a model disproportionately produces undesirable outcomes for a particular minority, then it is eminently possible to adjust model parameters until the bias is *neutralised*. This line of thinking, of course, is also used to support a popular counterargument to bias critiques: that if an image generation AI produces sexist images of male CEOs and female nurses, for example, then this is simply an objective representation of its training data, rather than "biased algorithms". In this case, "correcting" for bias is seen as an artificial adjustment away from objective reality.

We find here many of the persistent limitations that such a narrow understanding of bias imposes on critical evaluations of AI and algorithms. First, bias is rendered as an anthromorphic sin defined by intentional discrimination. This interpretation sequesters bias into a rather small and uncommon category, in which an algorithm is maliciously written to harass a group of people and betrays this intent transparently. This misguided focus on "bad actors" encourages a generally futile whodunnit exercise, which then allows the creators and users of those technologies to deflect responsibility through the claim that the algorithm, not being human, "cannot be racist or sexist" (Hoffmann 2019).

Secondly, efforts to "correct" bias often rely on a pervasive myth about AI and algorithms: that there exists a value-neutral, debiased "zero-point" that models can approach, and that contemporary data analytics can calculate their relation to this zero-point through objective assessments of social realities. Consider the rise of "debiasing" measures, such as IBM's Diversity in Faces (DiF) initiative. DiF sought directly to address the findings of the Gender Shades study, primarily by enlisting a larger pool of face images for AI datasets (Crawford 2021: 131–2). The problem, of course, was that this approach left the underlying task and definitions intact: it is taken as a given that craniometrics and facial recognition are depoliticised methods for objective assessments of human beings. In many cases, debiasing and other technical fixes attempt to hunt down exactly the kinds of model outputs singled out by landmark bias critiques – i.e. populational prejudice against protected characteristics like race or disability – and then to seek a computational adjustment to eliminate the "bad output". Subsequently, the algorithm may then be "certified" as unbiased, supporting its use in evolving social situations. The European Digital Rights institution (EDRi), for example, has argued that current EU policy overly relies on debiasing as a full and permanent corrective (Balayn and Gürses 2021; also see Scheuerman et al. 2021: 28). Broadly speaking, then, the growing focus on debiasing amounts to a "strategic concession ... that subdues the scale of the challenge" (Powles 2018), in which visible corrections of selected discriminatory outputs ultimately help legitimise the general project of ubiquitous facial recognition or automated hiring systems.

The imagination of "bias" as a needle skewed one way or another, to be put back into the zero, is less a model for really existing situations than a set of fragile and unsupported assumptions. Ben Green argues that the many slogans and projects around "AI for Good" often possess no robust definition of the social good, "relying on rough proxies such as crime = bad, poverty = bad, and so on" (2019: 1). The reliance on easily available proxies for complicated social phenomena, and a subsequent assumption of how these proxies are *connected*, is a broader fundamental issue in data science and machine learning, but especially pronounced in ethics and accountability, where "blue-sky" language about justice or human rights too often stands in for the lack of specific and enforceable measures (Munn 2023).

How notions like bias are (ill-)defined, and positioned as necessary or sufficient for ethical AI, thus has major ramifications for what kinds of real-world consequences get what kinds of corrective attention (or not). The language of bias is frequently exploited for performative gestures to "ethical" AI across much of applied AI research (both academic and industry), as well as policy circles. In a systematic study of two of the leading computer vision conferences, ICML and NeurIPS, Birhane et al. (2022) demonstrate how new, cutting-edge research papers overwhelmingly define their impact in terms like performance benchmarks, and largely eschew any discussion of societal needs or possible negative effects (for a similar study of computer vision datasets, see Scheuerman et al. 2021). Prominent public declarations for "ethical" AI and machine learning from major academic and industry practitioner groups also tend to co-opt the language of ethics, including bias, into a "limited, technologically deterministic, expert-driven view" (Greene et al. 2019: 1; also see Jobin et al. 2019; Rönnblom, Carlsson and Padden, Chapter 9 in this volume). Here, the kind of expertise sought after is predominantly technical, and aimed at producing computational solutions. Yet historically, it is expertise beyond the technical, and sensitivity to social and historical patterns that was required to bring bias and other concrete harms to the table. Luke Stark (2023) reminds us that until around 2015, the term "AI ethics" largely involved "metaphysical speculations about the status of machines". Increasingly, Big Tech companies are using showpiece ethics initiatives – high in public relations visibility, low in meaningful path to impact – borrowing from familiar playbooks of corporate social responsibility (CSR) and greenwashing. Google, for example, responded to growing worker unrest and public controversy over its participation in Project Maven (a computer vision project commissioned by the US Department of Defense for drone warfare) by publishing a set of ethical AI principles with no binding mechanisms for enforcement, and later, launching an external advisory council, the Advanced Technology External Advisory Council (ATEAC), which was shuttered after just a week due to controversy around its founding members (Phan et al. 2021).

Crucially, these definitional problems are being shaped not in the proverbial roundtable of independent thinkers engaged in good faith, but a quagmire of industry-funded lobby groups, Big Tech ethics teams at the mercy of corporate caprice, and active co-option of critical vocabulary into forms of "ethics washing" (Bietti 2020). In 2020, Timnit Gebru, a pioneering AI ethics researcher and the co-lead of Google's ethical AI team, was fired after co-authoring a paper, "Stochastic Parrots" (Bender et al. 2021), that outlined the environmental costs, biased and harmful output, and other general risks around natural language processing (NLP) applications. Yet the paper was not a sudden intervention into *terra nullius*; by 2020, such critical assessments had increasingly become commonplace in serious ethical discussions, and should have been common sense. Google's decision to fire Gebru – and soon after, another highly regarded co-author, Margaret Mitchell – demonstrated the company's insistence that "AI ethics" research should proceed strictly on their own terms only. In terms of funding, computational resources and prestige, Big Tech "make[s] the water in which AI research swims" (Whittaker 2021: 53) – as visible not only in signature projects like the Chan Zuckerberg Initiative's $500 million donation to Harvard, but also the rapid growth of corporate affiliated authorship in AI research (Birhane et al. 2022).

One constant in these forms of capture is to incorporate bias critique *into* boosterist narratives about the inevitability of technology. In such "criti-hype" (Vinsel 2021), criticism depends on taking AI hype at face value – such as the worry that large language models will revolutionise writing in exciting ways, *but* may reproduce hate speech against certain minorities. Here, AI continues to be treated with magical awe, with credulous speculation about whether a chatbot is truly "intelligent" or a text-to-image generation software spells the end of art (e.g. Bender 2022). A case in point is the rapidly growing fascination with "AI safety" (and alongside or sometimes subordinate to it, "AI alignment"). Contrary to safety's usual connotations around mundane, concrete and proven dangers, often considered "boring" but necessary, AI safety fixates on the coming of "truly" intelligent artificial general intelligence (AGI) as an overwhelming priority for human civilisation. With significant intellectual and financial connections to existential risk (x-risk) and long-termism communities (Tiku 2023), this approach leverages apocalyptic fears around AGI as an ever-ready rationale for further research and development (e.g. Beard and Torres, preprint; Torres 2021; Wong 2023). Such framing demarcates the limits of debate: by taking rapid technological progress resulting in AGI as a given, it forecloses many possible strategies, such as a slower, more rigorous and deliberative approach to technological adoption, as unrealistic – despite the fact that the current generation of machine learning approaches fundamentally are not able to, and do not even *try* to, replicate human intelligence or learning (processes which themselves remain underdefined). The focus on largest-scale existential threats has also been criticised as a turn to highly abstracted scenarios, distracting attention from actually existing harms – from "robodebt" algorithms that illegally garnished financially vulnerable Australians (McGowan 2021), to failure-ridden facial recognition systems that have already resulted in wrongful arrests of Black Americans (Hill 2020). Tellingly, the new generative AI systems hailed as a pathway to AGI continue to suffer from the same basic failures when it comes to algorithmic bias – for example, ranking white-associated names consistently higher in resume assessment tasks (Yin et al. 2024). As Emily Bender (2023) and others have noted, these "doomerist" warnings consistently work to displace existing genres of robust, independent research while providing little of their own. If the bias critique helped bring ethical concerns around AI above the surface of public visibility, this space for critical debate is today being recolonised by apocalyptic scenarios that ultimately return to more technology as the answer to all technological problems.

BEYOND BIAS

To reach beyond bias, then, is not to repudiate earlier efforts or to move "past" them, but to adapt their objectives to a changing – and often disingenuous or adversarial – public conversation. Where techno-optimist dismissiveness against rigorous attention to ethical considerations and disparate impacts had been the primary challenge (and often still remains the case), spaces like machine learning research and Big Tech increasingly impose their lenticular logic on bias, narrowing AI ethics into the task of correcting errors in data-driven models so that they can continue to be developed and deployed at scale. In this sense, emerging directions in critical AI research offer potential ways to reopen public and policy conversations towards at least minimal levels of genuine accountability.

The success of bias as lexicon – and its subsequent capture – testifies to the crucial role of language in coordinating public opinion and political agendas. Critical researchers are increasingly insisting on more capacious terminology, such as algorithmic justice or systemic harms, to emphasise actually occurring harms and their structural contributors rather than individuals and intent (e.g. Dave 2019; Dencik et al. 2019). In this approach, if algorithmic predictions in policing reproduce historical tendencies to suspect and litigate against a vulnerable group, a debate about whether the algorithm has "malicious intent", or is merely "accurately" replicating past patterns in the data, etc., is quite literally, *pointless*: the sometimes naïve, and often disingenuous, search for sinful machines or a zero-point of objectivity does not meaningfully address the growing record of concrete harms enacted through data-driven systems, and the historical pattern of asymmetries that these technologies often end up amplifying (e.g. Benjamin 2019; Burrell and Fourcade 2021). Some advise against the term artificial intelligence altogether, given that it remains fundamentally underdefined (Dick 2019), and that this very underdefinition has for decades been used to incite a sense of grandiosity and inevitability around the field – and along with it, a growing litany of misconceptions (e.g. Center on Privacy & Technology at Georgetown Law 2022).

Refreshing the critical vocabulary also requires reevaluating the concepts that might serve as tests and thresholds for evaluating the impact of AI and algorithms. In social decision-making situations like hiring or airport security stops, for example, there is always a pre-existing web of uncertainty, guesswork, intuition and organisational politics that governs how decisions are made – that is, a historically accumulated landscape of *discretion*. The ground-level impact of a predictive system depends not only on the biasedness of its own judgements, but how, say, it redistributes border officials' previously held levels of discretion (Côté-Boucher 2016). A social worker might understand very well that the algorithms scoring cases for likelihood of child neglect and abuse are imperfect, and that they as human experts are empowered to override these scores. But in practice, the workers often find that the very presence of the recommendations influences how they wield their discretion and justify it (Eubanks 2018). This redistribution of discretionary power is, as I argue elsewhere, a consistent outcome of actually deployed predictive AI and algorithmic systems (Hong 2023) – and an example of a broader structural effect that is not neatly reducible to individualised measures against an implicit point of objectivity. Analysing the redistribution of discretion is one way to move beyond technical adjustments and to focus on how AI systems interact with pre-existing social situations and their inequalities – work that is being undertaken across research labs such as the Automated Decision Making and Society (ADM+S) Centre in Australia.

Researchers are also working to recapture bias as a critical concept, harnessing the political momentum behind it and directing it towards a more expansive and historicised understanding of AI and society. The Center for Critical Race + Digital Studies (2022), for example, argues that "any algorithms that perpetuate the status quo and do not improve social equity for [...] marginalised groups are biased", noting that any act of datafication that presumes the existing status quo as a neutral zero-point thereby relegitimises whatever "biases" might already be present. A sense of *history*, in other words, is what is missing from the narrower, solutionist approaches to bias. Machine learning systems rely on compiling (highly partial and flawed collections of) past events into datasets, which are then used to train and predict future predictions – thus reproducing their biases and asymmetries while *disavowing* their historicity (e.g. Browne 2015; Chun 2021; Prabhu and Birhane 2020).

One way to put all this is that any AI technology that has a "bias problem" has a lot bigger problems than "just" bias. Correcting biased output alone often leaves intact more fundamental questions around how people and social situations get captured into data. The case of facial recognition is emblematic. The global conversation sparked by studies like Gender Shades implicitly positions *accurate identification* as a positive outcome – something statistically more likely for lighter-skinned men, in that study, than for other groups. Such critique focuses on what is functioning or broken *within* the self-defined objectives of the technology. Yet, as Nabil Hassein (2017) and others (e.g. Raji et al. 2020a; Stark 2019) have asked: is it even desirable for, say, Black Americans to demand that facial recognition detect their faces more accurately, given the historical pattern in which police are primary buyers of such technology, and US police's long record of disproportionate violence against Black Americans? Or consider the use of automated decision-making in hiring processes: quite aside from any biases and errors within the model itself, the key issue is that these tools are introduced into existing practices that *already* feature built-in biases, such as in the use of "nebulous criteria" like "cultural fit" (Ajunwa 2020). The definition of a "good" outcome must emerge from the historical conditions that skew who is likely to use such tools against whom: otherwise, a theoretically perfectly unbiased tool merely proves entirely accurate at extending pre-existing biases.

Even more fundamentally, the very notion of *identification* in facial recognition lacks scientific rigour, undermining the basic set of correlations upon which claims of bias or neutrality can be made in the first place. In practice, facial recognition software has tended to be oriented towards a particular set of identifications that are familiar figures in the history of surveillance: criminality, productivity and emotion. This orientation often crosses industry and research boundaries. A few notorious examples illustrate the trend: first, the Harrisburg University study (2020), which claimed to "predict if someone is a criminal based solely on a picture of their face", was led by a "Ph.D. student and NYPD veteran" Jonathan Korn, depicting one route by which policing as a way of seeing becomes built into this kind of research. Second, what became known as the "gaydar" study, by Stanford researchers Yilun Wang and Michal Kosinski, which claimed that facial recognition could be used to accurately identify sexual orientation (Davis 2017; Mattson 2017; also see Agüera y Arcas et al. 2017). Although the paper argued that it conducted this analysis to warn society of such capabilities, the predictable effect has been to further normalise the sense that if machine learning can be put to patently reckless uses, then it *will and must*.

Yet in each of these domains, there is a striking lack of rigorous evidence or even a coherent theory to support the idea that criminality, productivity or emotion can be identified using visual data of human faces in the first place. Facial emotion recognition (FER) suffers not only from unreliable output or the social harms caused by that output, but the inability to clearly define and prove the connection between emotion and faces. Emotion itself remains a contested concept, with thorny and unresolved theoretical problems around how one might stabilise it into a consistent measure (Stark and Hoey 2021). FER continues to rely overwhelmingly on Paul Ekman's work in the 1970s (Angerer and Bösel 2016), whose Basic Emotion Theory (BET) boiled it all down to nine universal categories like fear and disgust (labels which are now a familiar fixture on many FER interfaces) – despite the many documented problems with Ekman's research, from the wildly universalising impulses of BET, to his disastrous attempted fieldwork in Papua New Guinea that failed to produce any cross-cultural evidence (Crawford 2021). In addition, FER is affected by the unreliability of its ground truths – that is, the fact that existing human identifications of facial expressions of emotion are hardly consistent (Cabitza et al. 2022). Simply put, emotion lacks any robust evidence for a stable set of definitions, and it is also uncertain how or if it can be measured and quantified, especially via facial expressions. The challenge is not simply that the output may be biased, but that it remains misleading and nonsensical.

These fundamental problems recur in facial recognition's relationships with criminality and productivity, and indeed, more generally with many efforts to deploy machine learning for social and behavioural prediction (Narayanan 2019). Efforts to link facial images with criminality thus suppose that "criminality" exists as an objective quality, and that it can in some mysterious way be inferred through faces – mysterious, because a central tenet of machine learning prediction (or the "big data" paradigm) is that it is impractical and even unnecessary to know exactly how crime and faces are related, as long as the model somehow delivers the desired output. But if facial recognition for crime prediction justifies itself purely by its output accuracy rather than any theory of the relationship, in practice, their models often end up resembling historical efforts at anthropometrics and scientific racism, insofar as they collate human impressions of faces into categories (e.g. "untrustworthy") which are then presumed to objectively and independently "predict" crime (Agüera y Arcas et al. 2017). Explicitly physiognomic and phrenological objectives for profiling people by their faces is increasingly common in industry products and marketing, supported by compatible research in computer vision and proximate fields (Stark and Hutson 2022). Here again, computational systems end up replicating and extending longer historical patterns that would be entirely invisible in any narrow, model-internal view of bias: facial recognition is historically rooted in the later nineteenth- and early twentieth-century fascination with anthropometry, including phrenology and physiognomy, and since then has consistently been designed to profile "criminal types" of some form (Gates 2011).

A bias problem is thus symptomatic of more fundamental problems beyond bias, in which AI and algorithmic systems often proceed with poorly defined and scientifically dubious models of the human and social phenomena that they purport to identify or predict. In that "proceeding", these technologies naturalise their assumptions through the conceit of data's objectivity – enlisting narrow, instrumental definitions of bias in support of this obfuscation. What is at stake in the shifting conversations around bias is not just whether a tool of crime or emotion prediction is biased against certain groups, but what dubious definitions of criminality and emotion are being imposed as objective realities *such that* historical patterns of marginalisation cannot help but continue. Time and again, deploying techniques for automation, measurement and prediction into concrete social situations has resulted not in machines "learning" to understand and accompany humans, but imposing new standards of what "counts" – as a smiling or suspicious face, as a creditworthy consumer or cheating student – to which ordinary people adapt at their own peril (Alkhatib 2021; Birhane 2021; Hong 2020).

CONCLUSION

The success – and rapid co-option – of bias critiques testifies to how AI ethics cannot seek to simply describe its object in a vacuum, but must account for the political economic landscape around it. In the late 2010s, bias played a pioneering role in opening spaces for public and policy conversations around the limits of data's objectivity and the disparate impacts of algorithmic systems. Since then, many of its critical tools have been captured or obfuscated: by Big Tech's use of funding and media visibility for "ethics washing", by techno-solutionist approaches to debiasing as a computational solution and by strategies of "criti-hype", like AI safety and alignment discourses, which are saturating policy debates and the public momentum for change with apocalyptic scenarios divorced from concrete, real-life harms. This should not lead to the conclusion that the bias critiques have failed, or that it was some intellectual flaw in such research that is responsible for such failure. Rather, it was the stripping down of historical and structural patterns from that critique – enabled in large part by Big Tech's vast financial resources – that is diverting ethical and regulatory debates towards technological solutionism. Efforts like the European Union's AI Act, the United States' 2022 Blueprint for an AI Bill of Rights, and the widespread push for banning facial recognition tools do indicate that the past decade of critique has helped pave the way for policy efforts more attuned to the concrete social implications of technological systems. It is ever more important to cut beneath the technological assumptions built into the language of accuracy and objectivity, and to ask: how does the very act of measuring and predicting affect human lives and social structures? How are categories like criminality and emotion, or even the idea of "AI for Good", being defined – and by whom?

REFERENCES

Agüera y Arcas, B., M. Mitchell and A. Todorov (2017), 'Physiognomy's new clothes', accessed at https://medium.com/@blaisea/physiognomys-new-clothes-f2d4b59fdd6a.

Ajunwa, I. (2020), 'The paradox of automation as anti-bias intervention', *Cardozo Law Review*, **41** (5), 1671–742.

Alkhatib, A. (2021), 'To live in their utopia: Why algorithmic systems create absurd outcomes', in *CHI Conference of Human Factors in Computing*, Yokohama, Japan: ACM, pp. 1–9.

Angerer, M.-L. and B. Bösel (2016), 'Total affect control', *Digital Culture & Society*, **2** (1).

Angwin, J., J. Larson, S. Mattu and L. Kirchner (2016), 'Machine bias', accessed at https://www.propublica.org/article/machine-bias-risk-assessments-in-criminal-sentencing.

Balayn, A. and S. Gürses (2021), *Beyond Debiasing: AI Regulation and its Limits*, European Digital Rights (EDRi), accessed at https://edri.org/our-work/if-ai-is-the-problem-is-debiasing-the-solution/.

Beard, S. and P. Torres (n.d.), 'Ripples on the great sea of life: A brief history of existential risk studies', *SSRN Electronic Journal*.

Bender, E. M. (2022), 'On NYT magazine on AI: Resist the urge to be impressed', accessed at https://medium.com/@emilymenonbender/on-nyt-magazine-on-ai-resist-the-urge-to-be-impressed-3d92fd9a0edd.

Bender, E. M. (2023), 'Talking about a "schism" is ahistorical', accessed 10 July 2023 at https://medium.com/@emilymenonbender/talking-about-a-schism-is-ahistorical-3c454a77220f.

Bender, E. M., T. Gebru, A. McMillan-Major and S. Shmitchell (2021), 'On the dangers of stochastic parrots: Can language models be too big?', in *FAccT 2021 – Proceedings of the 2021 ACM Conference on Fairness, Accountability, and Transparency*, Virtual Event, Canada: ACM, pp. 610–23.

Benjamin, R. (2019), *Race After Technology: Abolitionist Tools for the New Jim Code*, Cambridge: Polity Press.

Bietti, E. (2020), 'From ethics washing to ethics bashing', in *FAT* '20: Proceedings of the 2020 Conference on Fairness, Accountability, and Transparency*, 27 January, Barcelona, pp. 210–19.

Birhane, A. (2021), 'The impossibility of automating ambiguity', *Artificial Life*, **27**, 1–18.

Birhane, A., P. Kalluri, D. Card, W. Agnew, R. Dotan and M. Bao (2022), 'The values encoded in machine learning research', in *2022 ACM Conference on Fairness, Accountability, and Transparency (FAccT '22)*, 21–24 June, Seoul, South Korea, pp. 173–84.

Broussard, M. (2018), *Artificial Unintelligence: How Computers Misunderstand the World*, Cambridge, MA: MIT Press.

Brown, S., J. Davidovic and A. Hasan (2021), 'The algorithm audit: Scoring the algorithms that score us', *Big Data & Society*, **8** (1).

Browne, S. (2015), *Dark Matters: On the Surveillance of Blackness*, Pittsburgh, PA: Duke University Press.

Buolamwini, J. and T. Gebru (2018), 'Gender shades: Intersectional accuracy disparities in commercial gender classification', in *Proceedings of the 1st Conference on Fairness, Accountability and Transparency*, vol. 81, pp. 77–91.

Burrell, J. and M. Fourcade (2021), 'The society of algorithms', *Annual Review of Sociology*, **47**, 1–25.

Cabitza, F., A. Campagner and M. Mattioli (2022), 'The unbearable (technical) unreliability of automated facial emotion recognition', *Big Data & Society*, **9** (2).

Campolo, A. and K. Crawford (2020), 'Enchanted determinism: Power without responsibility in artificial intelligence', *Engaging Science, Technology, and Society*, **6**.

Center for Critical Race + Digital Studies (2022), *What Is Algorithmic Bias?*, accessed at https://www
.criticalracedigitalstudies.com/peoples-guide-posts/what-is-algorithmic-bias.

Center on Privacy & Technology at Georgetown Law (2022), *Artifice and Intelligence*, accessed at
https://medium.com/center-on-privacy-technology/artifice-and-intelligence%C2%B9-f00da128d3cd.

Cheney-Lippold, J. (2017), *We Are Data – Algorithms and the Making of Our Digital Selves*, New York:
New York University Press.

Chun, W. H. K. (2021), *Discriminating Data: Correlation, Neighborhoods, and the New Politics of
Recognition*, Cambridge, MA: MIT Press.

Coeckelbergh, M. (2020), *AI Ethics*, Cambridge, MA: MIT Press.

Costanza-Chock, S., I. D. Raji and J. Buolamwini (2022), 'Who audits the auditors? Recommendations
from a field scan of the algorithmic auditing ecosystem', in *2022 ACM Conference on Fairness,
Accountability, and Transparency*, Seoul Republic of Korea: ACM, pp. 1571–83.

Côté-Boucher, K. (2016), 'The paradox of discretion: Customs and the changing occupational identity of
Canadian border officers', *British Journal of Criminology*, **56**, 49–67.

Crawford, K. (2021), *Atlas of AI*, New Haven, CT: Yale University Press.

Daston, L. J. and P. Galison (2007), *Objectivity*, New York: Zone Books.

Dave, K. (2019), 'Systemic algorithmic harms', accessed at https://points.datasociety.net/systemic
-algorithmic-harms-e00f99e72c42.

Davis, J. (2017), 'Rendering bodies out of rendered machines', accessed at https://thesocietypages.org/
cyborgology/2017/09/11/rendering-bodies-out-of-rendered-machines/.

Dencik, L., A. Hintz, J. Redden and E. Treré (2019), 'Exploring data justice: Conceptions, applications
and directions', *Information, Communication & Society*, **22** (7), 873–81.

Desrosières, A. (1998), *The Politics of Large Numbers: A History of Statistical Reasoning*, Cambridge,
MA: Harvard University Press.

Dick, S. (2019), 'Artificial intelligence', *Harvard Data Science Review*, **1** (1), 1–9.

Eubanks, V. (2018), *Automating Inequality: How High-Tech Tools Profile, Police, and Punish the Poor*,
New York: St. Martin's Press.

Finn, E. (2017), *What Algorithms Want: Imagination in the Age of Computing*, Cambridge, MA: MIT
Press.

Gates, K. A. (2011), *Our Biometric Future: Facial Recognition Technology and the Culture of
Surveillance*, New York: New York University Press.

Gitelman, L. and V. Jackson (2013), 'Introduction', in L. Gitelman (ed), *Raw Data is an Oxymoron*,
Cambridge, MA: MIT Press, pp. 1–14.

Green, B. (2019), '"Good" isn't good enough', in *NeurIPS 2019, AI for Social Good Workshop*,
Vancouver.

Greene, D., A. L. Hoffmann and L. Stark (2019), 'Better, nicer, clearer, fairer: A critical assessment
of the movement for ethical artificial intelligence and machine learning', *Proceedings of the 52nd
Hawaii International Conference on System Sciences*.

Harrisburg University (2020), 'HU facial recognition software predicts criminality', accessed at archive
.ph/N1HVe.

Hassein, N. (2017), 'Against black inclusion in facial recognition', accessed 11 March 2018 at https://
digitaltalkingdrum.com/2017/08/15/against-black-inclusion-in-facial-recognition/.

Hill, K. (2020), 'Wrongfully accused by an algorithm', accessed at https://www.nytimes.com/2020/06/
24/technology/facial-recognition-arrest.html.

Hoffmann, A. L. (2019), 'Where fairness fails: Data, algorithms, and the limits of antidiscrimination
discourse', *Information Communication & Society*, **22** (7), 900–915.

Hong, S. (2020), *Technologies of Speculation: The Limits of Knowledge in a Data-Driven Society*, New
York: New York University Press.

Hong, S. (2023), 'Prediction as extraction of discretion', *Big Data & Society*, **10** (1).

HU facial recognition software predicts criminality (2020), accessed at archive.ph/N1HVe.

Jardine, B. and M. Drage (2018), 'The total archive: Data, subjectivity, universality', *History of the
Human Sciences*, **31** (5), 3–22.

Jobin, A., M. Ienca and E. Vayena (2019), 'The global landscape of AI ethics guidelines', *Nature
Machine Intelligence*, **1** (2), 388–99.

Keyes, O. and J. Austin (2022), 'Feeling fixes: Mess and emotion in algorithmic audits', *Big Data & Society*, **9** (2).

Lemov, R. (2015), *Database of Dreams: The Lost Quest to Catalog Humanity*, New Haven: Yale University Press.

Mattson, G. (2017), 'Guest post: Artificial intelligence discovers gayface. sigh.', accessed 26 June 2023 at https://scatter.wordpress.com/2017/09/10/guest-post-artificial-intelligence-discovers-gayface-sigh/.

McGowan, M. (2021), '"Robodebt 2.0": NSW government unlawfully took money from financially vulnerable people, report finds', *The Guardian*, 30 November.

McPherson, T. (2012), 'US operating systems at mid-century: The intertwining of race and unix', in L. Nakamura and P. Chow-White (eds), *Race After the Internet*, New York: Routledge, pp. 21–37.

Morozov, E. (2013), *To Save Everything, Click Here: The Folly of Technological Solutionism*, New York: Public Affairs.

Munn, L. (2023), 'The uselessness of AI ethics', *AI and Ethics*, **3** (1–2), 869–977.

Narayanan, A. (2019), *How to Recognize AI Snake Oil*, Cambridge, accessed at https://t.co/iCpyFw5urN?amp=1.

Noble, S. U. (2018), *Algorithms of Oppression: How Search Engines Reinforce Racism*, New York: New York University Press.

O'Neill, C. (2016), *Weapons of Math Destruction: How Big Data Increases Inequality and Threatens Democracy*, New York: Crown.

Pasquale, F. (2015), *The Black Box Society: The Secret Algorithms that Control Money and Information*, Cambridge, MA: Harvard University Press.

Pasquale, F. (2019), 'The second wave of algorithmic accountability', accessed at https://lpeproject.org/blog/the-second-wave-of-algorithmic-accountability/.

Phan, T., J. Goldenfein, M. Mann and D. Kuch (2021), 'Economies of virtue: The circulation of "ethics" in big tech', *Science as Culture*, **31** (1), 121–35.

Powles, J. (2018), *The Seductive Diversion of 'Solving' Bias in Artificial Intelligence*, Medium, accessed at https://onezero.medium.com/the-seductive-diversion-of-solving-bias-in-artificial-intelligence-890df5e5ef53.

Prabhu, V. U. and A. Birhane (2020), *Large Image Datasets: A Pyrrhic Win for Computer Vision?*, accessed at https://arxiv.org/abs/2006.16923.

Raji, I. D., T. Gebru, M. Mitchell, J. Buolamwini, J. Lee and E. Denton (2020a), 'Saving face: Investigating the ethical concerns of facial recognition auditing', in *AIES 2020 – Proceedings of the AAAI/ACM Conference on AI, Ethics, and Society*, pp. 145–51.

Raji, I. D., A. Smart, R. N. White, M. Mitchell, T. Gebru, B. Hutchinson, J. Smith-Loud, D. Theron and P. Barnes (2020b), 'Closing the AI accountability gap: defining an end-to-end framework for internal algorithmic auditing', in *FAT* '20: Proceedings of the 2020 Conference on Fairness, Accountability, and Transparency*, 27 January, Barcelona, pp. 33–44.

Scheuerman, M. K., E. Denton and A. Hanna (2021), 'Do datasets have politics? Disciplinary values in ComputerVision dataset development', in *Proceedings of the ACM on Human-Computer Interaction*, vol. 5.

Snow, J. (2018), 'Amazon's face recognition falsely matched 28 members of Congress with mug-shots', accessed at https://www.aclu.org/news/privacy-technology/amazons-face-recognition-falsely-matched-28.

Stark, L. (2019), 'Facial recognition is the plutonium of AI', *XRDS: Crossroads, The ACM Magazine for Students*, **25** (3), 50–55.

Stark, L. (2023), 'Breaking up (with) AI ethics', *American Literature*, **95** (2), 365–79.

Stark, L. and J. Hoey (2021), 'The ethics of emotion in artificial intelligence systems', in *FAccT 2021 – Proceedings of the 2021 ACM Conference on Fairness, Accountability, and Transparency*, pp. 782–93.

Stark, L. and J. Hutson (2022), 'Physiognomic artificial intelligence', *Fordham Intellectual Property, Media & Entertainment Law Journal*, **32** (4), 922–78.

Statement on Principles and Prerequisites for the Development, Evaluation and Use of Unbiased Facial Recognition Technologies (2020), ACM US Technology Policy Committee, accessed at https://www.acm.org/binaries/content/assets/public-policy/ustpc-facial-recognition-tech-statement.pdf.

Tiku, N. (2023), 'How elite schools like Stanford became fixated on the AI apocalypse', accessed 10 July 2023 at https://www.washingtonpost.com/technology/2023/07/05/ai-apocalypse-college-students/.

Torres, E. P. (2021), 'The dangerous ideas of "longtermism" and "existential risk"', accessed at https://www.currentaffairs.org/2021/07/the-dangerous-ideas-of-longtermism-and-existential-risk.

Vinsel, L. (2021), 'You're doing it wrong: Notes on criticism and technology hype', accessed at https://sts-news.medium.com/youre-doing-it-wrong-notes-on-criticism-and-technology-hype-18b08b4307e5.

Whittaker, M. (2021), 'The steep cost of capture', *ACM Interactions* **6** (November–December), 51–5.

Wong, M. (2023), 'AI doomerism is a decoy', accessed 22 June 2023 at https://www.theatlantic.com/technology/archive/2023/06/ai-regulation-sam-altman-bill-gates/674278/.

Yin, L., D. Alba and L. Nicoletti (2024), 'OpenAI's GPT is a recruiter's dream tool: Tests show there's racial bias', accessed at https://www.bloomberg.com/graphics/2024-openai-gpt-hiring-racial-discrimination.

9. AI and ethics: policies of de-politicisation?
Malin Rönnblom, Vanja Carlsson and Michaela Padden

INTRODUCTION

The intense attention being directed towards how AI technologies (AITs) are increasingly permeating many aspects of society, as well as people's everyday lives, often ends in a call for ethics. The implementation of ethical AI, or responsible AI or trustworthy AI, is put forward, by both scholars and policymakers, as the answer to the potential risks that the implementation of different forms of AIT could bring. As UNESCO states on its website: 'In no other field is the ethical compass more relevant than in artificial intelligence' (https://www.unesco.org/ en/artificial-intelligence/recommendation-ethics). Although the implementation of AIT in the public sector is mainly presented as a way of increasing efficiency and cost-effectiveness, as well as securing the objective/non-biased treatment of all citizens (cf. Paul, Carmel and Cobbe, Chapter 1 in this volume; Heidelberg, Chapter 4 in this volume), i.e., mainly as beneficial to society, there is also an increased focus on the risks inherent in this transformation. Here, one central discussion concerns how the development and implementation of new technologies can produce bias and discrimination against social groups based on gender or skin colour (cf. Eubanks 2019). The response to these risks – from both the public sector and private tech companies – has been the development of ethical guidelines, to ensure what is often called 'an ethical and responsible AI' (Veale 2020; see also Carlsson and Rönnblom 2022). Similarly to the European Commission, which stresses 'the importance of ethics in the development and use of new technologies' (EC 2018, 12), both researchers and representatives of industry stress the need for agreement on ethical norms or standards. In addition, the need to educate AIT engineers in aspects of ethics and morality has been put forward as necessary in order to prevent risks when implementing AIT (Zhu and Clancy 2023).

A Scopus search on 'Ethics and AI' also reveals an intensified focus on this relationship, from 13 articles published in 2013 to 1,684 articles in 2021, mainly in the field of Computing Science (1,062 articles), but also in Social Sciences (602 articles). Thus, the risks of AIT in terms of ethics and responsibility is also a growing theme in research. Some researchers focus on how to make AIT 'more ethical' (see Dignum 2019) while others criticise 'AI ethics' for not addressing the core risks and problems that AIT brings (cf. Wagner 2018). Regardless of the different positions, it seems clear that ethics has become a dominant discourse in discussions about the risks of implementing AIT in the public sector (cf. Paul, Chapter 20 in this volume, on the dominance of 'applied ethics' perspectives in AIT regulation studies).

In parallel to this, and partly as a response to the intense focus on ethics and AIT, there is a growing critical discussion among scholars on what this 'ethification' of ICT in general, and of AI in particular, means in the context of democracy and governing (cf. van Dijk et al. 2021). 'Ethics washing' (cf. van Maanen 2022) is a term that was coined to illustrate how ethics are used, mainly by industry, to gloss over the risks involved in the implementation of AIT, such as discrimination and illegitimate profiling or surveillance. Ethics washing is also understood as a turn to self-regulation, whereby businesses are supposed to voluntarily follow ethical guidelines, instead of being regulated by the state. Thomas Metzinger, a member of the EU Commission's High-Level Expert Group (HLEG) in Artificial Intelligence (a group which had the mission of creating ethical guidelines for the EU and to develop policy recommendations), wrote a chronicle, on the same day as the group's guidelines were presented, in which he urged universities and civil society to: 'recapture the process and take the self-organized discussion out of the hands of industry' (Metzinger 2019, 5).

A growing body of scholarship explores the (potentially threatening) implications of AI and digitalisation for democracy more broadly (Duberry 2022; O'Neil 2019; Runciman 2019). There is also an emerging discussion on how different strands of critical policy studies could – and should – take on AIT and data-driven automation in public policy (e.g., Paul 2022) – and this *Handbook* adds to these debates. However, few studies so far have pinpointed the political dimension of AIT and related ethics debates (Öjehag-Pettersson, Carlsson and Rönnblom, Chapter 2 in this volume). As scholars in politics and policy studies, we find the strong focus on the ethics and responsibility of individual businesses partly puzzling, and partly worrying, as there seems to be a lack of political analysis or discussion on this fundamental transformation. Following the work of political theorist Chantal Mouffe (2013), we propose a more critical scrutiny of the political implications of the dominant ethics discourse that permeates the discussion on AIT, thus bringing forward the 'political', or agonistic, dimensions of this discussion.

In sum, this chapter brings together the state-of-the art regarding the discussions on AI and ethics in policy – with a focus on the growing strand of critical studies – with aspects of the critical studies of governing and policy. Consequently, we critically discuss what the strong scholarly and policy focus on ethics and AIT means if we focus on 'the political' and *how* ethics is used as a form of governing technology with the potential of de-politicising AIT. In doing so, we also demonstrate the analytical merit of a governmentality framework when focusing on the political implications of the prevailing 'ethics discourse'. This means that we do not seek to discuss different definitions of ethics; rather, our interest focuses on what ethics 'does' with and in policy, and what the political implications of these 'doings' are.

We begin the chapter by introducing the scholarly discussion on AIT and ethics, highlighting research that focuses on studies of what ethics 'does', but also including references to more 'mainstream' research on ethics, consisting of studies of ethical problems and their solutions. Then, we briefly present research on governing and the 'political' in order to suggest an analytical framework for a critical scrutiny of ethics in policy. In the section that follows, we provide some empirical illustrations of how ethics is articulated in different policy settings and by different policy actors in order to highlight how ethics could be seen as a de-politicising tool. We end the chapter with a concluding discussion on the relationship between ethics, 'the political' and democracy.

THE BROAD SCHOLARSHIP ON AI ETHICS

As stated in the introduction, there is increasing scholarly interest in questions related to ethics and technological change in general, as well as more specifically on ethics and AI. One indicator of this engagement is the journals that have a specific focus on ethics in relation to AIT and more broadly digitalisation and ICT; for example, *Ethics and Emerging Technologies* (originally launched by Nils Bostrom and David Pierce in 1998 under the title *The Journal of Transhumanism*), and *Ethics and Information Technology* which published its first issue in 1999. In 2021, a new journal was launched, *AI and Ethics*, which could be seen as an indicator of the strength of scholarly interest in ethics in relation to AI. The first few sentences of the description of this journal could be seen as a summary of the focus of this research, where the ambition to discuss different forms of ethical implications in relation to AI, and to suggest ethical solutions, is at the forefront: 'AI and Ethics seeks to promote informed debate and discussion of the ethical, regulatory, and policy implications that arise from the development of AI. It will focus on how AI techniques, tools, and technologies are developing, including consideration of where these developments may lead in the future' (https://www.springer .com/journal/43681). In a similar way, *Ethics and Information Technology* stresses its focus on answering ethical questions: 'The journal aims to foster and promote reflection and analysis which is intended to make a constructive contribution to answering the ethical, social and political questions associated with the adoption, use, and development of ICT' (https://www .springer.com/journal/10676). Thus, there is a wide range of research, emerging from a wide range of disciplines, focusing on the different ethical challenges and risks brought by AIT, as well as presenting potential solutions to resolve these challenges in order to avoid the potential harms of AIT. Another example is the work of the philosopher Mark Coecklebergh, who, among other titles, published the book 'AI Ethics' in 2020 as part of the MIT Press Essential Knowledge Series.

A comprehensive overview of this mainstream scholarship would of course generate a much more fine-grained picture, including different themes and different perspectives. Here, we are more interested in showing that this scholarship regards ethics as something that 'is' or 'should be' applied to AIT, research that is about defining and understanding ethics, as well as the risks that ethics needs to handle. We would like to stress that we have no intention of challenging the importance of scholars contributing to the discussion and analysing both the ethical challenges and answers in relation to AI. But we also see a need to scrutinise what this strong emphasis on ethics 'does' to both policy and politics, not least due to this emphasis among scholars. However, we also find a growing field of scholarship that engages in analysing the impact of this strong focus on ethics.

In an overview article on ethical guidelines, Hagendorff (2020) scrutinises 22 guidelines, opening his piece with the following observation: 'Do those ethical guidelines have any actual impact on human decision-making in the field of AI and machine learning? The short answer is: No, most often not' (2020, 99). His evaluation of these ethical guidelines reveals a tension between the interests of business and broader public and social dimensions. For example, few guidelines explicitly address aspects of democratic control, political abuse of AI systems or issues of public–private partnerships and industry-funded research. Hagendorff concludes by stressing the need to make ethics more situation-sensitive, based on virtues, and hence that ethics needs to be less abstract and detached from the actual technology, at the same time as it also needs to turn away from the purely technical and focus more strongly on personal and social aspects.

Hagendorff's piece is an illustrative example of the range of articles that scrutinise ethical guidelines, which are produced mainly by industry but also by public actors like the EU. Here, the lack of acknowledgement of the tension between business and the state comes through as a central aspect. For example, Veale (2020) highlights the need to challenge corporate governance when analysing the policy recommendations from the EU HLEG on AI, recommendations that to a large extent are framed in terms of ethics. Veale also highlights how the

HLEG 'foregrounds AI as a technological solution to completely inappropriate issues without considering the capacities needed to understand the problems which AI could potentially be applied to' (2020, 10). In short, Veale stresses the lack of problematisation of two central aspects: the infrastructure of AI, for example legal control over data collection or the building of machine learning models, and questions of power and control regarding the ownership of and responsibility for data (on concepts of power in AIT policy and scholarly work, see Ulbricht, Chapter 3 in this volume).

There are also scholars who combine a mapping and critical scrutiny of ethical guidelines with suggestions for how to improve ethical standards. For example, Delacroix and Wagner develop what they call 'a more robust ethics-regulation interface' and ask what it 'could look like' (2021, 1), while Jobin et al. (2019) mapped 84 documents on ethics and AI, from a range of countries, and found a global convergence on five ethical principles (transparency, justice and fairness, non-maleficence, responsibility and privacy). However, they also underline the differences in both how these principles are defined and the measures needed to implement them. Jobin et al. (2019, 396) also highlight the Eurocentric/Western dimension in the discussion of AI ethics: 'Further, the relative underrepresentation of geographic areas such as Africa, South and Central America and Central Asia indicates that the international debate over ethical AI may not be happening globally in equal measures' (also see: Omotubora and Basu, Chapter 17 in this volume).

Other scholars also emphasise how ethics becomes a soft alternative to law and other forms of regulation. In the article 'Ethics as an escape from regulation: From "ethics-washing" to ethics-shopping?' (2018), Wagner discusses how ethical frameworks could provide a way of moving beyond existing legal frameworks, but also an opportunity to ignore them. He points out a blurring of the distinction between ethics and rights, and also how the lack of what he calls 'thick ethics', which includes both human rights and transparent decision-making procedures, risks making ethics a substitute for fundamental human rights. A similar argument is made by van Dijk et al. (2021) in their analysis of the ethification of ICT governance and its effects on law, politics and democracy in the EU, where they highlight the vast range of ethification, but also argue for the need for 'ethicists to "stand up" for their practice' (2021, 13; see also Lauer 2021 on the complexity of ethics).

There are also a few scholars who emphasise the need to politicise data ethics, including van Maanen (2022), who discusses how the versions of ethics used close down the possibilities for politicising (see also Delacroix and Wagner 2021). In the next section, we elaborate on this by reviewing research on AI with a more specific focus on governing and politicisation.

ANALYSING ETHICS AS A TECHNOLOGY OF NEOLIBERAL GOVERNING

In sum, large parts of the scholarly critique of the ethics and AIT discourse are focused on how the state is subordinated to industry, and that the eagerness of business to further develop and marketise the technology is not paralleled by state regulation. Thus, the turn to ethics seems to play a central role in the state–industry nexus. From a governing perspective, we argue that this situation is made possible through the neoliberalisation of the state, where the rationalities of the market have become all-encompassing for the whole of society, including the public sphere (Brown 2019, 2015; Rönnblom et al. 2022). In short, the purpose of the state has to a large extent transformed into becoming a facilitator for the market, and through the contemporary rationalities of governing also functioning like the market. Wendy Brown describes this situation as a 'melt-down' of the border between the public and the market, whereby the rationalities of the public have been replaced by the rationalities of the market – a process that also undermines the construction of liberal democracy as we know it (Brown 2015).

This transformation could also be conceptualised as a process of de-politicisation. By making a distinction between 'politics' and 'the political', Mouffe takes the analysis beyond institutions and pinpoints the dimension of conflict in politics. Here, she stresses the importance of agonistic relations within which there is a mutual respect between adversaries, including an agreement on respecting 'politics', consisting of joint practices and institutions. In her work, Mouffe (2013) has also shown that both ethics and morality are replacing 'the political' in neoliberal forms of governing. This trend could be understood as meaning that the potential of 'the political' has been taken out of politics, highlighting the risk of de-politicisation. In a de-politicised situation, the goal – and the strategies – of politics becomes perceived as more or less self-evident and not something that needs to be debated.

This kind of situation resonates, for example, with the general development of Swedish politics, where the neoliberalisation of governing is increasingly taking the political out of politics through for example New Public Management procedures (Rönnblom et al. 2022). The agonistic differences in politics, or the struggles, have been replaced by increasing amounts of administration, including market rationalities like auditing and competition, making it increasingly difficult to articulate and thus address societal power relations in political work. In this way, informed by the framework of Foucauldian governmentality (Walters 2012), de-politicisation could be understood as a process of governing.

Thus, we argue that the turn to ethics could be elaborated further if it is seen as a governing tool, built into contemporary political rationalities. Following Brown (2015), political rationality, or governing rationality, are the terms used by Foucault to illustrate the ways in which the current turn to neoliberalism becomes 'self-evident':

> Political rationality is thus the term that Foucault uses to capture the conditions, legitimacy, and dissemination of a particular regime of power – knowledge that centers on the truths organizing it and the world it brings into being. (Brown 2015, 116)

Analysing governing through a focus on political rationalities also positions the analysis as part of a governmentality framework. Here the notion of governing is itself at the centre of the analysis, with no specific focus on 'government', or privileging the state (Walters 2012). Instead, governing is understood as a set of practices that take place across a vast range of sites, including the state, practices that could be understood in terms of political rationalities that in turn are produced through a range of political technologies (Miller and Rose 2008). In applying this framework, ethics is understood as a governing technology that takes part in (re) producing governing rationalities, such as marketisation or competition (cf. Rönnblom et al. 2022).

Using some empirical examples from our own earlier and ongoing work on AIT (Carlsson and Rönnblom 2022)[1] – based on EU policy documents, interviews with Data Protection Authorities (DPA), and policy documents from several global private actors – we seek to show how a governmentality analysis of AI ethics could illuminate what ethics 'does' in terms of political work, and how the ethics turn contributes to the de-politicisation of AIT. In our analysis, we found three modes in which ethics works as a de-politicising governing technology: (a) *individualisation and responsibilisation*, (b) *privatisation and commodification* and (c) *bureaucratisation and management*. We discuss them briefly in the next section, before summarising the implications for future critically oriented research on AI ethics.

ETHICS AS A GOVERNING TECHNOLOGY

During the last decade, it has been important for the EU to keep up with global developments in AIT. The first ethical guidelines were developed by the HLEG on AI and were called Ethics Guidelines for Trustworthy AI (2019). These guidelines have been important for defining an ethical approach at the European level. Interestingly, most EU policies which include the ethical guidelines lack a profound definition of the concept of ethics, and instead are often a mishmash of different conceptualisations (see the section on earlier research). However, ethics is generally used to address human interactions with AIT, labelled as 'human-centric AI' (EC 2018, 2019). The HLEG on AI (2019) states, for example, that human dignity and individual self-determination should be guiding the development and dissemination of AIT: 'respect for human dignity entails that all people are treated with respect due to them as moral subjects, rather than merely as objects to be sifted, sorted, scored, herded, conditioned or manipulated' (p. 10). Policies also refer to the fundamental rights guaranteed by the EU and based on the EU Treaty and Charter in the context of ethics, and the ethical challenge is described here in terms of fundamental rights being overlooked in AI development.

Similar aspects were raised by Data Protection Authorities (DPAs) when representatives were asked during interviews: 'what is ethical AI?' The answers listed a range of desirable features, including: transparency; understandable explanations of what is being done; being clear about what state authorities are 'optimising' with AITs; showing they have conducted prior assessments about the impact their AI could have on vulnerable groups; ensuring the possibility for 'human-interfaced based intervention' in AI decision-making processes; respect for fundamental rights; respect for existing laws, especially in relation to human rights, freedom of movement, freedom of speech, free elections and anti-discrimination; and that AIT use should not cause harm.

To dig deeper into understandings of what 'harm' may entail, we asked DPAs for examples of 'unethical AI'. One example provided was of a food delivery company, whose algorithm fired a worker for failing to deliver his assigned orders, the day after he had died whilst delivering food on his bicycle for the company. Whilst this may have been an 'unwanted mistake of the machine, … it shows how bad the automation of the machine [can be] without human intervention' (Interview 2). The DPA also raised the potential effects of algorithms on governing people's lives:

> What was also very striking was that the head of the company the day after commented, saying, 'it's not the algorithm which makes you run …', which in a way is true because it is not the algorithm – but the algorithm is conceived in such a way that you are obliged somehow to perform. Well, that's something which shows the impact on real lives of individuals, I think. (Interview 2)

In a sense, and as also shown in previous research (c.f., Wagner 2018), ethics is filled with varying meanings in our empirical examples, giving it a somewhat all-inclusive status. Yet, the focus on ethics places great hope in ethics per se ensuring individual fundamental rights and non-discrimination, human dignity and trust in a new era of AIT development. Thus, taking into account the fact that ethics is so widely used in addressing the problems and risks of AIT (as are similar concepts such as trust/trustworthiness or responsibility, see Gillis, Laux and Mittelstadt, Chapter 14 in this volume; Omotubora and Basu, Chapter 17 in this volume), we see an *individualisation* of these challenges as a way in which ethics 'works' in policy. As long as single individuals are not at risk, AIT is considered 'safe', and thus 'good' (see also Smuha 2021).

To further elaborate upon what ethics 'does', we looked into how the EU concretely sees these desirable ethical values as being integrated into the product design. The answer, according to EU AI policies, is through a method called ethics-by-design, in which ethical perspectives are incorporated into the design phase of AI products. Ethics-by-design, in turn, requires the good recruitment of product developers. It is expected that ethical perspectives will be secured by the fact that tech companies have a broad and diverse employee base, with employees from different social groups, among which women, the elderly and minorities are particularly important (EU Parliament 2019; EC 2019; HLEG on AI 2019).

In order to reduce the risk of algorithmic programming having a negative impact on individuals, such as systematic exclusion or discrimination in AI decision-making, tech companies are encouraged to recruit employees from marginalised social groups. The method is based on the assumption that an employee's own experiences of, for example, being a woman will automatically lead to a women's perspective being taken into account during product development. This method is also highlighted as important for increasing democratic participation in technological development. However, the ethics-by-design method results in a situation where democratic dilemmas and problems in digital technology production must be resolved through human resource management (HRM) within companies, rather than through public regulations or the work of public institutions. Here, ethics works as a *privatising* tool.

This approach to ethics has also been adopted by private business. For example, in one of its 'insight papers', Deloitte argues that diversity in the team is the most effective way of working with ethical tech (Deloitte 2019). In this way of implementing ethics in practice, ethics becomes the solution to a 'mis-representation' in AIT design. Thus, thinking with Bacchi (2009), the problem that is represented to be solved is a lack of 'minorities' in AIT design, and the solution is to increase their number, which in turn is presented as a responsibility of the industry and comes without public regulation. In turn, this *responsibilisation* of ethics is also placed on the individual representatives of 'diverse minorities', and thus works as a technology of governing that – in the end – places responsibility for ethics on the individual.

It is also clear that ethics has become a central feature for industry. For example, the so-called 'big four', the four largest accounting firms in the world (which also provide services beyond accounting) – Deloitte, Ernst & Young, KPMG and PwC – have all designed strategies for ethical and/or responsible tech. The drive towards private responsibility that is found in the EU documents thus also resonates with how these professional networks act in relation to tech and AIT. Among the 'big four', we can also find other versions of what ethics 'does'. In publicly available documents, both Ernst & Young and KPMG provide different versions of checklists and toolkits, with the ambition of creating 'responsible AI' (PwC 2023), or trust in AI: 'For AI solutions to be transformative, trust is imperative. This trust rests on four main anchors: integrity, explainability, fairness, and resilience' (KPMG 2021). Hence, the problem representation that emerges is a lack of checklists and toolkits to achieve ethical AI, meaning that ethics and trust turn into *bureaucratic* as well as *management* tools (rather than questions of democratic politics and contestable value judgements) (on a technical vs. a more contextual interpretation of accountability in AI: see Cobbe and Singh, Chapter 7 in this volume). In addition, these examples from private business also reveal how ethics becomes *commodified*, as something that both private and public actors can buy in order to become ethical.

CONCLUDING DISCUSSION

In this chapter, our ambition has been to demonstrate both how ethics has arisen as a key theme for scholars with an interest in AI policies, and where the main interest lies in addressing ethical 'challenges' within this field. We have also sought to identify the critical research that elucidates how this focus on ethics also works to de-politicise the societal transformation that AIT carries with it. Through a number of empirical examples, we have also shown how the use of an analytical strategy could help develop this critical perspective as well as making the critique more detailed, in terms of understanding the use of ethics in relation to AIT as governing technologies that have de-politicising effects for the wider discussion on AI and societal values and conflicts. We found that *individualisation and responsibilisation, privatisation and commodification*, and *bureaucratisation and management* are all technologies that resonate with key principles of neoliberal governing, such as the marketisation of the public, growth and competitiveness as self-evident political goals and 'the economic man' as the subject to be governed (cf. Rönnblom et al. 2022). Ethics seems to be an all-inclusive solution for what Mouffe (2013) calls 'pain-free politics', politics that promises 'good for all', politics that does not take societal conflicts or patterns of inequality into account, politics that is built on a notion of self-evident consensus. Policy priorities and policy instruments for digital developments that in the early 2010s were framed as political (Carlsson and Rönnblom 2022) are now handled in administrative, legal, moral or natural terms. This situation could be described as a form of governing where the political in terms of agonism is dismissed in favour of other rationalities, such as competition and efficiency.

Thus, the rapid implementation of AIT in the public sector, in conjunction with rising concerns about this development from both researchers and industry, makes the ethical turn appear somewhat worrying from a perspective that values democracy. The use of ethics as an all-inclusive solution to the challenges that AIT brings to society 'risks' positioning this development as something that lies 'outside democracy', due to a lack of space for 'the political'. Following Mouffe, we argue that a central dimension of a working democracy is precisely that space for the political, i.e., the opportunity to articulate different interests while simultaneously showing respect for your adversary. Hence, there is a need for politicisation without polarisation for democracy to work, where polarisation means that you reject your opponent's arguments as well as how politics is organised (Rönnblom et al. 2022). It is within this political context that the turn to AI ethics should be analysed and understood. Looking at the discussions on AI policies at different political levels – international, EU and national – it seems as though elected politicians are mostly involved in a discussion about the extent to which AIT should be regulated, i.e., they are taking a reactive position to technology, which also produces technological innovation and uses as something inevitable. If regulators and policymakers were instead to take a more proactive stance and also present what they want from technology for our future societies, ideological differences would occur, and in this way technology would become politicised. And, in politicising AIT, the space for polarisation, such as that increasingly seen, for example, on social media, would, if not disappear, then at least be more possible to meet with political means.

NOTE

1. These examples come from research by Vanja Carlsson and Malin Rönnblom in the project 'Artificial Intelligence – Destroyer or Enabler of Democracy and Self-determination?' funded by Marianne and Marcus Wallenberg Foundation, Grant/Award Number: MMW 2018.0116, and from Michaela Padden's ongoing dissertation work that includes interviews with Data Protection Authorities.

REFERENCES

Bacchi, C. (2009), *Analysing Policy: What's the Problem Represented to Be?*, Frenchs Forest, NSW: Pearson Education.

Brown, W. (2015), *Undoing the Demos: Neoliberalism's Stealth Revolution*, New York: Zone Books.

Brown, W. (2019), *In the Ruins of Neoliberalism: The Rise of Antidemocratic Politics in the West*, New York: Columbia University Press.

Carlsson, V. and M. Rönnblom (2022), 'From Politics to Ethics: Transformations in EU Policies on Digital Technology', *Technology in Society*, **71**, 102145. https://doi.org/10.1016/j.techsoc.2022.102145.

Coeckleberg, M. (2020), *AI Ethics*, Stanford, CA: MIT Press Direct. https://doi.org/10.7551/mitpress/12549.001.0001

Delacroix, S. and B. Wagner (2021), Constructing a Mutually Supportive Interface between Ethics and Regulation, *Computer Law & Security Review*, **40**, 105520. https://doi.org/10.1016/j.clsr.2020.105520

Dignum V. (2019), *Responsible Artificial Intelligence: How to Develop and Use AI in a Responsible Way*, Cham, Switzerland: Springer.

van Dijk, N., S. Casiraghi and S. Gutwin (2021), 'The "Ethification" of ICT Governance. Artificial Intelligence and Data Protection in the European Union', *Computer Law & Security Review*, **43**, 105597. https://doi.org/10.1016/j.clsr.2021.105597.

Duberry, J. (2022), *Artificial Intelligence and Democracy: Risks and Promises of AI-Mediated Citizen–Government Relations*, Cheltenham, UK and Northampton, MA: Edward Elgar Publishing.

Eubanks V. (2019), *Automating Inequality: How High-Tech Tools Profile, Police, and Punish the Poor*, New York: Picador, St Martin's Press.

Hagendorff, T. (2020), 'The Ethics of AI Ethics: An Evaluation of Guidelines', *Minds and Machines*, **30**, 99–120.

Jobin, A., M. Ienca and E. Vayena (2019), 'The Global Landscape of AI Ethics Guidelines', *Nature Machine Intelligence*, **1**, 389–399. https://doi.org/10.1038/s42256-019-0088-2.

Lauer, D. (2021), 'You cannot have AI ethics without ethics', *AI and Ethics*, **1**, 21–5. https://doi.org/10.1007/s43681-020-00013-4.

van Maanen, G. (2022), 'AI Ethics, Ethics Washing, and the Need to Politicize Data Ethics', *Digital Society*, **1** (9). https://doi.org/10.1007/s44206-022-00013-3.

Metzinger, T. (2019), EU Guidelines: Ethics Washing Made in Europe. Available at: https://www.tagesspiegel.de/politik/eu-guidelines-ethics-washing-made-in-europe/24195496.

Miller, P. and N. Rose (2008), *Governing the Present*, Cambridge: Polity Press.

Mouffe, C. (2013), *Agonistics: Thinking the World Politically*, London: Verso.

O'Neil, C. (2016), *Weapons of Math Destruction: How Big Data Increases Inequality and Threatens Democracy*, London: Penguin.

Paul, R. (2022), 'Can Critical Policy Studies Outsmart AI? Research Agenda on Artificial Intelligence Technologies and Public Policy', *Critical Policy Studies*, **16** (4), pp. 497–509. DOI: 10.1080/19460171.2022.2123018.

Runciman, D. (2018), *How Democracy Ends*, London: Profile Books.

Rönnblom, M., K. Alnebratt, M. Eduards, J. Johansson and A. Öjehag-Pettersson (2022), Trängd demokrati. Om politikens vardag och om att vara människa, Möklinta: Gidlunds förlag.

Smuha, N. (2021), 'Beyond the Individual: Governing AI's Societal Harm', *Internet Policy Review*, **10** (3). https://doi.org/10.14763/2021.3.1574.

Veale, M. (2020), 'A Critical Take on the Policy Recommendations of the EU High-Level Expert Group on Artificial Intelligence', *European Journal of Risk Regulation*, **11** (1), 1–10.

Wagner, B. (2018), 'Ethics as an Escape from Regulation: From "Ethics-Washing" to Ethics-Shopping?', in: E. Bayamlioglu, I. Baraliuc, L. Janssens, and M. Hildebrandt (eds), *Being Profiled: Cogitas Ergo Sum*, Amsterdam: Amsterdam University Press, pp. 84–89.

Walters, W. (2012), *Governmentality. Critical Encounters*, London and New York: Routledge.

Zhu, Q. and R. Clancy (2023), 'Constructing a Role Ethics Approach to Engineering Ethics Education' *Ethics and Education*, **8** (2), 216–229. DOI: 10.1080/17449642.2023.2249740.

Policy Materials

Deloitte Insights. (2019), *Innovating for All: How CIOs Can Leverage Diverse Teams to Foster Innovation and Ethical Tech*. https://www2.deloitte.com/us/en/insights/topics/value-of-diversity-and-inclusion/diversity-and-inclusion-in-tech/fostering-innovation-ethical-technology.html.

High-Level Expert Group on Artificial Intelligence. (2019), *Ethical Guidelines for Trustworthy AI*. EC.

EC. (2018), *Artificial Intelligence for Europe*.

EC. (2019), *Building Trust in Human-Centric Artificial Intelligence*.

EU Parliament. (2019), *A Comprehensive European Industrial Policy on Artificial Intelligence and Robotics*. C449/37.

KPMG. (2021), The Shape of AI Governance to Come. https://assets.kpmg.com/content/dam/kpmg/xx/pdf/2021/01/the-shape-of-ai-governance-to-come.pdf.

PwC Responsible AI. (2023), https://www.pwc.com/gx/en/issues/data-and-analytics/artificial-intelligence/what-is-responsible-ai.html.

10. Algorithm and code: explainability, interpretability and policy

David M. Berry

INTRODUCTION

Digital automation has become increasingly sophisticated and able to take on the kinds of learning, cognitive reasoning and synthesis that previously were thought only the preserve of human beings. Consequently, we see a growing use of computational systems to abstract, simplify and automate algorithms working with huge amounts of "Big Data". Put simply, algorithms tell a computer how to do something so that processes can be automated. This raises the problem of explaining our increasingly complex technical world which relies on algorithms and software to automate and manage many aspects of society, from everyday life to vast digital infrastructures. Additionally, algorithms often substitute artificial automated capacities by incorporating human cognitive rationality within software and code. A side-effect of this has been to reinforce a sense that human behaviour can be understood and predicted using causal and statistical models to map, understand and interpret complex social and cultural phenomena.

However, some of the newer machine learning systems are so complex that it becomes an extremely difficult challenge to explain their operation. One of the most difficult tasks facing the critical theorist today is, therefore, understanding this delegation and prescription of agency into these new algorithmic infrastructures. We hear, perhaps too much, about "opening the black box" of computing, as if by merely peering inside the innards of a computational system, we will thereby understand it. Unfortunately, we usually cannot either look into or understand these systems. If we want to explain a digital infrastructure or software system, it is therefore often characterised in terms of the kind of information it communicates, in which an output is an "explanatory product". The idea of an explanatory product is that the computer can present a static output which summarises or represents the algorithm processing, perhaps in a textual description or a data visualisation. Yet this method of explanation is increasingly thought of as insufficient to give a critical understanding of why a particular output or decision was made. Instead, displaying the computational *processes* dynamically or interactively gives a much better explanation of a computer system and enables a digitally literate public to be able to contest and challenge injustices, biases and errors in these systems. This challenge of how to explain automated processes, offers a unique potential for thinking about the policy issues raised by algorithms and code, but also to contribute reflexively to understanding what we are seeking from the attempt to explain the system.

ALGORITHM, CODE AND THE COMPLEXITY OF AUTOMATED SYSTEMS

Large-scale computer systems can be understood as systemic, themselves constructed from a number of component layers built from algorithms, but nonetheless constituting a distinct digital totality and increasingly structured through the data architecture made possible through the implementation of edge, core and cloud compute. The notion of layering in computational systems is very common – very much a logic of producing a "black box" that can handle machine learning processing but with a simplified interface for inputs and outputs. Internally, machine learning is structured rather like an onion, with the outside layers, usually programmed in a conventional computer programming language, creating an internal software machine (virtual machine) that constructs abstractions of data that can be created, linked, classified and weighted in a number of important ways. The infrastructural dimension of these algorithmic systems means that they can be scaled to the level of planetary technics: their physical location, particularly when presented as computational abstractions such as notions of compute, can be strategically placed and moved dynamically and geographically. For example, voice commands on a phone can be computed on the device itself (known as the edge), or uploaded to a computer server farm (called the cloud).[1]

Due to their size and complexity, algorithmic infrastructures are capital-intensive systems and hence tend to be developed by corporations or governments to combine multiple systems into a single unity. In this form, they point towards a unification of multiple grammars within a system of communication, such that they converge on a single ontology or technical stack. An ontology is a technical representation of a knowledge domain usually captured as a formal description of entities, properties and relations between things. A stack is an approach to writing software that explicitly abstracts a problem domain into a layered system of increasing abstraction so that it can be more easily addressed in a computer system (see Berry, 2014, p. 58).

Large-scale infrastructures also tend towards a logic of value extraction, particularly in large corporations, and this is part of the context that is often missing in technical explanation. That is, that due to their size and scale, the algorithms that make up these systems often intensify data capture to maximise rent-seeking behaviour for large tech corporations. This creates the possibility for monopoly rent from algorithms and hence drives the tendency towards gigantic informational systems, and monopoly-oriented corporations. It goes without saying that this is an extremely profitable means of extracting value, creating new forms of powerful companies, such as the "FAANG" corporations (Facebook, Apple, Amazon, Netflix, Google). By collecting user data, the owners of these infrastructural systems are able to capture trends, identify social tendencies and patterns, and to reincorporate this knowledge into their infrastructural ecology, and even feed this information back into circulation to amplify these tendencies in a profitable direction. The creation of an algorithmic infrastructure is, therefore, not just a digital logic, it is also a business logic.

Within popular culture, a wider social concern with algorithms can be seen in social media which have been used to highlight the inexplicable ways in which people's lives have been affected by an algorithmic decision. Sometimes these discussions reflect a confusion by users over the distinction between *noise*, where the decision is affected by incomplete or inaccurate data causing inconsistency or no decision being made, and *bias*, where the accuracy of a decision has been swayed by a predetermined or computed result affected by human biases (see

Jaume-Palasi, 2018). These have been used to justify a need for explanation to help the public understand algorithms. Bias in computer systems usually derives from (1) data-driven bias, where the biases are embedded in the data itself, (2) bias through interaction with humans, for example Microsoft's Tay chatbot which developed a fascist conversation style, (3) emergent bias, for example through likes and shares, (4) similarity bias, where filter bubbles can emerge and (5) conflicting goals bias, where stereotypes have been used in the development of the software in particular ways (Hammond, 2016) (also see Hong, Chapter 8 in this volume). Indeed, there are now many documented cases where algorithmic decision processes have discriminated against people on the basis of their names, their home address, gender or skin colour (Buranyi, 2017; Eubanks, 2018; Noble, 2018).[2] This is reflected in an "anxiety felt by those who fear the potential for bias to infiltrate machine decision-making systems once humans are removed from the equation" (Casey, Farhangi and Vogl, 2018, p. 4). It is in this context that public disquiet has risen in relation to the perceived unfairness of these, often unaccountable, automated algorithmic systems.

The most obvious example of automation that hides bias within its computation is Google Autocomplete on the search bar which tries to predict what a user will type before they have completed a sentence – and makes it easy for the user to just click rather than thinking through what they are writing. This technology has also been rolled-out to Gmail, where Google will write a user's emails by predicting what it thinks the user might be planning to write. Similarly, recent breakthroughs in artificial intelligence, such as GPT-3 also create long-form, remarkably competent, written texts based on a similar automated capacity. More recently ChatGPT has been developed which has created an impressive chatbot agent and enables conversational interfaces reminiscent of the original ELIZA chatbot from the 1960s, albeit much more capable (see Berry, 2023b). These techniques are increasingly being incorporated into many aspects of computer interfaces through design practices that predict, persuade or nudge particular behavioural outcomes. These technologies use the mobilisation of processes of selecting and directing activity through the automation of data from information collected from millions of users (Malabou, 2019, p. 52). Algorithms often compute much faster than human cognitive faculties by short-cutting individual decisions by making a digital "suggestion" or calculated intervention. One of the additional drivers for the attention given to algorithms has been a wider public unease with this emergence of machine learning in everyday life, resulting in calls for accountability in these systems (see Kuang, 2017; Sample, 2017; also see Cobbe and Singh, Chapter 7 in this volume). The social, economic, political implications of this ubiquity are key to addressing the wider public unease and social justice issues inherent in algorithms and code.

THE PROBLEM OF EXPLAINABILITY

The problem is that many of the algorithmic systems we have built, and are building, are becoming too complex for our understanding, and in some cases even too complex to explain. As described above, when these systems are accused of bias, unfairness or of being unequal in some sense, the problem of responding to these critiques can be difficult, whether querying the algorithms responsible or understanding their systemic integration. This explains, I think, the tendency to blame "bad data" or "biased data" or "data contamination" as an input to a system, which might be considered easier in many cases to check and "de-bias". This might also suggest why "ethics" has been proposed as another response, particularly in professional codes of ethics (see Berry, 2023a). For example, the OpenAI Generative Pre-trained Transformer 3 (GPT-3) has a capacity of over 175 billion machine learning parameters and is therefore extremely difficult to "explain" (Johnson, 2020). But explainable systems are not just about normative outcomes, they can also be about how to ensure the reliability of a system; how one can optimise it; and how one can check it is, indeed, doing what one wants (i.e. technical functional).

The concept of "explainability" attempts to close this interpretative gap. The key result of either explainable or interpretable systems is that they should create the conditions for contestability. Explainability is the use of computation to generate explanations, usually automatically by a computer. The idea of interpretability is that by making the source code human-readable the direct access to its technical function would make it easier to assess these criteria, although in practice, an algorithm can still be difficult to understand solely from its textual source code due to obscurity or designed obfuscation (Berry, 2011, p. 82). The aim for both is to enable the user of an algorithmic system to understand and challenge its processing or results. This might happen in a public sphere or through associational forms of protesting and lobbying, or media campaigns and educating politicians. This contestability is often claimed as a condition for (1) trusting these systems, (2) understanding the causality embedded in them, (3) acceptance of transferability of data models (e.g. credit rating based on other factors), (4) informativeness (to augment human decision-making), and (5) fair and ethical decision-making (see Lipton, 2017).

The first important question we need to consider is what counts as an explanation. Indeed, explanations are generally considered to be able to tell us how things work, thereby giving us the power to change our environment in order to meet our own ends. In this sense of explanation then, science is often supposed to be the best means of generating explanations (Pitt, 1988, p. 7). In relation to explanation, therefore, explainability needs to provide an answer to the question "why?". Scriven argues that "the right description is the one which fills in a particular gap in the understanding of the person or people to whom the explanation is directed". This can be seen as the value of explainability as "closing the gap in understanding (or rectifying misunderstanding)" (Scriven, 1988, p. 53). This, I argue, raises a new potential for an explainable form of life through *computational critique.* By "forms of life" I reference the idea of a non-instrumentalist notion of problem-solving processes as social practices developed by Rahel Jaeggi (Jaeggi, 2018). Jaeggi argues that where forms of life are anchored in the world, they provide a basis for affirming something like the appropriateness of social practices – they help answer the "why" questions. For example, the city as a form of life, which involves living in and around public spaces and the "open-mindedness, and independence invoked by the German saying 'City air makes you free'" (Jaeggi, 2018, p. 67). But for explainability to create this potential it must engage "forms of life" in reflection – as a collective self-education and a pattern of interpretation that becomes established. For someone to live an explainable form of life, society must educate them to facilitate a form of knowledge and reasoning through a process of identifying algorithmic problems and connecting them to social critique.

For this to happen, the answer to a "why" question cannot be just a technical description (e.g. of how an automated system is constructed). Instead, it should be connected to a number of complex secondary questions that explainability has only just begun to address. For example, what are the characteristics of the "subject" to which the explanation is offered? How is this theorised implicitly or explicitly within a theory of the subject? In what language?

At what level of competence? How technical? How metaphorical? In how much detail? Secondly, a more comprehensive answer might include: how long did the explanation take? Was it interrupted at any point? Who gave it? When? Where? What were the exact words used in the explanation? For whose benefit was it given? Indeed, it can be important to ascertain, who created the explanation originally? We might further pose the questions: is it very complicated? In what form or medium of communication was it given? And finally, who owns the explanation or explainability system? As can be seen, a response to a "why" question is therefore limited if explainability is understood through narrow technical criteria.

EXPLAINABILITY AND INTERPRETABILITY

The question of how an explanation should be constructed points to a debate within computer science as to whether it is better to offer an explanation of a technical system via explainability, or an interpretation, via interpretability. Although often confused or conflated they are different modes of understanding, with explainability tilted towards an automated production of an explanatory product from a model which can be represented to a human user, and interpretability which uses models that are human-readable across the stack, so that the black box can be opened, as it were.

Each of these approaches are normative in orientation. They contain an assumption that one can distinguish between good and bad readings, or appropriate uses, of the technology. But they have given support to a new public demand which has begun to crystallise in important critiques of computational opaqueness and algorithmic transparency. We see this, for example, in calls to restrict facial recognition systems, public unease with algorithmic judicial systems and challenges to algorithmic power. The two differing approaches of explainability and interpretability lead to quite different policy implications. Explainability insinuates a narrative and/or visual representation problem ("how to represent the underlying algorithmic processes to a user?") and interpretability suggests a technical literacy requirement and code access ("how to give access to the underlying algorithm and how to ensure the user has a sufficient technical literacy?"). The first is in many senses a communications problem, communicating complexity mediated through texts, the second is a digital literacy and open-source problem, mediated through technical knowledge and access to the underlying computer source code. This debate has huge implications, particularly for artificial intelligence systems, considering that these automated decision systems might have to develop a capacity to provide some form of explanation as a regulatory requirement.

With a stress on the importance of explanation, the European Union's *General Data Protection Regulation 2016/679* (GDPR) has become important as a benchmark of adequacy for satisfactory use of algorithmic decision systems within the European Union, and thereby legitimating their use in a multitude of settings.[3] The GDPR can help us to understand this new algorithmic problematic, as it is one legal formulation of how to deal with the problem of explainability, albeit not a completely satisfactory one. When instantiated in national legislation, the GDPR has created a new right in relation to automated algorithmic systems that requires the "controller" of an algorithm to supply an explanation of how a decision was made to the user (or "data subject"). The GDPR is a regulation in European Union law on data protection and privacy for citizens within the European Union and the European Economic Area.[4] The GDPR creates a new kind of subject, the "data subject" to whom a right to explanation (amongst other data protection and privacy rights) is given. The notion of a "data subject" has a range of very specific and unique rights as a "natural person", which distinguishes them from an artificial intelligence, machine learning system, algorithm or indeed a corporation. This definition creates what we might note as a return to the importance of being human by creating and reinforcing a boundary between humans, corporations and machines.[5] Additionally, it has created a legal definition of processing through a computer algorithm (GDPR, 2016, Art. 4).

In consequence, this has given rise to a notion of explainability which creates the right "to obtain an explanation of [a] decision reached after such assessment and to challenge the decision" (GDPR, 2016, Recital 71).[6] It has therefore been argued that the GDPR mandates a requirement for a representation of the processes of computation used in an automated decision – the calculative model for example – and for it to be presented to the data subject on request (Goodman and Flaxman, 2017; Selbst and Powles, 2017; cf. Wachter, Mittelstadt and Floridi, 2017).[7] It is crucial however to understand that this is not just an issue of (limited) legal rights, this has also created a wider normative demand for a social right to explanation. However, this notion of explanation does not provide guidance as to the form the explanation should take: explainability or interpretability?

Although the GDPR is limited to the European Union, in actuality, it has had global effects as it becomes necessary for global companies to standardise their software products and services but also to respond to growing public disquiet over these systems (Kuang, 2017; Sample, 2017; Turek, n.d.) (also see Mügge, Chapter 19 in this volume; Omotubora and Basu, Chapter 17 in this volume).[8] More recently, the EU has proposed an *Artificial Intelligence Act* (AIA) which revisits this issue and in Article 13 states that "High-risk AI systems shall be designed and developed in such a way to ensure that their operation is sufficiently transparent to enable users to interpret the system's output and use it appropriately." As Grady notes,

> The AIA demonstrates that the EU does not yet know if it wants "explainability" or "interpretability". While Recital 38 calls for "explainable" AI systems, Article 13 states that users should be able to "interpret" the system and requires human oversight measures that can facilitate the "interpretation" of its outputs. The distinction, however, is nontrivial: requirements for explainable and interpretable AI systems differ significantly; the consequences for the innovation ecosystem may be substantial. (Grady, 2022)

This has also become part of a wider public discourse. Explanation was one of the "rights" outlined in an "algorithmic bill of rights" published in 2019, for instance, which argued that, "we have the right to be given explanations about how algorithms affect us in a specific situation, and these explanations should be clear enough that the average person will be able to understand them" (Samuel, 2019) (also see Donoghue et al., Chapter 26 in this volume).

Consequently, developers and researchers working on explainable AI, transparent AI and responsible AI attempt to design AI systems whose actions can be easily understood by humans. These new AI systems are designed to produce more "explainable models, while still maintaining a high level of learning performance" and prediction accuracy thus helping humans to "understand, appropriately trust, and effectively manage the emerging generation of artificially intelligent partners" (Gunning et al., 2021).

This has become known as the "problem of explainability" in artificial intelligence research, and has led to the emergence of the subfield of Explainable Artificial Intelligence (XAI – see Turek, n.d. https://www.darpa.mil/program/explainable-artificial-intelligence). In 2016, the Defense Advanced Research Projects Agency (DARPA) sought to invest in "explainability" to create the XAI program to produce better explainable models, while maintaining a high level of learning performance (particularly prediction accuracy) whilst still enabling human users to understand, appropriately trust and effectively manage the emerging generation of artificially intelligent systems known as "third-wave AI systems".

This implies that XAI systems should have to have the ability to explain their rationale, characterise their strengths and weaknesses, and convey an understanding of how they will behave in the future in order to strengthen their public accountability. These requirements pose a very difficult challenge to the developers of these systems and remain aspirational in AI system design. This is starkly seen, for example in that explainable systems can produce radically different explanations of the same underlying machine learning system, which could lead to potential legal and regulatory issues in the future (Krishna et al., 2022).

Conversely, it is argued that not all systems require or would benefit from a purely interpretative approach (for a good discussion of this, see Grady, 2022). Interpretable systems have a performance cost on the design of the algorithms and code used in the system which can result in inefficiencies. This can be a real problem for critical infrastructure or real-time systems, such as fast-moving financial trading platforms. Similarly, some artificial intelligence or machine learning models are not amenable to being built through interpretative approaches, for example DALL-E and GPT-3 discussed below.

NEURAL NETWORKS AND THE LIMITS OF EXPLAINABILITY AND INTERPRETABILITY

I now want to briefly focus on these machine learning algorithms, particularly those which use neural networks and that are particularly difficult for humans to understand or to offer sufficient explanations for their operation.[9] The turn to machine learning has been driven by the limited capacities within disciplines to cope with an evergrowing mountain of digital data, so-called Big Data, combined with a political economy that sees huge economic potential in mining this data for insights and profit (cf. Gray, Chapter 15 in this volume; Paul, Carmel and Cobbe, Chapter 1 in this volume). Machine learning algorithms are used as powerful generalisers and predictors. Since the accuracy of these algorithms is known to improve with greater quantities of data to train on, the growing availability of such data in recent years has brought renewed interest to these algorithms. Machine learning is finding its way into a myriad of devices, from cloud computing centres, to translation services, televisions, phones and talking assistants. Indeed, the deployment of machine learning has increasingly begun to resemble other kinds of computational services.

I focus on these because neural networks have application in natural language processing but also in image and video recognition and, therefore, applicability in a wide range of computer systems. The wider public are becoming familiar with the generative capacities of so-called deep convolutional neural networks (CNNs), such as DeepDream, due to their appeal to popular culture in the generation of seemingly hallucinated images that are dreamlike in form. The software is designed to detect faces and other patterns in images, with the aim of automatically classifying images. CNNs work by modelling animal visual perception and have been applied to visual recognition automation. They are constructed from multiple layers of sensory neurons (so-called receptive fields, which are made up of clusters of these neurons). The word "convolution" comes from its use to describe a mathematical operation on two functions which produces a third function. For image analysis, convolutional filtering plays an important role in many important algorithms; for example, in edge detection, sharpening an image and adding blurring.

Another example of these systems is recurrent neural network (RNN), a class of artificial neural network where connections between networks form a directed cycle, the most common of which are called long short-term memory (LSTM). Unlike feedforward neural networks, RNNs can use their internal memory to process arbitrary sequences of inputs. This makes them applicable to tasks such as unsegmented connected handwriting recognition or speech recognition. Indeed, it is for these reasons that they are used by Google for speech recognition on the smartphone, for the smart helper Google Assistant and for Google Translate. Apple also used to use LSTM machine learning for the "Quicktype" function on the iPhone and for Siri, and Amazon similarly uses LSTM for Amazon Alexa.

In 2020 OpenAI, funded by Elon Musk and other venture capitalists, released the GPT-3 system, mentioned above. GPT-3 stands for Generative Pre-trained Transformer 3, which uses transformers, a technology that is particularly effective for natural language processing. Transformers were introduced by Google Brain in 2017 and have begun to replace the use of RNN models. They require huge training sets in order to match the performance of RNNs combined with an "attention mechanism" that allows the learning process to be made in parallel speeding up the process. RNNs were very slow to learn and often had problems being scaled to larger tasks (see Uszkoreit, 2017). Transformers on the other hand are very fast to learn and thus can be tweaked and scaled up with relative ease compared to the previous technologies. GPT-3 is able to produce strikingly convincing automated writing based on small samples that you provide to the system. This makes it ideal to produce certain types of written copy extremely quickly with much less time for the user to write it themselves (see Thunström, 2022). As one contributor to this *Handbook* documents, the perceived benefits of large language models already have wide use in judicial decision-making, for example in Latin America (Gutiérrez, Chapter 24 in this volume).

However, in terms of mapping the underlying structures beneath the GPT-3 textual interface, there has been some striking work on, for example, the perpetuation of biases in natural language generation (Sheng et al., 2019), such as the issues shown by intersectional occupational biases (Kirk et al., 2021), gender representation (Lucy and Bamman, 2021) and even anti-Muslim bias (Abid et al., 2021). So, for example, narratives generated by GPT-3 are more likely to have masculine characters and for them to play larger roles, feminine characters are correspondingly more likely to discuss family, emotions and the body (Lucy and Bamman, 2021, p. 50). Teasing these problems out is made harder due to the obscurity of the algorithms in the underlying GPT-3 system which remains proprietary.

The automated production of visual images is perhaps the most striking example of contemporary artificial intelligence systems. DALL-E (a name formed by combining WALL-E and Dali) and DALL-E 2 are transformer models developed by OpenAI to generate digital images from natural language descriptions. DALL-E was revealed by OpenAI in a blog post in January 2021 and is a 12-billion parameter version of GPT-3 modified to generate images (see Pereira, 2021). DALL-E works "by swapping text for pixels" in the GPT-3 platform, but the DALL-E model is a "smaller version of GPT-3 that has also been trained on text-image pairs taken from the internet" (Heaven, 2021). DALL-E is able to generate synthetic media from a text caption that is submitted to it but as it works in a similar way to GPT-3 it suffers from the same problems of memorising images that it has been fed and there is no understanding of what is being generated. It is a mechanical process of combination and synthesis. DALL-E 2 was released in 2022 and generates more realistic images by offering a resolution which is four times greater than the original DALL-E system.

CONCLUSION

These probes into machine learning systems are not meant to be exhaustive but rather to show the difficulties in describing complex technologies. We are at the beginning of getting to grips with understanding these systems, but it is likely that their underlying computer source code and models will remain hidden, leaving us with probing the surface of a system in order to reveal deeper structural formations. Whilst we are a long way from having a codified method or set of methods for engaging with these systems we are, nonetheless, already aware of the way in which they produce important social challenges, for example, generating gender, race or class biases in synthetic computations that are fast, invisible and at scale, and which we are only beginning to grapple with.

New policy and methods are needed for the critique of algorithmic infrastructures and how they might be examined in relation to different digital forms of life, and also interconnecting both explainability and interpretability to a wider political economy. This could include more reflexivity within computer science, questioning its own systems, tools and archives and making them self-explanatory so that they can be challenged and contested. Part of the responses we need to develop are about how we can think about computational infrastructures differently. As such, explainability and interpretability are concepts that can be critically deployed in relation to thinking *other computations*.

The key question is: what must be conveyed in order to have explained something? Currently, an "explanatory product" can usually be characterised in terms of the kind of information it communicates – no reference to the act of explaining is theorised. Crucially, this connection between an explanatory product and the legal regime that enforces it, has forced system designers and programmers to start to look for explanatory models that are sufficient to provide legal cover, but also at a level at which they are presentable and comprehensible to the user or data subject. But it is uncertain if the "right is only to a general explanation of the model of the system as a whole ('model-based' explanation), or an explanation of how a decision was made based on that particular data subject's particular facts ('subject-based' explanation)" (see also Ali et al., 2023, p. 42; Edwards and Veale, 2018, p. 4).[10] However, as argued in this chapter, a more comprehensive social critique might be appropriate in certain instances that takes account of contextual and political economic factors (e.g. as "infrastructural" explanation or "social" explanation) (see Berry, 2014, p. 2).

It will be interesting to see if the implementation of these systems results in an explanatory pragmatism where only a partial explanation, drawing on the notion of "good enough" results, is given, and how the legal system responds. This, of course, may lead to the danger of creating persuasive explanations rather than "transparent" explanations. It also raises questions related to the oversimplification of explanations or generating misleading explanations and how one might challenge them or even question their underlying explanatory model.[11]

There is a growing public concern over opacity in digital infrastructures and systems, whether intentional or not. The possible "right to explanation" is an attempt to mitigate these worries but also put in place legislative means to seek redress. This is increasingly a representational as much as a legal or reasoning challenge – how to represent an algorithmic decision to a data subject through the generation of synthetic explanations. In effect, the computer processing might be presented as a simplified model, or explanation. This might show the general contours of the algorithm used in a particular case to an assumed reader, but it also inevitably assumes a technically competent user who can understand an explanation.[12] There are huge implications of the problem of unaccountable and unreadable algorithmic systems that are increasingly part of people's everyday lives and serve as significant infrastructures for society.[13] The legal and regulatory frameworks around the question of explanation are an important part of the answer. But it is also absolutely key that the notions of explainability and interpretability are also connected to democratic participation, critique and digital inclusion. They can enable citizens to understand, debate and question policy decisions over the future direction of algorithmic societies and, crucially, to change them.

NOTES

1. Compute, in this sense, is an abstract unit of computation which tends to be priced at a particular level by cloud server companies so one can purchase a certain capacity of computation.
2. This has even resulted in families and groups being deliberately separated by algorithms for profit (Coffey 2018), or AI "scans" for a babysitter with "respect and attitude" (Harwell, 2018).
3. Regulation (EU) 2016/679 of the European Parliament and of the Council of 27 April 2016 on the protection of natural persons with regard to the processing of personal data and on the free movement of such data, and repealing Directive 95/46/EC (General Data Protection Regulation) (Text with EEA relevance, 2016).
4. Following the GDPR, in the UK, the enabling legislation for the European GDPR is the Data Protection Act 2018.
5. It appears that the idea is that only a "natural person" may ask for an explanation, preventing algorithms or corporations from requesting an explanation from other algorithms or corporations.
6. Whilst non-binding, the Recitals "dissolve ambiguity in the operative text of a framework", they provide a critical reference for future interpretations (Casey et al., 2018, p. 17).
7. Wachter et al. (2017) argue that the "GDPR does not, in its current form, implement a right to explanation, but rather what we term a limited 'right to be informed'", although this has been contested in the literature as their argument rests on a rather narrow reading of the effects of Recital 71 (see Edwards and Veale, 2018). But nonetheless "the GDPR's right of access only grants an explanation of automated decision-making addressing *system functionality*, not the rationale and circumstances of *specific decisions*" (Wachter et al., 2017, p. 19).
8. It is important to note that although this chapter has focused on the GDPR, explainability was also part of a Darpa research programme in 2016 (DARPA-BAA-16-53). More information can be found here: https://www.darpa.mil/attachments/DARPA-BAA-16-53.pdf.
9. The use of the term "algorithms" to talk about machine learning systems is a simplification, as technically the machine learning system creates its own "algorithm" based on calculated probabilities of weights between nodes in the network. Nonetheless, analytically I think it is still useful to use the concept of algorithm to understand, at least at an analytical level, the operation of these systems.
10. Ali et al. also identify "data explainability" as a category that highlights explainability as interpreting training data, "model explainability" as a method of explainability for understanding the inner working of AI models and "post-hoc explainability" as providing a human-understandable explanation of the AI model's decision (Ali et al., 2023, p. 42). To which we might append "political economic explainability" as an approach to explainability that encompasses the extra-algorithmic milieu that surrounds these systems.
11. For example, one could envision the user being able to challenge an explanation or appeal to a higher authority, such as a regulator, if it were considered inadequate.

12. This also raises questions about the potential for what we might call explainability regress, whereby explanations are sought for the explanation and so on ad infinitum. Until these cases are tested in practice, it is difficult to know what the limitations will be in relation to explanations provided by a system.
13. The rise of *synthetic infrastructures* that through diffusion models can create variation and abstractions based on their input prompts points towards new forms of generative AI architectures. Using vector representation, they are able to encode similarity in vector space which allows them to "blend-in" input context with their internal representation and create a wide range of synthetic media. The results of this are increasingly competent text, imagery, sound and video which can be created with variation and scale to flood social media and communications networks and which can only with difficulty be distinguished from intentional human cultural production.

REFERENCES

Abid, A., Farooqi, M. and Zou, J. (2021) 'Persistent Anti-Muslim Bias in Large Language Models'. arXiv. Available at: http://arxiv.org/abs/2101.05783 (Accessed: 31 October 2022).

Ali, S. et al. (2023) 'Explainable Artificial Intelligence (XAI): What We Know and What Is Left to Attain Trustworthy Artificial Intelligence', *Information Fusion*, **99**, 101805. Available at: https://doi.org/10.1016/j.inffus.2023.101805.

Berry, D. M. (2011) *The Philosophy of Software: Code and Mediation in the Digital Age*. Basingstoke, UK: Palgrave Macmillan.

Berry, D. M. (2014) *Critical Theory and the Digital*. 1st edn. New York: Bloomsbury Publishing Plc. Available at:https://doi.org/10.5040/9781501302114.

Berry, D. M. (2023a) 'AI, Ethics, and Digital Humanities', in J. O'Sullivan (ed.) *The Bloomsbury Handbook to the Digital Humanities*. London: Bloomsbury Publishing Plc, pp. 445–457. Available at: https://www.bloomsbury.com/uk/bloomsbury-handbook-to-the-digital-humanities-9781350232112/ (Accessed: 31 October 2022).

Berry, D. M. (2023b) 'The Limits of Computation: Joseph Weizenbaum and the ELIZA Chatbot', *Weizenbaum Journal of the Digital Society*, **3**(3). Available at: https://doi.org/10.34669/WI.WJDS/3.3.2.

Buranyi, S. (2017) 'Rise of the Racist Robots – How AI Is Learning All Our Worst Impulses', *The Guardian*, 8 August. Available at: https://www.theguardian.com/inequality/2017/aug/08/rise-of-the-racist-robots-how-ai-is-learning-all-our-worst-impulses (Accessed: 9 January 2023).

Casey, B., Farhangi, A. and Vogl, R. (2018) 'Rethinking Explainable Machines: The GDPR's "Right to Explanation" Debate and the Rise of Algorithmic Audits in Enterprise'. Rochester, NY. Available at: https://papers.ssrn.com/abstract=3143325 (Accessed: 9 January 2023).

Coffey, H. (2018) 'Airlines Face Crack Down on Use of "Exploitative" Algorithm that Splits Up Families on Flights', *The Independent*, 19 November. Available at: https://www.independent.co.uk/travel/news-and- advice/airline-flights-pay-extra-to-sit-together-split-up-family-algorithm-minister-a8640771.html.

Edwards, L. and Veale, M. (2018) 'Enslaving the Algorithm: From a "Right to an Explanation" to a "Right to Better Decisions"?', *IEEE Security & Privacy*, **16**(3), 46–54. Available at: https://doi.org/10.1109/MSP.2018.2701152.

Eubanks, V. (2018) *Automating Inequality: How High-Tech Tools Profile, Police, and Punish the Poor*. New York: St. Martin's Press.

Goodman, B. and Flaxman, S. (2017) 'European Union Regulations on Algorithmic Decision-Making and a "Right to Explanation"', *AI Magazine*, **38**(3), 50.

Grady, P. (2022) 'The EU Should Clarify the Distinction between Explainability and Interpretability in the AI Act', *Center for Data Innovation*, 31 August. Available at: https://datainnovation.org/2022/08/the-eu-should-clarify-the-distinction-between-explainability-and-interpretability-in-the-ai-act/ (Accessed: 8 January 2023).

Gunning, D. et al. (2021) 'DARPA's Explainable AI (XAI) Program: A Retrospective', *Applied AI Letters*, **2**(4), e61. Available at: https://doi.org/10.1002/ail2.61.

Hammond, K. (2016) '5 Unexpected Sources of Bias in Artificial Intelligence', *TechCrunch*, 10 December. Available at: https://techcrunch.com/2016/12/10/5-unexpected-sources-of-bias-in-artificial-intelligence/ (Accessed: 9 January 2023).

Harwell, D. (2018) 'Wanted: The "Perfect Babysitter". Must Pass AI Scan for Respect and Attitude', *The Washington Post*, 16 November. Available at: https://www.washingtonpost.com/technology/2018/11/16/wanted-perfect-babysitter-must-pass-ai-scan-respect-attitude/.

Heaven, W. D. (2021) 'This Avocado Armchair Could Be the Future of AI', *MIT Technology Review*. Available at: https://www.technologyreview.com/2021/01/05/1015754/avocado-armchair-future-ai-openai-deep-learning-nlp-gpt3-computer-vision-common-sense/ (Accessed: 23 October 2022).

Jaeggi, R. (2018) *Critique of Forms of Life*. Cambridge, MA: The Belknap Press of Harvard University Press.

Jaume-Palasi, L. (2018) *Blessed by the Algorithm: Computer Says NO!* Available at: https://media.ccc.de/v/froscon2018-2307-keynote (Accessed: 9 January 2023).

Johnson, K. (2020) 'OpenAI Debuts Gigantic GPT-3 Language Model with 175 Billion Parameters', *VentureBeat*, 29 May. Available at: https://venturebeat.com/ai/openai-debuts-gigantic-gpt-3-language-model-with-175-billion-parameters/ (Accessed: 9 January 2023).

Kirk, H. et al. (2021) 'Bias Out-of-the-Box: An Empirical Analysis of Intersectional Occupational Biases in Popular Generative Language Models'. arXiv. Available at: http://arxiv.org/abs/2102.04130 (Accessed: 31 October 2022).

Krishna, S. et al. (2022) 'The Disagreement Problem in Explainable Machine Learning: A Practitioner's Perspective'. arXiv. Available at: https://doi.org/10.48550/arXiv.2202.01602.

Kuang, C. (2017) 'Can A.I. be Taught to Explain Itself?', *The New York Times*, 21 November. Available at: https://www.nytimes.com/2017/11/21/magazine/can-ai-be-taught-to-explain-itself.html (Accessed: 9 January 2023).

Lipton, Z. C. (2017) 'The Mythos of Model Interpretability'. arXiv. Available at: http://arxiv.org/abs/1606.03490 (Accessed: 31 October 2022).

Lucy, L. and Bamman, D. (2021) 'Gender and Representation Bias in GPT-3 Generated Stories', in *Proceedings of the 3rd Workshop on Narrative Understanding*, Virtual: Association for Computational Linguistics, pp. 48–55. Available at: https://doi.org/10.18653/v1/2021.nuse-1.5.

Malabou, C. (2019) *Morphing Intelligence: From IQ Measurement to Artificial Brains*. Translated by C. Shread. New York: Columbia University Press. Available at: https://doi.org/10.7312/mala18736.

Noble, S. U. (2018) *Algorithms of Oppression: How Search Engines Reinforce Racism*. New York: University Press.

Pereira, D. (2021) 'OpenAI's DALL-E and CLIP 101: A Brief Introduction, Medium'. Available at: https://towardsdatascience.com/openais-dall-e-and-clip-101-a-brief-introduction-3a4367280d4e (Accessed: 23 October 2022).

Pitt, J. C. (ed.) (1988) *Theories of Explanation*. New York: OUP.

Regulation (EU) 2016/679 of the European Parliament and of the Council of 27 April 2016 on the protection of natural persons with regard to the processing of personal data and on the free movement of such data, and repealing Directive 95/46/EC (General Data Protection Regulation) (Text with EEA relevance) (2016) *OJ L*. Available at: http://data.europa.eu/eli/reg/2016/679/oj/eng (Accessed: 9 January 2023).

Sample, I. (2017) 'Computer Says No: Why Making AIs Fair, Accountable and Transparent Is Crucial', *The Guardian*, 5 November. Available at: https://www.theguardian.com/science/2017/nov/05/computer-says-no-why-making-ais-fair-accountable-and-transparent-is-crucial (Accessed: 9 January 2023).

Samuel, S. (2019) 'AI Experts Draft Algorithmic Bill of Rights to Protect Us from Big Tech', *Vox*. Available at: https://www.vox.com/the-highlight/2019/5/22/18273284/ai-algorithmic-bill-of-rights-accountability-transparency-consent-bias (Accessed: 9 January 2023).

Scriven, M. (1988) 'Explanations, Predictions, and Laws', in J. C. Pitt (ed.) *Theories of Explanation*. New York: OUP, pp. 51–74.

Selbst, A. D. and Powles, J. (2017) 'Meaningful Information and the Right to Explanation', *International Data Privacy Law*, 7(4), 233.

Sheng, E. et al. (2019) 'The Woman Worked as a Babysitter: On Biases in Language Generation', in *Proceedings of the 2019 Conference on Empirical Methods in Natural Language Processing and the*

9th International Joint Conference on Natural Language Processing (EMNLP-IJCNLP), Hong Kong, China: Association for Computational Linguistics, pp. 3405–3410. Available at: https://doi.org/10.18653/v1/D19-1339.

Thunström, A. O. (2022) 'We Asked GPT-3 to Write an Academic Paper about Itself—Then We Tried to Get It Published', *Scientific American*. Available at: https://www.scientificamerican.com/article/we-asked-gpt-3-to-write-an-academic-paper-about-itself-mdash-then-we-tried-to-get-it-published/ (Accessed: 31 October 2022).

Turek, M. (n.d.) *Explainable Artificial Intelligence (XAI)*. Available at: https://www.darpa.mil/program/explainable-artificial-intelligence (Accessed: 9 January 2023).

Uszkoreit, J. (2017) 'Transformer: A Novel Neural Network Architecture for Language Understanding', *Google AI Blog*. Available at: http://ai.googleblog.com/2017/08/transformer-novel-neural-network.html (Accessed: 21 October 2022).

Wachter, S., Mittelstadt, B. and Floridi, L. (2017) 'Why a Right to Explanation of Automated Decision-Making Does Not Exist in the General Data Protection Regulation', *International Data Privacy Law* [Preprint]. Available at: https://www.academia.edu/93498087/Why_a_Right_to_Explanation_of_Automated_Decision_Making_Does_Not_Exist_in_the_General_Data_Protection_Regulation (Accessed: 9 January 2023).

11. AI and interoperability

Matthias Leese

INTRODUCTION

Interoperability has been framed as a key challenge for contemporary forms of governance and public administration. Notably, apart from practical drivers in domains that require a high level of coordination between different actors, it is also seen as a cross-cutting requirement with regard to possible applications of machine learning and other forms artificial intelligence (AI) (Paul, 2022). In the European Union (EU), for example, interoperability is considered paramount in making knowledge infrastructures within a multi-level political architecture future-proof. The *New European Interoperability Framework (EIF)*, published by the European Commission (EC) in 2017 as a guideline for public administrations across the EU, calls to "avoid digital fragmentation" (European Commission, 2017b) and to link up information silos in order to achieve an optimal knowledge base for government–citizen interfaces and the single market. This strategy has more recently been followed up by a proposal for an *Interoperable Europe Act* that defines "measures for a high level of public sector interoperability across the Union" (European Commission, 2022). And while the political push for interoperability might currently be particularly strong in the EU, there is no shortage of interoperability projects in other part of the world (DeNardis, 2011), be it in North America (Vannijnatten, 2004; Dittmer, 2018), South America (Jimenez, Criado et al., 2011, Manda and Backhouse, 2016), Africa (Adebesin, Kotze et al., 2013, Gumbo and Moyo, 2020), or Australia (Sprivulis, Walker et al., 2007).

At times it does, however, remain vague what interoperability means in practice and how it relates to other concepts (Trauttmansdorff, 2022). The basic rationale of interoperability is as old as it is simple and intuitive. Its Latin origin translates to "to work between", indicating that it is concerned with the ways in which two or more different entities can function together and work towards a common goal. It thus speaks to fundamental questions of communication and coordination in complex environments that are characterized by specialization and division of labour. Literature from engineering, computer science, or management tends to break down interoperability into more specific layers, for example technical interoperability, syntactic interoperability, semantic interoperability, or organizational interoperability (Kubicek and Cimander, 2009; Roßnagel, Engelbach et al., 2012). Concrete interoperability challenges can then be addressed in research and practice with regard to concrete use cases. The *EIF*, for example, defines interoperability in public administration as "the ability of organisations to interact towards mutually beneficial goals, involving the sharing of information and knowledge between these organisations, through the business processes they support, by means of the exchange of data between their ICT systems" (European Commission, 2017b: 5). And the proposal for the *Interoperable Europe Act* frames it as "common rules and a framework for coordination [in the] public sector" (European Commission, 2022: 21).

As these examples illustrate, interoperability, while intuitively resonating with almost any form of public administration and governance, refuses to be defined easily and in a uniform way. As a high-level concept, it remains abstract enough for it to be an attractive political imaginary for regulation and practical improvement of cooperation structures that are considered to be insufficient. But at the same time, it needs to be substantiated in the context of concrete use cases. Only then can it be assessed in its meaning and implications, both in terms of the transformations that it brings to governance and public administration, but also in terms of its wider societal implications.

To do so, this chapter reconstructs how interoperability has been framed and is put into practice in the context of the European Area of Freedom, Security and Justice (AFSJ). In 2019, the EU adopted an interoperability framework for all major centralized databases that contain information regarding law enforcement, border control, and judicial cooperation (European Union, 2019a; European Union, 2019b: 28). This policy framework defines interoperability for EU internal security as the capacity to "facilitate the correct identification of persons" and "streamline access for the purposes of preventing, detecting or investigating terrorist offences or other serious criminal offenses" (European Union, 2019a). As will be argued, the case of AFSJ interoperability is illustrative of the politically perceived need to overhaul today's digital knowledge infrastructures and to render them ready for further technical advances such as AI applications. At the same time, as will be subsequently discussed, such an approach has sparked concerns regarding data protection infringements and disproportionate state surveillance and control capacities.

The chapter proceeds as follows. First, it engages the political imaginary that drives interoperability in the AFSJ. It then explores classification and standards as key considerations in interoperability efforts and discusses the related concept of data friction in the context of the costs that are required to overcome classification and standardization challenges. Finally, the chapter engages critique of the idea of interoperability and its practical implementations for research on public policy and AI technologies.

THE INTEROPERABILITY IMAGINARY

From a conceptual point of view, interoperability almost always indicates a policy aim in the form of a desirable future, i.e. it is presented as an imaginary that illustrates how things are supposed to work in contrast to current shortcomings (Hilgartner, 2015). In this sense, the interoperability agenda in the AFSJ speaks to alleged structural flaws in the information architecture that underpins law enforcement, border control, and judicial cooperation in the EU. In a largely digitized information environment, databases have come to be key tools for the execution of sovereign tasks (Ruppert, 2012) as they provide the information that is relevant for the (dis-)approval of border crossings, the production of intelligence about possible threats, and the intervention into potential illegal activities. However, as has been argued by the EC, AFSJ databases currently stand largely isolated from each other in a silo structure that prevents the connection of available information, thus leading to a suboptimal knowledge infrastructure that is riddled with "blind spots" (European Commission, 2017a: 33) and resulting intelligence that is "not always complete, accurate and reliable" (European Commission, 2017a: 9).

This perceived lack of knowledge production capacities stands in a sharp contrast to the increasing amount of AFSJ information systems and the data stored in them. There are currently three major systems that support information gathering and exchange in internal security matters in the EU: the Schengen Information System (SIS II) for law enforcement, border control, and judicial cooperation between the member states; the Visa Information System (VIS) for the exchange of data on visa applications and processes; and the European Asylum Dactyloscopy Database (EURODAC) for biometric data of asylum seekers and irregular border-crossers. In the future, these systems will be complemented by three additional ones that have been adopted but not yet implemented: the Entry-Exit System (EES) for the systematic recording of all border crossings into and out of the territory of the EU; the European Criminal Records System for third-country nationals (ECRIS-TCN) for information on individual criminal histories; and the European Travel Information Authorisation System (ETIAS) for the pretravel approval of entry criteria into the EU (analogous to similar systems in the US, Canada, and other parts of the world). As has been highlighted by the EC multiple times over the past decade, these systems are considered key in regard to the timely availability of accurate information, underpinning the regulation of mobility and the fight against terrorism and transnational crime (e.g. European Commission, 2014; European Commission, 2016b; European Commission, 2016a).

To make the most of the data and analytical capacities of these systems, interoperability is regarded as central to ensuring the accuracy and timely availability of information for national and supranational agencies involved in law enforcement, border control, and judicial cooperation in the EU. In its *Strategy Towards a Fully Functioning and Resilient Schengen Area*, the EC claims that "interoperability will connect all European systems for borders, migration, security and justice, and will ensure that all these systems 'talk' to each other, that no check gets missed because of disconnected information, and that national authorities have the complete, reliable and accurate information needed" (European Commission, 2021: 8). The political imaginary of interoperability in the AFSJ is thus one of uninterrupted information flow that addresses knowledge and awareness gaps and enables involved national and supranational actors to base their tasks on reliable and trustworthy data.

The way to achieve such a seamless information landscape is thereby presented in reductionist terms as a primarily technical challenge that deliberately brackets wider institutional, political, economic, and normative questions (also see on "trustworthiness": Gillis, Laux and Mittelstadt, Chapter 14; on "bias" discourses: Hong, Chapter 8; on "ethics": Rönnblom, Carlsson and Padden, Chapter 9, all in this volume). Practical interoperability between AFSJ databases is, in this perspective, supposed to be established through a cross-cutting layer that connects all systems without dissolving their actual structure, instead using biometric data to cross-match existing records, identify and merge multiple records tied to the same biometric identifiers, and facilitate searches and identification queries in a one-stop-shop fashion. To do so, the interoperability framework puts forward multiple technical components: a "Common Identity Repository" is in the future supposed to store biometric templates extracted from all AFSJ databases, whereas a "Multiple Identity Detector" is supposed to merge previously unconnected official records that pertain to the same person and detect fraudulent identities (European Union, 2019a; European Union, 2019b). These are to be complemented with a "European Search Portal", i.e. a unified query interface that can trigger simultaneous searches in all systems based on biometric or alphanumeric data (European Union, 2019a; European Union, 2019b). According to this rationale, implementing these features would raise informational awareness as involved authorities could obtain information on the availability of data in any of the six databases, whereas otherwise individual search queries would need to be run on each of the systems, with the additional hurdle of fragmented access rights.

Scholars have interpreted the interoperability imaginary in the domain of EU internal security as expressive of a deep-rooted sense of governmental failure and fear. Leese (2022) has argued that the political desire for interoperability refers to fundamental questions of (re-) establishing a proper interface between public agencies and the population – particularly with regard to third-country nationals about which by default less information is available and thus needs to be consolidated across different domains that relate to the administrative management of foreigners (e.g. tourism and business travel, asylum, customs, policing, border control). Similarly, Bellanova and Glouftsios (2022) have diagnosed the interoperability imaginary in EU internal security as being foundational to a politics that seeks to reform European knowledge infrastructures, notably in regard to the issue as to "what societal phenomena and subjects should be known and recorded" (Bellanova and Glouftsios, 2022: 460). For them, the interoperability imaginary in the AFSJ is the expression of political anxieties as to the governability of fleeting and elusive phenomena such as migration, crime, or terrorism. In this context, interoperability is considered to present a practical policy path that promises to remedy inadequate state actor capacities vis-à-vis these phenomena by reformatting the digital foundations of knowledge and intervention. Finally, Trauttmansdorff and Felt (2021) have retraced how interoperability aspirations tie in with a larger vision of digital transformation that is framed as an inevitable and unidirectional response to current and future crises. Overall, these accounts tie in with Carmel's (2017) diagnosis that the idea of interoperability is constitutive to the idea of Europe as a social (and governable) space in the first place.

CLASSIFICATION AND STANDARDIZATION

While, as the previous section has shown, from a policy perspective the establishment of interoperability in the AFSJ is framed as a logical and straightforward technical operation that, even in complicated cases, can be achieved if only sufficient resources and innovative engineering are applied, in practice things tend to be slightly more complicated. While purely technical issues might in fact be resolved comparatively easily, literature from Science and Technology Studies (STS) has shown that technology must not be understood as isolated from the larger societal contexts within which it is embedded (Latour and Woolgar, 1979; Pinch and Bijker, 1984). If interoperability in the AFSJ is about making knowledge infrastructures work together, attention must accordingly be paid to how both "knowledge" and "infrastructures" in EU internal security are shaped and come into being in different ways that may or may not render them compatible with others. Valuable conceptual hints regarding the social construction of knowledge infrastructures can be found in the literature on classification systems and standards.

Classification and standardization are closely related concepts, with the former usually preceding the latter. In other words, classification systems tend to become formalized in the form of standards that can be universally referred to in order to ensure the compatibility of material and non-material stuff across time and space. Bowker and Star (1999: 5), in their seminal work on the social ordering functions of classification, have highlighted the "work that classification does in ordering human interaction" by structuring the ways in which individuals and organizations make sense of the world. In its essence, classification refers to an agreed upon way of using the same categories and measurements for the description and quantification of empirical phenomena. As such, classification is an integral part of how humans perceive the world, allowing them to "sort things out" through a system of "spatial, temporal, or spatio-temporal segmentation" (Bowker and Star, 1999: 10). As an epistemic practice, for Bowker and Star (1999: 10) classification thus provides a "set of boxes (metaphorical or literal) into which things can be put to then do some kind of work – bureaucratic or knowledge production".

In regard to interoperability, the obvious issue with classification systems is that many different ones can exist alongside each other. Depending on choices regarding how to measure and quantify empirical phenomena, different forms of classification may lead to multiple different representations of the same phenomenon – and these might not be compatible (Stone, 2020). This is especially the case with regard to social phenomena such as mobility, crime, or terrorism – key categories in the field of EU internal security – that only come into being as governable phenomena through definition work and the subsequent operationalization of such definitions via data points (Law and Urry, 2004). Adam and Jeandesboz (2022) have shown, for example, how competing definitions of migration in EU external border control on the national level in the 1990s have hampered both operational awareness and the production of aggregate statistics, and how different classification systems were only resolved through the work of intergovernmental expert group meetings that harmonized definitions and corresponding data production. In the current landscape of EU AFSJ databases, legacy effects of their origins in legally separated domains have resulted in only partially compatible classification systems that currently present a major challenge.

The ways in which such epistemic incompatibilities are resolved is usually to formalize classification systems through standardization. Standards provide a common consensus as to how things should be categorized, counted, and measured that actors can refer to across different domains, cultures, and epochs (Lampland and Star, 2009). Arguably, the most well-known body for the establishment and distribution of standards today is the International Organization for Standardization (ISO) which aggregates national perspectives on standards to the global level, but there are many more specialized institutions for standard setting in almost any conceivable area or domain (Higgins and Larner, 2010). What they have in common is that if their work is successful, it tends to become invisible and, as Thévenot (2009) has argued, forms black boxes that govern life from the background where they are hardly noticed any longer. The common lack of visibility as well as the often technical appearance of standards do, however, conceal the work that goes into their construction and maintenance. Standardization work is in most cases by no means a smooth and straightforward operation but is, on the contrary, coined by the interest and power positions of multiple actors, rendering standardization processes fruitful sites for study of the socio-technical nature of politics and regulation (cf. Mügge, Chapter 19; Omotubora and Basu, Chapter 17; and Paul, Chapter 20, all in this volume). Leese (2018) has, for example, shown how in the EU the standardization of biometric modalities for border control largely revolves around business case considerations that prioritize cost-effectiveness over maximum accuracy. And Rommetveit (2016) has retraced how the introduction of biometric travel documents in the EU was largely preconfigured by industrial standards, notably the regulations provided by the International Civil Aviation Organization (ICAO).

As these considerations illustrate, interoperability is contingent on a number of seemingly unrelated and disparate issues in concrete use cases, and is moreover impacted by the legacies of choices made much earlier. In regard to the AFSJ, the significance of classification and standardization can, for example, be witnessed through the struggles for biometric matching capacities across multiple databases. As discussed earlier, such capacities are fundamental for the interoperability imaginary in EU internal security due to the role of biometrics as centralized link between administrative records located in multiple systems. The Joint Research Centre (JRC) of the EC has, for instance, in a study on fingerprint identification technology for the SIS II, explicated the socio-technical formations that determine whether biometric templates from fingerprints can be subjected to algorithmic matching processes. As the report outlines, such capacities are contingent, among other things, on the definition of standardized use cases, standardized performance requirements and indicators, database integrity, as well as the types and quality of biometric data that are to be processed (Joint Research Centre, 2015: 46).

Although there are already standards in place as to the specifications, formats, and minimum quality requirements of fingerprints for storage in the SIS II, the JRC highlights how these standards might in practice be undercut by messy conditions during the capture of biometrics with mobile devices (e.g. at refugee camps or at smaller border crossings points), the lack of quality-control processes to ensure that fingerprint images have a sufficient resolution for the capture of biometric templates, different practices of enrolment (e.g. when not all ten fingerprints are being captured), the non-compliance of ground personnel with best practice guidelines, or the lack of a common exchange standard for biometric data (Joint Research Centre, 2015: iii). As a consequence, the JRC (2015: ii) has called for further harmonization of the "selection of appropriate formats to collect, exchange and process data; production of statistics; identification of appropriate architecture options; application of rigorous procedures for biometric enrolment; selection of measures to foster quality; [and the] definition of use-case scenarios and introduction of regular performance evaluation actions". These recommendations highlight some of the epistemic stakes for interoperability projects in regard to the (digital) knowledge infrastructures that they usually target today. Interoperability processes, in this sense, must already start at the epistemic foundations that precede data and knowledge. Notably, these must not be reduced to technical questions, but instead comprise a wide variety of social, cultural, and organizational issues that must be excavated from "beneath layers of obscure representation" (Bowker and Star, 1999: 47).

In summary, interoperability considerations, while at the surface often presented as primarily technical challenges, are in fact rooted in more fundamental and long-standing ways of knowing and doing. Enabling public agencies and infrastructures to work together thus means harmonizing their ways of counting and measuring the phenomena that they are concerned with, as well as their ways of organizing and processing information. Analytically, accounting for the ordering capacities of classification systems and standards thus requires a broader understanding of interoperability as a socio-technical issue that relates to a multiplicity of organizational, institutional, political, economic, and normative considerations.

DATA FRICTIONS

Another concept that has particular relevance for interoperability questions is what Edwards (2010) has called "data frictions". In his work on climate data, he builds on the resistances that occur between poorly fitting parts in complex technical systems and "[reduce] the amount of work they can do with a given input" (Edwards, 2010: 83f.). Frictions are, however, not limited to the mechanical world, but also occur in computation. Such computational friction, according to Edwards, resists the transformation of data into knowledge and must thus from a practical perspective be reduced as best as possible. One particular form of friction that can frequently be experienced in computer systems relates to the intractability of data. As data moves from one place to another, it requires, as Edwards (2010: 84) frames it, "costs in time, energy, and attention" to ensure that it fits in with data from other sources, to convert its format, to check for consistency and integrity, and so on.

The EC offers a practical example of data friction in its Staff Working Document accompanying the legislative proposal for the interoperability framework for the AFSJ. Without interoperability between databases, so the argument goes, duplicates of the same information would need to be created individually for each system, leading to a multiplicity of records and potential error sources, for example concerning visa regulation where each "visa application contains application data valid at a given moment and data identifying the applicant that are mainly constant over time but which can undergo lawful changes under some circumstances. When not handling identification data distinctly, they are created again for each system" (European Commission, 2017a: 10). The branching off of one piece of master information (i.e. the issuing of a visa) into multiple separately handled records in unconnected systems would in this sense require additional workload to keep all records accurate and up-to-date if the master information changes (e.g. the issued visa has been extended). Moreover, data frictions can occur when data from different sources must be rendered compatible by re-formatting or re-coding it (Ruppert, Law et al., 2013), or when data from one domain/use case must be repurposed for another domain/use case (Glouftsios and Leese, 2023).

To reduce potential data frictions and the resources it would require to resolve them, actors in the AFSJ have attempted to harmonize infrastructures and data. As early as in 2003, during the design phase of the second-generation SIS II, the feasibility study conducted by private consultancy Deloitte contained a specific part on potential synergies between the SIS II and the VIS. The corresponding report made a number of recommendations as to the potential future interoperability of the two systems, including the use of the same formats and standards for alphanumeric and biometric data, the use of the same network for transmission and storage, the use of the same hardware and platforms for central system components, and not least the use of an identical high-level system architecture for both databases (Deloitte, 2003: 17f.). These considerations were, notably, made under the assumption that SIS II and VIS could be connected in the future, for example through the *ex post* implementation of a common Automated Fingerprint Identification Service (AFIS) as specified by the eventual legal regulation for the SIS II (European Union, 2006; European Union, 2007).

CRITIQUE

As the previous sections have outlined, interoperability is a complex socio-technical concept that has governmental as well as societal repercussions as it restructures knowledge infrastructures and intervention capacities. The case of EU internal security is a particularly pertinent one in this regard, as information stored in AFSJ systems could potentially affect the lives of the entire EU population and millions of third-country citizens. Making databases work together and linking up data on individuals is politically framed as a move towards increased accuracy and more effectiveness in security governance, but it also bears the risk of enabling unprecedented surveillance and control capacities for state authorities (Bigo, 2021). In regard to AFSJ interoperability, scholars have paid specific attention to the effects of interoperable databases for political and social ordering. As Bastos and Curtin (2020) have argued, the full realization of interoperability in EU internal security would have profound societal and political repercussions, for example in regard to new power constellations within the EU, in regard to the scope of data protection and fundamental rights, and not least in regard to the relations between the EU and third parties. Throughout this section, some of the most pertinent themes of critique throughout the literature will be discussed.

Firstly, as discussed earlier, in politics and policy-making, interoperability is often presented as a self-evident concept that addresses shortcomings in public administration and the knowledge infrastructures that underpin governance and regulation. Moreover, despite its genuinely socio-technical make-up, it is usually framed as a purely technical challenge that can be overcome if only sufficient resources are mobilized. As the EC has argued as early as in 2005, interoperability should be considered "a technical rather than a legal or political concept. This is disconnected from the question of whether the data exchange is legally or politically possible or required" (European Commission, 2005: 3). For Bigo, Ewert et al. (2020), such a technical framing is part of a larger strategy of the EC to depoliticize regulatory decisions, i.e. to conceal the impact on new technological tools for fundamental rights of both EU citizens and third-country nationals. As they argue, interoperability in the AFSJ is "entrenched in the paradox on freedom, technology, and surveillance" (Bigo, Ewert et al., 2020: 109) that goes back to the founding principle of the Schengen area and its underpinning rationale that free movement can only be safeguarded by enhanced surveillance and control capacities.

Such enhanced surveillance and control capacities tend to interfere with some of the fundamental legal and human rights principles that the EU is predicated upon. Vavoula (2020) has, for instance, pointed out that interoperability potentially interferes with the principle of purpose limitation, i.e. the fact that data generated for a particular use case must not without explicit permission be used in other contexts – an argument that, also in terms of access rights to data across different systems, resonates well with concerns put forward by the European Data Protection Supervisor (2018) and the EU Agency for Fundamental Rights (2018). For Vavoula (2020), fully interoperable AFSJ databases, in undermining purpose limitation, would contribute to what she deems a "Panopticon lens", or, in other words, the repurposing of existing data for as many different cross-domain use cases as possible, for example mobilizing asylum data for border control or visa data for law enforcement. From the perspective of EU citizens and third-country nationals, others have put forward concerns about individual privacy rights (Aden, 2020; Electronic Frontier Foundation, 2021) and have voiced concerns about interoperability further contributing to the pre-emptive regulation of crime and mobility (Giannakoula, Lima et al., 2020).

The latter argument ties in with the analysis of critical border scholars who see interoperability as yet another step towards a high-tech apparatus for surveillance and population control (cf. Antenucci and Meissner, Chapter 31 in this volume; Molnar, Chapter 23 in this volume). Dijstelbloem and Broeders (2015: 22) have in this sense advanced the argument that the EU border framework today is largely predicated on "monitors, computers, scans, cable networks, radars, [and] communication technology" that serve to "prevent the arrival of unwelcome migrants by tracking, tracing and blocking them, and facilitate their return". AFSJ interoperability, for them, thus speaks to larger trajectories of European migration policy and constitutes a political project that is geared towards the drawing together of "biometrics, information storage systems, risk profiles, migrant categories, and travel data [...] to a network in which references circulate" (Dijstelbloem and Meijer, 2011: 28). Notably, such a network could be accessed and mobilized at any given point in time and at any given location – at the border, inside the territory of the EU, and even outside of it.

CONCLUSIONS

In summary, this chapter has outlined how and why interoperability has become a key concept in public administration and governance that resonates closely with the continuing rise and importance of digital knowledge infrastructures and related questions of databases, information exchange, and analytical capacities, including AI applications. The first section argues that, as a high-level concept, interoperability has sufficient appeal to serve as a political imaginary that informs policy-making in many different domains. At the same time, however, the chapter has challenged the ways in which interoperability is commonly framed in the political arena. It is, as has been shown, not an exclusively technical matter, but rather connects to fundamental epistemic questions as well as social, cultural, and organizational aspects of knowledge and action.

The study of interoperability must then investigate its socio-technical composition within particular contexts. Only then can it be filled with meaning and assessed in its potentially transformative effects on public administration and governance. To do so, this chapter has engaged in more detail with the interoperability project in the EU AFSJ where it is supposed to make multiple large-scale databases for law enforcement, border control, and judicial cooperation work together through the biometrically mediated cross-matching of official records that pertain to different legal domains – without dissolving the actual silo structure of these databases. Understanding interoperability as a situated socio-technical phenomenon, as this chapter has argued, has significant repercussions for our understanding of governance and public administration. Rather than automatically being turned into more efficient and effective forms of cooperation, analytical attention must be paid to the wider epistemic and institutional surroundings within which interoperability is supposed to take place. As such, it challenges, among other things, techno-solutionist conceptualizations of AI as a means to address and resolve current challenges in the public domain. Instead, understanding interoperability as a relational and situated phenomenon foregrounds its entanglement with larger regulatory and societal issues.

Building on such an understanding, the chapter has discussed some of the most pertinent critiques of interoperability. While appearing intuitive and logical on the surface, as has been shown, the unrestricted availability of information can abet governmental aspirations that are predicated upon surveillance and control, undercutting both individual and collective normative and legal principles and, most importantly, serving to sort and discriminate populations and mobility flows almost independent of temporal and spatial constraints. Clearly, more empirical research on interoperability – in the EU AFSJ and elsewhere – is required to fully understand its (long-term) implications. As of the time of writing, interoperability of EU internal security databases remains a work in progress and even after eventual implementation, practical deviations from high-level policy can be expected. Nonetheless, interoperability can be expected to become real in one form or another in the near future. Therefore, the need to critically assess what such interoperability will look like and what effects it will have, both in the EU and beyond, is all the more pressing.

REFERENCES

Adam, P. and J. Jeandesboz (2022). 'Before Datafication: Quantification and Information Sharing on Migration and External Borders in the European Union', Paper presented at the EISA Pan-European Conference, 1–4 September, Athens.

Adebesin, F., et al. (2013). 'A Review of Interoperability Standards in e-Health and Imperatives for their Adoption in Africa', *South African Computer Journal*, **50** (1), 55–72.

Aden, H. (2020). 'Interoperability between EU Policing and Migration Databases: Risks for Privacy', *European Public Law*, **26** (1), 93–108.

Bastos, F. B. and D. M. Curtin (2020). 'Interoperable Information Sharing and the Five Novel Frontiers of EU Governance: A Special Issue', *European Public Law*, **26** (1), 59–70.

Bellanova, R. and G. Glouftsios (2022). 'Formatting European Security Integration Through Database Interoperability', *European Security*, **31** (3), 454–474.

Bigo, D. (2021). 'Interoperability: A Political Technology for the Datafication of the Field of EU Internal Security?', in D. Bigo, T. Diez, E. Fanoulis, B. Rosamond and Y. A. Stivachtis (eds), *The Routledge Handbook of Critical European Studies*, London/New York: Routledge, pp. 400–417.

Bigo, D., et al. (2020). 'The Interoperability Controversy or How to Fail Successfully: Lessons from Europe', *International Journal of Migration and Border Studies*, **6** (1–2), 93–114.

Bowker, G. C. and S. L. Star (1999). *Sorting Things Out: Classification and Its Consequences*, Cambridge, MA: MIT Press.

Carmel, E. (2017). 'Re-Interpreting Knowledge, Expertise and EU Governance: The Cases of Social Policy and Security Research Policy', *Comparative European Politics*, **15** (5), 771–793.

Deloitte (2003). *SIS II Feasibility Study. Additional Study: SIS-VIS Synergies*, 23 May.

DeNardis, L. (2011). *Opening Standards: The Global Politics of Interoperability*, Cambridge, MA/London: MIT Press.

Dijstelbloem, H. and D. Broeders (2015). 'Border Surveillance, Mobility Management and the Shaping of Non-Publics in Europe', *European Journal of Social Theory*, **18** (1), 21–38.

Dijstelbloem, H. and A. Meijer (2011). *Migration and the New Technological Borders of Europe*, Basingstoke, UK: Palgrave Macmillan.

Dittmer, J. (2018). 'The State, All at Sea: Interoperability and the Global Network of Navies', *Environment and Planning C: Politics and Space*, **39** (7), 1389–1406.

Edwards, P. N. (2010). *A Vast Machine: Computer Models, Climate Data, and the Politics of Global Warming*, Cambridge, MA: MIT Press.

Electronic Frontier Foundation (2021). *Privacy Without Monopoly: Data Protection and Interoperability*, San Francisco.

European Commission (2005). *Communication from the Commission to the Council and the European Parliament on Improved Effectiveness, Enhanced Interoperability and Synergies Among European Databases in the Area of Justice and Home Affairs*, COM(2005) 597 final, 24 November, Brussels.

European Commission (2014). *An Open and Secure Europe: Making it Happen*, COM(2014) 154 final, Brussels.

European Commission (2016a). *Delivering on the European Agenda on Security to Fight Against Terrorism and Pave the Way Towards an Effective and Genuine Security Union*, COM(2016) 230 final, Brussels.

European Commission (2016b). *Stronger and Smarter Information Systems for Borders and Security*, COM(2016) 205 final, Brussels.

European Commission (2017a). *Commission Staff Working Document Part 1/2: Impact Assessment Accompanying the Proposal for a Regulation of the European Parliament and the Council on Establishing a Framework for Interoperability Between EU Information Systems (Borders and Visa) and Amending Council Decision 2004/512/EC, Regulation (ED) No 767/2008, Council Decision 2008/633/JHA, Regulation (EU) 2016/399 and Regulation (EU) 2017/2226 and Proposal for a Regulation of the European Parliament and the Council on Establishing a Framework for Interoperability Between EU Information Systems (Police and Judicial Cooperation, Asylum and Migration)*, SWD(2017) 473 final, Brussels.

European Commission (2017b). *New European Interoperability Framework: Promoting Seamless Services and Data Flows for European Public Administrations*, Brussels: Publications Office of the European Union.

European Commission (2021). *Communication from the Commission to the European Parliament and the Council: "A Strategy Towards a Fully Functioning and Resilient Schengen Area"*, COM(2021) 277 final, Brussels.

European Commission (2022). *Proposal for a Regulation of the European Parliament and of the Council Laying Down Measures for a High Level of Public Sector Interoperability Across the Union (Interoperable Europe Act)*, COM(2022) 720 final, Brussels.

European Data Protection Supervisor (2018). *Opinion 4/2018 on the Proposals for Two Regulations Establishing a Framework for Interoperability Between EU Large-Scale Information Systems*, Brussels.

European Union (2006). *Regulation (EC) No 1987/2006 on the Establishment, Operation and Use of the Second Generation Schengen Information System (SIS II)*, Brussels: Official Journal of the European Union.

European Union (2007). *Council Decision 2007/533/JHA on the Establishment, Operation and Use of the Second Generation Schengen Information System (SIS II)*, Brussels: Official Journal of the European Union.

European Union (2019a). *Regulation (EU) 2019/817 of the European Parliament and of the Council of 20 May 2019 on Establishing a Framework for Interoperability Between EU Information Systems in the Field of Borders and Visa and Amending Regulations (EC) No 767/2008, (EU) 2016/399, (EU) 2017/2226, (EU) 2018/1240, (EU) 2018/1726 and (EU) 2018/1861 of the European Parliament and of the Council and Council Decisions 2004/512/EC and 2008/633/JHA*, Brussels: Official Journal of the European Union.

European Union (2019b). *Regulation (EU) 2019/818 of the European Parliament and of the Council of 20 May 2019 on Establishing a Framework for Interoperability Between EU Information Systems in the Field of Police and Judicial Cooperation, Asylum and Migration and Amending Regulations (EU) 2018/1726, (EU) 2018/1862 and (EU) 2019/816*, Brussels: Official Journal of the European Union.

European Union Agency for Fundamental Rights (2018). *Interoperability and Fundamental Rights Implications: Opinion of the European Union Agency for Fundamental Rights*, Vienna: European Union Agency for Fundamental Rights.

Giannakoula, A., et al. (2020). 'Combating Crime in the Digital Age: A Critical Review of EU Information Systems in the Area of Freedom, Security and Justice in the Post-Interoperability Era: Challenges for Criminal Law and Personal Data Protection', *Brill Research Perspectives in Transnational Crime*, **2** (4), 1–97.

Glouftsios, G. and M. Leese (2023). 'Epistemic Fusion: Passenger Information Units and the Making of International Security', *Review of International Studies*, **49** (1), 125–142.

Gumbo, T. and T. Moyo (2020). 'Exploring the Interoperability of Public Transport Systems for Sustainable Mobility in Developing Cities: Lessons from Johannesburg Metropolitan City, South Africa', *Sustainability*, **12** (15), 1–16.

Higgins, V. and W. Larner (2010). *Calculating the Social: Standards and the Reconfiguration of Governing*, Basingstoke, UK: Palgrave Macmillan.

Hilgartner, S. (2015). 'Capturing the Imaginary: Vanguards, Visions and the Synthetic Biology Revolution', in S. Hilgartner, C. A. Miller and R. Hagendijk (eds), *Science and Democracy: Making Knowledge and Making Power in the Biosciences and Beyond*, London/New York: Routledge, pp. 33–55.

Jimenez, C. E., et al. (2011). 'Technological e-Government Interoperability: An Analysis of Ibero-American Countries', *IEEE Latin America Transactions*, **9** (7), 1112–1117.

Joint Research Centre (2015). *JRC Science for Policy Report: Fingerprint Identification Technology for Its Implementation in the Schengen Information System II (SIS-II)*, Brussels: European Commission.

Kubicek, H. and R. Cimander (2009). 'Three Dimensions of Organizational Interoperability: Insights from Recent Studies for Improving Interoperability Frame-Works', *European Journal of ePractice* **6**, 1–12.

Lampland, M. and S. L. Star (2009). *Standards and their Stories: How Quantifying, Classifying, and Formalizing Practices Shape Everyday Life*, Ithaca, NY/London: Cornell University Press.

Latour, B. and S. Woolgar (1979). *Laboratory Life: The Social Construction of Scientific Facts*, Beverly Hills, CA: Sage.

Law, J. and J. Urry (2004). 'Enacting the Social', *Economy and Society*, **33** (3), 390–410.

Leese, M. (2018). 'Standardizing Security: The Business Case Politics of Borders', *Mobilities*, **13** (2), 261–275.

Leese, M. (2022). 'Fixing State Vision: Interoperability, Biometrics, and Identity Management in the EU', *Geopolitics*, **27** (1), 113–133.

Manda, M. I. and J. Backhouse (2016). 'Addressing Trust, Security and Privacy Concerns in e-Government Integration, Interoperability and Information Sharing Through Policy: A Case of South Africa', *CONF-IRM 2016 Proceedings* (67), n.p.

Paul, R. (2022). 'Can Critical Policy Studies Outsmart AI? Research Agenda on Artificial Intelligence Technologies and Public Policy', *Critical Policy Studies*, **16** (4), 497–509.

Pinch, T. J. and W. E. Bijker (1984). 'The Social Construction of Facts and Artefacts: Or How the Sociology of Science and the Sociology of Technology Might Benefit Each Other', *Social Studies of Science*, **14** (3), 399–441.

Rommetveit, K. (2016). 'Introducing Biometrics in the European Union: Practice and Imagination', in A. Delgado (ed.), *Technoscience and Citizenship: Ethics and Governance in the Digital Society*, Cham, Switzerland: Springer, pp. 113–126.

Roßnagel, A., et al. (2012). *SECUR-ED Deliverable 22.1: Interoperability Concept*.

Ruppert, E. (2012). 'The Governmental Topologies of Database Devices', *Theory, Culture & Society*, **29** (4–5), 116–136.

Ruppert, E., et al. (2013). 'Reassembling Social Science Methods: The Challenge of Digital Devices', *Theory, Culture & Society*, **30** (4–5), 22–46.

Sprivulis, P., et al. (2007). 'The Economic Benefits of Health Information Exchange Interoperability for Australia', *Australian Health Review*, **31** (4), 531–539.

Stone, D. (2020). *Counting: How We Use Numbers to Decide What Matters*, New York: Liveright.

Thévenot, L. (2009). 'Governing Life by Standards: A View from Engagements', *Social Studies of Science*, **39** (5), 793–813.

Trauttmansdorff, P. (2022). 'The Fabrication of a Necessary Policy Fiction: The Interoperability "Solution" for Biometric Borders', *Critical Policy Studies*, online first: 10.1080/19460171.2022.2147851.

Trauttmansdorff, P. and U. Felt (2021). 'Between Infrastructural Experimentation and Collective Imagination: The Digital Transformation of the EU Border Regime', *Science, Technology, & Human Values*, online first: 10.1177/01622439211057523.

Vannijnatten, D. L. (2004). 'Canadian–American Environmental Relations: Interoperability and Politics', *American Review of Canadian Studies*, **34** (4), 649–664.

Vavoula, N. (2020). 'Interoperability of EU Information Systems: The Deathblow to the Rights to Privacy and Personal Data Protection of Third-Country Nationals?', *European Public Law*, **26** (1), 131–156.

12. AI and environmental sustainability

Federica Lucivero

INTRODUCTION

AI-enabled technologies are often presented as tools to address global societal challenges, including the climate crisis. Machine learning enhances the capacity to discover patterns and predict outcomes that can be used to optimize supply chains or circular economies or to make renewable energy more efficient (Herweijer and Waughray, 2018). What gets lost in these visions of "AI for Good" and "AI for Sustainability" is that AI is not simply a technical solution, but is also part of the problem: storing large amounts of data, training models, running complex software, manufacturing and disposing of hardware all have significant environmental and social costs. This dual aspect of AI, as solution as well as problem for environmental sustainability, is nearly absent in documents on AI policy and regulation. As this chapter will argue, the scarce engagement with the environmental sustainability issue in the policy and regulatory context is a problem: first because environmental costs always have a social and ethical dimension, and secondly because ignoring such costs in debates on AI regulation creates a responsibility gap.

To develop this argument, the chapter starts with an overview of the relationship between AI and sustainability. It then introduces the concept of digital pollution, through examples that draw attention to the physical configuration of the infrastructures that enable AITs, the space occupied for data storage, the natural resources used for hardware manufacturing and energy production, and the toxic emissions discharged in the air and soil in informal recycling sites for electronic waste. These examples lead to a discussion of two sets of issues that are crucial for governing AITs in more sustainable ways, namely: the limits of cost–benefit analysis (CBA) in this area and the allocation of responsibility for the harmful effects of digital pollution. As I will argue, the search for solutions to the digital pollution of AI is not only a technological issue, but also a political and value-based one. It requires articulation of the plurality of values involved in decisions, a transparent evaluation of who benefits from and who is harmed by AIT development in environmental terms, and consideration of who has the responsibility to intervene.[1]

ENVIRONMENTAL SUSTAINABILITY, SUSTAINABLE DEVELOPMENT AND AI

In modern parlance, when we speak of "sustainable" practices, we refer to their ability to be sustained, or maintained, over time. Usually, the term has a positive connotation, but in its literal meaning it could also refer to practices, such as slavery, that are sustainable over time but morally problematic. In the context of environmental movements and ethics, the concept of sustainability refers to behavioural practices that last over time because they respect ecological limits, so as to bring benefits to the present and future generations (Attfield, 2013).

In sustainable fishing and agriculture, for example, fish or land resources are not treated as mere products to be exploited, but as ecosystems made to thrive. Although sustainable practices are considered as virtuous examples from an environmental point of view, it should be emphasized that the term is increasingly used in a generic way to refer to "good" commercial policies, practices or products, often ending up being used improperly and loosely.

The concept of sustainability is often associated with that of "development". In the definition that can be read in the Brundtland Report, published in 1987 by the World Commission on Environment and Development (WCED), sustainable development is "development that meets the needs of the present without compromising the possibility that future generations meet their own" (WCED, 1987). Related to this definition of sustainable development is that of "needs", represented in the report as a three-dimensional space which contemplates needs of an economic, social and environmental nature. Policies aimed at meeting these needs must therefore address not only problems of poverty and malnutrition – for example, through sustainable farming and fishing practices or through the promotion of renewable energies – but also issues of gender equality, access to primary education and basic health care, essential to ensuring the wellbeing of individuals in the present and the future. The Millennium Sustainable Goals (MSG, 2000–2015) and the Sustainable Development Goals (SDG, 2015–2030) are objectives set by the United Nations so that international policies move towards the realization of an ideal sustainable development.

It is important to note that the definition of sustainable development is grounded on a very broad concept of justice, which promotes a fair distribution of resources and wellbeing not only within the same society but also between different populations, species and ecosystems globally. A definition which, moreover, does not stop at assigning a certain moral status to individuals, animals and ecological systems in the present, but also considers the responsibilities of the present generation to ensure conditions of livability and prosperity for their descendants. This widening of the scope of sustainable practices (in space, time and dimensions) inevitably creates moral conflicts: for example, guaranteeing energy access to even the most vulnerable groups in poorer countries could imply an increase in greenhouse gas emissions globally and consequently harm future generations. On the other hand, there may be economists or politicians who believe that the responsibility for ensuring the wellbeing of the countries they represent (and the vulnerable groups within them) is more important than worrying about the wellbeing of other populations or even future generations. Although the concept of sustainable development suggests that the wellbeing of future and present generations, ecosystems and populations on a global scale is interconnected and should be promoted in a harmonized way, the delivery of this vision is not only practically difficult, but also raises ethical questions.

Sustainability and AI

AITs (artificial intelligence technologies) have the potential to contribute to sustainable development in general and environmental sustainability in particular. Sensors for environmental data collection, machine learning algorithms for processing energy consumption, models to support decisions to optimize cycles of consumption and waste recycling are all examples of how AITs can help us address environmental concerns and "save the planet" (Dauvergne, 2020). In parallel to these visions there has been a growing academic interest in the relationship between AI and sustainability in the context of AI governance. An exploratory search on Scopus for keywords such as AI, sustainability and governance[2] shows a steep increase in publications: the hits in 2022 have tripled compared to 2020 and grown even by a factor of ten when compared to 2019. The majority of these contributions explore the ways in which AI offers solutions to problems related to climate change, biodiversity and environmental degradation. However, scholars increasingly point to the need for a critical understanding of the relationship between AI and SDGs (Jobin et al., 2019; Dauvergne, 2020; Coeckelbergh, 2021). As van Wynsberghe (2021) puts it, there is a broad corpus of resources discussing "AI for sustainability" (where AITs are seen as tools to achieve the goals of sustainable development), with a comparatively limited number of contributions that address the issue of the "sustainability of AI" (showing how AI exacerbates unsustainable practices).

While the societal and ethical risks of AI have been widely discussed, its environmental "dark side" has only recently been acknowledged in policy and regulatory contexts, and often in a very timid way. The draft of the European AI Act, for example, originally only mentioned environmental sustainability as a value or principle innovators are encouraged to strive towards. The final version (March 2024) more explicitly states that the AI Office and Member States shall facilitate the development of codes of conducts for the voluntary application of specific requirements to "assessing and minimising the impact of AI systems on environmental sustainability, including as regards energy-efficient programming and techniques for the efficient design, training and use of AI".[3] In June 2019, the Chinese National Governance Professional Committee on New Generation AI released the "Governance Principles for the New Generation Artificial Intelligence – Developing Responsible Artificial Intelligence". Although this document states that the principles aim to better "promote sustainable development of economy, society and ecology", they are very abstract and come without a specific recommendation in this direction.[4] In order to understand why the lack of engagement with environmental sustainability issues, as well as the relegation of the issues to voluntary guidelines, in the AI policy and regulatory context is a problem, the next section articulates AITs' detrimental impacts for the environment.

DIGITAL POLLUTION: WHAT IS IT?

The terminology used to refer to AITs often refers to speed, to fluidity and the presumed immateriality of the network and IT systems underpinning AI solutions. The metaphor of the "cloud" (Hu, 2015) – the ethereal and limitless cloud, which can be extended according to customer needs for a few euros per month, and where data can be stored and made accessible from any location or networked device – is indicative of this misleading perspective on the digital as something immaterial. In reality, these systems require real industrial infrastructures which extract minerals, occupy land, alter urban and suburban landscapes, consume energy, release greenhouse gases into the atmosphere and end their life cycle in landfills.

The term "digital pollution" refers to the fact that the production and maintenance of AI technologies and their underpinning energy and data infrastructures have a significant environmental impact. This involves the production of greenhouse gases with negative consequences on the climate crisis, the depletion of natural resources used for AIT production, but also the release of toxic substances when they are decommissioned. The concept "digital pollution" shifts our attention towards the material infrastructure enabling AITs and their extractive nature (Crawford, 2021). For example, data centres, the core infrastructure of AI systems housing servers, storing data and supporting high-performance computing *processes* consume an increasing amount of energy to run their operations and cool the servers (Avgerinou et al., 2017). They also need diesel generators to keep the servers running in the event of a power outage, thus producing additional greenhouse gas emissions. The materiality of infrastructures and objects that make AITs become apparent in the (dirty) mining of lithium and other minerals which are needed for their manufacturing, as well as in the disposal of these materials through polluting practices such as incineration (Williams, 2011; Gabrys, 2013).

Another source of digital pollution relates directly to the development of AI systems. A group of researchers from the University of Massachusetts has calculated the energy consumption linked to the training of some deep neural networks used for natural language processing (Natural Language Processing, NLP). The study showed that training the GPT-2 system resulted in the emission of greenhouse gases equal to almost five times the emissions of a medium-sized car throughout its life cycle (including the production of the car itself) (Strubell et al., 2019). As ChatGPT has become available to the broader public in 2022, it has become clear that we not only need to account for the energy consumption of training language models with large amounts of textual data, but also the environmental costs of using them (in addition to their social and political implications).

In summary, Information and Communication Technologies (ICT) in general, and AI more specifically, involve high raw material and energy consumption and have a significant environmental impact (see also Hilty et al., 2013). It must be emphasized that these environmental impact estimates still entail elements of uncertainty and incompleteness. And yet, they give an idea of the extent of a less discussed problem in a context of constant growth in digital demand and supply (Freitag et al., 2020). These elements of uncertainty are not sufficient reason to overlook the problem. In fact, according to the Paris Agreements, to contain the rise in global temperature below 1.5°C, every productive sector must adapt and make significant changes. Even taking the most optimistic forecasts as a reference, it has been shown that the ICT and AI sectors cannot continue to produce the same amount of emissions, but must commit to a reduction to avoid an excessive increase in global warming (Blair, 2020). So, despite the lack of scientific consensus on the extent of digital pollution, there are legitimate reasons to predict irreversible damage in the event of inaction, especially given the growth rate of the industry.[5] As we will see later, this is only partly a technical-scientific problem (linked, for example, to improving the efficiency of the systems or to a more precise calculation of their environmental impact), but also (and perhaps above all) a problem of moral and political choices.

DIGITAL POLLUTION AND MORAL VALUES

In acknowledging and tackling the problem of digital pollution, we cannot rely on a mechanistic calculation of data, but must (1) consider value questions and political choices in regulating AI, and (2) reflect on how best to assign responsibilities for compensating for the environmental costs of AI production and use to the various interest groups. Let us examine these two aspects in turn.

Facts and Values

Building houses and heating them, eating, moving: it is reasonable to think that all human activities have an impact on the environment and on the climate crisis,[6] but this does not make us give up these activities. Only some of the most radical activists of the environmental cause recommend going to live in huts without heating, picking fruits spontaneously offered by nature and moving only on foot.[7] A more moderate (and more widespread) environmentalist approach consists in *evaluating the costs and benefits* of each of these activities, promoting the construction of houses with low energy consumption (never zero!), a diet based on products with a reduced carbon footprint (e.g. consuming fewer products of animal origin and more local products) and travelling by public transport or lower emission transport, such as hybrid cars or trains. A similar approach regarding digital pollution would involve seeking a reduction in the environmental impact of digital technologies and AI, but not a renunciation of their use. This approach is common in policy contexts where technologies' social costs are weighted against their potential benefits. While adopting a cost–benefit analysis (CBA) approach seems to be a more reasonable option than a complete renunciation of technology, it is not as straightforward as often implied (on risk analysis and AI, also see: Krutzinna, Chapter 29 in this volume). CBA is a valuable tool in contexts where the relationship between costs and benefits is calculated through the assignment of a monetary value. However, it has been debated whether monetizing options or assigning a quantifiable value to positive or negative consequences is a good approach in political decision making (Turner, 1979). First, quantifying costs or benefits can be difficult when the impact of a certain policy or technology cannot be determined with certainty. Secondly, CBA assumes a consensus on how to define a benefit (a consequence with a positive connotation) or a cost (a consequence with a negative connotation). This consensus is relatively easy to reach when considering monetary values that are easy to quantify, but becomes more complex when different evaluation criteria and perspectives come into play. Let us scrutinize the limits of CBAs in the concrete case of digital pollution in more depth.

To manage and reduce digital pollution it is important to know its extent, both in absolute terms (how much information technologies and AI pollute) and in relative terms (how much they pollute compared to the resulting environmental and social benefits). These two seemingly simple questions require complex answers. First, it is not easy to establish the extent of digital pollution in absolute terms. Let us take the example of data centres. Analyses of current energy consumption and forecasts of future development vary greatly. They depend primarily on data that is not always easy to acquire because it is often not publicly available and the metrics used to acquire it vary across contexts (Whitehead et al., 2014). Secondly, although the technologies used in data centres are constantly evolving and tending to become more efficient, the demand for access, sharing, storage and processing of data is increasing simultaneously. The picture becomes even more varied and complicated when other factors are considered. Energy consumption and greenhouse gas emissions from data centres are a *direct environmental impact* and relatively easier to measure once standard parameters are decided and data is made available. But a more realistic assessment of the environmental impacts of AI (or other digital) applications must also take into consideration their *indirect* effects on users' behaviours and practices (Berkhout and Hertin, 2004). For example, increases in the efficiency of AI models, combined with the promise of a reduction in the costs associated with experiments with animals, drive research on so-called digital twins (for the development of digital twins in the context of urban spaces, also see Antenucci and Meissner, Chapter 31 in this volume). Investments in this field (if not monitored with respect to their environmental impacts) could induce some energy consumption behaviours which have a negative impact on the environment: researchers could in fact run more experiments, repeat the same experiments and train their models for longer times with an overall countereffect in relation to the initial efficiency gain. Thus, even if the enhanced performance of a technology makes it more efficient and allows for a decrease in energy consumption and unit price, consumers might increase its use or use the savings achieved to use other technologies and develop new high-cost behaviours. Systemic effects of this type are also called "rebound effects" (Widdicks et al., 2023).

Indirect effects are quite difficult to evaluate because they require consideration of social and cultural behaviours and norms. Daily internet use practices, for example the times of day people stream video (or GPT applications), are an important variable to evaluate the demand for data and therefore to evaluate the corresponding energy consumption (Morley et al., 2018). All too often, however, effects related to social and cultural characteristics of the user and rebound effects are excluded from assessments of the environmental impacts of digital technologies (Pohl et al., 2019). This analysis becomes even more complex when we try to consider the entire life cycle of AI hardware and software systems, from the extraction of minerals that are used to build computers, to the development and use of software systems, to the disposing of hardware in landfills.[8] The limitations of existing methodologies for assessing all relevant variables and managing the corresponding factors of uncertainty require constant monitoring of AI developments and complicate CBAs.

It is also crucial to consider that a CBA not only requires having available numerical values that can be compared, but also having a reference system to evaluate the social significance of these values. As we have seen above, the concept of sustainable development refers not only to the environmental dimension, but also to the economic and social one. Therefore, to establish the sustainability of AITs we must not only be able to measure the numerical value of their environmental impacts,[9] but we must also ask ourselves about their "social value", for example the way in which they promote the satisfaction of needs such as access to education and basic health care, or foster a society with less inequality and discrimination. Based on a CBA, if the AIT in question has a higher social value, we may be more willing to justify a higher environmental impact. But from what (or whose) perspective is the social value of an AI service measured? How, for example, are we to quantify the value of communication services compared to services for online commerce or for the storage of electronic health records? Should we accept the environmental costs of producing life-improving AIs in a Global South context more readily than those developed to patrol Global North borders or even kill people in warzones (cf. Bode and Qiao-Franco, Chapter 21 in this volume; Molnar, Chapter 23 in this volume). And how do we evaluate the social value of different types of research or applications in AI and other fields of computing?

Social value is neither easily measurable, nor even determinable uniformly. It changes, for example, according to the population in reference to which the benefits are evaluated. For example, health data collection and processing services may be more important in highly computerized countries than they are for less computerized countries, where paper records are used less. Furthermore, the populations most vulnerable to the climate crisis are also those which currently benefit least from the digital revolution. Or, if they do benefit, as in the case of digital farming in Africa, the economic benefits of "digital inclusion" might still be reaped in the Global North (see the discussion of colonial "digital intrusion" by Brooks, Chapter 16; and of data colonialism by Gray, Chapter 15, as well as Omotubora and Basu, Chapter 17, all in this volume). The assessment becomes even more complicated if the needs and interests of future generations are taken into consideration, or if a less anthropocentric perspective with consideration of the needs of different ecosystems is assumed. An environmental assessment based on CBA is not easy to implement in this field, since the values of both environmental and social impact are difficult to measure and vary according to context.

These various elements of uncertainty and complexity suggest that current environmental impact assessment measures may not be sufficient to provide definitive answers or a clear weighting of benefits and costs. It is important to note that such conceptual and empirical difficulties do not provide a justification for neglecting the problem, since the climate crisis requires urgent action and measurements are important for this. Rather, they show that decisions and moral value judgements need to be made in a context of uncertainty and incomplete information. Any failure to attempt to tackle these issues is tantamount to an acceptance of the environmental (and social) costs of AITs' production and deployment. Furthermore, a critical reflection must consider not only quantitative aspects, but also more qualitative, social and moral dimensions of AI's sustainability. This is not a *one-off* exercise, but requires a continuous reflection that runs in parallel with the development of AITs.

Individual or Institutional Responsibility?

There are many related political, social and ethical issues that should be addressed for the sustainable design, deployment and governance of AI technologies. But by whom? In their article on energy consumption of model training for NLP, researchers from the University of Massachusetts in Amherst question the responsibilities of the industrial, academic and public sectors with respect to the environmental pollution of AI research. They suggest a more equal distribution of limited AI resources (which are currently largely in private hands in the Global North) and the development and use of more computationally efficient algorithms and devices with lower energy consumption. The recommendations move in the same direction as those of the European Commission's High-Level Expert Group on Artificial Intelligence, appointed to develop guidelines for a "Trustworthy AI".[10] Among the criteria identified by the group, they mention the environmental sustainability of AI: according to the group monitoring the environmental impact resulting from the development, the distribution and use of AI systems must be accompanied by appropriate measures to reduce their environmental impact throughout the life cycle. These requirements remain at such a high level of abstraction that they are difficult to implement. What measures of the life cycle environmental impact of an AI system are to be trusted? Who bears the costs of such monitoring, of the creation of more efficient systems and with a better overall environmental footprint? How is it possible to ensure that these costs do not further penalize small research centres, small and medium enterprises and users in favour of the already powerful multinationals in the sector? What incentive schemes – as in carbon emission certificate trading – should be designed to make AI developers and users consider and offset the environmental costs of their activities?

The fact that these ethically motivated requests in essence still translate into a self-regulatory system which is entirely voluntary, means that various questions regarding the distribution of responsibilities and compliance with certain environmental sustainability standards so far remain unanswered. If the moral and legal responsibilities for AI technologies' environmental impact are not well identified, any regulatory attempt to mitigate this impact loses strength and remains at the mercy of individual (profit-seeking) actors' decisions. For example, some large technology companies such as Microsoft, Google, Amazon and Apple have often made public commitments to reduce greenhouse gas emissions. While such commitments are commendable in principle, it is unclear in practice what these companies promise. Some propose to achieve a *carbon neutral objective*, which consists in offsetting *their* greenhouse gas emissions into the atmosphere with actions to eliminate these gases (such as reforestation activities, for example). Currently, however, there is no common standard to determine: (1) which elements of the supply chain are considered in the calculation of the emissions produced by a company (e.g. if only emissions produced by fossil fuels *in situ* are considered or if the measures include emissions produced by use of electricity and gas purchased from third parties, or if we also calculate the indirect emissions produced at different stages of the supply chain, such as extraction, manufacturing, transport, use, disposal); (2) how these emissions should be offset (e.g. through the use of renewable energies or the purchase of carbon credits); and (3) which compensation strategies are most effective (e.g. buying and conserving an existing forest or financing reforestation projects).

These ambiguities lead some activists and researchers to argue that a carbon neutral goal for AITs and digital technologies is not ambitious enough, because it merely offsets, but does not reduce all emissions *in absolute terms* (Freitag et al., 2020). According to this perspective, aiming for *zero net energy* is a more desirable goal, since it implies not only a compensation between gases emitted and removed, but also an absolute reduction of emissions throughout the supply chain. In theory, a company aiming for "carbon neutrality" could increase total emissions and thus not contribute to the effort to limit global warming to 1.5°C, a goal which requires reducing annual emissions by 50 per cent by 2030 and the achievement of "zero net emissions" (*net zero*) by 2050 (https://www.ipcc.ch/sr15/). Given these premises, companies that are committed to achieving *carbon negative targets* are even more commendable, because they intend to eliminate more greenhouse gases than they emit throughout the supply chain. Yet these goals are often presented without precise information on their implementation and have therefore led some commentators to speak of *greenwashing*, problematizing that companies may adopt a facade of ecologism to appease public opinion and disseminate a virtuous image of their environmental commitment. For example, some companies claim they want to use only renewable energy (solar, wind, hydro), but at the same time they do not specify if and how the transition to 100 per cent renewables will decrease their overall emissions and from which these energy sources *derive*. These examples show the limits of leaving issues of environmental impact reduction – in AIT development just as elsewhere – to the self-regulation of individual organizations.

Consensus on terminology, standards and indicators will be crucial for ensuring that policymakers can rely on robust measurements (OECD, 2022). The development of a shared framework for addressing AI environmental costs must be an international governance effort and cannot be left to the market. At the same time, such international efforts must also recognize that many aspects of AITs' environmental impacts are either difficult to measure (e.g. biodiversity assessments), or not readily comparable with other benefits and costs (e.g. health impacts on workers in informal e-waste sites). Public debate as to who benefits from AITs and who bears their environmental (but also wider social) costs thus remains crucial.

CONCLUSIONS

The use of AI-fuelled services and devices, and the collection and analysis of large amounts of data and the training of AI systems, undoubtedly contributes to social and economic development and the search for solutions to environmental problems. In this sense, these are technologies that can help achieve sustainable development and meet the needs of the global population, animal species and ecosystems. At the same time, the relationship between AITs and sustainability is highly ambiguous due to the inherent environmental costs and impacts of the technologies (Lucivero, 2020).

This chapter has reviewed the concept of digital pollution to capture different types of negative effects of AIT production and deployment for the environment. This includes energy consumption, the use of natural resources and greenhouse gas emissions by data centres, the emission of toxic substances during the disposal of electronic devices and the emissions produced by training neural networks in research on AI. Although it is difficult to collect data on the life cycle of these processes and products, and there are conflicting analyses and forecasts of future emissions, it is clear that the issue of the environmental sustainability of these technologies must be addressed.

As this chapter argues, the search for solutions to digital pollution is not an exclusively technological issue, but also a political and value-based one. In this sense, CBAs aiming to quantify the costs and benefits of AITs have limited use in a context where knowledge on the very costs and benefits are uncertain because they are closely linked to behavioural and social aspects. Rather than (merely) attempting to quantify the environmental implications of the AI production process and life cycle, it is important to articulate the plurality of values involved and to discuss relevant stakeholders' perspectives in such assessments (beyond a focus on corporate actors in the Global North). Moreover, the issue of digital pollution cannot be separated from any discussion of the assignment of responsibilities between the parties involved. Currently, solutions are often left to the market, with voluntary adoption of targets by the private sector to reduce its emissions (for a wider debate of regulatory capture in AI, see Paul, Chapter 20 in this volume). This leads to a lack of clear and effective standards on the environmental impact of AITs. To address this responsibility gap public, national and supranational organizations must have a more decisive role to play in setting up monitoring, control and verification mechanisms and in enforcing them.

At the moment there are several codes of self-regulation in the private sector and some legislation that specifies certain standards (e.g. regarding the improvement of the energy efficiency of data centres or the inclusion of electronic waste in special recycling and disposal plans),[11] but the approach of public institutions is fragmented and there is a lack of policies and regulations that address the issue of digital sustainability effectively, through incentives or sanctions. This is partially due to the lack of accurate data on AITs' environmental footprint. In line with these considerations, in a 2022 report regarding the AI footprint, the OECD recommends "the establishment of measurement standards, expanding data collection, identifying AI-specific impacts, looking beyond operational energy use and emissions, and improving transparency and equity to help policy makers make AI part of the solution to sustainability challenges" (OECD, 2022, p. 2). As the report explains, accurate measurements of AI's environmental impacts are key to guiding sustainable policy decision making. Although in agreement with this statement, this chapter argues that achieving these measurements may take time and may still be insufficient as it leaves aside societal and nonquantifiable values. Sustainable policy making is bound to act in this context of numeric uncertainty and request more transparency from relevant actors, while at the same time acknowledging the inadequacy of measurements and ensuring that complex and non-measurable aspects are taken into account in the decisional process. Questions of accountability must be addressed in this complex situation and cannot be postponed to the moment that we get the number right. Overall, we need a critical approach to guide a global AIT governance project capable of meaningfully addressing the sustainability of these technologies and defining the criteria that must form the basis of regulatory instruments. Critical reflections such as those shared in this chapter can help clarify the underlying concepts, diagnose problems, identify contradictions, explain conflicts between different values and needs, and offer a moral basis to justify such a global governance project.

NOTES

1. This chapter is a revised version of a text originally published (in Italian) in Fossa F., Schiaffonati, V., Tamburrini, G. (eds), *Automi e persone: Introduzione all'etica dell'Intelligenza Artificiale e della robotica*, Carrocci Editore, pp. 112–127.
2. Exact search: AI AND sustainab* AND (governance OR ethics OR regulation) AND PUBYEAR > 2006 AND PUBYEAR < 2024.
3. Chapter X, art. 95 of P9_TA(2024)0138, Artificial Intelligence Act, European Parliament legislative resolution of 13 March 2024 on the proposal for a regulation of the European Parliament and of the Council on laying down harmonised rules on Artificial Intelligence (Artificial Intelligence Act) and amending certain Union Legislative Acts (COM(2021)0206 – C9-0146/2021 – 2021/0106(COD)).
4. See https://ai-ethics-and-governance.institute/translation-series-on-ai-ethics-governance-and-sus tainable-development/#:~:text=And%20in%20June%202019%2C%20the,is%20safe%2C%20controllable%20and%20reliable%2C; https://www.loc.gov/item/global-legal-monitor/2019 -09-09/china-ai-governance-principles-released/; https://perma.cc/V9FL-H6J7.
5. This consideration refers to the precautionary principle, which is central to environmental reflection. According to the formulation of the Rio Declaration (1992), this approach aims to protect the environment and consists in adopting, in the event of risk of serious or irreversible damage, precautionary measures to prevent environmental degradation, even in the absence of a consensus of the scientific community on the extent of the risks: "Where there are threats of serious or irreversible damage, lack of full scientific certainty shall not be used as a reason for postponing cost-effective measures to prevent environmental degradation." The principle is often criticized because in its more rigid formulation it would require certain proof of the absence of risk before the approval of any innovation, thus causing a conspicuous slowdown in scientific-technological progress; however, in its softer formulation, it underlines the responsibility of States and interested parties to assess possible risks and costs for the environment and future generations. For further information on the precautionary principle, see Hanson (2018).
6. Although there is no consensus that human activity is the sole cause of global warming, the report published by the Intergovernmental Panel on Climate Change (IPPC) in 2013 establishes that it is highly probable that climate change is anthropogenic (caused by human activity).
7. An example of this approach is that adopted by some political movements in the 1960s and 1970s, in which environmentalist motivations were associated with the rejection of the capitalist ideology and the excesses of the industrial revolution (Smith, 2003).
8. Environmental scientists refer to methodologies that evaluate the environmental impacts associated with the different stages of the life cycle of a service, process or product as "Life Cycle Assessment" (LCA) or "cradle-to-grave".
9. It should be emphasized that there are different parameters for assessing the environmental impact. For example, the *carbon footprint* is a measure of the weight (in tons or kilograms) of the gas emissions responsible for global warming, while the *ecological* (or environmental) *footprint* has a more literal meaning, as it is an indicator of space that converts the consumption of natural resources and the production of resources into units of measure of area. Global hectares (gha) express the amount of environmental space (i.e. biologically productive area of sea and land) that would be necessary for the entire world population to maintain a given lifestyle. It has been calculated that it would take five "planet Earths" to support the average US individual's lifestyle, three and a half to support the

Italian lifestyle and a half to support the average Indian lifestyle (https://data.footprintnetwork.org/
#/?; accessed 18 February 2021).

10. High-Level Expert Group on Artificial Intelligence (https://ec.europa.eu/digital-single-market/en/
high-level-expert-group-artificial-intelligence; accessed 19 February 2021).

11. As regards self-regulatory codes, it is worth noting that of the International Telecommunication
Union (ITU) (https://www.itu.int/en/mediacentre/Pages/PR04-2020-ICT-industry-to-reduce-green
house-gas-emissions-by-45-percent-by-2030.aspx). As far as European regulations are concerned,
the *European Green Deal* partly discusses the need to reduce emissions from data centres
(https://ec.europa.eu/info/sites/info/files/european-green-deal-communication_en.pdf). Circular
economy policy issues for e-waste are addressed in the document: European Commission
(2020), *Changing how we produce and consume: New Circular Economy Action Plan shows the
way to a climate-neutral, competitive economy of empowered consumers* (https://ec.europa.eu/
commission/presscorner/detail/en/ip_20_420).

REFERENCES

Attfield, R. (2013), 'Sustainability', in H. Lafollette (ed.), *International Encyclopedia of Ethics*,
Chichester, UK: Wiley-Blackwell, p. 5092.

Avgerinou, M., Bertoldi, P., & Castellazzi, L. (2017), 'Trends in Data Center Energy Consumption under
the European Code of Conduct for Data Center Energy Efficiency', *Energies*, **10** (10), 1470.

Berkhout, F., & Hertin, J. (2004), 'De-materialising and Re-materialising: Digital Technologies and the
Environment', *Futures*, **36** (8), 903–920

Blair, G. S. (2020), 'A Tale of Two Cities: Reflections on Digital Technologies and the Natural
Environment', *Patterns*, **1** (5), 100068.

Coeckelbergh, M. (2021), 'AI for Climate: Freedom, Justice, and Other Ethical and Political Challenges',
AI and Ethics, **1**, 67–72. https://doi.org/10.1007/s43681-020-00007-2.

Crawford, K. (2021), *The Atlas of AI: Power, Politics, and the Planetary Costs of Artificial Intelligence*,
Yale, CT: Yale University Press. https://doi.org/10.2307/j.ctv1ghv45t.

Dauvergne, P. (2020), *AI in the Wild: Sustainability in the Age of Artificial Intelligence*, Cambridge,
MA: MIT Press.

Freitag, C., Berners-Lee, M., Widdicks, K., Knowles, B., Blair, G. S., & Friday, A. (2020), 'The Climate
Impact of ICT: A Review of Estimates, Trends and Regulations' (available at https://arxiv.org/abs/
2102.02622, accessed 5 February 2021).

Gabrys, J. (2013), *Digital Rubbish: A Natural History of Electronics*, Ann Arbor, MI: University of
Michigan Press.

Hanson, J. (2018), 'Precautionary Principle: Current Understandings in Law and Society', in D. A.
Dellasala & A. Goldstein (eds), *Encyclopedia of the Anthropocene*, Oxford and Waltham, MA:
Elsevier, pp. 361–366.

Herweijer, C., & Waughray, D. (2018), 'Harnessing Artificial Intelligence for the Earth' (https://www
.pwc.com/gx/en/services/sustainability/publications/ai-for-the-earth.html, consulted on 2 February
2021).

Hilty, L. M., Aebischer, B., Andersson, G., & Lohmann, W. (2013), *ICT4S 2013*, Proceedings of the First
International Conference on Information and Communication Technologies for Sustainability, ETH
Zurich, 14–16 February, 2013 (https://doi.org/10.3929/ETHZ-A-007337628, accessed 2 February
2021).

Hu, T.-H. (2015). *A Prehistory of the Cloud*. Cambridge, MA: MIT Press.

Jobin, A., Ienca, M., & Vayena, E. (2019), 'The Global Landscape of AI Ethics Guidelines', *Nature
Machine Intelligence*, **1** (9), 389–399.

Lucivero, F. (2020), 'Big Data, Big Waste? A Reflection on the Environmental Sustainability of Big
Data Initiatives', *Science and Engineering Ethics*, **26**, 1009–1030.

Morley, J., Widdicks, K., & Hazas, M. (2018), 'Digitalisation, Energy and Data Demand: The Impact of
Internet Traffic on Overall and Peak Electricity Consumption', *Energy Research & Social Science*,
38, 128–137.

OECD (2022), 'Measuring the Environmental Impacts of Artificial Intelligence Computing and Applications: The AI Footprint', *OECD Digital Economy Papers*, No. 341, OECD Publishing, Paris, https://doi.org/10.1787/7babf571-en.

Pohl, J., Hilty, L. M., & Finkbeiner, M. (2019), 'How LCA Contributes to the Environmental Assessment of Higher Order Effects of ICT Application: A Review of Different Approaches', *Journal of Cleaner Production*, **219**, 698–712. https://doi.org/10.1016/J.JCLEPRO.2019.02.018.

Smith, K. (2003), *Wendell Berry and the Agrarian Tradition: A Common Grace*, Lawrence, KS: University of Kansas Press.

Strubell, E., Ganesh A., & McCallum A. (2019), 'Energy and Policy Considerations for Deep Learning in NLP', arXiv preprint (arXiv:1906.02243).

Turner, R. (1979), 'Cost-benefit Analysis – A Critique', *Omega*, **7** (5), 411–419.

van Wynsberghe, A. (2021), 'Sustainable AI: AI for Sustainability and the Sustainability of AI', *AI and Ethics 2021*, **1** (3), 213–218. https://doi.org/10.1007/S43681-021-00043-6.

WCED (World Commission on Environment and Development) (1987), *Our Common Future* (https://www.un.org/ga/search/view_doc.asp?symbol=A/42/427&Lang=E , accessed 3 February 2021).

Whitehead, B., Andrews, D., Shah, A., & Maidment, G. (2014), 'Assessing the Environmental Impact of Data Centers part 1: Background, Energy Use and Metrics', *Building and Environment*, **82**, 151–159.

Widdicks K., Lucivero F., Samuel G., Croxatto L. S., Smith M. T., Holter C. T., Berners-Lee M., Blair G. S., Jirotka M., Knowles B., Sorrell S., Rivera M. B., Cook C., Coroamă V. C., Foxon T. J., Hardy J., Hilty L. M., Hinterholzer S., & Penzenstadler B. (2023), 'Systems Thinking and Efficiency under Emissions Constraints: Addressing Rebound Effects in Digital Innovation and Policy', *Patterns*, **4** (2), 100679.

Williams, E. (2011), 'Environmental Effects of Information and Communications Technologies', *Nature*, **479** (7373), 354–358.

13. AI and transparency

Ville Aula and Tero Erkkilä

INTRODUCTION

In this chapter we critically explore how the concept of transparency is used in the emerging scholarly and policy debates on AI systems, in particular, its political character. Calls for transparency are often motivated by an assumed link between transparency and accountability, but the relationship between the two is far from simple. Indeed, the concept of transparency has evolved over time, containing democratic and economic connotations, but is now gaining new technical interpretations in the context of AI systems.

This conceptual shift is important, because the emerging sociotechnical understandings of algorithmic transparency foregrounds specific framings of policy problems while deprioritizing others, therefore favouring the interests of some groups while others groups suffer negative consequences (cf. Bacchi 1999). How transparency is understood in the emerging AI policy debate therefore has far-reaching consequences to what solutions might be adopted and who they might benefit. Transparency of AI and algorithmic systems is therefore subject to a power struggle between actors that pursue different interests. As a political concept, algorithmic transparency hence carries the potential to be instrumentalized (Skinner 1989) for promoting technical and ethical solutions to AI instead of considering its broader democratic and economic aspects. The chapter identifies key ideas and arguments in these debates, paving way for further critical research into competing conceptualizations of algorithmic transparency in scholarly and policy debates.

We will begin our chapter by discussing the relevance of AI transparency. We will then contextualize the concept of transparency and its ideational history by discussing its development as a political ideal before discussing how it features in literature on AI systems and identifying emerging policies on AI transparency. We conclude that current debates on algorithmic transparency carry the promise of bringing societal and cultural aspects of AI to debates on accountability, but fall short on establishing actual institutional arrangements through which civil society actors and key stakeholders could control the use of algorithmic and AI applications.

WHY IS AI TRANSPARENCY RELEVANT?

There are several reasons why transparency of AI has emerged as a central theme in ethical and policy debates on AI. Here, we want to emphasize three interrelated drivers that have pushed transparency to the fore, with each driver prompting different responses: opacity of computational systems, platformization, and digital surveillance.

First, calls for AI transparency respond to algorithmic systems having become ubiquitous but remaining opaque to citizens. Data-driven algorithms and computational tools have been characterized as black boxes that can have a negative impact on citizens without their knowledge (Pasquale 2015). Calls for transparency have become stronger as more harms and injustices have been identified (O'Neill 2016; Noble 2018). Burrell (2016) distinguishes three varieties of AI opacity: (1) organizational opacity involved with secrecy of the organizations using AI, (2) technical opacity relating to the skills needed to make sense of new computational models, and (3) opacity of machine learning models and their operational environment. These varieties of opacity are relevant for public policy debate, because they indicate differences in what should be the object of interventions promoting transparency.

Second, transparency of AI has gained relevance also because of platformization: algorithmic systems are essential to digital businesses that collect, process, and monetize user data, but the ways this is done are often inscrutable for users (Srnicek 2017; van Dijck et al. 2018). Social media platforms became successful by establishing a digital infrastructure for social transactions, and corporations try to replicate this strategy of digital infrastructures in new fields (Plantin et al. 2018). Transparency of AI technologies therefore has a political economy element that cannot be reduced to the sociotechnical functioning of computational systems. Many policy interventions to promote AI transparency therefore target a handful of multinational corporations that control these platforms.

Third, calls for transparency respond to concerns of secretive government and corporate surveillance. The revelations by Edward Snowden in 2013 on the digital surveillance of the US National Security Agency initiated a critical debate on how online and digital data were used by governments (e.g. Lyon 2014). Domestic political surveillance and censorship by authoritarian governments increasingly relies on algorithmic solutions (e.g. King et al. 2012). However, the surveillance is no longer restricted to governments. When the business model of platform companies hinges on collecting as much data as possible, users become victims of corporate surveillance that monetizes online transactional data (Couldry and Mejias 2019; Zuboff 2015). Greater transparency has been called to curb both government and corporate surveillance as an infringement of citizens' rights.

Opacity, platformization, and surveillance are empirical developments that anchor debates on AI transparency. Their importance is evident in transparency becoming a leading theme in AI ethics frameworks that attempt to formulate principles that would guide use of AI to socially desirable outcomes and mitigate risks and harms (Mittelstadt et al. 2016; Tsamados et al. 2022). Indeed, Jobin et al. (2019) found transparency to be the most popular principle to be included in ethical frameworks. However, including transparency in ethical guidelines or proposing transparency as a policy response to opacity does not yet explain what transparency is meant to *achieve.*

One of the key goals of promoting transparency is accountability (Cobbe and Singh, Chapter 7 in this volume). When demands of transparency link with demands of accountability, their aim is to regulate the use of AI systems. Some argue that transparency of AI of itself is a method of accountability; others argue that transparency is a preliminary step; and yet others propose that forms of accountability are contingent on what aspects of AI systems are made transparent (for an overview, see Wieringa 2020). Indeed, algorithmic transparency, even if fully achieved on the level of individual algorithms or data sets, might have only limited effect as an accountability mechanism (Ananny and Crawford 2018). Furthermore, mere knowledge of problems and harms might not be useful as an accountability mechanism if it does not fall within the remit of existing legal protections. Selective transparency can even eschew real accountability if it lulls users into false sense of security or obfuscates user perception of the

AI systems. Because of such uncertainties, corporate interests play a major role in trying to shape public and policy debate on transparency.

In addition to accountability, transparency of AI systems can be used to promote trust in AI and the organizations using it (e.g. von Eschenbach 2021; Gillis, Laux and Mittelstadt, Chapter 14 in this volume). This goal has become prominent especially after the problems of opacity have eroded public trust, although trust would be needed for increased adoption of AI, which is a conundrum that the European Union AI Act tries to tackle with its goal of trustworthy AI (Laux et al. 2024). Trust as the goal of transparency has widespread currency in scholarly debate, although it has been criticized for its ambiguity, difficulty in terms of operationalization, and the uncertain implications of transparency (Felzman et al. 2019; Laux et al. 2024). Trust can be misused, and people can trust actors that are fundamentally untrustworthy, making trustworthiness a complicated goal for transparency (Reinhardt 2023). Furthermore, promotion of trust in AI differs significantly from the goal of accountability, because it aims at popular acceptance of AI. This means that rules and regulations relating to transparency are balanced against the goal of increased uptake, which creates tension with the goal of accountability.

Unpacking the trade-offs, stakeholder interests, and unintended consequences of concepts like transparency, trustworthiness, and accountability is a key priority for critical policy analysis on AI (Paul 2022). In the next section we show how the current framings of AI transparency have their roots in a longer trajectory of how transparency is understood as a political ideal, which is now being reinterpreted in the context of AI.

SHIFTS IN TRANSPARENCY AS A POLITICAL IDEAL

While the word transparency is fairly recent in its current popular meaning (Hood 2006), the concepts of openness and publicity have long histories. To put the debate on transparency of AI systems into the broader political context needed for critical analysis, it is necessary to identify key ideas that precede current debates on AI transparency.

Historical accounts of institutional openness or "transparency" are characterized by concern with social conflicts between the respective roles and authorities of markets, (state) institutions, and citizen rights (Emirbayer and Sheller 1999; Habermas 1989; Schulz-Forberg and Stråth 2010). Transparency as a political concept has its roots in the Enlightenment, when it came to be associated with a form of rule that can and should be scrutinized by citizens (Hood 2006). The lineages of openness and state secrecy differ between countries and have been discussed in terms of path dependence and its critical junctures (Knudsen 2003). Yet, the 1766 Swedish law on public access to state information was for a long time an exception to the prevailing practice of bureaucratic secrecy (Konstari 1977; Knudsen 2003; compare Gestrich 1994). The Swedish act was linked to the new printing techniques, and granted the right to publish information relating to the state and government documents, a development crucial to the emergence of the "public sphere". Here it is important to notice that new notions of publicity were connected to the introduction of new communication technologies, a situation analogous to current debates on AI systems and digital platforms.

Nevertheless, the practical implications of Enlightenment transparency ideals are different depending on whether they refer to publicity of the public sphere, transparency of state bureaucracy, liberalism of an open market economy, or budding political openness of republicanism and democracy. This makes transparency and openness themselves subject to a power struggle between actors with different interests.

Since the mid-twentieth century, politicization of government, the computerization of public administration, and transnational communication of policy innovations has led to the spread of government transparency (Bennett 1997; Schudson 2015). In addition, the end of the Cold War and the opening of the global market economy have also greatly contributed to the rise of transparency in public administration (Best 2005; Rose-Ackerman 2005). Since the 1990s, the rise of the internet has created pressures for transparency. More recently, big data, social media, and algorithmic governance have again influenced states' information strategies and transparency of public administration.

An important first link between computational technology and transparency was established in the emergence of Free Software/Open Source programming (Kelty 2008; Coleman 2012). Starting from the 1980s, software developers promoted the idea that programming source code should be publicly shared instead of being a private property. Initiatives like Open Science and Open Data grew out of the initial Open Source movement in the early 2000s, arguing that companies, researchers, and governments should share their data with the public. The motivation for these initiatives is the claim that openness leads to faster innovation and therefore to more benefits to society. In practice, however, attempts to promote open data have had ambiguous and even contradictory goals relating to democracy, the economy, and innovation (Janssen et al. 2012; Yu and Robinson 2011). Nevertheless, examples of the enduring appeal of these ideals is that one of the key AI development companies is called "OpenAI", and that AI researchers often collaborate in sharing some of their data sets and models.

The above ideals of transparency exercise ongoing influence on the struggle over AI policy and regulation. Citizens and civil society who face new harms from AI are locked in a power struggle with private corporations and developers who profit from AI systems, with each side using openness and transparency to make their case. Civil society can appeal to democratic ideals to demand regulation and transparency. Citizens can appeal to ideals of public scrutiny when resisting governmental decisions reached via AI. Private corporations using AI in their business can appeal to economic ideals to promote transparent market practices and resist regulation. Developers of AI can appeal to technological openness to accelerate the development of new products and services. Contrasting interests are clearly evident in this list of what transparency can be used to justify in debates on AI. This makes it necessary to apply a critical approach to the conceptualizations, political economy, and contingent applications of the (variable) ideals of AI transparency.

TRANSPARENCY IN LITERATURE ON AI SYSTEMS

A specialist literature on transparency of algorithmic and AI systems has emerged in the last ten years. In this section we further explore the political underpinnings of possible solutions to the problem of opacity in AI systems. Given the complex nature and vested interests in defining transparency in AI, it is no surprise that there are divergent views on *what* exactly should be transparent in AI systems. Most importantly, the technical and definitional details of AI transparency are far from trivial due to the contrasting interests they might serve. As argued by Amoore (2020), AI systems consist of various dependencies between humans and machines that constantly modify their interaction and operation, making it impossible to say what would be the ultimate point of origin whose transparency would *alone* reveal why an algorithm gives a specific output. Rather there are multiple elements whose transparency can each reveal a partial perspective on the operations of the moving puzzle of AI systems (see also Burrell 2016; Ananny and Crawford 2018). Yet pinning down these elements is crucial for successful AI policy, making the issue an ongoing political struggle.

Transparency of machine learning models is one of the most intensely debated technical aspects of AI. In research literature this is discussed as a question of model interpretability and explainable AI. These two concepts are discussed in detail elsewhere in this *Handbook* (see Berry, Chapter 10 in this volume) and we will here focus on their link to the transparency of AI more broadly. The debate on model transparency is driven by the technical characteristics of some machine learning techniques being near-impossible to understand by humans. Researchers have proposed various techniques to deal with the problem, but there is no consensus on what constitutes interpretability and explainability, or what metrics should be used to measure the success of individual techniques (Lipton 2018; Carvalho et al. 2019). In addition to the technical layer of model opacity, problematic outcomes of AI systems might follow from the way a fully transparent algorithm interacts with specific data sets in specific operational environments (Ananny and Crawford 2018). Although researchers have developed techniques that enhance the transparency of AI systems, this does not guarantee that they are meaningful for citizens at large. Developers, users, regulators, and the general audience all have a different rationale for dealing with AI systems and need different things from transparency (Felzmann et al. 2019). Furthermore, solutions promoting transparency often lack a critical audience that could effectively scrutinize and challenge algorithmic decisions most ordinary citizens lack the necessary knowledge or resources to do so (Kemper and Kolkman 2019). As a result, researchers must be critical of whether framing transparency solely around explainability or interpretability of machine learning models serves larger transparency goals. The literature on algorithmic transparency further considers accessibility, which not only refers to the public availability of source code, but also external experts' ability to analyse the algorithm. Tested in an experimental scenario, explainability had a more positive effect on citizen trust in algorithmic governance than mere accessibility (Grimmelikhuijsen 2023).

In the event that an AI system remains opaque, some information on its effects can still be reached externally with "algorithmic audits". The goal of algorithmic audit is often not direct access into the AI systems themselves, but exploration of whether systematic analysis of their outcomes can reveal discrepancies, biases, or injustices in their operation (Sandvig et al. 2014). Such audits are promoted especially by civil society actors which can use them to reveal biases and injustices, but algorithmic audits can also be used by government regulatory bodies to audit AI systems within government and in the private sector.

Research on AI systems often calls for transparency of the data used in AI systems. On one hand, there are demands for transparency into the data used to train AI systems (e.g. Hacker 2021; Bertino et al. 2019). Transparency of training data is meant to create opportunities to scrutinize the data sets and detect problems that would lead to systematic mistakes, inaccuracy, or bias in the models based on it. The assumption behind this is that detection of problems in the data will alleviate the problems and improve the AI systems. However, transparency of training data does not as such provide mechanisms of accountability. On the other hand, transparency has also been demanded to the operational data that guides individual decisions made by AI. This approach, however, faces obstacles because companies using AI systems are reluctant to share such data. Legitimate privacy concerns also limit the transparency of operational data beyond what can be handed to the information subjects. Furthermore, the business of collecting and monetizing personal data operates in a legal grey area where many politically suspect practices are not per se illegal, making transparency of data hardly a solution on its own (Crain 2018). The sheer volume and complexity of personal data used in AI systems, if made available to users, might in fact increase the *opacity* of the systems because it hides what matters for the algorithms in the seeming transparency of the data sets (Stohl et al. 2016). Transparency of data sets can therefore be a relevant avenue for developers of AI systems to improve their systems, but inadequate in providing a foundation for citizen redress or political action.

Calls for transparency in AI systems also extend to the corporate structures of the companies developing and using AI systems. The digital infrastructures and corporate dependencies underpinning the building, training, maintenance, and deployment of AI systems are highly complex and often hidden from the public. Not only are the structures geographically distributed across various jurisdictions, but also the complex vertical and horizontal dependencies across leading companies conceal key details of how AI systems are developed and who benefits from them (Ferrari 2023). Developers of AI systems can also obscure the human labour needed to train and maintain AI systems, making it unclear who is responsible for their development (Newlands 2021). Consequently, public authorities have difficulty in identifying AI systems as targets for policy intervention or regulation, and individual users have little understanding of what goes on behind the user interface. Lastly, public sector organizations using AI systems are often dependent on private technologies whose operational details their developers consider business secrets, making it difficult to determine responsibility for mistakes and harms caused by AI in the public sector.

The above discussion demonstrates that transparency of AI contains a variety of elements that provide a partial perspective to the working of the systems, with no guarantee that transparency alone will deliver the political goals that motivate the calls for openness. The issue as to which of these aspects are inscribed into policies and regulations is therefore very salient. In the next section we discuss the emerging literature on transparency in AI policies.

EMERGING POLICIES OF AI TRANSPARENCY

Although research literature on AI has developed new conceptual ideas of transparency, only some of them have started to make their way into practical policy. Governments across the world have taken different approaches to promotion and regulation of AI and it is not a given that transparency is treated as being important (Cath et al. 2018). The ways that governments address transparency in their AI policies are influenced by their political traditions and cultural values (Ahonen and Erkkilä 2020; on institutional filtering processes also see af Malmborg and Trondal, Chapter 5 in this volume). Furthermore, national policies can aim for transparency of different aspects of AI systems, making them a battleground for contrasting interests. Because the literature on AI transparency is still nascent and most policy interventions still in development, the coming years will provide a considerable opportunity for critical policy research.

First, there is scope to assess whether and how transparency is addressed in governmental policies promoting AI. Governments face contradictory pressures, both to promote the use of AI and to react to the challenges it poses. National AI strategies, for example, emphasize the opportunities of AI, discuss the need for ethical standards, and call for close public and private partnership (Radu 2021; Ulnicane et al. 2021). The notion of openness for the purpose of economic and technological progress can be more important in AI policies than the idea of transparency as political accountability. As discussed in this chapter and elsewhere in this volume, emphasis on ethics and a lack of government intervention can often undermine efforts to tackle the problems of AI systems.

In addition to the promotion of AI, some governments have crafted policies to regulate and deliberately increase transparency in AI systems. In the main, attempts to introduce algorithmic transparency have involved public descriptions of algorithm use in decision-making. In France, public bodies are expected to provide public descriptions of the algorithms they use in decision-making (Etalab 2021; Open Government Partnership 2021). There are also examples of public actors providing this information on their own initiative, for example the cities of Amsterdam and Helsinki (City of Amsterdam 2020; City of Helsinki 2020). The UK government has launched an Algorithmic Transparency Recording Standard (ATRS) that basically provides public organizations a format and mechanism for communicating their use of algorithmic tools in decision-making (UK Government 2023). This includes a centrally managed repository for reporting the functionality of the algorithm and the reason for its use.

In April 2023, the European Union launched the European Centre for Algorithmic Transparency (ECAT) to provide technical assistance and practical guidance (ECAT 2023). Residing under the European Commission's Joint Research Centre the ECAT aims to become an international hub for research and communicating best practices on algorithmic transparency (Bertuzzi 2023). The European Union General Data Protection Regulation (GDPR) was the first policy that directly tackled transparency of algorithmic systems (in addition to its primary goal of privacy), including goals regarding the right to explanation although this did not constitute a legal duty (Wachter et al. 2017). Nevertheless, the GDPR does include a duty of lawful, fair, and transparent processing of personal data, which also has implications for AI systems (Felzmann et al. 2019).

Overcoming the shortcomings of the GDPR is central to the proposed European Union AI Act, which takes a risk and harm-based approach to AI but might not contain explicit legal duties of transparency (Varošanec 2022). Further complications in relation to transparency arise from the fact that AI is often relevant in the context of digital platforms, which are subject to their own interventions by the European Union such as the Digital Services Act and Digital Markets Act (EUR-Lex 2022a; 2022b).

If the European Union has been active in regulating AI systems, the United States and China have opted for less interventionist policies. Academic research on how transparency is understood in these policies is, however, very limited. The dominant policy approaches in these countries have been the development and deployment of AI systems, not their regulation. Nevertheless, the different legal systems and regulatory cultures in Europe, the United States, and China mean that policymaking can also take different forms. The Chinese government has introduced several new policies on AI systems and digital platforms, but their practical implications for transparency are unclear. In the United States, AI policies have been developed in close collaboration with leading digital platforms and emphasize ethical frameworks. The development of such hybrid and networked forms of governance calls for critical policy analysis to examine how a transparency regime led by the private sector ultimately turns out and how its outcomes compare with other regimes. In the light of existing evidence, however, it is unlikely that private corporations that promote and profit from the proliferation of AI systems would voluntarily tackle the full complexity of problems relating to opacity, platformization, and surveillance (on AITs in labour regulation in these countries, see also Donoghue, Huanxin, Moore and Ernst, Chapter 26 in this volume).

Apart from regulating general use of AI systems, governments also have policies guiding transparency in their own use of AI. These discussions are a direct extension of classical debates and the rules of accountability and publicity in the governments context are often stronger in public administration than in private business. In the absence of access to private AI systems, governmental AI systems offer a unique window into how AI transparency policies and solutions work in practice. However, governments regularly use proprietary AI systems and outsource services to private companies, which can again place practices beyond scholarly and public scrutiny. Again, analysis of only the technical layer of transparency is inadequate when AI systems themselves constitute a complex governance structure between public and private entities. The transparency of corporate ties, procurement practices, and interdependencies of public and private computational systems are therefore crucial aspects of scrutinizing AI systems in the public sector.

Critical analysis of AI transparency policies must consider who is participating in the debates on AI transparency and informing government policy. So far debates on AI transparency have been led by researchers close to the development and operationalization of AI systems, information law specialists, social media researchers, and theorists developing normative frameworks. Political scientists and public policy scholars have been largely absent from the transparency debate, although there are tensions between different notions of transparency and uncertainty over the right policy instruments and governance structures.

CONCLUSION

As is clear from this chapter, literature on AI transparency often balances between improving transparency of AI systems and critiquing the opacity of AI systems. The transparency of AI remains caught between the sociotechnical complexity of algorithmic systems and the political ideals that make transparency desirable in the first place. Algorithmic transparency marks an ideational shift to the conceptual history of government transparency. While transparency has previously carried both democratic and market connotations, the debates on opacity of computational systems, platformization, and surveillance have added new technical elements to its conceptualization while highlighting the ethical issues of AI. This ideational shift is also apparent in the standing scholarship on the transparency of algorithmic and AI systems.

We identify a tension between the new sociotechnical conceptualization of transparency, adopted by scholars and practitioners alike, and the previous perceptions of transparency that perceived it primarily as a concept of democracy and markets. While the technological aspects of algorithmic transparency as well as the perspectives of AI bias, fairness, and equality are very important, these nevertheless frequently make the individual problems visible without providing a tangible mechanism of accountability (cf. Mulgan 2000). Scholars have argued that it is difficult to find a suitable audience for algorithmic transparency (Ananny and Crawford 2018; Kemper and Kolkman 2019), but it is even more challenging to further establish actual mechanisms through which algorithmic transparency is embedded in a broader accountability system (cf. Erkkilä 2007).

There is an apparent need to consider the broader democratic and economic aspects of algorithmic governance and AI in different institutional contexts. Here civil servants and private companies are key actors, but the inclusion of civil society actors should also be a priority. The sociotechnical perspective on algorithmic transparency carries the promise of bringing the societal and cultural aspects of AI to the debate on accountability. But the key challenge remains to establish institutional arrangements through which such transparency would include civil society actors and key stakeholders in the accountability system with actual mechanisms for controlling the use of algorithmic and AI applications.

REFERENCES

Ahonen, P., & Erkkilä, T. (2020). 'Transparency in algorithmic decision-making: Ideational tensions and conceptual shifts in Finland'. *Information Polity*, **25** (4), 419–432.

Amoore, L. (2020). *Cloud Ethics Algorithms and the Attributes of Ourselves and Others*. Durham, NC: Duke University Press.

Ananny, M., & Crawford, K. (2018). 'Seeing without knowing: Limitations of the transparency ideal and its application to algorithmic accountability'. *New Media & Society*, **20** (3), 973–989.

Bacchi, C. L. (1999). *Women, Policy and Politics: The Construction of Policy Problems*, London: Sage Publications.

Bennett, C. J. (1997). 'Understanding ripple effects: The cross-national adoption of policy instruments for bureaucratic accountability'. *Governance*, **10** (3), 213–233.

Bertino, E., Kundu, A., & Sura, Z. (2019). 'Data transparency with blockchain and AI ethics'. *Journal of Data and Information Quality (JDIQ)*, **11** (4), 1–8.

Bertuzzi, L. (2023). 'EU Launches Research Centre on Algorithmic Transparency'. www.Euractiv .Com. 19 April 2023. https://www.euractiv.com/section/platforms/news/eu-launches-research-centre -on-algorithmic-transparency/.

Best, J. (2005). *The Limits of Transparency: Ambiguity and the History of International Finance*, Ithaca, NY: Cornell University Press.

Burrell, J. (2016). 'How the machine "thinks": Understanding opacity in machine learning algorithms'. *Big Data & Society*, **3** (1).

Carvalho, D. V., Pereira, E. M., & Cardoso, J. S. (2019). 'Machine learning interpretability: A survey on methods and metrics'. *Electronics*, **8** (8), 832.

Cath, C., Wachter, S., Mittelstadt, B., Taddeo, M., & Floridi, L. (2018). 'Artificial intelligence and the "good society": The US, EU, and UK approach'. *Science and Engineering Ethics*, **24** (2), 505–528.

City of Amsterdam. (2020). 'Amsterdam Algoritmeregister'. https://algoritmeregister.amsterdam.nl/en/ ai-register/.

City of Helsinki. (2020). 'City of Helsinki AI Register'. https://ai.hel.fi/en/ai-register/.

Coleman, E. G. (2012). 'Coding freedom'. In *Coding Freedom*, Princeton, NJ: Princeton University Press.

Couldry, N., & Mejias, U. A. (2019). *The Costs of Connection: How Data Is Colonizing Human Life and Appropriating It for Capitalism*, Stanford, CA: Stanford University Press.

Crain, M. (2018). 'The limits of transparency: Data brokers and commodification'. *New Media & Society*, **20** (1), 88–104.

ECAT. (2023). 'European Centre for Algorithmic Transparency'. 9 October 2023. https://algorithmic -transparency.ec.europa.eu/index_en.

Emirbayer, M., & Sheller, M. (1999). 'Publics in history'. *Theory and Society*, **28** (1), 145–97.

Erkkilä, T. (2007). 'Governance and accountability – A shift in conceptualisation'. *Public Administration Quarterly*, **31** (1), 1–38.

Etalab. (2021). 'Fiche pratique: l'inventaire des principaux traitements algorithmiques'. 11 February. https://guides.etalab.gouv.fr/algorithmes/inventaire/#dans-quels-cas-une-administration-doit-elle -realiser-un-inventaire-de-ses-algorithmes.

EUR-Lex. (2022a). *Regulation (EU) 2022/1925 of the European Parliament and of the Council of 14 September 2022 on Contestable and Fair Markets in the Digital Sector and Amending Directives (EU) 2019/1937 and (EU) 2020/1828 (Digital Markets Act) (Text with EEA Relevance). OJ L.* Vol. 265. http://data.europa.eu/eli/reg/2022/1925/oj/eng.

EUR-Lex. (2022b). *Regulation (EU) 2022/2065 of the European Parliament and of the Council of 19 October 2022 on a Single Market For Digital Services and Amending Directive 2000/31/EC (Digital Services Act) (Text with EEA Relevance). OJ L.* Vol. 277. http://data.europa.eu/eli/reg/2022/2065/oj/eng.

Felzmann, H., Villaronga, E. F., Lutz, C., & Tamò-Larrieux, A. (2019). 'Transparency you can trust: Transparency requirements for artificial intelligence between legal norms and contextual concerns'. *Big Data & Society,* **6** (1).

Ferrari, F. (2023). 'Neural production networks: AI's infrastructural geographies'. *Environment and Planning F,* **2** (4), 459–476. https://doi.org/10.1177/26349825231193226.

Gestrich, A. (1994). *Absolutismus Und Öffentlichkeit. Politische Kommunikation in Deutschland Zu Beginn Des 18. Jahrhunderts,* Göttingen: Vandenhoeck & Ruprecht.

Grimmelikhuijsen, S. (2023). 'Explaining why the computer says no: Algorithmic transparency affects the perceived trustworthiness of automated decision-making'. *Public Administration Review* **83** (2), 241–262. https://doi.org/10.1111/puar.13483.

Habermas, J. (1989). *The Structural Transformation of the Public Sphere: An Inquiry into a Category of Bourgeois Society,* London: Polity Press.

Hacker, P. (2021). 'A legal framework for AI training data – From first principles to the Artificial Intelligence Act'. *Law, Innovation and Technology,* **13** (2), 257–301.

Hood, C. (2006). 'Transparency in historical perspective', in Hood, C., & Heald, D. (eds), *Transparency: The Key to Better Governance?,* Proceedings of the British Academy, Oxford: Oxford University Press, pp. 1–24.

Janssen, M., Charalabidis, Y., & Zuiderwijk, A. (2012). 'Benefits, adoption barriers and myths of open data and open government'. *Information Systems Management,* **29** (4), 258–268.

Jobin, A., Ienca, M. & Vayena, E. (2019). 'The global landscape of AI ethics guidelines'. *Nature Machine Intelligence,* **1**, 389–399. https://doi.org/10.1038/s42256-019-0088-2.

Kelty, C. M. (2008). *Two Bits: The Cultural Significance of Free Software,* Durham, NC: Duke University Press.

Kemper, J., & Kolkman, D. (2019). 'Transparent to whom? No algorithmic accountability without a critical audience'. *Information, Communication & Society,* **22** (14), 2081–2096.

King, G., Pan, J., & Roberts, M. E. (2013). 'How censorship in China allows government criticism but silences collective expression'. *American Political Science Review,* **107** (2), 326–343.

Knudsen, T. (2003). *Offentlighed i Det Offentlige. Om Historiens Magt,* Aarhus: Aarhus Universitetsforlag.

Laux, J., Wachter, S., & Mittelstadt, B. (2024). 'Trustworthy artificial intelligence and the European Union AI Act: On the conflation of trustworthiness and acceptability of risk'. *Regulation & Governance,* **18** (1), 3–32. https://doi.org/10.1111/rego.12512.

Lipton, Z. C. (2018). 'The mythos of model interpretability: In machine learning, the concept of interpretability is both important and slippery'. *Queue,* **16** (3), 31–57.

Lyon, D. (2014). 'Surveillance, Snowden, and big data: Capacities, consequences, critique. *Big Data & Society,* **1** (2), 2053951714541861.

Mittelstadt, B., Allo, P., Taddeo, M., Wachter, S., & Floridi, L. (2016). 'The ethics of algorithms: Mapping the debate'. *Big Data & Society,* **3** (2).

Mulgan, R. (2000). '"Accountability": An ever-expanding concept?'. *Public Administration,* **78** (3), 555–573.

Newlands, G. (2021). 'Lifting the curtain: Strategic visibility of human labour in AI-as-a-Service'. *Big Data & Society,* **8** (1), 20539517211016026.

Noble, S. U. (2018). *Algorithms of Oppression,* New York: New York University Press.

O'Neil, C. (2016). *Weapons of Math Destruction: How Big Data Increases Inequality and Threatens Democracy,* New York: Penguin Books.

Open Government Partnership. (2021). 'Building public algorithm registers: Lessons learned from the French approach'. Open Government Partnership. 12 May 2021. https://www.opengovpartnership.org/stories/building-public-algorithm-registers-lessons-learned-from-the-french-approach/.

Pasquale, F. (2015). *The Black Box Society: The Secret Algorithms that Control Money and Information*, Cambridge, MA: Harvard University Press.

Paul, R. (2022). 'Can critical policy studies outsmart AI? Research agenda on artificial intelligence technologies and public policy'. *Critical Policy Studies*, **16** (4), 497–509.

Plantin, J. C., Lagoze, C., Edwards, P. N., & Sandvig, C. (2018). 'Infrastructure studies meet platform studies in the age of Google and Facebook'. *New Media & Society*, **20** (1), 293–310.

Radu, R. (2021). 'Steering the governance of artificial intelligence: National strategies in perspective'. *Policy and Society*, **40** (2), 178–193.

Reinhardt, K. (2023). 'Trust and trustworthiness in AI ethics'. *AI Ethics*, **3**, 735–744. https://doi.org/10.1007/s43681-022-00200-5.

Rose-Ackerman, S. (2005). *From Elections to Democracy: Building Accountable Government in Hungary and Poland*, New York: Cambridge University Press.

Sandvig, C., Hamilton, K., Karahalios, K., & Langbort, C. (2014). 'Auditing algorithms: Research methods for detecting discrimination on internet platforms'. *Data and Discrimination: Converting Critical Concerns into Productive Inquiry*, **22**, 4349–4357.

Schudson, M. (2015). *The Rise of the Right to Know: Politics and the Culture of Transparency, 1945–1975*, Cambridge, MA: Belknap Press: An Imprint of Harvard University Press.

Schulz-Forberg, H., & Stråth, B. (2010). 'Soft and strong European public spheres', in R. Frank, H. Kaelble, M. Lévy, & L. Passerini (eds), *Building a European Public Sphere: From the 1950s to the Present*, Brussels: PIE-Peter Lang, pp. 55–76.

Skinner, Q. (1989). 'Language and political change', in T. Ball, J. Farr, & R. L. Hanson (eds), *Political Innovation and Conceptual Change*, Cambridge: Cambridge University Press, pp. 6–23.

Srnicek, N. (2017). *Platform Capitalism*, Polity. Cambridge.

Stohl, C., Stohl, M., & Leonardi, P. M. (2016). Managing opacity: Information visibility and the paradox of transparency in the digital age. *International Journal of Communication*, **15** (10), 123–137.

Tsamados, A., Aggarwal, N., Cowls, J., Morley, J., Roberts, H., Taddeo, M., & Floridi, L. (2022). 'The ethics of algorithms: Key problems and solutions'. *AI & Society*, **37** (1), 215–230.

Ulnicane, I., Knight, W., Leach, T., Stahl, B. C., & Wanjiku, W. G. (2021). 'Framing governance for a contested emerging technology: Insights from AI policy'. *Policy and Society*, **40** (2), 158–177.

UK Government. (2023). 'Algorithmic Transparency Recording Standard – Guidance for Public Sector Bodies'. GOV.UK. 5 January. https://www.gov.uk/government/publications/guidance-for-organisations-using-the-algorithmic-transparency-recording-standard/algorithmic-transparency-recording-standard-guidance-for-public-sector-bodies.

Van Dijck, J., Poell, T., & De Waal, M. (2018). *The Platform Society: Public Values in a Connective World*, Oxford: Oxford University Press.

Varošanec, I. (2022). 'On the path to the future: Mapping the notion of transparency in the EU regulatory framework for AI'. *International Review of Law, Computers & Technology*, **36** (2), 95–117, DOI: 10.1080/13600869.2022.2060471.

von Eschenbach, W. J. (2021). 'Transparency and the black box problem: Why we do not trust AI'. *Philosophy & Technology*, **34** (4), 1607–1622.

Wachter, S., Mittelstadt, B., & Floridi, L. (2017). 'Why a right to explanation of automated decision-making does not exist in the general data protection regulation'. *International Data Privacy Law*, **7** (2), 76–99.

Wieringa, M. (2020, January). 'What to account for when accounting for algorithms: A systematic literature review on algorithmic accountability', in *Proceedings of the 2020 Conference on Fairness, Accountability, and Transparency*, pp. 1–18. https://doi.org/10.1145/3351095.3372833.

Yu, H., & Robinson, D. G. (2011). 'The new ambiguity of open government'. *UCLA Law Review Discourse*, **59**, 178–208.

Zuboff, S. (2015). 'Big other: Surveillance capitalism and the prospects of an information civilization'. *Journal of Information Technology*, **30** (1), 75–89.

14. Trust and trustworthiness in artificial intelligence

Rory Gillis, Johann Laux and Brent Mittelstadt

INTRODUCTION

The concepts of trust and trustworthiness increasingly frame debates about how to approach advances in artificial intelligence (AI). Policy-makers have correctly recognised that introducing new technology can affect people's trust in public institutions and have become concerned about related issues such as disinformation, bias, and fairness (Laux et al. 2024; Vesnic-Alujevic et al. 2020). It is, therefore, not surprising that the need to ensure that AI is trustworthy has found high-level international consensus in Brussels, Washington, Beijing, and beyond, even if consensus on the meaning of trust and trustworthiness remains elusive. Concurrently, in the private sector, companies have recognised the importance of trust in AI systems, and have been keen to implement tools to improve their perceived trustworthiness including signing pledges, developing ethics frameworks and principles, and joining responsible AI networks such as the Partnership on AI (Mökander and Floridi 2021). Amidst these developments the effectiveness of such self-defined commitments to ensure trustworthy, responsible, or ethical development, usage, and governance of AI systems has been widely questioned by academia and civil society (Mittelstadt 2019).

In academic scholarship there are long-standing and wide-ranging debates on trust and trustworthiness in technology. The concepts are central to a wide range of questions concerning technology development, usage, and governance. A vast related literature has consequently emerged, spanning psychology to computer science (Taddeo and Floridi 2011). Unfortunately, one result of the sustained interest in the concepts of trust and trustworthiness across disciplines has been a variety of overlapping and complex definitions and discussions which hinders interdisciplinary dialogue and led to conceptual confusion. These aspects of the field continue to inhibit the extraction of clear and widely supported design and governance requirements to guide the development and usage of AI systems within institutions (McKnight and Chervany 2001). Some scholars and policy-makers have even proposed abandoning trust and trustworthiness as concepts due to this lack of precision and the seeming inevitability that they will be given drastically different meanings across AI use cases and jurisdictions (Simpson 2012).

This chapter nevertheless attempts to extract key lessons from this literature for ongoing policy debates around AI and examine whether existing theories of trust are fit for purpose, meaning that they can be extended to AI without modification. It draws upon the review methodology and results reported in a recent article by some of the authors (Laux et al. 2024). This article reported on results of a systematic literature review of normative and empirical research on trusting AI in the public sector. This chapter builds on this prior analysis and incorporates philosophical research and theories of trust and trustworthiness, most notably work on interpersonal and epistemic trust.

To provide some organising structure to the diverse literature on trust and trustworthiness in AI it is sensible to start by examining the philosophical underpinnings of the concepts in order to prise apart possible definitions and their implications. Section 2 starts by distinguishing trust from trustworthiness before presenting a brief overview of philosophical work on theories and definitions. Three approaches to trust are addressed: (1) interpersonal trust, (2) institutional trust, and (3) epistemic trust. Section 3 takes a more grounded approach, reviewing prior empirical research on trust and trustworthiness in information technologies. Methods for improving trustworthiness at both the individual level and in the public and private sector are highlighted. Finally, Section 4 proposes three recommendations for current debates about AI governance.

DEFINING TRUST

This section provides an overview of philosophical literature relevant to conceptualising and operationalising trust and trustworthiness in AI. Three approaches are considered: (1) inter-personal trust, or the possibility of extending traditional models of trust between humans to include AI systems; (2) institutional trust, which examines trustworthy AI through a societal and organisational lens; and (3) epistemic trust, according to which AI is trustworthy if its outputs are true or justified.

Interpersonal Trust

There are various reasons people trust each other such as personal knowledge or previously witnessed actions. The lens of interpersonal trust enables examination of how AI systems fit into traditional relationships and trust dynamics between people, and whether such approaches can be extended to AI, effectively treating the technology as a human analogue. This would be a *sociotechnical* approach according to which technologies do not exist and operate inde-pendently of people or institutions, but rather embedded within pre-existing social relation-ships and structures (Sartori and Theodorou 2022; on public sector institutional logics and discretion vis-à-vis the advent of AI, see af Malmborg and Trondal, Chapter 5 in this volume; Busch and Henriksen, Chapter 6 in this volume).

Extending the notion of interpersonal trust to include AI systems may seem intuitively sensible at first glance because AI often augments or replaces human intelligence and decision-making tasks, meaning that it can functionally fill the same role as a person. Additionally, a common theme in the literature on interpersonal trust emphasises the impor-tance of vulnerability to trusting relationships. This is pertinent given that people's well-being is increasingly affected by decisions made or influenced by AI systems concerning allocation of basic resources such as housing, visas, or healthcare, which suggests a growing vulnera-bility towards them (Baier 2014). These observations suggest that it is worth seriously con-sidering whether it can be functionally equivalent to a person in traditional interpersonal trust relationships. With that said, some authors would challenge this intuition, on the grounds that AI systems lack the requisite capacities expected in interpersonal relationships (Miller and Freiman 2020) such as intentionality or agency (Laux et al. 2024).

The literature on interpersonal trust addresses relationships in which people are the objects of trust. Here, *trust* is generally understood as an attitude and *trustworthiness* as a property

(McLeod 2021). Person X (the "trustor") trusts person Y (the "trustee") as part of a relationship. In contrast, person Y is trustworthy to the extent that they have some set of properties Z. Properties that can contribute to trustworthiness are explored throughout this chapter. It is helpful to draw an initial ontological distinction between properties that are inherent or objective, and those that are external or subjective that contribute to trustworthiness. The former are "real" properties that people can possess which are recognised as inherently contributing to trustworthiness according to some theoretical account. The latter are "subjective" properties that are evaluated or assigned by a third party in adopting an attitude of trust towards another person which contribute to their externally perceived trustworthiness, based for example on personal subjective opinions of the third party and other people. The former inform the latter insofar as trustors may assign different importance to inherent properties, resulting in the phenomenon of "trustworthy" people being trusted by some people but not others.

This initial distinction suggests that for trust to be "well-placed", person X should only trust person Y if they are actually trustworthy. However, given that trust is an attitude, the capacities of trustors are also relevant to predicting whether a person or technology will actually be trusted. Prior research has shown that some people may have a higher disposition towards being trusting than others (McKnight and Chervany 2001). Such dispositions may also exist for trusting technology in the form of "automation bias" in a positive sense, and "algorithm aversion" in the negative (Jones-Jang and Park 2023). Automation bias can be attributed to individuals overestimating an algorithm's performance, for example its perceived accuracy, consistency in its performance, or superiority to human expertise (Jones-Jang and Park 2023). Algorithm aversion occurs when people prefer human predictions over algorithmic ones, even when the technology is known to perform better (Dietvorst et al. 2015). Research on the existence and impact of both phenomena remains inconclusive (Alon-Barkat and Busuioc 2023; Laux 2023).

Literature on interpersonal trust reflects broad agreement that trust requires the trustor to be *vulnerable* and the trustee to be *competent* and *willing* (McLeod 2021). How to define these terms remains a key area of disagreement in the field. Some scholars have challenged the idea that a trustee must be competent in general, arguing instead that they need only be perceived as capable of performing one or more expected tasks (D'Cruz 2019).

Theories of interpersonal trust often emphasise the importance of distinguishing trust from "mere reliance" where vulnerability is not present (Goldberg 2020). For example, office workers rely on the coffee machine working every morning without being vulnerable to it. Trust can be distinguished from reliance through (1) motives-based and (2) non-motives-based theories. These schools of thought disagree on how to define "willingness" in a trust relationship.

Motives-based theories suggest that person X can only trust Y to perform an action if Y is acting from a particular incentive or reason. Will-based accounts of trust, for example, suggest that trust can only genuinely exist in cases where the trusted party is acting from goodwill (Jones 1999). This explains why, when someone breaks our trust, we feel a sense of betrayal. Breaking trust reveals that the person is not acting for the praiseworthy reason(s) that we initially assumed. More stringent goodwill approaches require that Y must *owe* us goodwill, not just *display* it, for trust to exist (Cogley 2012).

Moralistic motives-based theories suggest that Y can only be trusted when there is evidence that their goodwill arises out of a moral motivation. Trust here is based not solely on goodwill but also on a shared understanding that failure to perform an action would be morally wrong.

A variety of moralistic accounts have been proposed that correspond to ethical theories. Philip Nickel's deontological account claims that trust creates a moral obligation, making it appropriate to blame or sanction someone who fails to fulfil their obligation (Nickel 2007). Nancy Potter has advanced a virtue-based approach, according to which trustworthiness is a virtuous character trait that can be honed in personal relationships (Potter 2002).

Goodwill and moralistic motives-based accounts emphasise the importance of the trustee having a particular motivation to act. In contrast, non-motives-based theories do not make demands about the reason that Y is performing the particular action that X trusts them to do. One influential example is the "participant stance" theory proposed by Holton, who argues that trust involves adopting only a particular practical attitude towards the trustee, rather than requiring any particular belief in their trustworthiness (Holton 1994). In taking this stance the trustor must be prepared to be betrayed to distinguish trusting relationships from relationships of reliance. This account is not motives-based because the participant stance can be adopted while acting from a variety of reasons or motives. Another example is Hawley's commitment account of trust, which suggests that the importance of trust to a particular relationship need not be acknowledged or understood for a trusting relationship to exist (Hawley 2017). Rather, participants need only have a particular commitment and to act accordingly. This commitment encourages people to rely on others to perform actions and not betray their interests. Again, the reason why someone acts to fulfil this commitment is not important, making this a non-motives-based theory of trust.

Extending interpersonal theories of trust to AI systems is difficult because they require trustees and trustors to have moral agency, meaning they can autonomously determine their motivations, goals, or other commitments.[1] None of these properties self-evidently exist in current narrow AI systems, meaning they lack "artificial agency" (Floridi and Sanders 2004; Mittelstadt et al. 2016). While AI systems can set goals, plan and execute actions to achieve them, autonomous behaviour is distinct from having mental states, motives, or intent which are necessary to have goodwill or a sense of moral obligation.

AI can thus not be treated as a human analogue in interpersonal relationships in a straightforward manner. At their most demanding, motives-based theories require that trustors consciously understand the importance of goodwill or the relevant moral reasons for acting. Even if a hypothetical general AI system could achieve "consciousness" or artificial agency in the future, this does not change the fact that motives-based theories of interpersonal trust are poorly suited to examine possible trust relationships involving narrow AI systems. Comparatively speaking, non-motives-based theories might initially appear more promising. However, the reliance of these accounts on the adoption of stances also seemingly rules out narrow AI systems that lack moral agency or intentionality. Verifying that AI systems are acting from a "participant stance" or through a sense of commitment to the individuals they are interacting with is a complex philosophical and technical challenge that would require an agreed model of artificial agency, which currently does not exist practically or theoretically.

Interpersonal accounts of trust offer helpful insight for debates around trustworthy AI but cannot be easily extended to explain what makes an AI system trusted and trustworthy. An alternative approach would be to establish interpersonal trust by proxy for AI systems, by which AI systems would be trusted if the people building them are trusted. However, this approach can be challenged on the basis that AI developers often have insufficient control or oversight of projects to guarantee trustworthy systems in practice (Seger 2022). Given this limitation it may therefore be sensible to move away from individual, interpersonal trust and instead examine trust at an institutional level.

Institutional Trust

New technologies are often integrated into institutions with existing decision-making structures and hierarchies. The integration of AI into these structures can impact people's trust in institutions (Bodó 2021). AI being integrated into a healthcare institution might increase the institution's level of trustworthiness, for example, if it improves diagnostic accuracy in clinical settings.

Research on institutional trust addresses issues such as citizen trust in state institutions and its role in societal development (Sønderskov and Thisted Dinesen 2016; Spadaro et al. 2020). This section focuses on three ways of improving the trustworthiness of AI systems in institutions in the public and private sectors.

Demands for accountable AI are common in the public sector due to impacts on citizens' rights and interests. Citizens may be owed an explanation as to how AI makes decisions or why its usage is justified in a given public institution (Lazar 2022). If reasons are not offered, the roll-out of AI seems, for many authors, unacceptably authoritarian. A variety of proposals to improve accountability have been advanced, from general proposals to improve the transparency or fairness of AI systems, to more concrete ones including the creation of independent tribunals to review decisions or improved data management frameworks (Harrison and Luna-Reyes 2020; Kitsos 2020; Robinson 2020; Shah 2018; Wilson and van der Velden 2022; for a systematic summary of the debate, see Cobbe and Singh, Chapter 7 in this volume). This multiplicity of approaches to improve trustworthiness introduces a danger of "framework shopping", in which institutions choose means that best suit their interests rather than those that are ideal for citizens.

Creating accountable AI in practice faces many potential challenges. Transparency is a double-edged sword. While it is generally agreed that some degree of transparency is a necessary condition for accountability, greater transparency does not always increase accountability (de Bruijn et al. 2022). Disclosures may reveal inadequate implementations of AI or weaknesses in institutional structures and decision-making that erodes trust in practice. However, a lack of public knowledge about how AI operates, for example in cases where information cannot be shared due to privacy or intellectual property considerations, can also reduce confidence and trust in the system (de Bruijn et al. 2022). The utility of transparency can also be restricted by social context. AI systems making impactful decisions in a politicised environment may face public distrust regardless of how they are explained or justified. Achieving institutional trust is thus not a simple matter of increasing transparency to automatically increase accountability (for a wider discussion of transparency as a regulatory principle, see Aula and Erkkilä, Chapter 13 in this volume).

Consent is a core tenet of institutional trust in AI. At first glance the concept appears inherently desirable; the freedom of citizens to consent to or reject the usage of AI systems in the public sector respects both citizen autonomy and democratic principles (Wilson and van der Velden 2022). However, prior critiques of consent in other fields of research have shown that informed consent is often an impractical or impossible ideal, and may do more harm than good (Silverman 1989; Wachter and Mittelstadt 2019). It seems unrealistic, for example, to expect citizens to develop a detailed knowledge of how AI systems work to consent in an informed manner. Nonetheless, public implementation without consent could involve government coercion against the will of citizens. If the ability to use or access a public service is dependent on consenting to usage of AI and non-AI-based alternatives are lacking, consent risks being meaningless. Alternative notions of consent based on institutional trustworthiness rather than individual knowledge of AI functionality, such as "trust-based consent" (Pickering 2021) or stewardship-based models inspired by biobanks (Henderson et al. 2013), may prove better suited to public uses of AI.

Relatedly, literature on institutional trust also focuses on possible trust proxies for AI systems through the notion of mediated trust (Bodó 2021). According to this approach trust can be imbued in a varied set of "trust mediators", for example through platforms purpose-built to increase levels of trust in AI development or usage (Wilson and van der Velden 2022). To take this approach forward, further research will be needed to identify reliable institutional preconditions of trust. Take human oversight of AI systems as an example: while the assurance that a human is involved in the decision loop of an AI system can raise its perceived trustworthiness, proper institutional design is required to ensure oversight is meaningful and effective (Laux 2023b).

Epistemic Trust

Literature on epistemic trust begins from a different starting point than interpersonal and institutional trust by asking the practical question of when individuals are justified in trusting the decisions or outputs of AI systems. Trust is an epistemologically rich topic because reliance on individuals to tell the truth presumes a situation in which the trustor has insufficient evidence or knowledge to independently determine the truth of another person's statements. In such cases it is intuitively difficult to identify sufficient conditions to believe the statements. The same challenge exists for belief in the truth of predictions, classifications, or other AI outputs.

Truth-based accounts focus on the conditions that an individual must meet for someone else to trust or believe that their testimony or statements are truthful. A basic distinction in theories of epistemic trust is between internalist and externalist accounts of truth.[2] According to internalist accounts, person X will trust the decision or testimony of Y if good reasons exist to believe that Y is telling the truth. In practice this can mean making rough estimates of the trustworthiness of Y when considering the information at hand, and updating this assessment over time (Hardin 2002). Here, trust is an ongoing process rather than a static product or characteristic of a relationship. Decisions about trust remain open to revision as further evidence comes to light.

Externalist accounts focus on different factors to assess an individual's trustworthiness. For example, trust can be justified if statements are produced by a reliable thinking process (McLeod 2002). By this approach distrust is warranted of judgements that are too reliant on intuition. This differs from an internalist account when reasons play an operative role in determining a person's trustworthiness, such as their past actions or characteristics. Here, the processes through which our reasons for distrust are formed are the determining factor.

More recently, some authors have looked for ways to sidestep traditional debates in epistemology by foregrounding the notion that we can be justified in our beliefs that an individual is trustworthy without also needing to defend the view that our beliefs are true. One example of a nondemanding epistemic account of trustworthiness defines common identifiers of trust that can be considered when interacting with an individual (Goldman 1999). For AI these identifiers can be characteristics such as the transparency and accountability of systems.

Justification-based accounts avoid reliance on contentious epistemological premises found in truth-based accounts about which reasonable people may disagree, and thus may fit better with the introduction of AI into the public sector in pluralistic liberal societies (Rawls 1996). Some authors have, therefore, turned to the concept of justifiability rather than truth (Estlund 1998). For example, a "public reason" account of trust may be better suited to AI than truth-based accounts (Binns 2018). This approach sets limits on the types of reasons that can be given to justify the actions of an AI system. Justification must appeal to reasons that all citizens can accept, and not rely on contested philosophical, moral, or religious views (Binns 2018). Doing so sidesteps epistemological questions regarding truth in evaluating the trustworthiness of a system, but requires sufficient transparency to enable public assessment of the reasons behind AI outputs.

GAINING TRUST

In contrast to the theoretical literature reviewed above, this section discusses empirical research on determinants of institutional trust with a particular focus on the use of AI in public institutions. The literature reviewed here represents a wide range of research methods and disciplines, from attachment theory to papers in social psychology. Comparing results and generalising findings beyond individual studies is thus particularly difficult (Laux et al. 2024). Empirical determinants of institutional trust can be examined through (1) individual and (2) institutional lenses.

Starting with the individual level, one emerging theme in the literature concerns the existence and impact of "algorithm aversion" (AA) (Dietvorst et al. 2015). This concept addresses humans trusting AI outputs less than equivalent human statements, even if the system is shown to be more accurate or otherwise performs at a higher level. One study on AI in the legal system found that the perceived trust of human judges is higher than algorithmic judges amongst US residents (Yalcin et al. 2022). Technical and emotional complexities were found to reduce trust in human judges, whereas only emotional complexities reduced trust in algorithmic judges. The study also demonstrated the importance of contextuality for trust, as factors such as unbiasedness, fairness, and predictability played a particularly important role in determining citizens' levels of trust.

Other studies have cast doubt on the existence and impact of AA. One such study examined algorithmic systems used for forecasting geopolitical events and predicting recidivism in criminal justice (Kennedy et al. 2022). Their results did not wholly support the existence of AA, and instead found that respondents gave weight to advice from algorithmic systems. With that said, humans-in-the-loop were viewed as a means to increase trust, and some respondents preferred human involvement in a hybrid use case. A variety of other empirical studies have shown that people often choose not to rely on algorithmic advice, but this attitude cannot be unambiguously attributed to AA (Laux 2023a).

Through an institutional lens one suggested means of improving trustworthiness in institutions relevant to AI is increased open communication. Clear communication by government or public bodies of their reasons for introducing AI systems and benefits to citizens is hypothesised to improve citizens' trust of the technology. Prior studies have examined communication and trust in automated public services; a study on chatbots, for example, found difficulty in inspiring trust in sensitive areas like parental support (Aoki 2020). Another study on AI decision-making in the delivery of public services in the Japanese nursing sector highlighted the importance of communicating the intended purpose of AI and that a human is "in the loop" (Aoki 2021).

Clear communication of the added value of AI has also been proposed to improve trust in public sector AI. A study on Chinese citizens investigated whether usage of AI voice robot services can increase perceptions of government transparency or trust. The introduction of the "tax baby" AI voice system, designed to offer feedback to citizens about tax issues, was not found to significantly affect trust in government. In the UK, the Government Data Science Partnership reviewed empirical evidence on the acceptability of data science in government. They found that engagement can decrease when risks are communicated, showing how transparency and domain knowledge can reduce levels of trust and increase citizen scepticism (Drew 2016).

Empirical determinants of trust also vary by sector. Research on political economy has found that citizens have differing levels of trust towards governmental, corporate, and multi-stakeholder institutions in the development of AI. A survey of US residents revealed low to moderate level of trust in governmental, corporate, and multi-stakeholder institutions, higher trust in university researchers, and very low level of trust in organisations like Facebook (Zhang and Dafoe 2020).[3]

FURTHERING TRUST

The literature reviewed above suggests many ways that current debates in AI policy and governance can benefit from prior work on trustworthiness. Even if trustworthy AI is agreed upon as a desirable goal, there remain difficult decisions about how best to achieve it. A key distinction here is between "soft law" (or self-regulation) or "hard law". Soft law is often presented as more versatile and easily achievable, as it does not require passing new legislation or the political manoeuvring that such legislation involves. Self-regulation approaches that have been proposed to improve the AI trustworthiness include greater diversity in the technology workforce, ethics training, codes of conduct for data scientists, and greater reflexivity via independent deliberative bodies and think tanks (Shah 2018). Certification and accreditation programmes may likewise be helpful (Mittelstadt 2019).

Proponents of hard law often make two kinds of arguments. Firstly, there are many types and prior examples of harms that policy-makers may want to attribute to companies developing AI. These companies would not intuitively be the obvious choice to independently develop best practices around trustworthy and responsible AI. Biases in facial recognition systems have shown this problem in practice (Buolamwini and Gebru 2018). Rather than acknowledging or addressing known ethical problems, companies may instead prefer to avoid blame altogether or otherwise minimise their commitments to specific actions and reforms. This can occur, for example, through "ethics-washing" by adopting a framework of ethical principles for AI development, usage, or governance that map well onto their current capabilities to address known problems (Mittelstadt 2019; Morley et al. 2021; also see Rönnblom, Carlsson and Padden, Chapter 9 in this volume). To counter incentives for AI companies to avoid public interest interventions hard law can institutionalise reasonable distrust in AI oversight, for example by demanding evidence-based, public justifications of AI-safety provisions (Green 2022; Laux 2023b). In turn, institutionalised distrust in AI oversight may then further people's trust in AI systems (Laux 2023b; Sztompka 2000).

Legal provisions are also arguably better placed to address risks arising from power asymmetries in AI development and governance (Kuziemski and Misuraca 2020). The existence of power asymmetries has spurred thinking on how AI development could be restructured in a fairer manner (Gerdes 2021; Laux et al. 2021).

Other scholars have focused on extending existing legal statutes to cover the harms created by AI. Much discussion has centred on data protection law, non-discrimination law, and the role of sector specific regulations. Extending the foundations of non-discrimination law could, for example, help address types of bias and discrimination unique to AI (Wachter 2022; for a critical discussion of regulatory obsessions with bias, see Hong, Chapter 8 in this volume). AI can classify people into new kinds of unintuitive groups that have not previously been protected by non-discrimination law and yet experience similar harms to groups currently protected by the law.

Both hard and soft law approaches can help achieve trustworthy AI. The public and private sector are increasingly working together which creates opportunities to combine these approaches. Cybersecurity, which has traditionally been the domain of nation-states, provides a helpful model. AI companies have expressed concerns related to the security and safety of their products. In cybersecurity governments have worked successfully with private sector groups, such as through the UK's National Cyber Security Centre (Carr 2016), by sharing data about potential threats and co-developing defences. Governments can and are actively including industry in developing regulations and technical standards to meet legal obligations in practice (Laux et al. 2023); it remains to be seen, however, whether a public–private model of regulation improves or degrades the perceived trustworthiness of AI systems, manufacturers, and users.

The co-development of technical standards is particularly relevant for AI. Public–private standards setting initiatives are currently being led by standard-setting organisations such as the International Organization for Standardization (ISO), the European Committee for Standardisation (CEN) and the (European Committee for Electrotechnical Standardization (CENELEC). While counting as soft law, some standards offer certification and, as in the case of the EU Artificial Intelligence Act (AI Act), a presumption of conformity with hard law (cf. Art. 40 AI Act). Standardisation, however, regularly proceeds under the strong influence of industry representatives (Egan 1998). Largely a technical discourse, standards have also been found to be lacking in (democratic) legitimacy (Ebers 2021). At this point in time, it is an open question whether future AI standards will meaningfully address difficult ethical problems associated with the development and usage of AI systems. If, for example, standards were to include more stringent disclosure rules this would allow local AI stakeholders to make complex normative decisions regarding the deployment of AI systems and, hence, possibly increase their trust in the technology (Laux et al. 2023).

Policy levers not directly related to AI can also be applied holistically or indirectly to improve the trustworthiness of AI and address the technology's risks and impact. Integrating AI in a trustworthy manner into the public sector, for example, has been said to require greater focus on the trustworthiness of public institutions themselves. Poorly implemented and communicated policies can reduce estimations of government transparency and can therefore erode trust in future AI deployments (Robinson 2020).

CONCLUSION

This chapter has offered an introduction to some of the key debates around trust and trustworthiness, and highlighted the implications of such debates for discussions concerning policy and governance in AI.

Section 2 discussed the diversity and lack of uniformity in prior conceptualisations of trust and trustworthiness, and considered three ways of extending these concepts to account for AI systems through theories of interpersonal trust, institutional trust, and epistemic trust. Extending traditional models of motives-based and non-motives-based theories of trust to AI systems would be technologically demanding, but institutional approaches and epistemic approaches may fare better in concentrating on the social context of the technology and whether its outputs can be treated as true or justified. Section 3 surveyed empirical studies on means of gaining trust, including means to improve trust at the individual and institutional level. In the introduction of AI in the public sector, the importance of accountability and consent are particularly noteworthy. Difficulties facing AI in the private sector were also highlighted, in particular predispositions of citizens to be less trusting of the motivations of large organisations. Finally, in Section 4, the chapter identified promising contributions of this literature to modern debates around AI policy and governance focusing on soft law and hard law approaches, technical standardisation, and indirect policy levers to improve the trustworthiness of public institutions adopting AI.

Trust and trustworthiness have a long and diverse history in academic research, policy, and governance. AI can and will be used as a type of human analogue, augmenting, or replacing critical human expertise and decision-making at scale across the public and private sectors. While universal agreement on the meaning and requirements for trustworthy institutions and technology remains out of reach, this should not be used as a barrier to bring these concepts down to the ground and translate them into effective policy and governance with the utmost urgency.

NOTES

1. Even if it is not possible to extend theories of interpersonal trust to cover relationships between people and AI systems, this does not necessarily signal a failing of such theories. Many of the authors referenced here did not intend for their theories to cover technological trust.
2. Though this is the main division in the literature, there are important theories that do not fall under this categorisation. For a fuller exploration of divisions in the field, see Faulkner and Simpson (2017).
3. It is important to note that this study took place shortly after the Cambridge Analytica scandal.

REFERENCES

Alon-Barkat, S. and M. Busuioc (2023), 'Human-AI interactions in public sector decision-making: "Automation bias" and "selective adherence" to algorithmic advice', *Journal of Public Administration Research and Theory*, **33** (1), 153–69.
Aoki, N. (2020), 'An experimental study of public trust in AI chatbots in the public sector', *Government Information Quarterly*, **37** (4), accessed at https://doi.org/10.1016/j.giq.2020.101490.

Aoki, N. (2021), 'The importance of the assurance that "humans are still in the decision loop" for public trust in artificial intelligence: Evidence from an online experiment', *Computers in Human Behavior*, **114**, accessed at https://doi.org/10.1016/j.chb.2020.106572.

Baier, A. (2014), 'Trust and antitrust', in D. T. Meyers (ed.), *Feminist Social Thought*, New York: Routledge, pp. 604–29.

Binns, R. (2018), 'Algorithmic accountability and public reason', *Philosophy & Technology*, **31** (4), 543–56.

Bodó, B. (2021), 'Mediated trust: A theoretical framework to address the trustworthiness of technological trust mediators', *New Media & Society*, **23** (9), 2668–90.

Buolamwini, J. and T. Gebru (2018), 'Gender shades: Intersectional accuracy disparities in commercial gender classification', in *Conference on Fairness, Accountability and Transparency*, pp. 77–91.

Carr, M. (2016), 'Public–private partnerships in national cyber-security strategies', *International Affairs*, **92** (1), 43–62.

Cogley, Z. (2012), 'Trust and the trickster problem', *Analytic Philosophy*, **53** (1), 30–47.

D'Cruz, J. (2019), 'Humble trust', *Philosophical Studies*, **176** (4), 933–53.

de Bruijn, H., M. Warnier and M. Janssen (2022), 'The perils and pitfalls of explainable AI: Strategies for explaining algorithmic decision-making', *Government Information Quarterly*, **39** (2), 101666.

Dietvorst, B. J., J. P. Simmons and C. Massey (2015), 'Algorithm aversion: People erroneously avoid algorithms after seeing them err', *Journal of Experimental Psychology*, **144** (1), 114–26.

Drew, C. (2016), 'Data science ethics in government', *Philosophical Transactions of the Royal Society A: Mathematical, Physical and Engineering Sciences*, **374** (2083), accessed at https://doi.org/10.1098/rsta.2016.0119.

Ebers, M. (2021), 'Standardizing AI – The case of the European Commission's proposal for an Artificial Intelligence Act', in L. A. DiMatteo, C. Poncibò and M. Cannarsa (eds), *The Cambridge Handbook of Artificial Intelligence: Global Perspectives on Law and Ethics*, Cambridge: Cambridge University Press, pp. 321–44.

Egan, M. (1998), 'Regulatory strategies, delegation and European market integration', *Journal of European Public Policy*, **5** (3), 485–506.

Estlund, D. (1998), 'The insularity of the reasonable: Why political liberalism must admit the truth', *Ethics*, **108** (2), 252–75.

Faulkner, P. and T. Simpson (2017), *The Philosophy of Trust*, Oxford: Oxford University Press.

Floridi, L. and J. W. Sanders (2004), 'On the morality of artificial agents', *Minds and Machines*, **14** (3), 349–79.

Gerdes, A. (2021), 'AI can turn the clock back before we know it', in B. Caron, K. A. Schmitt, Z. Pearl, R. Dara and H. A. Love (eds), *Internatinonal Symposium on Technology and Society*, vol. 2021 – October, Institute of Electrical and Electronics Engineers Inc., accessed at https://doi.org/10.1109/ISTAS52410.2021.9629161.

Goldberg, S. C. (2020), 'Trust and reliance', in J. Simon (ed.), *The Routledge Handbook of Trust and Philosophy*, New York: Routledge, pp. 97–108.

Goldman, A. I. (1999), 'Internalism exposed', *Journal of Philosophy*, **96** (6), 271–93.

Green, B. (2022), 'The flaws of policies requiring human oversight of government algorithms', *Computer Law & Security Review*, **45**, 105681.

Hardin, R. (2002), *Trust & Trustworthiness*, New York: Russell Sage Foundation.

Harrison, T. M. and L. F. Luna-Reyes (2020), 'Cultivating trustworthy artificial intelligence in digital government', *Social Science Computer Review*, **40** (2), 494–511.

Hawley, K. (2017), 'Trustworthy groups and organizations', in P. Faulkner and T. Simpson (eds), *The Philosophy of Trust*, Oxford: Oxford University Press, pp. 230–50.

Henderson, G. E., T. P. Edwards, R. J. Cadigan, A. M. Davis, C. Zimmer, I. Conlon and B. J. Weiner (2013), 'Stewardship practices of US biobanks', *Science Translational Medicine*, **5** (215), 215cm7–215cm7.

Holton, R. (1994), 'Deciding to trust, coming to believe', *Australasian Journal of Philosophy*, **72** (1), 63–76.

Jones, K. (1999), 'Second-hand moral knowledge', *Journal of Philosophy*, **96** (2), 55–78.

Jones-Jang, S. M. and Y. J. Park (2023), 'How do people react to AI failure? Automation bias, algorithmic aversion, and perceived controllability', *Journal of Computer-Mediated Communication*, **28** (1), zmac029.

Kennedy, R. P., P. D. Waggoner and M. M. Ward (2022), 'Trust in public policy algorithms', *Journal of Politics*, **84** (2), accessed at https://doi.org/10.1086/716283.

Kitsos, P. (2020), 'The limits of government surveillance: Law enforcement in the age of artificial intelligence', in G. Giannakopoulos, E. Galiotou and N. Vasillas (eds), *CEUR Workshop Proceedings*, vol. 2844, CEUR-WS, pp. 164–68.

Kuziemski, M. and G. Misuraca (2020), 'AI governance in the public sector: Three tales from the frontiers of automated decision-making in democratic settings', *Telecommunications Policy*, **44** (6), accessed at https://doi.org/10.1016/j.telpol.2020.101976.

Laux, J. (2023a), *Institutionalised Distrust and Human Oversight of Artificial Intelligence: Toward a Democratic Design of AI Governance under the European Union AI Act*, accessed at https://doi.org/10.2139/ssrn.4377481.

Laux, J. (2023b), 'Institutionalised distrust and human oversight of artificial intelligence: Towards a democratic design of AI governance under the European Union AI Act', *AI & Society*, accessed at https://doi.org/10.1007/s00146-023-01777-z.

Laux, J., S. Wachter and B. Mittelstadt (2021), 'Taming the few: Platform regulation, independent audits, and the risks of capture created by the DMA and DSA', *Computer Law & Security Review*, **43**, 105613.

Laux, J., S. Wachter and B. Mittelstadt (2023), *Three Pathways for Standardisation and Ethical Disclosure by Default under the European Union Artificial Intelligence Act*, accessed at https://doi.org/10.2139/ssrn.4365079.

Laux, J., S. Wachter and B. Mittelstadt (2024), 'Trustworthy artificial intelligence and the European Union AI Act: On the conflation of trustworthiness and acceptability of risk', *Regulation & Governance*, **18** (1), 3–32.

Lazar, S. (2022), 'Power and AI: Nature and justification', in J. B. Bullock, Y.-C. Chen, J. Himmelreich, V. M. Hudson, A. Korinek, M. M. Young and B. Zhang (eds), *The Oxford Handbook of AI Governance*, Oxford: Oxford University Press.

McKnight, D. H. and N. L. Chervany (2001), 'Trust and distrust definitions: One bite at a time', in *Trust in Cyber-Societies: Integrating the Human and Artificial Perspectives*, Berlin: Springer, pp. 27–54.

McLeod, C. (2002), *Self-Trust and Reproductive Autonomy*, Cambridge, MA: MIT Press.

McLeod, C. (2021), 'Trust', in E. N. Zalta (ed.), *The Stanford Encyclopedia of Philosophy*, Fall 2021, Metaphysics Research Lab, Stanford University, accessed 3 January 2023 at https://plato.stanford.edu/archives/fall2021/entriesrust/.

Miller, B. and O. Freiman (2020), 'Trust and distributed epistemic labour', in J. Simon (ed), *The Routledge Handbook of Trust and Philosophy*, New York: Routledge, pp. 341–53.

Mittelstadt, B. (2019), 'Principles alone cannot guarantee ethical AI', *Nature Machine Intelligence*, **1** (11), 501–7.

Mittelstadt, B., P. Allo, M. Taddeo, S. Wachter and L. Floridi (2016), 'The ethics of algorithms: Mapping the debate', *Big Data & Society*, **3** (2), 2053951716679679.

Mökander, J. and L. Floridi (2021), 'Ethics-based auditing to develop trustworthy AI', *Minds and Machines*, **31** (2), 323–27.

Morley, J., A. Elhalal, F. Garcia, L. Kinsey, J. Mökander and L. Floridi (2021), 'Ethics as a service: A pragmatic operationalisation of AI ethics', *Minds and Machines*, **31** (2), 239–56.

Nickel, P. J. (2007), 'Trust and obligation-ascription', *Ethical Theory and Moral Practice*, **10** (3), 309–19.

Pickering, B. (2021), 'Trust, but verify: Informed consent, AI technologies, and public health emergencies', *Future Internet*, **13** (5), accessed at https://doi.org/10.3390/fi13050132.

Potter, N. N. (2002), *How Can I Be Trusted? A Virtue Theory of Trustworthiness*, Lanham, MD: Rowman & Littlefield.

Rawls, J. (1996), *Political Liberalism*, New York: Columbia University Press.

Robinson, S. C. (2020), 'Trust, transparency, and openness: How inclusion of cultural values shapes Nordic national public policy strategies for artificial intelligence (AI)', *Technology in Society*, **63**, 101421.

Sartori, L. and A. Theodorou (2022), 'A sociotechnical perspective for the future of AI: Narratives, inequalities, and human control', *Ethics and Information Technology*, **24** (1), 4.

Seger, E. A. (2022), *Experts & AI Systems, Explanation & Trust*, University of Cambridge.

Shah, H. (2018), 'Algorithmic accountability', *Philosophical Transactions of the Royal Society A: Mathematical, Physical and Engineering Sciences*, **376** (2128), accessed at https://doi.org/10.1098/rsta.2017.0362.

Silverman, W. A. (1989), 'The myth of informed consent: In daily practice and in clinical trials', *Journal of Medical Ethics*, **15**, 6–11.

Simpson, T. (2012), 'What is trust?', *Pacific Philosophical Quarterly*, **93** (4), 550–69.

Sønderskov, K. M. and P. Thisted Dinesen (2016), 'Trusting the state, trusting each other? The effect of institutional trust on social trust', *Political Behavior*, **38**, 179–202.

Spadaro, G., K. Gangl, J.-W. Van Prooijen, P. A. M. Van Lange and C. O. Mosso (2020), 'Enhancing feelings of security: How institutional trust promotes interpersonal trust', *PLoS ONE*, **15** (9), e0237934.

Sztompka, P. (2000), 'Trust, distrust and the paradox of democracy', *Polish Political Science Yearbook*, **29**, 5.

Taddeo, M. and L. Floridi (2011), 'The case for e-trust', *Ethics and Information Technology*, **13** (1), 1–3.

Vesnic-Alujevic, L., S. Nascimento and A. Pólvora (2020), 'Societal and ethical impacts of artificial intelligence: Critical notes on European policy frameworks', *Telecommunications Policy*, **44** (6), accessed at https://doi.org/10.1016/j.telpol.2020.101961.

Wachter, S. (2022), 'The theory of artificial immutability: Protecting algorithmic groups under anti-discrimination law', *Tulane Law Review*, accessed at https://doi.org/10.2139/ssrn.4099100.

Wachter, S. and B. Mittelstadt (2019), 'A right to reasonable inferences: Re-thinking data protection law in the age of Big Data and AI', *Columbia Business Law Review*, **1**.

Wilson, C. and M. van der Velden (2022), 'Sustainable AI: An integrated model to guide public sector decision-making', *Technology in Society*, **68**, accessed at https://doi.org/10.1016/j.techsoc.2022.101926.

Yalcin, G., E. Themeli, E. Stamhuis, S. Philipsen and S. Puntoni (2022), 'Perceptions of justice by algorithms', *Artificial Intelligence and Law*, accessed at https://doi.org/10.1007/s10506-022-09312-z.

Zhang, B. and A. Dafoe (2020), 'US public opinion on the governance of artificial intelligence', in *AIES – Proceedings of the AAAI/ACM Conference on AI, Ethics, and Society*, Association for Computing Machinery, Inc., pp. 187–93.

PART III

AI AND THE POLITICAL ECONOMY OF PUBLIC POLICY AND REGULATION

15. Decolonial critique in AI policy-making and policy analysis

Catriona Gray

INTRODUCTION

Whether it is in how we work, learn, care or move, AI technologies have become thoroughly embedded in our social and political lives. This chapter considers how decolonial thinking and practice can allow us to better understand, critique and contest their power. While it is generally accepted that technologies "have politics" (Winner, 1980), the meaning of such a proposition for AI technologies warrants further exploration. The term "artificial intelligence" has itself been subject to much critique – including decolonial critique (Mhlambi, 2021). While recognising that "AI" is something of a misnomer, we can nonetheless identify common attributes that allow us to delineate and study its conditions of possibility, as well as its techniques, processes and effects. AI technologies are often dependent on large volumes of social data, and are embedded in other systems, infrastructures and institutions. In other words, they are *sociotechnical* (Paul, Carmel and Cobbe, Chapter 1 in this volume). The axiomatic opacity and complexity of machine learning systems make their attributes, operations and effects particularly difficult to trace and characterise.

Out of this ever-denser thicket, critical AI research has attempted to reveal how power relations can be hidden or obscured in the design, integration and application of AI systems. It is now widely recognised that oppressive power relations shape the production and exchange of AI technologies (Kak, 2020), become encoded in their models (Benjamin, 2019; on notions of "bias", see Hong, Chapter 8 in this volume) and articulate with their effects (Noble, 2018). These relations can be doubly obscured, however, by our own use of inappropriate and overly reductive concepts, methodologies and empirics. The primary aim of this chapter is to set out how decolonial thinking can support our attempts to uncover these power relations (on different concepts of power in AI/policy settings also see Ulbricht, Chapter 3 in this volume).

From various disciplinary vantage points, recent scholarship has sought to uncover the colonial dynamics implicated in processes of digital transformation, datafication and automation (Birhane, 2020; Couldry and Mejias, 2019). Much of this work directly engages decolonial and postcolonial thinking (Adams, 2021). While opening important lines of inquiry for AI research and practice, these observations and critiques remain relatively scattered, and are not substantially pursued or reflected in formal policy-making. In the European Union (EU), for example, policymakers have, in line with the EU treaties, pursued the primary aim of market integration for AI products and services. Insofar as policymakers have attended to questions of justice and oppression, their focus has centred on relatively narrow notions of non-discrimination and the rights of EU citizens. These are, as any critical or decolonial analysis would hold, wholly inadequate as lenses with which to grasp the relationships between technologies and oppressive social relations.

In this chapter, I show how decolonial thinking can contribute to critical policy inquiry about AI by helping to better structure and expand the emancipatory potential of the field itself. I do this by first outlining what I mean by decolonial critique, and then showing how this can be mobilised to make sense of social transformations associated with AI. Various thinkers have detailed how colonial dynamics of wealth, power and knowledge are reflected in – and shape the production of – AI. I show that at least two further methodological and analytical advances are afforded: (1) a multiplication of the lenses we use to understand and recognise AI harms, and (2) a more critical account of the role of the state. To illustrate what a decolonial critique of "AI harms" can offer, I discuss the limitations of popular techniques for addressing "fairness" in AI, namely impact assessment and audit tools. To interrogate the place of the state in AI policy-making and analysis, I draw on the example of migration governance (see also Molnar, Chapter 23 in this volume).

DECOLONIAL CRITIQUE – A BRIEF INTRODUCTION

European colonial projects, which first emerged from around the late fifteenth century, have taken shape through many shifting and connected social processes, including extraction, dispossession, displacement, replacement, repression, enslavement, labour exploitation and reproductive alienation. Colonial rule would come in many guises, but all were subtended by relations of racial and gendered violence, cultural hegemony and varying forms of legal, political and economic control. Since these first encounters, colonial power relations have continued to shape global economic and political order. Key actors today include the Euro-American powers, international organisations like the World Bank, along with emerging global powers like China.

While any attempt to generalise about the entirety of decolonial thought – or indeed postcolonial and other anticolonial thought – would be futile (see Bhambra (2014) for a discussion of these distinctions), we can draw out some key analytical features of a broadly critical and decolonial approach. First, it is important to understand, and to take seriously, the fact that decolonial thinking and practice emerge not from within academic circuits of knowledge, but in sites of anticolonial struggle. Second, decolonial thinking offers a historicity not always available in the established Eurocentric canons, including that of social theory (Bhambra and Holmwood, 2021). Third, decolonial scholars are engaged in various ways in a de-universalisation of dominant ideas; in most cases via the displacement of Eurocentric Enlightenment thinking, and the excavation of alternative ways of knowing and being (Smith, 2021). Fourth, decolonial thinking can help us to connect different dimensions of oppression, including the material, the semiotic and the epistemic. That is, it can help us to better see how our structures of meaning and knowledge relate to our modes and methods of production and exchange. Finally, race is a central conceptual and empirical concern (though is not reducible to colonialism).

Perhaps the most central idea linking together these diverse bodies of thought is the importance of historicity. In other words, decolonial and other anticolonial perspectives allow us to see the contemporary world order as an outcome of contingent processes and events. This first requires recognition of the connectivities between the colonial present(s) and a past that is "imagined to be over but persists, reactivates, and recurs in transfigured forms" (Stoler, 2016, 33). Following a period of formal decolonisation, the reality of colonialism and its effects are far from negated. This historicised mode of inquiry also allows us to move beyond analogical thinking towards an understanding of how the contemporary world, even as it undergoes significant social and technological transformations (Gray, 2023), remains colonially ordered.

Aníbal Quijano (2007) first introduced the concept of "coloniality" to explain how colonialism has fostered power relations from the invention (Dussel, 1995) of "the Americas" in the fifteenth century onwards. For Quijano, and the Modernidad/Colonialidad research group, coloniality is modernity's mutually constitutive counterpart, and remains the most general form of domination across the globe. Walter Mignolo, who builds extensively on the concept, also conceptualises coloniality as maintained and enacted through a colonial *matrix* of power which encompasses appropriation as well as the imposition and control of authority, knowledge, subjectivity and economic orders (Mignolo, 2007).

Alongside these historicised analyses, many thinkers have sought to "decentre" or "provincialise" dominant European or Western ways of knowing and being. Colonialism inaugurated, whilst naturalising, ways of thinking about the world according to racial, cultural and epistemic hierarchies that are now thoroughly entangled in every domain of social life. In her influential essay *Can the Subaltern Speak?* postcolonialist feminist Gayatri C. Spivak explored the deep entanglements of knowledge and colonial violence. She developed the concept of *epistemic violence* to describe the "remotely orchestrated, far-flung, and heterogeneous project to constitute the colonial subject as Other" (Spivak, 1988, 280). This concept has been widely elaborated and applied (see e.g. Dotson, 2011), including to its own persistence as a feature of academic research. The Puerto Rican scholar Nelson Maldonado-Torres (2020) has summarised decolonial critique as pluriversal, intercultural and transdisciplinary. To resist and overcome epistemic violence, decolonial critique must encompass multiple registers of knowledge and expression, as well as plural methodologies.

An important point of disagreement for historians and sociologists, among others, has been the relationship between colonial rule and capitalist development. On this question, recent scholarship has put forward a revised interpretation that regards colonialism not as a mere "companion condition" (Bhambra, 2021, 308) to capitalist development, but as structurally and continuously integral to global capitalism and the very notion of "modernity". This recognition of the centrality of colonial histories and continuities within political economy offers a strong theoretical basis from which to study the colonial entanglements of information capitalism (Cohen, 2019) generally, and the place of AI technologies within those entanglements more specifically.

AI'S COLONIAL ENTANGLEMENTS – CONDITIONS OF POSSIBILITY AND PRODUCTION

Scholars of ICTs and digital technologies, including AI in particular, have drawn on decolonial critiques to study such technologies and their design, development, adoption and use. I organise these insights into those broadly concerned with the intellectual conditions of possibility for AI (including conceptions of the human and rationality) and those concerned with the material conditions of AI production (including the role of productive inputs such as labour, data and energy).

Intellectual Conditions of Possibility

As Adams (2021) observes, decolonial thought offers much more than simply a tool with which to problematise AI technologies or to enumerate the many harms associated with their design, adoption and use. It offers critical insights and methodologies for uncovering AI's very conditions of possibility. In this way, it is:

> an invocation to make intelligible, to critique, and to seek to undo the logics and politics of race and coloniality that continue to operate in technologies and imaginaries associated with AI in ways that exclude, delimit, and degrade other ways of knowing, living, and being that do not align with the hegemony of Western reason. (Adams, 2021, 190)

Despite its position at the conceptual core of AI, intelligence itself has been given surprisingly little attention in scholarship on AI. In one notable exception, Cave (2020) examines the highly problematic history and uses of intelligence, and intelligence testing, largely ignored in much AI discourse. The concept's trajectory can be traced through its applications in eugenicist and colonial projects.

The figure of the human is similarly ever-present in AI research and practice. It is central to how we think, metaphorically, about so-called machine intelligence, but also in our appeals for "human" oversight of AI systems (Williams, 2021). Our conceptions of what it means to be human cannot be thought of independently from the histories and legacies of colonialism or from "the technologies that made colonialism possible" (Risam, 2018, 84). Sylvia Wynter's creative and intellectual project of reimagining what it is to be human has aimed to unsettle the modern colonial episteme's (over)representation of the category of Man as human (Wynter, 2003). Wynter challenges the Western/European teleological conception of the human as constituted by biological properties; a conception that, she argues, gives rise to violent taxonomies and hierarchies of humanity, including those of race and gender. Citing Wynter, Parisi contends that we cannot approach the question of technology and what she calls "algorithmic thought" without accepting that mathematical and biological universalities are part of the global entanglements of technology and colonialism; that they are "enfolded in the neurocognitive neural networks of today's intelligent machines" (2021, 34). Reasoning based on these biocentric and mathematical universalisms can thus become taken for granted and concretised in AI technologies.

Colonial power dynamics have also been identified in many of the dominant techniques, logics and imaginaries of digital innovation and technological solutionism that underpin AI adoption (Madianou, 2019; Young, 2019; Khene and Masiero, 2022). This is particularly apparent in the fields of development and humanitarian action. Brooks (Chapter 16 in this volume) argues that the "platformisation" of global development and humanitarian action has not lived up to its promise of bridging digital divides. Instead, it has "extended surveillance of populations and prised open new markets while exacerbating inequalities and vulnerabilities". The "Data and AI for Good" movement which emerged over the past decade has strong continuities with earlier ICT4D initiatives. These kinds of initiatives, as Madianou argues, are developed in a way that "reworks colonial legacies of humanitarianism whilst also occluding the power dynamics at play" (Madianou, 2021, 851). A decolonial analysis, she goes on to argue, not only reveals these power relations but also renders visible AI's "genealogies of enumeration, measurement and classification" in prior projects to control imperial subjects (Madianou, 2021, 854).

In many cases, contemporary AI technologies, including central features of system architecture, can be traced to earlier examples of technologies and governmentalities developed under colonial rule. Taylor et al. (2023) show, for example, how the Mahalanobis Distance Function – used in modern facial recognition technologies – was originally created for the purpose of caste and ethnic classification by the British colonial bureaucracy in India. It is now, as they put it, a "mobile racialized technique" embedded in machine learning systems (Taylor et al., 2023, 663). Similarly, biometric technology, which nowadays tends to use AI techniques, was first developed in India under British colonial rule (Sengoopta, 2003), and developed in other contexts such as post-Second World War Kenya (Weitzberg, 2020) and South Africa (Breckenridge, 2014). India is now home to the world's largest biometric identification programme, *Aadhaar*. Scholarship has traced these contemporary data practices to reveal how biometric data collection practices have "shape-shifted" into new forms (Dattani, 2023).

Material Conditions of Production

Scholars and other commentators have directed increasing attention towards the material conditions under which AI systems, and their various inputs, are produced. Exploitative labour practices, widespread in the development of AI systems, represent the most prominent example. These practices include the general hidden "free" and "unwitting" work involved in the training and maintenance of AI systems by users (Morreale et al., 2023). They also include more specific sites of labour exploitation; namely the precarious, low-wage, hazardous annotation and moderation performed by workers in formerly colonised countries (Perrigo, 2023; Roberts, 2019). In their study of AI annotation workers outsourced from France to Madagascar, Le Ludec et al. found that outsourcing fosters "an increasingly precarious globalised workforce of underpaid pieceworkers" (2023, 2) selected to produce AI solutions in production processes controlled by firms in the Global North. At present, consideration of this global division of labour is all but absent in regulatory policy-making for AI.

Another key input constituting AI systems is data. Most AI systems are ultimately dependent on large volumes of data, including social data – that is, data about people, and their identities, bodies, activities and relationships to their environments (Ricaurte, 2019). Large language models (LLM) like ChatGPT, for example, tend to be trained on a corpus of data scraped from web sources. In many cases, machine learning models are produced and maintained using data from subjects who have not consented or even been notified. As Abebe Birhane has put it, the representation of social problems as solvable through data-driven solutions, and of African populations as data-rich and ripe for mining, is "reminiscent of the colonizer attitude that declares humans as raw material free for the taking" (Birhane, 2020, 397–398).

The production of AI technologies involves not just exploitation of labour and expropriation of social data, but also extraction of resources including energy, water and land – resulting in highly unequal distributions of AI's ecological harms. Environmental justice has not been a major topic of AI research or policy proposals. Current regulatory proposals, including the draft EU AI Act, do not include damage to environmental sustainability as a high-risk category, and there currently is no standard process to certify the sustainability of an AI model or product.

Relations of infrastructural domination and dependency can be seen across global digital value chains (Kwet, 2019; Thorat, 2019; Nothias, 2020), including in AI. These not only mirror but emerge out of global relations of exploitation and underdevelopment (Rodney,

2018). At the time of writing, global powers are engaged in what has been described as a "chip war" (Miller, 2022) over the development and production of key components of AI architectures, including graphics processing units (GPU). Control of AI components and manufacturing is emerging as a key index of geopolitical power.

DECOLONISING OUR UNDERSTANDINGS OF AI HARMS – THE EXAMPLE OF AUDITS

In the previous section, I surveyed literature that allows us to connect colonial histories and legacies to the conditions that make AI possible, and to the conditions that shape how it is produced today. I now turn to our understandings of AI's harmful effects. Decolonial thinking can help expand both our own understandings of AI's harmful effects, and the use of evidence about those harms in the evaluation of AI systems.

The discriminatory effects of AI technologies are well documented (Eubanks, 2019) and widely acknowledged across policy settings, including in almost all official policy instruments. In 2020, for example, the United Nations Special Rapporteur on contemporary forms of racism, racial discrimination and xenophobia, and related intolerance, E. Tendayi Achiume, published a report on emerging digital technologies which argued that AI technologies that classify and sort people are discriminatory "*at their core*" (paragraph 7; emphasis added), and that they compound existing inequalities existing along "racial, ethnic, and national origin grounds" (paragraph 4). Whilst this analysis is well grounded in real examples of AI adoption and their highly unequal effects, it nonetheless assumes the conceptual foundations of dominant policy discourses and practices. This includes the use of discrimination as the key lens to conceptualise, organise and frame responses to all instances of inequality associated with AI.

Within legal scholarship, it is recognised that antidiscrimination law frameworks are not equipped to handle all issues of fairness in AI (Hoffmann, 2019; Wachter et al., 2020). At the same time, within the field of AI ethics and governance, there is growing recognition of the limitations of a singular preoccupation with bias (also see Hong, Chapter 8 in this volume). In their paper *Studying Up Machine Learning Data: Why Talk About Bias When We Mean Power?* Miceli et al. argue that "the very understanding of bias and debiasing is inscribed with values, interests, and power relations that inform what counts as bias and what does not, what problems debiasing initiatives address, and what goals they aim to achieve" (2022). Amongst other things, this shortcoming points to the need for theoretical, methodological and empirical approaches that draw on decolonial and other critical emancipatory projects. Arguably, however, these critiques have so far not made full use of decolonial theoretical insights. Bringing these into critical policy analysis could allow us to contest the very terms on which these problems are addressed in policy, as well as the conditions under which knowledge is admitted as evidence in policy-making.

In response to many of the harms associated with AI, significant attention has been given, in research and practice, to various tools for accountability such as audits and impact assessments. The EU AI Act includes a requirement for conformity assessment of high-risk systems, while the New York City algorithmic hiring systems law mandates third-party audits. An audit can be understood as a tool for evaluating the reality of a system's behaviour with respect to "clearly articulated expectations, standards and claims" (Raji et al., 2022). An impact assessment has a more prospective outlook and generally focuses on measurable outcomes.

As Metcalf et al. (2021) outline, there are important differences between (1) impacts as "evaluative constructs that describe the unintended consequences of algorithmic systems in ways that make them amenable to assessment and regulatory control" and (2) the "unintended consequences themselves [...]" (2021, 740).

A concern only with what can already be *seen* and *measured* is clearly at odds with any approach that seeks to dismantle dominant ways of seeing and measuring. Harms that are harder to "audit" or to render legible and quantifiable in an *ex ante* impact assessment may go unrecognised. For example, with the adoption of AI and related technologies to support decision-making, the targets of those technologies can often become objectified (Origgi and Ciranna, 2017, 305), particularly when they are treated as mere sources of information to be extracted, rather than as informants. Aimé Césaire, in his essay, *Discourse on Colonialism*, stated the equation of "colonization = thing-ification" (Césaire, 2020). The dehumanising effects of logics and practices of abstraction and objectification are not easily accommodated in audits and similarly schematic tools.

AI audit tools are further limited by the categories of social division they employ. For example, we can understand the gender binary as a phenomenon that is, in part, colonially instituted and maintained. While AI audits can help us to identify gender disparities in AI generated outcomes, they do not enable any critique of the very use of AI technologies to identify and classify targets by gender, i.e., the enactment of "auto-essentialization" of racialised gender (Scheuerman et al., 2021).

By limiting what counts as harmful, which categories and measures are to be used, and which remedies are available, AI evaluation and assurance-based policies will be of very little use in addressing much of the violence enacted through the development and use of AI. These strategies and measures proceed from a flawed assumption that we can ontologise, represent and measure instances of oppression. They tell us very little about how algorithmic harm is actually *lived*. Moreover, they locate sources of harm in non-relational ways i.e., according to liberal individualist conceptions of subjectivity, agency and causation (see Raymen, 2023).

A more historicised and finely tuned analysis of AI technologies allows us to regard oppression as neither additive, nor made up of ontologically equivalent or stable phenomena. Relations, processes and structures of race, gender, class, disability, caste, sexuality, etc. do not emerge or operate across the same geographies, or according to the same logics. This insight calls for a reconsideration of the types of knowledge and techniques used to evaluate, and to place "guardrails" on, AI systems and their outputs. It suggests the need for an expanded, and indeed more sociological, notion of AI harms that can accommodate multiple dimensions of oppression and their interactions. To be effective in shaping policy outcomes, such a reorientation would need to be accompanied by a more inclusive global policy environment for AI governance that no longer marginalises communities of the majority (see Omotubora and Basu, Chapter 17 in this volume).

Instead of appealing to, and refining, positivist audit and impact assessment tools (for rational choice undertones of much AI regulation discourse also see Paul, Chapter 20 in this volume), critical and decolonial AI policy analysis can draw on and develop plural knowledges. In practice, this would entail developing ways of analysing and evaluating AI systems based on knowledge about AI harms not as an abstract set of categories but as lived knowledge. Through decolonial critique, we can expand our understanding of AI harms and engage in more critical, fruitful and equal relations of knowledge exchange between research, policy and the lived realities of people impacted by AI technologies. This could help to undo hierarchies of knowledge in AI research and pedagogy (Raji et al., 2021), and allow us to better understand the multidimensionality of AI's power beyond individualised, linear and falsely quantified accounts of harm.

DECOLONISING OUR UNDERSTANDINGS OF THE STATE – THE EXAMPLE OF TECH IN MIGRATION GOVERNANCE

Many violent, harmful and indeed controversial applications of AI systems are also products of state violence. AI-enabled systems such as live biometric facial recognition surveillance are now regularly used in policing. Risk profiling systems have been adopted in prison probation (see Kaufmann, Chapter 22 in this volume) and border control (see Molnar, Chapter 23 in this volume), and automated decision-making has been used to administer, and deny, basic services such as housing and social benefits (see Sleep and Redden, Chapter 27 in this volume). Whilst many of these governmental uses of AI have been identified as racist and authoritarian, there is less recognition of their global or colonial origins and entanglements. Meanwhile, many political and policy analyses tend to locate the violence enacted by governing authorities using AI technologies in a failure of liberal democratic institutions to properly constrain the exercise of public power, rather than any constitutive feature of modern statehood.

Axster et al. (2021) offer a useful corrective to the "colonial unknowing" that runs through most accounts of state surveillance and social control. Through their formulation of the *global colonial archipelago*, they show how what we might often regard as "domestic" policies are, in fact, forms of global control that persist throughout the *longue durée* of racialised and colonial accumulation by dispossession. Such an analysis allows us to understand authoritarian applications of AI in public policy settings like policing and prisons as part of global entanglements that extend across borders and that implicate citizens and non-citizens alike. As they put it, "once we take seriously the idea of entangled or connected histories, it becomes clear that immigration control and incarceration share common transnational roots" (Axster et al., 2021).

When, in June 2023, the European Parliament voted by an overwhelming majority to adopt its position on the AI Act, commentators noted the decision to ban the use of many public biometric surveillance tools. Yet, the reach of these prohibitions does not extend to protect people on the move, including people seeking asylum. The EU's border agency, Frontex, has meanwhile continued to increase its spending on surveillance technologies, including AI (Napolitano, 2023). Many people who seek to gain entry to EU territory lack access to the rights protections available to citizens. AI technologies are now widely used in the management of global mobilities (Beduschi, 2021), and the EU has been instrumental in funding, developing and implementing new and experimental applications of technology, including AI, to deepen and expand its external border regime (Molnar, 2022). Though a first wave of AI-specific European legislation is now emerging in the form of the AI Act, many of the very applications used to surveil, differentiate and prevent people entering EU territory, are specifically excluded from its scope. Here, we can mobilise the words of Fanon: "You are making us into monstrosities; your humanism claims we are at one with the rest of humanity but your racist methods set us apart" (Fanon, 1963, 8).

Calls for an unproblematically "rights-based" approach to AI regulation assume an optimistic view of what this could achieve when access to rights remains largely tied to European statehood, sovereignty and citizenship.[1] To make sense of ostensibly rights-violating exceptions to a supposedly rights-protecting instrument, we must understand Europe's place in the world. Europe's post-war integration was not just a project of peace but one designed to shore up colonial dispossession (Hansen and Jonsson, 2014; Brown, 2022). A more critical embrace of human rights discourse might mean, for example, assuming a more *agonistic* form of human rights-based contestation that takes the identity of "humanity" to be one of ambiguity, not of closure (Hoover, 2016). Doing so opens a space from which to question the very legitimacy of the terms of membership on which European policy-making is predicated.

This exclusion of non-citizens in our analyses is symptomatic of a more general overreliance on the state (including its supranational forms) as a unit of analysis in scholarship and commentary on AI ethics and governance. Cross-disciplinary research on AI governance even suffers from a type of methodological nationalism, i.e., "the assumption that the nation/state/society is the natural social and political form of the modern world" (Wimmer and Glick Schiller, 2002, 301). In most policy frameworks and soft law instruments, for example, norms establishing expectations for AI accountability and redress often assume some form of state oversight and administrative capacity. Despite parallel processes of privatisation of governance underway (Supiot, 2017; De Gregorio, 2022), where the citizens, subjects and targets of AI technologies are concerned, the state remains their only recourse.

CONCLUSION

This chapter has presented perspectives broadly defined as decolonial, and discussed how they help us to unearth and understand the many unjust, harmful and undemocratic outcomes arising from the use of AI in public policy contexts (and beyond). Decolonial critique allows us to situate social and technological transformations more accurately and firmly within their historical and geographical contexts. Decolonial appraisals of AI have uncovered many colonial entanglements in the genealogies and epistemologies of AI, and in the conditions of AI technology production, AI governance and AI uses in the policy world. I elaborated two analytical advances that decolonial thinking can offer critical policy inquiry: a more conceptually and methodologically plural understanding of AI harms; and a key framework for problematising the role of the state.

At the time of writing, lively debates about the global politics of AI are taking place. Policy actors are embroiled in discussions about the most appropriate venues and modalities for governing AI. What role should the United Nations play, for example? Do we need a new international agency to oversee AI development? How can we peacefully resolve the so-called "chip wars"? These debates are at once a site for contestation over knowledge – whose voices, and which knowledges, are validated or discarded – and a critical juncture in the reordering of the global political economy. Along with other critical and emancipatory frameworks (e.g. feminism or an antagonist approach to ethics, as in Rönnblom, Carlsson and Padden, Chapter 9 in this volume), decolonial critique is one important lens we have available to identify and challenge the structural exclusions and obfuscations in mainstream AI policy. If our critical policy research agenda is to be oriented to goals of greater democratic oversight, freedom, justice and repair – and to be capable of seeing things beyond the perspective of the OECD world – decolonial critique must be made more tractable in AI policy analysis, if not in policy-making.

NOTE

1.   For a discussion of citizenship as a technology of colonial violence, see Shahid and Turner (2022).

REFERENCES

Achiume, E. T. (2020), 'Racial discrimination and emerging digital technologies: A human rights analysis', *Report of the Special Rapporteur on Contemporary Forms of Racism, Racial Discrimination, Xenophobia and Related Intolerance*, A/HRC/44/57, Geneva.

Adams, R. (2021), 'Can artificial intelligence be decolonized?', *Interdisciplinary Science Reviews*, **46** (1–2), 176–197.

Axster, S. et al. (2021), 'Colonial lives of the carceral archipelago: Rethinking the neoliberal security state', *International Political Sociology*, **15** (3), 415–439.

Beduschi, A. (2021), 'International migration management in the age of artificial intelligence', *Migration Studies*, **9** (3), 576–596.

Benjamin, R. (2019), *Race after Technology: Abolitionist Tools for the New Jim Code*, Medford, MA: Polity.

Bhambra, G. K. (2014), *Connected Sociologies. Theory for a Global Age*, London: Bloomsbury Academic.

Bhambra, G. K. (2021), 'Colonial global economy: Towards a theoretical reorientation of political economy', *Review of International Political Economy*, **28** (2), 307–322.

Bhambra, G. K. and Holmwood, J. (2021), *Colonialism and Modern Social Theory*, Cambridge: and Medford, MA: Polity.

Birhane, A. (2020), 'Algorithmic colonization of Africa', *SCRIPTed: A Journal of Law, Technology & Society*, **17** (2), 389–409.

Breckenridge, K. (2014), *Biometric State: The Global Politics of Identification and Surveillance in South Africa, 1850 to the Present*, Cambridge: Cambridge University Press.

Brown, M. (2022), *The Seventh Member State: Algeria, France, and the European Community*, Cambridge, MA: Harvard University Press.

Cave, S. (2020), 'The problem with intelligence: Its value-laden history and the future of AI', in *AIES '20: Proceedings of the AAAI/ACM Conference on AI, Ethics, and Society*, February 2020, pp. 29–35.

Césaire, A. (2000), *Discourse on Colonialism*, New York: Monthly Review Press.

Cohen, J. (2019), *Between Truth and Power: The Legal Constructions of Informational Capitalism*, New York: Oxford University Press.

Couldry, N. and Mejias, U. (2019), *The Costs of Connection: How Data Is Colonizing Human Life and Appropriating It for Capitalism*, Stanford, CA: California.

Dattani, K. (2023), 'Spectrally shape-shifting: Biometrics, fintech and the corporate-state in India', *Journal of Cultural Economy*. First Online.

De Gregorio, G. (2022), *Digital Constitutionalism in Europe: Reframing Rights and Powers in the Algorithmic Society*, Cambridge Studies in European Law and Policy, Cambridge: Cambridge University Press.

Dotson, K. (2011), 'Tracking epistemic violence, tracking practices of silencing', *Hypatia*, **26** (2), 236–257.

Dussel, E. (1995), *The Invention of the Americas: Eclipse of 'the Other' and the Myth of Modernity*, translated by M. D. Barber, Continuum: New York.

Eubanks, V. (2019), *Automating Inequality: How High-tech Tools Profile, Police, and Punish the Poor*, New York: Picador.

Fanon, F. (1963), *The Wretched of the Earth*, New York: Grove Press.

Gray, C. (2023), 'More than extraction: Rethinking data's colonial political economy', *International Political Sociology*, **17** (2), https://doi.org/10.1093/ips/olad007.

Hansen, P. and Jonsson, S. (2014), *Eurafrica: The Untold History of European Integration and Colonialism*, London: Bloomsbury Academic.

Hoffmann, A. L. (2019), 'Where fairness fails: Data, algorithms, and the limits of antidiscrimination discourse', *Information, Communication & Society*, **22** (7), 900–915.

Hoover, J. (2016), *Reconstructing Human Rights: A Pragmatist and Pluralist Inquiry in Global Ethics*, Oxford: Oxford University Press.

Kak, A. (2020), '"The Global South is everywhere, but also always somewhere": National policy narratives and AI justice', in *Proceedings of the AAAI/ACM Conference on AI, Ethics, and Society (AIES '20), Association for Computing Machinery*, New York, pp. 307–312.

Kwet, M. (2019), 'Digital colonialism: US empire and the new imperialism in the Global South', *Race and Class*, **60** (4), 3–26.

Khene, C. and Masiero, S. (2022), 'From research to action: The practice of decolonizing ICT4D', *Information Technology for Development*, **28** (3), 443–450.

Le Ludec, C., Cornet, M. and Casilli, A. A. (2023), 'The problem with annotation: Human labour and outsourcing between France and Madagascar', *Big Data & Society*, **10** (2).

Madianou, M. (2019), 'Technocolonialism: Digital innovation and data practices in the humanitarian response to refugee crises', *Social Media + Society*, **5** (3), 1–13.

Madianou, M. (2021), 'Nonhuman humanitarianism: When "AI for good" can be harmful', *Information, Communication & Society*, **24** (6), 850–868.

Maldonada-Torres, N. (2020), 'What is decolonial critique?', *Graduate Faculty Philosophy Journal*, **41** (1), 157–183.

Metcalf, J., Moss, E., Watkins, E. A., Singh, R. and Elish, M. C. (2021), 'Algorithmic impact assessments and accountability: The co-construction of impacts', in *Proceedings of the 2021 ACM Conference on Fairness, Accountability, and Transparency (FAccT '21), Association for Computing Machinery*, pp. 735–746.

Mhlambi, S. et al. (2021), 'AI decolonial manyfesto', accessed 23 July 2023 at https://manyfesto.ai.

Miceli, M., Posada, J. and Yang, T. (2022), 'Studying up machine learning data: Why talk about bias when we mean power?', in *Proceedings of the ACM Human Computer Interaction*, September, 2022.

Mignolo, W. D. (2007), 'Introduction: Coloniality of power and de-colonial thinking', *Cultural Studies*, **21**(2–3), 155–167.

Miller, C. (2022), *Chip War: The Fight for the World's Most Critical Technology*, London: Simon & Schuster.

Molnar, P. (2022), 'Territorial and digital borders and migrant vulnerability under a pandemic crisis', in A. Triandafyllidou (ed.), *Migration and Pandemics*, IMISCOE Research Series, Cham, Switzerland: Springer, pp. 45–64.

Morreale, F., Bahmanteymouri, E. and Burmester, B. et al. (2023), 'The unwitting labourer: Extracting humanness in AI training', *AI & Society*, https://doi.org/10.1007/s00146-023-01692-3.

Napolitano, A. (2023), 'Artificial Intelligence: the new frontier of the EU's border externalisation strategy', accessed 29 July 2023 at https://euromedrights.org/wp-content/uploads/2023/07/Euromed_AI -Migration-Report_EN-1.pdf.

Noble, A. U. (2018), *Algorithms of Oppression*, New York: NYU Press.

Nothias, T. (2020), 'Access granted: Facebook's free basics in Africa', *Media, Culture & Society*, **42** (3), 329–348.

Origgi, G. and Ciranna, S. (2017), 'Epistemic injustice: The case of digital environments', in I. J. Kidd, J. Medina and G. Pohlhaus (eds), *The Routledge Handbook of Epistemic Injustice*, New York: Routledge, pp. 303–312.

Parisi, L. (2021), 'Interactive computation and artificial epistemologies', *Theory, Culture & Society*, **38** (7–8), 33–53.

Perrigo, B. (2023), 'The workers behind AI rarely see its rewards. This Indian startup wants to fix that', accessed 4 August 2023 at https://time.com/magazine/south-pacific/6301976/august-14th-2023-vol -202-no-5-international/.

Quijano, A. (2007), 'Coloniality and modernity/rationality', *Cultural Studies*, **21** (2–3), 168–178.

Raji, I. D. et al. (2021), 'You can't sit with us: Exclusionary pedagogy in AI ethics education', in *Proceedings of the 2021 ACM Conference on Fairness, Accountability, and Transparency (FAccT '21). Association for Computing Machinery*, New York, USA, pp. 515–525.

Raji, I. D. et al. (2022), 'Outsider oversight: Designing a third party audit ecosystem for AI governance', in *Proceedings of the 2022 AAAI/ACM Conference on AI, Ethics, and Society (AIES '22)*, 1–3 August, 2022, Oxford, United Kingdom. ACM, New York, USA, 16 pages.

Raymen, T. (2023), *The Enigma of Social Harm: The Problem of Liberalism*, Abingdon, UK: Routledge.

Ricaurte, P. (2019), 'Data epistemologies, the coloniality of power, and resistance', *Television and New Media*, **20** (4), 350–365.

Risam, R. (2018), 'Decolonizing the digital humanities in theory and practice', in J. Sayers (ed.), *The Routledge Companion to Media Studies and Digital Humanities*, New York: Routledge, pp. 78–86.

Roberts, S. T. (2019), *Behind the Screen: Content Moderation in the Shadows of Social Media*, New Haven, CT: Yale University Press.

Rodney, W. (2018), *How Europe Underdeveloped Africa*, London: Verso.

Scheuerman, M. K., Pape, M. and Hanna, A. (2021), 'Auto-essentialization: Gender in automated facial analysis as extended colonial project', *Big Data & Society*, **8** (2).

Sengoopta, C. (2003), *Imprint of the Raj: How Fingerprinting Was Born in Colonial India*, London: Macmillan.

Shahid, R. and Turner, J. (2022), 'Deprivation of citizenship as colonial violence: Deracination and dispossession in Assam', *International Political Sociology*, **16** (2).

Smith, L. (2021), *Decolonizing Methodologies: Research and Indigenous Peoples*, London: Zed Books.

Spivak, G. C. (1988), 'Can the subaltern speak?', in N. Carry and L. Grossberg (eds), *Marxism and the Interpretation of Culture*, Urbana-Champaign, IL: University of Illinois Press, pp. 271–313.

Stoler, A. (2016), *Duress: Imperial Durabilities in Our Times*, Durham, NC: Duke University Press.

Supiot, A. (2017), *Governance by Numbers: The Making of a Legal Model of Allegiance*, Oxford: Hart Publishing.

Taylor, S. M., Gulson, K. N. and McDuie-Ra, D. (2023), 'Artificial intelligence from colonial India: Race, statistics, and facial recognition in the Global South', *Science, Technology, & Human Values*, **48** (3), 663–689. https://journals.sagepub.com/doi/abs/10.1177/01622439211060839?journalCode=sthd.

Thorat, D. (2019), 'Colonial topographies of internet infrastructure: The sedimented and linked networks of the telegraph and submarine fiber optic internet', *South Asian Review*, **40** (3), 252–267.

Wachter, S., Mittelstadt, B. and Russell, C. (2020), 'Why fairness cannot be automated: Bridging the gap between EU non-discrimination law and AI', *Computer Law and Security Review*, **41**, 105567.

Weitzberg, K. (2020), 'Biometrics, race making, and white exceptionalism: The controversy over universal fingerprinting in Kenya', *The Journal of African History*, **61** (1), 23–43.

Williams, J. (2021), 'Locating LAWS: Lethal autonomous weapons, epistemic space, and "meaningful human" control', *Journal of Global Security Studies*, **6** (4).

Wimmer, A. and Glick Schiller, N. (2002), 'Methodological nationalism and beyond: Nation-state building, migration and the social sciences', *Global Networks*, **2** (4), 301–334. https://doi.org/10.1111/1471-0374.00043.

Winner, L. (1980), 'Do artifacts have politics?', *Daedalus*, **109** (1), 121–136.

Wynter, S. (2003), 'Unsettling the coloniality of being/power/truth/freedom: Towards the human, after man, its overrepresentation – an argument', *CR: The New Centennial Review*, **3** (3), 257–337.

Young, J. C. (2019), 'The new knowledge politics of digital colonialism', *Environment and Planning A: Economy and Space*, **51** (7), 1424–1441.

16. The platformisation of global development

Sally Brooks

INTRODUCTION

The techno-optimism accompanying calls to "bridge digital divides" and harness the potential of digital technologies as "liberation technologies" for development at the start of the millennium is giving way to concerns about "adverse digital incorporation" (Heeks 2022). The Data for Development (D4D) field has been transformed by technological advances in big data analytics and the emergence of "platform capitalism" (Langley and Leyshon 2016), in ways that have yet to be reflected in global governance frameworks (Mann 2018). This chapter draws on key areas of literature to provide a brief critical political economy analysis of emerging issues and trends. It is structured as follows: the next section traces the evolution of D4D from its origins in humanitarian spaces, particularly refugee camps, which have become "living laboratories" for new technologies of digital surveillance (Iazzolino 2021). "Financial inclusion" initiatives deploying fintech platforms are also highlighted, as more diffuse laboratories for experimentation with new types of privatised behavioural governance. The subsequent section focuses on the digital platform as a business model whose raison d'être is the extraction of monopoly rents. In development settings, transnational firms have been able to profit from platform infrastructures that extend and lock in market dominance, capture monetisable data streams and stifle domestic economic development (Mann and Iazzolino 2019). The final section discusses processes of subjectification underway in the platformisation of global development. The contemporary behavioural "turn" in global development aligns with the deployment of platforms that scale up enrolment through algorithm-driven behavioural manipulation. In this case, platforms function as infrastructures of "high-tech modernism" that reorder societies into segmented populations of "users" and erode human agency by design (Farrell and Fourcade 2023).

DATA FOR DEVELOPMENT: A LIVING LABORATORY

D4D is a field of knowledge and practice that emerged in the mid-2000s as international organisations (IOs) such as the United Nations (UN) Global Pulse and the World Economic Forum (WEF) became aware of the potential of "'big data' (high-volume, machine-readable data)". Initially deployed by humanitarian agencies in the design of emergency responses, these data are increasingly seen "as a developmental resource" that can be applied to all manner of development problems (Mann 2018, p. 4). In developing country contexts where capacity of public institutions has been eroded by successive structural adjustment reforms, development agencies rely increasingly on big data analysis to inform intervention design. Debates about the governance of D4D, however, tend to reflect its origins in top-down modes of humanitarian response. These debates centre on a reductive view of development subjects as "beneficiaries of better designed developmental solutions", rather than as social and economic agents (Mann 2018, p. 7). This solutionist mindset obscures the politically charged contexts into which digital technologies are often introduced. Within the humanitarian field, for example, the use of big data analytics amplifies tensions between care and surveillance resulting from the increasing securitisation[1] and privatisation of contemporary humanitarianism (Iazzolino 2021).

The following examples (all from 2019) provide snapshots of a reality very different to the one envisioned in the early 2000s by proponents of "Information and Communication Technologies for Development (ICD4D)" as "liberation technologies" of the future (Heeks 2010): The World Food Programme's (WFP) engagement of US data analytics firm Palantir to "help streamline delivery of food and cash-based assistance across its global operations"; the launch by Facebook, Mercy Corps (a global humanitarian nongovernmental organisation) and various other commercial and non-profit partners of a cryptocurrency and cross-border financial infrastructure to facilitate "financial inclusion" (of which more later); and the WFP's decision "to suspend food and distribution in parts of Yemen, following the Houthi authority's refusal to accept the introduction of a biometric registration system" (Martin et al. 2023, pp. 1363–1364). Biometric verification and digital "financial inclusion" are two areas of D4D intervention for which there is a high level of support among IOs, philanthropic foundations and governments, so these warrant further discussion before returning to issues of global governance.

The use of biometric systems of verification in refugee camps exemplifies logics of solutionism and securitisation that underpin a "humanitarian rationality tasked with both managing and policing populations in need" (Iazzolino 2021, p. 111; also see Molnar, Chapter 23 in this volume). Iazzolino draws on ethnographic research in Kakuma refugee camp in Northern Kenya to contrast the "rigid moral categories" of aid workers with the more nuanced moral economy of refugees who view formal rules and transactions though a lens of social relations and mutual obligations. Aid workers value the "efficiency" of biometric systems, which they justify in terms of "fairness" (understood as the ability to police "illicit" claims and activities). For marginalised refugee groups without access to remittances, informal "illicit" activities like trading surplus rations are essential livelihood strategies that are threatened by the intensified surveillance capacity of biometric systems. In this case a suggestion by elders that acceptance of biometric registration be reciprocated in the form of increased food rations showed, not a misunderstanding of the rationale for the system, but a realisation that it threatened to "exacerbate their condition of subordination to Somali traders from dominant clans" through increased indebtedness. In this way, technologies viewed by implementers as introducing accountability and "fairness" amplified the marginalisation and stigmatisation of disadvantaged groups within the refugee population. Moreover, biometric "precision" concentrated accountability checks on those beneficiaries, rather than more significant instances of fraud further upstream in the humanitarian ecosystem (Iazzolino 2021, p. 123).

Perspectives of poorer refugees anticipating introduction of a biometric verification system show how these technologies "introduce a new sociotechnical layer" that "exacerbate[s] existing biases, discrimination [and] power imbalances ... against a backdrop characterised by securitisation of refugee policies" and "steeped in the country's postcolonial history". The neocolonial foundations of digital infrastructures and their tendency to amplify inequalities are themes to which we will return throughout this chapter (cf. Gray, Chapter 15 in this volume; Omotubora and Basu, Chapter 17 in this volume). Indeed, humanitarian intervention has been described as the "canary in the coalmine" for reimagining power in the digital age (Martin et al. 2023, p. 1366). As Iazzolino (2021, p. 114) notes, refugee camps are "spaces of exception" that have been turned into "living labs for experimentation without properly accounting for the risks associated with each technological component of the biometric assemblage" (an assemblage integrating biometrics, artificial intelligence (AI), and blockchain). While these technologies, which are increasingly employed outside these spaces of exception, in immigration and asylum processing are new, they revive a much older, colonial practice of rendering populations legible and therefore manageable (Scott 1998).

The promotion of digital finance infrastructures in humanitarian spaces is indicative of "the attention that corporate-philanthropic actors are paying to the need to 'financially include' refugees" (Iazzolino 2021, p. 114). This financial inclusion imperative is not confined to refugees, however. Since the 2008 Global Financial Crisis a global consensus has formed around financial inclusion as an overarching development paradigm for the Sustainable Development Goals (SDGs) era (Lahaye, Abell and Hoover 2017). This agenda centres on the promise of the financial technology ("fintech") sector to reach "unbanked" populations on their mobile phones. The fintech boom capitalises on "disruptive" innovations in credit risk assessment of consumers with no banking history based on harvested online behavioural data, or "digital footprints" (Gabor and Brooks 2017) and an emergent "platform" business model (of which more later). "Fintech platforms are highly capitalized by venture capitalists, private equity and other forms of investment", for example, that of for-profit foundations like the Omidyar Network. "Their core rationale … is the reintermediation of monetary and financial relations", particularly in sub-Saharan Africa "which is home to roughly three-quarters of the estimated 1.7 billion 'unbanked' people across the globe" (Langley and Leyshon 2022, p. 403).

Vulnerabilities created by tying digital finance to biometric verification systems were revealed in a radical experiment undertaken by India's Modi administration in 2016, when the Indian state rolled out a rapid programme of demonetisation of Rs500 and Rs1,000 banknotes. India's *Aadhar* biometric ID system, in place since 2010, had been unevenly applied and was already selectively mandatory for marginalised groups such as poor people receiving food rations. Yet it was the poor who were routinely shut out of a system that requires "having legible fingerprints and irises [excluding older manual workers and individuals suffering from malnutrition], … possessing mobile phones, [and] having a stable family life where the same registrant can collect rations from week to week". These requirements "point to a middle-class standard for normality rather than the precarity and unpredictability of the lives of the poor" (Taylor 2017, p. 5). The disproportionate burden of *Aadhar* on the poor was thrown into sharp relief during the 2016 demonetisation rollout, which placed demands on automated payment systems that discriminated against the poor. Poor people without access to mobile phones and formal banking systems were more reliant on these systems than other groups, yet at the same time more likely to be shut out of those systems because "*Aadhaar*-related technologies failed to identify them correctly" (Taylor 2017, p. 5; Masiero 2017).

Particularly when linked to biometric ID systems, digital financial inclusion can be viewed as a more diffuse "living lab" for experimenting with new forms of privatised behavioural governance that erase informal practices and untraceable exchanges (cash transactions, "illicit" trading) and render economic activities of previously out-of-reach populations legible for the first time. Jain and Gabor (2020) have gone as far as to predict the reorganisation of financial systems in the Global South around "digital infrastructures" in a process they call "digital financialisation", which allows "new seams of profit [to] be generated from increasingly granular surveillance of individual behaviour" (Jain and Gabor 2020, p. 814). In this context, the introduction of *Aadhar* and the transition to digital finance (accelerated by demonetisation) in India showcases a reorientation of state power towards "creating surveillance infrastructures" and generating demand for (rather than providing or subsidising) digital financial services "often by coercive means" (Jain and Gabor 2020, p. 824).

The above examples demonstrate how D4D implementation is fraught with macro- and micro-politics in ways that could not have been envisaged by ICT4D advocates in the early 2000s (Heeks 2010). Yet their assumptions continue to underpin the recommendations of IOs. The UN Global Pulse and WEF have led debates that emphasise the "win-win" logic of governance frameworks that encourage data *emission, personalisation* and *centralisation* (Mann 2018, p. 3). While this formulation facilitates ease of data access and use for development agencies, it also creates advantages for private firms poised to capture the commercial value of big data in the Global South. For example, the WEF has discouraged the practice, common in many African countries, of owning several SIM cards, and made the case for "tying subscriptions to demographic information … to ensure data generated by mobile devices is as individualised as possible" (WEF, 2012, p. 5). Personalisation of data is at the same time a core requirement of private firms seeking to mine data for commercially useful insights. Similarly, their reports showcase projects like IBM's "Lucy, a US$ 100 million lab in Nairobi" as an exemplar of the benefits of centralisation, enabling data to be drawn from diverse sources and brought to bear on multiple development problems. However the "preference for centralisation has also helped firms like Facebook and Mastercard to position themselves at the centre of a growing information network" (Mann 2018, p. 9).

Transnational corporations are thus emerging as the clear winners in the D4D landscape, particularly in sub-Saharan African countries, where they have "position[ed] themselves as custodians of data" about emerging economies in the region (Mann 2018, p. 7). Governance frameworks promoted by IOs effectively function as a de facto industrial policy through which African governments are "facilitating the learning and innovation of [transnational] firms", rather than developing national innovation systems that can "foster technological learning and upgrading" of their own economies (Mann 2018, p. 9). This de facto industrial policy also prevents citizens from acquiring capacity to make informed decisions about sharing their own data (Mann 2018). The consequences of this are particularly severe for poor and marginalised groups who tend to be subjected to more intense digital surveillance than other social groups (as was highlighted earlier in the case of *Aadhar* in India). These groups are disadvantaged, not by digital *exclusion* (as current governance frameworks would have it) but by "adverse digital incorporation" in systems that enable "a more-advantaged group to extract disproportionate value from the work or resources of another, less-advantaged group" (Heeks 2022, p. 689). In other words, inclusion becomes intrusion (Kaminska 2015). While D4D frameworks undermine national development, however, they do not necessarily weaken state power. Rather, state power tends to be *strengthened* by the "overlap between commercial and governance surveillance". This also has implications for democratic politics, as efforts to make societies more legible to corporations and humanitarian agencies can also "make opposition groups more visible to regimes" (Mann 2018, p. 5). In this scenario, extension of state power becomes the corollary of value extraction by transnational businesses.

GLOBAL DEVELOPMENT IN THE AGE OF PLATFORM CAPITALISM

The framing of what Heeks (2008) has called ICT4D 1.0 around a problem of exclusion from opportunity reflected the techno-optimism of the Web 1.0 age. It was also consistent with the economic orthodoxy of the time. The failures of structural adjustment under what became known as the Washington Consensus (Williamson 1990) had led to a re-evaluation of the role of the state in economic development in favour of new institutional economics (NIE) (Fine 2012). This is "a branch of economics that conceptualises economic development as being held up by market barriers in the developing world". Rather than "leave it to the market", as the Washington Consensus advocated, NIE prescribed an, albeit limited, role for the state in removing domestic barriers that stood between the individual entrepreneur and the global marketplace. In this context, Information and Communication Technologies (ICTs) were viewed as "liberation technologies, levelling the playing field", removing transaction costs and ultimately "flattening the global economy" (Mann and Iazzolino 2019, p. 1). This incrementalist approach assumed that individual level productivity gains would aggregate up to macrolevel improvements in domestic economic performance. This ignored well-documented lessons of successful "developmental states" that had intervened directly in the economy to support strategic sectors and channel reinvestment back into the domestic economy (Mann and Iazzolino 2019; Mkandawire 2001; Leftwich 1995).

The 2008 financial crisis transformed the global development landscape. In the first instance it triggered a "profound loss of faith" in fundamentals of neoclassical economics such as the idea of the self-regulating market (Berndt and Boeckler 2017, p. 284). NIE, it should be noted, had been embraced by international financial institutions precisely because, unlike developmental state theory, it offered a policy fix that left tenets of mainstream neoclassical economics intact. In the aftermath of the 2008 financial crash, another branch of economics came to the rescue in a similar manner. Behavioural economists stepped in with concepts and tools "designed to correct for market failures in a way that reframed those failures in terms of shortcomings of market subjects themselves" (Brooks 2021, p. 376). Systemic failures were recast as the outcome of a crisis caused by the faulty decision-making of multiple borrowers. This narrative allowed the economic mainstream to continue its "meandering course" while retaining its "unifying principles of marginalism, methodological individualism, opportunity costs and the virtuous effects of market exchange" (Berndt and Boeckler 2017, p. 284).

The behavioural economics toolbox of "nudges" and adjustments to "choice architecture" (Thaler and Sunstein 2008) has since been absorbed into everyday governance in the Global North and into the programmes of development agencies and nongovernment organisations (NGOs) (Fine et al. 2016; Berndt 2015). This was acknowledged by the World Bank's selection of behavioural economics as the topic of its 2015 World Development Report (WDR): "Mind, society, and behavior" (World Bank 2015). The recommendations set out in the WDR combined the Bank's traditional pro-market stance with post-market elements that "recognise markets need a little help from 'incentive-compatible' mechanisms" (Klein 2017, p. 489). Poverty, the Bank argued, "poses constraints" on rational decision-making that can be remedied by direct interventions to *produce* more effective market behaviour. This was a departure from neoclassical assumptions that the poor are as rational as any other actor (Berndt and Boeckler 2017). Instead, poor people were cast as irrational agents who could be induced to *behave* rationally. This remained "a neoliberal approach", however, as the sole purpose of state intervention was to "advance human efficiency" to the benefit of the individual (Klein 2017, p. 489). Accordingly, NIE imperatives to adjust institutions to "make markets work for the poor" were set aside as the "behavioural turn" advocated by the WDR recast global development as a project of "producing responsible, efficient and effective subjects" primed for "inclusion" in existing market structures (Klein 2017, p. 490; Berndt 2015).

Alongside multilateral and bilateral development agencies, philanthropic foundations, notably the Gates Foundation and Omidyar Network, have also encouraged the reconception of global development in terms of micro-market adjustments to compensate for macro-market uncertainties (Mitchell and Sparke 2016). Their enthusiastic support for fintech platforms as a vehicle for financial inclusion in the Global South exemplifies the alignment of the behavioural turn in development with the emergence of platform capitalism (Langley and Leyshon 2016; Gabor and Brooks 2017). Here "the platform" is understood as a sociotechnical assemblage and business model with a "distinctive intermediary logic … which is to make multi-sided markets and coordinate network effects" which is becoming "incorporated into wider processes of capitalisation" (Langley and Leyshon 2016, p. 19). Platforms mobilise "infrastructures of participation" through processes of "*coding*, based on data and metadata; deploy[ment of] *algorithms* for processing relations between data points; use [of] *protocols* to script interactions; and configur[ation of] *interfaces*" with users (emphasis added). The emphasis on "'users' who 'co-create value'" rather than on consumers is key to a business model that "targets scale economies and seeks to extract rents from circulations and associated data trails" (Langley and Leyshon 2016, p. 14; see also Zuboff 2019). Techniques of behavioural manipulation are core to a business model that "*must invest in behaviour design*" to "ensure users stick around of their own accord" (Langley and Leyshon 2016, p. 17, original emphasis).

Platforms are modern tools for "the development of underdevelopment" in the Global South (Frank 1966), particularly in sub-Saharan Africa. Digital platforms built by transnational firms function as "privatised epistemic infrastructures" that capture learning as well as value to "lock in competitive technological advantage of rich countries" (Mann and Iazzolino 2019, p. 2). The example of fintech platforms in Africa exemplifies the emerging global consensus around development as "technologically-enabled inclusion" of market-ready subjects "within existing formal economic structures and relations" (Langley and Leyshon 2022, p. 403). Moreover, unlike US, European and Asian fintech sectors, which have been shaped by start-ups, banks and Big Tech platforms, platform architectures in African countries are built on distinctly neocolonial foundations. The emergence of fintech sectors in Africa has been seized by "neo-colonial telecommunications 'monoliths'" such as Vodacom, MTN, Airtel and Orange as an opportunity to "create platforms that build on their 'enclosure' of telecommunications … and enhance their capacity to extract rents" (Langley and Leyshon 2022, pp. 404–405). These platforms "renew and recast colonial relations in the present" as "populations excluded from formal financial relations under colonial regimes" are enrolled into infrastructures of "corporate neo-colonialism" (Langley and Leyshon 2022, p. 403).

The platform business model has also created opportunities for agribusiness firms to collaborate with fintech and telecoms providers in the design of platforms that "bundle" agricultural and financial products and related information for promotion to smallholder farmers (Brooks 2021). In addition to neocolonial telecommunications infrastructures, "digital farmer" platforms build on the legacy of the "long" Green Revolution (Patel 2013). This trajectory of agricultural modernisation and capitalisation has been driven by US philanthropic foundations which invested in public infrastructures of "high modernist" development in the Cold War era (Scott 1998; Cullather 2004), and the more recent Alliance for a Green Revolution in Africa (AGRA) whose aim is framed in NIE terms as enabling the inclusion of smallholders in global value chains (Alonso-Fradejas et al. 2015; Brooks 2016). Accordingly, "digital farmer" platforms enrol smallholders through mechanisms of data harvesting, digital profiling and micro-targeted nudging towards adoption of platform "bundles" designed around the commercial priorities of private sector partners (Brooks 2021).

Platform architects emphasise their "digital disintermediation" role, in which they claim to "reduce informational and market asymmetries to the benefit of all" (Iazzolino and Mann 2019, n.p.). Recent research indicates the reverse, however, as "platform developers actually *re-intermediate* the market and are able to reap profits through lock-in and control over market governance" (emphasis added). They reintroduce transaction costs in the form of "constraints, design values and updates of the user terms". Moreover, as market gatekeepers, platform developers are able to "pressure smaller actors into data sharing protocols that allow them to corral valuable data and determine the framework through which the data is transformed into tangible markets and assets". These platforms are not "neutral marketplaces" – far from it, as they reset economic relations and create new hierarchies (Iazzolino and Mann 2019, n.p.).

As platformisation continues, these processes of market consolidation, data capture and lock-in look set to intensify. Meanwhile programme bundles that mirror platform partnership structures are creating new vulnerabilities for smallholders. The inclusion of index-based insurance, despite an evident lack of demand (Johnson et al. 2019), illuminates the prioritisation of platform actors' interests over those of "beneficiaries". In this case, the promotion of index-based insurance reflects agribusiness partners' strategic interest in commodifying agricultural risk (Isakson 2015). The platform model allows businesses to sidestep crystal clear market signals and coerce farmers into adopting a product that individualises risk and weakens solidary relations that are an obstacle to market penetration. The bundling of index-based insurance with farming inputs "displaces informal systems of risk pooling linked to local institutions for seed saving and exchange that the long Green Revolution has long sought to render obsolete as 'backward'" (Brooks 2021, p. 388).

Fintech and "digital farmer" platforms share similar features, in that they: (i) render populations legible at a more granular level than was previously possible; (ii) generate behavioural data streams with potential for future monetisation; (iii) facilitate lock-in of economic advantage for dominant market actors; and (iv) equate "adverse digital incorporation" with development. In the case of agricultural platforms, a fourth feature can be added. As Langley and Leyshon (2016, p. 14) note, the platform business model is characterised by "future-facing processes of valuation and capitalisation" that "perform the structure of venture capital investment". This can be seen in the market effects of anticipated technological advances enabling monetisation of behavioural data (Zuboff 2019). What agricultural platforms offer in addition is the generation of micro-scale biophysical data on factors of agricultural production (soils, nutrients, water, climate, etc.). Demand for this type of digital knowledge is likely to grow as distant investors, particularly those with an interest in precision agriculture, calculate the value of land as an investible financial asset (Fraser 2018).

DEVELOPMENT SUBJECTS ON THE RISK FRONTIER

The "platformisation" of global development and humanitarian intervention advances the financialisation of development alongside its datafication (Langley and Leyshon 2022; Mann 2018). The pithy phrase "all data is credit data" (Aitken 2017) serves as a reminder of how intertwined these processes are, not only at the institutional level, but also in the daily lives of market subjects – whose data are "shared" with organisations through their "interpassive engagement" with digital platforms (Ruppert 2011). Antecedents of the financialisation of development, a term that refers to "the deepening nexus between financial logics, instruments and actors, and intentional 'development': that is, the ideologies, programmes and practices of the 'mainstream' international development community" (Mawdsley 2016, p. 265) go back a long way. Structural adjustment policies and privatisations of the 1980s and 1990s opened up economies in the Global South to "capital mobility required by investors" (Mawdsley 2016, p. 270) and generated income streams amenable to securitisation (pooled with other income-producing assets into investible financial products) (Fine 2012). The ubiquity of microfinance in community development over nearly three decades led to the reframing of empowerment as *economic* empowerment and the valorisation of individual self-reliance (Rankin 2001). Microcredit providers, meanwhile, evolved from revolving funds administered by community-based organisations to private microfinance institutions (MFIs) progressively exposed to global markets through processes of securitisation – promoted by the World Bank's International Finance Corporation (IFC) – that have driven up interest rates to punitive levels in the drive for profitability (Soederberg 2013; Aitken 2010).

Machine learning algorithms deployed by platforms also accelerate *internalisation* of logics of marketisation and financialisation. Returning to Scott's (1998) concept of legibility, the "high modernist" bureaucracies of the twentieth century "crafted categories and standardised processes" and "re-order[ed] society in ways that reflected its categorisations and acted them out". High modernism shaped markets, which were "standardised, as concrete goods like grain, lumber and meat were converted into abstract qualities to be traded at scale" (Farrell and Fourcade 2023, p. 226). As twentieth-century classification methods are superseded by digital techniques, high modernism has given way to "high-*tech* modernism". This term refers to "the body of classifying technologies based on quantitative techniques and digitised information that *partly displaces, and partly is layered over* the analogue processes used by high modernist organisations" (Farrell and Fourcade 2023, p. 227, emphasis added). Like bureaucracies, algorithms are "technologies of hierarchical ordering and intervention. But whereas bureaucracy reinforces human sameness … algorithms encourage human competition … High-tech modernism and high modernism are born from the same impulse to exert control, but are articulated in fundamentally different ways, with quite different consequences for the construction of the social and economic order" (Farrell and Fourcade 2023, p. 226).

The advent of high-tech modernism has transformed people's relationship with their classifications to limit their agency in ways that are invisible to them. Under high modernism, classifications were all too visible to publics who often resisted, albeit in limited ways, particularly under authoritarian regimes. "The pathologies of computational algorithms are more subtle. The shift to high-tech modernism allows the means of ensuring legibility to fade into the background of ordinary patterns of life" (Farrell and Fourcade 2023, p. 228). While bureaucratic classifications were often crude and inaccurate they were at least comprehensible, while "digital classification systems may group people in ways that are not always socially comprehensible". Political and social mechanisms through which people previously responded to their classification have been "replaced by closed loops in which algorithms assign people unwittingly to categories, assess their responses to cues, and continually update and reclassify them". These self-correcting, cybernetic categories are "automatically and dynamically adjusted in light of the reactions they produce" rather than in response to human intentions, decisions and actions (Farrell and Fourcade 2023, p. 229).

In the "living labs" of D4D, discussed earlier, classifications were invisible to affected groups but their material consequences were not: the introduction of a biometric verification system in a refugee camp in Northern Kenya exacerbated inequalities between Somali refugee groups, pushing poorer refugees into indebtedness (Iazzolino 2021); while, in India, a biometric ID system designed around middle-class lifestyles created a social catastrophe as poor people were denied access to funds in the aftermath of the government's rapid demonetisation intervention. In these cases, and many others, interventions have entrenched social hierarchies and exacerbated vulnerabilities of poor and marginalised groups (Martin et al. 2023). Furthermore, machine learning algorithms have more subtle, insidious effects as they "institutionalise competition between units (whether people, organisations, or ideas) by fostering a market-based vision of fairness" (Farrell and Fourcade 2023, p. 230). This was evident in humanitarian workers' association of the disciplinary function of biometric verification with "fairness"; despite outcomes that exacerbated inequalities and discouraged the redevelopment of solidary relations and cooperative survival strategies among marginalised groups (Iazzolino 2021).

In the case of fintech-powered financial inclusion, narratives about unqualified benefits of market inclusion circulate among members of an evolving "fintech-philanthropy-development (FPD) complex" of philanthropic foundations, government officials, development agencies and fintech and telecoms firms (Gabor and Brooks 2017). This optimistic framing belies the harsh disciplinary reality of fintech platforms in practice. The example of JUMO, a Cape Town-based fintech firm that partners with telecoms firms and banks to offer unsecured credit products in six African countries, is instructive. JUMO's algorithms gather data points from a range of sources to assess a customer's creditworthiness. These include driving data aggregated from the Uber app along with data points on mobile phone usage and mobile payments. Fraud risk, meanwhile, is calculated from a range of data including "data on mobile phone battery life and the frequency with which users 'let' their phone battery 'die' and how long the phone is off" (Langley and Leyshon 2022, p. 410). In this case, machineries of financial subject formation do not engage with (far less "empower") individuals, but with sets of data points:

> JUMO is fundamentally indifferent to singular individuals ... JUMO's platforms do not simply enrol individual subjects into formal credit–debt relations but, rather, enlist analytically-defined and segmented groups of users .... users figured by JUMO through data analytics only become known to the firm and its partners in terms of the behavioural and proxy credit history attributes that they share with others. Users are always already differentiated, that is, grouped, segmented, and scored by the platform as a result of its analysis of telecommunication and transaction data points. Put another way ... *users are abstract and data-derived figures produced by JUMO to be profitable, and without which they have no role or essential identity.* (Langley and Leyshon 2022, p. 408, emphasis added)

The promotion of fintech markets in the Global South as a "new risk frontier" for investors with an appetite for "high-risk, high profit" rewards is thus a more accurate depiction of platformised microfinance than is the narrative of inclusion that populates the websites of philanthropic foundations and development agencies (Gabor and Brooks 2017). The consensus around financial inclusion *as* development collapses what Hart (2010, p. 117) calls big-D and little-d development (where the former refers to "a post war international project" and the latter to "capitalist development as a highly uneven process of creation and destruction") into the consolidation of privatised infrastructures for coercive, financial*ised* inclusion and extraction of monopoly rents. Platforms function as infrastructures of "high tech modernism" (Farrell and Fourcade 2023) that "sort" customers into credit risk classifications based on harvested data on patterns of online behaviour (Aitken 2017) in a multi-tiered process of financial subject formation (Kear 2013). These classification processes are invisible to customers on the receiving end of algorithm-driven "nudges" towards products selected for them and priced according to their categorisation within an opaque, constantly fine-tuned hierarchical ordering of more or less risky market subjects (Gabor and Brooks 2017; Aitken 2017).

CONCLUSION

The deployment of digital technologies in global development has produced outcomes that have diverged dramatically from the hopes *and* fears that framed debates in the early 2000s, which centred on the urgency of bridging digital divides. The Global Financial Crisis, or, more specifically, the paradoxical institutional responses to it; technological advances in big data analytics and the diffusion of mobile devices; and the emergence of platform capitalism have transformed the field of D4D. The examples of humanitarian intervention, financial inclusion and technical assistance to smallholder farmers outlined in this chapter deploy platform infrastructures which have extended surveillance of populations and prised open new markets while exacerbating inequalities and vulnerabilities. The scaling up of reach and coverage achieved by these interventions coexists with a scaled-down development ambition (to paraphrase Taylor 2012, p. 604) of technologically enabled inclusion in structures that perpetuate conditions of inequality, marginalisation and exploitation.

The platformisation of global development is indicative of its incorporation into wider processes of capitalism. Beyond privatisation of discrete programme components, this points towards the potential absorption of "big-D development" into the "small-d" development (Hart 2010) of contemporary platform capitalism. As infrastructures of "high-tech modernism" (Farrell and Fourcade 2023) platforms render populations (and natural resources) legible to private firms and states, to a greater extent and degree than was previously possible, and in ways that are opaque to individuals so classified. Indeed, platforms do not engage with individuals as such, but with "users" that are "abstract and data-derived figures *produced*" by platforms "to be *profitable*" (Langley and Leyshon 2022, p. 408, emphasis added). These processes of subject formation erode human agency by design though continual fine-tuning and (re)classification. The platformisation of development poses particular risks to populations whose livelihoods depend on informal institutions of mutuality and reciprocity. Platforms are designed to perform accumulation strategies of their owners and these include the displacement of informal, solidaristic relations by vertical relations of market dependence.

NOTE

1. The term "securitisation" is used in this section to refer to the ways in which the post-September 11 "War on Terror" has transformed international refugee policy and increased the emphasis on surveillance.

REFERENCES

Aitken, R. (2010), 'Ambiguous incorporations: Microfinance and global governmentality', *Global Networks: A Journal of Transnational Affairs* **10** (2), 223–243.

Aitken, R. (2017), '"All data is credit data": Constituting the unbanked', *Competition and Change* **21** (4), 274–300.

Alonso-Fradejas, A., S. M. Borras Jr, T. Holmes, E. Holt-Giménez, and M. J. Robbins (2015), 'Food sovereignty: Convergence and contradictions, conditions and challenges', *Third World Quarterly* **36** (3), 431–448.

Berndt, C. (2015), 'Behavioural economics, experimentalism and the marketization of development', *Economy and Society* **44** (4), 567–591.

Berndt, C., and M. Boeckler (2017), 'Economic, experiments, evidence: Poor behavior and the development of market subjects', in V. Higgins and W. Larner (eds), *Assembling Neoliberalism: Expertise, Practices, Subjects*, New York: Palgrave Macmillan US, pp. 283–302.

Brooks, S. (2016), 'Inducing food insecurity: Financialisation and development in the post-2015 era', *Third World Quarterly* **37** (5), 768–780.

Brooks, S. (2021), 'Configuring the digital farmer: A nudge world in the making?', *Economy and Society* **50** (3), 374–396.

Cullather, N. (2004), 'Miracles of modernisation: The green revolution and the apotheosis of technology', *Diplomatic History* **28** (2), 227–254.

Farrell, H., and M. Fourcade (2023), 'The moral economy of high-tech modernism', *Daedalus* **152** (1), 225–235.

Fine, B. (2012), 'Neo-liberalism in retrospect? It's financialisation, stupid', in C. Kyung-Sup, B. Fine, and L. Weiss (eds), *Developmental Politics in Transition: The Neoliberal Era and Beyond*, Basingstoke, UK: Palgrave Macmillan, pp. 51–69.

Fine, B., D. Johnston, A. C. Santos, and E. Van Waeyenberge (2016), 'Nudging or fudging: The World Development Report 2015', *Development and Change* **47** (4), 640–663.

Frank, A. G. (1966), 'The development of underdevelopment', *Monthly Review* **18** (4), 17–31.

Fraser, A. (2018), 'Land grab/data grab: Precision agriculture and its new horizons', *The Journal of Peasant Studies* **46** (5), 893–912.

Gabor, D., and S. Brooks (2017), 'The digital revolution in financial inclusion: International development in the fintech era', *New Political Economy* **22** (4), 423–436.

Hart, G. (2010), 'D/developments after the Meltdown', *Antipode* **41**, 117–141.

Heeks, R. (2008), 'ICT4D 2.0: The next phase of applying ICT for international development', *Computer* **41** (6), 26–33.

Heeks, R. (2010), 'Do information and communication technologies (ICTs) contribute to development?', *Journal of International Development* **22** (5), 625–640.

Heeks, R. (2022), 'Digital inequality beyond the digital divide: Conceptualizing adverse digital incorporation in the Global South', *Information Technology for Development* **28** (4), 688–704.

Iazzolino, G. (2021), 'Infrastructure of compassionate repression: Making sense of biometrics in Kakuma refugee camp', *Information Technology for Development* **27** (1),111–128.

Iazzolino, G., and L. Mann (2019), 'Harvesting data: Who benefits from platformization of agricultural finance in Kenya?', *Developing Economics*, 14 April. https://developingeconomics.org/2019/03/29/harvesting-data-who-benefits-from-platformization-of-agricultural-finance-in-kenya/?blogsub=subscribed#subscribe-blog (accessed 30 April 2023).

Isakson, S. R. (2015), 'Derivatives for development? Small-farmer vulnerability and the financialization of climate risk management', *Journal of Agrarian Change* **15** (4), 569–580.

Jain, S., and D. Gabor (2020), 'The rise of digital financialisation: The case of India', *New Political Economy* **25** (5), 813–828.

Johnson, L., B. Wandera, N. Jensen, and R. Banerjee (2019), 'Competing expectations in an index-based livestock insurance project', *The Journal of Development Studies* **55** (6), 1221–1239.

Kaminska, I. (2015), 'When financial inclusion stands for financial intrusion', *Financial Times: FT Alphaville*, 31 July. http://ftalphaville.ft.com/2015/07/31/2135943/when-financial-inclusion-stands-for-financial-intrusion/ (accessed 30 April 2023).

Kear, M. (2013), 'Governing homo subprimicus: Beyond financial citizenship, exclusion, and rights', *Antipode* **45** (4), 926–946.

Klein, E. (2017), 'The World Bank on mind, behaviour and society', *Development and Change* **48** (3), 481–501.

Lahaye, E, T. E. Abell, and J. K. Hoover (2017), 'Vision of the future: Financial inclusion 2025', CGAP, https://www.cgap.org/sites/default/files/Focus-Note-Vision-of-the-Future-Jun-2017_0.pdf (accessed 30 April 2023).

Langley, P., and A. Leyshon (2016), 'Platform capitalism: The intermediation and capitalisation of digital economic circulation', *Finance and Society* **3** (1), 11–31.

Langley, P., and A. Leyshon (2022), 'Neo-colonial credit: FinTech platforms in Africa', *Journal of Cultural Economy* **15** (4), 401–415.

Leftwich, A. (1995), 'Bringing politics back in: Towards a model of the developmental state', *The Journal of Development Studies*, **31** (3), 400–427.

Mann, L. (2018), 'Left to other peoples' devices? A political economy perspective on the big data revolution in development', *Development and Change* **49** (1), 3–36.

Mann, L., and G. Iazzolino (2019), 'See, nudge, control and profit: Digital platforms as privatized epistemic infrastructures', *IT for Change*, https://projects.itforchange.net/platformpolitics/wp-content/uploads/2019/03/Digital-Platforms-as-Privatized-Epistemic-Infrastructures-_5thMarch.pdf (accessed 30 April 2023).

Martin, A., G. Sharma, S. P. de Souza, L. Taylor, B. van Eerd, S. M. McDonald, M. Marelli, M. Cheesman, S. Scheel, and H. Dijstelbloem (2023), 'Digitisation and sovereignty in humanitarian space: Technologies, territories and tensions', *Geopolitics*, **28** (3), 1362–1397. DOI: 10.1080/14650045.2022.2047468.

Masiero, S. (2017), Aadhaar, demonetisation, and the poor', *Perspectives*, https://www.ideasforindia.in/topics/money-finance/aadhaar-demonetisation-and-the-poor.html, 9 January 2017 (accessed 30 April 2023).

Mawdsley, E. (2016), 'Development geography II: Financialization', *Progress in Human Geography* **2** (2), 264–274.

Mitchell, K., and M. Spark (2016), 'The new Washington Consensus: Millennial philanthropy and the making of global market subjects', *Antipode* **48** (3), 724–749.

Mkandawire, T. (2001), 'Thinking about developmental states in Africa', *Cambridge Journal of Economics* **25** (3), 289–314.

Patel, R. (2013), 'The long green revolution', *The Journal of Peasant Studies* **40** (1), 1–63.

Rankin, K. N. (2001), 'Governing development: Neoliberalism, microcredit, and rational economic woman', *Economy and Society* **30** (1), 18–37.

Ruppert, E. (2011), 'Population objects: Interpassive subjects', *Sociology* **45** (2), 218–233.

Scott, J. C. (1998), *Seeing like a State: How Certain Schemes to Improve the Human Condition Have Failed*, New Haven, CT: Yale University Press.

Soederberg, S. (2013), 'Universalising financial inclusion and the securitisation of development', *Third World Quarterly* **34** (4), 593–612.

Taylor, L. (2017), 'What is data justice? The case for connecting digital rights and freedoms globally', *Big Data & Society* **4** (2), 2053951717736335.

Taylor, M. (2012), 'The antinomies of financial inclusion: Debt, distress and the workings of Indian microfinance', *Journal of Agrarian Change* **12** (4), 601–610.

Thaler, R. H., and C. R. Sunstein (2008), *Nudge: Improving Decisions about Health, Wealth, and Happiness*, New Haven, CT: Yale University Press.

WEF (2012), 'Big data, big impact: New possibilities for international development', New York: World Economic Forum. www3.weforum.org/docs/WEF_TC_MFS_BigData BigImpact_Briefing_2012.pdf (accessed 30 April 2023).

Williamson, J. (1990), *The Washington Consensus*, Washington, DC, https://books.google.co.uk/books ?hl=en&lr=&id=mpu-DAAAQBAJ&oi=fnd&pg=PA13&ots=MhNTQF8wz_&sig=iDMmW5E_dOt TdloTK6WM8Hvajec#v=onepage&q&f=false (accessed 30 April 2023).

World Bank (2015), *World Development Report 2015: Mind, Society, and Behavior*, Washington, DC: The World Bank.

Zuboff, S. (2019), *The Age of Surveillance Capitalism: The Fight for a Human Future at the New Frontier of Power*, London: Profile Books.

17. Decoding and reimagining AI governance beyond colonial shadows

Adekemi Omotubora and Subhajit Basu

INTRODUCTION

As the world contends with the proliferating influence of AI, there is a heightened imperative for regulatory measures, as evidenced by the intensified discourse among international legal scholars and policymakers. Underpinned by the foundational framework of the proposed EU AI Act, nations within the Global North (GN) are taking the lead in navigating this regulatory trajectory. However, we argue in this chapter that it is imperative to highlight the pressing necessity for inclusive international cooperation and governance instead of adopting an exclusionary approach. A limited set of influential countries and corporate giants within the GN has predominantly controlled the trajectory of AI's evolution and subsequent implementation. Post-colonial Global South (GS) countries often emulate the legal frameworks established by more advanced countries in the GN (and GN countries also experience deep regulatory interdependence, as discussed by Mügge, Chapter 19 in this volume). This dynamic has engendered a disproportionate consolidation of power, anchoring decision-making processes within these few entities. However, a more profound, historically grounded concern lies beyond these contemporary dynamics. The propensity for GS nations to emulate GN regulatory frameworks is not merely a response to present-day power imbalances. Instead, it echoes a long-standing legacy of colonialism, a past that has persistently moulded – and continues to shape – the legal and jurisprudential ethos of post-colonial states within the GS (for a discussion of decolonial approaches to AI and data more generally, see Gray, Chapter 15 in this volume). Therefore, beyond the rhetoric of the "gold standard" setting or the "Brussels effect"[1] that accompanies new digital laws from Europe, this chapter argues that colonial influence or coloniality of power plays a role in the often-rapid adoption of model laws in post-colonial GS countries.

This poses a significant risk: the broader global community might become passive recipients of a governance model developed by elite GN countries and corporations. Complicating this landscape further is the inherent intricacy of AI as a technology. Navigating its governance necessitates a blend of nuanced technical understanding and adept policy formulation – expertise that, yet again, is often monopolised by the very same GN powerhouses. Legislating to regulate AI presents particularly exceptional challenges. AI risks are diverse and impact cultures and societies differently. For example, AI systems are often trained on datasets biased towards certain cultural norms, languages and historical experiences, which can lead to cultural appropriation, misrepresentation and reinforcement of stereotypes. Ethical considerations also differ when AI technologies are deployed in regions with different cultural contexts. Local beliefs, traditions and social structures can influence their acceptance, regulation and governance. Therefore, while the law can deal with broader concerns around bias, privacy, unrepresentativeness, fairness and accountability, it must also consider the socio-cultural contexts and variances that influence the acceptance and perceptions of AI applications (see, for example, the discussion on contextual accountability in Cobbe and Singh, Chapter 7 in this volume). As part of a robust governance structure, laws must be culturally sensitive, respectful, and aligned with the values and aspirations of the communities they affect.

This chapter proposes that understanding the theoretical models for AI law-making from a decolonial perspective plays a critical role in realising these outcomes. It follows the growing literature on decolonising AI, suggesting that while formal colonisation may have ended, its logic, institutions and practices endure in AI development and deployment. In particular, it analogises to the "coloniality" (of power) – the decolonial lens that explains colonialism not just as a historical event but an ongoing system of domination that shapes societies, economies and cultures (Quijano 2007) – to demonstrate how the rationalistic, functionalist and conflict theories of law-making exhibit enduring relics of colonialisation. The chapter does not critique the EU AI Act, the process that produced it, or similar legislative initiatives. Instead, it is an exposition of a decolonial approach to challenge the underlying assumptions of objectivity, neutrality or universality embedded in such industries. It proposes decoloniality as an alternative epistemology for developing a self-reflexive approach that recognises the implicit biases and power imbalances in AI governance, including law-making.

The chapter is divided into four sections. Section two provides a brief iteration of the emerging discourse on the impacts of colonisation on datafication and AI design and governance. Section three demonstrates how colonialism influenced the jurisprudence and legal system of formerly colonised countries, using Nigeria as a case study. In section four, the chapter demonstrates the enduring influence of colonisation on the law-making process, leveraging the rationalistic, functionalistic and conflict theories (or models). It highlights the limits of the inherent assumptions about the applications of the functionalist and rationalistic theories in post-colonial and AI contexts and the insights for reforming global approaches to AI governance offered by the conflict model. The chapter concludes with suggestions for further research for decolonising the theoretical frames for making laws for AI.

DECOLONIAL THEORIES IN AI GOVERNANCE AND DISCOURSE

Decolonial perspectives on AI (cf. Gray, Chapter 15 in this volume) are not merely theoretical constructs but are a rallying call to confront AI's colonising footprints on the GS. These approaches push for an introspective lens, keenly attuned to the entrenched power disparities and inherent prejudices that ripple through AI systems (Miller 2019, 2023; Mohamed et al. 2020; Adams 2021; Mhlambi and Tiribelli 2023). At its heart, "decoloniality" is an analytical scaffold that challenges and deconstructs the intricate power edifices and ideological tenets that sustain and amplify colonialism and its accompanying inequities. Decolonial theories seek to excavate and spotlight knowledge systems and theoretical pathways that diverge from the traditional Eurocentric paradigms, giving voice to non-Western narratives. Integral to this scholarly dialogue is the understanding that the impacts of colonialism are not simply imprinted on the landscape but delineated through territorial acquisitions or expropriations. These influences penetrate cognitive frameworks, moulding perceptions and lived experiences, resulting in an intellectual and existential dominance indicative of Eurocentric ascendancy. Quijano's (2007) articulation of the "coloniality of power" encapsulates this idea, offering a poignant depiction of the persistent and intangible repercussions of colonial vestiges.

"Coloniality (of power)" explains colonialism as a historical event and an ongoing system of domination that shapes societies, economies and cultures. It is manifested as the violent imposition of ways of being, thinking and feeling that leads to the expulsion of human beings from the social order, denies the existence of alternative worlds and epistemologies and threatens life on Earth (Quijano 2007; Ricaurte 2019: 351). Coloniality endures far beyond the temporal confines of colonialism. It serves as the haunting echo of historical subjugations and persists as the residual power interplay between the privileged and the marginalised. It is anchored in the harrowing chronicles of dispossession, enslavement, appropriation and resource extraction that have been pivotal in sculpting our modern world (Bhambra et al. 2018). Ricaurte insightfully posits coloniality as the aftermath of colonial ventures that persistently taints our present day, elucidating the mechanisms that support Western hegemony (Ricaurte 2022). Within this framework, coloniality emerges as the realm of the "non-being", a space of detachment and redefinition, which subsequently opens avenues for recalibrating the epistemological paradigms dominant in the West. This recalibration especially revolves around critically interrogating what is hailed as legitimate "knowledge" and what is disregarded. Gillen and Ghosh (2007) further elucidates this concept by portraying coloniality as an encapsulation of continually regenerated racial, gendered or power-centric hierarchies. Initially crucial for asserting colonial dominance, these hierarchies have survived the end of explicit colonial rule and have been incessantly reanimated and fortified in post-colonial times.

AI as a technology is revealed in a stark new light through the prism of coloniality. This perspective allows us to discern how the collection and interpretation of data, the underlying design principles and the overarching governance models of AI can serve as conduits. These conduits can amplify and sustain the colonial edifices of knowledge acquisition, power dynamics, racial categorisations and identity constructs. It urges a critical examination of AI not just as a neutral technological advancement but as an instrument potentially imbricated with the legacy of colonial hierarchies. Couldry and Megias (2019, 2023) draw direct analogies between historical and data colonialism. They argue that the "data colonialism" thesis, credited to Thatcher et al. (2016), foregrounds the continuous extraction of economic value from human life.

Data colonialism is not a mere metaphor for capitalism, instead, it represents a tangible mechanism of capitalist accumulation. It bridges the ominous legacies of historic colonialism with present-day post-colonial realities. Deriving value from data is reminiscent of historical land usurpations that marked the onset of traditional colonial endeavours (Couldry and Mejias 2019: 339–341; 2023: 787–788). This modern-day "data grab" mirrors the historical concept of "terra nullius" – implying land unclaimed or uninhabited. Historically, this term was misapplied to territories teeming with indigenous populations (Miller 2019), painting them as devoid of rightful inhabitants and thereby ripe for exploitation. Contemporary narratives also portray data as a barren frontier – devoid of inherent value – until corporations, akin to colonial explorers, chart its expanses, unveiling its potential. These narratives posit corporations as the sole entities equipped to harness this data and frame their extractive endeavours as philanthropic missions.

Much like the justifications for historic colonialism, which painted it as a project to "civilise" the colonised, present-day discourses suggest that society at large stands to gain from these corporate data extractions, heralding them as modern-day civilisational endeavours (Couldry and Mejias 2019: 340). Perfunctorily, data has become a means of reconfiguring old hegemonies of power, with multiple layers of data colonialism forming part of a broader process of coloniality involving epistemic violence (Ricaurte 2019, 2022).

The idea of "data-centric rationality" articulated by Ricaurte (2019) champions the view that data faithfully mirrors reality. It posits that the analysis of such data invariably yields the most insightful and precise knowledge and that the conclusions drawn from processing this data inevitably lead to superior decision-making regarding our world. However, closer scrutiny reveals that this rationality is buttressed by knowledge production infrastructures largely cultivated by states, corporations and research entities predominantly rooted in the GN. This network operates within an economic framework favouring capital accumulation and economic expansion Consequently, the well-trodden colonial power dynamics can be re-envisioned within the context of "data colonialism" – positioning it as an epistemological system anchored in data (Ricaurte 2019: 351–356). This then necessitates a contemplative approach towards the phenomenon of "datafication", especially within the context of societies grappling with inherent inequalities. Drawing on Milan and Treré (2019), the South(s) can be perceived not merely as geographies but as symbolic spaces teeming with the potential for "resistance, subversion, and creativity" in the face of data-driven dominance.

The foundational challenges associated with data permeate all aspects of AI, from its design and development to its broader governance. Mohamed et al. (2020) dissect the intricate dimensions in which AI is entrenched in coloniality, terming this phenomenon "algorithmic coloniality". Drawing parallels between territorial and structural colonialism, they articulate how like the physical space, the digital environment is predisposed to becoming arenas of extraction and expropriation. Employing the prism of critical (decolonial) science theory, they develop a taxonomy tagged "decolonial foresight", characterised by institutionalised algorithmic oppression, exploitation and dispossession. Delving into this foresight, they earmark specific instances – ranging from algorithmic decision systems to national policies – as "sites of coloniality". These sites are emblematic of structural disparities with historical roots intertwined with the tendrils of colonial continuance (Mohamed et al. 2020: 659–684).

Expanding on this narrative, other scholars underline the colonial remnants in AI applications, such as facial recognition and predictive policing (Hao 2020). Buolamwini and Gebru (2018) demonstrate how algorithms trained on homogenous datasets magnify and sustain societal prejudices. The shortcomings of facial recognition technologies, particularly concerning black faces, serve as a poignant illustration of this concern. AI's data extraction venture further aggravates this imbalance. It siphons off economic benefits from the very communities that are data sources by embedding dominant GN perspectives into its core. This magnifies wealth disparities between the GN and GS – mirroring the extractive nature of European colonialism – and stifles the avenues for redressing historical wrongs.

In AI ethics discourses, the coloniality of power compels deeper introspection. While a handful of comprehensive ethical guidelines, such as the UNESCO Recommendations on the Ethics of AI – endorsed by an impressive roster of 193 States – stand out, a vast majority (approximately 173 as of 2019 as per the Algorithm Watch AI Ethics Global Inventory), emerge from the corridors of corporate behemoths. The critique here is profound. These ethical frameworks often mirror the ambitions and serve the interests of their creators (on the politics of AI ethics discourses, see Rönnblom, Padden and Carlsson, Chapter 9 in this volume). Consequently, they wield the power to dictate behavioural standards upon external entities, such as communities in the GS, while primarily addressing the concerns of the GN.

These dynamics foster a narrative that sees evolving ethical guidelines in two lights. From a more benign perspective, they are considered limited technical solutions to complex socio-technical challenges. However, a more critical standpoint posits them as mere instruments in an overarching stratagem of "ethics white washing" (Ricaurte 2022; Birhane 2020). The danger lies in their potential to camouflage deeper systemic issues under the veneer of ethical compliance, perpetuating a cycle where the dominant structures (of the GN) continue to benefit at the expense of the marginalised (GS) communities. Thus, there is a burgeoning consensus regarding the limitations of universal ethical guidelines, especially as they pertain to the GS, Africa, to be precise. While such guidelines have the potential to offer a shared ethical foundation bridging diverse cultures, they often falter in resonating with the unique socio-cultural configurations of African societies (Jobin et al. 2019; Mhlambi 2020; Gwagwa et al. 2022; Birhane 2020).

Gwagwa et al. and Mhlambi, among others, posit a compelling argument: the imperative to infuse AI ethics and policy with a decolonial perspective. They advocate for including distinctly African relational paradigms, spotlighting "ubuntu" as a quintessential ethical compass for AI. Rooted deeply in African communitarianism, "ubuntu" underscores the ethos of collective existence and engagement. It stands as a testament to the philosophy that one's humanity is intrinsically linked to the humanity of others, encapsulating the golden rule of treating others as one wishes to be treated. The intrinsic value of "ubuntu" lies in its amplification of interconnectedness and its emphasis on community and interpersonal relationships. It fosters traits like empathy, compassion and mutual respect – qualities that are indispensable in addressing the historical wrongs perpetuated by algorithms. By integrating "ubuntu" into the AI ethics narrative, there is an opportunity to champion the inclusion of African perspectives in the global AI ethics discourse, thereby fostering a more inclusive and holistic approach to AI development and governance (Gwagwa et al. 2022: 5; Mhlambi 2020).

Decolonial theories often face criticism for their perceived oversight of nuanced intricacies, particularly their tendency to generalise the "West and modernity" and inadvertently cast natives into static roles (Chibber 2013). It is undeniable that European societies exhibit multi-faceted differences. However, they also share a notorious legacy tied to the exploitation intrinsic to colonialist international laws. A salient example is the doctrine of discovery, including its elements of terra nullius, civilisation vis-à-vis Christianity, and the practical occupation of indigenous territories. This doctrine justified vast acquisitions of wealth and territories globally, which were then codified into property law (Cohen 2018). Regrettably, it continues to impede indigenous people's rights – encompassing sovereignty, trade and property rights (Miller 2019: 35–42), all underscored by contemporary datafication debates. Further, critics of decolonial perspectives on datafication claim that there is a misrepresentation, contending that, unlike traditional colonialism, datafication is not marked by overt physical violence (Segura and Waisbord 2019: 417). However, this critique seems myopic, neglecting the modern dispossession facilitated by data and AI. The prevailing narrative that data lacks inherent value until GN corporations exploit it underscores this dispossession.

Venturing into the relatively nascent realm of AI law-making through a decolonial prism can shed light on the interplay of ingrained values and the power dynamics in AI legislations, elucidating how colonial vestiges still pervade modern legal epistemologies. The intertwining of colonialism and jurisprudence has been extensively explored (Merry 2003; McBride 2016; Miller 2019; Miller and Siltz 2021), yet there is a glaring paucity of discourse concerning AI laws. To investigate more profoundly, we pivot to Nigeria in the ensuing section, exemplifying how the shadows of colonialism not only shape the legal ethos of countries once under colonial rule, but also persist in contemporary (AI) legislation.

THE COLONIALITY OF LOCAL AI GOVERNANCE – CASE STUDY OF NIGERIA'S LEGAL SYSTEM

A decolonial perspective is imperative when addressing AI law-making for two primary reasons. First, it challenges the prevailing notion that AI regulations emerging from the GN are universally applicable and beneficial for all. Secondly, it acknowledges that even when countries from the GS develop their AI regulations, the legislative process is often steeped in remnants of colonial thought and structures that demand re-evaluation. Embracing a decolonial perspective can yield invaluable insights for refining AI legislative processes and offers a crucial lens through which the influence of colonial legacies on post-colonial governance can be understood. Nigeria, having experienced British colonisation, serves as an illustrative example of these overarching themes in the GS.

Legislation is a dynamic process, a metamorphosis of conceptual law into enforceable statutes. It requires a deep comprehension of the motives behind laws and the mechanisms of their creation. Theoretical law-making models offer general insights into the impetuses behind legislation, guiding the process to ensure alignment with desired policy goals. While one might intuitively believe the legislative process to be driven by logic or specific objectives, with lawmakers aiming to craft the most effective regulations, reality often diverges. In post-colonial contexts like Nigeria, latent power dynamics within legislative processes can still sway what are perceived as independent or post-colonial regulations. Recognising this, examining the socio-cultural and legal backdrops of such legislation is essential, deepening our understanding of both the resulting laws and the underlying processes. Sebba (1999) observes that existing literature, predominantly anthropological, on colonial legal impositions, scarcely touches upon these legislative intricacies and their enduring post-colonial implications.

Considering the challenges posed by AI and other digital technologies, the African Commission on Human and Peoples' Rights introduced a resolution concerning Human Rights, AI and other New and Emerging Technologies in Africa in February 2021. This resolution acknowledges the dual nature of AI, robotics and other emerging technologies: they possess the potential to advance human and people's rights in Africa and the risk of undermining them. While organisations and businesses leveraging these technologies influence human rights protection in Africa, a cohesive governance framework to ensure their alignment with continental human rights obligations remains absent. The resolution stresses the imperative for a holistic governance system and emphasises the pivotal role African nations and citizens should play in shaping international AI policies and regulatory mechanisms. Moreover, it accentuates the importance of infusing African traditions, ethics, values and community-centred principles into creating these technological frameworks. It is incumbent upon African nations to ensure that AI development and application adhere to regional human rights norms, highlighting human dignity, privacy, equality, non-discrimination, inclusivity, diversity, safety, transparency, accountability and socio-economic progress (ACHPR/Res. 473, 2021, paras 1–4).

However, implementing such a clear-cut directive is challenging. Many African countries, due to their histories of colonial rule, still predominantly uphold the laws introduced by their former colonisers. Additionally, in the post-colonial era, they often emulate, assimilate or directly adopt legal frameworks from their former rulers. Shomade (2022) highlights this phenomenon, which aligns with Quijano's concept of the "coloniality" of power, denoting the persistent influence of colonialism. It seems there is a growing trend where Nigeria and potentially other African nations are modelling their data protection laws on the "global standards" set by the EU GDPR. Such an approach does not acknowledge the profound differences between African and European notions of privacy, economic maturity, market evolution and administrative and enforcement competencies. Instead, it perpetuates the historical power dynamics and colonial legacies in law-making. Omotubora (2021) and Omotubora and Basu (2020) argue that by mirroring these "global standards", the unique socio-cultural contexts of individual African societies may be overshadowed or overlooked. As a result, the so-called "local" laws enacted by sovereign post-colonial states may not truly resonate with or reflect the cultural and societal nuances of the communities they are meant to serve.

Nigeria's legal system is a classic example here. Nigeria operates a complex and dynamic legal system based on the common law of England, received (pre-1900) English laws and customary (indigenous norms that apply to personal and communal affairs) and Sharia law, based on Islamic principles. These legal systems collectively govern various aspects of Nigerian society, including constitutional, criminal, land, family and religious matters. Historically, before the colonial era, Nigeria boasted a rich mosaic of legal traditions, each echoing the distinct ethos of its multifarious ethnic and cultural clusters. These customary laws were not static, rigid frameworks but rather fluid constructs, ceaselessly evolving in response to the ebbs and flows of societal realities. Their essence encapsulated the distinct moralities, philosophies and worldviews of each ethnic group. The system emphasised restorative and communitarian justice rather than punitive and individualistic justice. The core intent behind settling disputes was not retribution, but restoring societal equilibrium and mending fractured relationships. Consequently, the adjudication process was highly inclusive, calling upon the collective wisdom of community elders, tribal leaders, extended family and neighbours, and prioritising community cohesion and harmony over punitive measures (Alkali et al. 2014).

Colonial intrusion significantly distorted these indigenous legal frameworks. The British superimposed their legal structures, founded on common law and equity, a system that often clashed with the ingrained local nuances. A glaring example was the institution of the "repugnancy test", which deemed any customary law null and void if it opposed natural justice, equity, good conscience or any pre-existing written law. This clause granted colonial courts ample liberty to disregard or reshape customary laws in line with their preferences and objectives. Consequently, the imposed legal system diminished the credibility of native institutions and eroded the previously prevalent societal harmony and unity. Although termed as "received law", the incorporation of English law was not a conscious choice by the indigenous people but rather an imposition stemming from colonisation. In essence, the will of the people was replaced by legal paternalism (Feinberg 1971).

While Nigeria embarked on a journey of legal assertion by revoking and reshaping several English statutes post-independence, the country's legal landscape remains heavily tinged with traces of English law. Many such laws, either untouched or slightly modified, persist. A notable example is the Bigamy Act, which deems polygamy illegal, even though the practice is common and broadly accepted in many Nigerian communities. This incongruity often results in ironic circumstance where the law is disregarded more than it is obeyed. Furthermore, principles rooted in English common law and equity remain relevant to Nigeria's legal system. English law still finds application in Nigerian courts. English court rulings are often invoked as persuasive reference points, and most strikingly, numerous Nigerian legislative instruments either emulate English laws or are directly adopted from them. The Defamation Law of Lagos State 2015 illustrates this trend, mirroring the English Defamation Act of 2013, especially in clauses concerning the single publication rule, platform liabilities and available defences. Arguably, as seen with the prevalent adoption of GDPR-like regulations, countries of the GS seem to have deferred the challenging task of framing laws for intricate technologies to the GN or perhaps yielded to external pressures to churn out regulations that pave their entry into the global trade arena.

Nevertheless, the tendency to mirror or adopt laws is not merely reactive to global market pressures or policy demands. Instead, it symbolises a deeper entrenchment of dominion via legal instruments, a lingering shadow of colonial influence. As highlighted previously, overt manifestations of such oppressive and exploitative dominance were evident in colonial era land and labour laws. Today, however, these manifestations have transitioned to the realms of data and technology. Domination and exploitation are intricately woven into the fabric of data handling and AI governance. Section 4 draws upon the rationalistic, functionalist and conflict paradigms of (GN-dominated) legal theory to elucidate the persisting "coloniality of power" within the context of legislative processes. We demonstrate that while all three theories are deeply rooted in colonial nuances, the conflict theory offers some perspectives for critical and self-reflexive approaches to AI governance.

LAW-MAKING THEORIES IN DECOLONIAL CONTEXTS

The theories and models underlying the legislative process offer insight into the motivations and considerations behind law-making, be it broadly or for specific subjects. However, it is posited here that these traditional models bear colonial imprints, which can distort the motivations for, and effectiveness of, laws regulating AI.

Rationalist and Functionalist Theories of Law-making

The "rationalist model" underscores logical, reasoned decision-making, framing laws as products of thorough analysis constructed in the spirit of fairness, justice and societal good. Proponents of this model believe that clear societal needs and aspirations drive legislation, and evidence-based decisions, broad expert consultations and rigorous regulatory impact analyses ideally mark this legislative process (Esptein 2014; Dascal and Wróblewski 1991). However, in reality, many laws deviate from this ideal of purpose and logic. This deviation is exemplified by colonial perspectives that perceive law as part of a "civilising mission", a generous offering from imperialists to their colonies (Sebba 1999; Rubin 1997). This colonial backdrop also underscores how wholesale legal systems, with their distinct cultural and social nuances, were imposed upon colonies. Post-colonial nations still wrestle with these overlapping systems, seeking ways to merge them or revert to their indigenous legal traditions (Merry 2003: 590).

This historical backdrop reveals limitations in the "rationalist" model when applied to AI governance and law-making. The model's emphasis on research and expert-driven processes can inadvertently favour technical insights from the GN, sidelining invaluable indigenous or localised knowledge (also see discussion on rationalistic auditing frameworks for AITs in the public sector by Gray, Chapter 15 in this volume). Such a tendency could foster an environment of elitism, potentially sidelining or ostracising marginalised communities. Moreover, while this model promotes comprehensive impact assessments, it often fails to consider intangible elements, such as cultural, historical or social contexts, which profoundly shape the quality and implications of laws. Thus, its inclination for simplification can render complex issues merely quantifiable metrics, potentially missing their nuanced intricacies.

For instance, pondering why a country like Nigeria has not formulated laws to mitigate AI threats despite being aware of associated risks, a plausible explanation can be traced to the lingering colonial impact, which instilled a propensity to mirror foreign legal frameworks in post-colonial states. Within the scope of the rationalistic model, it seems "logical" for countries to emulate European legislative precedents concerning AI, given the enduring perception of European cultural and epistemological supremacy.

The contemporary trajectory, contrasted with historical or territorial colonialism strategies, reveals a novel form which we call "governance colonialism". This concept is couched in the rhetoric of disseminating advanced scientific knowledge and enlightened governance. Under this prevailing perspective, non-Western nations, including their policymakers, specialists and academicians, are anticipated to adhere to these established benchmarks (Ricarture 2019: 35). The colonial mindset, which perceived lands as "terra nullius" or unclaimed if the indigenous communities governed them in unfamiliar or unapproved ways (Miller 2019, 2023), finds its modern parallel. It becomes convenient to promote the EU's methodical and "rational" legislative approach as a universally applicable benchmark. Quijano (2007) posits that the "coloniality of power" is evident in the pervasive mindset that views European culture as the pinnacle of rationality, capable of producing "subjects".

Conversely, non-European cultures are deemed irrational, rendering them incapable of producing comparable "subjects". This dichotomous view, positioning one as the subject and the other as the object, has stymied meaningful communication and exchange of knowledge between European and non-European cultures. As per this perspective, the relationship between a "subject" and an "object" is always one of distance and detachment. The European model of rational knowledge visibly embodies the coloniality of this power dynamic. Europe perceives itself as the guiding beacon for the future evolution of all other cultures, positioning itself as the epitome of the human species' progression (Quijano 2007: 174; Chakrabarty 2000).

The enduring dilemma is that Europe did not merely superimpose this illusion on most of the cultures it colonised and others outside its direct influence; these cultures continue to be captivated by this illusion (Quijano 2007: 176). This gives rise to what might be termed "internal colonialism", as state apparatuses, academic institutions and other entities perpetuate forms of colonisation, both domestically and internationally. They embed colonial influences in various spheres, from legal structures to public policies, even in deploying AI for public management (Ricaurte 2019: 350–365). While the concept of internal colonialism is not without its critics (Chaloult and Chaloult 1979; Turner 2018; Van de Grift 2015; Martins 2018), in this context, it is characterised by the wholesale adoption of European notions and classifications without tailoring them to fit the unique circumstances of formerly colonised nations. Casanova (1965: 29) points out the pressing need to move beyond this intellectual colonialism, emphasising the significance of analysing the interplay between political systems and social structures using concepts native to non-European nations.

The contention here is not that every nation should entirely reinvent its legal approach to AI, nor that a harmonised legal framework is inherently flawed. The argument is the potential inadequacy of the rationalistic model within a post-colonial setting. With AI presenting unique challenges like data extractivism, economic disparities and contextually varied ethical values, the assumption that externally sourced, albeit well-researched, AI laws – such as those emanating from Europe – can uniformly apply to GS countries like Nigeria is questionable at best. Compounding the issue is the persistent perception of the legal processes in post-colonial GS countries as lacking depth, rigour and sophistication (Pistor 2000; Weingast 2008). The rationalistic model inadvertently promotes a misleading sense of agency. Labelling African legal structures as reflections of European ones carries the implicit notion that legal reasoning and objectives are universally consistent. This implies that a singular model law could cater to the nuanced needs of diverse societies. However, as Quijano aptly notes, there is an inherent contradiction in touting the worldview of one ethnic or regional group as a universal yardstick for rationality. Elevating the Western European perspective to such a stature essentially portrays a regional understanding as a universal truth, a move Quijano critiques as an attempt to "impose provincialism as universalism" (Quijano 2007: 177).

The functionalist theory has similar shortcomings. At its core, functionalism views law as a means to foster social order, cohesion and stability. This approach emphasises the role of laws in fulfilling societal needs, preventing disarray and regulating behaviour to avoid conflicts. Functionalists regard laws as instrumental in affirming and upholding societal norms, values and expectations, acting as safeguards against disruptive behaviours. Additionally, this viewpoint acknowledges the law's pivotal role in resolving conflicts, which are seen as an unavoidable component of societal interactions and stability (Trevino 2008; Benditt 1975).

Nevertheless, this perspective can be critiqued for its potential oversights and simplifications. One main concern is its inadvertent or implicit disregard for power dynamics and vested interests within the law-making process. Contrary to the neutral lens that functionalism might suggest, laws frequently embody the interests of the prevailing class, serving to fortify their economic stronghold and facilitate societal control. Therefore, such a legal framework can often legitimise structures of capitalism – like property rights – while neglecting or minimising gender-related complexities, especially in societies historically influenced by male-centric institutions.

Moreover, the functionalist viewpoint seems to avoid the indelible mark of colonial history on legal systems. As previously highlighted, the laws and structures left behind by colonial powers do not operate in a vacuum. They often perpetuate systemic inequalities against the colonised, marginalising their unique cultural practices and traditions. Consequently, wholesale adoption of a legal framework like the EU's AI regulations by a nation such as Nigeria would not precisely align with the functionalist ideal. This is primarily because such a legal framework might lack the requisite inclusion of indigenous voices and knowledge systems.

Conflict Theory – Redefining Power Imbalances?

Although also tainted by colonial influence, the conflict theory is a more critical approach to the legal diffusion processes. It not only presents the most accurate depiction of the current power play in AI governance but also offers some insights into how the GS can address the imbalances. The conflict model views legislation as a product of social conflicts and power struggles. It suggests that the law reflects the distribution of power in society and serves the interests of dominant groups. Society is characterised by competing interests, values and goals held by different groups, and these conflicts manifest themselves in the legislative process, with different stakeholders seeking to influence the creation and content of laws to serve their interests. Law-making is, therefore, the result of ongoing negotiations and power struggles between different groups. Invariably, laws tend to reflect the interests and values of dominant groups; that is, the groups that possess greater social, economic or political power in society are more likely to shape legislation to their advantage, and laws are seen as tools that help maintain and reinforce existing power structures and social hierarchies (Bartos and Wehr 2002; Marx 2000; Wells 1979).

The previous analysis illustrates the predominance of the received English law and its eclipsing effect on indigenous legal systems in Nigeria, exemplifying the tendencies in colonial legislation where the colonising power imposes its laws upon the colonised people. Although there may be instances where a benevolent colonial administration attempts to consider the aspirations of the local inhabitants or specific segments thereof, such considerations might not be rooted in genuine democratic principles. Instead, they may be grounded in pragmatism, namely the desire that the law will be accepted and implemented with minimal friction and controversy (Merry 2003). This hierarchical structure also elevates the norms and institutions of former colonisers while downgrading or disregarding the values and cultural norms of the colonised people. Drawing from an extensive literature review on law and colonialism, Merry posits that "law frequently acts as an instrument of dominance, facilitating the establishment of novel systems of control and regulation" (2003: 917).

In AI governance, it is evident that laws are inclined to favour nations, communities and entities wielding significant power. This power can manifest in various forms: traditional metrics like economic strength, political clout and military might or contemporary indicators such as technological advancement and access to vast data repositories. Although a counter-argument suggests technology does not necessarily bestow power, the increasing relevance of a nation's or group's capacity to harness technology, drive innovation and assimilate emerging technologies is becoming a paramount indicator of global influence (Gu 2023). Indeed, power dynamics play a significant role in the fabric of international law. The process of crafting international laws – encompassing treaties, conventions and other agreements – is often punctuated by debates and negotiations, aiming to bridge differences and mitigate tensions among states of diverse power stature and interests. However, it is undeniable that influential states, measured by the criteria mentioned earlier, leverage their position to champion their agendas. In contrast, less powerful states, especially former colonies, might grapple with voicing their unique concerns effectively (Besson and Marti 2018). When it comes to AI governance, the equation becomes even more intricate. Non-governmental players, primarily tech behemoths, are pivotal to shaping international legal frameworks. This new dynamic intensifies the already existing power imbalances, influencing the trajectory of AI governance.

However, the conflict model offers unique insights when viewed through a decolonial lens. At its core, it underlines clashes, power imbalances and the contentious nature of law-making. It also provides a nuanced understanding of the dynamics influencing pre- and post-colonial systems and international law and standard-setting processes. The model aptly sheds light on the multifaceted aspects of colonisation and how they intersect, operating on internal, international and transnational levels. Thus, further perpetuating exploitative practices, erasure of distinct identities and threatening global biodiversity (Ricaurte 2019: 353). The model's essence lies in its inherent unpredictability, especially when predicting legislative outcomes, and identifying the victors and vanquished. This unpredictability becomes a crucial tool to examine and emphasise the viewpoints of often sidelined or underrepresented demographics, spotlighting potential biases, inequalities and injustices entrenched in legislative frameworks. It further underscores the need for more balanced, inclusive legislative processes.

Understanding the key aspects of conflict theory can lead to beneficial results in AI governance. It can accelerate the analysis of power dynamics, highlighting how the GN dominates and prioritises its interests over the GS. This recognition can trigger a redistribution of resources to support the GS in developing policies and technology and addressing biases that significantly impact them. Nevertheless, post-colonial GS nations, often perceived as weaker states, remain at a crossroads. One route involves a more passive approach, perhaps embracing established "gold standards" defined by influential entities like the EU. While this might seem like the path of least resistance, it is emblematic of the lingering shadow of colonial power dynamics. Rationalising the necessity of such laws, and pinpointing the specific issues they address, becomes an intricate task. Conversely, these states can choose a more assertive stance, rallying to promote their unique interests, challenging pre-existing power dynamics and advocating for reforms tailored to their distinct needs and ambitions. Achieving this necessitates a clear understanding of the required legal frameworks articulated via comprehensive, inclusive domestic legislative processes – effectively blending rationalist and functionalist theoretical models.

CONCLUSION

A decolonial approach to AI governance is not just a theoretical endeavour but a pragmatic and necessary step towards more inclusive global AI development. It offers a multidimensional approach that centres participation and deep respect for varied knowledge systems. At its core, the decolonial approach emphasises the involvement of communities directly impacted by AI. This ensures that the systems developed are not solely guided by the dominant perspectives of those with the most economic and political power and resources but are rooted in the rich tapestry of local knowledge and lived experiences. This is particularly important given the often-extractive nature of data and AI development, which might perpetuate historical injustices. Uncritical adoption of legal frameworks, especially those borrowed from former colonial powers or leading GN nations, often bypasses local contexts' unique challenges and aspirations. To avoid such oversights, grasping both the intrinsic merits and possible shortcomings of prevailing legislative paradigms is essential, especially in light of the enduring legacies of colonialism.

Adopting a decolonial lens provides a valuable foundation for AI law-making. It not only challenges the universality of GN-derived AI regulations but also recognises colonial influences in GS legislative processes. Yet the path towards inclusive AI governance is intricate and requires ongoing adjustments. Herein, empirical studies play a crucial role. By examining the translation of AI-related policy discussions in countries like Nigeria (or other GS nations) into tangible legal architectures, we can assess the real versus anticipated consequences of these policies. Such exploration will further illuminate dominant voices in these dialogues and those relegated to the periphery, shedding light on the prevailing dynamics. These assessments can subsequently be contrasted with established legal blueprints to pinpoint discrepancies and inefficiencies. This would allow for an informed debate as to the most apt models for future legislative endeavours as well as the necessary fine-tuning of existing structures, ensuring they are both efficacious and equitable. While the potential of a decolonial approach to AI governance is significant, actualising it demands an iterative strategy, persistently steered by scholarly inquiry, ongoing discourse and a dedication to comprehensive inclusiveness.

NOTE

1. The Brussels effect describes how the European Union indirectly extends its regulations globally through market forces. As a result, many entities, especially corporations, adhere to EU laws outside its borders.

REFERENCES

Adams, R. (2021), Can Artificial Intelligence be Decolonised?, *Interdisciplinary Science Reviews*, **46** (1–2), 176–197, https://doi.org/10.1080/03080188.2020.1840225.

Alkali, U., U. A. Jimeta, A. I. Magashi and T. M. Buba (2014), Nature and Sources of Nigerian Legal System: An Exorcism of a Wrong Notion, *International Journal of Business, Economics and Law*, **5** (4).

Bartos, O. J. and P. Wehr (2002), *Using Conflict Theory*, 1st ed., Cambridge: Cambridge University Press.

Benditt, T. M. (1975), A Functional Theory of Law, *University of Western Ontario Law Review*, **14** (149), 149–169.

Besson, S. and J. L. Martí (2018), Legitimate Actors of International Law-making: Towards a Theory of International Democratic Representation, *Jurisprudence*, **9** (3), 504–540, https://doi.org/10.1080/20403313.2018.1442256.

Bhambra, G. K., G. Dalia and K. Nişancıoğlu (2018), *Decolonising the University*, London: Pluto Press.

Birhane, A. (2020), Algorithmic Colonisation of Africa, *SCRIPTed*, **17** (2), http://dx.doi.org/10.2966/scrip.170220.389.

Bradford, A. (2012), The Brussels Effect. *Northwestern University Law Review*, **107** (1) (PDF); Columbia Law and Economics Working Paper No. 533. SSRN 2770634.

Buolamwini, J. and T. Gebru (2018), Gender Shades: Intersectional Accuracy Disparities in Commercial Gender Classification, https://www.classes.cs.uchicago.edu/archive/2020/winter/20370-1/readings/gendershadesAIbias.pdf.

Casanova, P. G. (1965), Internal Colonialism and National Development, *Studies in Comparative International Development*, **1**, 27–37.

Chakrabarty, D. (2000), *Provincializing Europe: Post-colonial Thought and Historical Difference*, 1st ed., Princeton, NJ: Princeton University Press.

Chaloult, N. B. and Y. Chaloult (1979), The Internal Colonialism Concept: Methodological Considerations, *Social and Economic Studies*, **28** (4), 85–99, https://www.jstor.org/stable/27861779.

Chibber, V. (2013), *Post-colonial Theory and the Specter of Capital*, 1st ed., New York: Verso Books.

Cohen, J. E. (2018), The Biopolitical Public Domain: The Legal Construction of the Surveillance Economy, *Philosophy & Technology*, **31**, 213–233, https://doi.org/10.1007/s13347017-0258-2.

Couldry, N. and U. Mejias (2019), Data Colonialism: Rethinking Big Data's Relation to the Contemporary Subject, *Television & New Media*, **20** (4), 336–349, https://doi.org/10.1177/1527476418796632.

Couldry, N. and U. Mejias (2023), The Decolonial Turn in Data and Technology Research: What Is at Stake and Where Is it Heading?, *Information, Communication & Society*, **26** (4), 786–802, https://doi.org/10.1080/1369118X.2021.1986102.

Dascal, M. and J. Wróblewski (1991), The Rational Lawmaker and the Pragmatics of Legal Interpretation, *Journal of Pragmatics*, **15** (1), 421–444, https://doi.org/10.1016/0378-2166(91)90047-2.

Epstein, D. Z. (2014), Rationality, Legitimacy, & the Law, *Washington University Jurisprudence Review*, **7** (1), http://dx.doi.org/10.2139/ssrn.1527590.

Feinberg, J. (1971), Legal Paternalism, *Canadian Journal of Philosophy*, **1** (1), 105–124, https://doi.org/10.1080/00455091.1971.10716012.

Gillen, P. and D. Ghosh (2007), *Colonialism and Modernity*. Kensington, Australia: UNSW Press.

Gu, H. (2023), Data, Big Tech, and the New Concept of Sovereignty, *Journal of Chinese Political Science*, 3 (1–22), https://doi.org/10.1007/s11366-023-09855-1.

Gwagwa, A., E. Kazim and A. Hilliard (2022), The Role of the African Value of Ubuntu in Global AI Inclusion Discourse: A Normative Ethics Perspective, *Patterns*, 3 (4), https://doi.org/10.1016/j.patter.2022.100462.

Hao, K. (2020, June 12), The Two-Year Fight to Stop Amazon from Selling Face Recognition to the Police, *MIT Technology Review*. https://www.technologyreview.com/2020/06/12/1003482/amazon-stopped-selling-police-face-recognition-fight/.

Jobin, A., M. Ienca and E. Vayena (2019), The Global Landscape of AI Ethics Guidelines, *Nature Machine Intelligence*, 1, 389–399. https://doi.org/10.1038/s42256-019-0088-2.

Martins, H. M. (2018), Internal Colonialism: Post-colonial Criticism and Social Theory, *Revue du MAUSS permanente*, 11 August 2018 [online], https://journaldumauss.net/./?Internal-Colonialism-Postcolonial-Criticism-and-Social-Theory.

Marx, K. (2000), *Selected Writings*, 2nd ed., Oxford: Oxford University Press.

McBride, K. (2016), *Colonialism and the Rule of Law in Mr. Mothercountry: The Man Who Made the Rule of Law*, online ed., New York: Oxford Academic.

Merry, S. E. (2003), Review: From Law and Colonialism to Law and Globalization, *Law & Social Inquiry*, 28 (2), 569–590, https://doi.org/10.1111/j.1747-4469.2003.tb00206.x.

Mhlambi, S. (2020), From Rationality to Relationality: Ubuntu as an Ethical & Human Rights Framework for Artificial Intelligence Governance, Carr Center Discussion Paper Series, 2020-009. Available at https://carrcenter.hks.harvard.edu/publications/rationality-relationality-ubuntu-ethical-and-human-rights-framework-artificial.

Mhlambi, S. and S. Tiribelli (2023), Decolonizing AI Ethics: Relational Autonomy as a Means to Counter AI Harms, *Topoi*, 42, 867–880, https://doi.org/10.1007/s11245-022-09874-2.

Milan, S. and E. Treré (2019), Big Data from the South(s): Beyond Data Universalism, *Television & New Media*, 20 (4), 319–335. https://doi.org/10.1177/1527476419837739.

Miller, R. J. (2019), The Doctrine of Discovery: The International Law of Colonialism, *The Indigenous Peoples' Journal of Law, Culture & Resistance*, 5 (1), 35–42, https://doi.org/10.5070/P651043048.

Miller, R. J. (2023), The International Law of Colonialism: Johnson v. M'Intosh and the Doctrine of Discovery Applied Worldwide, Canopy Forum, Center for the Study of Law and Religion, Emory University.

Miller, R. J. and O. Siltz (2021), The International Law of Colonialism in East Africa: Germany, England, and the Doctrine of Discovery, *Duke Journal of Comparative & International Law*, 32 (1), http://dx.doi.org/10.2139/ssrn.3798893.

Mohamed, S., M. T. Png and W. Isaac (2020), Decolonial AI: Decolonial Theory as Socio-technical Foresight in Artificial Intelligence, *Philosophy & Technology*, 33, 659–684, https://doi.org/10.1007/s13347-020-00405-8.

Omotubora, A. (2021), How (Not) to Regulate Data Processing – Assessing Nigeria's Data Protection Regulation (NDPR) 2019, *Global Privacy Law Review*, 2 (3), 186–199, https://doi.org/10.54648/gplr2021024.

Omotubora, A. and S. Basu (2020), Next Generation Privacy, *Information & Communications Technology Law*, 29 (2), 151–173, https://doi.org/10.1080/13600834.2020.1732055.

Pistor, K. (2000), The Standardisation of Law and its Effect on Developing Economies, *The American Journal of Comparative Law*, 50 (1), 97–130, https://doi.org/10.2307/840831.

Quijano, A. (2007), Coloniality and Modernity/Rationality Cultural Studies, *Cultural Studies*, 21 (2–3), 168–178, https://doi.org/10.1080/09502380601164353.

Ricaurte, P. (2019), Data Epistemologies, the Coloniality of Power, and Resistance, *Television & New Media*, 20 (4), 350–365, https://doi.org/10.1177/1527476419831640.

Ricaurte, P. (2022), Artificial Intelligence and the Feminist Decolonial Imagination, Bot Populi. Available at https://botpopuli.net/artificial-intelligence-and-the-feminist-decolonial-imagination/.

Rubin, E. (1997), Rational States?, *Virginia Law Review*, 83 (7), 1433–1451, accessed at https://doi.org/10.2307/1073763.

Sebba, L. (1999), The Creation and Evolution of Criminal Law in Colonial and Post-colonial Societies, *Crime, History & Societies*, 3 (1), 71–91, https://doi.org/10.4000/chs.936.

Segura, M. S. and S. Waisbord (2019), Between Data Capitalism and Data Citizenship, *Television & New Media*, **20** (4), 412–419, https://doi.org/10.1177/1527476419834519.

Shomade, S. A. (2022), *Colonial Legacies and the Rule of Law in Africa: Ghana, Kenya, Nigeria, South Africa and Zimbabwe*, 1st ed., London: Routledge.

Thatcher, J., D. O'Sullivan and D. Mahmoudi (2016), *Data Colonialism through Accumulation by Dispossession: New Metaphors for Daily Data, Environment and Planning D: Society and Space*, **34** (6), 990–1006, https://doi.org/10.1177/0263775816633195.

The African Commission on Human and Peoples' Rights (2021), Resolution on the Need to Undertake a Study on Human and Peoples' Rights and Artificial Intelligence (AI), Robotics and Other New and Emerging Technologies in Africa, ACHPR. Available at https://achpr.au.int/en/adopted-resolutions/473-resolution-need-undertake-study-human-and-peoples-rights-and-art.

Trevino, A. J. (2008), *Structural Functionalism in Sociology of Law*, 1st ed., London: Routledge.

Turner, J. (2018), Internal Colonisation: The Intimate Circulations of Empire, Race and Liberal Government, *European Journal of International Relations*, **24** (4), 765–790, https://doi.org/10.1177/1354066117734904.

Van de Grift, L. (2015), Theories and Practices of Internal Colonisation: The Cultivation of Lands and People in the Age of Modern Territoriality, *International Journal for History, Culture and Modernity*, **3** (2), 139–158, https://doi.org/10.18352/hcm.480.

Weingast, B. R. (2008), *Why Developing Countries Prove So Resistant to the Rule of Law in Global Perspectives on the Rule of Law*, 1st ed., London: Routledge-Cavendish.

Wells, A. (1979), Conflict Theory and Functionalism: Introductory Sociology Textbooks, 1928–1976, *Teaching Sociology*, **6** (4), 429–437, https://doi.org/10.2307/1317229.

18. Procurement and artificial intelligence
Cary Coglianese

INTRODUCTION

Public administrators seeking to improve their performance through the use of artificial intelligence (AI) avoid thinking about procurement at their peril. Consider how officials at the fourth most-populated city in the United States – Houston, Texas – learned about the importance of procurement several years ago, after the local teachers' union took the city's school district to court over an algorithmic tool used to assess teachers' performance (Houston Federation of Teachers, 2017). The algorithm generated a "value-added" teaching effectiveness score for each teacher, which school administrators then used to set teachers' terms of employment, including in making decisions about whether and when to terminate teachers who received low scores (Law Commission of Ontario, 2022). The union argued in court that teachers' due process rights were violated because the school district would not release to them the source code and computational structure of the algorithm. But the school district itself did not know how the algorithm worked. The software had been procured from a private firm which had claimed that information about its algorithm was protected as a proprietary trade secret – and the school district's licensing contract had failed to include any special terms that would require disclosure of any information (Houston Federation of Teachers, 2017).

Finding in favour of the teachers' union, the court concluded that the school district's use of the secret algorithm deprived teachers of their constitutional rights (Houston Federation of Teachers, 2017). Specifically, the court held that the school district had "flunk[ed] the minimum due process standard" because teachers were unable to access enough information about the algorithm to verify its accuracy or even to know how the scores it produced came about (Houston Federation of Teachers, 2017, p. 1178). Without any information about the algorithm used by the school district, it amounted to "a mysterious 'black box'" (Houston Federation of Teachers, 2017, p. 1179). The court ruled against the school district and concluded that "[w]hen a public agency adopts a policy of making high stakes employment decisions based on secret algorithms incompatible with minimum due process, the proper remedy is to overturn the policy, while leaving the trade secrets intact" (Houston Federation of Teachers, 2017, p. 1179).

But trade secrets need not always remain "intact". Although the machine-learning algorithms that characterize AI do have some inherent black-box elements to them, the secrecy surrounding the work of private contractors that develop and deploy these algorithms is not necessarily inherent to the technology.[1] It can be a function of contractual terms. Governments can instead require, through provisions in their contracts, that AI service providers release information to satisfy the public and courts that these tools are functioning fairly and responsibly – ultimately sparing public agencies the risk of lawsuits like the one in Houston and controversies that have surrounded the use of AI elsewhere in the world. These contract provisions can also require that contractors comply with specified standards governing how AI tools are developed and used (Coglianese and Ben Dor, 2021a).

Even in countries where litigation is not as common as in the United States, public officials who contemplate the possibility of future controversy over the fairness, accountability, and ethical concerns of their use of AI can use the contracting process as a vehicle for advancing the goals of responsible AI. Because technological innovation and data science expertise tend to be concentrated in private firms, governmental entities need private sector firms to provide many of the advanced data analytic services and AI tools that increasingly are being deployed with the aim of improving public sector performance. As Rubenstein (2022) has noted, outsourcing the development and deployment of AI tools allows governmental entities "to capitalize on industry's innovation, institutional know-how, and high-skilled workforce".[2] It is little exaggeration to observe that public sector use of AI is inextricably linked to procurement. As a result, contracts for AI services with private firms can establish the first line of defence against improper or ill-executed public sector use of algorithmic tools. When governmental institutions rely on private firms to build and deploy AI tools, procurement contracts provide an important avenue for governing the use of these tools (Coglianese and Ben Dor, 2021a). Procurement, in other words, can constitute policy with respect to the use of AI (Mulligan and Bamberger, 2019).

This chapter investigates the connections between procurement and AI in the public sector, highlighting the opportunities for developing procurement policies and contractual terms seeking to ensure the responsible deployment of AI by governmental agencies.[3] To provide a full account of the relationship between AI and procurement, the chapter begins by explaining how governments around the world are starting to rely on AI to improve their procurement processes. It proceeds by focusing on how procurement can be used as policy to govern the development and use of AI tools to perform a wide variety of public administration functions. It explains how careful attention to procurement contracts can in the first instance solve some of the first-level transparency concerns surrounding governmental use of AI. The chapter then turns to how procurement can help address not only deeper transparency and explainability concerns about AI (also see Aula and Erkkilä, Chapter 13 in this volume; Berry, Chapter 10 in this volume) but also concerns about fairness and accountability (Cobbe and Singh, Chapter 7 in this volume). In short, procurement can be an important source of AI governance.

PROCUREMENT AND AI: A TWO-WAY RELATIONSHIP

Although using procurement to govern AI is the central focus of this chapter, a complete accounting of the relationship between procurement and AI must begin by acknowledging that procurement offices, like other parts of government (Coglianese and Ben Dor, 2021b), are starting to find AI tools to be useful in helping improve their administrative efficiency and performance (Booth and Sharma, 2019). Procurement officials are exploring the possibilities for AI and other forms of "procuretech" to help reduce staff time in processing contracts and other related paperwork as well as to assist in making human judgements about contracting and sourcing decisions. They can also be used for supply chain management and the monitoring and auditing of contractual compliance.

The advantages deriving from automation in procurement can be potentially great because many public sector procurement processes involve the processing and review of substantial volumes of paperwork. This review either makes the procurement process slow or necessitates increasing the number of staff members devoted to contracting (Yama, 2018). At the bid selection stage, for example, every submitted proposal must be read, processed, and compared before any bid can be selected. If a validated natural language processing tool – a type of AI – can be used to process and assess a large volume of bids based on well-specified parameters, the bid selection process might not only be shortened, but it could also potentially become more accurate than relying solely on human paperwork review (ElectrifAi, 2020). If nothing else, automated tools can parse each proposal to determine how closely it fits within the parameters for bids, flagging items for further review (AI Data & Analytics Network, 2022).

Given the complexity of many countries' procurement rules, so-called knowledge bots can take advantage of generative AI to answer contracting officers' questions. One system being developed to support contracting within the US Air Force showed how it would be possible to use AI to answer specific procurement questions so that the contracting officer does not need to leaf manually through the pages of procurement regulations (Keegan, 2020, p. 57). According to one account, the Air Force's procurement project involved uploading "thousands of regulations, contract cases, acquisition training material and Defense Department policy to a database [and] AI technology then helped answer queries from federal contract officials and contractors about acquisition rules and regulations, such as how to proceed with a contract, what procedures to follow, and what contract a small business could bid on" (Chenok, 2022). When the officer did not know what to do with a specific set of facts, the AI-driven bot responded with focused guidance.[4]

AI tools can also provide other assistance to procurement officers. AI could be used, for example, to process past data to evaluate proposals for their risk exposure to the contracting agency or the likelihood of a potential contractor to miss a deadline or otherwise fail to meet contract terms (Tillipman, 2022). Procurement officials may benefit from reports on contractors based on their past performance, with AI helping identify relevant records or generate performance statistics or profiles (Larkin, 2021; Chenok, 2022).[5]

Finally, government officials must typically monitor implementation of and compliance with numerous contracts to ensure that contractual obligations are being met (AI Data & Analytics Network, 2022). Agencies have massive files or databases full of past contractor performance which can be used to train machine-learning algorithms to help officials forecast which contractors are likely in need of further investigation. AI tools that forecast the likelihood of delays and other risks can help optimize auditing and other oversight resources and practices (Reynolds and Norwood, 2020). In the same way that private sector firms are using AI tools to assist with supply chain management (Mayer, 2023), these same tools could be used by government agencies that have large supply chain responsibilities.

Integrating AI into the procurement process will undoubtedly require that procurement offices have sufficient data storage and analysis capabilities (Coglianese and Lai, 2022). The AI tools being developed to help with procurement will themselves likely need to be procured and then developed and deployed responsibly (Keegan, 2020). As with other governmental uses of AI, the use of AI in procurement poses potential concerns about transparency as well as the need for careful use and oversight (Reynolds and Norwood, 2020; Sievo, 2022).

PROCUREMENT AND ALGORITHMIC TRANSPARENCY

The transparency concerns underlying the use of AI derive in the first instance from the self-learning properties of machine-learning algorithms.[6] Unlike with traditional statistical algorithms, such as multivariate regression models, machine-learning algorithms do not depend on humans to select variables and mathematical relationships between them. As a result, even when a machine-learning algorithm generates a highly accurate result, it is not easy or intuitive to understand how it reached that result (Coglianese and Lehr, 2019). It is not possible, for example, to interpret results simply by pointing to identifiable variables in a specified model and showing that they account for some portion of the variation in the model's outputs (Busuioc, 2020). Nor are causal inferences capable of being drawn from the outputs of machine-learning algorithms in the ready fashion that they can from traditional statistical analysis in well-designed research. For these reasons, the machine-learning algorithms that drive AI systems have often been called "black-box" algorithms.

The intrinsic, relatively black-box nature of machine-learning algorithms has contributed to some unease about the use of AI across society and the economy (Pasquale, 2016). And when these black-box tools are used by governmental authorities, particular concerns have been raised that AI's inscrutability is antithetical to principles of due process and open government (Citron, 2008; Yeung, 2017; Calo and Citron, 2021). The teachers' union's lawsuit in Houston, for example, relied on an argument grounded in constitutional rights because the school district that used a teaching performance algorithm was a governmental institution – an argument that is not available to employees or customers of a private business who might object to the use of an algorithmic performance tool. In short, the harms alleged may be the same when public and private sector actors use AI technologies, but the law can differ between the two contexts, often imposing more stringent standards or affording aggrieved individuals more rights when governmental entities use these technologies.

Despite particular concerns over the opacity of AI tools used by governments, nothing about the intrinsic black-box nature of these algorithms would appear to bar their use by government authorities under existing law (Coglianese and Lehr, 2017; Coglianese and Appel, 2022). Even with the inherent black-box nature of a machine-learning algorithm, it is possible for governmental officials to describe what the algorithm was designed to predict, how it generally operates, what kind of data its results are based upon, and how it has been tested and validated. The disclosure of this kind of information is likely to be sufficient to withstand most requirements for transparency under existing legal standards (Coglianese and Lehr, 2019). Indeed, in response to a lawsuit challenging the use of a so-called black-box algorithm to assess the risk of a defendant in a criminal sentencing proceeding, the state supreme court in Wisconsin upheld the government's reliance on the algorithm in the face of a constitutional rights challenge. The Wisconsin court found that it was sufficient for the defendant to have basic information about the structure of the algorithm as well as the ability to confirm that the information about himself had been accurate (*State v. Loomis*, 2016).

Even if the law were to become more demanding about the disclosure of information about government-deployed algorithms, the ability to understand what these algorithms are doing is also increasing over time. Precisely because computer scientists appreciate and share concerns about the opacity of machine learning, they have been developing new techniques for understanding how these algorithms reach the results they do. Research keeps "accumulating that details technical methods for improving the ability to explain the inner workings of machine learning in more intuitive ways" (Coglianese and Lehr, 2019, p. 50).

Of course, even with these advances that reduce the intrinsic opacity of machine-learning algorithms, when algorithms are developed by a contractor an additional, qualitatively distinct black-box problem can arise. Contractors can claim that their algorithms are trade secrets or contain proprietary information, and then on this basis they can refuse to disclose any information about them. This creates a nested opacity problem, whereby the intrinsic black-box nature of machine-learning algorithms is compounded by claims of trade secret protection by the contractor that uses these tools. The risk of nested opacity often arises when government relies on AI tools, simply because few government agencies possess the necessary in-house capacity to design and operate AI tools (Coglianese and Lampmann, 2021). According to one estimate, at least half of the AI uses by the federal government in the United States are developed or carried out by private contractors (Rubenstein, 2021).

The nested opacity problem was central to the court's decision in the Houston school district case. The private contractor there treated its "algorithms and software as trade secrets, refusing to divulge them" to the teachers and even to its client, the school district (Houston Federation of Teachers, 2017, p. 1168). The court noted that "without access to [the contractor's] proprietary information – the value-added equations, computer source codes, decision rules, and assumptions – [the algorithmic system] will remain a mysterious 'black box,' impervious to challenge" (Houston Federation of Teachers, 2017, p. 1179).

The Wisconsin state supreme court in *State v. Loomis* (2016, p. 761) encountered a similar predicament in which a risk assessment scoring tool had been developed by a private contractor that considered the tool's algorithm to be "a trade secret" and therefore would "not disclose how the risk scores are determined or how the factors are weighed". But in *Loomis*, the contractor was at least willing to share some information about the algorithm, including all the variables used to generate the risk score used by the court in its sentencing decision. The *Loomis* court held that this disclosure was sufficient, and it upheld the government's algorithm.

The differing outcomes in the Houston and Wisconsin cases suggest an opportunity for procurement to play an important role in overcoming the nested opacity problem. If government contracting officials were to insist that their AI vendors disavow claims of absolute secrecy, and instead commit to disclosure of sufficient information to demonstrate the validity and proper functioning of an AI tool developed for governmental use, this would ensure public agencies could provide courts, other oversight entities, and the public with information needed to have trust in the design and use of AI tools. This could be accomplished either on an individual tender basis or through the adoption of general procurement policies that require disclosure by contracting firms sufficient to solve the nested opacity problem. Furthermore, by using procurement to require that contractors use emerging analytic techniques that enhance algorithmic explainability, the contracting process could even go some distance toward addressing the intrinsic opacity of machine-learning algorithms.

A total neglect during procurement of the need for information about how an AI tool operates would seem only to invite private contractors to assert excessively broad trade secret rights. After all, it is unclear if the kind of information needed to withstand legal challenges like the one in the Houston case would even qualify for legitimate trade secret protection (Coglianese and Lampmann, 2019, pp. 187–188). It may be sufficient to ensure the disclosure of general information about the algorithm's objective and sources of data, as well as efforts taken to validate and audit its performance. Some private sector firms are already following best practices and voluntarily disclosing "model cards" or "system cards" that contain such information about what AI tools can and cannot do, how they have been tested, and what risks they might pose (Mitchell et al., 2019; Coglianese, 2023), demonstrating that such information need not be viewed as a trade secret. But even for valid trade secret information, public contracts could specify that the contractor at least cooperate with a court to provide "in camera" review, a standard procedure that courts undertake to review protected information without it losing its protection.

If government contracts remain silent on these matters, private firms may have little reason not to claim expansive protection of secrecy over the algorithms they design and deploy, even if this might work to the detriment of their government clients in courts of law or in the court of public opinion. Such a predicament for government agencies would be to a large extent avoidable. It is possible, after all, to "specify public rights" to information about the objectives and operation of AI systems (Metcalf et al., 2023). In 2020, a government-wide statement on AI issued by the Administrative Conference of the United States made clear that federal "[a]gencies should not enter into contracts to use proprietary AI systems unless they are confident that actors both internal and external to the agencies will have adequate access to information about the systems" (ACUS, 2021, p. 6617). The New Zealand Law Foundation (2019) has issued a report recommending that "government agencies' procurement policies should give preference to companies which are open (i.e., publish information) about their algorithms, rather than those who hide behind proprietary code" (Gavaghan et al., 2019). In Canada, the federal government has issued a Directive on Automated Decision Making that calls for contractual provisions stipulating that the government always retains the right to access and audit proprietary software (Government of Canada, 2019).

As Brauneis and Goodman (2018) indicate, it is possible for government agencies to demand that access will be provided to information held by AI vendors. At the time of contracting, government procurement officers will often hold many advantages in terms of bargaining power over contractors eager to secure government work (Powles, 2017). The terms of government contracts for AI services and tools can call upon contractors to generate information needed to understand the operation of their algorithms and otherwise take into account future needs for transparency and explainability (Coglianese and Ben Dor, 2021a).[7] In this way, contracting can provide a necessary foundation for the kind of accountability that is expected in the realm of public administration.

GOVERNING AI THROUGH CONTRACTS

Contracts can do more than provide for the necessary condition of the transparency of AI systems. Government contracts can help more generally ensure that AI tools are ethically designed from the outset and used in a responsible manner. In short, contracts can provide a key source of governance with respect to the design and deployment of AI tools by public entities.

The use of contracts as governance is hardly a new phenomenon, nor is it a practice limited to the use of AI or even to governmental contracts. An extensive practice of what Lipson (2019) has called "contract social responsibility" has emerged in recent decades across both the public and private sectors and for a wide variety of contracts.[8] Contracts for many goods and services increasingly include "express promises to act (or to refrain from acting) in a way designed to have an important social or environmental impact in addition to, or apart from, the commercial interests of the parties" to the contract (Lipson, 2019, p. 1117). These practices include a wide variety of contractual provisions by private sector actors to ensure that the vendors with which they do business act in an environmentally responsible manner (Coglianese and Nash, 2006, pp. 10–11), treat workers fairly and safely (Fung, O'Rourke, and Sabel, 2001), and protect human rights (Ruggie, 2013).

In the public sector, procurement has long been relied upon to advance a host of public interest objectives that extend beyond the narrow, immediate provision of goods and services covered under the agreement. This reliance on contracting as governance – sometimes called social procurement (Ludlow, 2016) – occurs when procurement officials take "a full life-cycle approach, including the consideration of environmental and social costs", and then develop government contracts and oversee a contracting process with these overall impacts in mind (OECD, 2015). Such a life-cycle approach fits well in the context of AI, where problems can emerge at any stage of development and deployment of the technology. Indeed, the conversation around AI regulation more generally is sometimes framed specifically in life-cycle terms (Hwang, Kesselheim, and Vokinger, 2019; ICO, 2023; also see: Lucivero, Chapter 12 in this volume).

Today, a variety of standard public procurement policies seek to advance overall societal justice across all aspects of government contracting by including provisions that require sustainable business practices or that call for employing women or members of minority racial groups. Often these socially oriented contractual provisions incorporate by reference standards of social responsibility that have been developed by various nongovernmental, standards-setting organizations. As Lipson (2019, pp. 1118–1119) has noted, "[r]ather than design terms from scratch, the promisor may agree to adhere to social responsibility standards set by, for example, the International Organization for Standardization (ISO), the Global Reporting Initiative, or Social Accountability International" or "may agree to join an organization such as the Responsible Business Alliance, whose members must conform to that group's standards and code of conduct".

Against the backdrop of this larger use of government contracting as a form of public policy, it is hardly surprising that procurement has come to be viewed as an important vehicle for ensuring the responsible use of AI (Coglianese and Lampmann, 2021; Rubenstein, 2022; Marchant and Gutierrez, 2023, pp. 408–410). The Committee on Standards in Public Life (2020, p. 49) in the United Kingdom (UK), for example, has noted that procurement is "a crucial point in the AI lifecycle where provisions for ethical standards must be set". The Committee has specifically recommended the following with respect to government contracts for AI-related services:

> Government should use its purchasing power in the market to set procurement requirements that ensure that private companies developing AI solutions for the public sector appropriately address public standards. This should be achieved by ensuring provisions for ethical standards are considered early in the procurement process and explicitly written into tenders and contractual arrangements. (Committee on Standards in Public Life, 2020, p. 51)

In addition, the World Economic Forum (2020) has emphasized the importance of responsible contracting for AI, issuing a procurement "toolkit" aimed at encouraging governments around the world "to set the right policies, protocols, and perhaps even standards to facilitate effective, responsible and ethical public use of AI". In addition, a report by the Law Commission of Ontario (2021) has called for careful procurement practices so that governmental use of private contractors' AI tools will still meet public standards for transparency, due process, and the protection of human rights. A major nongovernmental standards development organization – the IEEE Standards Association – has launched a process aimed at developing a voluntary standard for AI procurement according to "which government entities can address socio-technical and responsible innovation considerations to serve the public interest" (IEEE, 2023).

Official governmental policies are starting to follow from these various reports and recommendations. The UK government, for example, has issued a set of best practices for procuring AI tools, including suggested contractual requirements that aim to "set the foundation for the effective, responsible, and ethical deployment of AI technologies" (UK Office for Artificial Intelligence, 2020). An executive order applicable to federal agencies in the United States specifically notes that its directives related to governmental use of AI tools also apply to all "agencies' procurement of AI applications" (Executive Order 13,960, 2020).

Even when procurement is not directly governed by official guidance, agencies can still use contract language to govern how their vendors develop and deploy AI tools. Just as in other contexts where contracts have incorporated third-party standards of social responsibility rather than containing their own distinctive terms, procurement officials can readily adopt third-party standards with respect to the responsible use of AI tools. Indeed, there appears to be little shortage in the number of possible standards that could potentially be incorporated into contracts for AI services. Through the OECD (2019), for example, a number of countries have concurred with a series of principles on the responsible use of algorithms, including those that call for transparency in the operation of algorithms and those that seek to ensure that AI tools are accountable as well as "robust, secure and safe". The non-profit organization, Responsible AI (RAI) Institute (2023), claims to have established "the first independent and community developed responsible AI assessment, rating, certification, and documentation system" that falls in line with the OECD principles. The Institute notes that

> [m]any procuring organizations are looking to the RAI Institute to help them define what their responsible AI procurement practices should be. By using our responsible AI maturity assessments for your AI-enabled systems you can assure customers that the AI-enabled system they are buying is built implemented and operated in a responsible manner and in accordance with their policies. (RAI Institute, 2023)

The OECD principles and RAI Institute's certification process are but two possible sources of substantive protections that can be built into AI-related contracts. Another example would be the IEEE Standards Association's P7000 standard, which outlines a process for "addressing ethical concerns" when building automated systems that rely on AI (IEEE, 2021). A standard issued jointly by the International Organization for Standardization (ISO) and the International Electrotechnical Commission (IEC) also provides guidance on managing risks from AI systems (ISO/IEC, 2023). One study has identified more than 600 other codes of conduct or other statements of best practices that articulate principles for the responsible use of AI (Marchant and Gutierrez, 2023). Although these various standards are non-binding – and considered to be "soft law" – they can become legally binding if incorporated into the agreements between vendors and government agencies.

In addition to incorporating substantive standards for AI responsibility into contracts, government officials can impose a variety of procedural requirements too. They can, for example, require that contractors conduct algorithmic impact assessments of new or modified AI tools and engage in regular auditing of these tools in practice (Kroll et al., 2017). Contracts can include requirements for compiling and sharing reports from these assessments and audits. As with substantive standards, procurement officers can incorporate by reference an externally developed set of guidelines for how these assessments and audits ought to be conducted, such as with the guidance developed by the US Government Accountability Office (2021) or reflected in a white paper issued by five countries' public auditing bodies (Supreme Audit Institutions, 2023). Contracts can also obligate vendors to convene or at least participate in public input sessions organized around the structure and operation of AI tools (Mulligan and Bamberger, 2019). In ways such as these, procurement can go well beyond the usual aspects of a contract, such as those related to prices, deadlines, and the like. Contracts can become a form of governance that seeks to promote AI accountability, safety, fairness, and transparency.

ASSESSING PROCUREMENT AS AI GOVERNANCE

Procurement will surely not be the only mechanism needed to govern AI. But using procurement as a means of governing AI does hold a variety of potential advantages. One chief benefit is that contractual governance can in most cases be adopted immediately, at least to some degree. In many countries, it will take considerably more time before legislators and regulators deliberate over what should appear in codified standards for governmental use of AI. In the meantime, procurement officials can begin to incorporate state-of-the-art principles and practices into contracts today. Indeed, the next time any government agency contracts for outside services related to AI, it can insist on transparency and careful development, testing and oversight of AI by its outside vendor. Because government officials typically possess discretion to define the terms of bid solicitations and ultimately the wording of contracts, they do not need to wait to begin using that discretion. By acting now, procurement officials can help ensure that their agencies do not end up in the kind of predicament that the Houston school district ultimately confronted when it was taken to court.

Beyond the ready availability of contractual provisions, using procurement as governance holds at least two other advantages. First, procurement's impact can spread beyond just the immediate confines of specific contracts. Simcoe and Toffel (2014) showed that when US cities set contractual benchmarks for energy efficiency of municipal construction, not only did it result in the targeted buildings being constructed in an energy-efficient manner, but it also was associated with more energy-efficient construction throughout these entire cities as well as even in neighboring ones. A similar spillover effect from the diffusion of best practices of responsible AI can be envisioned from public sector organizations' adoption of responsible procurement policies related to AI.

Second, contracting allows for bespoke governance. This is an advantage because AI tools can be highly varied, and the uses to which they are deployed vary even more widely. Bright-line rules and other blunt forms of regulation are generally unsuitable for governing AI tools because of the extreme heterogeneity of their designs, operations, uses, and potential harms and benefits (Coglianese, 2023). Contracts, though, can be customized to fit the specific circumstances and conditions surrounding particular uses of AI. Government contracts for the use of AI in law enforcement, for example, would presumably need different governing provisions than contracts for the use of AI in government-supported climate research.

Of course, just as with governance more generally, using procurement as a bespoke form of AI governance will not always be easy, nor is it likely by itself to be sufficient. In some government agencies, procurement officers do not yet possess a sufficiently sophisticated understanding of and experience with AI to craft concrete contractual language around AI tools (Sanchez-Graells, 2023). At least in the immediate term, contractual provisions may be limited to incorporating third-party standards and requiring conformity assessment by third-party auditors, rather than direct oversight by existing procurement teams. This may be necessary as a feasible first step, recognizing that it comes along with potential limitations, such as possible inconsistencies or insufficiencies in the underlying standards used or limitations in ensuring robust or consistent oversight performed by third-party auditors (McAllister, 2012). With time, however, it should be more reasonable to expect that agencies will develop both greater experience with AI and improved internal capacities to craft ever more sophisticated agreements with AI vendors. To get there, procurement teams will need "training and professional development to understand both technical and non-technical AI concepts" (Autio et al., 2023). Yet even without advanced training, procurement officers always should be on guard against inflated claims and sales pitches by government contractors about what their AI tools can do and how safe, transparent, and fair they will be (Coglianese and Lai, 2022; cf. Dekel and Schurr, 2014).

When it comes to governing AI through procurement, just as with governing AI through other means, a healthy dose of skepticism about AI's promises will be in order, as will be the need for careful planning and consideration of AI's potential negative consequences (Coglianese and Lai, 2022). It will also be important to remember that a government contract cannot fully substitute for truly vigilant managerial oversight. As Kroll (2022) has noted, "[r]esponsible AI is not merely responsibly sourced AI or AI contracted to follow an organization's internal controls" – it ultimately depends on a continuous process. Contractual governance can be helpful, and even essential (Rubenstein, 2022), but good governance of AI ultimately "requires an ongoing effort to understand an AI system's behaviors and sustain good outcomes" (Kroll, 2022). With ongoing vigilance by all government officials that interact with and rely upon AI – including procurement officers but also other agency staff members and upper-level management – the public can reap improvements in public sector performance from the proper use of AI tools, while also navigating around avoidable roadblocks like the kind that befell Houston's school officials when a court ruled against the algorithmic tool developed by their contractor.

NOTES

1. Although this chapter's analysis fits with a capacious definition of "artificial intelligence", the type of AI tools principally contemplated throughout the chapter are those that rely on machine-learning algorithms. These algorithms themselves can be highly heterogeneous, and they can be put to an even more varied set of use cases (Coglianese, 2023). In general, they are linked primarily by their self-learning properties, which allows them to discern patterns and make forecasts by processing large volumes of data without humans necessarily specifying the variables to consider or the functional form of the mathematical relationship between variables, as in conventional statistical analysis (Lehr and Ohm, 2017).
2. A US federal agency has noted that "[o]btaining AI systems from external sources might allow agencies to acquire more sophisticated tools than they could design on their own, access those tools sooner, and save some of the upfront costs associated with developing the technical capacity needed to design AI systems" (ACUS, 2021).
3. Although this chapter focuses on AI procurement in public administration, its principal discussion of contracting as a governance tool can also apply to private firms' procurement of AI-related services.
4. Similar tools provide essentially the same kinds of support for the management of contracting by private sector firms. One company, for example, markets "ProcurementGPT" that purports "not only to save time for procurement teams and for employees, but to actively reduce spend" (Tonkean,

2023). For a discussion of the role of AI in procurement processes generally, see Guida, Caniato, Moretto and Ronchi (2023).

5. The rejection of proposals on the basis of risk scores will inevitably raise concerns about due process treatment, with rejected bidders demanding an explanation for the government's decision. The so-called black-box nature of machine-learning algorithms can raise concerns about explainability which are addressed in the next section of this chapter. Suffice it to say here that, at least on the basis of current law, as long as procurement risk-scoring systems used by government agencies are well-calibrated and suitably validated, they are likely to withstand due process challenges by rejected bidders (Coglianese and Lehr, 2019).

6. Anastasopoulos and Whitford (2018) provide a helpful overview of machine learning in public administration.

7. The precise terms used could, in some settings, be standard ones that are reflected in general procurement policies that may be incorporated by reference into government contracts. In other settings, they may be more effective if customized to the particular use to which an AI tool is being put. Given the variety of AI tools that exist, and the multitude of uses to which they can be put, it may be difficult to craft general language that will always apply to all uses (Coglianese, 2023), a challenge discussed further in the next section of this chapter.

8. The reliance on bilateral contracts instead of top-down laws or regulations has sometimes been said to travel under the banner of "new governance". Although contracting does differ from the adoption of binding regulatory laws, it still relies on state power to enforce contractual terms and resolve disputes surrounding them. When the government itself is a contracting party, the distinction between contractual terms and regulation may be less pronounced, although the remedies for nonconformity with those terms will be different. For a more general discussion of governance, see Carmel (2019) and Carrigan and Coglianese (2011).

REFERENCES

Administrative Conference of the United States (ACUS) (2021) 'Agency use of artificial intelligence', *Federal Register*, **86** (13), pp. 6616–6617.

AI Data & Analytics Network (2022) *3 ways AI is changing procurement for the better*. Available at: https://www.aidataanalytics.network/data-science-ai/articles/3-ways-ai-is-changing-procurement-for-the-better (Accessed 3 January 2023).

Anastasopoulos, J. L. and Whitford, A. B. (2018) 'Machine learning for public administration research, with application to organizational reputation', *Journal of Public Administration Research and Theory*, **29** (3), pp. 491–510.

Autio, C., Cummings, K., Elliott, B. S., and Noveck, B. S. (2023) *A snapshot of artificial intelligence procurement challenges: Diagnosing perceived and actual risks impeding responsible AI acquisition in government*, The GovLab. Available at: https://files.thegovlab.org/a-snapshot-of-ai-procurement-challenges-june2023.pdf (Accessed 3 July 2023).

Booth, B. and Sharma, A. (2019) *Cognitive procurement: Seizing the AI opportunity*, IBM Institute for Business Value. Available at: https://www.ibm.com/downloads/cas/MV6LX6R2 (Accessed 29 June 2023).

Brauneis, R. and Goodman, E. P. (2018) 'Algorithmic transparency for the smart city', *Yale Journal of Law and Technology*, **20**, pp. 107–175.

Busuioc, M. (2020) 'Accountable artificial intelligence: Holding algorithms to account', *Public Administration Review*, **81** (5), pp. 825–836.

Calo, R. and Citron, D. K. (2021) 'The automated administrative state: A crisis of legitimacy', *Emory Law Journal*, **70** (4), pp. 1–50.

Carmel, E. (ed.) (2019) *Governance Analysis: Critical Enquiry at the Intersection of Politics, Policy and Society*. Cheltenham, UK and Northampton, MA, USA: Edward Elgar Publishing.

Carrigan, C. and Coglianese, C. (2011) 'The politics of regulation: From new institutionalism to new governance', *Annual Review of Political Science*, **14** (1), pp. 107–129.

Chenok, D. (2022) 'How can governments use AI to improve procurement', *The Regulatory Review* (30 June). Available at: https://www.theregreview.org/2022/06/30/chenok-how-can-governments-use-ai -to-improve-procurement/ (Accessed 27 June 2023).

Citron, D. K. (2008) 'Technological due process', *Washington University Law Review*, **85** (6), pp. 1249–1313.

Coglianese, C. (2023) 'Regulating machine learning: The challenge of heterogeneity', *TechReg Chronicle* (Feb.), pp. 17–27.

Coglianese, C. and Appel, S. M. (2022) 'Algorithmic administrative justice', in Hertogh, M., Thomas, R., and Tomlinson, J. (eds) *The Oxford Handbook of Administrative Justice*. Oxford: Oxford University Press, pp. 481–502.

Coglianese, C. and Ben Dor, L. M. (2021a) 'Procurement as AI governance', *IEEE Transactions on Technology and Society*, **2** (4), pp. 192–199.

Coglianese, C. and Ben Dor, L. M. (2021b) 'AI in adjudication and administration', *Brooklyn Law Review*, **86** (3), pp. 791–838.

Coglianese, C. and Lai, A. (2022) 'Algorithm vs. algorithm', *Duke Law Journal*, **72** (6), pp. 1281–1340.

Coglianese, C. and Lampmann, E. (2021) 'Contracting for algorithmic accountability', *Administrative Law Review Accord*, **6** (3), pp. 175–199.

Coglianese, C. and Lehr, D. (2019) 'Transparency and algorithmic governance', *Administrative Law Review*, **71** (1), pp. 1–56.

Coglianese, C. and Lehr, D. (2017) 'Regulating by robot: Administrative decision-making in the machine-learning era', *Georgetown Law Journal*, **105** (5), pp. 1147–1223.

Coglianese, C. and Nash, J. (2006) 'Management-based strategies: An emerging approach to environmental protection', in Coglianese, C. and Nash, J. (eds) *Leveraging the Private Sector: Management-Based Strategies for Improving Environmental Performance*, Washington, DC: Resources for the Future, pp. 3–30.

Committee on Standards in Public Life (2020) *Artificial intelligence and public standards*. Available at: https://assets.publishing.service.gov.uk/government/uploads/system/uploads/attachment_data/file/ 868284/Web_Version_AI_and_Public_Standards.PDF (Accessed 3 July 2023).

Dekel, O. and Schurr, A. (2014) 'Cognitive biases in government procurement: An experimental study', *Review of Law & Economics*, **10** (2), pp. 169–200.

ElectrifAi (2020) *Smarter procurement and significant savings with AI*. Available at: https://www .electrifai.com/blog/smarter-procurement-and-significant-savings-with-ai (Accessed 27 June 2023).

Executive Order 13,960 (2020) 'Promoting the use of trustworthy artificial intelligence in the federal government', *Federal Register*, **85** (236), pp. 78,939–78,943.

Fung, A., O'Rourke, D., and Sabel, C. (2001) 'Stepping up labor standards', *Boston Review*, **26** (1), pp. 4–10.

Gavaghan, C., Knott, A., MacLaurin, J., Zerilli, J., and Liddicoat, J. (2019) *Government Use of Artificial Intelligence in New Zealand*, Wellington: New Zealand Law Foundation [online]. Available at: https:// www.lawfoundation.org.nz/wp-content/uploads/2019/05/2016_ILP_10_AILNZ-Report-released-27 .5.2019.pdf (Accessed 3 July 2023).

Government of Canada (2019) Directive on automated decision making [online] Available at: https:// www.tbs-sct.canada.ca/pol/doc-eng.aspx?id=32592&section=html. (Accessed 3 July 2023).

Guida, M., Caniato, F., Moretto, A., and Ronchi, S. (2023) 'The role of artificial intelligence in the procurement process: State of the art and research agenda', *Journal of Purchasing and Supply Management*, **29** (2), pp. 1–21. Available at: https://doi.org/10.1016/j.pursup.2023.100823 (Accessed 24 September 2023).

Houston Federation of Teachers, Local 2415 v. Houston Independent School District (2017) United States District Court. *LexisNexis*. Available at: https://www.lexisnexis.com/community/casebrief/p/ casebrief-hous-fed-n-of-teachers-local-2415-v-hous-indep-sch-dist (Accessed 27 June 2023).

Hwang T. J., Kesselheim A. S., and Vokinger K. N. (2019) 'Lifecycle regulation of artificial intelligence – and machine learning-based software devices in medicine', JAMA, **322** (23), pp. 2285–2286.

IEEE Standards Association (2023) Project Authorization Request: Standard for the Procurement of Artificial Intelligence and Automated Decision Systems, https://development.standards.ieee.org/ myproject-web/public/view.html#pardetail/9448.

IEEE Standards Association (2021) IEEE Standard Model Process for Addressing Ethical Concerns during System Design, https://standards.ieee.org/ieee/7000/6781/.

Information Commissioner's Office (ICO) (2023) Annex A: Fairness in the AI Lifecycle, https://ico.org .uk/for-organisations/uk-gdpr-guidance-and-resources/artificial-intelligence/guidance-on-ai-and-data -protection/annex-a-fairness-in-the-ai-lifecycle/.

International Organization for Standardization/International Electrotechnical Commission (ISO/IEC) (2023) Artificial Intelligence: Guidance on Risk Management (ISO/IEC 23894), https://www.iso.org/ standard/77304.html.

Keegan, M. J. (ed.) (2020) *The future has begun: Using artificial intelligence to transform government*. Available at: https://www.businessofgovernment.org/sites/default/files/The%20Future %20Has%20Begun-Using%20Artificial%20Intelligence%20to%20Transform%20Government.pdf (Accessed 27 June 2023).

Kroll, J. A. (2022) 'Responsible AI is a management problem, not a purchase', *The Regulatory Review* (4 July). Available at: https://www.theregreview.org/2022/07/04/kroll-responsible-ai-is-a-management -problem-not-a-purchase/ (Accessed 3 July 2023).

Kroll, J. A., Huey, J., Barocas, S., Felten, E. W., Reidenberg, J. R., Robinson, D. G., and Yu, H. (2017) 'Accountable algorithms', *University of Pennsylvania Law Review*, **165** (3), pp. 633–705.

Larkin, G. (2021) *Artificial intelligence: Powerful procurement impact underway*. Available at: https:// www.targetgov.com/posts-by-gloria/artificial-intelligence-powerful-procurement-impact-underway (Accessed 27 June 2023).

Law Commission of Ontario (2022) AI decision-making: Protecting rights through litigation and regulation in Canada and the USA. Available at: https://www.youtube.com/watch?v=pHRaG8uu1iY&t= 2548s (Accessed 27 June 2023).

Law Commission of Ontario (2021) Legal Issues and Government AI Development [online]. Available: https://www.lco-cdo.org/wp-content/uploads/2021/03/LCO-Govt-AI-Workshop-Report-%E2%80 %94-March-2021.pdf (Accessed 3 July 2023).

Lehr, D. and Ohm, P. (2017) 'Playing with the data: What legal scholars should learn about machine learning', *UC Davis Law Review*, **51** (2), pp. 653–717.

Lipson, J. C. (2019) 'Promising justice: Contract (as) social responsibility', *Wisconsin Law Review*, **2019** (5), pp. 1109–1160.

Ludlow, A. (2016) 'Social procurement: Policy and practice', *European Labour Law Journal*, **7** (3), pp. 479–497.

Marchant, G. and Gutierrez, C. I. (2023) 'Soft law 2.0: An agile and effective governance approach for artificial intelligence', *Minnesota Journal of Law, Science & Technology*, **24** (2), pp. 375–424.

Mayer, M. (2023) ChatGPT-driven AI tool for supply chain management, *Supply & Demand Chain Executive* (21 April). Available at: https://www.sdcexec.com/software-technology/ai-ar/news/ 22834220/inspectorio-chatgptdriven-ai-tool-for-supply-chain-management (Accessed 29 June 2023).

McAllister, L. K. (2012) 'Regulation by third-party verification', *Boston College Law Review*, **53** (1), pp. 1–64.

Metcalf, J., Moss, E., Singh, R., Tafesse, E., and Watkins, E. A. (2023) 'Taking algorithms to courts: A relational approach to algorithmic accountability,' FAccT '23 Conference. Available at: https://dl .acm.org/doi/pdf/10.1145/3593013.3594092 (Accessed 3 July 2023).

Mitchell, M. et al. (2019) 'Model cards for model reporting', *Proceedings of the Conference on Fairness, Accountability, and Transparency*. Atlanta, 29–31 January. New York: Association for Computing Machinery, pp. 220–229.

Mulligan, D. K. and Bamberger, K. A. (2019) 'Procurement as policy: Administrative process for machine learning', *Berkeley Technology Law Journal*, **34** (3), pp. 773–851.

Organisation for Economic Co-operation and Development (OECD) (2019) Recommendation of the Council on artificial intelligence. Available at: https://legalinstruments.oecd.org/en/instruments/ OECD-LEGAL-0449 (Accessed 3 July 2023).

Organisation for Economic Co-operation and Development (OECD) (2015) Going green: Best practices for sustainable procurement [online]. Available at: https://www.oecd.org/gov/ethics/Going_Green _Best_Practices_for_Sustainable_Procurement.pdf (Accessed 3 July 2023).

Pasquale, F. (2016) *The Black Box Society: The Secret Algorithms that Control Money and Information*. Cambridge: Harvard University Press.

Powles, J. (2017) 'New York City's bold, flawed attempt to make algorithms accountable', *The New Yorker* (20 December). Available at: https://www.newyorker.com/tech/annals-of-technology/newYork-citys-bold-flawed-attempt-to-make-algorithms-accountable (Accessed 30 June 2023).

Responsible Artificial Intelligence (RAI) Institute (2023) Frequently asked questions [online]. Available at: https://www.responsible.ai/faq (Accessed 3 July 2023).

Reynolds, A. J. and Norwood K. P. (2020) *5 ways big data and artificial intelligence could change the landscape of government contracting.* Available at: https://www.wiley.law/newsletter-5-Ways -Big-Data-and-Artificial-Intelligence-Could-Change-the-Landscape-of-Government-Contracting (Accessed 27 June 2023).

Rubenstein, D. S. (2022) *Retooling the acquisition gateway for responsible AI.* Available at: https://www.theregreview.org/2022/06/28/rubenstein-retooling-the-acquisitiongateway-for-responsible-ai/ (Accessed 30 June 2023).

Rubenstein, D. S. (2021) 'Acquiring ethical AI', *Florida Law Review*, **73** (4), pp. 748–819.

Ruggie, J. (2013) *Just Business: Multinational Corporations and Human Rights.* New York: W.W. Norton and Company.

Sanchez-Graells, A. (2023) 'Procurement tools for AI regulation by contract. Not the sharpest in the shed', *Social Science Research Network* [online]. Available at: https://papers.ssrn.com/sol3/papers .cfm?abstract_id=4369297 (Accessed 3 July 2023).

Sievo (2022) *AI in procurement.* Available at: https://sievo.com/resources/ai-in-procurement#procure mentaisoftware-section (Accessed 27 June 2023).

Simcoe, T. and Toffel, M. W. (2014) 'Government green procurement spillovers: Evidence from municipal building policies in California,' *Journal of Environmental Economics and Management*, **68** (3), pp. 411–434.

State of Wisconsin v. Eric L. Loomis (2016) Supreme Court of Wisconsin, case 2015AP157-CR. *Leagle.* Available at: https://www.courts.ca.gov/documents/BTB24-2L-3.pdf (Accessed 30 June 2023).

Supreme Audit Institutions of Finland, Germany, The Netherlands, Norway and the UK (2023) *Auditing machine learning algorithms: A white paper for public auditors.* Available at: https://www .auditingalgorithms.net/ (Accessed 3 July 2023).

Tillipman, J. (2022) 'Using AI to reduce performance risk in US procurement', *The Regulatory Review* (29 June). Available at: https://www.theregreview.org/2022/06/29/tillipman-using-ai-to-reduce-per formance-risk-in-u-s-procurement/ (Accessed 27 June 2023).

Tonkean (2023) ProcurementGPT. Available at: https://www.tonkean.com/usecases/procurement-gpt (Accessed 24 Sept. 2023).

UK Office for Artificial Intelligence (2020) Guidelines for AI procurement [online]. Available at: https://assets.publishing.service.gov.uk/government/uploads/system/uploads/attachment_data/file/990469/Guidelines_for_AI_procurement.pdf (Accessed 3 July 2023).

US Government Accountability Office (2021) *Artificial Intelligence: An Accountability Framework for Federal Agencies and Other Entities* (GAO-21-519SP). Available at: https://www.gao.gov/products/gao-21-519sp (Accessed 30 June 2023).

World Economic Forum (2020) *AI Procurement in a Box: AI Government Procurement Guidelines* [online]. Available at: https://www3.weforum.org/docs/WEF_AI_Procurement_in_a_Box_AI_Gov ernment_Procurement_Guidelines_2020.pdf (Accessed 3 July 2023).

Yama, E. (2018) *How automation, AI can improve government contracting.* Available at: https://federalnewsnetwork.com/commentary/2018/04/how-automation-ai-can-improve-government-con tracting/ (Accessed 27 June 2023).

Yeung, K. (2017) 'Algorithmic regulation: A critical interrogation', *Regulation & Governance*, **12** (4), pp. 505–523.

19. Regulatory interdependence in AI
Daniel Mügge

INTRODUCTION

Much debate about the governance of artificial intelligence technologies (AITs) concentrates on the interplay between technological developments, their societal implications, and the legal guard rails necessary to manage those.[1] But both the shape and the effectiveness of domestic rules hinge on how other jurisdictions govern AITs – whether rules elsewhere are compatible with national ones, and whether they are more or less stringent. This regulatory interdependence is poorly reflected in most regulatory debates, which tend to discuss desiderata of regulation without heeding the global force field in which it plays out. Appreciating such interdependence thus helps us understand the real-world options jurisdictions have and the choices they make in AIT governance.

This chapter examines the different facets of this regulatory interdependence in AI, how they influence policy and its effectiveness, and in particular how regulatory interdependence is asymmetrical. Some jurisdictions feel its consequences much more than others, meaning that sovereignty in AIT regulation is distributed unevenly. Because of regulatory interdependence, many jurisdictions are de facto rule takers, rather than sitting in the regulatory driving seat themselves. Most obviously, this applies to many countries in the so-called Global South, or what Amrute et al. (2022) call the majority world (to which the minority world in the Global North rarely gives much thought, see Omotubora and Basu, Chapter 17 in this volume). But also the EU, for example, faces constraints. OpenAI's CEO Sam Altman openly mused about his company quitting the Continent if impending rules would prove too difficult to implement (Waters et al. 2023). Even though the threat was later retracted, it demonstrated the limits to EU leverage over an American tech behemoth before the latter just quits.

Where digital products can be freely traded across borders, relatively stringent national rules can put domestic firms at a disadvantage and trigger regulatory competition and a potential downward spiral in standards (Smuha 2021). Regulatory interdependence often pits economic rationales against regulatory aspirations (Lazer 2001; Simmons 2001; Singer 2004). Additional dynamics enter the picture for AITs: because many digital products can be supplied remotely, local regulation may fail to curtail their undesirable effects. And where indirect spillovers worry legislators, national rules may struggle to stop them – think for example of a global diffusion of oppressive technologies. AITs develop quickly, and estimates of their future capabilities vary widely (Ford 2018). That adds a speculative element to the regulatory politics that try to address those (Nordström 2022). For example, it is simply unclear how AI will transform geopolitical security dynamics. Some see a fundamental game-changer; others a transient hype. In consequence, whether governments embrace security logics in regulatory cooperation depends as much on successful AIT framings as on objective technological developments (Mügge 2023).

This chapter first introduces regulatory interdependence and competition as a lens on regulatory politics, before spelling out how these concepts apply to AITs and how they affect countries around the globe in very uneven ways.

REGULATORY INTERDEPENDENCE AND COMPETITION

Regulatory interdependence arises when one jurisdiction's regulation affects that in another (Lazer 2001, 2006; Newman and Posner 2011). In an open global economy, countries may confront a trade-off between competitiveness of domestic firms and the stringency of domestic rules. In many cases, tight rules make *production* more expensive: think of domestic banks having to hold big capital buffers to offset potential losses (Singer 2007) or companies having to adhere to tight safety standards in their factories.

Mismatches in regulation about *products* unleash a different dynamic. Here, all products sold in a jurisdiction have to fulfil specific requirements, no matter their provenance. Examples might include limits on chemicals used in foodstuff or obligatory car safety features. *Ex ante*, domestic and foreign firms would be affected equally, and companies from abroad may simply forgo market entry in the high-standards jurisdiction.

Finally, national rules on the permissible *use* of products may differ, too, for example through speed limits on highways. *Ceteris paribus*, use restrictions dent the demand for affected products, but beyond that, they have no competitiveness impact. Problems only surface when products whose use is banned outright are readily available for illegal import from abroad. Bans on citizen ownership of weapons or drugs, for example, are difficult to enforce with porous borders. A hard-to-control global digital space may pose similar challenges.

Jurisdictions have alternative strategies to tackle regulatory interdependence (cf. Müller et al. 2014). When the cross-border impact is low, one option is benign neglect. Once stringent standards do affect firms' competitiveness, a jurisdiction may embrace regulatory competition (Stigler 1971) and dilute its rules to benefit local firms. Or it may accept mismatched standards and sacrifice trade openness to safeguard regulatory goals or protect domestic producers (Sykes 1999).

Dynamics shift when a large jurisdiction can leverage access to its market (Vogel 1995). It can then arm-twist others to tighten regulations to avoid competitive disadvantage (e.g. Simmons 2001). The EU has often exercised such "market power" (Damro 2012, 2015), and it has externalized its policies both consciously and unintentionally (Bradford 2012; Lavenex and Schimmelpfennig 2009).

Jurisdictions can also cooperate to sidestep regulatory competition and solve coordination problems (Mattli and Woods 2009). Formats vary from international trade agreements, via trans-governmental networks (Eberlein and Grande 2005; Verdier 2009), to the implicit endorsement or embrace of privately set standards (Büthe and Mattli 2011), each with their own advantages and drawbacks.

Where harmonized standards are beyond reach, mutual recognition of local rules can facilitate cross-border market access. This strategy has been a cornerstone of the single European market (Egan 2001; Griffin 2001; Schmidt 2002), but also been used to manage transatlantic regulatory interdependence (Farrell and Newman 2019; Shaffer 2002), including in technically complex fields such as finance (Mügge 2014; Posner 2009).

Finally, when standard development is highly technical and the costs of standard creation loom large, it becomes attractive to outsource it to technical experts in transnational non-governmental organizations, or to delegate it to intergovernmental forums with few active participants (cf. Lorenz 2021). The same is true for standards that require frequent updating because of technologies' dynamism (Mandel 2007; Moses 2007), which is difficult for detailed international agreements (cf. Mügge and Linsi 2020).

The Character of Regulatory Interdependence for AITs

How do these dynamics play out for AITs? As a policy object, "AI" eludes unambiguous definition (Martinez 2019; Schuett 2023), and in debates around the EU AI Act for example, these ambiguities have themselves generated political discord. After all, more or less expansive AI definitions extend the regulatory net to more or fewer firms, pitting politicians eager to clamp down on AI against more permissive ones.

Nevertheless, many countries and international organizations have initiated regulatory programmes under the AI heading (Cath et al. 2018; Radu 2021), and the blurriness of AITs has not hampered international initiatives, at least at the level of general principles (von Ingersleben-Seip 2023). This chapter thus concentrates on those actors and technologies that commonly feature in AI policy debates.

AITs have five properties that shape regulatory interdependence: first, because of their digital character, the application of AITs is, *ex ante*, hardly territorially bound. Large language models (LLMs) for example run on high-performance computers, and the training of AI systems with many parameters – their production, as it were – requires enormous, and by now jealously guarded, quantities of hardware. With appropriate infrastructure, however, their services can be accessed from anywhere. For example, unless governments restrict access, OpenAI's ChatGPT can be used through a simple website from around the world through no more than a smartphone. AI *production* is territorially bound; AI *application* much less so.

Second, once systems have been trained (at considerable cost) and the required infrastructure is in place, they allow rapid scaling and at least temporary market domination unless legal restrictions come in the way.[2] Based on the speed with which ChatGPT could be rolled out globally, it became synonymous with LLMs within weeks. These oligopolistic tendencies remain particularly pronounced for generative AI, as extensive deployment by users itself improves the algorithm, locking in first-mover advantages. They also thrive off the platform and marketing power of companies like Microsoft or Google, which dominate subsegments of the market for digital products into which generative AI can profitably be integrated (Staab 2019). To be sure, the strength of centripetal dynamics depends on specific use cases and the model complexity required to make an algorithm successful. Using locally generated data – say, weather observations – to train predictive models for agriculture may also be commercially viable for niche companies. Patterns from other technology- and capital-intensive sectors point to possible future consolidation: large digital firms that identify synergies between AI and its existing products have incentives to acquire AIT start-ups. It is unclear how long niche companies would survive market consolidation unless competition policy gets in the way.

Third, AITs are broadly applicable, inviting comparisons with electricity or the steam engine (Brynjolfsson and McAfee 2014). AIT governance with an eye to one use case may thus have unintended consequences for others. The collateral damage that both excessively loose and tight regulation may do is disproportionately large, making targeted regulation difficult even when we ignore the global context – a tension that has fuelled heated debates about "general purpose AI" in the European Parliament. It is amplified by the dual-use (joint civilian and military) applications that many AITs have (cf. Mügge 2023).

Fourth, AIT development is quick. Generative AI performance has improved enormously year on year; capabilities a decade from now are anybody's guess (Nordström 2022). AITs therefore require particularly adaptable regulatory frameworks, able to evolve with technology and our understanding of it (Mandel 2007; Moses 2007). Such adaptability, however, may be difficult to square with rigid international agreements that might otherwise help solve collective action problems.

Finally, AIT development is unpredictable, also regarding successful real-world application (Marcus and Davis 2019). Autonomous driving was long heralded as imminent, whereas generative AI hopes were much lower. In the event, the former faltered while the latter thrived. The regulatory interdependence that shapes real-world policy therefore includes speculation about future technologies and developments (cf. Berten and Kranke 2022), creating openings for authoritative actors in AI to frame debates, problems, and solutions in self-interested ways.

The AI Competitiveness Discourse

One key facet of regulatory interdependence is a potential tension between regulatory stringency and economic competitiveness. Such arguments animate AI debates, as well. The EU *Coordinated Plan on Artificial Intelligence* (European Commission 2018) or its updated version, *Fostering a European Approach* (European Commission 2021), ceaselessly underline that homegrown AITs are crucial for EU economic success. Debates in the European Parliament have frequently pitted a pro-economic innovation camp, fearful of excessively tight rules, against lawmakers eager to weave a tight regulatory net. The anticipated commercial dynamics surrounding AITs are thus one side of the regulatory interdependence coin, as stringent regulation might hand companies from laxer jurisdictions a competitive advantage. In a global market for digital products, including AITs, the economic price tag of regulation depends on what other jurisdictions do.

While these economic dynamics are crucial to regulatory politics, they are also highly speculative, because just what there is to be won or lost economically remains disputed: Brynjolfsson and McAfee (2014) had famously presaged a *Second Machine Age*; other observers suspect that the transformative impact of digital technologies has been overhyped, an intuition buttressed by the dismal performance of the digital tech sector in 2022 after several prodigious years. (AI companies have largely bucked that trend.) Similar disagreement characterizes debates about AITs' economic downsides, in particular job losses and rising inequality: some predict massive job destruction and hence crumbling bargaining power for workers (Dyer-Witheford et al. 2019; Frey 2019; Frey and Osborne 2017); others see those fears as large exaggerations (Autor 2015; cf. Campbell-Verduyn and Hütten 2022), pointing to continuing labour market shortages across many sectors and countries.

While the extent of economic transformations is unclear, AITs concentrate the ability to extract surplus among the companies in control of them and enable the monetization of personal information, creating incentives for large-scale commercial data collection and analysis (Beer 2019; Zuboff 2019). And they offer profit opportunities by commodifying hitherto untapped societal and personal domains (Couldry and Mejias 2019). Taken together, profit-concentration, labour market disruption, and personal data commodification creates both winners and losers.

Widespread AIT application may thus have contradictory effects: it may simply shift profits from the non-AI sector to the most advanced digital companies occupying strategic links in a particular production chain – akin to rent extraction by the financial and real estate sector (Krippner 2005, 2011; Staab 2019; Stockhammer 2007). As capital's share in national income would increase at the expense of wages, aggregate demand would suffer, too (cf. Gordon 2016). A boon for individual firms might be a bane for the macroeconomy. AI-powered productivity increases may only generate sustainable economic growth if accompanied by redistributive policies that counteract the wealth-concentrating dynamics digitization entails.

The unpredictable *specific* economic impact of AITs, however, creates discursive flexibility: the weight attached to different economic aspects in policy discourse thrives on extrapolation of short-term trends far into the future. Economic AI-discourse – including the potential costs of losing out in global regulatory competition (Bryson and Malikova 2021; Smuha 2021) – is prone to hyperbole (Ulnicane 2022). The impact of AI regulatory interdependence on actual policies is therefore not direct; instead, it is mediated by whatever discourses about it dominate policy debates (Bareis and Katzenbach 2022).

Two implications for regulatory interdependence follow: first, it is variegated across different actors in national economies. For companies eager to access foreign markets, a misaligned regulatory regime might be an obstacle, because it could impede market access. For uncompetitive local incumbents and their workers, in contrast, such misalignment might be a blessing as it could shelter their business from foreign market intruders. The economic dimension of the regulatory interdependence equation varies with the economic actor in question. Countries do not either win or lose as a whole, but rather find within them winners and losers in terms of any policy options.

Second, as policymakers confront uncertainty surrounding AITs and their economic impact (Wirtz et al. 2020), they are heavily dependent on those actors closest to their application for information – the companies that develop AITs. Uncertainty opens the door to lobbying from the corporate sector, disguised – whether consciously or not – as expertise. In that discursive environment, the argument that "missing out now on AI will lock in economic disadvantage indefinitely" can develop substantial force (Bareis and Katzenbach 2022; Lee 2018), and in consequence temper regulatory ambitions. The uncertain AIT future hands an advantage to tech companies, also in terms of international regulatory policy, with potentially adverse consequences for other stakeholders.

Dimensions of Regulatory Interdependence in AITs

The economic dimension of regulatory interdependence in AITs is the backdrop against which countries evaluate and develop their policies, also relative to others. As I will argue further below, the high concentration of leading AIT firms – particularly in the US and China – creates a steep hierarchy among the world's nations in international AI policy: some occupy a position of strength; many others are weak, to different degrees. Their economic strategies and policies bear the imprint of that position.

That said, many policymakers do recognize specific public policy concerns that AITs create and debate useful regulatory interventions to curtail those. Prominent examples include breaches of privacy, poor machine safety, automated discrimination, manipulation of the spreading of fake digital content, and so on (Smith and Browne 2019; West and Allen 2020). As jurisdictions regulate AITs with an eye to these harms, how does regulatory interdependence enter the picture? How, in other words, does it matter for local rules what others do? These effects can be ordered along four kinds of effects: market fragmentation, loss of regulatory effectiveness, remote provision of undesirable AI-powered services, and AITs' indirect effects.

Equivalent but incompatible product standards mean that products made for one market cannot be sold in another – an example would be an AI system certified as bias-free following a domestic testing regime that is not recognized abroad. The effect of such mismatches is limited as long as, compared to the commercial opportunities a market offers, it is not too costly for AIT developers to tailor systems to local requirements (cf. Siegmann and Anderljung 2022). If it is costly, however, private companies may simply shun that market. Governments could then acquiesce or embrace a more widely accepted foreign standard.

A jurisdiction's ability to use market access as a lever to impose onerous rules on foreign companies unilaterally is largely a function of domestic market size and the adaptation cost companies would face to bridge the gap between companies' home country rules and those envisaged in the host market. Large jurisdictions such as the EU clearly have an advantage here (Damro 2015).

The importance of market size – rather than population size – hands a regulatory advantage to rich countries. Governments can leverage their citizens' purchasing power to secure compliance with exacting domestic rules. Countries whose citizens or companies are less attractive as direct or indirect customers are at the mercy of regulatory deals struck elsewhere and face incentives to embrace a regulatory regime to whose specifications companies already tailor their products. Colonial legacies are thus reproduced in global regulatory dynamics for AITs (cf. Carmel and Paul 2022). That said, only time will tell to what degree even the EU can force a company such as OpenAI to tweak its algorithms to produce different outputs for a European audience than for those elsewhere in the world. As noted earlier, the company's CEO has openly mused about quitting the EU altogether should regulatory demands be too high (Waters et al. 2023).

AI-powered services that can be supplied at a distance generate additional challenges. Whenever AITs are built into physical products, the latter can be taken off a market in case of non-compliance with domestic rules. Examples would be semi-autonomous vehicles or devices with AI-powered voice assistants that fail domestic safety tests. Restrictions are much harder to enforce on digital products sold through a fibre-optic cable. As an example, consider the general prohibition on real-time biometric identification in the EU, as envisaged at the time of writing. Somebody eager to identify individuals as they are being filmed – say, at a political demonstration – could still share a live feed with a company abroad, if necessary through a VPN connection, and have individuals identified in real time. Even the Chinese government frequently struggles to enforce digital censorship, despite significant infrastructure to that end. Circumventing local regulations by accessing AI-powered digital services abroad will remain attractive especially for malevolent users, who do not mind breaching host country laws if that enables them to use a banned service. This problem therefore concerns only a subset of AIT uses, but an important and potentially crucial one.

The final category of regulatory interdependence concerns second-order effects of AIT diffusion, for example the export of oppressive surveillance or automated weapons systems around the world (Polyakova and Meserole 2019). Jurisdiction A cannot directly block the sale of harmful AITs from jurisdiction B to jurisdiction C, however much it may oppose it. This dynamic transcends what is normally considered regulatory interdependence, but it is a key channel through which one country's rules have effects on others. It incentivizes countries to seek global accords, akin to non-proliferation or environmental agreements, which equally seek to limit externalities (Głowacka et al. 2021).

However, cooperation is more difficult for AITs than for environmental collective action problems, in which everyone could benefit from cooperation. China may have little to lose from surveillance tech exports to third countries; indeed, if they would solidify other governments' grip on political power, China could create technological dependencies and political alliances through them (Feldstein 2019). Considered in isolation, the incentives to join comprehensive export bans would remain meagre.

Global Asymmetries

Regulatory interdependencies are rarely balanced: they constrain some countries much more than others. How do they play out for countries at different levels of the global AI hierarchy? Five factors matter in particular (cf. Bradford 2012; Damro 2015; Siegmann and Anderljung 2022): first, countries with a large homegrown AIT sector have much more immediate regulatory leverage over the companies in question, and they depend less on foreign firms to supply AI-powered services domestically. Second, domestic market size shapes the regulatory concessions a jurisdiction can extract from foreign market entrants in exchange for access. Third, its regulatory capacity (Bach and Newman 2007) determines to what degree a jurisdiction is able to use its own enforcement mechanisms rather than having to rely on those of home countries. For many countries, a comprehensive domestic auditing regime to monitor the products and services of global AI firms is implausible. Fourth, jurisdictions may be able to leverage other political or economic resources to counter regulatory disadvantage. And finally, it matters whether countries favour relatively lower or higher levels of stringency than others. When regulatory ambitions are low, a lack of political leverage may matter little; it does matter, however, when aspirations are high.

How do these criteria map onto the current global AIT landscape? By most measures, the US and China are the clear global frontrunners (Lee 2018). AIT investment is most extensive there, and they host the largest AIT companies. Indeed, given the transatlantic economic integration in digital products, the predominance of large American companies also in Europe perpetuates itself; potential competitors confront hard-to-beat winner-takes-all dynamics. American strength, in other words, is a source of European weakness.

For the US and China, the effects of regulatory interdependence are relatively limited, because they can simply exclude each other's AIT firms from their domestic markets. China tries, with varying success, to control cross-border digital traffic, so that remote provision is a lesser challenge. At the same time, both countries seek to diffuse domestic AIT projects abroad, for both commercial and geopolitical reasons, and are therefore invested in regulatory cross-border harmonization which would facilitate such access. China, for example, is strongly represented in transnational expert forums for AIT standard setting such as the International Standardization Organization and the International Electrotechnical Commission; the USA leverages the transatlantic Trade and Technology Council (TTC) for US–EU alignment of AIT policy. Both forms of engagement seek to shape cross-border regulatory spaces to the advantage of domestic firms and technologies.

The EU occupies a very different position. Its regulatory capacity is high and access to its large market prized by foreign companies (Siegmann and Anderljung 2022). At the same time, most companies dominating the European AIT market are foreign (largely American), and its regulatory ambitions are higher than those of most other jurisdictions. That generates a complex challenge: relatively strict domestic rules, for example about data gathering and use, may hamper the development of a European AI sector that could rival US firms. At the same time, the subsequent dominance of those American firms reinforces EU dependence on regulatory policies abroad. Current intra-European negotiations regarding appropriate regulation reflect these opposing forces. At the time of writing, in June 2023, this dynamic is mirrored by two parallel policy processes: negotiations within the European Parliament about a political common position on AI regulation on the one hand, and the EU Commission's TTC negotiations with the US government about shared AI standards on the other. It is unclear how far these two processes can be reconciled without subordinating one to the other.

Smaller jurisdictions with similar levels of regulatory aspirations have significantly fewer levers to impose their preferences and may therefore opt to copy whatever regime the EU adopts (Siegmann and Anderljung 2022). In the AI version of Bradford's Brussels Effect (2012), they could free-ride on the EU's unique capacity to impose high standards on foreign firms who may enjoy laxer rules in their home jurisdictions. That said, the EU itself is not an autonomous agent in AI regulation, heeding as it must its regulatory and technological dependence on the US. The Brussels Effect plays out, in other words, in the shadow of US and Chinese dominance of the sector. Economically relatively small countries that are de facto niche developers of AI-powered products are a different category again – for example Israel, Canada, or Russia. For commercial success, they depend on market access abroad, creating strong incentives for regulatory alignment with the main envisaged export markets and for a permissive regime at home.

Akin to financial secrecy jurisdictions (Palan 2002; Shaxson 2012), regulatory havens for AIT use and development may become sorts of black holes in the global web of rules. Depending on just how tight major jurisdictions' rules and enforcement capacities are, companies could circumvent regulatory intentions by selectively outsourcing or relocating specific parts of their AI development to jurisdictions that offer little more than data storage, computing capacity, or even only legal residence for subsidiaries or contractors (Scasserra and Foronda 2022). Examples would include outsourcing of human data labelling, content moderation, or other inputs to train or police algorithms – work that is frequently draining and harmful, while poorly paid under bad working conditions (Gray and Suri 2019). To what degree these jurisdictions will undermine regulatory restrictions imposed elsewhere is still hard to say, as that will depend not only on corporate business models and scope for regulatory arbitrage, but also the technological possibilities that future AIT development may itself afford. Nevertheless, just as has been true for financial regulation and taxation, the availability of regulatory escape hatches to circumvent limits on data storage and analysis may seriously damage the effectiveness of rules elsewhere.

Countries that fall into neither of the categories above will rely on overseas providers for their digital technologies, including AI-powered applications, but have limited leverage themselves to enforce significantly higher regulatory standards that have been set in one of the other major jurisdictions. With potentially limited monitoring and enforcement capacities, their best bet may be to piggy-back on other major regimes including, as potentially the most stringent one emerging, the European one.

In practice, this means that much of what Amrute et al. (2022) have called the majority world – what others have called the Global South – may de facto become rule takers in AITs, with limited scope to shape the development and application of technologies beyond standards devised and agreed elsewhere (cf. Brooks, Chapter 16; Gray, Chapter 15; Omotubora and Basu, Chapter 17, all in this volume). For most countries outside the circle of technologically or economically privileged countries, digital sovereignty – and by implication at least a modicum of AIT sovereignty – is likely to remain beyond reach.

CONCLUSION

Current regulatory debates about AITs rarely heed the interdependencies that characterize the field – even though both the shape and the effectiveness of national rules will depend heavily on what other jurisdictions do. When they are considered, they typically feature as economic or geopolitical competitors to be beaten through ingenious policies and regulatory interventions. That, beyond such narratives, the global economic political force field in which countries find themselves simply limits what government policy can achieve, is rarely acknowledged – even though it is essential both for understanding current policies and their effects, and for maximizing the effectiveness of public interventions in AI.

This interdependence generates strong incentives for cooperation, not least to evade regulatory competition that might otherwise generate undesirably low regulatory standards. On the other hand, the asymmetry in interdependence means that some countries can largely afford to ignore what others do, and use regulatory alliance building as a geopolitical tool. The US in particular has led attempts to forge an anti-China coalition in AI regulation, using both the TTC to consolidate an integrated transatlantic regulatory space and multilateral organizations such as the Organisation for Economic Co-operation and Development for broader standard design that excludes Beijing.

Regulatory interdependence therefore curtails the potential for digital sovereignty that different countries enjoy. Most of them will be at the receiving end of the economic and geopolitical competition that unfolds between and within a handful of leading global AIT powers (cf. Gray, Chapter 15 in this volume for a wider discussion of AI, old and new forms of colonialism). To the degree that AITs will be a defining feature of future societies, asymmetrical regulatory interdependence is therefore likely to cement the economic and technological imbalances we see around the globe today.

NOTES

1. Artificial intelligence (AI) is also a contested concept in regulatory debates (Schuett 2023). To do justice to the blurry edges of AI as a policy object, this chapter follows Paul, Carmel and Cobbe's suggestion (in the introduction to this volume) and talks of artificial intelligence technologies, in the plural, instead.
2. Just training GPT3, ChatGPT's precursor, reportedly cost $5 million, and answering the millions of queries ChatGPT now receives was estimated to consume $700,000 per day, mostly due to high server costs (Mok 2023). Maintaining and expanding ChatGPT's services – initially without charge to private users – requires deep pockets, and Microsoft's $10 billion investment in OpenAI is indicative of the resources required to create an early market leader (Bass 2023).

REFERENCES

Amrute, S., R. Singh and R. L. Guzmán (2022), *A Primer on AI in/from the Majority World: An Empirical Site and a Standpoint*, accessed at http://dx.doi.org/10.2139/ssrn.4199467.

Autor, D. H. (2015), 'Why Are There Still So Many Jobs? The History and Future of Workplace Automation', *Journal of Economic Perspectives*, **29** (3), 3–30.

Bach, D. and A. Newman (2007), 'The European Regulatory State and Global Public Policy: Micro-Institutions, Macro-Influence', *Journal of European Public Policy*, **14** (6), 827–46.

Bareis, J. and C. Katzenbach (2022), 'Talking AI into Being: The Narratives and Imaginaries of National AI Strategies and Their Performative Politics', *Science, Technology, & Human Values*, **47** (5), 855–81.

Bass, D. (2023), 'Microsoft Invests $10 Billion in ChatGPT Maker OpenAI', accessed 10 June 2023 at https://www.bloomberg.com/news/articles/2023-01-23/microsoft-makes-multibillion-dollar-investment-in-openai.

Beer, D. (2019), *The Data Gaze. Capitalism, Power and Perception*, London: Sage.

Berten, J. and M. Kranke (2022), 'Anticipatory Global Governance: International Organisations and the Politics of the Future', *Global Society*, **36** (2), 155–69.

Bradford, A. (2012), 'The Brussels Effect', *Northwestern University Law Review*, **107** (1), 1–67.

Brynjolfsson, E. and A. McAfee (2014), *The Second Machine Age*, New York: W.W. Norton.

Bryson, J. J. and H. Malikova (2021), 'Is There an AI Cold War?', *Global Perspectives*, **2** (1), accessed at https://doi.org/10.1525/gp.2021.24803.

Büthe, T. and W. Mattli (2011), *The New Global Rulers. The Privatization of Regulation in the World Economy*, Princeton, NJ: Princeton University Press.

Campbell-Verduyn, M. and M. Hütten (2022), 'Governing Techno-Futures: OECD Anticipation of Automation and the Multiplication of Managerialism', *Global Society*, **36** (2), 240–60.

Carmel, E. and R. Paul (2022), 'Peace and Prosperity for the Digital Age? The Colonial Political Economy of European AI Governance', *IEEE Technology and Society Magazine*, **41** (2), 94–104.

Cath, C., S. Wachter, B. Mittelstadt, M. Taddeo and L. Floridi (2018), 'Artificial Intelligence and the "Good Society": The US, EU, and UK Approach', *Science and Engineering Ethics*, **24** (2), 505–28.

Couldry, N. and U. Mejias (2019), *The Costs of Connection. How Data Is Colonizing Human Life and Appropriating It for Capitalism*, Stanford, CA: Stanford University Press.

Damro, C. (2012), 'Market Power Europe', *Journal of European Public Policy*, **19** (5), 682–99.

Damro, C. (2015), 'Market Power Europe: Exploring a Dynamic Conceptual Framework', *Journal of European Public Policy*, **22** (9), 1336–54.

Dyer-Witheford, N., A. M. Kjosen and J. Steinhoff (2019), *Inhuman Power. Artificial Intelligence and the Future of Capitalism*, London: Pluto Press.

Eberlein, B. and E. Grande (2005), 'Beyond Delegation: Transnational Regulatory Regimes and the EU Regulatory State', *Journal of European Public Policy*, **12** (1), 89–112.

Egan, M. (2001), *Constructing a European Market: Standards, Regulation and Governance*, Oxford: Oxford University Press.

European Commission (2018), *Coordinated Plan on Artificial Intelligence [COM(2018) 795 Final]*, Brussels.

European Commission (2021), *Fostering a European Approach to Artificial Intelligence*, Brussels.

Farrell, H. and A. Newman (2019), *Of Privacy and Power. The Transatlantic Struggle Over Freedom and Security*, Princeton, NJ: Princeton University Press.

Feldstein, S. (2019), 'The Road to Digital Unfreedom: How Artificial Intelligence Is Reshaping Repression', *Journal of Democracy*, **30** (1), 40–52.

Ford, M. (2018), *Architects of Intelligence. The Truth about AI from the People Building It*, Birmingham, UK: Packt Publishers.

Frey, C. B. (2019), *The Technology Trap: Capital, Labor, and Power in the Age of Automation*, Princeton, NJ: Princeton University Press.

Frey, C. B. and M. A. Osborne (2017), 'The Future of Employment: How Susceptible Are Jobs to Computerisation?', *Technological Forecasting and Social Change*, **114**, 254–80.

Głowacka, D., R. Youngs, A. Pintea and E. Wołosik (2021), *Digital Technologies as a Means of Repression and Social Control*, Brussels.

Gordon, R. (2016), *The Rise and Fall of American Growth. The US Standard of Living Since the Civil War*, Princeton, NJ: Princeton University Press.

Gray, M. and S. Suri (2019), *Ghost Work. How to Stop Silicon Valley from Building a New Global Underclass*, New York: Harper Business.

Griffin, P. B. (2001), 'The Delaware Effect: Keeping the Tiger in Its Cage – The European Experience on Mutual Recognition in Financial Services ', *Columbia Journal of European Law*, **7** (3), 337–54.

Krippner, G. (2005), 'The Financialization of the American Economy', *Socio-Economic Review*, **3** (2), 173–208.

Krippner, G. (2011), *Capitalizing on Crisis. The Political Origins of the Rise of Finance*, Cambridge, MA: Harvard University Press.

Lavenex, S. and F. Schimmelpfennig (2009), 'EU Rules Beyond EU Borders: Theorizing External Governance in European Politics', *Journal of European Public Policy*, **16** (6), 791–812.

Lazer, D. (2001), 'Regulatory Interdependence and International Governance', *Journal of European Public Policy*, **8** (3), 474–92.

Lazer, D. (2006), 'Global and Domestic Governance: Modes of Interdependence in Regulatory Policymaking', *European Law Journal*, **12** (4), 455–68.

Lee, K.-F. (2018), *AI Superpowers. China, Silicon Valley, and the New World Order*, Boston, MA: Houghton Mifflin.

Lorenz, P. (2021), *AI Standardization and Foreign Policy. How European Foreign Policy Makers Can Engage with Technical Standardization*, Berlin.

Mandel, G. (2007), 'History Lessons for a General Theory of Law and Technology', *Minnesota Journal of Law, Science & Technology*, **8** (2), 551–70.

Marcus, G. and E. Davis (2019), *Rebooting AI. Building Artificial Intelligence We Can Trust*, New York: Pantheon.

Martinez, R. (2019), 'Artificial Intelligence: Distinguishing between Types & Definitions', *Nevada Law Journal*, **19** (3), 1015–41.

Mattli, W. and N. Woods (2009), *The Politics of Global Regulation*, Princeton, NJ: Princeton University Press.

Mok, A. (2023), 'ChatGPT Could Cost Over $700,000 Per Day to Operate. Microsoft Is Reportedly Trying to Make It Cheaper', accessed 11 June 2023 at https://www.businessinsider.com/how-much -chatgpt-costs-openai-to-run-estimate-report-2023-4.

Moses, L. B. (2007), 'Recurring Dilemmas: The Law's Race to Keep up with Technological Change', *University of Illinois Journal of Law, Technology & Policy*, **2** (Fall 2007), 239–86.

Mügge, D. (2014), *Europe and the Governance of Global Finance*, Oxford: Oxford University Press.

Mügge, D. (2023), 'The Securitization of the EU's Digital Tech Regulation', *Journal of European Public Policy*, **30** (7), 1431–46.

Mügge, D. and L. Linsi (2020), 'The National Accounting Paradox: How Statistical Norms Corrode International Economic Data', *European Journal of International Relations*, **27** (2), 403–27, accessed at https://doi.org/10.1177/1354066120936339.

Müller, P., Z. Kudrna and G. Falkner (2014), 'EU–global Interactions: Policy Export, Import, Promotion and Protection', *Journal of European Public Policy*, **21** (8), 1102–19.

Newman, A. and E. Posner (2011), 'International Interdependence and Regulatory Power: Authority, Mobility, and Markets', *European Journal of International Relations*, **17** (4), 589–610.

Nordström, M. (2022), 'AI under Great Uncertainty: Implications and Decision Strategies for Public Policy', *AI & Society*, **37** (4), 1703–14.

Palan, R. (2002), 'Tax Havens and the Commercialization of State Sovereignty', *International Organization*, **56** (1), 151–76.

Polyakova, A. and C. Meserole (2019), *Exporting Digital Authoritarianism. The Russian and Chinese Models*, Washington, DC, available at https://www.brookings.edu/wp-content/uploads/2019/08/FP _20190827_digital_authoritarianism_polyakova_meserole.pdf.

Posner, E. (2009), 'Making Rules for Global Finance: Transatlantic Regulatory Cooperation at the Turn of the Millennium', *International Organization*, **63** (4), 665–99.

Radu, R. (2021), 'Steering the Governance of Artificial Intelligence: National Strategies in Perspective', *Policy and Society*, **40** (2), 178–93.

Scasserra, S. and A. Foronda (2022), *Banking on Data. How the World's Tax Havens Became the Data Centres for the Digital Economy*, Amsterdam: Transnational Institute.

Schmidt, S. (2002), 'The Impact of Mutual Recognition – Inbuilt Limits and Domestic Responses to the Single Market', *Journal of European Public Policy*, **9** (6), 935–53.

Schuett, J. (2023), 'Defining the Scope of AI Regulations', *Law, Innovation and Technology*, **15** (1), 60–82.

Shaffer, G. (2002), 'Reconciling Trade and Regulatory Goals: The Prospects and Limits of New Approaches to Transatlantic Governance Through Mutual Recognition and Safe Harbor Agreements', *Columbia Journal of European Law*, **9** (1), 29–77.

Shaxson, N. (2012), *Treasure Islands: Uncovering the Damage of Offshore Banking and Tax Havens*, New York: Palgrave Macmillan.

Siegmann, C. and M. Anderljung (2022), *The Brussels Effect and Artificial Intelligence: How EU Regulation Will Impact the Global AI Market*, London.

Simmons, B. (2001), 'The International Politics of Harmonization: The Case of Capital Market Regulation', *International Organization*, **55** (3), 589–620.

Singer, D. (2004), 'Capital Rules: The Domestic Politics of International Regulatory Harmonization', *International Organization*, **58** (3), 531–65.

Singer, D. (2007), *Regulating Capital. Setting Standards for the International Financial System*, Ithaca, NY: Cornell University Press.

Smith, B. and C. A. Browne (2019), *Tools and Weapons. The Promise and Peril of the Digital Age*, London: Penguin.

Smuha, N. A. (2021), 'From a "Race to AI" to a "Race to AI Regulation": Regulatory Competition for Artificial Intelligence', *Law, Innovation and Technology*, **13** (1), 57–84.

Staab, P. (2019), *Digitaler Kapitalismus. Markt und Herrschaft in der Ökonomie der Unknappheit*, Frankfurt am Main: Suhrkamp.

Stigler, G. (1971), 'The Theory of Economic Regulation', *Bell Journal of Economics*, **2** (1), 113–21.

Stockhammer, E. (2007), *Some Stylized Facts on the Finance-Dominated Accumulation Regime*, Amherst, MA: Political Economy Research Institute WP 142, University of Massachusetts Amherst.

Sykes, A. (1999), 'Regulatory Protectionism and the Law of International Trade', *University of Chicago Law Review*, **66** (1), 1–46.

Ulnicane, I. (2022), 'Emerging Technology for Economic Competitiveness or Societal Challenges? Framing Purpose in Artificial Intelligence Policy', *Global Public Policy and Governance*, **2** (3), 326–45.

Verdier, P.-H. (2009), 'Transnational Regulatory Networks and their Limits', *Yale Journal of International Law*, **34** (1), 113–72.

Vogel, D. (1995), *Trading Up. Consumer and Environmental Regulation in a Global Economy*, Cambridge, MA: Harvard University Press.

von Ingersleben-Seip, N. (2023), 'Competition and Cooperation in Artificial Intelligence Standard Setting: Explaining Emergent Patterns', *Review of Policy Research*, **40** (5), 781–810, accessed at https://doi.org/https://doi.org/10.1111/ropr.12538.

Waters, R., M. Murgia and J. Espinoza (2023), 'OpenAI Warns Over Split with Europe as Regulation Advances', *Financial Times*, accessed at https://www.ft.com/content/5814b408-8111-49a9-8885-8a8 434022352.

West, D. and J. Allen (2020), *Turning Point. Policymaking in the Era of Artificial Intelligence*, Washington, DC: Brookings Institution Press.

Wirtz, B. W., J. C. Weyerer and B. J. Sturm (2020), 'The Dark Sides of Artificial Intelligence: An Integrated AI Governance Framework for Public Administration', *International Journal of Public Administration*, **43** (9), 818–29.

Zuboff, S. (2019), *The Age of Surveillance Capitalism: The Fight for a Human Future at the New Frontier of Power*, New York: Public Affairs.

20. The politics of regulating AI technologies: towards *AI competition states*

Regine Paul

INTRODUCTION

The regulation of artificial intelligence technologies (AITs) has recently become the subject of intense discussions. Initially dominated by industry self-regulation and soft ethical guidelines (Hagendorff 2020; Jobin et al. 2019), demands have grown for more stringent state-run regulation in the AIT domain, seeing that the "reckless" development and deployment of AITs could bring "social and political instability" with the potential to threaten "freedom, self-determination, human rights, and fundamental values" (de Almeida et al. 2021: 507). More recently, the arrival of coercive and more concrete regulation by public actors (statutory regulation) seems to put an end to the "Wild West" phase of disruptive innovation. In 2019, the US proposed an Algorithmic Accountability Act and China published the Beijing Artificial Intelligence Principles; in 2020 Canada established an Algorithmic Impact Assessment tool; and the European Commission proposed a first set of legally binding rules for AI, including prohibited applications in 2021, with a compromise text adopted by Council and Parliament in February 2024. Understanding the drivers and functioning of AIT regulation is a key scholarly and societal endeavour.

This chapter introduces and critically evaluates alternative conceptualizations of AIT regulation. The first half of the chapter offers a systematic review, suggesting that so far dominant accounts fall into three camps: (a) *applied ethics prescriptions* for "effective" and "good" regulation; (b) *technocratic rational choice approaches* with "risk-based" and "proportionate" interference in business freedoms; (c) *political economy accounts of big tech capture* in AI regulation. I argue that the former two camps apply problematically apolitical concepts of AIT regulation which hide the *politics* of value choices in rule-setting and enforcement. As the latter camp depicts a more *political conceptualization of regulation* – as an exchange of lean regulation by the state against political support by businesses – it invites us to reflect on the wider politics of regulating AITs (cf. Paul 2022).

The second half of the chapter develops a competition state lens of AIT regulation. This assumes that as "technological advances have always been a source of national power and economic competitiveness" (Rühlig 2022), states' technology regulation will always also seek to *regulate into being*[1] their own strategic innovation and competitiveness projects – both in general and specifically in the AI sector. I outline three specific research avenues for examining the role of "AI competition states" in future research on public policy and AI: (1) the explanatory role of states' strategic competitiveness projects as part of regulatory efforts, (2) variations of national/regional regulatory strategies and their interaction with economies' variable position in global AIT production processes, and (3) critical inquiry of the states' own interest in using AITs for enhancing their administrative and governance capacities as part of contemporary regulatory projects.

THE REGULATION OF ARTIFICIAL INTELLIGENCE TECHNOLOGIES: THREE STYLIZED ACCOUNTS

To review the state-of-the-art on emergent statutory AIT regulations systematically, on 3 July 2023, I searched the *web of science* Social Science Citation Index[2] with the four alternative keyword combinations "regulat* artificial intelligence" OR "regulat* AI*" OR "regulat* automated decision* OR "regulat* algorithm* decision*" in the title of the article. I thus identified 58 published research articles (see Table 20A.1 in the Appendix), with the earliest article published in 2014. Research intensified (at a still comparatively low level) over time: six web-of-science-indexed research articles written in 2020 were followed by nine in 2021, nineteen in 2022, and another fourteen already in the first half of 2023. An important meta-structural observation concerns the sheer dominance of articles from US- and UK-based authors (fifteen and eleven, respectively), followed by China and Belgium (five each), Australia, Canada, and Germany (four each). Only Brazil-based authors perturb the relative absence of the Global South in these English-speaking journal publications (three works).

A limitation of this search strategy, besides the focus on English-language research risking reification of existing biases towards Global North and Chinese dominance in academic and regulatory debates about AI, is that it does not cover work which mentions the search words in the articles' key words or full texts. However, the goal here was to identify those studies for review which deal with AIT regulation and/or the regulation of ADM (automated decision-making) systems as a central concern for research. To offer a more general flavour of how scholars conceptualize and explain AIT regulation beyond this systematic review, I will situate it in wider scholarly debates of technology regulation as well as illustration from existing regulatory proposals and debates in the policy world, drawing on a larger set of articles and monographs in the field.

The systematic review identified research works which conceptualize AIT/ADM regulation in largely three different ways (11 articles do not apply a social science concept of regulation):[3] as a *normative project of applied ethics* (19), as a *technocratic rational choice endeavour* (17), or as a *politico-economic struggle over influence* characterized by powerful interests (8). The remainder of the section introduces these three stylized accounts of AIT regulation and situates them in wider, and older, debates in regulation studies and political economy. This review work lays the foundation for problematizing the relative dominance of apolitical concepts of regulation – and public regulators' role – in existing scholarly accounts of AIT regulation.

AIT Regulation as Applied Ethics Project

Almost half of the articles identified through a systematic search discuss AIT regulation from a normative perspective as a project of applied ethics (cf. Appendix Table 20A.1). Written mostly by lawyers and ethicists, they consider specific regulatory proposals – such as the EU's General Data Protection Regulation (GDPR) or AI Regulation – and examine how effectively these protect specific rights such as non-discrimination, legibility, or explainability of decisions (inter alia: Forgo 2023; Goodman and Flaxman 2017; Lee 2020; Malgieri and Comande 2017; Van Kolfschooten 2022; Wachter et al. 2017). The normative orientation of these works is visible in their providing advice on how to "improve" regulation by protecting ethical principles and fundamental rights "better", in their efforts to review existing regulatory proposals and developing an "integrated governance framework" (de Almeida et al. 2021), but also in analyses of whether the EU's (allegedly) ethically motivated AI regulation can spread globally given its technological and economic lagging behind China and the US (Feldstein 2023).

Overall, these works conceptualize regulation as a normative project where ethical principles ought to be adhered to and implemented properly through suitable governance structures. Their laudable goal is to contribute to the development of an a priori normative baseline for developing and using AI in liberal democratic societies (none of the publications considers regulation outside the EU/Northern America): as the most cited of these works proposes, their goals is to assist in "designing algorithms and evaluation frameworks that avoid discrimination and enable explanation" (Goodman and Flaxman 2017: 50). With their detailed discussions of ethical principles and prescriptions of how they ought to be effectively designed and implemented through law and regulation, these studies certainly provide relevant inputs for regulatory practice. For example, some of the authors have served as advisers on the EU Commission's AI High Level Expert Group, and two studies advising regulators on how to codify ethical standards are the most cited[4] by far in my sample (with 663 citations: Goodman and Flaxman 2017; with 355 citations: Wachter et al. 2017).

However, a key limitation of these works is the absence of accounting for political struggles over the exact meaning of normative precepts for regulation (what constitutes "fairness" or "transparency" for whom and whose interpretation of these principles comes to dominate regulation?; cf. debates in Part II of this *Handbook*) both on paper and in practice. Critics of applied ethics approaches to AIT regulation (Gyulai and Ujlaki 2021) argue that the constant attempt to develop more fine-grained legal and technical fixes for problems such as bias or lack of explainability rules – though well intended – can be complacent in disguising the deeply political nature of rule-setting and enforcement. The close examination of struggles over norm interpretation and practice is therefore vital. In addition, this literature's well-meant fixation on improving the regulatory and technical design of AITs from an ethics platform can be unconsciously complacent of industry's suspected efforts in diverting attention from underlying political questions about the production and use of AITs in our societies (on the discussion over "bias": Powles 2018; cf. Hong, Chapter 8 in this volume; on the ethics discourse: Rönnblom, Carlsson and Padden, Chapter 9 in this volume). To understand and explain regulatory development and enforcement in the AIT domain, it is therefore vital to situate (struggles over) normative prescriptions of applied ethics in their wider political and economic context.

AIT Regulation as Technocratic Rational Choice Endeavour

Another – equally large – part of the emerging literature on AIT regulation conceptualizes regulation as a technocratic rational choice project in which the ethical principles and harm-minimization strategies portrayed by scholars in the first camp are (to be) balanced with innovation and economic growth goals. Central to these accounts – often authored by scholars of law and economics, political economists, but also political scientists – is the normative-ideological conviction that "over-regulation" ought to be avoided because it raises compliance costs for firms (but also public sector users) and thus hinders the development and deployment of AIT/ADM systems (most explicitly in: Han et al. 2020, 2022; Krafft et al. 2022; Tschider 2018): "Adequate regulation is key to maximize the benefits and minimize the risks stemming from AI technologies." (Erdélyi and Goldsmith 2022). Some articles in this camp focus more pragmatically on the effects of regulation on companies and manager perceptions

(Candelon et al. 2021; Cuellar et al. 2022), but their assessment of "trade-offs" between firms' willingness to invest and their information on AIT regulation as well as companies' effective preparation for such regulation entails a similar normative ambition for regulation as the optimal balance between risk mitigation and innovation. More political questions about how regulation defines risks, harms, and innovation, who does so, to whose benefit and to whose detriment do not feature.

Several studies in the sample prescribe specific regulatory approaches which they deem fit to ensure that regulation interferes in business freedom in "proportionate" ways (in general: Krafft et al. 2022; for the Food and Drug Administration (FDA) in the US: Sharma and Manchikanti 2020; for the internet of things: Tschider 2018; for healthcare regulation: Johnson 2022; McKee and Wouters 2022; Wang et al. 2022). Authors assume the goal of state regulation is, and indeed should be, to mitigate risks incurred through market failure only if such failure occurs and in ways that avoid overly burdensome requirements for developers, sellers, and users of the technology. Technocratic risk assessment would help provide *rational* answers to the question whether "to regulate or not" (Han et al. 2020), whereby rationality is achieved through the *pareto-optimal* allocation of costs and benefits of AI innovation for society, regardless of whether this implies distributional inequalities, human suffering, and/ or a crossing of moral red lines (see discussion of lethal weapons: Bode and Qiao-Franco, Chapter 21 in this volume).

The article by Krafft et al. (2022) offers the most explicit version of this rational choice recipe, proposing that ADM systems – also those drawing on AI and machine learning– "can be embedded in very different settings and vary widely in terms of their purposes as well as the decision consequences and the risks involved" so that "a higher risk … warrants greater regulatory efforts for ensuring algorithmic accountability" (Krafft et al. 2022: 2, 12). This differentiation could entail prohibitive approaches towards unacceptably harmful uses where fundamental human rights or people's physical or psychological safety are threatened, tight risk mitigation and controls for high-risk uses, and permissive regulation for low-risk adoptions (Krafft et al. 2022). For example, automation in war technology is likely to trigger human deaths, while an automated email filter used by a social service provider will most likely not. Similarly, the use of AI-based social scoring systems in the public sector (the ranking of people due to their social media uses, purchasing behaviour, etc. which determines access to public services) might be deemed more unacceptable than the automatic sorting of phone calls to specific social service experts in call centres. The key message here is that optimal regulatory responses to AITs and AI-based ADM – the optimal mix of regulatory tools (Covarrubias et al. 2022) – can and *ought to be* identified through risk analysis and other methods of so-called evidence-based regulation.

Similar managerialist arguments feature beyond the sample (cf. Taeihagh 2021). They are representative of a wider debate in regulation studies about proportionate and *risk-based regulation* (cf. summary of debate in Paul 2021), building on the assumption that "absolute safety cannot be a sensible regulatory goal" (Majone 2010: 94) and risk-based regulation should intervene only against the highest risks and otherwise keep compliance costs for firms low (Sunstein 2009). Proportionate regulation is conceived of as an optimizing conciliator between ethical and safety-related considerations vs. innovation and economic growth goals. Such thinking moves beyond scholarly ivory towers: a recent policy review by Ernest & Young, written jointly with the OECD, specifies the benefits of risk-based regulation in the

AIT domain (Etziani et al. 2021: 4) and the EU Commission's AI Act proposal also adopts a "proportionate" and risk-based approach.

Despite their commonsensical articulation and impact on regulation, rational choice conceptualizations of proportionate AIT regulation feature two major limitations. Similar to applied ethics approaches, they depict a merely normative vision of how we *ought to* regulate AIT rather than explaining the outcomes of really existing regulatory struggles. The prescription of technocratic AIT risk regulation entails an apolitical concept of regulation. In particular, the failure to acknowledge the political nature of regulatory decisions – over whether to adopt risk-based regulatory frameworks in the first place, how to frame risks and whose costs and benefits of using AI to consider, how to calculate harm, costs, and benefits, but also which specific rules and sanctions to tie to such risk assessments – contributes to a problematic depoliticization (cf. Stone 2020 on the politics of numerical analysis). Articulating regulatory judgements as straightforwardly "rational" and "evidence-based" precludes much-needed societal dialogue and political debate over interpretations and allocations of harms and benefits of developing and using AIT. It also glosses over globally highly diverse base norms about the "acceptability" of AIT uses in different contexts, for example between liberal democracies and authoritarian states (Rühlig 2022), but also countries in the so-called Global North vs. the Global South (Gray, Chapter 15 in this volume; Omotubora and Basu, Chapter 17 in this volume), thus problematically universalizing "Western" concepts of rationality.

AIT Regulation as a Political Struggle between Powerful Interests

The third broad set of perspectives in the systematic review depicts regulation as a political struggle in which powerful private interests seek to counter the state's regulatory efforts (and often succeed). Their interest is less in prescribing recipes for "ethical" or "rational" regulation, but to understand the politics of regulating AITs and digital tech in specific empirical cases. The eight studies identified in this camp are quite diverse in their depiction of *what constitutes politics* and the role of business interests in the context of AI regulation. Five works discuss the influence of corporate actors explicitly (Bode and Huelss 2023; Boubker 2021; Dignam 2020; Grzeszczak and Mazur 2021; Kokshagina et al. 2023), while Justo-Hanani (2022) mentions global economic competition norms as one of three explanatory factors for AIT regulation outputs (next to institutions and domestic politics). Krzywdzinski and colleagues (2023) focus on trade union strategies for countering corporate anti-regulation lobbying, whereas Gyulai and Ujlaki (2021) develop a Hobbesian realist political theory of AI regulation without focusing much on business interests.

They also vary in their empirically enriched understanding of why regulation takes specific forms. A study on the regulation of content display and moderation on social media platforms in Australia, for example, conceptualizes regulation as the outcome of "institutional tussles between governments, digital platforms and third parties", with platforms seeking to "delegitimize regulatory efforts and narrow the scope of regulation" (Kokshagina et al. 2023). Another describes the corporate governance, financing, and networking structures of big tech firms in the Silicon Valley as "autocratic" and oligopolic to an extent where the public interest in regulating AITs is severely compromised (Dignam 2020; cf. for the wider argument: Petit 2020). Boubker (2021: 453) shows that Silicon Valley's "usual practice of 'do first, ask for forgiveness later'" severely jeopardizes the FDA's regulation of medical AI applications. Grzeszczak and Mazur's study (2021) on the implementation of the GDPR highlights that the right not to be subject to ADM – among other rights – has *not* considerably shifted "regulatory power" from tech businesses and large users of ADM systems (including the state) towards citizens and consumers. Bode and Huelss' (2023: 1233) analysis of EU approach to military AIT uses finds that "corporate actors, understood as technical experts, construct and perform particular discourses and practices of military AI and thereby limit EU decisions".

These accounts concur with wider discussions of industry self-regulation of AITs through ethical guidelines as a successful corporate strategy for avoiding stricter, "truly binding legal framework[s]" (Hagendorff 2020: 100). They also speak to reports of big tech firms' strong interest in shaping regulation because "the political-economic benefits of personal data depend on turning it into an asset (i.e., capitalized property) and ensuring that its financial value – based on expected future revenues – are not threatened by future political and policy changes" (Birch et al. 2020: 479). Examples of successful lobbying by tech companies have been widely discussed for the EU's GDPR with its focus on individual privacy at point of data collection (Bygrave 2019; Mantelero 2016) which, as some argue, "privileges economic growth" over a more comprehensive notion of individual rights (Padden and Öjehag-Pettersson 2021: 486). Another study on competition effects of the GDPR shows that, while potentially well meant, the regulation strengthened the technological and market dominance of key corporations rather than tackling it, for example by enabling big tech firms to restrict access to data for competitors on grounds of data protection (Geradin et al. 2021).

More generally, these debates echo works which have explored the power of economic interests in regulation and policy since at least the eighteenth century, when James Madison expressed fears over how powerful interest groups' influence on US policymaking could undermine the common good (Stewart 1990). Rather than viewing regulation as a normative project of applied ethics or a technocratic response to market failure, political economists have highlighted the deeply political nature of regulation as a struggle with and over corporate power. Prominently, Nobel laureate George Stigler (1971: 8), has identified a "correspondence between regulations and economic interests" which he explains with a focus on "the political process by which regulation is achieved". Capture theory holds that industry would turn to the state to increase its profitability and seek regulatory measures to control market entry (e.g., definitions of product standards or professions, pricing strategies, tariffs). Regulation becomes a means to keep competitors out and avoid constraints on corporate business models.

More specifically for AITs, recent works in political economy portray a powerful tech industry, mainly located in the iconic Silicon Valley, and castigate the ability of firms such as Amazon, Alphabet, Meta, or Microsoft to avoid or water down regulation, and/or to shape it in their own interest (e.g., Birch et al. 2020; Cohen 2018; Pasquale 2015; Zuboff 2019). Taken jointly, these works explore the business models of big tech companies in the age of "informational", "platform", or "surveillance" capitalism, suggesting that corporate strategies for shaping AIT regulation have a dual purpose: firstly, to ensure the relatively unfettered continuation of the mass generation, extraction, and processing of user (and other) data at the heart of these firms' business models; and secondly, to avoid the tighter scrutiny of monopoly endeavours and business models which rely on network effects and monopoly rents, as well as the exclusive ownership of data and technical infrastructures.

Certainly, their concentrated market power and big tech corporate interest in unregulated mass data extraction, trading, and use in the design of AITs render accounts of regulatory capture highly plausible. And yet, when read against a rich and long-standing literature on the politics of regulation, the conceptual narrowing of the politics of AIT regulation to capture is misleading, for at least three reasons. Firstly, we need to account *for national/regional varieties* of state-economy structures, interests and strategies of different socio-economic and political actors, and their role in shaping regulatory strategies (cf. Guidi et al. 2020). Depending on the structure of a national economy and its relative position on the global AIT market, it might seem apt to regulate (certain elements of) AITs more – rather than less – strictly.[5] For example, given their strategic disadvantage vis-à-vis US big tech players in accessing data for AIT development and use, European tech start-ups might lobby for EU regulation that shields them from US-American dominance. Indeed, the works in the sample by Kokshagina et al. (2023) and Krzywdzinski et al. (2023) highlight the crucial role of institutional context in shaping actors' much diverse regulatory strategies and interactions.

Secondly, if we relax rational choice assumptions and take a more constructivist view, regulation is likely shaped not only by regulators' profit-maximization calculations (political support by big tech companies in exchange for lean regulation or by consumers/SMEs in exchange for stricter regulation), but also their "ideology, beliefs about the proper role of government, and visions of sound regulatory policymaking" (Croley 2011: 58). Such *ideational undercurrents* of regulation will also vary across contexts (cf. Borraz et al. 2022; Rothstein et al. 2020).

Thirdly, and relatedly, accounts of regulatory capture arguably draw on a *flawed dichotomy of state vs. economic interests*. The economic, social, and political power of big tech companies over regulatory agendas, outputs, and outcomes must certainly be acknowledged; but so must state regulators' very own agency and interest in producing the conditions for the national economy's AI competitiveness on a global market, in shaping global competition according to their ambitions and visions, and in incorporating private sector interests and expertise in their regulatory projects.

THE CRITICAL POLITICAL ECONOMY OF AIT REGULATION: A *COMPETITION STATE* LENS

In response to the problematizations in the previous section, I go on to develop a *critical political economy of AIT regulation*: as part of competition state projects in which state regulators articulate, and seek to *regulate into being*, their own future visions of the national (or regional) economy in global capitalism. In this section, I will briefly dwell on cues from the review – few as they are – to then develop a more critically oriented political economy framework for exploring the politics of AIT regulation as part of competition state endeavours.

Towards *AI Competition States*

Though there are very few cures in the systematic review overall, three studies in the sample do adopt a more proactive and strategic view of the state's incorporation of economic interests. Dignam (2020) suggests that while "in both the UK and USA, deregulation and self-regulation have formed key parts of nationalist AI strategies" due to the dominance of financial capitalism and its strong focus on shareholder value (Dignam 2020: 47), stricter regulation goals feature in the US Democrats' agenda as well as a coercive approach in the EU. Capture by big tech companies is no automatism then; its relative weight depends on national regulators' own strategic interests and appetite for navigating between economic competitiveness goals and a wider "public interest" in regulating AITs. A second study stresses the state's effort to gain a "decisive strategic advantage" over other states in the "AI race" (Gyulai and Ujlaki 2021: 39; citing the work of Bostrom 2014). As technological progress and competition is tightly linked to state capacity, power, fiscal revenues, and the ability to generate wealth for its citizens, states' regulatory projects are more endogenous but also more multidimensional and ambivalent than capture theory would predict. Last, but not least, Bode and Huelss' work (2023) on EU regulation of military AITs highlights the co-constitution of public and private legitimacy and power through an EU-level staging of corporate actors as the holders of technocratic expertise who are officially granted "epistemic authority" in ways which, in turn, are meant to boost the legitimacy and capacity of the EU as a global statutory security actor.

These studies – though few in number in the sample – speak to a growing body of work in critical policy and regulation studies which explore the economic orientations of different AIT-related policies as a *performative* enactment of states' future visions of their own economy's competitiveness in a global AIT market and innovation race (af Malmborg 2023; Bareis and Katzenbach 2022; Krarup and Horst 2023; Paul 2023). Much can be gained, I suggest, if this emerging literature tapped more explicitly into longer-standing debates in critical political economy about the state's strategic incorporation of capitalist competitiveness logics (Cerny 1997, 2010; Hirsch 1995; Jessop 2002; Sum and Jessop 2013).

Critical political economists propose that economic globalization and the increased exposure of national (and regional) economies to global competition have led to a restructuration of states into "competition states" (Cerny 1997). Neither are these weak states who lost sovereignty vis-à-vis powerful business interests and mainly engage in deregulation, nor are they entirely de-territorialized by the logics of global markets. Rather, states have substantially transformed: they have reduced their direct provision of public goods and services all while expanding interventions and regulation "in the name of competitiveness and marketization" (Cerny 1997: 251; for a similar argument cf.: Jessop 2002). At the same time, states' continued territorial fixation provides a key reference point for the diversification, segmentation, and proliferation of markets and thereby arguably enables capitalist accumulation in the first place (Hirsch 1995: 33).

A substantial difference to capture theory, competition states are *active* forces, operating as "both the engine room and the steering mechanism" (Cerny 1997: 274) in global capitalism. Competition states use research and development policy, industrial policy and inflation control, as well as education and migration policies, to boost private investment in, and the international competitiveness of, the national economy (Cerny 1997, 2010), and they do so in inevitably *selective* ways. From this lens, regulation evolves as always *embedded* in wider discourses and structures of socio-economic accumulation (most often shaped by the contemporary capitalist formation). At the same time, regulators wield considerable influence as they select, vary/combine, and retain (elements of) existing discourses and material structures into specific (re-)articulations of the social world (Sum and Jessop 2013; cf. Paul 2012, 2023 for a more detailed discussion of Sum and Jessop's work). This implies that state regulation is unlikely to cater to business interests on an individualistic vote-seeking basis in a purely exogenic manner. Instead, regulation always also articulates and seeks to bring into being the state's own perceptions and future visions of the national economy's global competitiveness.

Three Research Avenues on *AI Competition States*

From a competition state lens, eventually, AIT regulation can be approached as a case of *AI competition states* which seek to regulate into being their own specific visions of macro-economically desirable tech futures in global capitalism. Building on this conceptualization of AI competition states, I propose at least three research avenues to explore, explain, and critically assess AIT regulation beyond the state-of-the-art: (1) explore the explanatory role of states' strategic competitiveness projects in the domain, (2) explain how variable national/regional regulatory strategies interact with economies' variable position in the global production of AITs, and (3) incorporate critical inquiry of states' own interest in using AITs for enhancing their administrative and governance capacities as part of their regulatory projects.

Firstly, an AI competition state perspective firmly situates explorations of AIT regulation in states' perception of, and relative position in, the global "race to AI". AIT development and applications are marked by fierce global competition between mainly Chinese, European, and US-American providers, with countries now portraying the need to "win" the "race to AI" as "an almost existential necessity" due to hopes of stellar economic gains, but also the assumed societal and geopolitical costs of lagging behind technological developments (Smuha 2021: 3; cf. Mügge 2023). For example, the European Commission, in 2018, expressed an "ambition … for Europe to become the world-leading region for developing and deploying cutting-edge, ethical and secure AI, promoting a human-centric approach in the global context" (European Commission 2018: 1). Observers suggest that leapfrog ambitions to forge a common European AI market which is globally competitive already co-shape the EU's regulatory agenda (Krarup and Horst 2023; Paul 2023). A competition state perspective can further unpack the imprint of such imaginations of different economies' position in globally competitive markets on AIT regulation.

Importantly, critical political economy highlights that the regulatory enactment of future visions of markets can trigger material implications but also remains subject to ideational contestation of the "best way forward". Materially, AI regulation shapes the conditions for competition through product and production standards, quality certification schemes, as well as its ties with investment in research and development of AITs, including the establishment of interdependent conditions for regulatory projects in other jurisdictions (Mügge, Chapter 19 in this volume). The literature on the EU as a global regulatory power highlights how Brussels product regulation structures global markets, both unintentionally and as a strategic project, in ways that aid the European economy's international competitiveness (Bradford 2012; Damro 2012). AIT regulation will shape business models through the formulation of prohibited uses, ethical principles, and risk mitigation requirements – that define the realm of legitimate use cases hence shaping profitable product development strategies for the data and behavioural models which companies seek to sell, including for new market entrants. In this context, regulators also engage in ideational power struggles because they propose potentially competing norms, instruments, and processes for enforcement. The EU AI Act, for example, introduces bans on certain AIT uses in an explicit attempt to set the Union apart from Chinese-style social scoring and mass surveillance and promote both a vision of more "trustworthy" and "ethical" AITs and of the EU as a morally credible regulator which can also shape global norms (Paul 2023).

This latter point connects to a *second avenue* for critical political economy research on AIT regulation: to explore and explain the variability of AI competition states. The longer-standing literature on regulatory competition assumes that states apply different regulatory "styles" – some stricter and some more lenient, some more hierarchical and some more open to self-regulation (more generally: Vogel 2003). This literature explains well how different regulatory "styles" emerge from different state traditions of balancing safety vs. risk-taking and the relative role of states vs. markets. It also discusses the effects of the resulting coexistence of variable regulatory approaches in terms of interaction and interdependence dynamics (Bradford 2012; specifically for AITs: Smuha 2021; cf. Mügge, Chapter 19 in this volume). We need closer interrogation of how dominant interpretations of AI competitiveness build on, or break with, previous articulations of – and struggles over – competitiveness in different jurisdictions.

Cursorily, research on varieties of AI competition states could explore how the large finance and venture capital sector and its demand for fast innovation and monopoly rents in liberal market economies has shaped a laissez-faire and deregulatory approach to AIT – and to platform economy giants and their data generation and business models – in the US and the UK. By contrast, does the EU "behave" more like a coordinated market economy which sees its competitive edge in the AIT world in its high-tech industrial sector (e.g., for robotics, machinery, and medical devices) and competes on high-quality products, expert know-how, and industrial clusters which include SMEs, research institutions, and public sector organizations? To what extent does the EU approach to regulating AITs as a matter of CE-certified product standards, and its efforts to curb US-style platform capitalism through the acts on digital markets and digital services, represent a strategic attempt to boost the EU's more coordinated market economy and constrain the laissez-faire US competition strategy in the race to AI? At the same time, observers of Chinese technology regulation argue that the country has "successfully utilized its party-state-permeated economy to increase its technical standardization power" vis-à-vis the US and the EU (Rühlig 2021; cf. Rolf and Schindler 2023; Donoghue et al., Chapter 26 in this volume). How does the Chinese state-capitalist configuration with state-owned AI enterprises and tightly controlled private firms, state-driven research and innovation, and massive investment in national and international standardization bodies interact with its AI-related regulatory strategies, at home and more globally? Pointing to another example, more recent work on drivers of Brazilian AI regulation highlights ambitions of establishing regional leadership – economically, technically, and politically – in a domain dominated by "Western" and "Northern" rule (Silva 2023), suggesting that contestations of global power asymmetries and inequalities have also become part of AIT competition state projects in the Global South (cf. Omotubora and Basu, Chapter 17 in this volume).

The *third research avenue* expands the perspective to explore how states' non-economic governance projects co-shape AIT regulation and get intermingled with economic competitiveness agendas. This takes cues from Bode and Huelss' (2023) paper in the sample on the military-research-regulation complex in European security and defence matters. As AITs are relevant to a very wide range of security and military applications, including domestic infrastructure security, cybersecurity, and access to data on citizens (including for elections) and would-be-residents (in the realm of border control), the regulation of such technologies is not just about risk mitigation and competitiveness, but also crucially about the state's more traditionally security-oriented governance projects and capacities (for the EU also see: Carmel 2017; Mügge 2023). Moreover, the increasing mutual dependence of (1) states on the corporately organized, designed, and partially also owned AIT infrastructure (such as the private "minting" of data/patterns for public governance: Fourcade and Gordon 2020), and of

(2) private actors on large-scale public funding, academic education and research, and technological experimentation, blurs any neat analytical distinction of public vs. private interests.

The case of EU migration governance shows, for example, that AIT development is powerfully fuelled by an industry "eager to cater to real and perceived needs of governments in the field of border management" (Broeders and Hampshire 2013: 1208). Research and development for diverse security technologies is conceptualized and funded in the EU (through Horizon and other funding streams) to develop and enhance European security technology markets in line with corporate interests, to meet public agendas for promoting investment in these technologies, but also to advance the EU's own control ambitions through AIT uses (Carmel 2017). The EU does not "just" regulate AITs from a distance, it proactively creates markets, "testing grounds" (Molnar 2021), and "business cases" (Leese 2018) for such innovation *through and for* its own uses of AITs in migration and border control. Leese (2018) suggests that such public development of tech business cases problematically contributes to the *ex-post* permissive mainstreaming of thus-trialled technology uses by those supposed to regulate it. The EU's AI regulation actively supports "regulatory sandboxes" for AIT developers to deploy applications – including in public sector use cases – and test whether and how they can comply with ethical and safety standards (European Commission 2021). While we do not yet have conclusive evidence on the constitutive logic of such testing grounds for specific AIT-regulation-marketization configurations, this brief illustration certainly evokes the necessity to critically explore how states' desire to use technology in their own governance projects co-shapes AIT regulation beyond purely economic agendas, and how, in turn, potentially self-empowering state regulation shapes AIT development and uses on the ground.

CONCLUSION

This chapter critically discussed existing conceptualizations of AIT regulation and, on that basis, proposed a novel concept of *AI competition states* to better grasp the politics of regulatory projects. I argued that both applied ethics and rational choice accounts – the most dominant and visible perspectives identified in a systematic review – entail problematically apolitical concepts of AIT regulation. Works on the relative capture of AI regulation by corporate interests, by contrast, provide a welcome invitation to reflect on the wider politics of regulating AITs. But unlike standard accounts of capture suggest, more constructivist takes on tech regulation highlight that regulators do not straightforwardly receive and filter business interests or somewhat "neutrally" balance them against wider societal concerns over ethical AI. Neither are they the reluctant victim of big tech capture. Instead, from the competition state perspective detailed in this chapter, regulators proactively try to *regulate into being* conditions under which AI innovation in their respective economy can be globally competitive, pursuing their specific ambitions and visions of such competitiveness.

I identified three manifestations of competition states in AIT regulation which require more critical scholarly work in the future. Firstly, we need to explore how AI competition states promote competitiveness aims through regulatory discourses and interventions alongside specific visions of their techno-economic but also geopolitical future (how successfully they do this is yet another question). Secondly, we ought to better understand how and why different AI competition states vary in their articulation of competitiveness and how such variation is shaped by – and shapes in return – different economies' position in the "global race to AI".

The role of new state-capitalist endeavours might play a crucial role here (Rolf and Schindler 2023). Thirdly, we must reveal interactions between AIT regulation's strong competitiveness undertones with states' very own AIT-fuelled governance projects. Where AI competition states promote public sector AITs as "testbeds" or "sandboxes" for innovation and technology deployment (see Sleep and Redden, Chapter 27 in this volume; Whitfield, Wright and Hamblin, Chapter 28 in this volume) as part of a self-serving regulatory agenda, the effective protection of the rule of law and democratic governance risk becoming secondary concerns.

NOTES

1. This formulation draws on work by Bareis and Katzenbach (2022) on how AI policies "narrate into being" specific AI futures.
2. This includes works in Sociology, Political Science, and Public Administration, and also from related disciplines of interest to this *Handbook*. Of the 58 identified articles, web of science categorized 20 in Law, eight in Information Science, five each in Computer Science and Education, and four each in Business, Management, and Political Science (other disciplines were mentioned less often). This disciplinary patterning of AI regulation research foreshadows my analytical arguments about the relative lack of more political conceptualizations.
3. The majority of these explore the use of AI in "self-regulated" learning settings from a technical optimization lens while a few also study the "regulatory" effects of AITs on individual and organizational decision-making.
4. Web of science calculates these citation figures across all databases (date: 3 July 2023).
5. Indeed, Stigler's original capture theory (1971) already acknowledges that businesses might not have a default preference for lean regulation or deregulation but instead push for strict product standards or price-fixing rules where they disable market access for unwanted competitors.

REFERENCES (EXCLUDING WORKS IDENTIFIED IN SYSTEMATIC REVIEW WHICH ARE IN THE APPENDIX)

af Malmborg, F. (2023), 'Narrative dynamics in European Commission AI policy – Sensemaking, agency construction, and anchoring', *Review of Policy Research*, **40** (5), 757–80.
Bareis, J. and C. Katzenbach (2022), 'Talking AI into being: The narratives and imaginaries of national AI strategies and their performative politics', *Science, Technology, & Human Values*, **47** (5), 855–81.
Birch, K., M. Chiappetta and A. Artyushina (2020), 'The problem of innovation in technoscientific capitalism: Data rentiership and the policy implications of turning personal digital data into a private asset', *Policy Studies*, **41** (5), 468–87.
Borraz, O., A.-L. Beaussier, M. Wesseling, D. Demeritt, H. Rothstein, M. Hermans, M. Huber and R. Paul (2022), 'Why regulators assess risk differently: Regulatory style, business organization, and the varied practice of risk-based food safety inspections across the EU', *Regulation & Governance*, **16** (1), 274–92.
Bradford, A. (2012), 'The Brussels Effect', *Northwestern University Law Review*, **107** (1), 1–67.
Broeders, D. and J. Hampshire (2013), 'Dreaming of seamless borders: ICTs and the pre-emptive governance of mobility in Europe', *Journal of Ethnic and Migration Studies*, **39** (8), 1201–18.
Bygrave, L. A. (2019), 'Minding the machine v2.0: The EU General Data Protection Regulation and automated decision making', in K. Yeung and M. Lodge (eds), *Algorithmic Regulation*, New York: Oxford University Press, pp. 248–62.
Carmel, E. (2017), 'Re-interpreting knowledge, expertise and EU governance: The cases of social policy and security research policy', *Comparative European Politics*, **15** (5), 771–93.
Cerny, P. G. (1997), 'Paradoxes of the competition state: The dynamics of political globalization', *Government and Opposition*, **32** (2), 251–74.

Cerny, P. G. (2010), 'The competition state today: From *raison d'État* to *raison du Monde*', *Policy Studies*, **31**, 5–21.

Cohen, J. E. (2018), 'The biopolitical public domain: The legal construction of the surveillance economy', *Philosophy & Technology*, **31** (2), 213–33.

Croley, S. P. (2011), 'Beyond capture: Towards a new theory of regulation', in D. Levi-Faur (ed.), *Handbook on the Politics of Regulation*, Cheltenham, UK and Northampton, MA, USA: Edward Elgar Publishing, pp. 50–69.

Damro, C. (2012), 'Market power Europe', *Journal of European Public Policy*, **19** (5), 682–99.

Dignam, A. (2020), 'Artificial intelligence, tech corporate governance and the public interest regulatory response', *Cambridge Journal of Regions, Economy and Society*, **13** (1), 37–54.

Etziani, G., A. Koene, R. Kumar, N. Santiago and D. Wright (2021), *A Survey of Artificial Intelligence Risk Assessment Methodologies. The Global State of Play and Leading Practices Identified*, available at https://www.trilateralresearch.com/wp-content/uploads/2022/01/A-survey-of-AI-Risk-Assessment -Methodologies-full-report.pdf.

European Commission (2018), *Coordinated Plan on Artificial Intelligence*, COM(2018) 795 final, Brussels.

European Commission (2021), *Proposal for a Regulation Laying Down Harmonised Rules on Artificial Intelligence and Amending Certain Union Legislative Acts*, Brussels.

Fourcade, M. and J. Gordon (2020), 'Learning like a state: Statecraft in the digital age', *Journal of Law and Political Economy*, **1** (1), 78–108.

Guidi, M., I. Guardiancich and D. Levi-Faur (2020), 'Modes of regulatory governance: A political economy perspective', *Governance*, **33** (1), 5–19.

Hagendorff, T. (2020), 'The ethics of AI ethics: An evaluation of guidelines', *Minds and Machines*, **30** (1), 99–120.

Hirsch, J. (1995), *Der nationale Wettbewerbsstaat: Staat, Demokratie und Politik im globalen Kapitalismus*, Berlin: Id-Verlag.

Jessop, B. (2002), *The Future of the Capitalist State*, Cambridge: Polity.

Jobin, A., M. Ienca and E. Vayena (2019), 'The global landscape of AI ethics guidelines', *Nature Machine Intelligence*, **1** (9), 389–99.

Krarup, T. and M. Horst (2023), 'European artificial intelligence policy as digital single market making', *Big Data & Society*, **10** (1), 20539517231153812.

Leese, M. (2018), 'Standardizing security: The business case politics of borders', *Mobilities*, **13** (2), 261–75.

Majone, G. (2010), 'Strategic issues in risk regulation and risk management', in *OECD Reviews of Regulatory Reform*, Organisation for Economic Co-operation and Development, pp. 93–128.

Mantelero, A. (2016), 'Personal data for decisional purposes in the age of analytics: From an individual to a collective dimension of data protection', *Computer Law & Security Review*, **32** (2), 238–55.

Molnar, P. (2021), *Technological Testing Grounds. Migration Management Experiments and Reflections from the Ground Up*, EDRi and Refugee Law Lab, p. 57.

Mügge, D. (2023), 'The securitization of the EU's digital tech regulation', *Journal of European Public Policy*, **30** (7), 1431–46.

Padden, M. and A. Öjehag-Pettersson (2021), 'Protected how? Problem representations of risk in the General Data Protection Regulation (GDPR)', *Critical Policy Studies*, **15** (4), 486–503.

Pasquale, F. (2015), *The Black Box Society: The Secret Algorithms that Control Money and Information*, Cambridge, MA: Harvard University Press.

Paul, R. (2012), 'Limits of the competition state: The cultural political economy of European labour migration policies', *Critical Policy Studies*, **6** (4), 379–401.

Paul, R. (2021), *Varieties of Risk Analysis in Public Administrations*, London: Routledge.

Paul, R. (2022), 'Can critical policy studies outsmart AI? Research agenda on artificial intelligence technologies and public policy', *Critical Policy Studies*, **16** (4), 497–509.

Paul, R. (2023), 'European AI "trusted throughout the world": How risk-based regulation fashions a competitive common market for artificial intelligence', *Regulation & Governance*. First Online.

Petit, N. (2020), *Big Tech and the Digital Economy: The Moligopoly Scenario*, Oxford: Oxford University Press.

Powles, J. (2018), 'The seductive diversion of "solving" bias in artificial intelligence', accessed 21 June 2022 at https://onezero.medium.com/the-seductive-diversion-of-solving-bias-in-artificial-intelligence -890df5e5ef53.

Rolf, S. and S. Schindler (2023), 'The US–China rivalry and the emergence of state platform capitalism', *Environment and Planning A: Economy and Space*, 0308518X221146545.

Rothstein, H., R. Paul and D. Demeritt (2020), 'The boundary conditions for regulation: Welfare systems, state traditions, and the varied governance of work safety in Europe', *Governance*, 33 (1), 21–39.

Rühlig, T. (2021), *China, Europe and the New Power Competition over Technical Standards*, accessed at https://www.ui.se/globalassets/ui.se-eng/publications/ui-publications/2021/ui-brief-no.-1-2021.pdf.

Rühlig, T. (2022), *The Rise of Tech Standards Foreign Policy*, accessed 3 July 2022 at https://dgap.org/ en/research/publications/rise-tech-standards-foreign-policy.

Silva, G. C. (2023), 'Articulating AI futures for Brazil: AI policy between technological solutionism, development and dependency', paper presented at the International Public Policy Conference, 27–29 June, Toronto.

Smuha, N. A. (2021), 'From a "race to AI" to a "race to AI regulation": Regulatory competition for artificial intelligence', *Law, Innovation and Technology*, 13 (1), 1–28.

Stewart, R. B. (1990), 'Madison's Nightmare', *The University of Chicago Law Review*, 57 (2), 335–56.

Stigler, G. J. (1971), 'The theory of economic regulation', *The Bell Journal of Economics and Management Science*, 2 (1), 3–21.

Stone, D. (2020), *Counting: How We Use Numbers to Decide What Matters*, New York: Norton.

Sum, N.-L. and B. Jessop (2013), *Towards a Cultural Political Economy. Putting Culture in Its Place in Political Economy*, Cheltenham, UK and Northampton, USA: Edward Elgar Publishing.

Sunstein, C. (2009), *Laws of Fear: Beyond the Precautionary Principle*, Cambridge: Cambridge University Press.

Taeihagh, A. (2021), 'Governance of artificial intelligence', *Policy and Society*, 40 (2), 137–57.

Vogel, D. (2003), 'The hare and the tortoise revisited: The new politics of consumer and environmental regulation in Europe', *British Journal of Political Science*, 33 (4), 557–80.

Zuboff, S. (2019), *The Age of Surveillance Capitalism: The Fight for a Human Future at the New Frontier of Power*, 1st ed., New York: PublicAffairs.

APPENDIX

Table 20A.1 *Published articles on AIT/ADM regulation identified through systematic review*

No.	Author(s)	Article Title	Source Title	Year	Concept of REG
1	Eroglu, M.; Kaya, M. K.	Impact of artificial intelligence on corporate board diversity policies and regulations	*European Business Organization Law Review*	2022	none
2	Hytha, D. A.; Aronson, J. D.; Eng, A.	Technology innovation and the rebirth of self-regulation: How the internet of things, cloud computing, blockchain, and artificial intelligence solve big problems managing environmental regulation and resources	*International Journal of Communication*	2019	none
3	Henkel, A. P.; Bromuri, S.; Iren, D. et al.	Half human, half machine – augmenting service employees with AI for interpersonal emotion regulation	*Journal of Service Management*	2020	none
4	Santos-Arteaga, F. J.; Di Caprio, D.; Tavana, M.	A self-regulating information acquisition algorithm for preventing choice regret in multi-perspective decision making	*Business & Information Systems Engineering*	2014	none
5	Xia, Q.; Chiu, T. K. F.; Chai, C. S.	The moderating effects of gender and need satisfaction on self-regulated learning through Artificial Intelligence (AI)	*Education and Information Technologies*	2022	none
6	Dohl, F.	Artificial intelligence, law and cultural heritage on the potential for strategic dynamics in the current legal policy discourse on the upcoming EU AI regulation for libraries	*Zeitschrift für Bibliothekswesen und Bibliographie*	2021	none
7	Jarvela, S.; Nguyen, A.; Hadwin, A.	Human and artificial intelligence collaboration for socially shared regulation in learning	*British Journal of Educational Technology*	2023	none
8	Hilpert, J. C.; Greene, J. A.; Bernacki, M.	Leveraging complexity frameworks to refine theories of engagement: Advancing self-regulated learning in the age of artificial intelligence	*British Journal of Educational Technology*	2023	none
9	Wang, C. Y.; Lin, J. J. H.	Utilizing artificial intelligence to support analyzing self-regulated learning: A preliminary mixed-methods evaluation from a human-centered perspective	*Computers in Human Behavior*	2023	none
10	Xia, Q.; Chiu, T. K. F.; Chai, C. S.; Xie, K.	The mediating effects of needs satisfaction on the relationships between prior knowledge and self-regulated learning through artificial intelligence chatbot	*British Journal of Educational Technology*	2023	none
11	Hsu, T. C.; Chang, C.; Jen, T. H.	Artificial intelligence image recognition using self-regulation learning strategies: effects on vocabulary acquisition, learning anxiety, and learning behaviours of English language learners	*Interactive Learning Environments*	2023	none

No.	Author(s)	Article Title	Source Title	Year	Concept of REG
12	Ouyang, F.; Wu, M.; Zhang, L. Y.; Xu, W. Q.; Zheng, L. Y.; Cukurova, M.	Making strides towards AI-supported regulation of learning in collaborative knowledge construction	*Computers in Human Behavior*	2023	none
13	Baek, T. H.; Kim, M.	AI robo-advisor anthropomorphism: The impact of anthropomorphic appeals and regulatory focus on investment behaviors	*Journal of Business Research*	2023	none
14	Stuurman, K.; Lachaud, E.	Regulating AI. A label to complete the proposed Act on artificial intelligence	*Computer Law & Security Review*	2022	normative/applied ethics
15	Etzioni, A.; Etzioni, O.	Should artificial intelligence be regulated?	*Issues in Science and Technology*	2017	normative/applied ethics
16	de Almeida, P. G. R.; dos Santos, C. D.; Farias, J. S.	Artificial intelligence regulation: A framework for governance	*Ethics and Information Technology*	2021	normative/applied ethics
17	Van Kolfschooten, H.	EU regulation of artificial intelligence: challenges for patients' rights	*Common Market Law Review*	2022	normative/applied ethics
18	Lee, J.	Access to finance for artificial intelligence regulation in the financial services industry	*European Business Organization Law Review*	2020	normative/applied ethics
19	Farisco, M.; Evers, K.; Salles, A.	On the contribution of neuroethics to the ethics and regulation of artificial intelligence	*Neuroethics*	2022	normative/applied ethics
20	Opderbeck, D. W.	Artificial intelligence in pharmaceuticals, biologics, and medical devices: present and future regulatory models	*Fordham Law Review*	2019	normative/applied ethics
21	Ingles, I. M.	Regulating religious robots: Free exercise and RFRA in the time of superintelligent artificial intelligence	*Georgetown Law Journal*	2017	normative/applied ethics
22	Clarke, R.	Regulatory alternatives for AI	*Computer Law & Security Review*	2019	normative/applied ethics
23	Ferryman, K.	Addressing health disparities in the Food and Drug Administration's artificial intelligence and machine learning regulatory framework	*Journal of the American Medical Informatics Association*	2020	normative/applied ethics
24	Malgieri, G.; Comande, G.	Why a right to legibility of automated decision-making exists in the General Data Protection Regulation	*International Data Privacy Law*	2017	normative/applied ethics
25	Wachter, S.; Mittelstadt, B.; Floridi, L.	Why a right to explanation of automated decision-making does not exist in the General Data Protection Regulation	*International Data Privacy Law*	2017	normative/applied ethics
26	Bayamlioglu, E.	The right to contest automated decisions under the General Data Protection Regulation: Beyond the so-called right to explanation	*Regulation & Governance*	2022	normative/applied ethics

No.	Author(s)	Article Title	Source Title	Year	Concept of REG
27	Tosoni, L.	The right to object to automated individual decisions: resolving the ambiguity of Article 22(1) of the General Data Protection Regulation	*International Data Privacy Law*	2021	normative/applied ethics
28	Goodman, B.; Flaxman, S.	European Union Regulations on algorithmic decision making and a right to explanation	*AI Magazine*	2017	normative/applied ethics
29	Forgo, N.	To regulate artificial intelligence, also in law enforcement	*Monatsschrift für Kriminologie und Strafrechtsreform*	2023	normative/applied ethics
30	Bradley, F.	Representation of libraries in artificial intelligence regulations and implications for ethics and practice	*Journal of the Australian Library and Information Association*	2022	normative/applied ethics
31	Ploug, T.; Holm, S.	The right to a second opinion on artificial intelligence diagnosis – Remedying the inadequacy of a risk-based regulation	*Bioethics*	2023	normative/applied ethics
32	Feldstein, S.	Evaluating Europe's push to enact AI regulations: how will this influence global norms?	*Democratization*	2023	normative/applied ethics
33	White, J. M.; Lidskog, R.	Ignorance and the regulation of artificial intelligence	*Journal of Risk Research*	2022	rational choice
34	Jago, R.; Gaag, A. V.; Stathis, K. et al.	Use of artificial intelligence in regulatory decision-making	*Journal of Nursing Regulation*	2021	rational choice
35	Sharma, K.; Manchikanti, P.	Regulation of artificial intelligence in drug discovery and health care	*Biotechnology Law Report*	2020	rational choice
36	Tschider, C. A.	Regulating the internet of things: Discrimination, privacy, and cybersecurity in the artificial intelligence age	*Denver Law Review*	2018	rational choice
37	Cuellar, M. F.; Larsen, B.; Lee, Y. S. et al.	Does information about AI regulation change manager evaluation of ethical concerns and intent to adopt AI?	*Journal of Law Economics & Organization*	2022	rational choice
38	Kumar, A.; Finley, B.; Braud, T. et al.	Sketching an AI marketplace: Tech, economic, and regulatory aspects	*Ieee Access*	2021	rational choice
39	Candelon, F.; di Carlo, R.C.; De Bondt, M. et al.	AI regulation is coming: How to prepare for the inevitable	*Harvard Business Review*	2021	rational choice
40	Han, T.A.; Lenaerts, T. C.; Santos, F. C. et al.	Voluntary safety commitments provide an escape from over-regulation in AI development	*Technology in Society*	2022	rational choice
41	Han, T. A.; Pereira, L. M.; Santos, F. C. et al.	To regulate or not: A social dynamics analysis of an idealised AI race	*Journal of Artificial Intelligence Research*	2020	rational choice
42	Krafft, T. D.; Zweig, K. A.; König, P. D.	How to regulate algorithmic decision-making: A framework of regulatory requirements for different applications	*Regulation & Governance*	2022	rational choice

No.	Author(s)	Article Title	Source Title	Year	Concept of REG
43	Covarrubias, J. Z. L.; Enriquez, O. A. M.; Guerrero, M. G.	Regulatory approaches to artificial intelligence (AI)	Revista Chilena de Derecho	2022	rational choice
44	Erdelyi, O. J.; Goldsmith, J.	Regulating artificial intelligence: Proposal for a global solution	Government Information Quarterly	2022	rational choice
45	Johnson, S. L. J.	Artificial intelligence in health care: The challenge of effective regulation	Journal of Legal Medicine	2022	rational choice
46	Belli, L.; Zingales, N.	Data protection and artificial intelligence inequalities and regulations in Latin America	Computer Law & Security Review	2022	rational choice
47	Wang, C.; Zhang, J. Y.; Lassi, N.; Zhang, X. H.	Privacy protection in using artificial intelligence for healthcare: Chinese regulation in comparative perspective	Healthcare	2022	rational choice
48	McKee, M.; Wouters, O. J.	The challenges of regulating artificial intelligence in health care; comment on clinical decision support and new regulatory frameworks for medical devices: Are we ready for it? – a viewpoint paper	International Journal of Health Policy and Management	2022	rational choice
49	Belli, L.; Curzi, Y.; Gaspar, W. B.	AI regulation in Brazil: Advancements, flows, and need to learn from the data protection experience	Computer Law & Security Review	2023	rational choice
50	Currie, W. L.; Seddon, J. J. J. M.; Van Vliet, B.	From decision optimization to satisficing: Regulation of automated trading in the US financial markets	Information & Management	2022	rational choice
51	Dignam, A.	Artificial intelligence, tech corporate governance and the public interest regulatory response	Cambridge Journal of Regions Economy and Society	2020	politics/political economy
52	Justo-Hanani, R.	The politics of artificial intelligence regulation and governance reform in the European Union	Policy Sciences	2022	politics/political economy
53	Gyulai, A.; Ujlaki, A.	The political AI: A realist account of AI regulation	Információs Társadalom	2021	politics/political economy
54	Boubker, J.	When medical devices have a mind of their own: The challenges of regulating artificial intelligence	American Journal of Law & Medicine	2021	politics/political economy
55	Grzeszczak, R.; Mazur, J.	Regulating without Regulation? Regulating without the sovereign? The good governance concept versus automated decision-making in Poland in the light of European Union Law	Review of Central and East European Law	2021	politics/political economy
56	Krzywdzinski, M.; Gerst, D.; Butollo, F.	Promoting human-centred AI in the workplace. Trade unions and their strategies for regulating the use of AI in Germany	European Review of Labour and Research	2023	politics/political economy

No.	Author(s)	Article Title	Source Title	Year	Concept of REG
57	Kokshagina, O.; Reinecke, P. C.; Karanasios, S.	To regulate or not to regulate: Unravelling government institutional work towards AI regulation	*Journal of Information Technology*	2023	politics/political economy
58	Bode, I.; Huelss, H.	Constructing expertise: the front- and back-door regulation of AI's military applications in the European Union	*Journal of European Public Policy*	2023	politics/political economy

PART IV

AI AND PUBLIC POLICY ON THE GROUND: PRACTICES AND CONTESTATIONS

21. The geopolitics of AI in warfare: contested conceptions of human control

Ingvild Bode and Guangyu Qiao-Franco

INTRODUCTION

The use of artificial intelligence technologies (AIT) in the military, more generally, and in weapon systems, more specifically, develops at a constant pace while the international community is wrestling with what arms control for AIT could look like. This development occurs along a trajectory that started with integrating automated and autonomous technologies into targeting functions of weapons such as air defence systems or guided missiles in the 1960s. In recent years, weapon systems that use sensor-based machine analysis to track and attack targets have been developed and used in conflicts. Different types of so-called loitering munitions, for example, were used by conflict parties in the Syrian Civil War (2011–), the Libyan Civil War (2014–2020), the 2020 Nagorno-Karabakh War and the War in Ukraine (2022–) (Bode and Watts 2023).

Attempts to regulate AIT in warfare have, however, so far been bogged down by geopolitics. In 2016, the Group of Governmental Experts (GGE) on lethal autonomous weapon systems (LAWS) was created to discuss challenges raised by and the potential governance of AIT in warfare under the framework of the United Nations Convention on Certain Conventional Weapons (CCW).[1] While the substance of GGE debate deepened significantly over the past six years, this progress has, by and large, not translated into the group's written outputs, i.e. its final reports. That these reports remain akin to a lowest common denominator has much to do with the fact that the GGE operates via a consensus procedure. If even a single state party disagrees, the GGE cannot move forward on matters of substance. The group therefore has yet to secure a mandate moving beyond discussion and towards negotiating a legally binding instrument. The GGE debate has decided geopolitical undercurrents that have become more pronounced in line with the deteriorating relations between China, the US and Russia. Notably, these are also the states with the most significant research and development (R&D) plans in military AIT, including its integration in weapon systems (Haner and Garcia 2019).

The GGE's main achievement to date has been the 2019 Guiding Principles on LAWS. These principles feature a broad agreement that "human responsibility for decisions on the use of weapons systems must be retained since accountability cannot be transferred to machines" (UN-CCW 2019: III). But states parties continue to put forward different understandings about the technical, operational and decision-making components of human control (Automated Decision Research 2023; Human Rights Watch and International Human Rights Clinic 2021: 12–17). Substantive debate about an "appropriate" quality of human control at the GGE appears to be increasingly structured by the rise of several coalitions of states that work in the form of loose formations rather than tight-knit communities. Two of the most vocal coalitions notably feature states parties respectively chiefly associated with the Global North and the Global South (Bode 2019). A group of Global North countries around the US has argued in favour of increasing autonomy in the targeting functions of weapon systems based on humanitarian justifications as well as military advantages. By contrast, a Global South alliance (represented by the Group of 11) has joined forces with international civil society actors such as the Campaign to Stop Killer Robots in refusing on (moral) principle to accept delegating kill decisions to machines.

This chapter scrutinises the "scientific" knowledge base that underpins these competing views of "appropriate" human control in the development and use of AIT in weapon systems. Following a particular strand of scholarship in Science and Technology Studies (STS), we argue that the boundaries of the scientific knowledge that underpins the debate are socially constructed demarcations (Bijker and Law 2010; Gieryn 1983; Jasanoff 1995; Mitchell 2002). Rather than treating such knowledge bases as objective, we therefore treat them as deeply social and political, as shaped by complex, contested and ongoing manifestations of socio-economic contexts. We focus specifically on the question of how social structures are reflected in "scientific" knowledge surrounding LAWS. We contend that such a focus is necessary to understand how the persistent, inequitable divide between the Global North and the Global South produces competing bodies of "knowledge" on the development, deployment and use of AIT and thereby on what constitutes adequate governance of AIT in warfare (on the wider discussion of Global South approaches to regulating AITs, see Omotubora and Basu, Chapter 17 in this volume). By analysing past and present intersections of science and North–South relations (Harding 2009) and the geopolitical dynamics therein, we open both new and familiar – but neglected – possibilities and imperatives for AI arms control interventions.

To do so, we proceed in three steps: first, we outline two distinct understandings of human control at the GGE and chart the two main coalitions around these discourses in the period from 2017–2023. Second, we examine the geopolitics of knowledge about AIT in weapon systems and how its production across diverging social and political contexts sustains competing expectations about "appropriate" forms of human control. Here, we identify three dynamics shaping "knowledge" production: (1) defence R&D capability, (2) availability of resources in international negotiations and (3) historical exposure to and experience of weapon testing. We conclude by reflecting on the implications for research and practice.

GGE COALITIONS AND COMPETING UNDERSTANDINGS OF HUMAN CONTROL

Human control has been an underlying issue in discussions about the potential regulation of LAWS since the creation of the GGE. The notion of "meaningful human control" was initially coined by the NGO Article 36 as an effort of moving beyond the increasingly circular definitional debates about what constitutes autonomy or automation as technologies animating LAWS (Article 36 2013). Since, human control or human–machine interaction have quickly become main reference points for states parties, leading to much more substantive discussion. States parties have *inter alia* referred to appropriate or effective human control of LAWS although "what that involves, concretely, remains to be clarified" (Brehm 2017: 8). The current vagueness of the concept may go some way towards explaining why it has been readily taken up by many states parties.

There have been various efforts to define human control, including in operational terms. Many states parties underline that human control should extend across the entire life cycle of

LAWS from R&D, to testing, deployment and use. In fact, principle (c) of the 2019 Guiding Principles speaks to the possibility of integrating human–machine interaction at "various stages of the life cycle of a weapon" (UN-CCW 2019: III). This distributed approach to human control is also visible in the iceberg diagram, a publication by the UN Institute for Disarmament Research which distinguishes between political, strategic, operational and tactical planning phases each featuring human control (UNIDIR 2020).

In 2020, the Stockholm Peace Research Institute (SIPRI) in collaboration with the International Committee of the Red Cross (ICRC) published a further operationalisation of human control (Boulanin et al. 2020). This distinguishes between three dimensions of human control: (1) a technological dimension that enables human control via the design of weapon parameters, for example, limits on target type; (2) a situational dimension that sets operational limits to the ways weapon systems are used to enhance human control, for example through setting geographical or temporal restrictions; and (3) a decision-making dimension that sets out acceptable forms of human–machine interaction through ensuring appropriate human supervision, for example by making certain that human operators or decision-makers understand how the weapon systems function (Bode and Huelss 2022: 161). These more nuanced and intricate understandings of human control have clearly and usefully informed states' thinking about the multiple components across various dimensions. At the same time, much remains to be explored. Along the decision-making dimension of human control, for example, simply keeping a human in the loop to authorise the release of force may only lead to nominal rather than meaningful control if the human operator is unable to exercise critical deliberation (Bode and Watts 2021, 2023).

Different understandings of human control and the role and significance of integrating autonomy in targeting have sustained the formation of various coalitions at the GGE. These coalitions represent loose affiliations without formal lists of group members. States parties within the same coalition work together in general terms to establish common positions. We highlight outputs by two coalitions that have produced substantive proposals for what a normative framework to regulate LAWS could look like for the 2022 GGE sessions.[2] First, a group of Global North states parties (Australia, Canada, Japan, the UK, the US, Republic of Korea) support a series of non-binding principles and "good practices" on LAWS rather than any new binding international law. These states parties argue in favour of the supposed humanitarian advantages represented by integrating autonomy into targeting. Second, a group of Global South states parties (Argentina, Costa Rica, Ecuador, Guatemala, Kazakhstan, Nigeria, Panama, Peru, the Philippines, State of Palestine, Sierra Leone and Uruguay) propose a roadmap towards a new, specific and binding international protocol to govern LAWS. Most Global South states parties have expressed their opposition to autonomous targeting functions inferring moral, legal and security concerns about the loss of meaningful control over the use of force.[3] These documents represent the most substantive articulation of shared positions on human control and autonomy in weapon systems as expressed by two key coalitions featuring Global South and Global North actors and therefore serve as an ideal window into their understandings.

To provide some necessary backdrop to these positions, some basic information about the CCW is warranted. Having entered into force in 1983, the CCW is composed of a framework document and five protocols. It has 125 high contracting parties, 72 of which are Global South states parties. While a majority of CCW states parties are therefore from the Global South, that majority is not as pronounced as at the UN General Assembly. Eighty states parties have

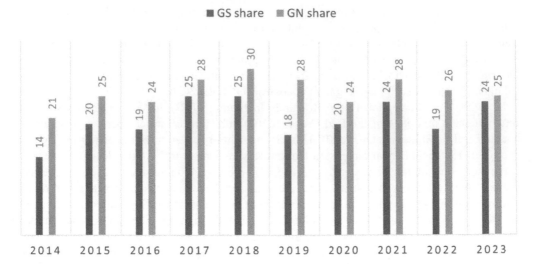

Figure 21.1   States parties contributing to the CCW debate on LAWS 2014–2023

formally contributed to the CCW meetings on LAWS from 2014 to 2022: 36 states parties of the Global North and 44 states parties of the Global South. While there is a slight majority of Global South states parties contributing overall, as Figure 21.1 shows, only around 20 Global South states parties contribute on a regular basis. These numbers remain relatively stable over time, with Global North states parties contributing to slightly bigger numbers over time.

Global North Coalition around the US

Entitled "Principles and Good Practices of Emerging Technologies in the Area of Lethal Autonomous Weapon Systems", the proposal presents an essentially permissive list of practices for integrating autonomous technologies into the targeting functions of weapon systems that is to be implemented via voluntary national measures. Here, the development and use of AWS rather than the potential regulation or even prohibition of such systems is the starting point of discussion. The proposal is framed as seeking to "strengthen the implementation of international humanitarian law (IHL)" and to promote "responsible behaviour" in relation to designing, developing, deploying and using AWS (Acheson 2022: 1). This argument is based on the supposed humanitarian benefits of AWS: the Republic of Korea has therefore argued that "AWS could reduce human mistakes and enhance targeting", while Japan connected the better implementation of IHL to utilising AWS by mitigating harm to civilians (Acheson 2022: 1). The proposal's use of the notion of "good practices" throughout can be remarked upon as assuming inherent benefits in autonomous technologies (Acheson 2022: 2). Further, the proposal does not include new principles or restrictions but reiterates the sufficiency of current IHL to govern LAWS. Notably, the proposal "seems to permit autonomous weapons systems that select targets without a human operator" (Acheson 2022: 2).

States parties in this coalition support ensuring that weapons operate as intended in a fashion predictable to users and in accordance with legal and policy requirements (e.g. through rigorous hardware and software verification and validation; realistic system development and operational testing and evaluation) and that human users of these weapons systems are properly trained on how to use them. But they oppose formulating new or categorical limitations on autonomy and AI in targeting, as well as on target duration and scope (see operational and technical components of human control). They also hold that human involvement is just one type of control that can be used to ensure compliance with IHL. They further argue that control measures can be implemented across the life cycle of a weapon: processes of design, development, training and usage thus all count as human touchpoints, not only the human operator in specific use of force situations.

Global South Coalition (Group of 11): Roadmap towards a Binding Protocol

This proposal holds that there is a legal gap in IHL when it comes to LAWS that needs to be filled (Acheson 2022: 2). This is why it champions the negotiation of a legally binding instrument in the form of an additional CCW protocol rather than proposing non-binding practices or principles. The protocol could follow a two-tier approach that prohibits some LAWS, while the development and use of others would be restricted and regulated (Acheson 2022: 4). So-called fully AWS that "by their nature cannot comply with IHL would be prohibited", while the use of partial AWS "would be regulated to ensure compliance with IHL, as well as international human rights law (IHRL), international criminal law (ICL), the UN Charter, and ethics" (Acheson 2022: 2).

The Group of 11 holds that fully autonomous machines that target, engage and apply force, *inter alia* in deciding on the life or death of human beings are unacceptable. More specifically, they argue that the use of target profiles to identify and use force against humans should also be prohibited because it is legally and morally unacceptable. As a consequence, the use of LAWS to target human beings should be ruled out through a prohibition on systems that are designed or used to apply force against persons. Further, they argue that sufficient levels of predictability, foreseeability, reliability, oversight and explainability of weapon systems as well as spatial and temporal constraints are needed to enable operators to exercise meaningful human control, ensure legal compliance and avoid technical vulnerabilities (Republic of Costa Rica et al. 2021).

THE SOCIAL SHAPING OF TECHNOLOGY

To make sense of these different understandings of human control, we draw on insights from a particular constructivist strand of scholarship in STS, an interdisciplinary body of knowledge focusing on the social, cultural and political dynamics that inform and shape science and the development of technology (Jasanoff 1987; MacKenzie and Wajcman 1985; Bijker and Law 2010). Constructivist STS scholarship emerged through a critique of "technological determinism" that assumes technology to be a phenomenon progressing out of its own inner logic (e.g. Bloor 1991; Latour 2001). Instead, constructivist STS scholars characterise science and technology as incorporating and coevolving with its social context (Jasanoff 1987, 2005). They have argued for opening the "black-box" of technology to understand the socio-economic patterns embedded in both the content of technologies and the processes of innovation (Bijker and Law 2010; MacKenzie 2001; MacKenzie and Wajcman 1985). To be more specific, such scholarship emphasised that every step of technology innovation and implementation involves a set of, essentially political, choices between different technical options. In addition to narrow "technical" considerations, a variety of social factors – economic, political, cultural and institutional – influence the selection of these options. Therefore, technological development and social change are understood as being deeply intertwined and should not be examined in isolation from each other (Collins and Evans 2007).

The GGE represents active efforts by decision-makers to influence technological trajectories according to various societal needs. It is a complex forum that brings together experts across professions and occupations as part of states parties' delegations, including but not limited to military officers, computer specialists, legal scholars, diplomats, engineers, technicians and political scientists. Within the GGE, the knowledge (presented) about LAWS is a constant work in progress where relevant social groups with different interests negotiate how new artefacts should be interpreted, including what should count as the "appropriate" quality of human control over the use of force. These discussions thereby open up new socio-technical options for military applications of AIT. In this process, coalitions are attempts by social groups to increase their relative power positions at the GGE and make their claims stick, an aspect that has been highlighted by scholars focusing on power relations in the production of scientific knowledge (Lidskog and Sundqvist 2015; Weiss 2005).

In what follows, we offer some reflections on the nature of competing knowledge practices that sustain the various claims on human control across Global North and Global South coalitions. We outline their different grounds for claiming scientific truth, ranging from defence R&D capability, the availability of resources in international negotiations, and historical exposure to and experience of weapon testing or use.

Defence R&D Capability

Many states of the Global North, in particular but not exclusively, are deeply committed to technological innovation not only for the purpose of advancing their domestic economy, but also to sustain a strong military defence. There is a frequent consensus among political, military and industrial elites in favour of the importance of technology for upgrading national defence systems, including through the development of new forms of weaponry. Starting in the 1970s, many states parties began to invest heavily in military applications of automation, autonomy and AI, including all states parties associated with the Global North coalition around the US, various EU member states, as well as Russia, Israel, Turkey and China (Bode and Huelss 2018; Haner and Garcia 2019; Payne 2021; Scharre 2018). For the time being, weapon systems that integrate autonomy in targeting remain operated in human "in-the-loop" modes. This can take the form of decision-aids for human operators or of implementing certain targeting tasks autonomously but under the supervision of human operators.

While acknowledging some level of unpredictability, proponents of weapons integrating autonomy or AI have argued for the benefits of physically separating human operators from the battlefield. They hold that increasing autonomous technologies in weapon systems, plus the use of AIT in data collection and analysis, command and control, and decision-making have the potential to make attacks faster and allegedly more precise, reduce the loss of human lives and contribute to civilian protection (e.g. Mission of the United States 2018, 2021).

For societies with relatively scarce labour, a problem facing most developed countries of the Global North, the trend of increasing autonomy in weapon systems is especially appealing.

There is also a clear strain of disingenuity in positions expressed by states parties that are developing weapon systems integrating autonomous technologies while at the same time expressing their scepticism towards negotiating new binding legislation on LAWS. States parties associated with the Global North group, e.g. the Republic of Korea, have characterised any shared understanding of what constitutes LAWS at the GGE to be at the early stages.[4] Yet, today there are a variety of weapons integrating automated, autonomous and, to a limited extent, AI technologies in the arsenals of military forces of many states (Bode 2023; Boulanin and Verbruggen 2017). Furthermore, reports of recent wars show that such weapons, for example loitering munitions, have already begun to supplant human soldiers on the battlefield (Bode and Watts 2023).

Perhaps unsurprisingly, enthusiasm for integrating AI technologies in weapons systems has not been universal. For some less developed countries, even a modest AI weapon programme is unobtainable without significant aid because they lack access to the necessary materials, expertise and training data. Newly industrialised countries that have gone through a period of economic and industrial development have also faced persistent challenges to transit from arms importers to independent weapon developers. Competition in international arms markets that favours major weapon producers[5] has become a major factor for these countries to turn to foreign weapons acquisition, which further erodes their R&D capability (Jan and Jan 2000).

Defence R&D capability is a major factor generating competing knowledge over human control since, first of all, some determination of the effects of weapons and of what controls need to be in place require assessments of who employs them. What seems a means of ensuring capability extension for those with the ability to develop LAWS could just be seen as a source of vulnerability for those on the receiving end. Along these lines, the efforts by some countries to develop extensive protective measures for their troops and populations through integrating AIT into weapon systems are taken by others as dangerous moves that lower the threshold for war. In short, one person's desirable outcome is another's unwanted consequence. In light of this geopolitical situation, it is thus not surprising to see that while most Global North countries seek a regulatory approach flexible enough to accommodate new technologies and that does not limit the use of AI technologies for benign purposes, Global South countries strive for a legally binding instrument to elaborate what is and is not permissible.

Moreover, the defence research capability of states is directly associated with the roles that can be accorded to their views in weapon innovation. Developing countries have long been marginalised in the arms control decision-making process. The debate regarding what "appropriate" military AI looks like never surfaced before concerns over LAWS or "killer robots" arose around 2013. Even the current debates on LAWS are generally future-oriented (Bode 2023). Many actors that are against the integration of AIT are no longer fully able to exercise agency in shaping the technological direction because of the ways in which the automation of particular tasks related to targeting have already been normalised (Bode and Watts 2021). What exacerbates the trend towards AIT is the ever-expanding deployment of "smart" weapons, including in operations outlined above, which seems only to deliver grounds for justifying the further integration of AIT in weapons.

Availability of Resources in Negotiations

It is also necessary to examine whether states parties have sufficient resources to participate in the multilateral negotiations on equal terms, the reason underlying the *missing* and *misrepresented* voices on human control at the GGE. Any CCW states parties participating in GGE negotiations on LAWS face numerous challenges. Not only do delegates need to be well versed in the complex ethical and legal issues related to LAWS, but they also need extensive specialised knowledge (e.g. on machine learning, AI training data, natural language processing, etc.) to fully understand the issue under negotiation and articulate their positions. States parties associated with the Global South face an additional key challenge that hinders their ability to participate effectively in the negotiations: the lack of human, technical and financial resources, as obviously reflected in their small delegation size or even absence in GGE meetings. While the CCW has, for example, 25 African states parties, only eight African delegations have ever contributed to the GGE debate. And out of these eight, only Sierra Leone and South Africa have contributed to the debate substantively on several occasions.

Inadequate resources have negatively affected the ability of smaller Global South states parties to exercise political will and develop substantive positions on human control in international negotiations. The broader literature on small state diplomacy has provided rich analysis of the struggles many states have to go through to effectively participate in multilateral diplomacy. For instance, understaffed bureaucracies, small delegation sizes, language differences and inconsistency in delegation composition have all put smaller states and especially those of the Global South at a disadvantage in trying to influence decision-making (Chan 2021; Chasek 2001; Corbett and Connell 2015; Panke 2012; also see Omotubora and Basu, Chapter 17 in this volume; Mügge, Chapter 19 in this volume). As data collected by the NGO Article 36 across international disarmament fora show: "the lower a country's income category, the less likely they will [...] attend, speak or hold formal roles at any given meeting" (Article 36 2016: 6).

The authors observed such struggles clearly at GGE meetings. Many states parties of the Global South were passive or not even present at sessions. Some states were represented by a single delegate or even an intern. Small delegations were not able to adequately participate in GGE meetings if there were parallel meetings on other issues. Many found themselves relying on states parties within the same regional group (e.g. African Union and the Arab Group), or coalitions such as the Non-Aligned Movement to represent their viewpoints and interests. Notwithstanding that negotiations on LAWS may not be considered vital to the interests of some Global South countries, their inaction more often arises from inadequate resources to allow them to send delegations to every single UN conference or meeting. It is also notable that vocal Global North states parties include academic researchers, some with nationally funded research projects, as part of their delegations. This kind of collaboration is financially not feasible for their Global South counterparts. Relative Global South passivity can therefore also be associated with a focus on different priorities considering tight resources: "for many states, LAWS is just not a priority".[6] Further, the information imbalance is associated with resources. A cynicism among the Global South diplomatic disarmament community may also play a role: how helpful are these discussions when "the powerful countries still do whatever they want in terms of weapon systems".[7]

Even for Global South states parties that were able to send delegations to the GGE, many of them do not have adequate capacity to conduct systematic research and collect sufficient data to inform a strong position on LAWS. Some delegations are overstretched when it comes to evaluating the implications of proposals made by other states parties. Some states rely on information published by active civil society organisations such as Reaching Critical Will, Human Rights Watch, the Campaign to Stop Killer Robots and various research institutes (mostly based in the Global North countries) to develop positions. There have also been cases where smaller states proactively reach out to NGOs and other international organisations and accredit certain individual NGO representatives as advisors to their delegations (Bode 2019). As one Global South diplomat remarked, the civil society campaign can therefore also be "used as a resource".[8] The dynamic of drawing on NGOs must therefore not necessarily be one-sided, as the case of Pakistan illustrates. One of the earliest states parties to call for a ban on LAWS, Pakistan finds itself on the same side as human security-oriented, civil society organisations that it usually does not interact with constructively. In prior arms control negotiations, Pakistan has tended to follow an orthodox perspective in security politics. These practices of forging coalitions with NGOs are in line with those associated with Western-liberal democracies in scholarship on how small states engage in norm-making (Behringer 2005; Finnemore and Sikkink 1998; Nadelmann 1990). Notably, such strategies are here also pursued by Global South states parties, something that we have already seen in relation to the Nuclear Weapons Prohibition Treaty (Bode 2019; Potter 2017; Thakur 2017).

While the support of NGOs and drawing on academic resources can help overcome informational gaps, it must also be noted that information provided to serve advocacy goals or mandates will not necessarily keep Global South contexts in mind. Positions developed without proper accounts of national contexts will likely affect compliance negatively – whether in terms of subsequent ratification, or in terms of a commitment to effective implementation (Chan 2021; Chasek 2001). Scholarship has associated the underrepresentation of the Global South at disarmament negotiations with decreased effectiveness of such processes and decreased legitimacy of norms resulting from such processes as they may not be framed with Global South priorities in mind (Borrie and Thornton 2008; Nash 2015). Therefore, the long-term effects of inadequate participation of the Global South at the GGE for meaningful control of autonomous weapons can be quite serious.

Historical Experience of Weapon Testing or Use

Another major source of disagreement between coalitions has been the uneven consequences of the development of weapon technologies that different countries or regions have experienced. Government representatives of the Global South coalition have, for instance, articulated various points of critique concerning the extra harm of weapon testing and development on countries of the Global South.

The potential for weapons to cause injury deemed unacceptable is often linked to assessments of their destructiveness. The greater the potential for harm, the more numerous the situations in which the resort to autonomous weapons cannot be justified. International law, especially IHL, stipulates limits to the means of combat that cause "unnecessary suffering or superfluous injury" to combatants. Formalised definitions of these terms have never been set out.

However, it may readily be acknowledged that historically weapons have caused greater injury to humans in certain countries and regions than others. Global South countries have not only been the primary field for testing of new weapons featuring emerging or new technology, but also for the deployment of such weapons. Examples of this are numerous. South Pacific

Island countries have been testing grounds for nuclear weapons starting with the US in 1946, the UK in 1957, followed by France in 1966 with serious consequences for public health and the environment and, in turn, the destruction of livelihoods (Fry 1986). Remotely piloted uncrewed aerial vehicles (UAVs), which for many states parties of the Global South represent another part of the trajectory towards autonomous weapon systems, have been extensively used by the US in Afghanistan, Pakistan, Yemen, Somalia and Iraq.

Developers of weapon systems integrating autonomous technologies have tested and used these platforms in countries of the Global South – sometimes with the permission of contested state authorities. Russian officials have on a number of occasions publicly declared that they tested more than 600 weapons, including weapon systems reportedly integrating AI technologies in Syria since 2015 (Russian News Agency 2017). LAWS are therefore another case illustrating how Global South territories "may become the testing ground for new technologies".[9]

At the GGE, some states parties have made this link of the Global South serving as a testing and deployment ground explicit. Pakistan has drawn explicitly on the history of targeted killing via drone strikes on its territory[10] and connected this to the regulatory position of some Global North states parties: "technology-holders prefer to do nothing at this stage, but the international community is not content with staying idle".[11] The Palestinian delegation, for example, explicitly spoke of the Global North developing LAWS and their testing and use in the Global South (Acheson 2022: 2).[12] Other Global South states parties have been more implicit in their statements, speaking, for example, of major concerns that particularly countries in the South have about the uses of LAWS and the consequences,[13] of potential regional and international arms races,[14] arguing that a legally binding instrument on LAWS is necessary to "prevent the rise of *inequality* and instability".[15]

CONCLUSION

This chapter has suggested that understandings of what counts as an "appropriate" level of human control over the use of force as expressed at the GGE debate need to be unpacked. We argued that accounts of prohibitions for technologies associated with LAWS differ across coalitions associated with, respectively, the Global South and the Global North. Their different interpretations of human control are contingent on particular social contexts, comprising such elements as defence R&D capability, the availability of resources in international negotiations and historical experience of weapon testing or use. Moving beyond summarising the numerous grounds for disagreement among states parties about how to regulate LAWS, our analysis illustrated the contrasting ways that states make sense of the issues at stake and the geopolitical undertones therein. In this, we highlighted some fundamental disagreements between the Global North and the Global South. Our investigation is not meant to suggest that attempts to regulate military applications of AIT will be counter-productive or rejected. Instead, we sought to clarify how geopolitics affects how states define human control and influence attitudes towards regulation. Stakeholders to the GGE debate will need to recognise and work through these issues to establish doable and legitimate standards to prohibit/regulate the integration of AIT in weapon systems.

A number of scholars have insightfully pointed to the possibility of intervening into socio-technical transformation processes (Bareis and Katzenbach 2022; Paul 2022; Sørensen and Williams 2002). Building on this scholarship, some modes of intervention to steer technological trajectories surrounding LAWS may be possible. These include providing protected spaces for social learning about new technologies and their implications (such social learning should include not only an examination of the actual effects of technologies but instead build on approaches sensitive to the considerations under which interpretations are made); establishing communication channels to promote understandings of the diverse visions between users and developers of AIT;[16] supporting the expansion of coalitions and networks thereby facilitating the alignment of elements into new socio-technical configurations. Whichever approaches are adopted, detailed insights into the different social-technical transformation processes that sustain the variated Global South and North human control claims are necessary for informing international efforts towards regulating AIT in warfare.

ACKNOWLEDGEMENT

Research for this chapter was supported by funding from the European Union's Horizon 2020 research and innovation programme (under grant agreement No. 852123, AutoNorms).

NOTES

1. The precise mandate of the GGE covers emerging technologies in the area of LAWS.
2. There are at least two other key coalitions at the GGE to have put forward different ideas about the "appropriate" quality of human control: (1) A South–North coalition including states parties such as Austria, Belgium, Brazil, Chile, Mexico and New Zealand that also support the two-tier approach to regulation/prohibition; (2) a group of chiefly European states parties such as France, Germany and the Netherlands which favour a middle ground in starting with a set of non-binding principles that could eventually lead to the negotiation of new international law at a later stage. Some states parties, such as China, India, Israel and Russia, have chosen to intervene in their individual capacities instead of joining coalitions, despite there being some overlap with positions expressed elsewhere (Nadibaidze 2022; Qiao-Franco and Bode 2023). For the purpose of this chapter, we will only concentrate on the two coalitions mentioned above as they include some of the most vocal contributors to the GGE debate over the past six years.
3. In February 2023, 30 countries in Latin America and the Caribbean adopted a statement "to promote the urgent negotiation of an international legally binding instrument with prohibitions and regulations with regard to autonomy in weapons systems" (Latin American and the Caribbean Conference of Social and Humanitarian Impact of Autonomous Weapons 2023).
4. Remarks by the Republic of Korea, 9.03.2022.
5. Countries responsible for the largest shares of global arms export between 2017 and 2021 are: the US (38.6%), Russia (18.6%), France (10.7%), China (4.6%), Germany (4.5%), Italy (3.1%), the UK (2.9%) and South Korea (2.8%) (SIPRI 2022).
6. Expert interview #3, 27.04.2017.
7. Expert interview #1, 25.04.2017.
8. Expert interview #1, 25.04.2017.
9. Expert interview #2, 26.04.2017.
10. Remarks by Pakistan, 13.11.2017.
11. Remarks by Pakistan, 28.08.2018.
12. See also Remarks by Palestine, 25.07.2022.
13. Remarks by Cuba, 28.08.2018.
14. Remarks by Iraq, 28.08.2018.
15. Remarks by Sri Lanka, 31.08.2018.

16. In the first half of 2023, open letters calling for a moratorium on developing generative AI technologies garnered significant attention. Triggered by developments in large language models (LLMs), developers and researchers of AI drew attention to the existential risks these technologies posed. These letters, in turn, triggered policy responses on potential regulatory approaches, often prominently featuring Big Tech CEOs. While we do not want to rule out the potential of AIT posing existential risks, we agree with scholars who see the growing prominence of this framing as distracting from existing, present forms of societal harm caused by AIT, including in the military space, which could be addressed by Big Tech (Gebru 2023; Whittaker 2021).

REFERENCES

Acheson, R. (2022), 'Intersessional meeting on autonomous weapons highlights two paths forward, and the urgency of action', *CCW Report*, **10** (3), 1–4, 28 April.

Article 36 (2013), *Killer Robots: UK Government Policy on Fully Autonomous Weapons*, accessed at http://www.article36.org/wp-content/uploads/2013/04/Policy_Paper1.pdf.

Article 36 (2016), *Development, Disarmament and Patterns of Marginalisation in International Forums*, April, accessed 24 May 2018 at http://www.article36.org/wp-content/uploads/2016/04/A36-Disarm-Dev-Marginalisation.pdf.

Automated Decision Research (2023), *Convergence in State Positions on Human Control*, Automated Decision Research, May, accessed at file:///C:/Users/bode/Downloads/ADR_Convergences-in-state-positions-on-human-control.pdf.

Bareis, J. and C. Katzenbach (2022), 'Talking AI into being: The narratives and imaginaries of national AI strategies and their performative politics', *Science, Technology, & Human Values*, **47** (5), 855–81.

Behringer, R. M. (2005), 'Middle power leadership on the human security agenda', *Cooperation and Conflict*, **40** (3), 305–42.

Bijker, W. E. and J. Law (eds.) (2010), *Shaping Technology/Building Society: Studies in Sociotechnical Change*, Cambridge, MA: MIT Press.

Bloor, D. (1991), *Knowledge and Social Imagery*, 2nd ed., Chicago: University of Chicago Press.

Bode, I. (2019), 'Norm-making and the Global South: Attempts to regulate lethal autonomous weapons systems', *Global Policy*, **10** (3), 359–64.

Bode, I. (2023), 'Practice-based and public-deliberative normativity: Retaining human control over the use of force', *European Journal of International Relations*, online first, accessed at https://doi.org/10.1177/13540661231163392.

Bode, I. and H. Huelss (2018), 'Autonomous weapons systems and changing norms in international relations', *Review of International Studies*, **44** (3), 393–413.

Bode, I. and H. Huelss (2022), *Autonomous Weapon Systems and International Norms*, Montreal: McGill-Queen's University Press.

Bode, I. and T. Watts (2021), *Meaning-Less Human Control. The Consequences of Automation and Autonomy in Air Defence Systems*, Oxford and Odense: Drone Wars UK & Center for War Studies, February.

Bode, I. and T. Watts (2023), *Loitering Munitions and Unpredictability: Autonomy in Weapon Systems and Challenges to Human Control*, Odense and London: SDU Center for War Studies, Royal Holloway Centre for International Security, May.

Borrie, J. and A. Thornton (2008), *The Value of Diversity in Multilateral Disarmament Work*, UNIDIR/2008/16, New York and Geneva: United Nations Institute for Disarmament Research, accessed 19 June 2023 at http://www.unidir.org/files/publications/pdfs/the-value-of-diversity-in-multilateral-disarmament-work-344.pdf.

Boulanin, V., N. Davison, N. Goussac and M. Peldán Carlsson (2020), *Limits of Autonomy in Weapon Systems. Identifying Practical Elements of Human Control*, SIPRI & ICRC, June.

Boulanin, V. and M. Verbruggen (2017), *Mapping the Development of Autonomy in Weapon Systems*, Stockholm: SIPRI, November.

Brehm, M. (2017), *Defending the Boundary: Constraints and Requirements on the Use of Autonomous Weapons Systems under International Humanitarian and Human Rights Law*, Academy Briefing No. 9, Geneva Academy, May.

Chan, N. (2021), 'Beyond delegation size: Developing country negotiating capacity and NGO "support" in international climate negotiations', *International Environmental Agreements: Politics, Law and Economics*, **21** (2), 201–17.

Chasek, P. S. (2001), 'NGOs and state capacity in international environmental negotiations: The experience of the Earth Negotiations Bulletin', *Review of European Community & International Environmental Law*, **10** (2), 168–76.

Collins, H. M. and R. Evans (2007), *Rethinking Expertise*, Chicago: University of Chicago Press.

Corbett, J. and J. Connell (2015), 'All the world is a stage: Global governance, human resources, and the "problem" of smallness', *The Pacific Review*, **28** (3), 435–59.

Finnemore, M. and K. Sikkink (1998), 'International norm dynamics and political change', *International Organization*, **52** (4), 887–917.

Fry, G. (1986), 'The South Pacific nuclear-free zone: Significance and implications', *Bulletin of Concerned Asian Scholars*, **18** (2), 61–72.

Gebru, T. (2023), 'Don't fall for the AI hype', accessed 19 June 2023 at https://techwontsave.us/episode/151_dont_fall_for_the_ai_hype_w_timnit_gebru.

Gieryn, T. F. (1983), 'Boundary-work and the demarcation of science from non-science: Strains and interests in professional ideologies of scientists', *American Sociological Review*, **48** (6), 781–95.

Haner, J. and D. Garcia (2019), 'The artificial intelligence arms race: Trends and world leaders in autonomous weapons development', *Global Policy*, **10** (3), 331–37.

Harding, S. (2009), 'Postcolonial and feminist philosophies of science and technology: Convergences and dissonances', *Postcolonial Studies*, **12** (4), 401–21.

Human Rights Watch and International Human Rights Clinic (2021), *Areas of Alignment. Common Visions for a Killer Robots Treaty*, accessed at https://www.hrw.org/sites/default/files/media_2021/07/07.2021%20Areas%20of%20Alignment.pdf.

Jan, T. S. and C. G. Jan (2000), 'Development of weapon systems in developing countries: A case of long range strategies in Taiwan', *Journal of the Operational Research Society*, **51** (9), 1051–1050.

Jasanoff, S. (1987), 'Contested boundaries in policy-relevant science', *Social Studies of Science*, **17** (2), 195–230.

Jasanoff, S. (1995), *Science at the Bar: Law, Science, and Technology in America*, Cambridge, MA: Harvard University Press.

Jasanoff, S. (2005), 'Technologies of humility: Citizen participation in governing science', in A. Bogner and H. Torgersen (eds), *Wozu Experten? Ambivalenzen Der Beziehung von Wissenschaft Und Politik*, Wiesbaden: VS, Verlag für Sozialwissenschaften, pp. 307–89.

Latin American and the Caribbean Conference of Social and Humanitarian Impact of Autonomous Weapons (2023), *Communiqué of the Latin American and the Caribbean Conference of Social and Humanitarian Impact of Autonomous Weapons*, accessed 19 June 2023 at https://www.rree.go.cr/files/includes/files.php?id=2261&tipo=documentos.

Latour, B. (2001), *Science in Action: How to Follow Scientists and Engineers through Society*, 9th ed., Cambridge, MA: Harvard University Press.

Lidskog, R. and G. Sundqvist (2015), 'When does science matter? International relations meets science and technology studies', *Global Environmental Politics*, **15** (1), 1–20.

MacKenzie, D. A. (2001), *Inventing Accuracy: A Historical Sociology of Nuclear Missile Guidance*, 4. pr, Cambridge, MA: MIT Press.

MacKenzie, D. A. and J. Wajcman (eds.) (1985), *The Social Shaping of Technology: How the Refrigerator Got Its Hum*, Milton Keynes, UK and Philadelphia, PA: Open University Press.

Mission of the United States (2018), 'CCW: US Opening Statement at the Group of Governmental Experts Meeting on Lethal Autonomous Weapons Systems', accessed 19 June 2023 at https://geneva.usmission.gov/2018/04/09/ccw-u-s-opening-statement-at-the-group-of-governmental-experts-meeting-on-lethal-autonomous-weapons-systems/.

Mission of the United States (2021), '3rd Meeting – 1st Session Group of Governmental Experts on LAWS 2021', accessed 19 June 2023 at https://media.un.org/en/asset/k1k/k1klog2whq.

Mitchell, T. (2002), *Rule of Experts: Egypt, Techno-Politics, Modernity*, Berkeley, CA: University of California Press.

Nadelmann, E. A. (1990), 'Global prohibition regimes: The evolution of norms in international society', *International Organization*, **44** (4), 479–526.

Nadibaidze, A. (2022), 'Great power identity in Russia's position on autonomous weapons systems', *Contemporary Security Policy*, **43** (3), 407–35.

Nash, T. (2015), 'The technologies of violence and global inequality', *Sur International Journal on Human Rights*, **12** (22), 115–22.

Panke, D. (2012), 'Dwarfs in international negotiations: How small states make their voices heard', *Cambridge Review of International Affairs*, **25** (3), 313–28.

Paul, R. (2022), 'Can *critical policy studies* outsmart AI? Research agenda on artificial intelligence technologies and public policy', *Critical Policy Studies*, **16** (4), 497–509.

Payne, K. (2021), *I, Warbot: The Dawn of Artificially Intelligent Conflict*, London: Hurst & Company.

Potter, W. C. (2017), 'Disarmament diplomacy and the nuclear ban treaty', *Survival: Global Politics and Strategy*, **59** (4), 75–108.

Qiao-Franco, G. and I. Bode (2023), 'Weaponised artificial intelligence and Chinese practices of human–machine interaction', *The Chinese Journal of International Politics*, **16** (1), 106–28.

Reaching Critical Will (2023), *Convention on Certain Conventional Weapons (CCW)*, accessed 19 June 2023 at http://reachingcriticalwill.org/disarmament-fora/ccw.

Republic of Costa Rica, Republic of Panama, Republic of Peru, Republic of the Philippines, Republic of Sierra Leone and Eastern Republic of Uruguay (2021), *Joint Working Paper*, accessed at https://documents.unoda.org/wp-content/uploads/2021/06/Costa-Rica-Panama-Peru-the-Philippines-Sierra-Leone-and-Uruguay.pdf.

Russian News Agency (2017), *Russia/Syria: More than 200 Weapons Tested in Syria Prove to Be Highly Effective*, 28 August.

Scharre, P. (2018), *Army of None: Autonomous Weapons and the Future of War*, New York and London: W. W. Norton.

SIPRI (2022), 'SIPRI Arms Transfers Database', accessed 20 April 2022 at https://www.sipri.org/databases/armstransfers.

Sørensen, K. H. and R. Williams (2002), *Shaping Technology, Guiding Policy: Concepts, Spaces, and Tools*, Cheltenham, UK and Northampton, MA, USA: Edward Elgar Publishing.

Thakur, R. (2017), 'The nuclear ban treaty: Recasting a normative framework for disarmament', *The Washington Quarterly*, **40** (4), 71–95.

UN-CCW (2019), *Report of the 2019 Session of the Group of Governmental Experts on Emerging Technologies in the Area of Lethal Autonomous Weapons Systems. UN Document No. CCW/GGE.1/2019/3*.

UNIDIR (2020), *The Human Element in Decisions about the Use of Force*, accessed at https://unidir.org/sites/default/files/2020-03/UNIDIR_Iceberg_SinglePages_web.pdf.

Weiss, C. (2005), 'Science, technology and international relations', *Technology in Society*, **27** (3), 295–313.

Whittaker, M. (2021), 'The steep cost of capture', *Interactions*, **28** (6), 50–55.

22. AI in policing and law enforcement

Mareile Kaufmann

INTRODUCTION

One late October 2015 in Manchester, New Hampshire, Connor Deleire waited in his friend's car for him to return. What he did not know was that the car was parked in a "predictive hot spot", which is why he was singled out by the police. Not being able to give a legitimate reason for being there he became victim of a violent police arrest, as journalist Shane Kavanaugh describes (2017). Stories like this keep surfacing in public discussions about predictive policing. Official accounts of predictive policing summarize it as the use of AI or algorithmic tools to "harness the power of information, geospatial technologies and evidence-based intervention models to reduce crime and improve public safety" (National institute of Justice 2014). There is a trend to summarize the upsurge of algorithms and machine learning in predictive policing under the notion of Artificial Intelligence (AI) (e.g. McDaniel and Pease 2022). Since AI is an ambiguous concept, this chapter follows the understanding of AI suggested in this book's introduction: a "cluster of technologies" that is socially embedded. This chapter will focus specifically on the use of *databases* and *algorithms* which, together with humans, matter in predictive policing and other algorithmic tools for law enforcement.

Originally a US-based approach, variants of predictive tools emerged, for example in China (e.g. Sprick 2020), Iraq (e.g. Perry et al. 2013), India (e.g. Marda and Narajan 2020), and Europe, including the UK (e.g. Mohler et al. 2016), Germany and Switzerland (e.g. Egbert and Leese 2021) and the Netherlands (e.g. Meijer et al. 2021). In most cases it involves the services of private companies that develop the design of such tools, structure processes (such as the flow of data required for the tool to work) and provide the software. One go-to provider for these services is the US-based company Palantir[1] that specializes in predicting patterns of most kind. In Norway, for example, Palantir was hired to develop a local version of their "super-weapon" (Gjerding and Andersen 2017) for police use. The system "omnia" literally sought to integrate any available data in Norway's landscape of public management, ranging from addresses, health data, transport, data on sentencing, pictures, to a broad range of biometric information, including DNA, in order to "upgrade" law enforcement (Trædal 2017). Palantir's project, however, was discontinued in Norway without success after 11 years and investments of 100 million Norwegian kroner (Røise 2020). The reasons for this are unclear: did such a large-scale system simply not meet Norway's social realities? Was there too little data for the tool to work efficiently? Or did the emerging European pushback initiated by anti-discrimination initiatives and civil liberty unions factor into the decision (e.g. Fair Trials 2022)?

This chapter will dive into these issues and others when it explains the assumptions, decision-making processes and technological models that drive predictive policing today. It will summarize how predictive processes and techniques are discussed and describe how they materialize and are made to matter in policing (Kaufmann 2023). What is more, the chapter will also provide a brief outlook into new areas of prediction within policing. It brings the discussion into the field of genomic predictions for crime investigation. Here, algorithms are used to derive predictions about genealogy (familial relations) and physiognomy from DNA in order to identify suspects. The chapter will focus on the latter. This field is chosen, because it no longer relates to the "territory" of geographic models, but it ties prediction to suspicious groups based on biological factors. To this extent, it is a technological practice that exacerbates the already sensitive context of law enforcement in which predictive technologies are used.

STATE OF THE ART: DEBATES ON PREDICTIVE POLICING

Considering the history of predictive techniques, Connor Deleire could have had the same experience without the use of algorithms. The origins of predictive policing are analogue, where police data were translated into hotspots marked with pins on a map. Such techniques were part of the project to scientize police patrol (Manning 2008) and gave rise to the idea of evidence-based policing (Sherman 1998). Rational Choice Theory (Cornish and Clarke 1986) is one of the first and best-known theoretical attempts to conceptualize projects of this kind. The theory is based on the assumption that offenders follow patterns of spatial and temporal proximity of their original offence when they commit the next crime, because they are familiar with the scene and local habits. The Near-Repeat Hypothesis (e.g. Townsley et al. 2003) emerged in relation to this model and was tested in the field of domestic burglary. Proponents of predictive policing, then, argue that such patterns are useful to focus police efforts. Officers would be able to focus attention on crime-prone areas (Kennedy et al. 2011). According to these expectations, predictions would render police work more efficient and provide relief for overworked police officers – all based on statistical knowledge (Beck and McCue 2009). This logic also corresponded with managerialist reforms of police work and the rising focus on cost-efficiency. Digitization, then, enabled the relaunch of "geographically applied criminology" (cf. Kaufmann et al. 2019), because one could include more data, more parameters (population density, events, architecture and environmental characteristics, weather forecasts, etc.), as well as sophisticated algorithmic models to find patterns. Not least, digitization provided a certain degree of automation. This development is welcome among some communities, because it bears the promise of enhancing the precision of prediction and providing speedy, actionable results. Efficient information processing and a prioritization of police actions are the main drivers for the use of algorithms for predictive policing (ibid.).

The development of these models, related technocratic approaches and the arguments for adopting these tools do, however, meet criticism. Critique is advanced, for example, by police professionals who are sceptical of algorithmic solutions (Sandhu and Fussey 2021). Their doubt includes ethical and moral concerns (Gundhus et al. 2017). Officers also point to challenges such as technology failures (Kaufmann 2018) and cost-inefficiencies. Further, some officers feel insecure due to a lack of digital literacy or fear that their competences may be replaced by automated systems (ibid.). A more fundamental concern relates to the role of the state and democratic accountability (for a systematic review of this concept in the context of AIT uses, see Cobbe and Singh, Chapter 7 in this volume). Mark Andrejevic argues, for example, that predictive policing nurtures a logic of "data collection without limits" (2018), which leads to a general increase in surveillance. Linked to that problem is the critique that only those with access to data and processing power will be able to create and access insights (Andrejevic and Gates 2014). Especially in the sensitive context of crime governance, such practices enhance already existing power imbalances. Limited access to and knowledge of databases and mathematical models is a central problem. This, paired with the fact that most software solutions involve commercial players, leads to a lack of transparency that is difficult to address (Meijer and Wessels 2019). Many solutions are owned by private companies and a close collaborative process between companies and clients is not necessarily a given. Sometimes algorithmic designs are even treated as business secrets. This lack of transparency and the multitude of stakeholders involved in the process, again, entail problems of accountability (Bennett Moses and Chan 2018; for a discussion of transparency principles in AIT uses, see Aula and Erkkilä, Chapter 13 in this volume). Accountability is, however, particularly relevant as the status of neutrality that algorithmic technologies enjoy is challenged by a variety of problems at a systemic level (for a critique see Wilson 2018). Feedback loops (created by sending police officers back to the already well-policed and stigmatized areas) shape databases, which leads to a perpetuation of social imbalances and injustices (Gill 2000; Harcourt 2007; Brayne 2017). The result is over-patrolling of poor and minority neighbourhoods (Marda and Narayan 2020). This problem interlinks with racial biases and skewed datasets that create the basis for algorithmic predictions (Ferguson 2017; Richardson et al. 2019), which leads to *systematic* forms of unfair and discriminatory treatment (Alikhademi et al. 2022). Beyond that, the social life of a prediction, which is how and when officers take action based on them, could also produce problems (Richardson et al. 2019) as we saw in the case of Connor Deleire. Many problems of bias are dependent on the software type used, the databases involved to train them and human-decision making.

UNDERSTANDING HOW PREDICTION ALGORITHMS COME ABOUT AND CO-CREATE SOCIETY

Using predictive technologies in law enforcement is part of a larger trend towards a "pre-crime society" (Zedner 2007; Mantello 2016). This trend implies an epistemological shift: the problem of criminality is relocated into the future with the ambition of governing crime before it occurs (this is also true, for example, when predicting child abuse with risk factors: Krutzinna, Chapter 29 in this volume). Prediction and prevention are epitomes of this shift, where the problem of "prepression" (repression as a result of prediction, Schinkel 2011) and a drift towards crime preemption emerge, too (Egbert and Krasmann 2020). Within this pre-crime approach in public policy, large databases and algorithmic calculation engender a governance by patterns and categorizations that are the basis for predictions. Patterns and categories, however, perform their own politics (Kaufmann et al. 2019). In order to serve as an argument for intervention, patterns reduce, simplify and discriminate (in the sense of *distinguishing entities from each other* and *discriminating against*). The decision-making processes that inform these patterns are a part of complex technological developments and remain largely invisible. This underlines the relevance of studying the social life of prediction algorithms, their emerging agencies (see the introductory chapter to this volume), as well as the collaborations between humans, datasets and machines in creating predictions (Kaufmann 2018; 2023), to which we turn now. Already in the early 1990s Stephen Ackroyd et al. pointed out that the integration of policing with information systems is shaped by many aspects, such as "the nature of that work, how it is organized day-to-day, what tacit understandings are built into this organization, its situatedness within a network of other organizational arrangements" (1992: 26).

Following the *algorithm's life cycle* is one approach to study the functionalities, different forms of agency and politics of algorithms in context (ibid.). Tracing a life cycle allows researchers to determine those points at which important design decisions are taken (which often cascade through the entire prediction process), but also those moments where algorithms exhibit agencies that influence predictions (Kaufmann and Leese 2021). Indeed, the concept of the life cycle carries the ontology of data and algorithms as lively (Lupton 2016) and dynamic (Barad 2003). As opposed to analytics that focus on the role of humans in "mastering" technologies, the life cycle draws a more complex picture of predictive processes. It suggests that things, including algorithms, live their own life and intersect with the many life cycles of others in processes of mattering (Kaufmann 2023). Together, humans, data and technologies also define whatever may be considered efficiency and situations that require action by law enforcement representatives. The remainder of this chapter is used to sketch out a prototype life cycle of a predictive policing algorithm, before giving an outlook into a new area for predictions in law enforcement that involve DNA.

THE LIFE CYCLE OF AN ALGORITHM IN PREDICTIVE POLICING

An algorithm's life begins before it is written, namely with *imaginaries* and preconceptions about its purpose and abilities. The purpose of the algorithm is linked to the data that developers believe are best to train algorithms. Ruha Benjamin (2019) addresses such imaginaries when she writes about names as data. What lies in a name comes with an expectation or association, in the worst case a prejudice. If software developers believe that names can capture a group's heritage or a type of neighbourhood, names would be used as data with the aim of distinguishing neighbourhoods for prediction.

Imaginaries also drive *data generation*, *curation* and *cleaning*. Already the ways in which data is first collected, according to specific protocols and on-site routines, are integral to the dataset which is later used to train algorithms. In predictive policing, for example, one would need data about crime. Already the (analogue) form that police officers fill out determines what type of information will be available for the algorithm's training. This analogue form is embedded in social and policing processes. Not only do forms express police protocol that has developed over many years, but also incorporate ideas about what data are needed for police work. In most cases, such data are generated with the intention of a *specific* usage (via registration or surveys). Other datasets were generated with a different or more general aims in mind (e.g data about number plates), but are reused for the purpose of creating predictions (cf. Palantir's approach).

This illustrates that *data storage* influences predictive tools, too. In predictive policing we find a broad spectrum that starts out with small, highly cleaned datasets that are chosen according to specific theories (Kaufmann 2019). When tools, for example, draw on Townsley's Near-Repeat Hypothesis, predictions would be based on data that capture where, when and what type of crime occurred. Such data may be extracted from existing datasets or are collected during police patrol. At the other end of the spectrum we find approaches that are interested in most types of stored data from weather data to population density. In that case, data from many public and private databases are combined, because the approach is to create algorithms that correlate "very big" datasets with each other in order to identify new types of patterns (this approach is also reflected in the notion of "interoperability", see Leese, Chapter

11 in this volume). Here, the role of commercial databases makes a difference since their rules for storage tend to be less strictly regulated. However, as the abovementioned example of Palantir's "omnina" showed, big data predictions can also include public sector databases. A known and obvious challenge are datasets that are based on discriminatory data collection practices (cf. Magnet 2011). Such biases are then carried throughout the entire design of the algorithm (Mann and Matzner 2019). The fact that data cascade and influence predictions illustrates how datasets assume agency. Other examples of the agencies of datasets are the moments at which algorithms identify surprising patterns, for example when they start to predict crime in accordance with phases of the moon (Kaufmann 2019). This pattern may be spurious, or it may predict well. *Why* the pattern would predict well is not necessarily explored. In such models, theory and causality are no longer important as long as actionable patterns are produced. This goes to show that the dataset used to train algorithms has epistemological implications: some datasets are used to predict according to a specific theoretical model. A different approach is to "let the data speak for themselves", that is to infer new patterns without being guided by a specific hypothesis.

For the algorithm to *emerge* police officers and developers must select content parameters (such as *time*, *space* and *type of crime* for algorithms based on Near-Repeat models). The team would first have to agree on the type of data that expresses these parameters. Such parameters are then translated into mathematic form. Though the expertise of those writing the algorithm's mathematic "code" is central at this stage, it is not a given that those who define content parameters and those who translate them into mathematic variables understand each other (Kaufmann 2018). Here, decision-making processes and frictions can occur that determine the entire process all the way to the algorithm's outputs.

Predictive policing algorithms emerge when they are trained. One such (simplified) training process could look like this: the mathematic parameters are put to use on datasets where the correct hits for a pattern are known. Developers follow the correlation process and give feedback about which result is considered an actual result. Note that giving feedback is here also an influential decision-making process, where "correct" hits based on (potentially biased) databases and value statements guide the training of the algorithm. When the algorithm identifies a pattern that is considered to be wrong, the parameters are adjusted. Here, algorithms can provoke frictions, for example when they identify ambiguous patterns (Kaufmann 2019).

The algorithm is considered *mature* when it has become good enough at identifying the results that match the algorithm's predefined aims and the patterns considered a correct hit. It can now be run on datasets where the "correct" hits are not known. Its agency becomes very pertinent at this stage as it now provides new insights to police officers the origins of which are no longer easily traceable. Algorithms do not disclose the arguments about how they have reached a specific result, which complicates the accountabilities involved when taking action based on algorithmic results. What is more, algorithms can now start to delete parameters that they identify as irrelevant. These concrete influences do change police cultures as they literally guide police patrol and foster new knowledge practices based on patterns (Kaufmann 2019).

What happens to prediction algorithms at the end of a life cycle? Do they reach a natural limit, are they ever retired? Whether algorithms *die*, that is, whether they will stop computing or identifying predictions, is mathematically speaking an unknown. The answer to this question is not computable (ibid.). The respective algorithm has to be run. However, whether the algorithm stops computing or not, whether it is taken out of work or not, is not necessarily tied to its capacity to act. Their agency is still present in decision-making. Training data or parameters can also be reused in new policing algorithms, venturing from one context to the next. Such instances of reuse raise new concerns about systemic biases that cascade across systems. The death of an algorithm would be the moment at which all of its elements no longer matter, which is rarely the case.

Following the life cycle of a predictive policing algorithm can assist in the identification of key moments at which collaborations occur that impact the entire prediction process, including the ethics, politics and values predictions perform.

Algorithmic policing technologies are not reduced to geographic predictions. Algorithms are also used in crime investigations to create predictions about familial relations and physical appearance from DNA. In the next part I will focus on the latter.

THE LIFE CYCLE OF AN ALGORITHM IN DNA ANALYSIS

In the forensic landscape of the late 1980s DNA emerged as a competitor to fingerprinting. Contrary to its role in the criminal justice system today, the suitability of DNA for forensic investigation was so contested that proponents borrowed authority from fingerprinting to argue for the evidentiary value of DNA (see *DNA fingerprinting*; Aronson 2007). The main aim of using DNA in forensics, then, was to establish matches between two DNA samples – one from a crime site, one from a database – for the sake of identification.

In order to match two samples, DNA first needs to be sequenced. Sequencing is to prepare DNA samples in a way that allows forensic scientists to identify four regions of the genome (so-called Short Tandem Repeats, STRs) that distinguish individuals from each other. Over the years, this number of regions rose to over 24 STRs, which means that by today, DNA profiles are more comprehensive, changing the possibilities for finding a match. A second important factor for identification is the growing availability of databases. Without the storage of DNA data, there would be no option to compare samples. A third factor that influences the identification of matches concerns the use of statistics to express the likelihood of two DNA samples stemming from the same person. In the struggle to establish procedure for DNA use, debates among the forensic and legal community revolved around the statistical forms and models used to express the likelihoods (Gigerenzer and Hoffrage 1995; NRC 1992). Different statistical models would lead to considerably different results, which had a direct impact on sentencing (cf. Lynch et al. 2008). This example emphasizes that any use of new data analyses in law enforcement sparks discussions about the "correct" analytic models, each of which creates different societal impacts – as we have also seen in predictive policing.

This brief history of DNA analysis in law enforcement is important to appreciate that DNA samples first had to become a trusted and reliable source for knowledge production in the law enforcement system. For these imaginaries and expectations to emerge, concrete scientific discourses and framing efforts were undertaken (Lynch et al. 2008). Only when these were established would DNA collection and analysis become a viable policy. Nowadays, DNA is considered the "gold standard" of forensic science. DNA has become a "truth machine" (ibid.). This *imaginary* heavily influences the use of DNA in investigations and in court today. What is more, it is also a driver for scientific endeavour to develop DNA analysis further and integrate it with more advanced computational practices. Algorithms are used at many stages and for many different reasons in DNA analysis today (to create profiles, analyse DNA mixtures, calculate probabilities, etc.). In what follows I focus on the use of algorithms for phenotypic predictions that increasingly inform police work. Phenotyping is the process of predicting physiognomic characteristics from a DNA sample.

An important moment in the rise of such predictions was the arrival of Next-Generation Sequencing (NGS), also called Massive Parallel Sequencing (MPS). These sequencing techniques no longer focus on STRs, but on other regions of the genome. These are also called "coding regions", because they code for proteins, which again shape gene expression. Coding regions are, for example, analyzed to identify proneness to illnesses, but they are also increasingly integrated with forensic work. As the names for the technique signal: these sequences contain different, and *much more*, information than STR profiles. The expressions "Massive" and "Next Generation" capture this considerable increase in information. Hence, this shift has been described as the beginning of "big genome data" (Murphy 2018) – the rise of genomic data so large that it has to be analyzed with more complex algorithms.

As we have seen above, the functionality of algorithms is highly integrated with the data and data imaginaries they analyze. Together, they form a "cluster of technologies". In order to understand the social life of an algorithm for DNA analysis, one needs to already take account of DNA sampling, because it creates the base data for analysis. DNA sampling, for example, involves a lot of "low tech" equipment, such as analogue forms that give context about the origin of the trace containing DNA. In the laboratory, traces are extracted and apparatuses such as centrifuges and thermo-regulators prepare DNA for the subsequent range of biochemical processes which eventually result in a sequence. This sequence eventually appears as a code on a computer screen. As illustrated with the case of predictive policing, these early steps are relevant, because they create the data to be stored and analyzed. The development of protocol for DNA sampling is also always a negotiation between humans and technologies.

Now that a DNA sample is sequenced and exists as digital data, it can be integrated with computation. In order to train and use algorithms to analyze DNA and create predictions, sequences have to be *stored* at a large scale. Some DNA databases are owned by the National Crime Investigation Services or different law enforcement institutions, others are owned by forensic departments in hospitals, or commercial actors. In relation to STR datasets Erin Murphy found that the storage and categorization of DNA data varies across institutions, and data-exchange between different database providers is not necessarily streamlined (Murphy 2018). Databases, then, emerge as "inventive, sometimes unruly" sites (Nadim 2016: 516), where data work, such as negotiations about the type of information stored and cleaning processes are needed to create consistent datasets. Yet, even if the algorithm is trained on one specific dataset, it is not a given that these data stem from a database where storage and curation is streamlined. Such socio-technical processes also need to be taken into account when building databases with NGS profiles.

Datasets containing DNA profiles and details about their owners can now be used for *training* algorithms that predict physiognomic features from DNA. This process is called phenotyping. Phenotyping software is advocated as an investigative tool of use to the police when a "classic" STR profile does not yield a match. The company Parabon, for example, offers a software called "Parabon Snapshot" that predicts a "typical" facial image from DNA, similar to a classic identikit picture. Officers would then be able to use such predictions to focus their investigations on a group with specific physiognomic expressions. Parabon is, however, a commercial solution and not yet broadly accepted among police officers.

The training of an algorithm to predict a facial image based on DNA is not too dissimilar from that for predictive policing described above. I will draw on Rose Hopman's work to explain the process. In order to estimate eye, hair and skin colour, genes known to impact pigmentation are correlated with DNA profiles of individuals whose geno- and phenotype is known (Hopman 2021). The algorithm, then, correlates pigmentation genes with physiognomic expressions. From these correlations, it is inferred which genomic pattern expresses what type of pigmentation. The size and the quality of the database decides, however, what type of correlations can be established and what patterns can be found. The next step is then to link the continuous reading of colour (a scale that is not subdivided into colour categories), to grades of, for example, skin colour for the sake of prediction (Hopman 2021). This work of categorizing skin colour as "white", "intermediate" and "black" is done by humans, who perform a highly political act, because these grades express generalizations that are now part of identification processes (ibid.).

In order to complete the "snapshot" image, a similar process is used to predict the morphology of the face. Here, a dataset is needed featuring records of individuals whose facial morphologies and genomic profiles are known. Biometric imaging is used to capture facial morphologies. These images are then standardized and symmetrized, which involves the cleaning of irregularities in order to render the morphologies comparable (ibid.). This is again a highly political process, because it involves templates of human "types". These morphological types are then linked to similarities in the respective genomes. Eventually, the algorithm *emerges* when it integrates these two pattern-based approaches to predict the facial features of a DNA owner. Again, not only the available datasets, but also the processes of categorizing skin colour and "cleaning away" morphological "deviances" are practices that influence the prediction. Most phenotyping instruments still focus on eye, hair and skin colour, with new features being added throughout. It is mainly the product Parabon Snapshot (Parabon, n.d.) that already offers a prediction of the entire face.

Phenotyping of eye, hair and skin colour is used as a tool for intelligence in the US and in an increasing number of European countries, which represents an epistemological shift. DNA is no longer used to express a likely match, but analyzed to offer physiognomic expressions to guide investigations. However, the use of phenotyping is debated. Arguments about new possibilities for efficient intelligence are countered by concerns about reliability and discrimination. The above life cycle illustrates that outputs are highly dependent on a range of different actors that influence prediction processes; predictions involve biased databases that emerge from discriminatory policing practices (e.g. Skinner 2020) and concrete value statements about physical appearance (Hopman 2021) (for wider discussion of bias: see Hong, Chapter 8 in this volume). The intention of phenotyping is no longer to ascertain an individual's identity, but to enlarge the pool of suspects from which new investigative leads can be inferred. Phenotypic predictions, then, offer physiognomic predictions in order to draw groups with a specific physiognomic profile into the realm of suspicion (Hopman and M'charek 2020).

While some of these criticisms remind us of the debates about geospatial predictions, phenotyping introduces an entirely new level of challenges, because it generates predictions about groups of people based on their physical appearance. Moreover, the involvement of DNA represents a new form of data capture and biometric surveillance that opens the door for entirely new policing practices.

CONCLUSION

The histories of public policy, policing and their relationship to information technologies are more integrated than one may expect. From the fifteenth to the seventeenth century "polizey" represented the moral oversight in a state and was derived directly from the concept of "policy" (Weatherby 2016). Before public policy and the police became established as more distinct fields, they already organized many areas of life by aid of information (ibid.). Statistics, for example, were relevant instruments for administration and governance back then and today (cf. Foucault 1977–78).

While there are continuities in doing (public) administration by means of counting, calculating and data processing, the rise of large datasets and new tools for data processing introduced qualitative shifts – also in fields that we define as policing today. This chapter has documented how the "clusters of technology" involved in predictive policing and DNA phenotyping create new epistemological practices in law enforcement. Predictive instruments strengthen the role of patterns in the governance of crime. While geospatial patterns define vulnerable areas to be policed, physiognomic patterns are used to direct crime investigations. The generation of patterns is a highly complex process that combines a vast range of decisions and agencies. What is more, in their function as actionable, "efficient" knowledge patterns also exercise their own agency. They guide the police to vulnerable areas and people of a specific physical appearance. The creation of territorial markers or pheno-*types* of potential suspects plays into the desire for efficient, technologically upgraded and evidence-based policing. Yet, these patterns hide the imaginaries, practices and hypotheses that guide the adoption of new technologies, data collection, the decisions that direct data generation and cleaning, the structural designs and inconsistencies of databases, the parameters that are defined to train algorithms and the mathematic models that guide analyses.

All of these elements determine the knowledge algorithmic technologies create and the politics they exercise (Kaufmann et al. 2019). Identifying and addressing these relationships is particularly relevant in the sensitive domain of law enforcement, where predictions produce concrete security and juridical implications.

ACKNOWLEDGEMENT

This project has received funding from the European Research Council (ERC) under the European Union's Horizon 2020 research and innovation programme (grant agreement No. 947681).

NOTE

1. Other known companies are Predpol (n.d) which bought Australian HunchLab, Azavea (n.d.) and Precobs (Institut für musterbasierte Prognosetechnik n.d.).

REFERENCES

Ackroyd, S., Harper, R., Hughes, J. A. and Shapiro, D. (1992) *New Technology and Practical Police Work. The Social Context of Technical Innovation*, Buckingham, UK/Philadelphia, PA: Open University Press.

Alikhademi, K., Drobina, E., Prioleau, D. et al. (2022) 'A review of predictive policing from the perspective of fairness', *Artificial Intelligence and Law*, **30** (3), 1–17.

Andrejevic, M. (2018) 'Data collection without limits: Automated policing and the politics of frameless-ness', in A. Završnik (ed.) *Big Data, Crime and Social Control*, Abingdon, UK/New York: Routledge, pp. 93–107.

Andrejevic, M. and Gates, K. (2014) 'Big data surveillance: Introduction', *Surveillance & Society*, **12** (2), 185–196.

Aronson, J. D. (2007) *Genetic Witness: Science, Law, and Controversy in the Making of DNA Profiling*, New Brunswick, NJ: Rutgers University Press.

Azavea (n.d.) *Azavea*, accessed 7 April 2021 at https://www.azavea.com.

Barad, K. (2003) 'Posthumanist performativity: Toward an understanding of how matter comes to matter', *Signs*, **28** (3), 801–831.

Beck C. and McCue, C. (2009) 'Predictive policing: What can we learn from Wal-Mart and Amazon about fighting crime in a recession?', *Police Chief*, **76** (11), 18–24.

Benjamin, R. (2019) *Race After Technology. Abolitionist Tools for the New Jim Code*, Medford, MA: Polity Press.

Bennett Moses, L. and Chan, J. (2018) 'Algorithmic prediction in policing: Assumptions, evaluation, and accountability', *Policing and Society*, **28** (7), 806–822. https://doi.org/10.1080/10439463.2016.1253695.

Brayne, S. (2017) 'Big data surveillance: The case of policing', *American Sociological Review*, **82** (5), 977–1008.

Cornish, D. B. and Clarke, R. V. (1986) *The Reasoning Criminal: Rational Choice Perspectives on Offending*, New York: Springer-Verlag.

Egbert, S. and Leese, M. (2020) *Criminal Futures. Predictive Policing and Everyday Police Work*, London: Routledge.

Egbert, S. and Krasmann, S. (2020) 'Predictive policing: Not yet, but soon preemptive?', *Policing and Society*, **30** (8), 905–919.

Fair Trials (2022) 'Leading European Parliament figures agree to ban predictive policing and justice AI', accessed 9 December 2022 at https://www.fairtrials.org/articles/news/leading-european-parliament-figures-agree-to-ban-predictive-policing-and-justice-ai/.

Foucault, M. (1977–78) *Security, Territory, Population. Lectures at the College de France, 1977–78*, M. Senellart, F. Ewald and A. Fontana (eds), London: Palgrave.

Ferguson A. G. (2017) *The Rise of Big Data Policing: Surveillance, Race, and the Future of Law Enforcement*, New York: New York University Press.

Gigerenzer, G. and Hoffrage, U. (1995) 'How to improve Bayesian reasoning without instruction: Frequency formats', *Psychological Review*, **102** (4), 684–704.

Gill, P. (2000) *Rounding Up the Usual Suspects? Developments in Contemporary Law Enforcement Intelligence*, Aldershot, UK: Ashgate.

Gjerding, S. and Andersen, L. S. (2017) 'Nyt "supervåben" skal gøre politiet bedre til at snage i face-bookprofiler. Information', accessed 20 April 2022 at https://www.information.dk/indland/2017/03/nyt-supervaaben-goere-politiet-bedre-snage-facebookprofiler.

Gundhus, H. O., Rønn, K. V. and Fyfe, N. R. (2017) *Moral Issues in Intelligence-led Policing*, London/New York: Routledge.

Harcourt, B. H. (2007) *Against Prediction: Profiling, Policing, and Punishing in an Actuarial Age*, Chicago/London: The University of Chicago Press.

Hopman, R. (2021) 'The face as folded object: Race and the problems with "progress" in forensic DNA phenotyping', *Social Studies of Science*. Online First. https://doi.org/10.1177/03063127211035562.

Hopman, R. and M'charek, A. (2020) 'Facing the unknown suspect: Forensic DNA phenotyping and the oscillation between the individual and the collective', *BioSocieties*, **15** (3), 438–462.

Institut für musterbasierte Prognosetechnik (n.d.) *Precobs*, accessed 7 April 2022 at http://www.ifmpt .de.

Kaufmann, M. (2018) 'The co-construction of crime predictions: Dynamics between digital data, software and human beings', in H. O. Gundhus, K. V. Rønn and N. R. Fyfe (eds), *Moral Issues in Intelligence-led Policing*, London/New York: Routledge, pp. 143–160.

Kaufmann, M. (2019) 'Who connects the dots? Agents and agency in predictive policing', in M. Hoijtink and Leese, M. (eds), *Technology and Agency in International Relations*, London: Routledge, pp. 141–163.

Kaufmann, M. (2023) *Making Information Matter. Understanding Surveillance and Making a Difference*, Bristol: Bristol University Press.

Kaufmann, M. and Leese, M. (2021) 'Information in-formation. Algorithmic policing and the life of data', in A. Završnik and V. Badalič (eds), *Automating Crime Prevention, Surveillance, and Military*, Cham, Switzerland/New York: Springer, pp. 69–83.

Kaufmann, M., Egbert, S. and Leese, M. (2019) 'Predictive policing and the politics of patterns', *British Journal of Criminology*, **59** (3), 674–692.

Kavanaugh, S. D. (2017) 'This teen's story is your worst "predictive policing" nightmare', accessed 9 December 2022 at https://www.vocativ.com/418541/predictive-policing-nightmare/index.html.

Kennedy L. W., Caplan, J. M. and Piza, E. (2011) 'Risk clusters, hotspots, and spatial intelligence: Risk terrain modeling as an algorithm for police resource allocation strategies', *Journal of Quantitative Criminology*, **27** (3), 339–362.

Lupton, D. (2016) 'Digital companion species and eating data: Implications for theorizing digital data-human assemblages', *Big Data & Society*, **3** (1), 1–5.

Lynch, M., Cole, S. A., McNally, R. and Jordan, K. (2008) *Truth Machine. The Contentious History of DNA Fingerprinting*, Chicago: The University of Chicago Press.

Magnet, S. A. (2011) *When Biometrics Fail. Gender, Race, and the Technology of Identity*, Durham, NC: Duke University Press.

Mann, M. and Matzner, T. (2019) 'Challenging algorithmic profiling: The limits of data protection and anti-discrimination in responding to emergent discrimination', *Big Data & Society*, **6** (2).

Manning, P. K. (1992) 'Technological dramas and the police: Statement and counterstatement in organizational analysis', *Criminology*, **30** (3), 327–346.

Mantello, P. (2016) 'The machine that ate bad people: The ontopolitics of the precrime assemblage', *Big Data & Society*, July–December, 1–11.

Marda V. and Narayan, S. (2020) 'Data in New Delhi's predictive policing system', in *Proceedings of the 2020 Conference on Fairness, Accountability, and Transparency*, pp. 317–324.

McDaniel, J. and Pease, K. (2022) *Predictive Policing and Artificial Intelligence*, Abingdon, UK: Routledge.

Meijer, A. and Wessels, M. (2019) 'Predictive policing: Review of benefits and drawbacks', *International Journal of Public Administration*, **42** (12), 1031–1039.

Meijer, A., Lorenz, L. and Wessels, M. (2021) 'Algorithmization of bureaucratic organizations: Using a practice lens to study how context shapes predictive policing systems', *Public Administration Review*, **81** (5), 837–846.

Mohler, G. O., Short, M. B., Malinowski, S., Johnson, M., Tita, G. E., Bertozzi, A. L. and Brantingham, P. J. (2015) 'Randomized controlled field trials of predictive policing', *Journal of the American Statistical Association*, **110** (512), 1399–1411.

Murphy, E. (2018) 'Law and policy oversight of familial searches in recreational genealogy databases', *Forensic Science International*, **292**, e5–e9.

Nadim, T. (2016) 'Data labours: How the sequence databases GenBank and EMBL-Bank make data', *Science as Culture*, **25** (4), 496–519.

National Institute of Justice (2014) 'Overview of predictive policing', accessed 9 December 2022 at https://nij.ojp.gov/topics/articles/overview-predictive-policing.

NRC (National Research Council) (1992) *DNA Technology in Forensic Science*, Washington, DC: National Academy Press.

Parabon (n.d.) *Parabon Snapshot* (R), accessed 21 April 2021 at https://snapshot.parabon-nanolabs.com/.

Perry, W. L., McInnis, B., Price, C. C., Smith, S. C. and Hollywood, J. S. (2013) 'Predictive policing: The role of crime forecasting in law enforcement operations', RAND Safety and Justice Program, accessed 14 May 2024 at https://www.rand.org/content/dam/rand/pubs/research_reports/RR200/RR233/RAND_RR233.pdf. Predpol (n.d.) *Predpol*, accessed 7 April 2021 at https://www.predpol.com.

Richardson R., Schultz J. and Crawford, K. (2019) 'Dirty data, bad predictions: How civil rights violations impact police data, predictive policing systems, and justice', *94 New York University Law Review*, online, 192.

Røise, M. B. (2020) 'Prestisjeprosjekt avsluttet etter 11 år: – Ser ut som 100 millioner er brukt uten å gi resultater', accessed 20 April 2022 at https://www.digi.no/artikler/prestisjeprosjekt-avsluttet-etter-11-ar-ser-ut-som-100-millioner-er-brukt-uten-a-gi-resultater/491448.

Sandhu, A. and Fussey, P. (2021) 'The "uberization of policing"? How police negotiate and operationalise predictive policing technology', *Policing and Society*, **31** (1), 66–81.

Schinkel, W. (2011) 'Prepression: The actuarial archive and new technologies of security', *Theoretical Criminology*, **15** (4), 365–380.

Sherman, L. B. (1998) 'Evidence-based policing. Ideas in American policing', *Police Foundation*, July 1998, 1–16.

Skinner, D. (2020) 'Race, racism and identification in the era of technosecurity', *Science as Culture*, **29** (1), 77–99.

Sprick, D. (2020) 'Predictive policing in China', *Naveiñ Reet: Nordic Journal of Law and Social Research* (9), 299–324.

Townsley, M., Homel, R. and Chaseling, J. (2003) 'Infectious burglaries: A test of the near repeat hypothesis', *British Journal of Criminology*, **43** (3), 615–633.

Trædal, T. J. (2017) 'Kan søke gjennom flere hundre millioner fingeravtrykk i løpet av sekunder', *Politiforum*, accessed 9 March 2022 at https://www.politiforum.no/nyheter/kan-soke-gjennom-flere-hundre-millioner-fingeravtrykk-i-lopet-av-sekunder/136521.

Weatherby, L. (2016) 'Police psychology: E. T. A. Hoffmann, Johann Beckmann, and technological narration', *Romantic Circles*, accessed 13 April 2022 at https://romantic-circles.org/praxis/german/praxis.2016.german.weatherby.html.

Wilson, D. (2018) 'Algorithmic patrol: The futures of predictive policing', in A. Završnik (ed.) *Big Data, Crime and Social Control*, Abingdon, UK/New York: Routledge, pp. 108–127.

Zedner, L. (2007) 'Pre-crime and post-criminology?', *Theoretical Criminology*, **11** (2), 261–281.

23. AI in border control and migration: techno-racism and exclusion at digital borders[1]

Petra Molnar

US VS. THEM IN A DIGITAL WORLD: AN ETHNOGRAPHIC VIGNETTE FROM THE POLISH/BELARUSSIAN BORDER

"Why did we have to freeze in the forest? The blood that comes out of all people is the same colour." Ibrahim is a Syrian refugee who crossed into Poland from Belarus, and who was stuck in the freezing November forest. He made it safely to Germany and reflects on his experiences a few months later: "Why are bombs falling on Ukraine more important than bombs falling on Syria?" (The New Humanitarian 2022b)

We have been walking in this same forest for hours. The dark sky hangs heavy on a cold and damp November afternoon. We are quickly losing the light. "Marhaba! Hello? We are friends," we shout into the darkening woods that separate Poland from Belarus, the newest site of border violence. In 2021, the Lukashenko regime has been encouraging hundreds of asylum seekers from Iraqi Kurdistan and Syria to enter the European Union through its land border with Poland. There are even rumours of flights from various cities in the Middle East to Minsk, the capital city of Belarus. But unfortunately, Poland had other ideas. A hastily erected barbed wire fence and hundreds of police now separate the two countries in a violent standoff. Hundreds of families remain trapped as winter comes closer with each passing day. Poland's policy creates create a 5km wide exclusion zone that human rights monitors and journalists are not allowed to enter (Politico 2021). Poland is also constructing what some Members of the European Parliament have called a "fence of shame" at its Belarus border (Politico 2022). It includes a fortified wall and border surveillance (AP News 2022) to aid in the efforts of keeping non-Europeans out, copying some of the technologies first piloted at the Greek-Turkey border (Reuters 2021). It also cuts through the ancient Białowieża Forest, the only surviving patch of Europe's primeval forest. As the weather worsens and people continue to try and cross into the EU, they remain trapped in this no-man's land. Some die (Fallon n.d.).

A few months later, after the full-scale invasion of Ukraine in February 2022, I am once again at the Polish border. Mere hours away from where people continue to freeze in Poland's Białowieża Forest, I weave my way through small towns, soup kitchens, living rooms, stadiums and border crossings and are moved by the tremendous outpouring of humanity to the millions of people fleeing Russia's brutal crackdown on Ukraine. Reminiscent to the solidarity and kindness shown to Syrian refugees at the height of 2015 and 2016 when thousands were coming to Europe to seek asylum, open borders during a war near the EU are clearly very possible. Especially when the refugees fleeing are blonde and blue eyed (Davis 2022).

But even among this incredible solidarity and show of support for Ukraine, already the cracks begin to show – after just three weeks of being at various borders along the warzone, racism, discrimination, human trafficking and even old tropes about Ukrainians not being "true Europeans" are beginning to surface (Deutsche Welle 2014). The fatigue that so commonly set in after the adrenaline of a crisis wears off is palpable. And unfortunately this often manifests in racial violence. Groups of Middle Eastern medical students studying in the Ukrainian city of Kharkiv told me about being denied boarding on trains speeding across the border into Hungary. Hungary has weaponized its open-door response to secure the Orban government another term in power (Zeit 2022). Romani families were the only ones surrounded by hordes of police in Slovakia (Popoviciu 2022). According to an official statement by then – United Nations Special Rapporteur on Discrimination Tendayi Achiume: "non-white migrants and refugees face deadly discrimination all over the world as they attempt to cross international borders. The images and testimonies from non-white people attempting to flee Ukraine attest to this fact" (OHCHR n.d.).

Sociologist Heba Gowayed warns that "If the war on Ukraine continues, the reality is that Ukrainians too will likely enter this sad and familiar cycle: wards of a system intended to protect the displaced but predicated on the humanitarian goodwill of countries who define their sovereignty by borders meant to keep people out" (The New Humanitarian 2022a). Indeed, as the conflict in Ukraine drags on, will its borders also become yet another lucrative space for the growing border industrial complex, fuelled by surveillance and disaster capitalism? Big Tech stands to benefit from crises.

MIGRATION MANAGEMENT AT THE DIGITAL FRONTIER

Today, there are millions of people on the move[2] due to forces of colonialism and imperialism, conflict, instability, environmental factors and economic reasons. As a result, in the last few years, states and international organizations involved in migration management have expanded their use of technological experiments in various domains such as border enforcement, decision-making and data mining. Mobile populations have historically been seen as trackable, intelligible and controllable (Macklin 2005, De Genova 2002, Blommaert 2009, Inda 2004, Ahmed 2004, Appadurai 2006, Lemberg-Pedersen and Haioty 2020). Now, through every point of a person's migration journey, they are impacted by risky, unregulated technologies used to control movement and manage migration. Decisions such as whether to grant a visa or detain someone, which would otherwise be made by administrative tribunals, immigration officers, border agents, legal analysts and other officials are now made by machines through algorithms. Predictive analytics which use large data sets to make predictions about human behaviour are used both in humanitarian emergencies to deliver aid but also to see where people may be crossing borders, leading to violence or even death at the border. There is also the rise in the use of biometrics, or the automated recognition of individuals based on their biological and behavioural characteristics. Biometrics can include fingerprint data, retinal scans and facial recognition, as well as less well-known methods such as the recognition of a person's vein and blood vessel patterns, ear shape and gait, among others. Even more experimental are lie detectors relying on AI as to deciding who is telling the truth at the border, while voice-printing technologies analyze accents and pattern of speech. The surveillance dragnet is also expanding, with a growing arsenal of cameras, blimps, loud sound cannons and even experimental robo-dogs deployed to control borders.

From smart border walls to unpiloted drones used to prevent people from reaching the safety of European shores, to artificial-intelligence (AI) lie detectors at various airports worldwide, to proposed robo-dogs patrolling the US–Mexico corridor, people on the move are getting caught in the crosshairs of an unregulated and harmful set of technologies touted to control borders and "manage migration",[3] bolstering a multi-billion-dollar industry. Thousands have already died. The rest experience old and new traumas provoked and compounded by surveillance and automation (Molnar 2021). These technologies separate families, push people into life-threatening terrain and exacerbate the historical and systemic discrimination that is a daily reality for people on the move and other marginalized communities. Border spaces serve as testing grounds for new technologies (Molnar 2020), places where regulation is deliberately limited and where an "anything goes" frontier attitude informs the development and deployment of surveillance at the expense of people's lives.

There has been a proliferation of research in recent years on the use of various technologies at borders,[4] including discussions of the need to create more robust regulations for the governance of high-risk border technologies. This chapter builds on this corpus of work and argues that an increasingly global and lucrative panopticon of migration control exacerbates discrimination and obfuscates responsibility and liability through the development and deployment of increasingly hardline border technologies. These technological experiments play up the "us" vs. "them" mentality at the centre of migration management policy. Unbridled techno-solutionism (Molnar and Naranjo 2020) and migration surveillance exacerbates deterrence mechanisms already so deeply embedded in the global migration management strategy, as at the Polish Belarusian border, making things as difficult as possible for people so as to set an example and to prevent others from coming. But what is the logic underpinning these technological border logics and the spectacles of increasingly higher risk border technologies? As writer and activist Harsha Walia reminds in *Border and Rule*, it boils down to racist nationalism, imperialism and privatization of migration management which lie at the heart of border control.

Wealth is allowed to flow to the centres of global capital, but never outward. The mobility of capital never applies to the wretched of the earth, who are forced to traverse deadly water and land passages across borders, not of their making, and are unwelcome in countries that may have destroyed theirs. Only punishment awaits them. Their mobility is made criminal, their existence made illegal. While it is framed as a migrant or refugee crisis, it is really a crisis of humanity, the failure of the current system to offer any real alternative other than the demonization of the other (Walia 2020).

For western states build on white supremacy and racial exclusion embedded in their nation-building projects; states justify increasing technological experiments in migration precisely because unwelcome people on the move,[5] like Ibrahim from Syria at the Polish border, have been historically rendered as a population which is intelligible, trackable and manageable.[6]

Whether retinal scans or AI lie detectors at the airport, the primary purpose of these projects is to collect data, make decisions and report to the state the necessary information on a potentially unsafe or unknown migrant body, transforming them into security objects and data points to be analysed, stored, collected and rendered intelligible.[7] Yet all this experimentation deliberately occurs in a space that is largely unregulated, with weak oversight and governance mechanisms, driven by the private sector innovation. Various jurisdictions including Canada, the US and the UK, so-called receiving states for migration, deliberately create and re-create opaque laws and introduce exemptions and ministerial discretion into an already discretionary decision-making system. With the push to innovate and digitize migration, the creation of such legal black holes without accountability and oversight is very deliberate to allow for the creation of opaque zones of technological experimentation that would not be allowed to occur in other spaces in the same way (Molnar and Naranjo 2020) like our local grocery store or doctor's office. The use of border technologies reinscribes the way that powerful actors make decisions that affect thousands of people on the margins of society. The growing opacity of border zones and increased transnational surveillance transform migration into a site of potential criminality that must be surveilled and managed to root out the ever-present spectre of terrorism and irregular migration (IOM 2020; PR Newswire 2020). The very concept of a "border" is also shifting, with policies of "border externalisation", or the transfer of border controls to foreign countries, becoming one the main instrument through which the EU seeks to stop unwelcome migration to Europe (Akkerman 2018). Through aerial surveillance, the EU border is extended and disaggregates various enforcement practices as far away from the physical EU border as possible.

THE BORDER IS SUSPENDED FROM THE SKIES

EU spending on border security in third countries has increased vastly. The research group the Transnational Institute (TNI) estimates that the border industrial complex is estimated to reach $65–68 billion USD by 2025 with the largest increase in global biometrics and AI (TNI 2021: 1). The EU's locus of power is in Brussels, with more powerful member states in Western Europe able to wield power over weaker members, creating buffer zones in the non-EU member states in the Balkans and even using Greece as a "shield".

Israeli technologies again make an appearance. Starting in May 2021, Crete, Airbus-run Israel Aerospace Industries Heron drone became a tool for Frontex (Loewenstein 2023: 99), the EU's border force. The EU has spent approximately $91 million USD on drones patrolling the Mediterranean. Iceland has also started deploying Israeli Heron drones for surveillance, while Hungary and Bulgaria explicitly cited their interest in wanting to use Israeli companies to build walls (Loewenstein 2023: 106): "[E]uropean countries] all want solutions and see the relevance of [Israeli] technologies" (Times of Israel 2015). The EU's research and development funding scheme, Horizon 2022, has also backed various border-control systems and surveillance projects by Israel. Interoperable biometric databases and data sharing such as EUROSUR and other international agreements make information sharing easier (on interoperability discourses in the EU, see Leese, Chapter 11 in this volume). There are also other extreme ways of pushing the border back, such as the reliance on space satellite surveillance through programmes with scientific names like Galileo or Kopernikus, perhaps deliberately using these names to lend an air of objectivity and scientific legitimacy to these efforts (Statewatch and TNI 2009).[8]

Frontex, the pan-jurisdictional border force of the EU, is a major player in the outsourcing of borders. Not only does it rely on Israeli drone surveillance to monitor boats that cross the Mediterranean, Frontex also renewed a contract with Israel's Windward project, which makes a maritime analysis tool that "catches bad guys at seas" – digital aggregation, vessel tracking evaluation, maritime surveillance data to track ships. Frontex has long had a securitization agenda at its core. It began operations in May 2005 after significant political impetus for an EU-wide border mechanism to combat terrorism after 9/11, growing more powerful after the subsequent Madrid and London bombings and the 2015 movement of Syrian refugees. There has been a huge expansion at Frontex over the years, from 70 staff to hundreds, blowing up its budget from €6 million to €11.3 billion for 2021–2027. The EU has also increased the remit and power of Frontex, expanding its standing corps by thousands of officers and increasing its funding, with few checks and balances and the somehow impervious ability to withstand investigations into pushbacks, corruption and even the resignation of its former chief Fabrice Leggieri in 2022. From a backstage player to the central star of border operations in EU, its 2019 mandate explicit that "combatting cross-border crime" lay at its core, all the while implicated in illegal pushback operations themselves.[9]

These types of technological expansion of both EU and US borders are also directly implicated in political manoeuvring and war profiteering, destabilizing entire regions all the while shutting Europe's doors to the refugees who are forced to flee as a result.

"WE ARE HERE BECAUSE YOU WERE THERE"[10]

Surveillance technologies and practices developed and used by the most advanced surveillance agencies in the world are being spread globally. Surveillance is being used to entrench political control, and also to spy on activists, journalists, dissidents and any opposition. These transfers of surveillance are driven by governments and institutions aiming to outsource ongoing wars on migration, terror and drugs to other countries (Privacy International 2020; Greenfield 2020).

Entire books have been written about US warmongering. One recent example is the invasion of Afghanistan and the state-building projects inherent in the US's involvement, and the subsequent hasty departure after the fall of Kabul into Taliban control in August 2021. Many of us sprang into action as thousands were attempting to flee the capital and surrounding regions, forming lawyer coalitions and information networks, as official communications from governments were unclear. Images of people rushing to the last remaining planes on the tarmac and falling to their death after clinging to the wings remain burned into the memory. While many were successfully evacuated, thousands remain stranded with valid visas, including translators and support staff who did vital work for governments like the US, Canada and the UK. And there is as always a technological component here too. During their hasty withdrawal, the US government and various international organizations left behind high-risk biometric identification equipment (The Intercept 2021), which pretty much immediately fell straight into the hands of the Taliban. It also includes a huge database of around 40 data points/person, including demographic information and iris scans (MIT Technology Review 2021) – perfect for a violent regime to optimize its strategies of repression with US technology.

The EU and US are increasingly advancing their defence and security agendas by militarizing their own borders and pushing them further afield. After the Syrian war forced millions of people into the EU, the EU Commission attempted to redraft its migration policy, culminating in its New Pact of Asylum and Migration, a comprehensive set of policies which envisages highly restrictive border control policies, increased militarization and externalization, detention, normalization of surveillance and widespread removal/deportation proceedings. There is again a clear conflation between migration control with national defence and homeland security.

The EU also directly funds and sometimes donates military and security equipment as well as exerting political pressure on third countries to strengthen their border-security capacities, boosting the border-security market in places like Africa. For example, the lobby organization AeroSpace and Defence Industries Association of Europe (ASD) has started to focus on EU border externalization. Large arms companies like Airbus and Thales have also set their eyes on the growing African and Middle Eastern market. The decision-making on and implementation of border externalization at an EU-level has been marked by unusual speed and has by-passed democratic control by the European Parliament. Several important agreements with third countries, including the Compacts under the Partnership Framework and the migration deal with Turkey, have excluded or sidelined European parliamentary oversight (Akkerman 2018).

The growth in border-security spending has also benefited a wide range of companies, in particular arms manufacturers and biometric security companies. French arms giant, Thales, also a major arms exporter to the region, is one prominent player, providing military and security equipment for border security and biometric systems and equipment (Akkerman 2018). Significant biometric security corporate suppliers include Veridos, OT Morpho and Gemalto (which will soon be taken over by Thales). Meanwhile, Germany and Italy fund their own arms firms – Hensoldt, Airbus and Rheinmetall (Germany) and Leonardo and Intermarine (Italy) – to underpin border-security work in a number of MENA countries in particular Egypt, Tunisia and Libya. In Turkey, substantial border-security contracts have been won by Turkish defence companies, in particular Aselsan and Otokar, who are using the resources to subsidize their own defence efforts that also underpin Turkey's controversial attacks on Kurdish communities (Akkerman 2018). Their involvement is enabled by the adoption of ad hoc funds, like the controversial "EU-Turkey deal", an agreement which saw €6 billion given to Turkey in exchange for its commitment to seal its border with Greece and Syria (Biella 2016). Hidden within these policies is also the EU's Internal Security Fund and the benignly named US Trust Fund for Africa (Privacy International 2020) – aimed at bolstering the mandate and capacity of third countries to militarize their borders, essentially outsourcing the EU's bordering mechanism by directly funding border-control practices aimed at keeping people withing the African continent.

Not only are powerful global actors trying to prevent migration and push their borders as far away as possible, they are also actively engaged in political destabilization for profit, through the use of new technologies of power and surveillance. TNI's 2018 report "Expanding the fortress: The policies, the profiteers and the people shaped by EU's border externalization" examines the systematic strengthening of dictatorships and repressive regimes, undermining local political and economic stability, such as in Libya, where the EU and member states like Malta continue funding, training and cooperating with militias actively killing and detaining people on the move in torture centres and detention facilities. Another TNI report, *Smoking Guns*, draws a direct line between the exportation of arms, military equipment, technology and training and their devastating effects which actively destabilize entire regions. TNI reports that world military spending has risen to $2 trillion USD (TNI 2021) with the US, China, India, Russia and the UK accounting for 62 per cent, while the EU accounts for about 36 per cent. Arms trade is not only causing mass displacement, it is also a highly lucrative industry profiting from conflict and the militarization of borders: "War is highly profitable, and the war on migrants is becoming increasingly so" (TNI 2021: 3). More people on the move that need to be controlled means more lucrative high-tech projects developed by the private sector.

Israel is also of course a major player here, with Israeli security companies among the most successful – and lucrative – in the world. With its world-class weapons industry consistently tested out on Palestinians and then marketed as "battle-tested", as journalist Antony Loewenstein argues, "the Palestine laboratory is a signature Israeli selling point" (Loewenstein

2023). Israel has actively supplied weapons to myriad repressive regimes, including South Sudan, the Ceausescu regime in Romania, Russia and the Assad regime in Syria (Loewenstein 2023: 81), Sri Lanka (Loewenstein 2023: 53) and the Duvalier regime in Haiti, among many others. Elbit Hermes drones are even patrolling the Canadian arctic, supposedly for environmental monitoring. And right after the invasion of Ukraine, Elbit stocks rose up by 70 per cent (Loewenstein 2023: 12) – war is indeed very profitable.

There are also smaller players such as Bulgaria, Croatia and Romania that sell arms and other technologies. For example, Bulgaria and Romania have increased their exported ammunition from €1 million per year in 2012 to €82 million in 2016 after the start of the war in Syria (TNI 2021: 1). Bulgaria also exported missile tubes and rockets to Saudi Arabia and the US, which then ended up in the hands of ISIS fighters in Iraq during the Ramadi crisis displacing over half a million people from the Anbar province between November 2015 and February 2016 and damaging around 80 per cent of housing (TNI 2021: 2). Serbia and Bulgaria have also been exporting assault rifles, weapons and grenade launchers to the Democratic Republic of Congo (DCR), while Italian helicopter components have been exported to Turkey and used in the Afrin districts of Northern Syria, displacing approximately 180,000 people including 80,000 children (TNI 2021: 2). While very little accountability exists, a case from February 2029 in Germany, currently being appealed, argued that German arms export Heckler and Koch sent weapons to Mexico and was complicit in the killing of six people and the forced disappearance of 43 students in the Ayotzinapa region.

TNI, Human Rights Watch and journalists like the EU's collective Lighthouse Reports have also shed light on the cooperation between the EU and Libya. For example, Italy donated at least four patrol boats to the Libyan Coast Guard, which were then used for pullback operations and subsequent detention. At least one boat had a machine gun retrofitted by the Libyan National Army:

> many of those fleeing Libya had most likely already fled other conflicts in other African and West Asian countries that may have purchased or were in receipt of European arms, so that at each step along their journey from displacement to migration, the European arms trade is making massive profits by first displacing them, and then later deterring and pushing them back. (TNI 2021: 2)

European arms are also used in internal conflicts (TNI 2021: 32) and the EU has trained the Libyan Coast Guard to intercept refugees to make sure people do not reach European territory, but all the while it is recognized internationally that Libya is not a safe country of return. And in an absurd twist, while the EU is proud to publicly commit to rooting out human smuggling, the Libyan Coast Guard often directly cooperates with human traffickers or is sometimes directly involved. According to Mark Akkerman, a specialist in armed conflict:

> refugees pay smugglers to go to Europe, only to be picked up by the sometimes pre-alerted coast guard and detained in Libya, having to pay again to be released and make another attempt to cross the Mediterranean. The EU and some member states, primarily Italy, pour money into all actors in this horrific system – the internationally recognized [Libyan] government with its brutal human rights record and various militia groups, and by extension, the smugglers and traffickers among or cooperating with them. (Akkerman 2018, see also Wintour 2018 and Michael et al. 2019)

The EU cannot easily plead ignorance– official documents show the EU is well aware of these risks (Human Rights Watch 2006), calling into question what the real motivation is here. Under the guise of saving people from drowning, the EU's Operation IRINI actively supplies information on rafts to the Libyan Coast Guard, enabling it to return people to detention centres in Libya. Similar operations also occur along the Atlantic route, with Frontex's operation HERA sending people picked up in the Atlantic to Senegal (Frontex 2020).

TECHNO-RACIAL LOGICS OF EXCLUSION

Racism, technology and borders create a cruel intersection that traps people on the move in high-risk technological experiments. In an increasingly destabilized world, when national sovereignty appears under threat, states justify their control over populations through repeated spectacles, performances and messaging around necessary national security and border control at the exclusion of the Other. Often, the "Other" is a person of colour from countries outside of North America and Europe.

While some people continue to be able to move freely and buy their way across borders through enhanced security screenings, Nexus and other expediencies, others remain excluded and actively discouraged from exercising their right to freedom of movement. As Hannah Arendt reminds us, we are able to tolerate the contradictions inherent in the differentiation of rights precisely because the normalization of increased surveillance, data collection and augmentation of decision-making become ingrained in everyday actions and experiences (Arendt 1994). The concept of Giorgio Agamben's "inclusive exclusion", wherein the state is able to divide and separate populations based on the figure of the "outlaw" who is outside the boundaries of the social and political life of the state further entrenches how we imagine the differentiation of rights to be natural (Agamben 2006) when used to justify interventions and experimentations on the margins for the so-called common good. Making mobile populations the ultimate Other justifies unregulated technological experimentation under the guise of efficiency and security. The state justifies this experimentation through "permanent vigilance, activity, and intervention" (Foucault 2008: 131). These practices also perpetuate the so-called Global North as the locus of power and technological development, to be deployed in the Rest of the World.

However, not all migration is the same. In cross-border migration management, certain mobilities are made legitimate while others are made illicit (Amoore 2006, Sparke 2006). An investor immigrant – or indeed, a product like an iPhone – travels across borders with relative ease, while other migrants are incarcerated, surveilled and tracked. Wealthy immigrants can move their families, assets and financial capital at will, while the vast majority of people in situations of displacement from the Global South are actively prevented from doing so. The authority of the state and its legitimacy to make these decisions are cleverly manufactured and constantly supported (Butler 2005), and migration management spaces are particular locales where sovereignty intersects with notions of threat, security and power. Certain bodies become the ones upon which experimentation is not only permissible but necessary, as the population must be controlled, managed and used in the performance of sovereignty and security at the border and beyond. Importantly, as theorist Peter Andreas reminds us, "[p]ublic perception is powerfully shaped by the images of the border which politicians, law enforcement agencies, and the media project" (Andreas 2009: 9). Coupled with the push to innovate in the global technological arms race, the theatre of conspicuous performance of power manifests in the equating of one particular group – migrants – with the necessity to manage, catalogue, experiment and innovate. There is a profound fear of mobility and of the uncontrollable migrant that motivates the proliferation of border technologies.

For sociologist Didier Bigo (2008), the securitization of migration actually creates a paradox: by creating a permanent state of emergency, the state is able to lean in on insecurities and fears of a chaotic future at the hands of undesirable migrants coming to take over: smart is safe and surveillance is freedom. By creating a closed loop where law enforcement, immigration control and national security intelligence processes conflate, states sell their vision of predictive, preventive and protective policies – presented as a depoliticized necessity in an increasingly unsafe and fractured world. Law professor and former UN Special Rapporteur on Discrimination E. Tendayi Achiume (2021) evocatively speaks about the "legal conjuring" that goes on when norms and law are stretched to accommodate increasing exclusion.

Migration management is inherently a deeply political exercise. The rise of anti-migrant xenophobic sentiments, the justification of surveillance and online media monitoring, and the rise of extreme right and neo-fascist groups and political organizations globally also impacts how migration management technologies function. A major geopolitical tragedy full of fear, the COVID-19 pandemic has also normalized widespread surveillance (Molnar and Naranjo 2020). As governments moved toward biosurveillance (Cliffe 2020) to contain the spread of the COVID-19 pandemic, there was an increase in tracking projects and automated drones (Privacy International 2020). Once again, refugees and people crossing borders are disproportionately targeted and negatively affected. Pandemic responses are political (Khatib 2020) and refugees and people on the move have historically been tied to the spread of illness and disease. COVID-19 was weaponized and used as a justification to keep people contained, and in the summer of 2020 the Greek authorities kept people locked in refugee camps (MSF 2020) much longer after the reopening of the country. As the "Feared Outsiders", refugees, immigrants and people on the move have long been linked with bringing disease and illness (The World 2019) across borders. In the media and politics today, people crossing borders, whether by force or by choice, are described in apocalyptic terms like "flood" or "wave" (Kainz 2016), underscored by growing xenophobia and racism (OHCHR n.d.). Elected leaders like Poland's Kaczynski and Hungary's Órban capitalize on incendiary rhetoric of immigrants carrying "parasites and protozoa" (Cohen 2018) and blame various diseases on refugees – not dissimilar to historical examples such as people being detained at Ellis Island when they first arrived for fear of disease. Of course, no list would be complete without the former US President Trump's violent rhetoric against people on the move, including their apparent "tremendous medical problems" (Rodrigo 2018) that necessitate building that costly border wall and smart surveillance. Not only are these links blatantly incorrect (Herrera 2019), but they also legitimize far-reaching state incursions and increasingly hardline policies of surveillance and novel technical "solutions" to manage migration. The pandemic accelerated the growth of a migration management industry that now has yet another reason to thrive. Proposed and far-fetched tools such as virus-targeting robots (CBC 2020), cellphone tracking (Romm 2020) and AI-based thermal cameras (Cox 2020) can all be used against people crossing borders, with far-reaching human rights impacts. In addition to violating the rights of the people subject to these technological experiments, the interventions themselves do not live up to the promises and arguments used to justify them. This use of COVID-tracking technology to manage and control migration was also shielded from scrutiny because of its emergency nature – a seeming necessity during a global health crisis which has now become difficult to dislodge during the increasing digitization of daily life.

Emergencies and fears of being overrun by undesirable (and racialized) Others also fuel the so-called war on migration from the far right. Far-right groups have been long engaged in violence again migrants around the world, including in the US, mainland Europe and Canada. In border frontiers such as Greece, far-right extremism and anti-migrant sentiments have been reaching boiling point, with the island of Lesbos becoming the epicentre for extreme right groups all across the EU (Fallon 2020). However, in a repudiation of the extreme right, the Greek Supreme Court ruled on 7 October 2020 that Golden Dawn, a political party which previously held a minority position in parliament, acted as a criminal organization and found various of its members guilty of murder and assault (BBC 2020). These attacks included multiple assaults on migrants, stoking of xenophobia, inciting hatred and attempted murder. This "criminal organization" designation is the first time since the Nuremberg trials that a political party has been designated as such, sending a strong message globally. However, since this verdict, in Greece, the targeting of people on the move and those working on human rights issues have intensified, including state-sponsored surveillance (Markham and Emmanouilidou 2022).

Fears of uncontrollable migration also require data to operationalize fear-based policies. States have long politicized migration data to justify greater interventions in support of threatened national sovereignty and to bolster xenophobic and anti-migrant narratives (Scheel and Ustek-Spilda 2018). The so-called "Politics of Numbers" show that entities like the EU's border force Frontex and various states overblow the numbers of people crossing borders, inflating statistics and stoking panic around huge groups of people coming to our borders. The Trump Administration also more recently capitalized on these ideas by suggesting that a huge caravan of people was about to arrive, in the same way as the Greek government publicly tweeting and sharing information about a similar caravan which never materialized. But often the reality does not matter – the fear of racialized and unwanted groups is enough to support a burgeoning industry of border technologies.

Technologies impinge on the very definition of "humanness" in the digital era (Zureik and Hindle 2004), which once again breaks down among racial lines. The experiences of people on the move who are racialized bring into sharp relief the importance of utilizing critical analysis to pick apart why these violent technologies are allowed, practised and perpetuated. Borders have long been sites of racial violence. And today, systemic racism and oppression of Black and Brown bodies on the move become the practices which underpin surveillance and automation without meaningful public debate, as an undebatable given when used at the border.

CONCLUSIONS: DIGITAL EXCLUSION IN AN INCREASINGLY DESTABILIZED WORLD

Seventy-seven border walls and counting are now cutting across the landscape of the world. They are both physical and digital, justifying broader surveillance under the guise of detecting illegal migrants and catching terrorists, creating suitable enemies we can all unite against (Fekete 2009). The use of military, or quasi-military, autonomous technology bolsters the connection between immigration and national security. These technological practices have also justified the expansion of other technologies that manage migration. None of these projects and sets of decisions are neutral. All technological choices – choices about what to count, who counts and why – have an inherently political dimension and replicate biases that render certain communities at risk of being harmed, communities that are already under-resourced, discriminated against and vulnerable to the hardening of borders all around the world (for a wider discussion of bias, see Hong, Chapter 8 in this volume; on the politics of AI choices in the public sector: Paul, Carmel and Cobbe, Chapter 1 in this volume; Paul 2022).

At the Polish border, Ibrahim from Syria asks: "How is it possible that on one border you beat people, and yet on the other you give them soup and cookies? Isn't this racist?" Why does Ibrahim have to freeze in the forest between Poland and Belarus while mere hours south the border is open for Ukrainian refugees streaming into the EU? Critiquing the deep systemic racism inherent in this differentiation is not a repudiation of Ukrainians needing to seek safety. Why is migration and refugee protection a zero-sum game? Borders are inherently racist and discriminatory. While we open doors to Ukraine, we must also critique the violence and exclusion which animates border policies all around the world. Solidarity and critique can and must be practised simultaneously.

Once solidarity wanes, it will not be long before this border zone becomes yet another lucrative area for technological experiments, signs of which are already beginning, with Ukraine using the controversial facial recognition firm Clearview AI to uncover Russian assailants, for combat misinformation and to identify the dead (CNBC 2022). Biometrics have also been used in various countries like Moldova along the Ukrainian border to gather data on people crossing over (Ataii 2022). There are always people with rich and complicated lives who are caught in the web of private sector money-making, racist state policies and the weakening of human solidarity. There is big money to be made in the hardening of borders. "Robo-dogs", drones with tazers (Biddle 2021) and border AI lie detectors (Gallagher and Jona 2019) all funnel money into a global and lucrative multi-billion dollar border industrial complex, involving everyone from Israeli surveillance companies (Privacy International 2020) to well-known players like Airbus, Accenture and Thompson Reuters, to single out but a few. (Higgins 2021). Transnational private security companies have made major inroads (Privacy International 2020), with lucrative contracts procured by governments for shiny new tech experiments presented as a way to strengthen border security. Big Tech interests are given free reign to develop and deploy technologies at the border and set the agenda of what counts as innovation and whose perspectives really matter when conversations around borders happen in national, regional and international policy circles. Governments wishing to control mobile populations benefit from these technological experiments.

In a crowded train station in Poland's border town of Przemysl, Yulia, a willowy 18-year old digs her hands out of her pockets to show us: she had her nails done just before the occupation – sky blue with clouds: "They give me hope." There are also other treasures people keep, like Calvin, a 26-year-old medical student from Nigeria who has been studying in Ukraine for six years. He fled his apartment with just a backpack and his medical diploma stuffed inside. Calvin arrived after a harrowing three-day journey, unsure of what comes next. But for Calvin, the hope of return remains: "My keys are still in my pocket."

NOTES

1. A portion of this chapter and ethnographic work appears in Molnar (2024).
2. The choice of terminology throughout this chapter is deliberate. While in law and policy, rigid categories of "refugee", "asylum seeker" and "migrant" are used to create particular narratives, in reality, these categories often elide. As such, wherever possible, this chapter uses the term "people

on the move" or "people crossing borders" to try to expand the terminology that is commonly used when discussing the many complexities inherent in human migration and how migration management technologies are experienced. This more inclusive terminology also highlights that we may all be in one way or another affected by migration management technologies as we cross borders and move across the world. While high-risk applications have the greatest ramifications on communities traditionally marginalized such as refugees and asylum seekers, the ecosystem of migration management technologies affects us all. See also Molnar (2020) and EDRi and Refugee Law Lab, https://edri.org/wp-content/uploads/2020/11/Technological-Testing-Grounds.pdf.

3.   Migration management is a theoretically contested term, yet is widely used in the literature on global governance of migration by various international organizations. For a broad overview of the concept, see Geiger and Pécoud (2012). Migration management has also been widely critiqued by various scholars and linked to broader theories such as biopower (see Mbembe (2003)) and state performativity (Butler (2004)), some of which inform the analysis in this chapter.

4.   See for example Molnar (2019) and Beduschi (2020). UN Special Rapporteur (2021), Molnar (2021), 66–82, at 70, McAuliffe, Blower and Beduschi (2021), Ozkul (2023), Ghezelbash (2022) and others.

5.   See broadly Atak and Simeon (2018).

6.   See for example the work of Macklin (2005), De Genova (2002), Blommaert (2009), Inda (2004), Ahmed (2004) and Appadurai (2006) 49–85. See also Lemberg-Pedersen and Haioty (2020).

7.   Molnar (2019) and Beduschi (2020). See also the work of Amin Parsa, Lund University.

8.   And as early as 2009, various proposed automated surveillance projects such as SECTRONIC and AMASS were being implemented, which have later expanded into member state projects like Greece's HERA project, SIVE, which expands Spain's omnipresence into Gibraltar and North Africa as well as their Seahorse programme (see Statewatch and TNI (2009), at 37 and 39).

9.   This type of deterrence policy is very evident in Greece, Italy and Spain, countries which are on the geographic frontiers of Europe and increasingly rely on violent deterrence and "push back" policies to prevent people from reaching Europe's shores. See for example Statewatch (2017) and EFAD (2020). For example, as recently as 23 October 2020, a consortium of journalists, investigators and researchers revealed that Frontex has been actively complicit in illegal pushbacks in the Aegean, intercepting boats and forcing them into opposing territorial waters instead of facilitating maritime rescue. See Investigation by Bellingcat, Lighthouse Reports, Der Spiegel, ARD Online, Asahi News, the DisInfaux Collective and freelance journalists: Nick Waters, Emmanuel Freudenthal and Logan Williams (Waters et al. 2020).

10.   An often-cited sentiment in migrant justice and border critique, "we are here because you were there" reminds us of colonial and imperial histories which have plundered regions outside of the EU and North America, giving justification to global migration northwards as perhaps an atonement for western imperialism. See for example Patel (2021).

REFERENCES

Agamben, G. (2006). *State of Exception*. Chicago: University of Chicago Press.

Ahmed, S. (2004). 'Affective economies', *Social Text*, **22** (2), 117–39.

Akkerman, M. (2018). 'Expanding the fortress' (The Transnational Institute, 11 May) https://www.tni.org/en/publication/expanding-the-fortress.

Amoore, L (2006). 'Biometric borders: Governing mobilities in the war on terror', *Political Geography*, **25** (3), 336.

Andreas, P. (2009). *Border Games: Policing the U.S.–Mexico Divide*, 2nd edn, Ithaca, NY and London: Cornell University Press.

AP News. (2022). Poland installs monitoring gear on Belarus border wall [Online]. Available at: https://apnews.com/article/technology-poland-migration-belarus-alexander-lukashenko-8ebb2a449d0a3e39 5c571dc13e79daa7 [Accessed 2 Nov. 2023].

Appadurai, A. (2006). *Fear of Small Numbers: An Essay on the Geography of Anger*. Durham, NC: Duke University Press.

Arendt, H. (1994). *Eichmann in Jerusalem: A Report on the Banality of Evil*. New York: Penguin Books.
Ataii, T. (2022). Why is the UN collecting the biometric data of Ukrainian refugees? [Online]. Infosecurity Magazine. Available at: https://www.infosecurity-magazine.com/opinions/un-biometric -data-ukrainian/ [Accessed 3 Nov. 2023].
Atak, I. and Simeon, J. (eds) (2018). *The Criminalization of Migration: Context and Consequences*. Montreal: McGill-Queens University Press.
BBC (2020). Greece Golden Dawn: Neo-Nazi leaders guilty of running crime gang, 7 October [Online]. BBC News. Available at: https://www.bbc.com/news/world-europe-54433396.
Beduschi, A. (2020). 'International migration management in the age of artificial intelligence', *Migration Studies*, **9** (3), September 2021, 576–96, https://doi.org/10.1093/migration/mnaa003.
Biddle, S. (2021). Startup pitched tasing migrants from drones, video reveals [Online]. The Intercept. Available at: https://theintercept.com/2021/12/13/brinc-startup-taser-drones-migrants/ [Accessed 3 Nov. 2023].
Biella, D. (2016). L'accordo Ue-Turchia viola i diritti umani, ci sono le prove, 28 June [Online]. Vita. Available at: http://www.vita.it/it/article/2016/06/28/laccordo-ue-turchia-viola-i-diritti-umani -ci-sono-le-prove/139960/ [accessed 19 Mar. 2020].
Bigo, D. (2008). The globalized security field: The ban-opticon [Online]. Available at: https://www .taylorfrancis.com/chapters/edit/10.4324/9780203926765-7/globalized-security-field-ban-opticon- didier-bigo.
Blommaert, J. (2009). 'Language, asylum, and the national order', *Current Anthropology*, **50** (4), 415.
Butler, J. (2004). *Precarious Life: The Powers of Mourning and Violence*. London: Verso Books.
Butler, J. (2005). *Precarious Life: Powers of Violence and Mourning*. London: Verso Books.
CBC. (2020). COVID-19: Helping the most vulnerable Canadians, technology deployed to fight pandemic, a warning from Italy [Online]. Available at: https://www.cbc.ca/listen/live-radio/1-63-the- current/clip/15765854-covid-19-helping-the-most-vulnerable-canadians-technology-deployed-to -fight-pandemic-a-warning-from-italy.
Cliffe, J. (2020). The rise of the bio-surveillance state [Online]. New Statesman. Available at: https:// www.newstatesman.com/science-tech/2020/03/rise-bio-surveillance-state [Accessed 3 Nov. 2023].
CNBC. (2022). Ukraine has started using Clearview AI's facial recognition during war [Online]. Available at: https://www.cnbc.com/2022/03/13/ukraine-has-started-using-clearview-ais-facial-recog nition-during-war.html.
Cohen, R. (2018). How Viktor Orban bends Hungarian society to his will, 6 April [Online]. The New York Times. Available at: https://www.nytimes.com/2018/04/06/opinion/sunday/orban-hungary -kaczynski-poland.html.
Cox, J. (2020). Surveillance company says it's deploying 'coronavirus-detecting' cameras in US [Online]. Vice. Available at: https://www.vice.com/cn_us/article/cpg8xc/surveillance-company- deploying-coronavirus-detecting-cameras [Accessed 3 Nov. 2023].
Davis, H. (2022). At Poland's borders, Ukrainians are welcomed while refugees from elsewhere face a growing crackdown [Online]. The New Humanitarian. Available at: https://www.thenewhumanitarian .org/news-feature/2022/05/26/Poland-borders-Ukraine-refugees-crackdown.
De Genova, N. (2002). 'Migrant "illegality" and deportability in everyday life', *Annual Review of Anthropology*, **311**, 419.
Deutsche Welle (2014). Well trained, poorly paid – DW – 02/17/2014 [Online]. Available at: https:// www.dw.com/en/study-eastern-europeans-underpaid-in-germany/a-17431961 [Accessed 2 Nov. 2023].
EFAD (2020). Italy [Online]. Available at: https://www.efadrones.org/countries/italy/ [Accessed 23 October 2020].
Fallon, K. (2020). How the Greek island Lesbos became a stage for Europe's far right, 6 May [Online]. Al Jazeera. Available at: https://www.aljazeera.com/features/2020/5/6/how-the-greek-island-lesbos -became-a-stage-for-europes-far-right.
Fallon, K. (n.d.). In Poland's forests, refugees fall gravely ill amid border row [Online]. Al Jazeera. Available at: https://aljazeera.com/news/2021/11/15/in-polands-forests-refugees-fall-gravely-ill-amid -border-row [Accessed 2 Nov. 2023].
Fekete (2009). *A Suitable Enemy: Racism, Migration, and Islamophobia in Europe*. London: Pluto Press.

Foucault, M. (2008). *The Birth of Biopolitics: Lectures at the Collège de France 1978–1979*, Basingstoke, UK: Palgrave Macmillan.

Frontex (2020). Annual report on the implementation of Regulation (EU) 656/2014 of the European Parliament and of the Council of 15 May 2014 establishing rules for the surveillance of the external sea borders in the context of operational cooperation coordinated by Frontex 2018. Available at: https://data.consilium.europa.eu/doc/document/ST-6294-2020-INIT/en/pdf (retrieved 9 March 2020).

Gallagher, R. and Jona, L. (2019). We tested Europe's new lie detector for travelers – and immediately triggered a false positive [Online]. The Intercept. Available at: https://theintercept.com/2019/07/26/europe-border-control-ai-lie-detector/.

Geiger, M. and Pécoud, A. (2012). 'The politics of international migration management', in M. Geiger and A. Pécoud (eds), *The Politics of International Migration Management*. Basingstoke, UK: Palgrave Macmillan, pp. 1–20.

Ghezelbash, D. (2022). 'Technology and countersurveillance: Holding governments accountable for refugee externalization policies', *Globalizations*, https://papers.ssrn.com/sol3/papers.cfm?abstract_id=4420423.

Greenfield, C. (2020). As governments build advanced surveillance systems to push borders out, will travel and migration become unequal for some groups?, Migration Policy Institute, available at https://www.migrationpolicy.org/article/governments-build-advanced-surveillance-systems.

Herrera, J. (2019). Studies show fears about migration and disease are unfounded [Online]. Pacific Standard. Available at: https://psmag.com/news/studies-show-fears-about-migration-and-disease-are-unfounded.

Higgins, M. (2021). How the $68 billion border surveillance industrial complex affects us all, 11 June [Online]. Vice. Available at: https://www.vice.com/en/article/k7873m/how-the-dollar68-billion-border-surveillance-industrial-complex-affects-us-all.

Human Rights Watch (2006). Stemming the flow: Abuses against migrants, asylum seekers and refugees. Available at: https://www.hrw.org/reports/2006/libya0906/libya0906webwcover.pdf (retrieved 9 March 2020).

Inda, J. (2004). *Targeting Immigrants: Government, Technology, and Ethics*. Oxford: Blackwell.

IOM, Terrorism and Migration (IOM) (2010). https://www.iom.int/jahia/webdav/shared/shared/mainsite/activities/tcm/international_terrorism_and_migration.pdf.

Kainz, L. (2016). Posts from February 2016 [Online]. Available at: https://www.law.ox.ac.uk/research-subject-groups/centre-criminology/centreborder-criminologies/blog/2016/02/people-can%E2%80%99t.

Khatib, L. (2020). COVID-19 impact on refugees is also political, 31 March [Online]. Chatham House. Available at: https://www.chathamhouse.org/expert/comment/covid-19-impact-refugees-also-political.

Lemberg-Pedersen, M. and Haioty, E. (2020). Re-assembling the surveillable refugee body in the era of data-craving (Taylor & Francis Online, 5 July). https://www.tandfonline.com/doi/full/10.1080/13621025.2020.1784641.

Loewenstein, A. (2023). *The Palestine Laboratory: How Israel Exports the Technology of Occupation Around the World*, London and New York: Verso.

Macklin, A. (2005). 'Disappearing refugees', *Columbia Human Rights Law Review*, **36** (2), 101.

Markham, L. and Emmanouilidou, L. (2022). How free is the press in the birthplace of democracy?, 26 November [Online]. The New York Times. Available at: https://www.nytimes.com/2022/11/26/business/greece-journalists-surveillance-predator.html.

Mbembe, A. (2003). 'Necropolitics', *Public Culture*, **15** (1), 11–40.

McAuliffe, M., Blower, J. and Beduschi, A. (2021). 'Digitalization and artificial intelligence in migration and mobility: Transnational implications of the COVID-19 pandemic', *Societies*, **11** (4), 135.

Médecins Sans Frontières (MSF) International (2020). Coronavirus COVID-19 is excuse to keep people on Greek islands locked up [Online]. MSF Available at: https://www.msf.org/covid-19-excuse-keep-people-greek-islands-locked.

Michael, M., Hinnant, L. and Britto, R. (2019). 'Making misery pay: Libya militias take EU funds for migrants', AP News. Available at: https://apnews.com/article/9d9e8d668ae4b73a336a636a86bdf27f (retrieved 7 March 2021).

MIT Technology Review (2021). The US left Afghanistan with the world's biggest biometric database [Online]. Available at: https://www.technologyreview.com/2021/08/30/1033941/afghanistan-biometric-databases-us-military-40-data-points/.

Molnar, P. (2019). 'Technology on the margins: AI and global migration management from a human rights perspective', *Cambridge Journal of International Law*, **8** (2), 305–30.

Molnar, P. (2020). Technological testing grounds: Migration management experiments from the ground up, EDRi and Refugee Law Lab, https://edri.org/wp-content/uploads/2020/11/Technological-Testing-Grounds.pdf.

Molnar, P. (2021). 'Surveillance sovereignty: Migration management technologies and the politics of privatization', in A. Itak and G. Hudson (eds), *Migration, Security, and Resistance: Global and Local Perspectives*. London: Routledge, pp. 66–82.

Molnar, P. (2024). *The Walls Have Eyes: Surviving Migration in the Age of Artificial Intelligence*. New York: The New Press.

Molnar P. and Naranjo, D. (2020). Surveillance won't stop the coronavirus (The New York Times, 15 April) https://www.nytimes.com/2020/04/15/opinion/coronavirus-surveillance-privacy-rights.html.

OHCHR (n.d.). Ukraine: UN expert condemns racist threats, xenophobia at border [Online]. Available at: https://www.ohchr.org/en/press-releases/2022/03/ukraine-un-expert-condemns-racist-threats-xenophobia-border.

Ozkul, D. (2023). 'Automating immigration and asylum: New technologies in migration and asylum governance in Europe', Oxford: Refugee Studies Centre, and AFAR.

Patel, I. S. (2021). *We're Here Because You Were There: Immigration and the End of Empire*. London and New York: Verso.

Paul, R. (2022). 'Can critical policy studies outsmart AI? Research agenda on artificial intelligence technologies and public policy', *Critical Policy Studies*, **16** (4), 497–509.

POLITICO (2021). Poland's persistent forbidden zone on the border with Belarus [Online]. Available at: https://www.politico.eu/article/polands-persistent-forbidden-zone-on-the-border-with-belarus/ [Accessed 21 Feb. 2022].

POLITICO (2022). MEPs blast Brussels inaction on Poland's 'fence of shame' in protected forest [Online]. Available at: https://www.politico.eu/article/meps-blast-brussels-inaction-on-polands-wall-of-shame-in-protected-forest/.

Popoviciu, A. (2022). Ukraine's Roma refugees recount discrimination en route to safety, 7 March [Online]. Al Jazeera. Available at: https://www.aljazeera.com/news/2022/3/7/ukraines-roma-refugees-recount-discrimination-on-route-to-safety.

PR Newswire (2020). Smart borders, immigration enforcement & border security markets in Europe 2017–2022, 4 April [Online]. PR Newswire. Available at: https://www.prnewswire.com/news-releases/smart-borders-immigration-enforcement--border-security-markets-in-europe-2017-2022-300434690.html.

Privacy International (2020). Challenging the drivers of surveillance, https://privacyinternational.org/challenging-drivers-surveillance [Accessed 13 May 2020].

Reuters (2021). Poland seeks to bolster border with new tech amid migrant influx, 4 May [Online]. Reuters. Available at: https://www.reuters.com/world/europe/poland-seeks-bolster-border-with-new-tech-amid-migrant-influx-2021-10-04/ [Accessed 2 Nov. 2023].

Rodrigo, C. M. (2018). Trump: Border wall needed to stop 'tremendous medical problem' coming into US [Online]. The Hill. Available at: https://thehill.com/homenews/administration/420870-trump-border-wall-needed-to-stop-tremendous-medical-problem-coming [Accessed 3 Nov. 2023].

Romm, T. (2020). White House asks Silicon Valley for help to combat coronavirus, track its spread and stop misinformation [Online]. Washington Post. Available at: https://www.washingtonpost.com/technology/2020/03/11/white-house-tech-meeting-coronavirus/ [Accessed 3 Nov. 2023].

Scheel, S. and Ustek-Spilda, F. (2018). Why big data cannot fix migration statistics, 5 June [Online]. News Deeply. Available at: https://www.newsdeeply.com/refugees/community/2018/06/05/why-big-data-cannot-fix-migration-statistics [Accessed 3 Nov. 2023].

Sparke, M. (2006) 'A neoliberal nexus: Economy, security, and the biopolitics of citizenship on the border', *Political Geography*, **25** (2), 151.

Statewatch (2017). EU-Spain: New report provides an 'x-ray' of the public funding and private companies in Spain's 'migration control industry', 23 November [Online]. Available at: https://www

.statewatch.org/news/2017/november/eu-spain-new-report-provides-an-x-ray-of-the-public-funding-and-private-companies-in-spain-s-migration-control-industry/.

Statewatch and TNI (2009). NeoConOpticon: The EU security industrial complex [Online]. Available at: https://www.tni.org/en/publication/neoconopticon.

The Intercept (2021). How the US built the Taliban's war chest and left biometrics data behind [Online]. Available at: https://theintercept.com/2021/08/17/afghanistan-taliban-military-biometrics/.

The New Humanitarian (2022a). The human toll of war [Online]. Available at: https://www.thenewhumanitarian.org/opinion/2022/02/28/human-toll-war [Accessed 2 Nov. 2023].

The New Humanitarian (2022b). Why did we have to freeze in the forest? [Online]. Available at: https://www.thenewhumanitarian.org/first-person/2022/03/15/ukraine-poland-syria-refugee-welcome-forest.

The World from PRX (2019). For centuries, migrants have been said to pose public health risks. They don't [Online]. Available at: https://www.pri.org/stories/2019-05-23/centuries-migrants-have-been-said-pose-public-health-risks-they-don-t.

Times of Israel (2015). Hungary, Bulgaria ask Israel about barrier to keep out migrants [Online]. www.timesofisrael.com. Available at: https://www.timesofisrael.com/hungary-bulgaria-ask-israel-about-barrier-to-keep-out-migrants/ [Accessed 2 Nov. 2023].

TNI (2018). Expanding the fortress: the policies, the profiteers and the people shaped by EU's border externalization [Online]. Available at: https://www.tni.org/en/publication/expanding-the-fortress.

TNI (2021). Smoking guns: How European arms exports are forcing millions from their homes [Online]. Available at https://www.tni.org/en/publication/smoking-guns.

UN Special Rapporteur (2021). 'Racial and xenophobic discrimination and the use of digital technologies in border and immigration enforcement: Report of the Special Rapporteur on contemporary forms of racism, racial discrimination, xenophobia and related intolerance, E. Tendayi Achiume' A/HRC/48/76 (22 September).

Walia, H. (2020). *Border and Rule*. New York: Haymarket.

Waters, N., Freudenthal, E. and Williams, L. (2020). Frontex at fault: European border force complicit in 'illegal' pushbacks, 23 October [Online]. Bellingcat. Available at: https://www.bellingcat.com/news/2020/10/23/frontex-at-fault-european-border-force-complicit-in-illegal-pushbacks.

Wintour, P. (2018). UN accuses Libyan linked to EU-funded coastguard of people trafficking', 8 June [Online]. The Guardian. Available at: https://www.theguardian.com/world/2018/jun/08/un-accuses-libyan-linked-to-eu-funded-coastguard-of-people-trafficking.

ZEIT (2022). Suddenly hospitable: Refugees in Hungary. Available at: https://www.zeit.de/politik/ausland/2022-03/gefluechtete-ungarn-ukraine-krieg-aufnahme [Accessed 2 Nov. 2023].

Zureik, E. and Hindle, K. (2004). 'Governance, security and technology: The case of biometrics', *Studies in Political Economy*, **73**, 113.

24. Critical appraisal of large language models in judicial decision-making

Juan David Gutiérrez

INTRODUCTION[1]

In a radio interview, a judge from Colombia who used ChatGPT to write almost 30 per cent of a ruling that dealt with the fundamental rights of a minor claimed that "the drafting of texts through artificial intelligence is welcome, because (…) the tool will do it in an organized, simple and structured manner, and this could improve response times in the judicial branch". The radio interview was held on 2 February 2023, hence the judge was a very early adopter of large language models (LLMs) as means for supporting the drafting of rulings.

The Colombian judge's quote echoes a key element of the techno-solutionist discourse that is used by the different stakeholders around the globe to justify the use of artificial intelligence (AI) by the judiciary: the need to relieve judicial congestion by finding ways to (semi)automate human activities to speed decisions (for this more general argument in the public sector see: Paul, Carmel and Cobbe, Chapter 1 in this volume). More specifically, these narratives promote the use of LLMs to generate synthetic text that supports judicial decision-making, including the process of drafting rulings.

However, LLMs should not be considered as a source of trustworthy information and users should not expect "truth" from these systems. As explained in this chapter, the output generated by these models can be inaccurate and biased. LLMs are systems trained with massive datasets with the aim of "predicting the likelihood of a token (character, word or string) given either its preceding context or … its surrounding context" (Bender et al. 2021: 611). Bender et al. describe LLMs as "stochastic parrots" because this type of language model stitches "together sequences of linguistic forms it has observed in its vast training data, according to probabilistic information about how they combine, but without any reference to meaning" (2021: 616).

While the use of certain AI tools may contribute to improving the efficiency of certain judicial activities and complement the work of judicial operators, as other digital technologies already do, the use of LLMs in judicial decision-making carries risks at a social, organizational, and individual level (Flórez Rojas 2021; Flórez Rojas et al. 2022; Gutiérrez and Flórez 2023). The risks include the violation of different fundamental rights, such as the right to due process, fair trial, access to justice, personal data protection and privacy, and non-discrimination, among others (Gutiérrez 2020, 2023a, 2023b, 2023c; Gutiérrez and Flórez 2023).

LLMs can be particularly risky, when compared to other AI systems, due to two main reasons. First, most LLMs are available through freemium models that provide basic access free of charge. Hence any judicial operator with internet access can use these technologies for professional purposes. The widespread access of LLMs contrasts with the lack of training, guidance and rules offered by the bodies that govern the judiciary to their judicial operators. Second, judicial congestion and the burdens faced by judicial operators can make these tools very attractive for automating core tasks while being unaware of the LLM's flaws (privacy and cybersecurity issues), limitations (inaccurate outputs), and risks (biased outputs).

The main objective of this chapter is to provide an account of how judiciaries around the world, but especially in Latin America, have used LLMs to draft rulings and/or take decisions during court hearings and to problematize such uses by judges and their clerks and how they have justified these applications. The chapter argues that current LLMs cannot be regarded as trustworthy sources of information even if their capacity to produce language outputs mimics human ones in often seemingly convincing ways. LLMs should hence only be used – with the utmost care – when other more effective and safe options for judicial decision-making are not available. Moreover, the chapter contends that the judiciary should promote digital literacy and an informed, transparent, ethical, and responsible use of AI tools, to reap its potential benefits and prevent risks.

This chapter is divided in four sections. The first section briefly overviews how different types of AI systems are being used by the judiciary and what makes LLMs a special case in wider discussions of such AI uses in the field. The second documents in detail how judges in Latin America used LLMs to draft part of their written rulings and to support decisions in court hearings. This thirdly leads to a reflection on the risks associated with the illustrated uses of LLMs by the judiciary. The chapter closes with a discussion on the implications for critically minded research on state uses of AI and how they may be regulated.

HOW JUDGES USE AI IN GENERAL AND LLMS IN PARTICULAR

While courts in European states are gradually exploring the implementation of AI systems (Terzidou 2022; also see Mark, McInerney and Morison, Chapter 25 in this volume), in other areas of the world their adoption appears to advance at a faster pace and has a broader scope. In Latin America, for example, since September 2017, the Prosecutor's Office of Buenos Aires, Argentina, adopted an AI system called "Prometea" that has two main functionalities: (i) to facilitate the search and classification of documents that may be relevant to draft an opinion and, in general, support case management; and (ii) to produce draft opinions (Saavedra and Upegui 2021).

Furthermore, in Colombia, Gutiérrez and Muñoz-Cadena (2023) found that at least 18 per cent of the automated decision-making systems adopted or piloted by the state were used by different organizations of the judicial sector, including courts, the general prosecutor's office, administrative agencies with judicial functions, and the state's judicial defence agency. The tools mapped in Colombia included systems that aimed to facilitate the search and classification of legal documents, chatbots that provided information about case law, and systems that aimed at predicting judicial outcomes, among others (Gutiérrez et al. 2023).

Additionally, Shi et al. (2021) reported that China had planned to establish a "smart court" since 2016 and that since then different AI initiatives have been implemented, such as systems that facilitate the search of case law and drafting judgments. They also noted that these developments were not devoid of concerns, particularly "issues linked to automated judgments, digital divide issues, judicial independence, as well as concerns linked to privacy and data protection" (Shi et al. 2021: 19).[2]

A broad range of automated and semi-automated decision-making systems are being tested or implemented by judicial operators that can be used in different stages of the life cycle of a judicial procedure, including pre-trial, hearing, and post-sentencing proceedings (Terzidou 2022). In October 2023, the European Commission for the Efficiency of Justice (CEPEJ) mapped 92 AI systems and other "cyberjustice tools" used by judicial operators in Europe, the United States, Australia, and Latin America. Four types of tools represented 85 per cent of the systems that were mapped: case management tools that automated certain activities (e.g. assigning levels of priority to tasks); tools to support search of case law or to process electronic documents; tools that partially or fully automate decision-making processes (e.g. tools that aim at analysing recidivism); and, natural language processing systems which include speech to text conversion and chatbots like ChatGPT (CEPEJ 2023). The dataset of CEPEJ also includes systems that aim at "predicting" litigation outcomes and anonymization tools that remove personal data included in the texts of the judicial files.[3]

While some of these tools may not classify as AI systems, because some seem to be powered by rules-based algorithms, the use of these types of tools by judicial operators may have significant implications for the parties in any given court case, third parties, and the public in general (Gutiérrez 2020; Gutiérrez and Muñoz-Cadena 2023). For example, Terzidou, who assessed the implications of implementing AI systems "for the automation of judicial administration under the right to a fair trial", warned that "[c]ertain AI algorithms may impede access to courts, as is the case with predictive justice algorithms enabling the prediction of the outcome of a case based on the analysis of previous case law" (2022: 159). Furthermore, she highlighted that outsourcing the development of AI systems "may interfere with judges' independence since companies are profit driven and want to deliver efficient algorithmic systems that can perform the task determined by their clients, without necessarily embedding values like fairness" (Terzidou 2022: 161). These clashes of public values and purposes with profit-orientation in the development and deployment of AI technologies are also discussed for other use cases in this *Handbook* (this volume: Kaufmann, Chapter 22 on policing; Antenucci and Meissner, Chapter 31 on urban planning; Pot and Prainsack, Chapter 30 on healthcare; Whitfield, Wright and Hamblin, Chapter 28 on social care).

Additionally, Terzidou also argued that the impartiality of justices could also be compromised by AI systems' potential pre-existing bias (e.g. societal biases that are immanent in the data with which the algorithms were trained), technical bias (e.g. computation limitations due to unbalanced datasets, biased models), and emergent bias ("when the algorithm embeds values that become redundant by the time it is used") (2022: 161) (on policy discussions around bias cf. Hong, Chapter 8 in this volume).

Terzidou (2022) also pointed out that certain AI systems used in the context of criminal cases, such as those which aim to calculate the probability of recidivism, would diminish the principle of "equality of arms" and "fair balance", since defendants would not be able effectively to challenge judges' decisions due to the opacity of the algorithms (on wider issues with accountability in AI-driven public decision-making: Cobbe and Singh, Chapter 7 in this volume). The opaqueness of these algorithms may be the result of the type of technique used to develop it (e.g. machine learning), but also the proprietary rights and confidentiality agreements that may protect the computer code from being disclosed (Gutiérrez 2020).

The launch of ChatGPT by OpenAI in November 2022 triggered a new phase in the use of AI technologies by the judiciaries. Although by 2022 the LLMs were not a new technology (Bender et al. 2021), the novelty was that the *freemium* business model that OpenAI implemented placed the technology in the hands of anyone who had an internet connection and who registered in its platform. During 2023, other chatbots became available such as Microsoft's

Bing (now called *Copilot*), Google's *Bard* (now called *Gemini*), Anthropic's *Claude* and Meta's *Llama*, among others. In practice, lay users access LLMs through these chatbots by entering text to obtain a string of natural language text as an output. Current models are available at myriad online platforms and applications and allow users to produce strings of paragraphs through their prompts.

Hence, since late 2022, judges and their staff all over the world have been able to use LLMs on their own and have not had to depend on the governing bodies of the judicial system to obtains licences to access an AI system developed through natural language processing and deep learning. Meanwhile the governing bodies of the judiciary have been slow to produce guidelines or rules on how judges may (or may not) use these systems.[4]

ILLUSTRATIONS OF CHATGPT USES IN THE JUDICIARY IN LATIN AMERICA

This section describes cases of Latin American judges and magistrates from Argentina, Bolivia, Brazil, Colombia, Mexico, and Peru that used ChatGPT to support decision-making processes.[5] However, it is worth mentioning that similar cases have emerged in other countries of the Global South, including India – in a criminal trial in the Chandigarh High Court – and Pakistan – a criminal case that involved a minor and a civil law case (Tamim 2023). Additionally, news outlets from Singapore have reported that "courts are testing the use of generative AI in the small claims tribunal first – which sees about 10,000 cases a year – with an eye to expanding it to other areas such as divorce maintenance and civil claims" (Lam 2023). Finally, there are also known cases from Global North countries, for example, a British Court of Appeal judge claimed that he used ChatGPT to write a judgment on intellectual property law (Corfield 2023).[6]

Use of LLMs to Draft Rulings

Latin American judges have submitted legal and technical questions to chatbots powered by LLMs and used the answers to draft their judicial decisions. Judges have also used LLMs to summarize the main conclusions of their rulings in clear and accessible language. This section portrays these types of uses in constitutional, administrative, criminal, and family law cases in Brazil, Colombia, Peru, and Argentina. A critical evaluation of the described use cases is discussed in a later section of the chapter.

On 31 January 2023, Judge Juan Manuel Padilla García issued a seven-page ruling on a case in which the fundamental right to health of a child, diagnosed as being on the autism spectrum, was at stake (Padilla García 2023). It was a relatively simple second instance case decided by a judge in Cartagena, Colombia, in which the key legal question was whether a health insurance company's request for co-payments or a fee for authorizing a medical procedure infringed on the child's fundamental rights to health and dignified life. Judge Padilla upheld the first instance ruling that favoured the child.

The ruling would have been one of thousands of health-related judicial decisions adopted in Colombia every year, but for the fact that the judge decided to transcribe his interactions with ChatGPT, which he had used to come to his verdict. In a matter of hours, the ruling made its way into the Colombian national media and has now been registered by media outlets all over the world.[7]

Only ten days later, magistrate María Victoria Quiñones from the Administrative Tribunal of the Magdalen, also in Colombia, similarly issued a court order in which ChatGPT prompts were also transcribed (Quiñones Triana 2023). The interactions of magistrate Quiñones with the chatbot aimed to answer technical questions that helped her to decide on how to carry out a judicial hearing in a metaverse. The metaverses are "immersive three-dimensional virtual worlds (VWs) in which people interact as avatars with each other and with software agents, using the metaphor of the real world but without its physical limitations" (Mitchell et al. 2009: 91). The judicial process concerns a direct remedy claim (*reparación directa*) requested by a contractor of Colombia's National Police. On 15 February, the hearing was held through Meta's *Horizon Workrooms* and was livestreamed through the magistrate's personal *YouTube* channel (Audiencia Inicial en el Metaverso 2023).

The texts of the ruling and court order issued by the Colombian judges were not a simple copy/paste of the queries introduced to ChatGPT and the chatbot's answers. On the one hand, the decision of Judge Padilla succinctly explained the facts of the case, described the logic of the first instance decision, stated the main constitutional issues at stake, listed the relevant articles of the Colombian Constitution, and cited a ruling of the Constitutional Court that addressed a very similar case.[8] On the other hand, the court order of magistrate Quiñones explained that the parties agreed to carry out the initial hearing of the administrative procedure in the metaverse, cited legal provisions and case law that justified the use of information technologies in judicial procedures, and explained what the metaverse is and how the hearing would be conducted.

In the two Colombian cases, the answers of ChatGPT were not incidental but determinant for the decisions adopted by the courts. In Judge Padilla's ruling, two of the seven pages consisted of a transcription of four ChatGPT's responses to prompts. This means that about 29 per cent of the ruling consists of text generated by ChatGPT. Hence, although the answers of ChatGPT were not the sole legal basis of the ruling, they were a key component of the decision. Moreover, the four questions posed by the judge to ChatGPT dealt with key legal issues required to decide the case:

1. Is an autistic child exempt from co-payments for therapy?
2. Should tutela [constitutional] actions in these cases be granted?
3. Is requiring a co-payment in these cases a barrier to access to health services?
4. Has the jurisprudence of the Constitutional Court made favourable decisions in similar cases?

Hence, Judge Padilla prompted ChatGPT to address core legal questions that are very specific to the Colombian legal system.

In the case of magistrate Quiñones' court order, the questions dealt with issues that were not substantive for the cause of action. The three questions aimed at supporting procedural decisions required to carry out the hearing in the metaverse:

1. What is an avatar?
2. What is the most effective method to verify the authenticity of those connecting to a meeting and/or virtual hearing.
3. Method for verifying the authenticity of the avatar in the metaverse?

Although these questions appear to be merely technical, they deal with how the magistrate makes sure that the people who participate in the hearing legitimately represent the parties, a matter that is essential for ensuring access to justice and due process. The statements included in the court order illustrate the point: "Thus, for a better understanding of some concepts about the metaverse and the administration of the hearing in this environment, this judicial agency will rely on AI, using ChatGPT."[9]

In the Peruvian case, the use of ChatGPT appeared to be very limited (Flores García 2023). A Specialized Judge of the Transitory Civil Court of San Juan de Miraflores, of the Judicial District of South Lima, decided a second instance case related to the determination of the child support obligations that a mother and a father had with respect to their daughter, who was born in December 2021. The judge "invoked" ChatGPT in the motivation section of the ruling, in which he had to calculate the value of the child support obligation that corresponded to the father and the mother in proportion to their "economic possibilities and personal conditions". In the eleventh recital, the judge reported that:

> through the assistance of the Artificial Intelligence platform of Open AI – Chat GTP[1] [*sic*], it is appropriate to apply the technique of mathematical proportion, in order of establishing what is the contribution that corresponds to each parent, according to their income, to meet the living expenses of their daughter. (Flores García 2023)

In other words, the judge apparently consulted on what mathematical operation was required to calculate the proportion of child support that each parent should assume according to his and her capacity. At this point it is worth adding that the judge was not entirely transparent about how he used the system because he did not reveal the prompt or prompts he used, nor the answer(s) he received from the system. We also do not know if he prompted ChatGPT to do the calculation directly.

The Peruvian judge has not been the only justice who has used LLMs to obtain answers that require arithmetic operations. In a ruling issued on 3 April 2024, the Superior Tribunal of the Judicial District of Pereira in Colombia included ChatGPT's answer to the following question: "The presence of 20 milligrams per 100 millilitres of ethanol in the blood is equivalent to how many glasses of wine, aguardiente, rum or beer?". This second instance ruling decided a criminal case where a pedestrian had been killed by a motorcyclist while crossing the road at midnight. The first instance ruling had concluded that the victim's attempt to cross the road was impaired by alcohol consumption. The Superior Tribunal needed to determine the effects of certain levels of ethanol found in the blood of the pedestrian because the first instance ruling claimed that the victim's death was her fault even though the motorcyclist had exceeded the speed limit. After copy-pasting ChatGPT's answer in the ruling, the Superior Tribunal concluded that there was "no doubt that the percentage of ethanol that the victim had in her blood could not be classified as significant or relevant enough to be able to conclude that it had a negative impact on her cognitive, motor and sensory functions" (Yarzagaray, 2024: 24).[10]

In Argentina, a Justice of the Peace exemplified a different use case of LLMs: to transform text that may be complex for lay persons into a text that is more accessible. On 14 June 2023, Judge José Osvaldo Ledesma decided a family law case in which the main arguments of the ruling were summarized with the support of an LLM. The final pages of the judgment included a section titled "The judgement in easy reading" followed by the following statement "I am going to explain to you, in easy words, this sentence" (Ledesma 2023: 8). The 150-word synthesis of the judge's arguments was printed in bold letters and appeared just before the verdict.

The nine-page ruling did not explain how the summary was prepared, but a press release issued by the Judicial Power of the province of Corrientes informed that Judge Ledesma had used ChatGPT, using the following prompt: "Summarize in simple and easy language, in one paragraph, the following text in quotation marks" (Dirección de Prensa 2023). Then, according to the press release, the judge copy-pasted the legal motivations that he had previously drafted to complement his prompt.

In a radio interview, Judge Ledesma explained that he did not transcribe the exact output produced by ChatGPT, but that he inserted the synthetic text in the ruling with minor edits (Mucho Humo 2023). In the radio interview, the judge argued that rulings written with "clear language" and that are "easy to read" would help people "with some vulnerability factor and/or with a very low education level" to understand the decisions. In the specific case of the ruling where he used ChatGPT to synthesize the reasons for his decision – to deny the request – the judge also highlighted that the petitioner had not been represented by a lawyer. Judge Ledesma claimed that the LLM's output "condensed the nine pages of the ruling into one paragraph that could be understood by a person with a very limited level of education".

Finally, a recent case in Brazil depicts the risk that judges include false information in their rulings due to copy-pasting answers generated by LLMs without checking their veracity. In late 2023, the National Council of Justice announced that a judge would be investigated due to a ruling that cited non-existent jurisprudence. According to press reports, the investigated judge stated that "the case was a 'mere mistake' due to work overload and that part of the ruling was drafted by a subordinate" (Consultor Jurídico 2023). Due to this case, the Federal Regional Court of the 1st Region issued a circular letter recommending justices "not to use open generative AI tools to search for jurisprudential precedents that the Judiciary's control bodies have not approved" (Guedes 2023: 2).

Use of LLMs during Court Hearings

Magistrates have also consulted LLMs during hearings to support their arguments about factual issues and have used these technologies to inquire about legal questions. This section illustrates such uses by documenting two cases of Mexico and Bolivia that involved judicial procedures about electoral and constitutional issues. A critical appraisal of these use cases is discussed in the next section of the chapter.

At the hearing of the SUP-JE-21/2023 process, held on 29 March 2023, Magistrate Reyes Rodríguez Mondragón, president of the Superior Chamber of the Electoral Tribunal of the Mexican Judiciary, indicated that he had consulted ChatGPT on his phone (TEPJF 2023). He read some of the outputs that he obtained from the chatbot to illustrate how a ruling could be easily motivated with the help of ChatGPT.

Before explaining how ChatGPT was used by the magistrate and the discussion that ensued in the tribunal, it is pertinent to provide the context of the case. In this process, the Electoral tribunal had to decide about an appeal filed against a first judgment that dealt with the use of the expression "you know who" (in Spanish, "ya sabes quién") as part of the electoral pre-campaign advertisements of the Morena party in the State of Mexico (López Ponce 2023). The legal question addressed by the Electoral Tribunal was whether the use of the expression could generate a situation of imbalance in the pre-campaign, since it could be interpreted as a signal of support by President Andrés Manuel López Obrador.

In the hearing in which the first instance ruling of the local electoral court was examined, Judge Rodríguez Mondragón argued that the judgment should be revoked since it did not include a contextual analysis of the use of the expression "you know who" and, therefore, there was a legal defect due to lack of completeness.

To illustrate how a ruling could be motivated, Justice Rodríguez Mondragón stated the following:

> For example, here on the cell phone, I have been making consultations to PT Chat [*sic*] […] if you know who "you know who" is and the answer is that in the Mexican political context it is the president […] they refer to President Andrés Manuel López Obrador and it gives us an explanation that this reference was popularized in 2018 in the campaign.

The magistrate did not stop there. He made additional queries to ChatGPT which he referenced during the hearing:

> I also asked PT Chat [*sic*] … who was referred to as the "unnamable" or 'the one who is not named', and it answers that to Voldemort in the Harry Potter series. […] I think that if I also use the same paragraphs, I could ask whether this is an act in anticipation of a campaign or pre-campaign and it provides an explanation, that is, if the artificial intelligence gives us an explanation of context with motivations, this is what is expected from a court that reasons about the expressions that are analysed.

Then the magistrate continued his argument that the courts of first instance should offer arguments and reasons to justify their rulings and insisted on his comparison between ChatGPT's supposed ability to reason. The magistrate ended with an implicit invitation to use systems such as ChatGPT to draft judicial rulings:

> […] the Electoral Tribunal of the State of Mexico reiteratively is not complying with the principle and duty of exhaustiveness … it is not providing sufficient reasons … when even technology now facilitates a series of information, obviously processing databases and all the knowledge that is available to the courts.

Afterwards, Justice José Luis Vargas took the floor to criticize the way in which his colleague proposed that judges use tools such as ChatGPT:

> I would like to think that what you have just told us is simply an isolated example and is not a forecast of what will be the jurisprudence of this court … because I would be concerned that now our resolutions will be taken based on what ChatGPT says.

Then Justice Vargas expressed his concern about what role the courts would have if in the future ChatGPT were to define cases from start to finish, arguing that this type of system "still has quite a few errors" and that "that is the reason why I think we human beings will be in charge of this kind of positions for a good while".

Finally, in the Bolivian case, two magistrates of a tribunal consulted ChatGPT at the intermission of a court hearing, just before they announced their decision against three journalists. According to press reports, the trial dealt with a case of "a victim of [domestic] violence who decided to retract her complaint against a former government official and accused the journalists of violation of privacy" (Página Siete 2023). The journalists were accused of violating the privacy of the woman who, according to the defendants, had sent them pictures of herself with bruises allegedly produced by her partner and had consented to publish the photos (Erbol 2023).

According to one of the defendants, after the intermission, the magistrates announced "that they were going to make history by consulting an Artificial Intelligence about the sanctions" that the tribunal should impose (Página Siete 2023). The hearing took place through an online platform and the magistrates shared their screen to show the answers provided by ChatGPT about the legal issues consulted by the magistrates (Erbol 2023; Los Tiempos Digital 2023; Página Siete 2023). The magistrates prompted ChatGPT to answer questions such as the following:

> What is the legitimate public interest in case of disclosure of photos of a woman's body parts on social networks such as Facebook, by the media and without the consent and/or authorization of the woman?
> In case there is no consent for the publication of images, videos and photos of parts of a woman's body by the social networks Facebook, could the possibility of ordering the deletion or removal of the same by the tribunal be considered as a violation of the right to information?

In a press conference after the court hearing, two of the magistrates explained and justified how they used ChatGPT to decide the case. First, Judge Jimmy López compared the process of developing new pharmaceuticals, in which the drugs are first tested on animals and then they are tested in humans, with the way the tribunal tested ChatGPT. Judge López declared: "Did we first try it internally [the chatbot]? Yes. How we tested it later? With you" (El Deber 2023). Then, Judge Diego Ramírez claimed that in other countries of Latin America judges had used LLMs to decide cases and that they could not "ignore what is happening in other countries". Furthermore he claimed that *Prometea*, the system used by the Prosecutor's Office of Buenos Aires, had "incremented the automation of repetitive works, that [such systems] optimized the time spent [to draft legal documents]" (El Deber 2023).

RISKS ASSOCIATED WITH TECHNO-SOLUTIONIST APPROACHES TO THE USE OF LLMS IN THE JUDICIARY

The last two subsections of the chapter aimed at describing how judges from different countries of Latin America have used LLMs to draft decisions and support decision-making processes without assessing the implications of such uses. This subsection addresses the risks and potential harms associated with most of the uses described above.

It is a cause for concern that most of the judges used ChatGPT's answers to motivate their decisions without thoroughly examining whether the information was correct. Given the way in which some of the judges used LLMs it seems that they were unaware that these technologies are not a reliable source of information about legal, technical, or factual issues. For example, Judge Juan Manuel Padilla, from Colombia, claimed in a radio interview that "what ChatGPT does is to help us choose the best of these texts from the Internet and compile them in a very logical and very short way to what we need" (León 2023).

Moreover, some of the judges described in this chapter seemed to assume that LLMs can perform tasks that are beyond the capacity of this type of system. For example, Judge Juan Manuel Padilla claimed in a radio interview that ChatGPT could be used to anticipate how a judge would rule (León 2023).

Moreover, there is a risk that the judges and their clerks become over-reliant on the AI's recommendations, incurring what is known as "automation bias". As explained by Flórez Rojas (2023a), "(d)ue to an overconfidence in the impartiality or certainty of the AI system, such as ChatGPT, judges may be hindered in their ability to make exact judgments and understand their surroundings. This could lead to an over-reliance on the outputs of automated systems." Justice José Luis Vargas, from the Electoral Tribunal of the State of Mexico, is right to be concerned about the risk of judicial officers relying on ChatGPT to determine legal, technical, and factual questions. The tool may be useful to explore topics, but it is not suitable to use its answers to motivate rulings without a detailed verification of each sentence included in the synthetic text generated by the system.

Automated or semi-automated decision systems used by states to perform their public functions should always be subject to close human scrutiny and control. This is especially important in the context of judicial functions, as certain uses of some AI tools may have negative consequences for the fundamental rights of the parties to the proceedings, and of third parties. Hence, the argument is not that ChatGPT or other LLMs should not be used for supporting judicial work. The point is that any content produced by these systems, which is meant to be used directly or indirectly to draft rulings or take decisions in court proceedings, should be subjected to a rigorous and through examination.

The latter echoes an argument made by Judge Jorge Osvaldo Ledesma, the Argentinian Justice of the Peace who used ChatGPT to generate text written in more accessible terms, in a radio interview: "ChatGPT was not designed for writing entire rulings" and he explained that "human supervision is necessary, [the LLM] does not replace human work. People should not believe that that we press a button and the decision is ready, this involves intellectual work" (Mucho Humo 2023).[11]

Another concerning aspect of how judges used LLMs in the cases described in this chapter relates to the varying degrees of opacity that such uses entailed. With the exception of the Peruvian case, all the judges and tribunals provided information about the type of questions they made to the chatbots and identified the synthetic text produced by the LLM. But even in these cases there were open questions about their modus operandi. For example, some of the judgments stated that the information offered by ChatGPT was corroborated, but there was no explicit trace in the rulings which proved that the judges effectively checked whether ChatGPT's responses were accurate. Furthermore, OpenAI has not fully disclosed the data used to train its latest models (GPT 3.5 and GPT 4), hence the judges lack key information to assess precisely whether the datasets are biased and/or outdated, how so and to what extent.

The case of the Peruvian judge using ChatGPT is more extreme, because he was not transparent about how he used the system to support his decision. He only documented his interaction with ChatGPT by footnoting the platform's URL. However, the URL he provided did not grant access to his chat history with the chatbot. This point is not trivial, because it indicates that the judge was not familiar with how the tool works, which may imply that he was unaware of its limitations and risks. Moreover, if he asked ChatGPT to do the calculation, it suggests he was unaware that these types of LLMs are not trained to perform precise mathematical calculations. The inability of ChatGPT to resolve these types of queries is notorious and it is not difficult to identify the high frequency of errors it produces when faced with these types of questions.

Most of the judges justified the use of LLMs in terms of the possibilities to speed judicial procedures. In the two Colombian case, for example, both the ruling and the court order explicitly claim that emerging technologies can help to streamline judicial processes. For example, Judge Padilla's ruling stated: "The purpose of including these AI texts is not in any way to replace the Judge's decision. What we are really looking for is to optimize the time spent in writing sentences" (Padilla García 2023). Further, in a radio interview, Judge Padilla claimed that: "my only concern is to improve the justice system's timings […] (T)hat string of text that the artificial intelligence provided me with could also have been provided by a clerk when he or she submits a draft ruling to me, now ChatGPT is providing that initial text" (León 2023). Moreover, he stated in a radio interview that judges from all over Colombia would be "very happy" because ChatGPT could save "many hours transcribing things that are already on the Internet" (León 2023).

Paradoxically however, and exposing a somewhat naïve techno-solutionist belief in this case, since ChatGPT and other currently available LLMs tend to produce inaccurate and biased outputs, the judges would require significant amounts of time to check the validity of any AI-generated content, thereby undoing any significant "time savings". As happens with AI in other areas, under the narrative of such supposed "efficiencies", fundamental rights can be put at risk.

Finally, another narrative in some of the judges' justifications for using these tools was the need to experiment to find new ways to fulfil their objectives. For example, the Bolivian magistrates who used ChatGPT to research legal issues during a court hearing, defended their approach by framing it as "revolutionary" and as "an experiment" that aimed at "changing how justice is administered". However, from a rule of law perspective, experimental tools should not be deployed in state-related activities which affect human rights and if judges currently have access to more effective and safe tools, the latter should be preferred over untested ones. The stakes in judicial rulings are too high – especially when human rights are involved – to justify the use of unreliable and insufficiently tested technologies.

CONCLUSIONS

This chapter examined the use of AI tools by the judiciary and focused on documenting how judges from Latin American have used chatbots powered by LLMs to draft judicial rulings and support their decisions during hearings. Moreover, the chapter analysed the dangers of using this type of emerging technology in judicial activities and illustrated how techno-solutionist approaches dominate judges' justifications for using LLMs. The Latin American cases could contribute to a global discussion of the importance of digital literacy of judges, their aides, and attorneys, as well as the need for clear guidelines of when and how to use AI systems in the judicial system and how to critically countercheck any synthetic outputs. This final section discusses the policy implications of the widespread use of LLMs by the judiciary.

There is a tendency towards greater access to chatbots powered by LLMs offered by different companies through web and app-based platforms around the globe. Hence, the uninformed use of these systems by judges may expand to regions beyond Latin America. There is a high risk that judges and their clerks all over the world start transcribing outputs of LLMs in draft rulings etc. as if they were a reliable source.

While most of the judges in the cases described in this chapter were transparent about the fact that they used an LLM, their lack of understanding of how LLMs work illustrates why ensuring digital literacy among the judiciary is critical. Moreover, plaintiffs and defendants may also use LLMs, to the detriment of their clients' interests, without informing them of such use. All judicial operators should have basic knowledge of how LLMs work, how they were developed, when they can be suitable support tools, and what limitations and risks they entail.

A chatbot powered by an LLM should not be used as if it was an oracle – a trustworthy source of knowledge that does not require thorough verification. As has been widely reported and documented, the outputs produced by these systems often present strings of text that seem coherent but which in fact are inaccurate, incorrect, and/or biased. LLMs may be useful for exploring topics, summarizing texts, and even for inspiration, but they are not suitable tools for answering factual, technical, or even legal questions. Additionally, the output produced by LLMs is not neutral: the model and the data with which they were trained embody certain values. However, judges may not be aware of which values are being promoted or limited by the company which has developed a given system since most companies do not disclose how the models were developed, or the datasets with which the systems were trained.

Furthermore, AI tools should only be used in judicial matters where such tools have been sufficiently tested, when their potential impact on human rights has been thoroughly assessed, and when the tools are adequate to meet the required ends. Hence, it is crucial that the bodies in charge of governance of the judiciary open a dialogue on the conditions in which LLMs may be used as support tools for the drafting of judicial decisions or taking decisions in judicial procedures. It will be necessary to have an open and public discussion to decide which types of AI and which uses of these technologies are appropriate, and which should be avoided.

The Constitutional Court of Colombia, for example, is currently studying the case of the judge who used ChatGPT to write a second instance ruling that involved the fundamental rights of a minor. Both the petitioners of the revision and the Ombudsman office argued that the way in which the judge used ChatGPT, in an unregulated context, could have violated fundamental rights, particularly the right to a due process (Gutiérrez 2023d). In this process Lorena Flórez and I submitted an amicus curiae, by request of the Constitutional Court, where we argued that certain uses of LLMs could negatively affect due process as well as other fundamental rights, such as the right to a fair trial and data protection. We also contended that the independence of judges could be compromised due to a lack of information on how these systems were trained. Additionally, we recommended that the bodies that govern the judiciary should consider the development of their own AI systems, instead of acquiring off-the-shelf products, to ensure that the tools would be compliant with cybersecurity standards and that the design process would be centred on the protection of human rights (Gutiérrez and Flórez 2023).

Finally, the bodies that manage the judiciary should design guidelines and policies on how and when certain AI tools, including LLMs, can be introduced into judicial processes. The guidelines could establish certain standards and best practices for judges, clerks, and attorneys who wish to use AI tools. For example, an informed, transparent, ethical, and responsible use of AI tools by judges, clerks, and attorneys should comply with the following standards: (i) that the user understands how the technology works, acknowledges its limitations and risks, and makes sure that the tool is adequate for the required task (*informed use*); (ii) that the user is transparent about the use of the technology in its proceedings (*transparent use*); (iii) that the user distinguishes clearly which sections of the judicial decision or legal document are AI-generated text (*ethical use*); and (iv) that the user rigorously checks information retrieved from the AI system against reliable sources, explicitly documents the results of such examination and shares them transparently, and that the user refrains from using prompts that contain personal data or confidential information (*responsible use*) (Gutiérrez 2023b, 2023e).

NOTES

1. The author acknowledges that parts of the description of the cases described throughout the chapter were previously published in three different short articles (Gutiérrez 2023a, 2023b, 2023c).
2. For a short article on the implications of the adoption of AI systems for the principle of judicial independence in the European Union, see Gentile (2022).
3. For a review of the automation tools used by European Union Member States' courts to anonymize published rulings and the technical and administrative challenges of implementing these systems, see Terzidou (2023).
4. In December 2023, the judiciaries of the United Kingdom, New Zealand and Canada issued the first guidelines for using AI – especially generative AI – in courts and tribunals (Gutiérrez 2024).
5. I am not aware of documented cases of Chilean judges who have used LLMs to draft rulings, but in March 2023 several of the Court of Appeals judges which participated in a process to fill one of the vacancies of the Supreme Court of Chile discussed the use of AI in the judiciary and one of them even referred to the case of the Colombian judge who transcribed four prompts and answers from ChatGPT to motivate his ruling (Zúñiga 2023). Furthermore, in Paraguay a defendant claimed that a decision of an Appeals Tribunal included synthetic text produced by ChatGPT. However, neither the tribunal nor its magistrates were informed about the alleged use, nor it has been proven (ABC 2023).
6. Lord Justice Colin Birss remarked at a Law Society conference: "I asked it to give me a summary of an area of law I was writing a judgment about. I thought I would try it. I asked ChatGPT can you give me a summary of this area of law, and it gave me a paragraph. I know what the answer is because I was about to write a paragraph that said that, but it did it for me and I put it in my judgment. It's there and it's jolly useful" (Castro and Hyde 2023).
7. The section of this chapter that analyses how the media framed the ChatGPT use by Colombian judges accounts for over 200 publications from Colombia and other countries of the world.
8. For a more thorough description of the facts and of the *tutela* constitutional action, see Flórez Rojas (2023a).
9. See Flórez Rojas (2023b), for a discussion on the legal and equity implications of using the metaverse for a court hearing and the need to assess the necessity of the tool and to implement user-centered approaches (design thinking) to decide how to conduct judicial activities.
10. The prompt used by the Tribunal and ChatGPT's response can be consulted here: https://chat.openai.com/share/643c1b20-d46b-421a-bb82-7d7cbbf5ac2c.
11. The press release of the Judicial Power of the province of Corrientes also acknowledged the limitations of LLMs: "It is important to emphasize that these technologies are not infallible, so they do not replace the intellectual work of the magistrates, but rather enhance it. Like any other tool, they contribute to a better and more efficient achievement of the proposed objectives, without displacing the control and human intervention that are as necessary as they are unavoidable. In this case, the judge analysed the summary provided by the chatbot and considered that it adequately condensed the grounds for the decision, which is why he decided to incorporate it into his sentence" (Dirección de Prensa 2023).

REFERENCES

ABC (2023), *Abogados denuncian que juez usó inteligencia artificial para dictaminar en resolución judicial – Policiales – ABC Color*, accessed 17 October 2023 at https://www.abc.com.py/policiales/2023/08/31/abogados-denuncian-que-juez-uso-inteligencia-artificial-para-dictaminar-en-resolucion-judicial/.

Audiencia Inicial en el Metaverso (2023), Colombia, 15 February, accessed 16 October 2023 at https://www.youtube.com/watch?v=LXi2TX9OBmQ.

Bender, E. M., T. Gebru, A. McMillan-Major and S. Shmitchell (2021), 'On the Dangers of Stochastic Parrots: Can Language Models Be Too Big?', in *Proceedings of the 2021 ACM Conference on Fairness, Accountability, and Transparency*, New York, NY, USA: Association for Computing Machinery, pp. 610–23.

Castro, B. and J. H. Hyde (2023), 'Solicitor condemns judges for staying silent on "woeful" reforms', accessed 16 October 2023 at https://www.lawgazette.co.uk/news/solicitor-condemns-judges-for-staying-silent-on-woeful-reforms/5117228.article.

CEPEJ (2023), *Resource Centre Cyberjustice and AI*, European Commission for the Efficiency of Justice (CEPEJ), 9 October, accessed at https://public.tableau.com/app/profile/cepej/viz/ResourceCentre CyberjusticeandAI/AITOOLSINITIATIVESREPORT?publish=yes.

Consultor Jurídico (2023), 'CNJ vai investigar juiz que usou tese inventada pelo ChatGPT em decisão', 12 November, accessed 19 April 2024 at https://www.conjur.com.br/2023-nov-12/cnj-vai-investigar -juiz-que-usou-tese-inventada-pelo-chatgpt-para-escrever-decisao/.

Corfield, G. (2023), 'British judge uses "jolly useful" ChatGPT to write ruling', *The Telegraph*, 14 September, accessed 16 October 2023 at https://www.telegraph.co.uk/business/2023/09/14/british -judge-uses-jolly-useful-chatgpt-to-write-ruling/.

Dirección de Prensa (2023), 'Utilizando inteligencia artificial dictaron sentencia en lenguaje claro y lectura fácil', accessed at https://www.juscorrientes.gov.ar/prensa/utilizando-inteligencia-artificial -dictaron-sentencia-en-lenguaje-claro-y-lectura-facil/.

El Deber (2023), 'Vocales admiten uso de ChatGPT en juicio contra tres periodistas y una asociación anuncia demanda por prevaricato', accessed 17 October 2023 at https://eldeber.com.bo/santa -cruz/vocales-admiten-uso-de-chatgpt-en-juicio-contra-tres-periodistas-y-una-asociacion-anuncia- demanda-po_322224.

Erbol (2023), 'Un tribunal utiliza el ChatGPT para consultar criterios jurídicos en un proceso contra peri-odistas', accessed 17 October 2023 at https://erbol.com.bo/seguridad/un-tribunal-utiliza-el-chatgpt -para-consultar-criterios-jur%C3%ADdicos-en-un-proceso-contra.

Flores García, F. P. (2023), *Sentencia de Segunda Instancia – Resolución Nro. 4*, accessed at https://img .lpderecho.pe/wp-content/uploads/2023/03/Expediente-00052-2022-18-3002-JP-FC-01-LPDerecho .pdf.

Flórez Rojas, M. L. (2021), 'Toolkit ético legal', accessed 2 September 2022 at https://gecti.uniandes.edu .co/qsm_quiz/toolkit-etico-legal-es/.

Flórez Rojas, M. L. (2023a), 'A judge in Cartagena (Colombia) claims to have used ChatGPT as support tool to resolve a guardianship for health care neglect', accessed 16 October 2023 at https:// forogpp.com/2023/02/03/a-judge-in-cartagena-colombia-claims-to-have-use-chatgpt-as-support-tool -to-resolve-a-guardianship-for-health-care-neglect/.

Flórez Rojas, M. L. (2023b), 'Colombian judge holds a court hearing in the metaverse', accessed 16 October 2023 at https://forogpp.com/2023/02/22/colombian-judge-holds-a-court-hearing-in-the -metaverse/.

Flórez Rojas, M. L., R. M. Felipe, D. O. Niño Muñoz and A. M. Rey Grajales (2022), *La Adopción de Tecnologías Disruptivas en Las Organizaciones a Partir de la Creación e Implementación de un Toolkit Ético-Legal*, Bogotá, accessed at https://doi.org/10.1007/s11948-019-00146-8.

Gentile, G. (2022), 'AI in the courtroom and judicial independence: An EU perspective', accessed 26 October 2023 at https://euideas.eui.eu/2022/08/22/ai-in-the-courtroom-and-judicial-independence-an -eu-perspective/.

Guedes, N. (2023), 'Inteligência artificial generativa – Utilização não recomendada para pesquisa jurisprudencial – Deveres de cautela, de supervisão e de divulgação responsável dos dados do pro-cesso quanto ao uso de IA em decisões judiciais', Tribunal Regional Federal da 1a Região, Circular Coger 33/2023, accessed at https://www.conjur.com.br/wp-content/uploads/2023/11/SEI_19283798 _Circular_Coger_33.pdf.

Gutiérrez, J. D. (2020), 'Retos éticos de la inteligencia artificial en el proceso judicial', in ICDP (ed.), *Derecho Procesal. #NuevasTendencias. XLI Congreso Colombiano de Derecho Procesal*, Bogotá DC: Instituto Colombiano de Derecho Procesal (ICDP) y Universidad Libre, accessed at https://papers .ssrn.com/sol3/papers.cfm?abstract_id=4011179.

Gutiérrez, J. D. (2023a), 'ChatGPT in Colombian Courts: Why we need to have a conversation about the digital literacy of the judiciary', accessed at https://verfassungsblog.de/colombian-chatgpt/.

Gutiérrez, J. D. (2023b), '¿Están los jueces en capacidad de usar modelos de lenguaje a gran escala (LLMs)?', *Revista EXCEJLENCIA*, **7**, 10–15.

Gutiérrez, J. D. (2023c), 'Judges and magistrates in Peru and Mexico have ChatGPT fever', accessed 16 October 2023 at https://techpolicy.press/judges-and-magistrates-in-peru-and-mexico-have-chatgpt -fever/.

Gutiérrez, J. D. (2023d), 'La Corte Constitucional de Colombia está revisando el caso del juez de segunda instancia que utilizó ChatGPT para sustanciar una sentencia que decidió sobre los derechos fundamentales de menor de edad', accessed 26 July 2023 at https://forogpp.com/2023/09/09/la -corte-constitucional-de-colombia-esta-revisando-el-caso-del-juez-de-segunda-instancia-que-utilizo -chatgpt-para-sustanciar-una-sentencia-que-decidio-sobre-los-derechos-fundamentales-de-menor-de -edad/.

Gutiérrez, J. D. (2023e), 'Lineamientos para el uso de inteligencia artificial en contextos universitarios', *GIGAPP Estudios Working Papers*, **10** (270), 416–34.

Gutiérrez, J. D. and M. L. Flórez (2023), *Intervención de Profesionales Expertos/as En El Uso de Tecnologías de La Información En El Ámbito Jurídico En El Proceso de Referencia*, Amicus curiae Expediente No. T-9301656, Bogotá, 8 September, accessed at https://juangutierrezco.files.wordpress .com/2023/09/20230908-intervencion-corte-constitucional-gutierrez-y-florez.pdf.

Gutiérrez, J. D. and S. Muñoz-Cadena (2023), 'Adopción de sistemas de decisión automatizada en el sector público: Cartografía de 113 sistemas en Colombia', *GIGAPP Estudios Working Papers*, **10** (270), 365–95.

Gutiérrez, J. D., S. Muñoz-Cadena and M. Castellanos-Sánchez (2023), *Sistemas de decisión automatizada en el sector público colombiano [Dataset]*, accessed at https://doi.org/10.34848/YN1CRT.

Lam, L. (2023), 'Generative AI being tested for use in Singapore Courts, starting with small claims tribunal', accessed 16 October 2023 at https://www.channelnewsasia.com/singapore/artificial-intelligence -court-small-claims-singapore-chatgpt-3801756.

Ledesma, J. O. (2023), *G.M.C. s/ Información Sumaria (Convivencia)*, accessed at https://www .diariojudicial.com/uploads/0000053024-original.pdf.

León, A. (2023), 'Sentencia la tomé yo, ChatGPT respaldó argumentación: juez de Cartagena usó inteligencia artificial', text, Blu Radio, accessed 17 October 2023 at https://www.bluradio.com/judicial/ sentencia-la-tome-yo-chatgpt-respaldo-argumentacion-juez-de-cartagena-uso-inteligencia-artificial -pr30.

López Ponce, J. (2023), 'TEPJF valida que Morena use la frase "ya sabes quién" en Edomex – Grupo Milenio', accessed 17 October 2023 at https://www.milenio.com/politica/tepjf-valida-morena-use -frase-edomex.

Los Tiempos Digital (2023), 'Procesan por la vía penal a tres periodistas y juez usa ChatGPT en audiencia', accessed 17 October 2023 at https://www.lostiempos.com/actualidad/pais/20230418/procesan -penal-tres-periodistas-juez-usa-chatgpt-audiencia.

Mitchell, A., J. Murphy, D. Owens, D. Khazanchi and I. Zigurs (2009), 'Avatars, people, and virtual worlds: Foundations for research in metaverses', *Journal for the Association for Information Systems*, **10**, accessed at https://doi.org/10.17705/1jais.00183.

Mucho Humo (2023), Argentina: Diario El Litoral, 16 June, accessed at https://podcasters.spotify.com/ pod/show/diarioellitoral/episodes/Jos-Ledesma-en-Mucho-Humo-e25qara/a-aa0q7f7.

Padilla García, J. M. (2023), *Sentencia No. 032*, accessed at https://forogpp.files.wordpress.com/2023/ 01/sentencia-tutela-segunda-instancia-rad.-13001410500420220045901.pdf.

Página Siete (2023), 'Sin considerar la Ley de Imprenta, juzgan a 3 periodistas en la vía penal y con "inteligencia artificial"', accessed 17 October 2023 at https://www.paginasiete.bo/sociedad/sin -considerar-la-ley-de-imprenta-juzgan-a-3-periodistas-en-la-via-penal-y-con-inteligencia-artificial -LY7265519.

Quiñones Triana, M. V. (2023), *Auto que resuelve solicitud de realización de audiencia en el metaverso*, accessed at https://forogpp.files.wordpress.com/2023/02/2020-014-siett-vs-nacion-policia-nacional -solicitud-audiencia-en-el-metaverso-1.pdf.

Saavedra, V. and J. C. Upegui (2021), *PretorIA y La Automatización Del Procesamiento de Causas de Derechos Humanos*, Colombia: Derechos Digitales América Latina y Dejusticia, March, accessed at https://www.derechosdigitales.org/wp-content/uploads/CPC_informe_Colombia.pdf.

Shi, C., T. Sourdin and B. Li (2021), 'The smart court – a new pathway to justice in China?', *International Journal for Court Administration*, accessed at https://doi.org/10.36745/ijca.367.

Tamim, B. (2023), *Pakistani Court Utilizes ChatGPT-4 to Grant Bail in a Juvenile Kidnapping Case*, accessed 16 October 2023 at https://interestingengineering.com/culture/pakistani-court-utilizes -chatgpt-4-to-grant-bail.

TEPJF (2023), *Sesión Pública de Resolución*, accessed at https://www.youtube.com/watch?v= OwaZg3quyls&t=3679s.

Terzidou, K. (2022), 'The use of artificial intelligence in the judiciary and its compliance with the right to a fair trial', *Journal of Judicial Administration*, **31** (3), 154–68.

Terzidou, K. (2023), 'Automated Anonymization of Court Decisions: Facilitating the Publication of Court Decisions through Algorithmic Systems', in *Proceedings of the Nineteenth International Conference on Artificial Intelligence and Law*, New York, NY, USA: Association for Computing Machinery, pp. 297–305.

Yarzagaray, M. (2024), Sentencia de 2° instancia, 3 April, Tribunal Superior del Distrito Judicial de Pereira, Rad. Núm. 76 001 60 00193 2013 80734 01.

Zúñiga, A. (2023), 'Abogados valoran uso de inteligencia artificial para fallos, pero sin que reemplace ponderación del juez', accessed 16 October 2023 at https://prensa.udd.cl/files/2023/03/pedro-pablo -vergara-el-mercurio.png.

25. Regulating automated decision-making in the justice system: what is the problem?

David Mark, Tomás McInerney and John Morison

INTRODUCTION: A NEW REGULATORY SPACE?

The permeation of Artificial Intelligence (AI) into legal processes is in some ways unsurprising (Felten et al., 2023). Many tasks fundamental to legal practice, such as the analysis and interpretation of precedents and legislative texts, align well with AI's proficiency in data analysis, pattern recognition and predictive tasks (Yu & Alì, 2019; Surden, 2014). Indeed, a 2023 report by Goldman Sachs argues that up to 44 per cent of legal operations could be automated through AI (Briggs & Kodnani, 2023). Moreover, scholars have long posited that this technology has the potential to streamline judicial procedures; indeed 25 years ago predictions highlighted how AI could reduce costs and increase predictability by aiding in aspects of document and case management, thereby alleviating resource constraints within the judiciary (Sartor & Branting, 1998). Now advances in AI, particularly in the realm of large language models, text analysis and text generation, are further encouraging this techno-optimist view of progress (for a critical review of judicial uses of large language models, see Gutierréz, Chapter 24 in this volume). Moreover, the use of AI is not just limited to preparatory and research functions; it is increasingly becoming a part of Alternative Dispute Resolution (ADR) and Online Dispute Resolution (ODR) mechanisms (Alessa, 2022), thereby inching closer to the core of judicial proceedings. China appears to be leading this innovation (Shi et al., 2021; Ji, 2020), but the trend is undoubtably global (UNESCO, 2023).

Amid this emerges a multifaceted and contested landscape of governance (Veale, 2023). This chapter seeks to examine how a conspicuous lack of sector-specific legislation has engendered a complex landscape of debate, with contrasting stakeholder perspectives, that arguably undermines the coherence and efficacy of AI policy around judicial decision-making. As such, we seek to sketch out the complexities of AI's integration into judicial decision-making and the accompanying evolving regulatory environment.

WHY? PREDICTIVE POWER

The burgeoning confidence in the potential of AI in adjudication arguably revolves predominately around AI's predictive prowess (Surden, 2014). Proponents argue that the extensive body of legal documents – legislation, case law, policy documents – constitutes a massive corpus of unstructured data (Custers & Leeuw, 2017). When processed with Machine Learning (ML) algorithms, this data can potentially predict case outcomes before court proceedings. Katz et al. (2017) uses similar methods to claim prediction accuracies of over 70 per cent for studied US Supreme Court decisions, and litigation analytics platforms like Lex Machina offer further evidential support (Harbert, 2013). All this suggests, despite certain cognitive limitations, that these AI tools can showcase remarkable predictive prowess under certain conditions (Surden, 2014).

In this context, some advocates believe this shift towards algorithmic prediction in the judicial arena will eventually lead to algorithms handling all judicial decision-making tasks, rendering human judges obsolete (Xu, 2022). Of course, such projected developments necessitate not only technical advances but also discussions around infusing judicial norms and societal values into these systems (Morison & Harkens, 2019). Critics of such an algorithmic-centric judiciary of the future often underscore the absence of a unified consensus on guiding judicial values (Winter et al., 2023). They question the impact of these technologies on a legal system's legitimacy and efficiency, and express concerns about potential threats to core legal values (Pasquale & Cashwell, 2017; Morison & McInerney, 2024). Arguing the inherent complexity of law, encompassing unquantifiable sociocultural dimensions which are necessary for a decision to be both lawful and constitutive of law, is beyond algorithmic replication (Ross, 2001; Binns, 2020).

Notwithstanding this, there are irresistible imperatives coming from the speed, efficiency and cost reduction that AI may bring. Against this potentially transformative change our interest is in why and how this might be regulated.[1] More particularly, how is the phenomenon of regulating technology within judicial decision-making perceived by those thought responsible for regulating it? What are the issues and problems identified that require solving? What risks do these technologies pose and who should be responsible for resolving the problems and on what basis?

CURRENT REGULATION

Within the regulation of AI technologies, frameworks devised by national governments and supranational bodies like the European Union (EU) are increasingly recognised as pivotal policy instruments (Veale et al., 2023). Here it is noteworthy to observe the trends among key Western stakeholders, such as the EU, United States (US) and United Kingdom (UK) (Hutson, 2023). For example, the EU's imminent AI Act adopts a precautionary, risk-based approach to regulation, mandating that certain AI systems be safe, transparent and non-discriminatory, with similarities that can be broadly drawn to Canada's Artificial Intelligence and Data Act. The US, which has no broad federal AI related law, offers an executive order on Safe, Secure and Trustworthy AI, building upon a White Paper delineating similar foundational principles guiding AI's deployment, an approach largely echoed by the UK's own 'pro-innovation', principle-based proposal.

Notably, these concepts are very similar in identifying core regulatory goals – safety, non-discrimination, transparency, etc. However, intriguingly across many of these jurisdictions there is a conspicuous lack of focused sector-specific legislation implementing these overarching policy principles. Take for example the UK, which is a useful case study given the notably proactive approach towards the integration of AI in judicial decision-making. In 2019, the Lord Chief Justice of England and Wales founded an advisory group specifically to equip senior judges with guidance regarding the deployment of AI technologies (Hilborne, 2019). Indeed, AI has been enthusiastically welcomed at high levels into what has been termed the 'digital justice system' (Vos, 2022; 2023b). Despite this, the arena remains somewhat under-regulated, a view previously underscored by several contributors to an investigation by the House of Lords Justice and Home Affairs Committee (2022) exploring the application of emerging technologies in the justice system. Recent guidance from the Courts and Tribunals Judiciary provides an overview of guiding principles for judicial office holders but this remains high level (Courts and Tribunals Judiciary, 2023).

Overarching AI regulation within the UK[2] endorses AI as a 'general purpose' technology that cuts across a variety of regulatory remits (UK AI White Paper, 2023). The overall approach is characterised as 'deliberatively agile and iterative [to] learn from experience and continually adapt to develop the best regulatory regime' (UK AI White Paper, 2023: 6; Vallance, 2023). It largely eschews sector-specific legislation, instead providing an overarching set of regulatory principles: safety/security, transparency/explainability, fairness, accountability and contestability/redress (see the chapters in Part II of this volume for critical accounts of these concepts and their political work). However, these remain guiding concepts rather than codified regulations. Indeed, the paper specifically notes that they will not be implemented in statute initially, for fear that 'new rigid and onerous legislative requirements on businesses could hold back AI innovation' (UK AI White Paper, para 11). The reluctance to codify such principles into industry-specific policy, ostensibly to avoid hindering innovation, has perhaps contributed to an absence of detailed domain-focused governance.

Even considering the wider European context, whilst there are some exceptions (Chesterman, 2023; Artificial Lawyer, 2019), regulation is similarly limited. There is the European Commission for the Efficiency of Justice (CEPEJ) who have produced a *European Ethical Charter on the Use of Artificial Intelligence in Judicial Systems and their Environment* (2018), which provides a taxonomy of use cases with varying degrees of caution required for each type of deployment. However, such initiatives are exceptional, and the main control comes from Article 22 of the GDPR, which prohibits the full automation of decisions that produce legal or similarly significant effects (subject to certain exceptions). This approach partly frames the regulation of automated decisions through the prism of 'effect' (suggesting that the effect of the decision is integral to regulatory endeavours). There is a clear distinction here – but admittedly this may be in terminology only – between regulatory attempts that frame problematic automated decision-making practices through the *effect* of the decision (Article 22 GDPR); the *risk* the AI system poses (the EU Artificial Intelligence Act); and/or the *impact* automated systems may have on fundamental *principles* (UK AI White Paper). Nonetheless, despite a difference in language at regulatory level in terms of how government actors are problematising AI, a commonality is a lack of sector-specific regulation governing the arena of AI in judicial decision-making.

The result is a cacophony of stakeholder voices contributing to a multifaceted, contested regulatory landscape. This fragmentation is largely attributable to the disparate ways in which these stakeholders in judicial decision-making frame the risks, challenges and opportunities of AI in adjudication.

REVEALING THE 'PROBLEM'

Against this background of fragmented discourse, we seek to delineate the different conceptualisations of the challenges inherent in the area and subsequently explore the policy approaches employed by key actors to address these challenges. Here we understand policy in a broad sense, encompassing any prescriptive documents that influences the arena (frameworks, guidance, research, written responses, speeches, etc.). This analysis relies heavily upon the Foucauldian concept of 'problematisation'. This suggests that issues are not predefined or monolithically understood. Instead, phenomena are perceived as challenges or issues requiring intervention and management (Foucault, 1984; Lawlor & Nale, 2015). It is a useful way of removing the self-evidence of the term 'problems' by designating the concept as a process, and investigating how this perception of issues as problematic came to be made.[3] Moreover, the importance of problematisation extends beyond mere identification of challenges; it inherently demands, and suggests, solutions (Miller & Rose, 2008). Drawing upon this understanding that problems within an arena 'are not pre-given, lying there waiting to be revealed' but rather 'issues and concerns have to be made to appear problematic, often in different ways … by different agents' (Miller & Rose, 2008: 14), it becomes evident that the differing perspectives of various stakeholders yield divergent identifications and formulations of what constitutes a 'problem'. Simply put, the issues and problems that key actors see are determined by the lens through which they view the arena as 'the way we see things is affected by what we know or what we believe' (Berger, 2008).

Such an analysis accounts for the diverse array of policy and regulatory suggestions articulated by different stakeholders from distinct professional and academic backgrounds and allows for the recognition of varying conceptual frameworks that dictate what is seen as a 'problem' and what is considered an 'adequate solution'. These frameworks are not mere abstract constructs; rather, they are informed by values that differ based on the stakeholders involved. What makes this discourse fascinating is that multidimensional stakeholders not only view the issues through their unique prisms but also engage in a dynamic negotiation to shape policy and practice.

TRENDS, PATTERNS AND CONTESTATIONS

Despite the multifaceted nature of the public policy discourse surrounding AI in judicial systems, there is an undeniable trend amongst stakeholders to present AI enhanced systems as superior in some respects (Kuppala, 2022; Unesco, 2023; Eurojust, 2022; Aidinlis et al., 2020). These systems are often juxtaposed against a backdrop of traditional judicial systems, which are frequently problematised as inefficient, presenting instead as antiquated, ineffective systems that lag behind more modern approaches. Moreover, whilst key actors may view the arena through different lenses and with different perspectives, there is a general acceptance of the potential benefits of AI technologies in this arena.

Consider for instance, the narrative of '*efficiency*' which is pervasive in stakeholder discussions surrounding AI in judicial proceedings (Ji, 2020; Zeleznikow, 2017; Xu, 2022; The Law Society, 2019; Public Law Project, 2023a; Vos, 2018; Susskind, 2019) and enjoys a somewhat universal appeal across the regulatory landscape. This narrative champions the transformative potential of AI, proponents highlight the technology's capability to reduce the time and costs associated with many legal tasks, potentially alleviating pressure on already stretched judiciary resources. In other words, such technologies make for a better, more efficient system (Vos, 2022). As a corollary, a primary argument at the heart of the AI judicial decision-making discourse is the proposition that such technology can improve efficiency exponentially, thereby enhancing access to justice. Indeed, entities that witness these technologies first-hand (judicial institutions, legal professional associations) have noted with some enthusiasm the potential here of AI and related technologies. Continuing with the UK as a case study, both the Law Society of England and Wales (2018) and the Bar Council (2022) underline that AI's deployment will aid in 'improving efficiency, increasing profit or saving cost, upholding the rule of law and promoting access to justice' (Bar Council, 2022: 1), a sentiment reciprocated by the Council of Bars and Law Societies of Europe (Homoki, 2022). Significant judicial figures too have endorsed the added values (Burnett, 2018; Vos, 2022), as has the forward-looking review offered by the Law Society's Future Worlds 2050 project (Chittenden, 2021).

Similarly, the UK government's more general stance on AI in this field arguably aligns with these views, often seeing AI as a catalyst for cost-effectiveness and resource optimisation (UK AI White Paper, 2023; Government Response, 2022; Dories, 2022). This enthusiasm, particularly around efficiency gains, is echoed by other legislative bodies in the UK (House of Lords Justice and Home Affairs Committee, 2022), and at a European level as well (European Commission for the Efficiency of Justice, 2021; Eurojust, 2022; Council of the EU, 2020). Beyond this, many non-governmental organisations (NGOs) in this field, like 'Justice' (Justice, 2023), the 'Public Law Project' (Public Law Project, 2023b) and 'Fair Trials' (Fair Trials, 2021), are likewise quick to acknowledge the transformative effects of AI technologies on the UK's judicial system. Here too the narrative is about recognising 'the promise of greater efficiency and accuracy' (Public Law Project, 2023b: 2). Yet, it is not just about efficiency. Ethical norms, risk and social justice are also part of the narrative. Key stakeholders in this arena, particularly judicial institutions and professional associations, alongside independent oversight bodies, charities and NGOs often stress the need to ensure that AI technologies used in decision-making processes do not perpetuate existing social biases or inequalities (Public Law Project, 2023a). For instance, the seminal 2021 report entitled 'Automating Injustice', published by global justice watchdog 'Fair Trials' (2021) catalogues examples across policing and criminal justice throughout Europe where AI and automated decision-making results in discrimination, lack of transparency and bias.

Such critiques often underscore a disparity; while efficiency gains in the justice system might be palpable, the associated risks may, for some stakeholders, appear to considerably overshadow these benefits. It is within this tension, between risk and reward, that we see how different key actors problematise AI in judicial decision-making and how their perception of risks shapes their regulation and policy approaches.

RISK/REWARD

This chapter aims to elucidate the varying perceptions and problematisations of risks associated with AI in judicial decision-making. And whilst we are not focused on identifying harms or resolutions per se, we do acknowledge that risks generally pertain to intertwined concerns at the data level, which impact downstream at the model level, and consequently present broader challenges concerning the legal business and overall governance of such systems. Concurrently, there are accompanying apprehensions of AI extending beyond ancillary functions to replace human judgement.

Once again, these risks are generally widely acknowledged by key stakeholders (Veale, 2019b; Sales, 2019b; Bar Council, 2022; Public Law Project, 2023a), but their individual problematisation of these issues, informed by their own perception and understanding of risk, leads to a variety of proposed regulation. For instance, from the perspective of certain stakeholders, the risks associated with AI significantly outweigh the potential benefits. The Council of Europe aptly illustrates these apprehensions in the justice-focused section of its review of global AI regulations, stating that 'given the degree of potentially affected interests … the risks remain high in the case of equitable justice and seem disproportionate to the benefits largely in terms of efficiency for the justice system' (2020: 87). Certainly, for many charities, NGOs and oversight bodies, the associated risks seem to overwhelm the benefits. Indeed, in June 2023, around 30 UK civil society groups, including 'Fair Trials' and the 'Public Law Project', voiced these concerns in response to the UK government's pro-innovation approach (Public Law Project, 2023c). Their approach strongly advocates for transparency and accountability. They assert, in consonance with Frank Pasquale's critiques on black box algorithms (Pasquale, 2015), that the opaque nature of such technologies impedes meaningful accountability and explicability (Edwards & Veale, 2018). Moreover, when applying such a regulatory approach specifically to the realm of adjudication, concerns encompass fears of a generalised justice framework that might discriminate against marginalised groups (Big Brother Watch, 2020). The signatories of the alternative AI white paper argue that 'without transparency, individuals and parliamentarians cannot hold decision-makers to account when AI systems produce harmful or discriminatory outcomes' (Public Law Project, 2023a).

These issues of 'explainability' and opacity have previously been cited as obstacles to AI's utilisation in judicial decision-making (Wang, 2020; Future of Life, 2017; also see Berry, Chapter 10 in this volume). Now, with the increasing use of such systems, 'transparency' has emerged as a buzzword among UK NGOs in this arena (Big Brother Watch, 2023; Fair Trials, 2021; Public Law Project, 2023a) and the lens through which many solutions are framed (ICO & Alan Turing Institute, 2022). This viewpoint is exemplified by the charity 'Justice', whose response to the UK government's pro-innovation approach to AI regulation contained five key messages. Central amongst them was that 'transparency is a gateway principle: opacity undermines the ability for civil society and directly impacted individuals to assess the safety and fairness of AI systems, and in turn undermines the accountability and contestability of AI' (Justice, 2023).

Such perspectives, and apparent focus upon transparency and accountability, are perhaps shaped by how these groups perceive the concept of justice and the role of judicial decision-making, which in turn informs their problematisation of the issues and risks associated with AI in this domain. It is notable that many watch groups and NGO's take issue with the general nature of justice in many of these mechanisms, expressing concerns about a lack of individualised justice leading to fears of discrimination, particularly against socially disadvantaged groups (Big Brother Watch, 2020). There is an emphasis on the importance of ensuring that AI works for public good, and that justice involves the protection of fundamental rights and democratic values (Public Law Project, 2023a). Fears centre on the ways that automated decision-making may infringe upon an individual's rights, particularly when those technologies are opaque and unaccountable – terms that are often used broadly and interchangeably across these various publications.

In their pursuit of transparency and accountability, these key stakeholders emphasise the indispensable nature of human involvement in decision-making processes, valuing the unique qualities of human judgement and discretion that cannot be replicated by algorithms. This appreciation of human judgment is a recurring theme, pervasive among many of the central stakeholders and informing many policy recommendations stressing both accountability and transparency. For instance, the signatories of the 'Key principles for an alternative AI white paper' argue that 'decision-making which has significant implications for people, and which may affect their rights, should be undertaken with a human meaningfully in the loop' (Public Law Project, 2023a).

Similar sentiments are echoed by professional legal organisations. Both the Council of Bars and Law Societies of Europe (2023) and members of the judiciary in England and Wales (Vos, 2023b) have emphasised the right to a human judge. Whilst such entities are perhaps more trusting of the legal system, remaining somewhat keen to take advantage of the opportunities afforded by these technologies (Law Tech UK, 2022; Veale, 2019a), many legal professionals also express concerns about the ethical and regulatory implications of AI. Understandably, they are additionally uniquely concerned about the impact upon their professions and the potential of these technologies to change or reduce work for practitioners (Mylvaganam & McMillan, 2020; Cross, 2017; Chittenden, 2021; Homoki, 2022). Overall, the concepts of 'transparency' and 'accountability' once again emerge as pivotal themes in this discourse (cf. Aula and Erkkilä, Chapter 13 in this volume; Cobbe and Singh, Chapter 7 in this volume), evidenced by the representations that legal professional bodies made to the House of Lords Justice and Home Affairs Committee where trust, transparency, accountability and individual rights feature strongly (House of Lords, 2022).

Delving deeper into this emphasis on transparency and accountability by legal practitioners, organisations and the judiciary, a distinct narrative emerges, and when held in comparison with entities considered to be NGO's, charities or watch groups, it is evident that there is a difference in how legal professionals may frame issues and rationalise solutions. The desire for transparency and accountability by legal actors appears to extend beyond a wish to ensure procedural propriety or protect the rights of the individual, albeit these concerns are certainly acknowledged. It appears there is an additional broader goal of legitimising the process (Tyler, 2006) and ensuring that the use of AI in the judicial system is perceived as appropriate, fair and just by those directly impacted (Veale, 2019a). This narrative of trustworthiness and legitimacy reverberates in multiple jurisdictions (Bakst et al., 2022; also see Gillis, Laux and Mittelstadt, Chapter 14 in this volume). Interestingly, this focus upon validity and trust might dovetail with the call for maintaining a human element in judicial decision-making. In the UK, Vos (2023b) argues 'for there always to be the option of taking a case to appeal to allow it to be scrutinised by a human judge', echoing the Information Commissioner's Office who state, 'human oversight remains a fundamental factor in appropriating responsibility and retaining trust in new technologies and the sectors that use them' (Information Commissioner's Office, 2022). In other words, the focus on human oversight could be understood as an endeavour to preserve transparency and trust in the legal system, thus facilitating broader acceptance of digital judicial tools, ensuring the successful evolution of the digital justice system in England and Wales. These aspirations seem to align with some of the UK government's views in this arena, as explored below.

While overall the UK government approach to regulation in the area emphasises innovation and cost-cutting and focuses on ethical and governance principles rather than firm rules, there is at least a recognition of many of the same risks, as evidenced in the response to the *Technology Rules?* report (Government Response, 2022). However, as the response document suggests, the UK government is perhaps comparatively more inclined to advocate for the use of AI technologies within the judicial system, dismissing numerous concerns about a lack of minimum standards, evaluation and transparency in AI technologies as raised in the report (Government Response, 2022). Interestingly, to disregard some of these fears, the government's response affirmed its commitment to human decision-making in key legal processes, stating that AI would augment rather than replace existing processes to improve the justice system. Again, this idea of 'human-in-the-loop' raised by most stakeholders in this arena is seen as the answer to concerns that arise.

While the nuances of the government approach remain somewhat opaque there is the often-stated desire of the Sunak government to establish the UK as a hub for future AI regulation (Reuters, 2023). Unfortunately, this regulation has been somewhat slow to appear and there is a notable lack of sector-specific government policy dealing with AI in the judicial system. Rather, we are left to assess the government's framing of issues in this area by analysing overarching regulatory frameworks such as the recent light touch, 'pro-innovation' guidance (UK AI White Paper, 2023) and the UK government's 'Roadmap to an effective AI assurance ecosystem' (Centre for Data Ethics and Innovation, 2021). In such documentation, it is made clear that 'well designed regulation can drive growth and shape a thriving digital economy and society' (Centre for Data Ethics and Innovation, 2021: 2). Indeed, it becomes apparent that the government views the concept of regulation through the lens of economic prosperity, hoping that any regulatory framework can result in 'the UK [becoming] a global leader in a new multi-billion-pound industry' (Centre for Data Ethics and Innovation, 2021: 2). This approach as it translates to the justice system is perhaps summarised succinctly by the committee report: 'the aim behind the introduction of these technologies is to do the job (whatever it may be) better, faster, and more cheaply than was previously possible' (House of Lords, 2022).

HUMAN-IN-THE-LOOP: A PANACEA?

As noted, one theme that clearly runs through these varying sectoral approaches to AI regulation is the human-in-the-loop: seemingly regarded as a panacea for the use of AI systems in judicial processes (and other high-stakes areas). Whilst stakeholders arrive at this suggestion through different methods and contrasting reasons, they commonly agree that having a human making the final decision is key to tackling problematised issues.

Current regulatory approaches stress the utility of this approach. For example, Article 22 of the GDPR prohibits the use of *fully* automated decision-making in certain contexts, thus inadvertently framing human-in-the-loop decisions as potentially less severe. Additionally, guidance from the Article 29 Working Party (now the European Data Protection Board) notes that human intervention is a crucial component, and that this should be carried out by someone 'who has the authority and competence to change the decision'.[4] Human involvement must be more than a 'token gesture' (Article 29 Working Party, 2017: 10, 15). The Justice and Home Affairs Committee also state a human should 'always be the ultimate decision maker – as a safeguard for when the algorithm gets things wrong' (Justice and Home Affairs Committee, 2022: 5).

We are not convinced that the human-in-the-loop approach sufficiently ameliorates the anxieties of relying on AI in the judicial context, primarily because such responses omit consideration of the role AI systems can play in crystallising problematic perceptions of problems and their solutions (Morison & Harkens, 2019). Rather, we believe the totalising and often seductive nature of these technologies can undermine meaningful human involvement, and that human-in-the-loop AI might leave deeper considerations behind, including the impact these systems can have on human autonomy (Morison, 2020). It is much more revealing to view human-in-the-loop AI as an intricate entanglement of human and machine – with no clear demarcation between where one ends and the other begins – within which it is hard to properly locate or attribute responsibility (Amoore, 2020). These configurations reinforce ways of seeing; suggesting that it is in fact a composite form of human and AI that drives both the problems stemming from the reliance on machines alone, as well as those issues arising from attempts to plug a human meaningfully in the sequence. Framing solutions in this way undoubtedly shapes the narrative on AI in judicial decision-making (and propagates a sort of AI-augmented reality).

CONCLUSION: THE PUBLIC POLICY NEXUS

The advent of AI in judicial decision-making has created an intricate discourse around public policy shaped by varying perspectives of key stakeholders. On one hand, there is wide recognition across the spectrum of stakeholders, from governments to professional associations and NGOs, of the substantial benefits that AI can offer the judicial system. These include efficiency gains, cost savings and the subsequent increase in access to justice (for a discussion of such positive framings of AIT potentials in the public sector, see Paul, Carmel and Cobbe, Chapter 1 in this volume). However, counterbalancing these advantages are significant risks and concerns. Including fears of inherent data bias, technical challenges such as data privacy and broader systemic issues such as the explainability of AI-driven outcomes or the potential shift in judicial power with AI extending beyond supporting roles to impact human judgement. It is within this interplay of potential risks and rewards that we can discern how various stakeholders problematise AI in the judicial decision-making domain. Stakeholder interpretations and prioritisation of associated risks influence their responses, which in turn guide the ensuing policy views and suggestions in this sector.

Whilst acknowledging this is a somewhat general overview, it appears that the UK government and other international bodies often focus on wider regulatory and compliance aspects. The light touch, pro-innovation guidance (UK AI White Paper, 2023) offers an example of a principles-based approach to regulation that often favours economic prosperity when balancing pros and cons of AI technologies. Conversely, judicial institutions and professional associations are perhaps more concerned with the ethical and regulatory issues associated with AI. Whilst understandably occupied with the implications of this technology on their practices, they additionally seek to legitimise AI technologies, making sure that their deployment in the judicial system is viewed as appropriate, proper and just by those they impact. Furthermore, independent oversight bodies, charities and NGOs often emphasise the risks, and express reservations, particularly pertaining to individualised justice. The principle-based response to the government's own regulatory framework which emerged from the Public Law Project (2023a) reflects a more risk-averse approach to AI in judicial decision-making.

There are, however, some intriguing similarities traversing the regulatory preferences of key stakeholders, particularly when suggesting solutions to problematised issues. A universally recognised theme emerges clearly: the importance of transparency, accountability and subsequently the indispensable role of human oversight. Regardless of whether different actors are motivated by transparency and accountability, or efficiency and access to justice, the regulatory consensus clearly seems to be that the human-in-the-loop remains paramount.

AI systems can assist judges – but they should not replace them. Whether this is sufficient is perhaps less clear.

NOTES

1. Here in a sense, we are following the approach suggested by Cobbe in her review of technochauvinism and her development of key questions, whenever it is suggested technology is brought in to solve a 'problem'. See further-Jennifer Cobbe, *Technochauvinism* (2022) https://www.sciencespo.fr/public/chaire-numerique/wp-content/uploads/2022/06/Jennifer-Cobbe-TECHNOCHAUVINISM-Policy-Brief-.pdf.
2. See 'patchwork of legal requirements' – https://www.gov.uk/government/publications/ai-regulation-a-pro-innovation-approach/white-paper, Box 2.1.
3. As Foucault puts it, 'Problematization doesn't mean the representation of a pre-existent object, nor the creation through discourse of an object that doesn't exist. It's the set of discursive or nondiscursive practices that makes something enter into the play of the true and false, and constitutes it as an object for thought (whether under the form of moral reflection, scientific knowledge, political analysis, etc.)' (Foucault, 1988: 257).
4. Whilst an EU guideline, the ICO states: 'Although these guidelines relate to the EU version of the GDPR, they are also a useful resource for understanding the requirements of the UK GDPR.' https://ico .org .uk/ for -organisations/ uk -gdpr -guidance -and -resources/ accountability -and -governance/ guide-to-accountability-and-governance/accountability-and-governance/data-protection-officers/.

REFERENCES

Aidinlis, S., Smith, H., Adams-Prassl, A., & Adams-Prassl, J. (2020). Building a justice data infrastructure: Opportunities and constraints. https://www.law.ox.ac.uk/sites/default/files/migrated/ukri_justice _data_report_fv_0.pdf.
Alessa, H. (2022). The role of artificial intelligence in online dispute resolution: A brief and critical overview. *Information & Communications Technology Law*, **31** (3), 319–334.
Amoore, L. (2020). *Cloud Ethics: Algorithms and the Attributes of Ourselves and Others*. Durham, NC: Duke University Press.
Article 29 Working Party (adopted on 3 October 2017). *Guidelines on Automated Individual Decision-making and Profiling for the Purposes of Regulation 2016/679*. European Union.
Artificial Lawyer. (2019, 4 June). France bans judge analytics, 5 years in prison for rule breakers. https://www.artificiallawyer.com/2019/06/04/france-bans-judge-analytics-5-years-in-prison-for-rule -breakers/.
Bakst, J., Harden, M., Jankauskas, T., McMurrough, M., & Morril, M. (2022). Artificial intelligence and arbitration: A US perspective. https://www.cov.com/-/media/files/corporate/publications/2022/05/ artificial-intelligence-and-arbitration-a-us-perspective_bakst-harden-jankauskas-mcmurrough-morril .pdf.
Bar Council. (2022). *Written Evidence to the Justice and Home Affairs Committee (NTL0048). Technology Rules? The Advent of New Technologies in the Justice System.* https://committees .parliament.uk/writtenevidence/39768/pdf/.
Berger, J. (2008). *Ways of Seeing*. London: Penguin Books.
Big Brother Watch. (2020). Briefing on algorithmic decision making in the criminal justice system. https://bigbrotherwatch.org.uk/wp-content/uploads/2020/02/Big-Brother-Watch-Briefing-on-Algo rithmic-Decision-Making-in-the-Criminal-Justice-System-February-2020.pdf.
Big Brother Watch. (2023). Big Brother Watch's response to the government's consultation the 'A pro-innovation approach to AI regulation', White Paper. https://bigbrotherwatch.org.uk/wp-content/uploads/2023/06/Big-Brother-Watch-response-to-Govt-White-Paper-on-AI.pdf.

Binns, R. (2020). Analogies and disanalogies between machine-driven and human-driven legal judgement. *Journal of Cross-Disciplinary Research in Computational Law*, **1** (1). https://journalcrcl.org/crcl/article/view/5.

Briggs, J., & Kodnani, D. (2023). The potentially large effects of artificial intelligence on economic growth. https://www.key4biz.it/wp-content/uploads/2023/03/Global-Economics-Analyst_-The-Potentially-Large-Effects-of-Artificial-Intelligence-on-Economic-Growth-Briggs_Kodnani.pdf.

Burnett, Lord (2018). *The Age of Reform*. https://www.judiciary.uk/wp-content/uploads/2018/06/speech-lcj-the-age-of-reform.pdf.

Centre for Data Ethics and Innovation. (2021). The roadmap to an effective AI assurance ecosystem. https://assets.publishing.service.gov.uk/media/61b0746b8fa8f50379269eb3/The_roadmap_to_an_effective_AI_assurance_ecosystem.pdf.

Chesterman, S. (2023). All rise for the honourable robot judge? Using artificial intelligence to regulate AI. *Technology and Regulation*, 45–57. https://ssrn.com/abstract=4252778.

Chittenden, T. (2021). *Future Worlds 2050: Images of the Future Worlds Facing the Legal Profession 2020–2030.* https://www.lawsociety.org.uk/topics/research/future-worlds-2050-images-of-the-future-worlds-facing-the-legal-profession-2020-2030#report.

Cobbe, J. (2022). *Technochauvinism.* https://www.sciencespo.fr/public/chaire-numerique/wp-content/uploads/2022/06/Jennifer-Cobbe-TECHNOCHAUVINISM-Policy-Brief-.pdf.

Council of Bars and Law Societies of Europe. (2023). CCBE statement on the use of AI in the justice system and law enforcement. https://www.ccbe.eu/fileadmin/speciality_distribution/public/documents/Statements/2023/EN_ITL_20230525_CCBE-Statement-on-the-use-of-AI-in-the-justice-system-and-law-enforcement.pdf.

Council of Europe. (2020). *Towards Regulation of AI Systems.* https://rm.coe.int/prems-107320-gbr-2018-compli-cahai-couv-texte-a4-bat-web/1680a0c17a.

Courts and Tribunals Judiciary. (2023). Artificial intelligence guidance for judicial office holders. https://www.judiciary.uk/wp-content/uploads/2023/12/AI-Judicial-Guidance.pdf.

Cross, M. (2017). Law Society predicts 'savage reduction' in legal jobs as AI takes over. https://www.lawgazette.co.uk/news/law-society-predicts-savage-reduction-in-legal-jobs-as-ai-takes-over/5108772.article.

Custers, B., & Leeuw, F. L. (2017). Legal big data. *Nederlands Juristenblad*, **2017** (34), 2449–2456.

Dories, N. (2022). Establishing a pro-innovation approach to regulating AI. https://www.gov.uk/government/publications/establishing-a-pro-innovation-approach-to-regulating-ai/establishing-a-pro-innovation-approach-to-regulating-ai-policy-statement.

Edwards, L., & Veale, M. (2018). Enslaving the algorithm: From a 'right to an explanation' to a 'right to better decisions'? *IEEE Security & Privacy*, **16** (3), 46–54. https://doi.org/10.1109/MSP.2018.2701152.

Eurojust. (2022). *AI Cross Border Cooperation.* https://www.eurojust.europa.eu/sites/default/files/assets/artificial-intelligence-cross-border-cooperation-criminal-justice-report.pdf.

European Commission for the Efficiency of Justice. (2018). *Ethical Charter on the Use of Artificial Intelligence in Judicial Systems.* https://rm.coe.int/ethical-charter-en-for-publication-4-december-2018/16808f699c.

European Commission for the Efficiency of Justice. (2021). *Ethical Charter.* https://rm.coe.int/ethical-charter-en-for-publication-4-december-2018/16808f699c.

Fair Trials. (2021). *Automating Injustice.* https://www.fairtrials.org/app/uploads/2021/11/Automating_Injustice.pdf.

Felten, E. W., Manav, R., & Seamans, R. (2023). How will language modelers like ChatGPT affect occupations and industries? https://papers.ssrn.com/sol3/papers.cfm?abstract_id=4375268.

Foucault, M. (1984). Michel Foucault, polemics, politics, and problemizations: An interview. In P. Rabinow (ed.), *The Foucault Reader*. New York: Pantheon, p. 257.

Foucault, M. (1988). The concern for truth, in Foucault, M., Sheridan, A. and Kritzman, L. (eds), *Politics, Philosophy, Culture: Interviews and Other Writings*. New York: Routledge, pp. 255–67.

Future of Life Institute. (2017). *The Asilomar AI Principles.* https://futureoflife.org/open-letter/ai-principles/.

Government Response. (2022). Response to Justice and Home Affairs Committee report 'Technology rules? The advent of new technologies in the justice system'. https://committees.parliament.uk/publications/22773/documents/167387/default/.

Harbert, T. (2013). The law machine. *IEEE Spectrum,* **50** (11), 31–54.

Hilborne, N. (2019). Susskin named chair of expert group to advise judges on AI. Legal Futures. https://www.legalfutures.co.uk/latest-news/susskind-named-chair-of-expert-group-to-advise-judges-on-ai.

Homoki, P. (2022). Guide on the use of artificial intelligence-based tools by lawyers and law firms in the EU. https://www.ccbe.eu/fileadmin/speciality_distribution/public/documents/Events/20220331_AI4L/EN_IT_Law_2022_Guide-AI4L_web.pdf.

House of Lords Justice and Home Affairs Committee. (2022). *Technology Rules? The Advent of New Technologies in the Justice System.* https://publications.parliament.uk/pa/ld5802/ldselect/ldjusthom/180/180.pdf.

Hutson, M. (2023). Rules to keep AI in check: Nations carve different paths for tech regulation. *Nature,* 620 (7973), 260–263. https://doi.org/10.1038/d41586-023-02491-y.

ICO & Alan Turing Institute. (2022). *Explaining Decisions Made with AI.* https://ico.org.uk/media/for-organisations/uk-gdpr-guidance-and-resources/artificial-intelligence/explaining-decisions-made-with-artificial-intelligence-1-0.pdf.

Information Commissioner's Office [ICO]. (2022). *Written Evidence to the Justice and Home Affairs Committee (NTL0016). Technology Rules? The Advent of New Technologies in the Justice System.* https://committees.parliament.uk/writtenevidence/38632/html/.

Ji, W. (2020). The change of judicial power in China in the era of artificial intelligence. *Asian Journal of Law and Society,* **7** (3), 515–530. https://doi.org/10.1017/als.2020.37.

JUSTICE. (2023, June). *A Pro-Innovation Approach to AI Regulation.* https://justice.org.uk/white-paper-a-pro-innovation-approach-to-ai-regulation/.

Katz, D. M., Bommarito, M. J. II, & Blackman, J. (2017). A general approach for predicting the behavior of the Supreme Court of the United States. *PLoS ONE,* **12** (4), e0174698. https://doi.org/10.1371/journal.pone.0174698.

Kuppala, J., Srinivas, K. K., Anudeep, P., Kumar, R. S., & Vardhini, P. A. H. (2022). Benefits of artificial intelligence in the legal system and law enforcement. In *2022 International Mobile and Embedded Technology Conference (MECON),* pp. 221–225. doi: 10.1109/MECON53876.2022.9752352.

Law Tech UK. (2022). *Adoption of Machine Learning in Legal Services Case Studies.* https://lawtechuk.io/our-reports/.

Lawlor, L., & Nale, J. (2014). Problematization. In L. Lawlor & J. Nale (eds), *The Cambridge Foucault Lexicon.* Cambridge: Cambridge University Press, pp. 399–403.

Miller, P., & Rose, N. (2008). *Governing the Present: Administering Economic, Social and Personal Life.* Cambridge: Polity.

Morison, J. (2020). Towards a democratic singularity? Algorithmic governmentality, the eradication of politics – And the possibility of resistance. In S. Deakin & C. Markou (eds), *Is Law Computable? Critical Perspectives on Law and Artificial Intelligence.* Oxford and New York: Hart, pp. 85–106.

Morison, J., & Harkens, A. (2019). Re-engineering justice? Robot judges, computerised courts and (semi) automated legal decision making. *Legal Studies,* **39** (4), 618–635.

Morison, J., & McInerney, T. (2024). When should a computer decide? Judicial decision-making in the age of automation, algorithms and generative artificial intelligence. In S. Turenne & M. Moussa (eds), *Research Handbook on Judging and the Judiciary.* Cheltenham, UK and Northampton, MA, USA: Edward Elgar Publishing (forthcoming).

Mylvaganam, M., & McMillan, S. (2020). Legal tech: Gamechanger or ethical dilemma? https://www.barcouncil.org.uk/resource/legal-tech-gamechanger-or-ethical-dilemma.html.

Pasquale, F. A. (2015). *The Black Box Society: The Secret Algorithms that Control Money and Information.* Cambridge, MA: Harvard University Press.

Pasquale, F. A., & Cashwell, G. (2017). Prediction, persuasion, and the jurisprudence of behaviorism. University of Maryland Legal Studies Research Paper, No. 2017-34.

Public Law Project. (2023a). Key principles for an alternative AI white paper. https://publiclawproject.org.uk/content/uploads/2023/06/AI-alternative-white-paper-in-template.pdf.

Public Law Project. (2023b). Government 'behind the curve' on AI risks. https://publiclawproject.org.uk/latest/government-behind-the-curve-on-ai-risks/.

Public Law Project. (2023c). *Written Evidence to the Justice and Home Affairs Committee (NTL0046).* Technology rules? The advent of new technologies in the justice system. https://committees .parliament.uk/writtenevidence/39761/html/.

Reuters. (2023, June 12). UK PM Sunak pitches Britain as future home for AI regulation. https://www .reuters.com/technology/uk-must-seize-opportunities-ai-remain-tech-capital-pm-sunak-2023-06-11/.

Ross, H. (2001). *Law as a Social Institution.* Oxford: Hart Publishing.

Sales, Lord (2019). Algorithms, artificial intelligence and the law: The Sir Henry Brooke Lecture for BAILII, Freshfields Bruckhaus Deringer, London, 12 November. https://www.supremecourt.uk/docs/ speech-191112.pdf.

Sartor, G., & Branting, K. (1998). *Judicial Applications of Artificial Intelligence.* https://doi.org/10 .1007/978-94-015-9010-5.

Shi, C., Sourdin, T., & Li, B. (2021). The smart court – A new pathway to justice in China? *International Journal for Court Administration*, **12** (1), https://iacajournal.org/articles/10.36745/ijca.367.

Surden, H. (2014). Machine learning and law. *Washington Law Review*, **89** (1), 87–101. https:// digitalcommons.law.uw.edu/wlr/vol89/iss1/5.

Susskind, R. (2019). *Online Courts and the Future of Justice.* Oxford: Oxford University Press.

The Council of the EU. (2020). Access to justice – Seizing the opportunities of digitalisation. [Online]. https://www.europeansources.info/record/access-to-justice-seizing-the-opportunities-of -digitalisation/.

The Law Society. (2018). Artificial intelligence (AI) and the legal profession. https://www.lawsociety .org.uk/topics/research/ai-artificial-intelligence-and-the-legal-profession.

The Law Society. (2019). *Algorithm Use in the Criminal Justice System Report.* https://www.lawsociety .org.uk/topics/research/algorithm-use-in-the-criminal-justice-system-report.

Tyler, T. (2006). Psychological perspectives on legitimacy and legitimation. *Annual Review of Psychology*, **57**, 375–400. https://doi.org/10.1146/annurev.psych.57.102904.190038.

UK AI White Paper. (2023). *AI Regulation: A Pro-Innovation Approach.* https://www.gov.uk/gov ernment/publications/ai-regulation-a-pro-innovation-approach.

UNESCO. (2023). *AI and the Rule of Law.* https://www.unesco.org/en/artificial-intelligence/rule-law/ mooc-judges.

Vallance, P. (2023). *Pro-Innovation Regulation of Technologies Review: Digital Technologies Report.* https://www.gov.uk/government/publications/pro-innovation-regulation-of-technologies-review-digi tal-technologies.

Veale, M. (Lead Author). (2019a). Algorithm use in the criminal justice system report. https://www .lawsociety.org.uk/topics/research/algorithm-use-in-the-criminal-justice-system-report.

Veale, M. (2019b). A critical take on the policy recommendations of the EU high-level expert group on artificial intelligence. *European Journal of Risk Regulation*, **11** (e1), 1.

Veale, M., Matus, K., & Gorwa, R. (2023). AI and global governance: Modalities, rationales, tensions. *Annual Review of Law and Social Science*, **19** (1), 255–275.

Vos, G. (2018). Speech at the Foundation for Science and Technology. UK Judiciary. https://www .judiciary.uk/wp-content/uploads/2018/06/speech-chc-the-foundation-for-science-and-technology .pdf.

Vos, G. (2022). The future for dispute resolution: Horizon scanning. UK Judiciary. https://www.judi ciary.uk/wp-content/uploads/2022/03/MR-to-SCL-Sir-Brain-Neill-Lecture-2022-The-Future-for-Dis pute-Resolution-Horizon-Scannings-.pdf.

Vos, G. (2023a). Law and technology conference. UK Judiciary. https://www.judiciary.uk/wp-content/ uploads/2023/06/Law-Society-Scotland-Law-and-Tech-Conference-2023.pdf.

Vos, G. (2023b). 20th Annual Law Reform Lecture. Judiciary of England and Wales. https://www .judiciary.uk/speech-by-the-master-of-the-rolls-to-the-bar-council-of-england-and-wales/.

Wang, N. (2020). 'Black box justice': Robot judges and AI-based judgment processes in China's court system. In *2020 IEEE International Symposium on Technology and Society (ISTAS)*, pp. 58–65. https://doi.org/10.1109/ISTAS50296.2020.9462216.

Winter, C., Hollman, N., & Manheim, D. (2023). Value alignment for advanced artificial judicial intel-ligence. *American Philosophical Quarterly*, **60** (2), 187–203. https://doi.org/10.5406/21521123.60.2 .06.

Xu, Z. (2022). Human judges in the era of artificial intelligence: Challenges and opportunities. *Applied Artificial Intelligence*, **36** (1). https://doi.org/10.1080/08839514.2021.2013652.

Yu, R., & Ali, G. (2019). What's inside the black box? AI challenges for lawyers and researchers. *Legal Information Management*, **19** (1), 2–13. https://doi.org/10.1017/S1472669619000021.

Zeleznikow, J. (2017). Can artificial intelligence and online dispute resolution enhance efficiency and effectiveness in courts. *International Journal for Court Administration*, **8** (2), 30–45.

26. AI, regulation, and the world of work: the competing approaches of the US and China

Robert Donoghue, Luo Huanxin, Phoebe Moore and Ekkehard Ernst

INTRODUCTION

A burgeoning area of concern for researchers, policymakers, trade unions and workers is the impact that AI technologies (AITs) will have in the workplace. Some argue that AITs will herald a new world of work, where boring and dangerous jobs will be automated away by algorithms and intelligent robots – leaving more pleasant and creative jobs for us humans (Hyman, 2023). Others are optimistic about the skyrocketing productivity and innovation that may result from the expansion of AITs into the production process (The Economist, 2023). AITs, it is argued, will eliminate wasteful human expenditure, and self-learning algorithms will continue to discover ever-more efficient production pathways (Mariani and Vega-Lozada, 2022).

But some foresee, and are already observing, a much darker story. First, the deployment of AITs in workplaces is already having numerous adverse macro-economic effects. One concern is the politically salient question of whether AITs will bring forth a "job apocalypse" or simply create new jobs as old ones are automated away, and experts are sharply divided (Levy, 2018; Cappelli, 2020). It seems only time will tell, although large numbers of workers are already gripped by automation anxiety fearing that their jobs will be lost to AI in the near future (Smith and Anderson, 2017).

In addition, AITs are changing the management and governance of workplaces. Increasingly, managerial tasks and duties are being delegated to automated decision-making (ADMs) and algorithmic management systems (AM). This managerial transformation poses significant new risks for workers, especially privacy invasions. In order for AITs to function effectively, vast volumes of data must be collected through a significant surveillance operation. Ajunwa (2018) argues that legal systems will find it difficult to balance privacy rights of workers and employer interests in the use of these technologies at work. Other noted problems with AM systems is their lack of transparency, lack of accountability in their use and their generation of biased or prejudicial outcomes (Donoghue and Vieira, 2022; for wider discussion of regulatory concepts such as accountability or bias, see contributions in Part II of the *Handbook*).

Third, AITs are also changing the nature of work and how we experience it. The deployment of AITs creates highly "quantified" workplaces, made possible by wearable technologies and productivity-monitoring software (Lustig et al., 2016; Moore, 2017). This quantification of work creates high-pressure work environments, where workers are pushed to satisfy ever-higher performance metrics. Amazon Warehouses, for instance, have become (in)famous examples of this dynamic, as the company monitors "the activity of each workers' handheld package scanner to determine whether that worker is spending 'time off task'", and keeps a "tally of each worker's TOT down to the minute" (Ashworth, 2022). This kind of work intensification exacerbates a number of occupational health and safety (OSH) risks including greater fatigue, burnout, stress and anxiety (Moore, 2019).

This wide range of observed issues associated with AITs demands actionable policy solutions. To date, the solutions that have been adopted vary significantly by country. What follows is a critical comparison of the main regulatory approaches taken by China and the US to regulate AITs in the workplace. The cases of the US and China stand out as a natural juxtaposition not only because they are the two leading powers in the world, but because they are taking sharply different approaches to the regulation of AITs. In this chapter, we argue that the Chinese government has adopted an aggressive and top-down intervention. The consequences of this approach in China is indeterminate as it relies on effective implementation, but it does offer the possibility of emergent new social and labour rights: around explanation, transparency and consultation in use of algorithms. In the US, the patchwork regulation is rather focused on reinforcing existing rights to non-discrimination, rather than wider harms.

CHINA

The State of AIT Regulation in China

China is making an ambitious bid to be a global leader in AIT regulation, with a flurry of policy enactments over the last decade. This new regulatory era within China commenced with the "New Generation Artificial Intelligence Development Plan" (AIDP) published in July 2017, announcing the government's sweeping intention to "Establish an AI security supervision and evaluation system".[1] Two years later, in June 2019, an expert committee established by China's Ministry of Science and Technology (MOST) released a document outlining eight principles for AI governance and "responsible AI".[2] These declaratory documents signal that government leaders seek to shape digital space into a realm that they believe best promotes the public interest.

Government bodies tasked with regulating the internet and AITs have focused on digital labour platforms, as posing significant risks to the rights of gig workers. In September 2020, a report called "Delivery Rider, Trapped in the System" went viral on social media. This triggered a heated nationwide discussion on how Chinese citizens, including workers, are likely subjected to algorithmic manipulation (Youxuan, 2020), and prompted intense criticism of delivery platforms. These displays of public outrage have played a role in motivating government to pursue more robust regulation of AITs at work.

To date, most of the laws and policies regarding data and AI governance have taken an omnibus approach, meaning they apply across sectors, with the workplace being just one of the targets (Cai and Chen, 2022). Below, we focus on the most prominent laws and policies likely to be most important for workplaces. The Chinese government is constructing a regulatory infrastructure that can aggressively intervene to minimize the social risks caused by AITs. However, interpreting the exact consequences of this effort is complicated. There is still considerable ambiguity surrounding the substantive implications of these initiatives and laws for the workplace. The implementation of new laws, regulations and policies may vary across provincial and local jurisdictions, and the legal system will play a crucial role in clarifying how they are to be implemented in the workplace.

National Laws: PIPL

Since China has yet to initiate AI legislation by the National People's Congress, its Personal Information Protection Law (PIPL) passed and effective from 2021, is the main legal source of AIT regulation for branches of the State Council. PIPL is "a special legislation on personal information protection … [that] contains the basic principles, requirements and related systems for the protection of personal information" (Xiao and Shen, 2023). It is often described as a Chinese version of the EU's GDPR, given the similarities between them. This legislation is expected to have a significant impact because it "adopts a centralized and comprehensive model, which indicates that all the collecting and processing activities of personal information, regardless of the diverse purposes, subjects, or industries, shall fall into their jurisdiction and, consequently, are treated equally by the law" (Shi and Wang, 2023). PIPL thus establishes a basic framework for personal information protection across all industrial sectors. The regulations must be followed when using AITs to process personal information.

Moreover, Article 24 of the PIPL explicitly regulates the common application of AITs as part of automatic decision-making systems. It requires transparency, justification and fairness when data processors use ADM to make decisions, and bans unreasonable treatment through price discrimination or any other practices. Article 24 PIPL also empowers an individual access to clarifications on the ADM process and the right to deny results solely made by the ADM system when the results could significantly impact their rights and interests. This right is also recognized as "a right to explanation" and it has aroused heated discussion in both the US and the EU[3] (see Berry, Chapter 10 in this volume). China's PIPL is the first legislation to legislate explicitly for data processors' duty to explain algorithms while the EU has only described such a requirement in GDPR Recital 71.[4]

Companies utilizing AITs in the workplace, whether for traditional or platform work, should abide by PIPL rules since they generally apply to all industries. For example, Article 24 PIPL empowers workers to ask for explanations of algorithmic decision-making which significantly affect their labour rights. If a delivery rider or car-hailing driver has questions or complaints on the order distribution or service ratings, s/he can exercise a right to explanation of automatic decisions. According to the PIPL, platform workers may also submit a lawsuit against platform companies that refuse to guarantee the data rights of platform workers.

National Regulations: ARP

China's algorithm-specific regulation went into effect in March 2022 – the "Internet Information Service Algorithmic Recommendation Management Provisions (ARP)". It is claimed to be the first regulation of this kind in history (Yin, 2022). The ARP has one article which specifically deals with labour algorithms. The tech company that manages platform work has been recognized as a provider of "algorithmic recommendation services". It indicates that all ARP rules must be followed by platform work companies.

A central theme running through the ARP is enhancing the capacity of individuals to interact with algorithms or platforms on their own terms. Considerable emphasis is placed on the "protection of user rights", which includes appeals to user notification, norms disclosure, procedures for obtaining consent, provisions for opting out of monitoring and surveillance, and control over personal data. These protections constitute a considerable set of tools for individuals to circumscribe and resist the power of algorithms and contest their outputs. This may have major implications for workers, as labour is increasingly pushed into digitalized space. Workers confront a future characterized by heightened surveillance and management by smart technologies, and key provisions within the ARP can – in principle – be leveraged by employee representatives to limit and, in some cases eliminate, exploitative and dominating workplace practices. Examples include deleting user tags that signal personal characteristics; demanding explanation of algorithmic practice that influence worker interests; as well as amplified enforcement of existing labour rights.

The ARP also commits to aligning algorithmic recommendation services to the promotion of the "common good". For the field of labour in China, the "common good" means a harmonious relationship between employers and employees. It remains contentious as to whether platform work should be recognized as standard employment protected by labour law. This has proved a source of tension as the government seeks to promote harmony between tech companies and platform workers. The "common good" objective underscores the Chinese government's intention to implement a social model of governance that directly oversees the adoption of algorithmic and AITs. Furthermore, the duties imposed on algorithmic recommendation service providers mandate explicitly socially oriented observances like advancing "the social public interest", respecting "national security", not "upsetting the economic or social order", and preventing "addiction or excessive consumption" among other imperatives related to the general welfare. Again, this policy goal may be utilized to promote worker well-being, because improved working conditions are ostensibly in the social interest and provide stability to the economic order.

National Policies: Document No. 56

In July 2021, a guideline called "Guiding Opinions on Protecting the Labour Rights and Interests of Workers under New Forms of Employment" (hereinafter as "Document No. 56") was published by the Ministry of Human Resources and Social Security (MOHRSS) together with seven other departments.[5] This is the first time China's labour department has issued a normative legal document that mentions labour algorithms directly. Document No. 56 emphasizes the need to increase algorithmic transparency, requiring that companies using algorithms which affect workers' rights and interests must consult on the development of those algorithms with trade unions or workers' representatives.

Subsequently, another, more detailed document regulating labour algorithms for online catering was published.[6] In China, the most prominent companies that employ gig workers are online catering platforms. In accordance with the requirement for transparency in Document No. 56, the guidance for online catering stipulates that algorithmic rules affecting the vital interests of food delivery workers must be made public in advance so that food delivery workers, unions and other parties can provide their input. Such advice may include how they want the platform to improve the algorithms. For example, gig workers and the trade union can provide feedback on how to improve the algorithms, such as by predicting more reasonable delivery times in order to preserve a balance between efficiency and safety.

Soon after the two documents were launched, on 10 September 2021, MOHRSS and four other governmental departments, met with the ten leading food delivery and ride-sharing platform companies including Meituan, Didi and Eleme, in order to get them to follow the new regulations, and to enhance working conditions, such as improving income distribution, and ensuring rest periods. On the same day as the "910 meeting", Chinese food delivery giant Meituan explained its algorithms to the public for the first time.

The China Approach: Aggressive but Ambiguous Efforts to Create New Protections (for Workers)

Some general observations can be drawn about the Chinese approach to regulating AITs in the world of work. First, the state is seeking to ensure that existing labour rights (e.g. entitlement to wages, rest, workplace safety, etc.) remain inviolate with the spread of AITs. For example, Document No. 56 stipulates that platform workers have a legally mandated claim to the minimum wage. This will play a crucial role in stemming some of the previously discussed risks like work intensification.

Second, the state is laying the foundation for a new kind of social and workplace right, what might be called "the right to explanation". The Chinese government seems to be reacting to the problem of transparency (Ajunwa, 2020; also see Aula and Erikkilä, Chapter 13 in this volume), by pursuing policies like PIPL and ARP that will require labour algorithmic systems to become trustworthy and accountable. As we have seen, these omnibus regulations equip workers with additional tools for resisting domination by AITs that are opaque or hard to understand. The strongest of these tools is the right to an explanation of automatic decisions. Failure to act on workers' requests could result in costly litigation and reputational harm to companies. This constitutes a strong incentive for companies to meet their legal obligations to avoid government sanctions.

Third, the Chinese approach includes efforts to improve worker input to contest AIT abuse and overreach. The importance of empowered worker input has been emphasized in numerous regulatory documents. For example, the most recent revision of China's Trade Union Law makes clear that gig workers are entitled to join unions (Huld, 2022). This is critical, as at the moment, such workers are often precluded from such representation due to their legal classification as independent contractors or self-employed. Furthermore, the new requirement (Document No. 56) that digital labour platforms consult workers on algorithm design and use, when those algorithms directly affect labour rights, may eventually lead to the co-determination of algorithmic rules, that better track the interests of workers.

In practical terms, however, the impact of many of the new directives and laws on workers remains unclear. Some of these bills were written with consumers in mind more so than workers. For example, the PIPL has given individuals a right to refuse decisions made solely by automatic decision-making systems. This is good for consumers, but it is impossible for a platform worker to exercise such right as the automatic decision-making system is the technical premise of platform work. It is believed that the everyday significance of these regulatory efforts will be clearer when workers marshal policies like ARP and PIPL directly to challenge workplace malpractice in the courts. When the courts begin to adjudicate employee suits in reference to these policies, the rights conferred by them will become clearer[7] – but this has yet to happen in any substantive way, adding to the overall state of ambiguity.

UNITED STATES

The United States (US) is not a standard setter in AI regulation. This is likely due to a couple of overarching factors. Firstly, wider public policy norms endorse a pro-business and anti-regulation approach in relation to AI development and use, valuing the freedom of entrepreneurship above other potential social objectives like user protections (Thierer, 2022; Solowey, 2023). Attention focuses on wining the "AI race" by attracting substantial (foreign) capital investment, among arguments that excessive regulation might discourage investments and impede innovation, as has been an alleged outcome in Europe with the AI Act (O'Sullivan, 2017; Toh, 2023); also see Mügge, Chapter 19 in this volume; Paul, Chapter 20 in this volume).

There is no clear governmental arm tasked with regulating AITs in the US. The distribution of power between public authorities has resulted in a confused and patchwork regulatory landscape. The most robust advances in AI regulation stem from executive regulatory agencies and state and local governments. This contrasts with the centralized and intentional approach demonstrated by other great powers like China and the EU. Despite the US's noted lack of a grand strategy, there is an overarching and consistent theme amongst all efforts so far to regulate AITs in the world of work. Federal, state and local actors are all rushing to protect individuals from the harm of discrimination in ADM processes. The focus is on the extension of long-existing rights and protections against new technologies.

The Federal Level: Executive Orders, Legislation and Agency Directives

At the time of writing, there are no bills or laws directly targeted at regulating the development or use of AITs – except for the National AI Initiative Act which does not contain regulatory implications per se.

The most significant development is the Algorithmic Accountability Act of 2022 with a focus on transparency (Chu, 2022) (see Aula and Erkkilä, Chapter 13 in this volume). If enacted into law, it will require organizations deploying ADM to "take several concrete steps to identify and mitigate the social, ethical, and legal risks" (Mökander et al., 2022). As workers are often subjected to the determinations of ADS, this bill presents some beneficial opportunities if eventually enacted, and it has inspired comparisons with the EU's AI Act. However, its application and scope are limited to large companies, it lacks the specificity of the EU AIA and is focused exclusively on "equal treatment of decision subjects and equal outcomes for different protected groups". Moreover, there are serious limitations that may prevent the Federal Trade Commission (FTC: the body tasked with enforcing this law) from effectively enforcing these objectives (Gursoy et al., 2022).

An early federal-level intervention was an Executive Order of the Trump administration, but this focused on AI as an economic and security good; the workforce is addressed as productive potential not as persons at risk of domination by AITs. The Biden White House did publish a non-binding white paper proposing an "AI Bill of Rights" in October of 2022. Described as a "blueprint" it contains five core principles that should guide the responsible development and deployment of AI systems in the US:

- safe and effective systems;
- algorithmic discrimination protections;
- data privacy;

- notice and explanation;
- human alternatives, consideration and fallback.

This blueprint constitutes a major step forward in thinking about how future policy could be designed to protect workers from AITs. Data privacy and notice and explanation may offer tools for workers to contest unlawful automated decisions when subjected to them. The right to human alternatives and fallback could provide insight to avoid automated sanctioning and identifying legally prohibited algorithmic activity, but this is not a statute.

A third federal avenue is the decision-making power of executive agencies. For example, through the *Joint Statement on Enforcement Efforts Against Discrimination and Bias in Automated Systems* the Consumer Financial Protection Bureau (CFPB), the Civil Rights Division of the Justice Department, the Equal Employment Opportunity Commission (EEOC) and the Federal Trade Commission[8] have started to clarify their regulatory power to regulate AITs, and articulate what this could mean for businesses, consumers, workers, debtors, and among other data subjects.

As AITs continue to be integrated into business activities, the scope for FCT enforcement in relation to AITs grows, with some potential impacts for workers. DiResta and Sherman (2023) argue that the FTC has two specific powers with implications for workers:

- *Section 5 of the FTC Act* prohibits unfair or deceptive practices. That would include the sale or use of – for example – racially biased algorithms.
- *Fair Credit Reporting Act may take effect* where an algorithm is used to deny people employment, housing, credit, insurance or other benefits.

In October of 2021, the EEOC launched its own "initiative to ensure that AI used in hiring and other employment decisions complies with federal civil rights laws" (US Equal Employment Opportunity Commission, 2022a). This was followed by official guidance on 12 May 2022 that, "provides practical tips to employers on how to comply with the Americans with Disabilities Act ('ADA'), and to job applicants and employees who think that their rights may have been violated" (Cain et al., 2022). According to the EEOC, these might commonly include:

- the employer not providing "reasonable accommodation" necessary for a job applicant or employee to be rated fairly and accurately by the algorithm;
- the employer relying on an algorithmic decision-making tool that intentionally or unintentionally "screens out" an individual with a disability, even though that individual is able to do the job with a reasonable accommodation;
- the employer adopting an algorithmic decision-making tool for use with its job applicants or employees that violates the ADA's restrictions on disability-related inquiries and medical examinations (US Equal Employment Opportunity Commission, 2022b).

These examples underscore that executive agencies are starting to accept responsibility for applying their regulatory powers to the use of AITs, but their focus is limited to using existing powers. This means that workers generally stand to benefit from the civil rights protections they currently enjoy against discriminatory treatment along protected characteristics. Whilst the maintenance of such protections is important, it does not constitute a new form of workplace regulation spurred by the immersion of AITs into the world of work.

State and Local Legislation and Initiatives

Across the US, numerous state and local governments are taking up initiatives to regulate AI, especially harms typically associated with AI systems of discriminative ADM, privacy and data ownership.[9] New York City Council passed Local Law 144 (enforceable since 5 January 2023) which "requires enterprises to obtain bias audits of automated employment decision tools (AEDTs)" (Hilliard, 2023). The City Council was prompted to act due to "increasing concerns about the risks of using automated tools to make employment decisions" by New York City employers (Levine and Hilliard, 2023).

The state of California is also taking steps to curb the potential abuses of AI in workplaces. In March 2022, the California Fair Employment and Housing Council published "draft modifications to its employment anti-discrimination laws that would impose liability on companies or third-party agencies administering artificial intelligence tools that have a discriminatory impact" (Ochs and Betts, 2022). They note that these modifications to existing laws would make it:

> it unlawful for an employer or covered entity to 'use … automated-decision systems, or other selection criteria that screen out or tend to screen out an applicant or employee … on the basis' of a protected characteristic, unless the 'selection criteria' used "are shown to be job-related for the position in question and are consistent with business necessity".

Several other states are passing similar types of legislation. A notable example is the Artificial Intelligence Video Interview Act passed by the state of Illinois that took effect in January 2020. The central aim of the law is to protect prospective applicants' privacy through three primary requirements: (a) by requiring consent from applicants prior to the use of AI software, (b) prohibiting the distribution of interview materials with third parties and (c) requiring the deletion of materials submitted by applicants within a month of their request (Heilweil, 2020). Other pending regulatory efforts include the Washington DC's proposed Stop Discrimination by Algorithms Act, Connecticut's Senate Bill SB 1103 ("An Act concerning artificial intelligence, automated decision-making and personal data privacy"), and New Jersey's Assembly Bill 4909 (requiring bias audits for ADM systems).

The US Approach: Patchwork Efforts to Reinforce Existing Protections

The sections above demonstrate a consistent theme when it comes to US regulation of AI and its impact on the world of work: there is simply no systematized approach to regulating how this kind of technology can and will be used in the workplace. For now, a patchwork approach dominates with federal, state and local legislatures and agencies taking their own measures where they can. At the federal level, in both the US Congress and the Executive branch, there appears to be serious uncertainty over how to proceed beyond spending money on research and development. Again, this is probably due to a combination of corporate influence, a fear of hampering innovation and investment, and even a lack of confidence about how to regulate these technologies (Koopman and Chilson, 2023).

However, what does remain consistent across initiatives from federal legislation to executive agencies, to state and local laws, however, is a focus on protecting individuals from discrimination against legally protected characteristics. Indeed, none of the developments cited above indicate a regulatory objective that extends (meaningfully) beyond protecting individuals from having to engage with or be subjected to the determinations of a biased or discriminatory AIT – although, the non-binding advisory principles of the AI Bill of Rights do articulate a more comprehensive regulatory agenda. The regulatory agenda of the US, thus far, is committed to a very circumscribed remit of concern: namely, that AITs do not make automated decisions that contravene already existing protections around key characteristics.

Overall, this approach offers very little protection for workers. The core promise is that "employment related decisions" should be rendered "non-arbitrary", but only in a very specific way: namely, workers can expect not to be prevented from accessing opportunities or be sanctioned by employers based on their protected characteristics (as defined in current US law). In the face of revolutionary technological advances, US lawmakers and regulators are not responding with equally revolutionary rules. They are merely denying employers the opportunity to use AITs as an excuse for discriminatory behaviour. Even this promise of social justice is itself highly tenuous for workers as it is not universally nor rigorously enforced, given the absence of federal legislation.

The AI Bill of Rights published by the White House does bring a wider spectrum of protections for workers into consideration. Framing this as a Bill of Rights indicates that these rights are universal and inalienable. Moreover, it would extend rights beyond the limited "protected characteristics" focus with commitments to "safe and effective systems, "data privacy", "notice and explanation" and "human alternatives, consideration, and fallback". These other aims present a suite of new rights that workers could leverage when confronting domination in the workplace.

CONCLUSION: TWO DIVERGENT APPROACHES TO AIT REGULATION IN THE WORLD OF WORK

Based on our reading of recent policy developments in China and the US, we can see that these nations are approaching the regulatory question of AITs in starkly different ways.

We categorize their different approaches along three axes, as visualized in Table 26.1. Their first point of divergence is their respective "regulatory spirit", by which we mean how government leaders generally conceptualize their role in relation to the issue. China's leaders demonstrate a preference for aggressive intervention in the economy and business institutions to set clear, strong and (what they consider) prosocial boundaries on the applications of AITs. In contrast, the US is gripped by a laissez-faire regulatory spirit, continuing its tendency to support industry-self regulation and limited government interference.

Another noted distinction is the regulatory approaches of these two countries. China is capitalizing on its aggressive spirit by taking an expressly top-down approach in setting the regulatory agenda surrounding AITs. The Communist Party of China (CPC) and the government (both central and local) are integrating themselves into key economic structures in order

Table 26.1   *A comparative overview of AIT regulation in China and the US*

China	USA
Regulatory spirit: aggressive	Regulatory spirit: laissez-faire
Regulatory approach: top-down	Regulatory approach: patchwork
Regulatory logic: social harmony	Regulatory logic: social justice

to guide the development of AITs so as to maintain technological safety and align with the public good. The reconfiguration of government agencies in recent years, such as the creation of the Cyber Administration of China (CAC), underscores this approach. Meanwhile, we have seen that the US approach is best characterized as a "patchwork", given the uncoordinated activity of numerous different authorities at different jurisdiction levels. Unlike China, the US lacks a federal, cohesive position on how AITs ought to be regulated.

The third axis captures the loftiness of the efforts taken by regulators and legislators in each country. China's policy measures seek not only to reinforce already existing worker rights, but potentially foster new ones such as the right to explanation and improved worker voice in the development and use of AITs. The requirement that workers be consulted in the creation of algorithms is unique, because it constitutes an "active right" to participate in the development of workplace managerial practices, as opposed to merely a "passive right" of protection against some particular harm.

The US approach, on the other hand, aligns with its tendency towards industry/employer self-regulation coupled with a reaffirmation of civil rights presently held by workers in relation to protected characteristics. Workers are not active participants in shaping how these new technologies function in the workplace. It seems, then, that the Chinese government is pursuing a more active agenda to proactively prevent social disharmony that may erupt over the dominating effects and experiences associated with AITs (as occurred with the "Delivery Rider, Trapped in the System" report). Whereas US lawmakers demonstrably prefer a light-touch approach that still encompasses a commitment to social justice understood as fairness and equality in automated-decision making process along certain individual characteristics.

NOTES

1. See "V. Guarantee measures" of AIDP.
2. The eight principles are I. Harmony and friendliness; II. Fairness and justice; III. Inclusivity and sharing; IV. Respect privacy; V. Secure/safe and controllable; VI. Shared responsibility; VII. Open collaboration; VIII. Agile governance.
3. One of the most notable articles discusses "a right to explanation": see Wachter et al. (2017).
4. GDPR Recital 71, "In any case, such processing should be subject to suitable safeguards, which should include specific information to the data subject and the right to obtain human intervention, to express his or her point of view, to obtain an explanation of the decision reached after such assessment and to challenge the decision."
5. More analysis of Document No. 56, see Popov (2022).
6. It is called "Guidance on the implementation of the responsibility of online catering platforms to effectively safeguard the rights and interests of take-away food delivery personnel". It was published by the State Administration for Market Regulation (SAMR) with other government departments.
7. The judicial cases so far have mainly focused on whether the platform workers are employees. Few workers have filed lawsuits over data or algorithmic rights. See Wang et al. (2023).
8. Available from: https://www.ftc.gov/system/files/ftc_gov/pdf/EEOC-CRT-FTC-CFPB-AI-Joint-Statement%28final%29.pdf.
9. Available from: https://www.uschamber.com/technology/state-by-state-artificial-intelligence-legislation-tracker.

REFERENCES

Ajunwa, I. (2018) 'Algorithms at Work: Productivity Monitoring Applications and Wearable Technology', *Faculty Publications*, p. 21.

Ajunwa, I. (2020) 'The "Black Box" at Work', *Big Data & Society*, **7** (2), https://doi.org/10.1177/2053951720938093.

Ashworth, B. (2022) 'Amazon Watches Its Workers and Waits for Them to Fail', *Wired*, 6 April. Available at: https://www.wired.com/story/amazon-worker-tracking-details-revealed/ (Accessed: 24 September 2023).

Cai, P. and Chen, L. (2022) 'Demystifying Data Law in China: A Unified Regime of Tomorrow', *International Data Privacy Law*, **12** (2), 75–92.

Cain, P. et al. (2022) 'EEOC Issues Artificial Intelligence Guidance', *JD Supra*, 6 February. Available at: https://www.jdsupra.com/legalnews/eeoc-issues-artificial-intelligence-2457882/ (Accessed: 25 September 2023).

Cappelli, P. (2020) *The Consequences of AI-based Technologies for Jobs*. Brussels: European Commission Directorate-General for Research and Innovation. Available at: https://research-and-innovation.ec.europa.eu/knowledge-publications-tools-and-data/publications/all-publications/consequences-ai-based-technologies-jobs_en (Accessed: 24 September 2023).

Chu, K. (2022) *Wyden, Booker and Clarke Introduce Algorithmic Accountability Act of 2022 to Require New Transparency and Accountability for Automated Decision Systems*, Ron Wyden United States Senator for Oregon. Available at: https://www.wyden.senate.gov/news/press-releases/wyden-booker-and-clarke-introduce-algorithmic-accountability-act-of-2022-to-require-new-transparency-and-accountability-for-automated-decision-systems (Accessed: 25 September 2023).

DiResta, A. and Sherman, Z. (2023) 'The FTC Is Regulating AI: A Comprehensive Analysis | Insights', *Holland & Knight*, 25 July. Available at: https://www.hklaw.com/en/insights/publications/2023/07/the-ftc-is-regulating-ai-a-comprehensive-analysis (Accessed: 25 September 2023).

Donoghue, R. and Vieira, T. (2022) 'Horrible Bosses: How Algorithm Managers Are Taking Over the Office', *The Conversation*. Available at: http://theconversation.com/horrible-bosses-how-algorithm-managers-are-taking-over-the-office-191307 (Accessed: 24 September 2023).

Gursoy, F., Kennedy, R. and Kakadiaris, I. (2022) 'A Critical Assessment of the Algorithmic Accountability Act of 2022'. Rochester, NY. Available at: https://doi.org/10.2139/ssrn.4193199.

Heilweil, R. (2020) 'Illinois Says You Should Know If AI Is Grading Your Online Job Interviews', *Vox*, 1 January. Available at: https://www.vox.com/recode/2020/1/1/21043000/artificial-intelligence-job-applications-illinios-video-interivew-act (Accessed: 25 September 2023).

Hilliard, A. (2023) 'Assembly Bill A07859: New York's Steps Towards Transparency in HR Tech', *Holistic AI*, 7 October. Available at: https://www.holisticai.com/blog/new-york-assembly-bill-a07859 (Accessed: 25 September 2023).

Huld, A. (2022) 'China Trade Unions: Requirements for Employers Under Amended Law', *China Briefing News*, 17 February. Available at: https://www.china-briefing.com/news/china-trade-unions-considerations-for-employers-under-new-amended-law/ (Accessed: 25 September 2023).

Hyman, L. (2023) 'Opinion | It's Not the End of Work. It's the End of Boring Work', *The New York Times*, 22 April. Available at: https://www.nytimes.com/2023/04/22/opinion/jobs-ai-chatgpt.html (Accessed: 24 September 2023).

Koopman, C. and Chilson, N. (2023) 'Pausing AI Development Would Be a Mistake. Congress Shouldn't Meddle – For Now', *USA TODAY*, 22 May. Available at: https://www.usatoday.com/story/opinion/2023/05/22/ai-pause-mistake-us-tech/70235637007/ (Accessed: 25 September 2023).

Levine, L. and Hilliard, A. (2023) 'The Evolution of NYC Local Law 144: An Overview of the Key Changes', *Holistic AI*, 19 May. Available at: https://www.holisticai.com/blog/nyc-local-law-144-key-changes (Accessed: 25 September 2023).

Levy, F. (2018) 'Computers and Populism: Artificial Intelligence, Jobs, and Politics in the Near Term', *Oxford Review of Economic Policy*, **34** (3), 393–417. Available at: https://doi.org/10.1093/oxrep/gry004.

Lustig, C. et al. (2016) 'Algorithmic Authority: The Ethics, Politics, and Economics of Algorithms that Interpret, Decide, and Manage', in *Proceedings of the 2016 CHI Conference Extended Abstracts on*

Human Factors in Computing Systems. New York: Association for Computing Machinery (CHI EA '16), pp. 1057–1062. Available at: https://doi.org/10.1145/2851581.2886426.

Mariani, K. and Vega-Lozada, F. (2022) 'The Use of AI and Algorithms for Decision-making in Workplace Recruitment Practices'. Rochester, NY. Available at: https://papers.ssrn.com/abstract= 4544420 (Accessed: 24 September 2023).

Mökander, J. et al. (2022) 'The US Algorithmic Accountability Act of 2022 vs. the EU Artificial Intelligence Act: What Can They Learn from Each Other?', *Minds and Machines*, **32** (4), 751–758. Available at: https://doi.org/10.1007/s11023-022-09612-y.

Moore, P. V. (2017) *The Quantified Self in Precarity: Work, Technology and What Counts*. Abingdon, UK and New York: Routledge.

Moore, P. V. (2019) 'OSH and the Future of Work: Benefits and Risks of Artificial Intelligence Tools in Workplaces', in V. G. Duffy (ed.), *Digital Human Modeling and Applications in Health, Safety, Ergonomics and Risk Management. Human Body and Motion*. Cham, Switzerland: Springer International Publishing (Lecture Notes in Computer Science), pp. 292–315. Available at: https://doi .org/10.1007/978-3-030-22216-1_22.

Ochs, D. and Betts, J. (2022) 'California's Draft on Use of AI for Employment Decisions', *The National Law Review*, 13 May. Available at: https://www.natlawreview.com/article/california-s-draft -regulations-spotlight-artificial-intelligence-tools-potential-to (Accessed: 25 September 2023).

O'Sullivan, A. (2017) 'Don't Let Regulators Ruin AI', *MIT Technology Review*, 24 October. Available at: https://www.technologyreview.com/2017/10/24/3937/dont-let-regulators-ruin-ai/ (Accessed: 25 September 2023).

Popov, G. (2022) 'China and International Labor Standards: New Guidelines Extend Labor Protections to Platform Workers', *NYU Journal of International Law & Politics*, https://www.nyujilp.org/wp -content/uploads/2022/04/Popov_online_formatted-131-138_final.pdf.

Shi, Z. and Wang, Y. (2023) 'China's Risk Approach to Data Privacy: Analyzing China's New Personal Information Protection Law Under a Comparative Perspective'. Rochester, NY. Available at: https:// doi.org/10.2139/ssrn.4432303.

Smith, A. and Anderson, M. (2017) *Americans' attitudes toward a future in which robots and computers can do many human jobs*. Washington, DC: Pew Research Center. Available at: https:// www.pewresearch.org/internet/2017/10/04/americans-attitudes-toward-a-future-in-which-robots-and -computers-can-do-many-human-jobs/ (Accessed: 25 September 2023).

Solowey, J. (2023) 'Regulators Must Avert Overreach When Targeting AI', Cato Institute, 13 September. Available at: https://www.cato.org/commentary/regulators-must-avert-overreach-when-targeting-ai (Accessed: 25 September 2023).

The Economist (2023) 'Your Job is (Probably) Safe from Artificial Intelligence', *The Economist*, 5 July. Available at: https://www.economist.com/finance-and-economics/2023/05/07/your-job-is-probably -safe-from-artificial-intelligence (Accessed: 24 September 2023).

Thierer, A. (2022) 'Why Is the US Following the EU's Lead on Artificial Intelligence Regulation?', *The Hill*, 21 July. Available at: https://thehill.com/opinion/technology/3569151-why-is-the-us-following -the-eus-lead-on-artificial-intelligence-regulation/ (Accessed: 25 September 2023).

Toh, M. (2023) '"Serious Concerns": Top Companies Raise Alarm over Europe's Proposed AI Law', *CNN*, 30 June. Available at: https://www.cnn.com/2023/06/30/tech/eu-companies-risks-ai-law-intl -hnk/index.html (Accessed: 25 September 2023).

Wachter, S., Mittelstadt, B. and Floridi, L. (2017) 'Why a Right to Explanation of Automated Decision-making Does Not Exist in the General Data Protection Regulation', *International Data Privacy Law*, **7** (2), 76–99.

Wang, Q., Chen, Y. and Yang, Y. (2023) 'Unpacking the Legal Status of Platform Workers in China: An Empirical Analysis of Judicial Attitudes and Challenges in the Food Delivery Sector', *Asia Pacific Law Review*, **32** (1), 149–171.

Xiao, F. and Shen, R. (2023) *Analysis of the Highlights of the Personal Information Protection Law*. Deloitte. Available at: https://www2.deloitte.com/cn/en/pages/risk/articles/personal-information-pro tection-law-analysis.html (Accessed: 25 September 2023).

US Equal Employment Opportunity Commission (2022a) 'Artificial Intelligence and Algorithmic Fairness Initiative', 31 January, https://www.eeoc.gov/ai.

US Equal Employment Opportunity Commission (2022b) 'The Americans with Disabilities Act and the Use of Software, Algorithms, and Artificial Intelligence to Assess Job Applicants and Employees', 12 May, https://www.eeoc.gov/laws/guidance/americans-disabilities-act-and-use-software-algorithms-and-artificial-intelligence.

Yin, L. (2022) 'The World's First Legal Document Dedicated to Algorithms Has Been Officially Released', *Legal Weekly*, 1 April. Available at: http://mp.weixin.qq.com/s?__biz=MzI3MTYzODg0Mg==& mid=2247530305&idx=3&sn=745bbd1f84855d6b152a94fce0d615cc&chksm=eb3cff14dc4b7602 667e3f160869ae8121430b7637ccb54247b808dcaa548e8aa63c8d9f04db#rd.

Youxuan, L. (2020) 'Delivery Rider, Trapped in the System', *Weixin Official Accounts Platform*. Available at: http://mp.weixin.qq.com/s?__biz=MjEwMzA5NTcyMQ==&mid=2653119915&idx =1&sn=419be88865569ed1e39f806ffaa919ec&chksm=4eb2836d79c50a7bf2b628d8af2c4c42fe36 288829e217dbaaa95d17ce8c70ef0435bfe3c236#rd (Accessed: 25 September 2023).

27. Reimagining failed automation: from neoliberal punitive automated welfare towards a politics of care

Lyndal Sleep and Joanna Redden

INTRODUCTION

Social policy refers to the policies and practices created to provide welfare and services to support the health, dignity and needs of populations. While social policy encompasses a range of policies that relate to education, health care, ageing and social assistance, it is particularly necessary to address inequalities. Those serviced by social policy can be the most marginalised in a society, meaning that changes in social service can have an enormous impact on individual and family life chances, as well as on levels of equality and fairness in any society. The use of automation in social welfare has a different nuance to its application in other domains like taxation or consumer law because those that are impacted by policy shortfalls and technological glitches are often already economically and socially marginalised and often have fewer resources to challenge harms experienced and errors made, compounding already stressful and challenging living circumstances. When a family is one pay cheque from eviction, the smallest change in their welfare payment can mean the difference between paying the rent and homelessness.

This chapter discusses the automation of social welfare as an example of the increasing digitisation of government administrative processes, which must be viewed in connection with the wider social policy contexts that shape how systems are developed and implemented. This chapter takes the reader on a journey through some of the ways automation has manifested in different social policy contexts. It begins with a focus on the neoliberal social policy environments of Australia, the UK and the US where the move to increasing punitive approaches to welfare means that AI and automated technologies used in social policy are also geared towards punishment and personalisation of hardship as an individual responsibility.

In 2019, former UN Special Rapporteur Philip Alston said he was worried we were stumbling zombie-like into a digital welfare dystopia after researching how government agencies around the world were turning to digital, and largely automated, systems to inform welfare decision making and service administration (Alston 2019). The automation of fraud detection is part of this trend. Australia had Robodebt (Sleep et al. 2022), the Netherlands had the Systeem Risico Indicatie ('SyRI', Risk Indication System) (Redden 2018; Ng 2020) and Michigan in the US the Michigan Integrated Data Automated System (MiDAS) (Redden et al. 2022). This pattern continues outside wealthy Western neoliberal governments. South Korea also has a digital fraud detection programme in operation as part of its Social Security Information System (SSiS) (Korea Social Security Information Service 2022; Sleep et al. 2024). Serbia began automating some of its social protection programmes in 2022 as part of the new *socijalna karta*, social card system (Meaker 2023). Alston's research into Western welfare states found that while the intentions had been to cut costs, increase efficiency and target resources, they had in practice led to wide-ranging negative effects and harms. He raised concerns about the kind of shared dystopian futures we were moving into.

The use of automation in welfare fraud detection has been particularly prominent and problematic in this context, and we consider some disrupting and disrupted uses of automation for fraud detection – Robodebt in Australia and MiDAS in the US. We outline some significant policy lessons that can be learned from these well-known cancelled automated fraud detection applications. We then move on to consider an application of automated technologies in a social policy domain that appears to provide an alternative social, political and cultural context to the neoliberal punitive approach – the welfare Blind Spot Identification System (BSIS) in South Korea. We highlight some ways that AI technologies may manifest outside neoliberal aims which provide some foundations for imagining a move from punitive automated welfare in countries like the UK, US and Australia towards a politics of care. The crises of automation identified in this chapter are deeply connected to neoliberal assaults on social welfare, as well as longer histories of oppression and inequality (Milner and Traub 2021; Hoffmann 2020; Sleep 2022). A politics of care approach is informed by activists and academics arguing for politics and policy that prioritises meeting peoples' needs, promoting health and well-being for all while also recognising our interdependence on each other and the natural world (Woodly et al. 2021; Chassmen and Cohen 2020). This approach explicitly counters logics of austerity which maintain existing orders of privilege, and instead views practices of care as a necessary and interdependent survival strategy (Woodly et al. 2021). Some practices are detailed in the final discussion, and include an emphasis on decision making that is historically and contextually informed while centring social, economic and human rights. The importance of critical refusal as practice is stressed as a key component of any alternative approach to not just decision making around automation but our collective futures (Gangadharan 2021; Cifor et al. 2019; Hoffmann 2021).

PUNITIVE WELFARE EQUALS PUNITIVE AUTOMATED WELFARE DELIVERY

Previous empirical research on the automation of welfare services has demonstrated how the way automated systems are implemented and used in the US, the UK and Australia is directly tied to their neoliberal and austerity-driven contexts (Eubanks 2018; Dencik and Kaun 2020; Dencik et al. 2019). Understanding these contexts is important to our discussion of how it is that the harms we link to automating fraud detection in the following chapters occur.

Political turns towards neoliberalism in the 1970s and 1980s in Western democracies were often facilitated through shifts from wars on poverty to wars on the poor (Bashevkin 2002; Finkel 2006). Business lobbyists and others attempted to influence policy-makers by attacking Keynesian economics and government spending on social services, arguing that the discipline of the market was required across all areas to "smarten" civil society up (Finkel 2006). Political leaders in the US, the UK and Canada abandoned goals of full employment and also language that stresses the collective, mutual dependency and social justice (McGuigan 2009). Neoliberal discourses become dominant politically, which emphasise market values, individualisation and responsibility for the self (Harvey 2007; Foucault 2008; Bourdieu and Wacquant 2001).

In the 1980s, Western democracies like the US, the UK and Australia implemented wide-ranging welfare reforms that effectively transformed the post-World War II welfare state to align with and support neoliberal values, with an emphasis on individual responsibility and marketisation. In broad terms, these reforms seek to reframe how we understand the welfare state and the safety net it provides. Instead of a post 1930s depression-era recognition that macro and micro crises are a regular part of a capitalist system and that regulated and collective approaches are required to prevent harm and ensure equal opportunity, the welfare state is framed as bloated and unnecessary. Individuals who must access unemployment insurance or childcare subsidies are framed as "welfare dependent". Punitive approaches to welfare administration are introduced, including restricting access to welfare payments and imposing conditions on welfare receipt to encourage or compel recipients to take up any kind of paid employment, including low-paid, insecure work (Kingfisher 2013; Marston 2008; Mosher et al. 2010). In Australia, for example, the reform agenda has followed the lead of the US towards a "work-first" welfare state (Marston and McDonald 2007). This includes the introduction of onerous reporting obligations and compulsory participation in approved welfare-to-work activities, including for single mothers when their youngest child turns six. These welfare-to-work policies have been accompanied by new measures to regulate and scrutinise welfare recipients to guard against non-compliance and fraud (Grahame and Marston 2012; Marston and McDonald 2007).

While neoliberalism was a political and economic project, those advocating it understood the necessity of also changing the way people think and speak (Foucault 2008; Brown 2008). Critics noted early how neoliberal speak constrained communication by limiting discussions on key issues to neoliberal terms (Bourdieu and Wacquant 2001). Former UK Prime Minister Tony Blair's 1999 "Beveridge Lecture" which outlined his government's plans to reform welfare, focused on differentiating between people who are deserving of government assistance such as children versus the many people he identified as taking advantage of the welfare state (Redden 2014). This focus on child poverty over poverty more generally across Western democracies like the UK, the US and Canada reinforces the longstanding binary of deserving versus presumed undeserving people, while also undermining the idea that freedom from poverty should be a universal right (McKeen 2004). A focus on child poverty narrows debate from poverty as a structural and systemic issue connected to low wages, underemployment, job insecurity, exploitation, rising costs of housing, discrimination, differential access to opportunities like quality education and health care and a lack of affordable childcare (Redden 2014).

The term 'welfare dependency' has been long criticised as a neoliberal construct that places the responsibility of economic disadvantage, ill health or trauma onto the individual, rather than locating it in broad social structures of intersectional inequality, capitalism or colonialism (Marston and McDonald 2007; Mendes 2017; Zanoni 2023). It entrenches the stigma and exclusion of those who utilise welfare services, labelling them with harsh stereotypes like the "welfare queen" in the US and elsewhere (Hancock 2004; Baekgaard et al. 2023), and "dole bludger" in Australia (Archer 2009; Mendes 2017). The individualisation and stigmatisation of welfare was facilitated through often stereotypical representations of welfare users and felt by welfare users themselves. For example, Dean (1991) explains how welfare users in the UK feel so surveilled and distrusted that, despite there being means for administrative review of decisions, few pursue appeals because they fear the additional scrutiny. Similarly, in Canada the man-in-the-house rule, which denies or reduces payment to women who are in a relationship with a man, means in practice that women's relationships were scrutinised by the state and the general community were encouraged to report on welfare users who they suspected to be breaking the rule (Little and Morrison 1999). Cuts to the social welfare sector following the ascendancy of neoliberal-driven governance were accompanied by increasing resources to the penal system and prison populations in Australia, the US, the UK and Canada (Wacquant 2009; Walmsley 2005, 2009). The punitive solution became to change welfare users, to make them "better", and a raft of carrot-and-stick policies followed. In Australia, this became the Mutual Obligations reforms, based on the McClure reports, which emphasised that in return for receiving social security payments, recipients, who were reconstituted as "clients", were required to give back through various "agreed" activities. A series of punishments, in the form of breaches, were instigated to provide the "stick", if they wanted to keep receiving the "carrot" of payment. These measures were justified as a way to decrease "welfare dependency", and it was argued would force people on welfare to behave in a way that would develop values of independence and self-sufficiency. However, in reality, these policies were experienced as punishment by service users, often made life harder and reinforced the stigma and shame of receiving payments and services from the government (or the quasi-government bodies that were created during this period).

These "welfare reforms" were partnered by increasing digitisation in governmental administration in the UK, US, Australia and Canada. Krystle Maki (2011) details how the introduction of new technologies such as the consolidated verification procedure in Canada in the 1990s has led to economic exploitation, stigmatisation and marginalisation of poor families while deterring people from applying for support (Maki 2011). In Australia the Welfare Payment Infrastructure Transformation (WPIT) aims to "simplify" payments and services for a "customer centric ... flexible, modern welfare delivery system" (Services Australia 2022). However, social welfare recipients are not "customers" in the traditional market sense. They do not have the freedom to choose another provider, or other rules and regulations that suit them better, and they are subjected to harsh penalties if they do not comply despite often needing to access services in times of crisis. The WPIT overhaul entrenches the neoliberal focus on the individual, retracting services through punitive policies, in a new digitised and round-the-clock interface with carefully designed colours, hyperlinks and self-service (Sleep 2023).

While the digitisation of welfare states is often presented and promoted as a means of improving social services, the recent UN investigation into this phenomenon found that such shifts are often accompanied by major reductions in welfare budgets, a narrowing of who is eligible for services and support, service cuts as well as new and intrusive forms of conditionality (Alston 2019). Against the background of increasing digitisation of government administrative processes, the move from welfare as a citizenship right to welfare as punishment means that AI and automated technologies used in social policy in Western neoliberal welfare states are also geared towards punishment and personalisation of hardship as an individual responsibility. In a retracted welfare state social service users are often society's most (temporarily or structurally) marginalised and therefore vulnerable, unlike some other public services that provide for the wider population (cf. discussion on child protection by Krutzinna, Chapter 29 in this volume). Studying AITs in social policy has a very different nuance to studying them in other sectors (Sleep 2022). As Brown (2020, p. 115) observes:

Governments talk about trust being built into their systems (DTA 2018), and the Department wants to ensure "that customers trust their information is secure" (DHS 2016a, s. 20.5). But such assurances are usually made in the context of protecting personal data from external threats, rather than what bureaucrats might do lawfully with their data.

In these contexts distrust between the welfare provider and the service user is deep, and governments score political points by retracting services, openly punishing its "customers" according to neoliberal ideologies. AI technologies amplify and accelerate the neoliberal punitiveness of the Australian social security apparatus (Carney 2019).

Automated social security systems in the US and Europe have also been found to amplify and accelerate punitive practices with little accountability. Previous research details how fraud detection systems have wrongly targeted thousands of people in the US and Australia. This has meant people have been wrongly targeted by debt collectors and collection agencies, faced wrongful persecution, been bankrupted by being forced to pay debts they did not owe and faced stress, family breakdown and illness. In the Netherlands, after a coalition-led legal challenge, a government-run fraud detection system known as SyRI was ruled to cease immediately by the Court of First Instance in The Hague as being in violation of the right to privacy under the European Convention of Human Rights in February 2020 (Redden et al. 2022; van Bekkum and Borgesius 2021).[1] This was one of the first court rulings anywhere that halted a digital welfare initiative on human rights grounds (UN Special Rapporteur on Extreme Poverty and Human Rights 2020).

CASE STUDY 1: AUSTRALIA ROBODEBT

Australia's social security payment system is a series of payments administered by the national government and resourced by national taxation revenue. It is heavily means-tested, with significant apparatus in place to verify service users' eligibility.

The Online Compliance Intervention (OCI), colloquially known as Robodebt, was a fraud detection system that was operational between 2016 and 2020. It was part of an "integrated package of compliance and process improvement initiative including improved automation and targeted strategies for fraud prevention in areas of high risk" in an attempt to make the social security system more fiscally sustainable (Commonwealth of Australia 2016, p. 116).

The OCI matched annual Australian Tax Office income data with Department of Human Services fortnightly income records. When an apparent discrepancy between these amounts was identified, a letter was automatically sent to social security recipients asking them to confirm or update their income details online. Users were required to provide evidence of income for periods of up to ten years previously. If the service user did not update their earning details online by the due date, a debt was raised and the system automatically generated an account payable notice (a debt notice).

The scale of the OCI was significantly larger than the department's previous debt raising and recovery processes; approximately 700,000 debts per year compared to approximately 20,000 per year under the previous manual process (Glenn 2017).

However, serious issues soon emerged which led to Robodebt becoming internationally known as a "debacle" of automation in social policy. The OCI was revealed to be based on a flawed algorithm, which, in instances where income information was missing, made a calculation of annual income based on sporadic weekly income. This meant the annual income of workers in short term, casual or sporadic employment was overestimated and hundreds of thousands of social services users were issued incorrect debts (Commonwealth of Australia 2020). The scheme has been shown to be illegal, socially and politically unacceptable, and was disbanded in 2022 with some debt payments returned to service users after a class action against the government settled out of court and multiple Commonwealth Ombudsman and Senate enquiries. A Royal Commission into the administration of the scheme was competed in July 2023.

Harm, Injustice and a Lack of Accountability and Transparency

Stories of the stress caused by the debt notices, aggravated mental health issues, homelessness and suicides emerged in various media channels, with a collective sympathy towards social security recipients that is rare in Australian media (Carney 2019). In addition, an interactive website was set up by advocates for service users and invited people to share their Robodebt stories – notmydebt.com.au (#notmydebt.com 2022). In one case, in retaliation for this negative publicity, the government "publicly released personal information about people who spoke about the [OCI] process", compounding the trauma caused to service users impacted by the programme (Senate 2017, p. 107).

Government Investigation and Review

The Australian Commonwealth Ombudsman highlighted issues with the "accessibility, usability and transparency of the system, including quality of services delivery and procedural fairness" (2017, 2021). They found that the initial letter was "unclear" and omitted "crucial information". Further, "many complainants did not realise their income would be averaged across the employment period if they did not enter their income again each fortnight" (Commonwealth Ombudsman 2017, p. 2). The Ombudsman also identified that "many of the OCI's implementation problems could have been mitigated through better project planning and risk management at the outset" (2017, p. 3). The system was also criticised for placing the onus of proof onto service users, who needed to prove the calculation was incorrect or be served a debt to repay unentitled funds. At the same time, avenues for correcting incorrect estimates were unclear.

In July 2023, the Royal Commission into Robodebt was completed, reporting a blatant failure of administrative care, calling it a failure of public service culture when such widespread harms to citizens as well as legal processes are ignored for ideological politics.

CASE STUDY 2: MICHIGAN INTEGRATED DATA AUTOMATED SYSTEM (MIDAS)

In 2013 Michigan's Unemployment Insurance Agency launched the Integrated Data Automated System to administer and process unemployment benefits, and to also automate fraud assessment. After MiDAS was implemented, the system began generating wrong accusations of fraud. It has been reported that as many as 40,000 false accusations were made within the first two years the system was used (de la Garza 2020).

The MiDAS system was developed by three private vendors: the SAS Institute, FAST Enterprises LLC and CSG Government Solutions, although FAST Enterprises is reported as the main developer. The company was awarded a $47 million contract to build the system (Wykstra 2020). This is in addition to $18 million awarded to CSG Government Solutions to provide onsite project management and $14 million to SAS Analytics to integrate fraud detection software into the system.

The MiDAS system was used to determine the eligibility of unemployment insurance claims by analysing data from past and present claimants, searching for wage-record irregularities and discrepancies between claimants and their employers accounts for the reasons employment ended. The entire process was automated. An inconsistency in the data would lead to the claimant being flagged for potential fraud and an email notice would be sent to the claimant's unemployment insurance email address, not the person's personal address (Shaefer interview 2020 referenced in Redden et al. 2022, p. 14; see also Shaefer and Gray 2015). The claimant was given ten days to respond and if there was no response, the system automatically issued a charge for repayment as well as quadrupling the penalty. After a 30-day appeal period the state was able to garnish a person's wages and income tax refunds as well as make a criminal referral if payments were not made (Wykstra 2020). The Agency has acknowledged that the system ran from 2013 to 2015, for the most part, without any human review (Wykstra 2020).

As with Robodebt, one of the main problems with the system was that the method used for detecting inconsistencies was flawed. The system was not developed in a way that recognised that many claimants work varying hours due to insecure, contractual and temporary work (Shaefer interview 2020 referenced in Redden et al. 2022, p. 14). For example, the system would average how much was earned across hours worked for three months and use that figure as the weekly average, which was often different to the amounts reported each week by claimants. If the hours reported by the claimant differed from MiDAS averaging, the claimant would be flagged for fraud (Shaefer interview 2020 referenced in Redden et al. 2022, p. 14). The inability of automated fraud detection systems to account for, and be responsive to, the complexity and precarity of claimants' lives seems to be a key feature of many of these systems. For example, this has also been identified as a significant problem with the UK's automated universal credit system and with similar systems introduced across the US (Griffiths 2021; Gilman and Madden 2022). Another key feature of these systems is that developers do not consult with system users about either the assumptions informing development, or system design and impact.

An impact assessment was not done before or after the MiDAS system was implemented, with system administrators describing the system as being developed and deployed "in record breaking time". The impact of the system on those falsely flagged has been reported in legal challenges and media reports. Negative effects include personal trauma, evictions, house foreclosures, homelessness, bankruptcies and ruined credit (Charette 2018). In some cases it would take years for the Unemployment Insurance Agency to admit that the fraud allegations were made in error, which meant that any repayment of wrongly captured funds would come nowhere near covering the costs and impacts associated with a wrongful charge.

Contestation, Mobilisation and Legal Action

Community-level push-back has been ongoing and widespread. People wrongly accused of fraud contacted the Michigan Unemployment Insurance Clinic as well as other community organisations (Redden et al. 2022). Members of these organisations responded by taking a number of actions. These actions included writing to the US Department of Labor urging investigation. There was critical media coverage (Felton 2015). Two audits were conducted which provided key details and also reported 40,000 false fraud cases, a 93 per cent inaccuracy rate and that 96 per cent of people who made calls to the Agency that were ignored (Redden et al. 2022).

Mobilisation led to political action as Michigan's state representative wrote to the Governor urging a review of claims of fraud and that people harmed by inaccurate determinations be fully reimbursed (Levin 2016). A number of lawsuits were filed against the Unemployment Insurance Agency. While many were dismissed, *Zynda et al. v. Arwood et al.* has been noted as a key case because it resulted in a settlement that ordered the Unemployment Insurance Agency to stop automating adjudications and introduce human oversight (Michigan Eastern District Court 2017; Redden et al. 2022).

One of the lawyers involved in challenging the system has argued that a lack of due process was a fundamental flaw in the system, because the state was accusing people and taking their money without due process. It has been argued that the combined efforts of community mobilisation, political outcry including federal government pressure and legal challenges led the Unemployment Insurance Agency to admit there was a problem (Charette 2018, Fleming and Fournier 2015). The Michigan State legislature passed a law in 2017 requiring fraud detection be done manually (de la Garza 2020). At the time of writing, legal proceedings were continuing to seek remuneration to people for the damage caused due to charges and financial penalties made in error.

CASE STUDY 3: SOUTH KOREA BLIND SPOT IDENTIFICATION SYSTEM

Our overview of automation highlighted above as well as in previous research (Redden et al. 2022) demonstrates the widespread harm caused by automating social services which affect people's access to necessities for life and well-being. By pointing to South Korea in the following paragraphs our aim is not to argue for automation, but to demonstrate how alternative imaginaries can inform alternative uses of technology by governments. Examples like this demonstrate that our technologically mediated present and future are not inevitable, but shaped by different values, visions and context-specific struggles.

In contrast to the punitive approaches to automation outlined above, in South Korea data systems have been used to provide increased access to social support. The identification of welfare blind spots, households and neighbourhoods that have not accessed social services despite need, has been a public issue in South Korea for many decades (Nam and Park 2020). An ongoing series of media reports of suicides due to financial hardship has problematised the need for vulnerable people to apply for social services in order to receive support and the Korean government, in partnership with the private sector, has implemented an array of in-person and digital systems to identify and locate individuals and families who may become the next tragedy if left unsupported (Lee and Koo 2010).

In 2009 the Korean SSiS, which is responsible for operation of the social security information system (Haengbok-E-eum[2]) e-government platform, was established by the Ministry of Health and Welfare (Yeong-Ran 2023). Haengbok is an e-government platform that manages social benefits for low income and marginalised people, and also personalised welfare services. It has various components, including a welfare blind spot identification system which identifies families in crisis by using deep learning to collect and analyse big data, such as losing power and water over unpaid bills, and social insurance default records (Social Security Information Service 2023). Families are then contacted by departmental officers and linked in with services. The first version of the BSIS was introduced in 2015 and used traditional predictive modelling regression. In 2018, the system adopted an ML model based on XGBoost, a tree-based ensemble algorithm using large-volume datasets. In the first year the system led to 2.28 million initial consultations on welfare crises cases, 2,400,000 integrated case conferences and 1.75 million simple service connections (Min 2020). Supported by legislation the indicators used expanded from 37 sets of data from the SSiS database, to 44 indicators from government and private company databases in April 2023 (Ministry of Health and Welfare 2023). This approach is used in conjunction with other more analogue systems.

While efficiency and fraud detection are also part of the broader SSiS's role, a feature of the BSIS is that, unlike the Australian and US system, it does not solely rely on the initiative of the service users to apply for social services. It tries to locate people according to need and bring them into the welfare net. While proactive automations have been used elsewhere, including in Norway where Government Child Payments and Covid Payments have been automatically paid into eligible people's bank accounts using an automated process (Haldar and Larsson 2021), this system relies on the individuals already being in the administrative system. The Korean BSIS, in contrast, brings in individuals who are currently outside the administrative system. A particular concern is to locate individuals who are not aware of the government help available, including North Korean defectors who flee across the border to South Korea and are at particular risk because they do not have the skills, networks or knowledge to access South Korean government services.

The South Korean media reported an array of tragedies relating to single-parent family suicide. In these cases some parents were found leaving letters apologising for not being able to pay small debts, such as the Suwon Three Mother and Daughter Incident. The families were found to be living in heart-wrenching poverty, and to have been in very poor health prior to the suicide with evidence of starvation. In a targeted top-down policy response to suicides linked to economic hardship, South Korea's SSiS has utilised AI to try to identify individuals who are in welfare blind spots. While the system does link in with child protection (see the chapter on child protection services by Krutzinna, Chapter 29 in this volume) and automated care for older Koreans who live alone (see the chapter on social care by Whitfield, Wright and Hamblin, Chapter 28 in this volume), economic vulnerability is also a focus of the Korean BSIS. AI is used to identify proxies, such as an unpaid power bill, to bring individuals and families who are currently not receiving support into support systems (Korea Social Security Information Service 2023).

FROM PUNITIVE AUTOMATION TO A POLITICS OF CARE

Both the Australian Robodebt case and the American MiDAS case present examples of punitive automation. In these cases thousands of people who applied for social services were wrongly subjected to assumptions of guilt and burdened with proving their own innocence. As argued by Philip Alston, the previous UN Special Rapporteur on Extreme Poverty and Human Rights:

> The presumption of innocence is turned on its head when everyone applying for a benefit is screened for potential wrongdoing in a system of total surveillance. And in the absence of transparency about the existence and workings of automated systems, the rights to contest an adverse decision, and to seek a meaningful remedy, are illusory. (Alston 2019)

The automated shifts of the burden of proof seen in these systems are, we argue, an extension of the punitive, blame and shame logics and practices informing welfare services in Australia and the US. With these two examples we see government agencies using automated fraud detection systems, that will always come with error, without consideration of impact. The examples we reference are part of longer neoliberal and austerity-driven welfare practices of exclusion and limitation. The Robodebt and MiDAS examples demonstrate the urgent need to rethink and politicise not only the automation of fraud detection, but also the logics driving social service provision.

Despite public criticisms, review, media coverage, legal challenges and advocacy work, both systems detailed in this chapter continued for years. In both cases there was a failure to design fraud detection systems that reflect the complex realities of people's lives at a most basic level, for instance by recognising that people applying for social support have fluctuating income due to precarious and fluctuating employment. Both systems demonstrate a failure by those in charge to listen and respond to the experiences being voiced by those wrongly targeted (on AITs clashes with professional values in street-level bureaucracy, see Busch and Henriksen, Chapter 6 in this volume). Further, in both cases, the automation of fraud detection was done by removing human oversight and making it the responsibility of those receiving an automated notice to prove their innocence.

These case studies reveal a significant disconnection between government decision makers and people relying on social services. Neoliberal shifts in welfare state governance compound long-standing deserving and undeserving binaries. Such stereotypical thinking can be embedded in system design, as was the case with systems considered in this chapter.

A different approach will require significant changes to social policy and practices as well as the logics underpinning both. There are many people suggesting changes that could lead to more humane and equitable datafied futures. Alston (2019) has stressed the importance of social policy and legislative oversight that is grounded in respect for human rights and the protection of political, economic and social rights. The right to a life with dignity, he argues, is at particular risk with the digitisation of the welfare state.

There is now an overwhelming amount of research documenting the fact that automated decision-making systems can be used in ways that cause significant harm through encoded bias, discrimination, the exacerbation of inequality, the infringement of people's rights, the wrongful denial of access to necessary services and benefits, and the intensification of surveillance (Gandy 2005; Lum and Isaac 2016; Lyon 2002; Gangadharan et al. 2014; Benjamin 2019; Eubanks 2018; O'Neil 2016; Hu 2016; for a wider discussion of "bias" also see Hong, Chapter 8 in this volume).

Given this body of evidence, there is a need for government agencies who want to make use of automated decision-making systems to address how they have taken into consideration the way problems have occurred elsewhere. Jason Lewis and colleagues (2020) have argued that a way to ensure decision making about potential uses of automation is done with trust, care and responsibility is by engaging all relevant communities, particularly those who stand to be most affected by any potential application. Costanza-Chock (2020) stresses the importance of a design justice approach, one that emphasises collective design principles and practices. Costanza-Chock argues:

> A paradigm shift to design that is meant to actively dismantle, rather than unintentionally reinforce, the matrix of domination requires that we retool. This means that there is a need to develop intersectional user stories, testing approaches, training data, benchmarks, standards, validation processes, and impact assessments, among many other tools.

Others have argued the importance of going beyond stories of success told by promoters and insiders to ensuring expert and external critique, as well as rigorous review (Collins 2021, Garvey 2021). As argued by Karen Yeung, Rapporteur for the Council of Europe's Expert Committee on human rights and automated data processing:

> If we are to take human rights seriously in a hyperconnected digital age, we cannot allow the power of our advanced digital technologies and systems, and those who develop and implement them, to be accrued and exercised without responsibility … This includes obligations to ensure that there are effective and legitimate mechanisms that will operate to prevent and forestall violations to human rights which these technologies may threaten …

The extensive human and financial cost detailed in this chapter demonstrate the need for those making decisions about whether or not to use automations in welfare systems DS to ask questions about the potential impact of systems, particularly as related to inequality, before embarking on any system.

There are a range of costs that occur when any system goes wrong that extend far beyond financial costs, these include deepening inequality, loss of public image and trust, and the considerable strain placed on individuals and community organisations who must use time and resources to redress negative effects. Responsibility must extend to system legality, accuracy and effectiveness (Cobbe et al. 2020). The systems referenced in this chapter were inaccurate, ineffective and deemed unlawful. As argued by Lewis (2020), the need for greater attention to care and community is essential to addressing blind spots in computation and system development and use. Part of attending to community must also include the ability for community members to decide there are some areas where there should not be automation because of potential harm and risk. There is a strong and growing body of work stressing the importance of rights of refusal and how this could be built into democratic processes (Gangadharan 2022; Cifor et al. 2019; Gilman and Madden 2022). For example, this could be facilitated through expanded review and resourced third-party auditing to ensure communities have decision-making power, it could also include citizen juries, citizen assemblies or deliberative polling (Hintz et al. 2023; Raji et al. 2023). Social movement building and mobilisation is another way refusal is being operationalised. The Stop LAPD Spying Coalition is just one example of community-led movements against automation that have led to systems being stopped, in this case predictive policing, as well as holding governments and technologies to account (Benjamin 2019 and 2016; Gangadharen 2021; Redden et al. 2022).

Welfare fraud detection appears an almost universal application of automated technologies; however, there are different nuances across jurisdictions, providing alternative imaginaries to the punitive approach in neoliberal governance cultures. For example, the BSIS uses technology in an explicit policy articulation to expand access to welfare by including those who are not receiving support. When paired with Confucian administrative culture, which values collectivism and family and responsibility (Shamsul Haque 2018, p. 43), a different language and tone emerges in digital welfare transformation. In the department website, Haengbok-E-eum, there is a tone of care, and acknowledgment that deciding who can access welfare can be a life and death issue for those who are most vulnerable. Phrases like "SSIS will build a seamless social safety net to address the welfare blind spot and for proactive identification and support for families-in-crisis" and "Social security will contribute to national happiness with social security information services" softly place "the realization of warm welfare" at its centre (Korea Social Security Information Service 2023).

CONCLUSION

Inspired by Carmel's (2019) notion of governance as being constituted through "regimes of governance practices", this chapter introduced some ways that AI technologies have been used and constituted in different social policy contexts, with varying socio-political-historical administrative approaches. It opened with an outline of the punitive neoliberal social policy context in countries like Australia, the UK and the US. It then discussed two cases of failed automation within this regime of governance practices – Robodebt (Australia) and MiDAS (US). It then moved on to further demonstrate how context has informed approaches to automation by focusing on the example of the South Korean BSIS. The goal was to argue that the now cancelled Robodebt and MiDAS systems, and the different approach to automation taken in South Korea, make clear that our datafied futures are not determined and can be shaped by different logics.

The BSIS contrasts markedly with the neoliberal aims and priorities that currently dominate neoliberal Western welfare articulation of AI and automated technologies in welfare administration, which focus on self-reliance and market-driven decision making (Mendes 2017). That there are different approaches to administering welfare among states is not a new observation; Esping-Andersen's (1990) seminal work on worlds of welfare has led to a rich and empirically detailed literature comparing different types of welfare states. Exploring the cases of the neoliberal forerunners of automated welfare provision is also meaningful more generally, given that often these countries also serve as impulse givers for the Global South. However, as this chapter has demonstrated there is an urgent need to reimagine and develop alternative modes of welfare administration. We argue for a recognition and refusal of automated welfare provision approaches informed by neoliberal and austerity logics (Eubanks 2018). A politics of care-informed approach to considerations of automation would involve resourcing public agencies to support greater transparency and accountability which would include meaningful public engagement and rigorous review. Such review would need to involve impact assessments that attend to systemic injustice, as well as community involvement including the right to decide no-go areas. Responsibility would involve recognition of the numerous examples of automated failures as well as harm caused. An alternative approach would also involve rethinking the use of technology in welfare, a shift from thinking about technology as a means to assist with punishment to thinking about how technology might be used to help human and societal flourishing and foster connections between people.

NOTE

1. *NJCM et al. v. The Dutch State* (2020), The Hague District Court ECLI: NL: RBDHA:2020:1878
    (SyRI). English translation available at: http:// deeplink .rechtspraak .nl/ uitspraak ?id = ECLI: NL:
    RBDHA:2020:1878.
2. 'Haengbok' means 'happiness' in English.

REFERENCES

Alston, P. (2019), 'Report of the Special Rapporteur on Extreme Poverty and Human Rights, United Nations', accessed 2 September 2021 at: https://www.ohchr.org/en/press-releases/2019/10/world-stumbling-zombie-digital-welfare-dystopia-warns-un-human-rights-expert.

Archer, V. (2009), 'Dole Bludgers, Tax Payers and the New Right: Constructing Discourses of Welfare in 1970s Australia', *Labour History*, **96**, 177–190.

Baekgaard, M., Herd, P., and Moynihan, D. P. (2022), 'Of "Welfare Queens" and "Poor Carinas": Social Constructions, Deservingness Messaging and the Mental Health of Welfare Clients', *British Journal of Political Science*, **53** (2), 594–612. https://doi.org/10.1017/S000712342200031X.

Bashevkin, S. B. (2002), *Welfare Hot Buttons: Women, Work and Social Policy Reform*, Toronto: University of Toronto Press.

Benjamin, R. (2016), 'Informed Refusal: Toward a Justice-Based Bioethics', *Science, Technology, & Human Values*, **41** (6), 967–990. https://doi.org/10.1177/0162243916656059.

Benjamin, R. (2019), *Race After Technology: Abolitionist Tools for the New Jim Code*, Cambridge, MA: Polity Books.

Bourdieu, P. and Wacquant, L. (2001), 'Neoliberal Newspeak', *Radical Philosophy*, **105**, 1–6.

Brown, D. L. (2020), 'Digital Government: Ideology and New Forms of Power', PhD thesis, Deakin University.

Brown, W. (2009), 'Neoliberalism and the End of Liberal Democracy', in *Edgework: Critical Essays on Knowledge and Politics*, Princeton, NJ: Princeton University Press, pp. 37–59. https://doi.org/10.1515/9781400826872.37.

Carmel, E. (2019), 'Regimes of Governing Practices, Socio-Political Order and Contestation', in *Governance Analysis: Critical Enquiry at the Intersection of Politics, Policy and Society*, edited by E. Carmel, Cheltenham, UK and Northampton, MA, USA: Edward Elgar Publishing, pp. 24–46.

Carney, T. (2019), 'Robo-Debt Illegality: The Seven Veils of Failed Guarantees of the Rule of Law?', *Alternative Law Journal*, **44** (1), 4–10. https://doi.org/10.1177/1037969X18815913.

Charette, R. N. (2018), 'Michigan's MiDAS Unemployment System: Algorithm Alchemy Created Lead, Not Gold, IEEE Spectrum', accessed 4 August 2021 at: https://spectrum.ieee.org/michigans-midas-unemployment-system-algorithm-alchemy-that-created-lead-not-gold.

Chassmen, D. and Cohen, J. (2020), *The Politics of Care: From Covid 19 to Black Lives Matter*, New York: Verso.

Cifor, M., Garcia, P., Cowan, T. L., Rault, J., Sutherland, T., Chan, A., Rode, J., Hoffmann, A. L., Salehi, N., and Nakamura, L. (2019), 'Feminist Data Manifest-No', accessed 1 May 2023 at: https://www.manifestno.com/.

Cobbe, J., Deakin, S., and Markou, C. (2020), 'Legal Singularity and the Reflexivity of Law', in *Is Law Computable: Critical Perspectives on Law and Artificial Intelligence*, edited by S. Deakin and C. Markou (eds), Oxford and New York: Hart Publishing, pp. 286–290.

Collins, H. (2021), 'The Science of Artificial Intelligence and Its Critics', *Interdisciplinary Science Reviews*, **46** (1–2), 53–70, DOI: 10.1080/03080188.2020.1840821.

Commonwealth of Australia (2016), 'Budget 2015–16: Budget Measures – Budget Paper No. 2', accessed at: https://archive.budget.gov.au/2015-16/bp2/BP2_consolidated.pdf.

Commonwealth of Australia (2020), 'The Senate. Community Affairs References Committee. Centrelink's Compliance Program. Second Interim Report', September, accessed at: https://www.aph.gov.au/Parliamentary_Business/Committees/Senate/Community_Affairs/Centrelinkcompliance/Second_Interim_Report/section?id=committees%2freportsen%2f024338%2f72633.

Commonwealth Ombudsman (2017), 'Centrelink's Automated Debt Raising and Recovery System: A Report about the Department of Human Services' Online Compliance Intervention System for Debt Raising and Recovery (No. 2)', Commonwealth of Australia, accessed at: https://www.ombudsman .gov.au/__data/assets/pdf_file/0022/43528/Report-Centrelinks-automated-debt-raising-and-recovery -system-April-2017.pdf.

Commonwealth Ombudsman (2021), 'Services Australia's Income Compliance Program: A report about Services Australia's implementation of changes to the Program in 2019 and 2020 (No. 2)', Commonwealth of Australia, accessed at: https://www.ombudsman.gov.au/__data/assets/pdf_file/ 0014/112442/Services-Australias-Income-Compliance-Report.pdf.

Costanza-Chock, S. (2020), *Design Justice: Community-Led Practices to Build the Worlds We Need*, Cambridge MA: MIT Press.

Dean, H. (1991), *Social Security and Social Control*, New York: Routledge.

de la Garza, A. (2020), 'Automated Systems Trapping Citizens in Bureaucratic Limbo', *TIME* Magazine, accessed 20 August 2021 at: https://time.com/5840609/algorithm-unemployment/.

Dencik, L. and Kaun, A. (2020), 'Datafication and the Welfare State,' *Global Perspectives*, **1**, (1), https:// doi.org/10.1525/gp.2020.12912.

Dencik, L., Redden, J., Hintz, A., and Warne, H. (2019), 'The "Golden View": Data-Driven Governance in the Scoring Society', *Internet Policy Review*, **8** (2), https://doi.org/10.14763/2019.2.1413.

Esping-Andersen, G. (1990), *The Three Worlds of Welfare Capitalism*, Princeton, NJ: Princeton University Press.

Eubanks, V. (2018), *Automating Inequality*, New York: Macmillan.

Felton, R. (2015), 'Criminalizing the Unemployed', *Detroit Metro Times*, accessed 20 August 2021 at: https://www.metrotimes.com/news/criminalizing-the-unemployed-2353533.

Finkel, A. (2006), *Social Policy and Practice in Canada: A History*, Waterloo, ON: Wilfred Laurier University Press.

Fleming, L. N. and Fournier, H. (2015), 'Class-Action Lawsuit Filed Over Seized Tax Refunds', *The Detroit News*, available at: https://www.detroitnews.com/story/news/local/michigan/2015/09/14/class -action-lawsuit-filed-tax-refunds/72255478/ (accessed: 26 August 2021).

Foucault, M. (2008), *The Birth of BioPolitics: Lectures at the Collège de France 1978–1979*, New York: Palgrave Macmillan.

Gandy, O. (2005), 'Data Mining, Surveillance, and Discrimination in the Post-9/11 Environment', in *The New Politics of Surveillance and Visibility*, edited by K. D. Haggerty and R. V. Ericson, Toronto: University of Toronto Press, pp. 363–384.

Gangadharan, S. P. (2021), 'Digital Exclusion: A Politics of Refusal', in *Digital Technology and Democratic Theory*, edited by L. Bernholz, H. Landemore, and R. Reich, Chicago: University of Chicago Press, pp. 113–140. https://doi.org/10.7208/9780226748603-005.

Gangadharan, S. P., Eubanks, V., and Barocas, S. (2014), 'Data and Discrimination: Collected Essays', Open Technology Institute and New America, accessed 9 September 2015 at: https://www.ftc.gov/ system/files/documents/public_comments/2014/10/00078-92938.pdf.

Garvey, S. C. (2021), 'Unsavory Medicine for Technological Civilization: Introducing "Artificial Intelligence & Its Discontents"', *Interdisciplinary Science Reviews*, **46** (1–2), 1–18, DOI: 10.1080 /03080188.2020.1840820.

Gilman, M. E. and Madden, M. (2022), 'Digital Barriers to Economic Justice in the Wake of COVID-19', *Data & Society*, University of Baltimore School of Law Legal Studies Research Paper, available at SSRN: https://ssrn.com/abstract=4012133.

Glenn, R. (2017), 'Centrelink's Automated Debt Raising and Recovery System. A Report about the Department of Human Services' Online Compliance Intervention System for Debt Raising and Recovery. April. Commonwealth Ombudsman', accessed at: https://www.ombudsman.gov.au/_ _data/assets/pdf_file/0022/43528/Report-Centrelinksautomated-debt-raising-and-recovery-system -April-2017.pdf.

Grahame, T. and Marston, G. (2012), 'Welfare-to-Work Policies and the Experience of Employed Single Mothers on Income Support in Australia: Where are the Benefits?', *Australian Social Work*, **65** (1), 73–86.

Griffiths, R. (2021), 'Universal Credit and Automated Decision Making: A Case of the Digital Tail Wagging the Policy Dog?', *Social Policy and Society*, 1–18.

Haldar, M. and Larsson, K. K. (2021), 'Can Computers Automate Welfare? Norwegian Efforts to Make Welfare Policy More Effective', *Journal of Extreme Anthropology*, **5** (1), 56–77.

Hancock, A. M. (2004), *The Politics of Disgust: The Public Identity of the Welfare Queen*. New York: NYU Press.

Harvey, D. (2007), 'Neoliberalism as Creative Destruction', *The ANNALS of the American Academy of Political and Social Science*, **610** (1), 21–44.

Hintz, A., Dencik, L., Redden, J., and Trere, E. (2023), 'Civic Participation in the Datafied Society: Introduction', *International Journal of Communication*, **17**, 3549–3561.

Hoffmann, A. L. (2020), 'Terms of Inclusion: Data, Discourse, Violence', *New Media & Society*, **23** (12), 3539–3556.

Hoffmann, A. L. (2021), 'Even When You Are a Solution You Are a Problem: An Uncomfortable Reflection on Feminist Data Ethics', *Global Perspectives*, **2** (1), 21335. https://doi.org/10.1525/gp .2021.21335.

Hu, M. (2016), 'Big Data Blacklisting', *Florida Law Review*, **67** (5), 1735–1809.

Kingfisher, C. (2013), *A Policy Travelogue: Tracing Welfare Reform in Aotearoa/New Zealand and Canada*. New York: Berghahn Books.

Korea Social Security Information Service (2022), accessed 2 September 2022 at: http://www.ssis.or.kr/ eng/lay1/S6T37C38/contents.do.

Lee, S. and Koo, I. (2010), 'Social Welfare Programs and Poverty Blind Spots: Roles of the Government and the Private Sector', *Health and Social Welfare Review*, **30** (1), 29–61.

Levin, S. (2016), 'MiDAS Politician Letter', available at: https://drive.google.com/file/d/1CtCt8V5KP -JQGZMCsavhdsomxBCPAHXQ/view?usp=sharing&usp=embed_facebook (accessed 20 August 2021).

Lewis, J. E. (ed.) (2020), 'Indigenous Protocol and Artificial Intelligence Position Paper', Honolulu, Hawai'i: The Initiative for Indigenous Futures and the Canadian Institute for Advanced Research (CIFAR), accessed at: https://www.indigenous-ai.net/position-paper.

Little, M. H. and Morrison, I. (1999), '"The Pecker Detectors are Back": Regulation of the Family Form in Ontario Welfare Policy', *Journal of Canadian Studies*, **34** (2), 110–136. https://doi.org/10.3138/jcs .34.2.110.

Lum, K. and Isaac, W. (2016), 'To Predict and Serve', *Significance*, **13** (5), 14–19, accessed 9 September 2017 at: https://rss.onlinelibrary.wiley.com/doi/full/10.1111/j.1740- 9713.2016.00960.x.

Lyon, D. (ed.) (2002), *Surveillance as Social Sorting: Privacy, Risk and Automated Discrimination*, New York: Routledge.

Maki, K. (2011), 'Neoliberal Deviants and Surveillance: Welfare Recipients under the Watchful Eye of Ontario Works', *Surveillance & Society*, **9** (1/2), 47–63.

Marston, G. and McDonald, C. (2007), 'Assessing the Policy Trajectory of Welfare Reform in Australia', *Journal of Poverty and Social Justice*, **15** (3), 233–245.

McGuigan, J. (2009), *Cool Capitalism*, New York: Palgrave Macmillan.

McKeen, W. (2004), *Money in Their Own Name: The Feminist Voice in Poverty Debate in Canada, 1970–1995* (Vol. 19), Toronto, Buffalo and London: University of Toronto Press.

Meaker, M. (2023), 'The Fraud-Detection Business Has a Dirty Secret', *Wired UK*, 7 March, accessed 21 May 2023 at: https://www.wired.co.uk/article/welfare-fraud-industry.

Mendes, P. (2017), *Australia's Welfare Wars: The Players, the Politics and the Ideologies* (3rd edition), Sydney: New South Publishing, UNSW Press.

Michigan Eastern District Court (2017), *Zynda et al. v. Arwood et al.*, https://www.govinfo.gov/app/ details/USCOURTS-mied-2_15-cv-11449/summary.

Milner, Y. and Traub, A. (2021), 'Data Capitalism and Algorithmic Racism', Data for Black Lives and Demos, accessed 2 January 2023 at: https://www.demos.org/research/data-capitalism-and-algorithmic -racism.

Min, Y. A. (2020), 'A Study on the Application of Distributed ID Technology Based on Blockchain for Welfare Blind Spot Management', *The Journal of The Institute of Internet, Broadcasting and Communication*, **20** (6), 145–150. https://doi.org/10.7236/JIIBC.2020.20.6.145.

Ministry of Health and Welfare (2023), 'Government to Increase the Number of Indicators for Warning Signs of Household Crisis to 44 to Better Reduce Welfare Blind Spots', Press Release, 3 May 2023.

https://www.mohw.go.kr/eng/nw/nw0101vw.jsp?PAR_MENU_ID=1007&MENU_ID=100701&page=1&CONT_SEQ=376107.

Mosher, J., Brockman, J., and Bertrand, M.-A. (2010), 'Welfare Fraud: The Constitution of Social Assistance as Crime', in *Constructing Crime: Contemporary Processes of Criminalization*, edited by J. Mosher and J. Brockman, Vancouver and Toronto: UBC Press, pp. 17–52. https://doi.org/10.1515/9780774818216-003.

Nam, J. and Park, H. (2020), 'The 2015 Welfare Reform of the National Basic Livelihood Security System in South Korea: Effects on Economic Outcomes', *International Journal of Social Welfare*, **29** (3), 219–232. https://doi.org/10.1111/ijsw.12416.

Ng, Y.-F., O'Sullivan, M., Paterson, M., and Witzleb, N. (2020), 'Revitalising Public Law in a Technological Era: Rights, Transparency and Administrative Justice', *University of New South Wales Law Journal*, **43** (3), 1041–1077. https://doi.org/10.53637/YGTS5583.

#NotMyDebt (2022), #NotMyDebt Stories, accessed at: https://www.notmydebt.com.au/stories/notmydebt-stories.

O'Neil, C. (2016), *Weapons of Math Destruction: How Big Data Increases Inequality and Threatens Democracy*, New York: Crown Publishing.

Raji, I. D., Chock, S. C., and Buolamwini, J. (2023), 'Change from the Outside: Towards Credible Third-Party Audits of AI Systems', in *Missing Links in AI Governance*, edited by B. Prud'homme, C. Régis, G. Farnadi, V. Dreier, and S. Rubel, Paris and Montreal: UNESCO/Mila – Québec Institute of Artificial Intelligence, pp. 5–26.

Redden, J. (2014), *The Mediation of Poverty: The News, New Media and Politics*, New York: Lexington.

Redden, J. (2018), 'The Harm that Data Do', *Scientific American*, **319** (5), https://www.scientificamerican.com/article/the-harm-that-data-do/.

Redden, J., Brand, J., Sander, I., and Warne, H. (2022), 'Automating Public Services: Learning from Cancelled Systems', Carnegie UK Trust and Data Justice Lab, October, accessed 12 January 2023 at: https://www.carnegieuktrust.org.uk/publications/automating-public-services-learning-from-cancelled-systems/.

Senate Community Affairs References Committee (2017), 'Design, Scope, Cost–Benefit Analysis, Contracts Awarded and Implementation Associated with the Better Management of the Social Welfare System Initiative', Commonwealth of Australia, accessed at: https://www.aph.gov.au/Parliamentary_Business/Committees/Senate/Community_Affairs/SocialWelfareSystem/~/media/Committees/clac_ctte/SocialWelfareSystem/report.pdf.

Services Australia (2022, 2 February), Welfare Payment Infrastructure Transformation (WPIT) programme, accessed at: https://www.servicesaustralia.gov.au/welfare-payment-infrastructure-transformation-wpitprogramme?context=.

Shaefer, L. and Gray, S. (2015), 'Michigan Unemployment Insurance Agency: Unjust Fraud and Multiple Determinations' [Memo to US Department of Labor].

Shamsul Haque, M. (2018), 'Rethinking Public Governance in the Asian Century: Grand Discourse vs. Actual Reality', in *Public Policy in the 'Asian Century': Concepts, Cases and Futures*, International Series on Public Policy, edited by S. Bice, A. Poole, and H. Sullivan, London: Palgrave Macmillan, pp. 41–63.

Sleep, L. (2022), 'From Making Automated Decision Making Visible to Mapping the Unknowable Human: Counter-Mapping Automated Decision Making in Social Services in Australia', *Qualitative Inquiry*, **28** (7), 848–858.

Sleep, L. (2023), 'Female Dependents, Individual Customers and Promiscuous Digital Personas: The Multiple Governing of Women through the Australian Social Security Couple Rule', *Critical Social Policy*, **43** (2), 193–213.

Sleep, L., Coco, B. A., and Henman, P. (2022), 'Mapping ADM in Australian Social Services', *ADM+S Working Paper 006*, available at: https://apo.org.au/node/321337.

Sleep, L., Coco, B. A., Rodrigeuz, G., Min, J., Nguyen, D., Henman, P., Moon, C., and Nugroho, R. (2024), *Mapping Automated Decision Making in Social Services in Australia and the Asia Pacific* (forthcoming).

Social Security Information Service (2023), Social Security Information System (Haengbok-E-eum), http://www.ssis.or.kr/eng/lay1/S6T37C38/contents.do.

UN Special Rapporteur on Extreme Poverty and Human Rights (2020), 'Landmark Ruling by Dutch Court Stops Government Attempts to Spy on the Poor – UN Expert', available at: https://www.ohchr .org/EN/NewsEvents/Pages/DisplayNews.aspx?LangID=E&NewsID=25522.

van Bekkum, M. and Borgesius, F. Z. (2021), 'Digital Welfare Fraud Detection and the Dutch SyRI Judgment', *European Journal of Social Security*, **23** (4), 323–340. https://doi.org/10.1177/ 13882627211031257.

Wacquant, L. (2009), *Punishing the Poor: The Neoliberal Government of Social Insecurity*. Durham, NC: Duke University Press.

Walmsley, R. (2005), 'World Prison Population List' (sixth edition), International Center for Prison Studies, London, wppl.3.indd (brown.edu).

Walmsley, R. (2009), 'World Prison Population List' (eighth edition), International Center for Prison Studies, London, www.kcl.ac.uk/depsta/law/research/icps/worldbrief/.

Woodly, D., Brown, R. H., Marin, M., Threadcraft, S., Harris, C. P., Syedullah, J., and Ticktin, M. (2021), 'The Politics of Care', *Contemporary Political Theory*, **20**, 890–925. https://doi.org/10.1057/ s41296-021-00515-8.

Wykstra, S. (2020), 'Government's Use of Algorithm Serves Up False Fraud Charges', *Undark Magazine*, accessed 26 August 2021 at: https://undark.org/2020/06/01/michigan-unemployment -fraud-algorithm/.

Yeong-Ran, P. (2023), 'ICT and Social Welfare in Korea', in *Digital Transformation and Social Well-Being: Promoting an Inclusive Society*, edited by A. López Peláez, S.-M. Suh, and S. Zelenev, London: Routledge, pp. 128–138. https://doi.org/10.4324/9781003312208-12.

Yeung, K. (2018), 'A Study of the Implications of Advanced Digital Technologies (Including AI Systems) for the Concept of Responsibility within a Human Rights Framework', MSI-AUT 05, accessed 2 September 2022 at: https://ssrn.com/abstract=3286027.

Zanoni, A. (2023), 'Remembering Welfare as We Knew It: Understanding Neoliberalism through Histories of Welfare', *Journal of Policy History*, **35** (1), 118–158. https://doi.org/10.1017/S08980 30622000318.

28. AI in care: a solution to the 'care crisis' in England?

Grace Whitfield, James Wright and Kate Hamblin

INTRODUCTION

In recent years, discussions about the use of AI technologies in the context of long-term care provision have been gathering momentum, and examples of their actual deployment are also on the rise. Industry stakeholders and governments have sought to portray AI as a technology that will improve care delivery and increase efficiency in a policy domain which is, in many countries, in crisis, with concerns about care quality and quantity (UN 2018). Significant numbers of people are not receiving the care they need: a systematic review and meta-analysis reported that globally one in four older adults' long-term care needs were unmet (Rahman et al. 2022). Across the European Union (EU), in 2022, Eurostat found that 45 per cent of people aged 55 and over with care needs report a 'lack of assistance' (Eurostat 2022). The European Public Services Union highlights 'poor government decisions, decades of cost-driven neo-liberal reforms and austerity that have reduced capacity in health and social services with disastrous effect' (Florek 2021: 36, 21). AI is often presented as a way to save the increasingly scarce care labour, cut costs, and improve the quality of care by predicting and preventing the need for care or by optimally targeting its provision. In the EU, digital technologies have been framed as 'transformative' (European Commission 2018), with AI viewed as a 'key enabling technology' for public services (European Parliament 2021). However, the uses of AI technology raise a host of social, ethical, political and legal concerns: from questions around the use of data to fears that workers and their 'human touch' will be replaced by robots intro-duced to carry out intimate care labour for sometimes vulnerable people. Debate has focused on whether regulatory frameworks could safeguard both those receiving and providing care, as well as those engaged in labour within AI supply chains, working 'behind the curtain' (Sadowski 2018).

This chapter uses the illustrative example of England's long-term care – or 'adult social care' – sector to explore how AI is framed and enacted in relation to care policy and practice across the levels of national government, local authorities and industry, including technology companies and care providers. While grounded in the case of England, our analysis has impli-cations for other countries facing similar cost pressures and labour shortages in the care sector that are also considering introducing AI technologies as a central part of a future technology 'solution'. Overarching this tendency towards techno-positivism in Europe are New Public Management-influenced priorities of efficiency, economy and effectiveness (Power 1999), which have been entrenched in England's approach to public policy for the past 40 years (Connolly and Van der Zwet 2021).

This chapter explores which forms of AI are actually being deployed in care, and how decisions around implementation are shaped by New Public Management principles (cf. af Malmborg and Trondal, Chapter 5 in this volume; Paul, Carmel and Cobbe, Chapter 1 in this volume). We begin by describing the policy domain, including how adult social care is funded, commissioned and regulated in England, how national bodies seek to drive technology implementation, and how AI is being introduced in policy terms. We then analyse how AI technologies are portrayed in policy documents and discourse as fundamental to delivering efficiencies in the struggling adult social care sector, and contend that this focus on technology as 'transformative' is not (yet) well evidenced. Furthermore, emphasis on the 'three Es' of New Public Management (economy, efficiency and effectiveness) can neglect (and worsen) inequalities related to ethics (Bringselius 2018) and equity (Norman-Major 2011). New Public Management aligns with marketisation of the 'exchange' of care and expanding private sector, processes formalised in policy since the 1980s (Hudson 2021). Emphasising these structural dynamics – which have been less of a focus in existing literature – we suggest that the case for AI in policy documents is driven by a motivation to construct notions of care as something which should be *fast*. This is done without regard for specificities of care needs and labour processes. In particular, our analysis highlights limited recognition of environmental costs and exploitative labour practices in the government approach to promoting a 'global market' of care technologies.

POLICY, INVESTMENT AND PRACTICAL APPLICATIONS IN ENGLAND

Responsibility for legislation, standards and funding allocation for adult social care in the UK is devolved to the four nations, and within those nations care provision is organised by local authorities, councils and trusts. In England 152 local authorities are responsible for the provision of adult social care services, the delivery of which is generally contracted out to private and third sector providers. Centrally allocated funding levels stagnated in the 2010s, with real-terms spending power of local authorities lower in early 2020 (pre-pandemic) than it was in 2010/11 (Bottery and Ward 2021). The care workforce, which faces precarious employment terms and low pay, is struggling to meet the increasing care needs of an ageing population (Turnpenny and Hussein 2021). As of the time of writing (spring 2023), the approach of the UK government to the care crisis has been erratic, despite former Prime Minister Boris Johnson's promise in 2019, on the first day of his premiership, to 'fix the crisis in social care once and for all' (Johnson 2019). Discontinuities in national-level political leadership have exacerbated problems of strategic planning, with the Secretary of State for Health and Social Care changing six times since 2018, including three changes in 2022 alone.

   At a national level, funding to support the use of AI in the health sector has been prioritised over adult social care, with the latter often framed as an indirect or downstream beneficiary of National Health Service (NHS) uses of AI (cf. Pot and Prainsack, Chapter 30 in this volume). The organisations that were responsible for funding and implementing 'transformative' technologies in the context of health and social care until 2019 – NHS Digital and NHSX – collaborated on only a small number of care-related projects. These include the Digital Social Care 'virtual hub' and the Social Care Programme initiative, which provided funding opportunities for local authorities to explore the potential of digital technologies, including AI, but had a comparatively modest budget of £22.8 million for the period 2016–2021. After the Social Care Programme came to an end, NHS Digital and NHSX were integrated into the NHS Transformation Directorate and in 2022 the Digitalising Social Care Fund was launched.

This fund is 'drawing on' (Digital Social Care 2022) £150 million in funding announced in the long-awaited 2021 White Paper 'People at the Heart of Care' (Department of Health and Social Care [DHSC] 2021). The fund was announced to 'drive greater adoption of technology and achieve widespread digitisation across social care' (DHSC 2021: 7), yet appears to have been diverted towards combined 'health-and-social-care' activities. Up until 2022/23, £25 million had been allocated to Integrated Care Systems – partnerships between health and social care services.

In 2019, £250 million of investment was announced for the NHS 'AI Lab', part of the NHS England Transformation Directorate which pools data across health and social care services, but it is unclear how much of this resource was allocated to social care. The NHS AI Lab is included in the UK's National AI Strategy, published in 2021. The strategy refers to a key short-term action to '[b]egin engagement on the Draft National Strategy for AI-driven technologies in Health and Social Care, through the NHS AI Lab'. While the draft strategy was intended to have been launched in early 2022, at time of writing it has not been published.[1] Several of the projects listed as case studies on the website of the NHS AI Lab so far, however, report practical challenges related to data sharing across different providers (on the mythical notion of interoperability, see Leese, Chapter 11 in this volume). This aligns with a general lack of clarity about how technology can drive transformation when collaboration between health and social care services is difficult (Wade-Gery 2021). As Simon Bolton, interim CEO of NHS Digital, notes, 'the link between healthcare and social care in digital is really unclear and the models are massively different' (quoted in Say 2022).

Few applications of AI are currently deployed in social care practice in England beyond prototypes or pilots – a situation that is shared in many other countries in Europe, North America and beyond (Molinari et al. 2021). However, this seems to be changing as the quantity of data collected and stored by governments, companies and healthcare providers continues to grow, particularly with the nationwide switch from analogue to digital telecommunications infrastructure (Hamblin 2020). Private providers and local authorities are increasingly trying to use AI to manage, plan and predict care needs and provision across fragmented social care systems and at the level of individuals. Platforms providing data modelling and predictive analytics via machine learning claim to identify where care needs are unfulfilled and where they might increase. Some, such as Cera's AI-powered 'Concern Predictor', claim to be able to analyse both structured and free-text health and care data to predict risk at the individual level. Other projects like TRIBE[2] combine census data, adult social care data, health data and data collected via their platform to map geographical 'care deserts' where there are likely to be high levels of unmet need, to allow local authorities and providers to take mitigating action.

Care companies also increasingly utilise AI to monitor and manage care labour, and tools have been developed to assist staff and unpaid carers in providing care. For example, the NHS AI Lab website features a case study of an 'AI-powered Dynamic Tasks tool' developed by Cera that 'suggests the next best actions' for care workers to take, by analysing the care recipient's recent health and care data. A growing number of sensing devices with care applications are available and in active use in the UK, ranging from specialist equipment such as Vayyar Care's fall detection and home monitoring products, to environmental sensors and smart home devices, to consumer wearables, such as Fitbit. The data from such devices is increasingly being combined and analysed to yield insights into user behaviour, flag early signs of health issues and predict risks, as for example in Access Health and Social Care's ARMED fall prediction system and others. The company PainChek, featured as an NHS AI Lab case study, uses an AI-powered facial recognition app to detect and score user pain. Local authorities in England are also exploring the application of smart speakers to access information from the internet and control internet of things (IoT) or networked smart devices around the home to support care and care tasks (Wright 2021b, Hamblin 2022b).[3]

Social robots continue to be developed that make use of AI to converse with users and provide cognitive training, support and a sense of companionship. Several social robots, for example Intelligent System's PARO or Intuition Robotics' ElliQ, use AI for tasks such as natural language processing or facial recognition to personalise interactions with the user. The now-discontinued humanoid robot Pepper was customised by the CARESSES research project to deliver 'culturally sensitive' care in the UK and Japan (Papadopoulos et al. 2020). While the EU and Japan notably have invested large sums in the development and deployment of care robots, adoption levels remain relatively low (Wright 2021a, Wright 2023) and technologies utilised tend to be less complex. For example, one of the most commonly used social robots in the UK, Ageless Innovation's Joy For All companion pets, does not use highly sophisticated AI. Chatbots (which are far less expensive) are used on a larger scale than robots – such as the Woebot app, which applies a cognitive behavioural therapy approach in response to users' inputted concerns. As with the Emma chatbot used by the US Citizenship and Immigration Service and highlighted in this volume's Introduction (Paul, Carmel and Cobbe, Chapter 1 in this volume), the aim of applying this type of AI to social care is to manage increased user demand that human workers are struggling to meet. The release of a new generation of powerful large language models such as OpenAI's ChatGPT and Google's Bard is also likely to lead to their accelerated use across a range of care applications (Business Wire 2023).

The COVID-19 pandemic also spurred on the uptake of services that use AI to make outbound calls via natural language processing. Hampshire County Council worked with Amazon Web Services (AWS) to make 185,000 automated wellbeing calls[4] to 53,000 people who were shielding during the COVID-19 lockdowns. Each automated call was calculated to cost under 60p. The council reported 'overwhelmingly positive feedback' from citizens who were called via the service, and the local authority estimated that this would have taken six months to complete with their existing workforce (TSA 2021, Carefull 2021). Given the growing importance of proactive wellbeing calls beyond the pandemic as councils try to keep more older people living in their own homes to reduce costs, this large-scale proof of concept for mass data collection could prove highly persuasive to other councils, aligning with ambitions towards efficacy and low-cost care.

FRAMING AI IN CARE CONTEXTS: EFFICIENCY, ECONOMY AND EFFECTIVENESS

The imperative to spend less has intensified across national government and local authorities under the aegis of austerity following the 2008 financial crisis. In social care this can be achieved by off-loading care responsibilities onto friends and family members (Dowling and Harvie 2014), reducing the amount of care provided, and keeping staffing numbers and wage levels low. AI is often presented in public discourse in England in ways that are aligned with the nation's characterisation as an 'audit society' and the rise of New Public Management (Power 1999), with a focus on the three 'Es' of economy (spending less), efficiency (spending better) and effectiveness (spending well) (Byrne 2000). The 2021 White Paper connects technology with reduced demand: 'continued investment in technologies to support and reduce demand for care has resulted in the deployment of equipment in people's homes to predict interventions and prevent longer term demand' (DHSC 2021: 81). Similarly, NHS Digital described how a government-funded Pathfinder project between Central Bedfordshire Council and PredictX developed a proof of concept for a machine learning tool to predict where 'costly' care packages might be required and to 'reduce their future care needs' (NHS Digital 2022).

Efficiency, while closely linked to economy, seems more evident in AI and care-related policy and governance discourse than economy. Spending social care budgets *better* is, perhaps, more palatable than just spending *less*. The 2022 policy paper 'A Plan for Digital Health and Social Care' (DHSC 2022) refers to machine learning and data visualisation as tools for both economy and efficiency, able to 'show staff when to take pre-emptive action to prevent care needs arising or escalating, enabling staff to work more efficiently'. However, in practice, the delivery of applications that use machine learning are stymied by sectoral fragmentation – in England alone there were 17,900 organisations providing or organising adult social care in 2021/22, delivering care at 39,000 locations (Skills for Care 2022). Similarly, efficiencies related to technologies which monitor and assist are not straightforward. Strategy documents tend to ignore external, additional human labour including microwork (Jones 2021), and labour of installing, instructing updating and maintaining even supposedly 'light-touch' technological solutions. Additional labour and wraparound services are rendered deliberately invisible to maintain the 'automation charade' (Taylor 2018). Furthermore, purported workforce efficiencies are dubious as even fully 'autonomous' AI technologies require human intervention. In the case of care robots, care workers typically have to perform a variety of additional tasks, including explaining the robot to care recipients and teaching them how to use it, troubleshooting software or hardware issues, moving the robot into the correct position and storing it after use, and disinfecting it regularly. These 'care' practices for the robot itself then reduce the time available for interacting with care recipients (Wright 2019, Hamblin 2022a, Wright 2023).

The 'effectiveness' of these technologies is thus debateable: efficiencies are assumed to improve quality of care, e.g. the organisation OptifAI uses the tagline, 'the more efficiently you work, the more you can care', but such contentions are not yet well evidenced. In addition, while consulting groups present the solution as 'upskilling' labour to accommodate new technologies (Schlogl et al. 2021), such practices could lead to a *de*skilling and degradation of job quality (Wright 2023). For example, the company UniqueIQ (n.d.) presents monitoring as evidence of valuing staff: '[i]f a Care Professional missed a call, they would now feel valued and appreciated when their manager would give them a quick call to check everything was alright'. But a 'quick call' may equally constitute a surveillance mechanism akin to 'big brother' (Brown and Korczynski 2010), and act as a fruitless and potentially damaging attempt to rationalise and instrumentalise an inherently unpredictable labour process (MacLeavy 2021: 145). Monitoring can also impact whether workers 'trust' technology (Engelsen et al. 2020); England's care system is reliant on unpaid and underpaid labour and goodwill among staff (Allard and Whitfield 2023, Community Integrated Care 2022, Glasby et al. 2022b), rendering 'trust' important. Questions also remain about mechanisms of accountability and redress, including whether there is a human in/on the loop to monitor the results of the algorithms in real time, and who can be held responsible if mistakes are made. This is particularly important in emergency situations, but also in the use of predictive algorithms to allocate care resources or initiate disciplinary proceedings against care workers perceived to have neglected a care recipient.

Overall, there is a lack of research addressing the implications of AI on care workforce roles. A review by Consilium Research & Consultancy (2018: 7) on behalf of Skills for Care (the workforce development body in England) suggests that assertions regarding its labour-saving properties may be aspirational rather than evidenced. Resources within care organisations must also be put towards training staff to use these technologies, and providing time for staff to work with residents and users of home care services to learn and adapt to their use. Yet resources are scarce. A recent rapid review of the use of sensor technology with AI capabilities in adult social care in England noted that these devices are introducing 'prevention into an environment which is focused on dealing with crises' (Glasby et al. 2022b: 12), with limited scope and resources for the necessary service redesign, training and culture change within care organisations.

As with the lack of research into the care workforce implications, the evidence base related to the effectiveness of AI applications in adult social care is 'under-developed' (Consilium Research & Consultancy 2018: 7). The NHS AI Lab emphasises capacity to 'improve outcomes and increase choices for adult social care service users', prevent escalating need and associated moves into residential or healthcare settings, and 'target and prioritise' the deployment of scarce resources (NHS AI Lab 2020). Yet it remains unclear whether these technologies do what companies and governments claim they do, and whether they do so precisely, accurately, safely, securely and consistently. For example, how accurate are fall risk prediction algorithms? How secure from hacking are automated welfare calling systems? How effective are virtual assistants in calling for help in emergency situations when the user has a strong regional accent or cognitive or speech-related disability? Do chatbots consistently provide suitable healthcare advice as intended and escalate to a human expert serious concerns or complex cases? How are these applications being tested and audited, against what criteria or by what methodology, and by whom? Are the results publicly available? And when care and technology providers aim to utilise AI in 'effective' ways, are they adhering to relevant legal standards, regulatory rules and government guidance?

BEYOND THE 'THREE ES': EQUITY, ETHICS, REGULATION AND PRODUCTION

The focus on the 'three Es' in the framing of AI in adult social care in England neglects other important issues, such as equity and ethics (c.f. in other domains of enquiry, Norman-Major 2011, Bringselius 2018). Reflecting on equity, much of the discourse related to the use of technology broadly and AI specifically in adult social care emphasises its potential in delivering efficiencies and facilitating 'fast' care. 'Fast' or time-limited care has been argued to be at odds with the 'natural rhythms' (Hayes 2018: 174) and 'changing and adaptive human body' (Hayes and Moore 2017: 333–334). Though extensively critiqued, 15-minute time-and-task focused care visits remain a reality of statutory-funded care in England, with electronic monitoring technology used to facilitate the payment of care 'by the minute' (Hamblin et al. Goodlad 2023) to create savings for commissioning local authorities (Hayes and Moore 2017). Raising questions of equity as to who is in receipt of this rationed and time-bound 'fast' care, those with the means to privately fund their own care have access to 'slow' care. They can access a market of care providers offering care visits of not less than one hour, or flexible appointments where the client is able to negotiate with the care worker in real time (Burns et al. 2023). The size of this self-funded care market in England is difficult to capture (Brown 2021), but currently anyone with assets over £23,250 is required to finance their own care provision and estimates from 2014 indicated there could be between 170,000 and 290,000 people in this situation in England (Baxter and Glendinning 2015).

Regarding ethics and regulation, the UK government has laid out a 'pro-innovation' approach to AI regulation premised on flexibility, encouraging greater industry access to public data and avoiding regulating too early (UK Government 2023). UK regulators are also facing 'significant readiness gaps' in relation to issues increasingly being thrown up by AI, with some at a far more advanced state of readiness and capacity than others to enforce even already existing regulations (Aitken et al. 2022). In the absence of a clearly defined framework for regulating AI as a general technology or in specific sectors, various ethical frameworks have been presented as a stopgap measure until more detailed regulation is developed. The UK government has contributed to and formally adopted international agreements on ethical principles for AI, including the G20 'AI Principles', the OECD 'Principles on AI' and the UNESCO 'Recommendation on the Ethics of AI'. Examples of national ethical frameworks include the Department for Culture, Media and Sport's 'Data Ethics Framework' (2018) and the 'Guide to Using AI in the Public Sector' (2019), co-written by the Office for AI, the Government Digital Service and the Alan Turing Institute, as well as 'Guidelines for AI Procurement' (2020) by the Office for AI in partnership with the World Economic Forum. In 2020, the Local Government Association published a commissioned report entitled 'Using predictive analytics in local public services', while DHSC published a 'Code of Conduct for Data-Driven Health and Care Technologies' that integrated AI ethics with pre-existing medical and public standards. A recent report by Glasby et al. (2022a) – 'co-badged' by Digital Social Care and the NHS England Transformation Directorate – also provides guidelines for decision makers on implementing AI.

The proliferation of ethical frameworks has been critiqued for delaying the introduction of enforceable regulation and, in doing so, serving corporate interests. This can amount to 'a dangerous distraction, diverting immense financial and human resources away from potentially more effective activity' (Munn 2022). Obfuscation and a multiplicity of codes and guidance then 'confuses the landscape and undermines attempts to make any set of ethical principles authoritative' (Committee on Standards in Public Life 2020: 32). Indeed, it is unclear to what extent frameworks are being taken into account in local authority efforts to develop, procure or implement AI-powered services or applications such as Amazon Alexa-enabled devices or automated welfare calls, and there seems very little likelihood that they were taken into account by the non-UK companies that developed many of these AI services. The King's Fund (2021: 41) contends that the 'complex picture' of digital technologies 'requires boundaries to be agreed and rules to be articulated and clearly understood'.

Even with a lack of hard regulation of AI, partnerships between government, the NHS and technology companies have on several occasions broken existing data protection laws. For example, in 2017, the Royal Free Hospital was found to have breached the UK Data Protection Act in its deal with DeepMind, an AI company owned by Alphabet (the parent company of Google). Government partnerships with corporations in the use of data have also fallen foul of ethical expectations of public bodies. For example, criticism was directed towards NHS Digital and NHSX's partnership with Amazon that afforded the corporation free access to copyrightable data (Walker 2019; for a critical discussion of tech corporations' interactions with public authorities in the case of urban governance, see Antenucci and Meissner, Chapter 31 in this volume; and in the case of policing, see Kaufmann, Chapter 22 in this volume). The contract for the NHSX 'Covid-19 Data Store', aimed at combining health and social care data to predict trends using AI, was awarded to Palantir, a firm which provides 'predictive policing' for US military and police forces. When Palantir lost the contract, the data was then transferred to a system developed by the arms manufacturer BAE Systems. Ethical considerations also arise when technologies developed for care are subsequently utilised in other contexts: monitoring platforms developed by tech companies Oxehealth and Tunstall have been used in prisons (the former having received public funding to develop the technology); Anthropos' monitoring technology is used in probation services (Whitfield and Hamblin 2022). Another multifunctional product is the tracking device 'Buddi', used both in care provision and in migration policing of asylum seekers (Privacy International 2022).

Questions of ethics and regulation often tend to focus on the use of data and algorithms rather than the polluting and energy-intensive material production processes involved in the technology which stores and processes the data and trains the AI model (on sustainability discourses in AI domain, see Lucivero, Chapter 12 in this volume). This includes so-called 'ghost work' – data cleaning, coding and classifying content[5] – and the supply chains producing technology used in care contexts. Guidance for local authorities on purchasing was developed as part of the Digital Social Care Programme, but reference to supply chain practices is only in relation to a prohibition on using labour resulting from slavery or human trafficking. Yet production processes are often *un*ethical in ways that may not fall under the category of 'slavery or human trafficking'. Despite the fact that many care technologies are publicly procured, there is little in the way of regulation or guidance to deter partnerships with stakeholders that are engaged in unethical practices – even in the Office for AI's 'Guidelines for AI Procurement'. For example, concerns have been raised regarding Amazon Echo technology (which has been adopted by multiple local authorities) in relation both to the company's relationship with the UK tax system (Hamblin 2020, Wright 2021b) and the material processes of its production (Crawford 2021).[6] A report on Foxconn, Amazon's supplier, describes the employment conditions of a young person working at the factory as part of her studies:

> Xiao Fang, a 17-year-old studying computing, started work on the Amazon Echo production line last month and was given the job of applying a protective film to about 3,000 Echo Dots each day. She told researchers that her teacher initially said she would be working eight hours a day, five days a week but that this had since changed to 10 hours a day (including two hours of overtime) for six days a week. (Chamberlain 2019)

Xiao Fang's experience contrasts with the experience of another young person, Georgie, described in a report on consumer devices in adult social care:

> At just 20-years-old, Georgie's neurological diagnosis changed her life dramatically [...] not being able to do things she could before was very upsetting. But thanks to the Amazon Echo and its tailored skills, her newfound sense of independence is making everyday life that little bit better. (PA Consulting 2019: 9)

Such contrasting experiences are obscured because, once purchased, technology seems to assume a semblance of never having been produced. Supply chains are overlooked in a form of 'machine fetishism': technology is imbued with the quality of *contributing to productivity* instead of the quality of being a material (produced) good. Technology also becomes 'a local achievement, rather than as a product of the confluence of global flows' (Hornborg 2001: 486). For example, in UK government policy, care technologies are presented as a British achievement, e.g. '[a] new generation of British businesses will be thriving in the growing global market for age-related products and services' (DBEIS 2019). Little mention is made of the 'global market' necessary for the creation and maintenance of 'British' technologies. The fetish belief in technology *as innovation* becomes a key driver in the 'spiral of perpetual growth and expansion of capitalism' (Harvey 2017: 120, 21), as reflected in the policy paper quote, '[a] brighter future depends on a stream of transformative technologies being developed and spreading fast through the health and social care system' (DHSC 2022).

Also omitted from this 'hopeful' vision is the potential that businesses developing AI technology or analysing data may fail. Using massive data sets to develop AI currently entails a dependence on a small number of private companies, often based in the US, that have the expertise and compute resources to train machine learning models with billions or even trillions of parameters. This creates risk: for AI services that have already been embedded in commercial products, such as Amazon's Alexa, integration of such tools into care systems could leave users vulnerable to the precarity of corporate infrastructures (Wright 2021b). For example, amid widespread layoffs in the tech sector, it was reported that Amazon's Alexa unit was on track for a $10 billion loss, and Amazon planned to cut 10,000 jobs (Amadeo 2022). While there is currently no sign of Alexa's services being withdrawn, this remains a possibility amid disruption in the sector.

CONCLUDING COMMENTS

This chapter has illustrated debates surrounding the use of AI in social care. We have used the example of England, where policy rhetoric frames AI as part of the digital technology 'solution' for the sector, ensuring that resources are deployed economically, efficiently and effectively. Similar critical framings of AI and robots as solutions to crises of care can, however, be found in other countries with ageing populations (e.g. Lipp 2019, Wright 2023, Wright and De Togni forthcoming). Building on previous work (Hamblin 2022a, Wright 2023), we suggest that rather than straightforwardly 'replacing' workers with technology, AI is more likely to lead to the reconfiguration of existing jobs in terms of tasks and quality (cf. Donoghue et al., Chapter 26 in this volume). Facilitative work is also still required, such as training users to operate and understand technology, and troubleshooting, checking on, updating and replacing technology. Far from augmenting the capacity of care workers and giving them more time to relate to care recipients, job quality could further deteriorate with increased AI-powered monitoring of staff. We also contribute to the debate on ethics in AI use of care data. In particular, we highlight ethically questionable partnerships and the sharing of data by NHSX with private companies, which can erode public confidence in an area where trust is vital for the consensual collection and analysis of data. Fears regarding rights violations in data collection are, we suggest, exacerbated by a reluctance on the part of the government in England so far to regulate AI. This reluctance extends into the *production* of AI technologies. In a process of technological fetishisation, not only is AI presented as part of the technological silver bullet solution (Eccles 2021), it is also detached from the resource extraction and human labour required to produce, implement and run the technology.

Policy discourse justifies the use of light regulation by setting regulation in opposition, or at least as subordinate, to innovation (e.g. UK Government 2023), presenting the nation as business friendly. AI is thus inserted into the existing discursive focus on 'innovative' markets – despite this marketised solution having so far failed to resolve unmet care needs. In addition, within the framing of debates in England, questions of economic accessibility and the systemic factors that lead to requiring 'efficient' AI solutions are rarely voiced. That is, rhetoric does not question *why* England's largely marketised social care system often allocates home care in accordance with 'time-to-task' commissioning, with visits in 15-minute slots (or whether it *should*). Instead, rhetoric focuses on *how* AI tools can assist workers in carrying out care within those 15 minutes. There is little challenge within government to the assumption that faster care is better care – despite the potential for 'slower' care to alleviate loneliness, enable workers to better identify issues and improve job quality. Overall, lack of coherent leadership, a 'confused picture' of technology use and funding deficiencies (Maguire et al. 2021) have led to problems in the sector which are too extensive and complex for an AI 'fix' to solve.

NOTES

1. Instead, a series of case studies (14 at the time of writing) of the application of AI in social care has been made available via the NHS AI Lab website.
2. See https://tribeproject.org/.
3. In the US, Amazon has directly targeted the care market with its 'Alexa Together' service, combining the smart speaker's standard functionalities with a 24/7 response service, fall detection and tools for caregivers to remotely monitor and 'check in' with care recipients.
4. Wellbeing calls carried out by Hampshire County Council used a feminine voice – consistent with the allocation of women's names and feminine voices to voice assistants (e.g. Siri, Alexa and Cortana). This tendency has been criticised for embedding and reproducing existing gendered relations in care and 'feminizing AI' (Manasi et al. 2022).
5. See www.ghostwork.org.
6. See also: https://anatomyof.ai.

REFERENCES

Aitken, M., D. Leslie, F. Ostmann, J. Pratt, H. Margetts, and C. Dorobant (2022), Common regulatory capacity for AI. *The Alan Turing Institute*, accessed at https://doi.org/10.5281/zenodo.6838946.
Allard, C. and G. J. Whitfield (2023), Guilt, care, and the ideal worker: Comparing guilt among working carers and care workers. [Online first]. *Gender, Work & Organization*.
Amadeo, R. (2022), Amazon Alexa is a 'colossal failure,' on pace to lose $10 billion this year. Ars Technica. 21 November, accessed at https://arstechnica.com/gadgets/2022/11/amazon-alexa-is-a-colossal-failure-on-pace-to-lose-10-billion-this-year/.
Baxter, K. and C. Glendinning (2015), People who fund their own social care: Findings from a scoping review. *SSCR Scoping Review*. NIHR School for Social Care Research, London, accessed at https://www.sscr.nihr.ac.uk/publication/sr011/.
Bottery, S. and Ward, D. (2021), Social care 360. King's Fund, accessed at https://assets.kingsfund.org.uk/f/256914/x/609306b60e/social_care_360_2021.pdf, p. 9.
Bringselius, L. (2018), Efficiency, economy and effectiveness – but what about ethics? Supreme audit institutions at a critical juncture. *Public Money & Management*, **38** (2), 105–110.

Brown, E. (2021), Social care: Estimating the size of the self-funding population. Office of National Statistics, accessed at https://blog.ons.gov.uk/2021/02/03/social-care-estimating-the-size-of-the-self-funding-population/.

Brown, K. and M. Korczynski (2010), When caring and surveillance technology meet: Organizational commitment and discretionary effort in home care work. *Work and Occupations*, **37** (3), 404–432.

Business Wire (2023), ChatGPT with Wonderful Platform's Seniorcare robot 'Avadin', accessed at https://www.businesswire.com/news/home/20230306005831/en/ChatGPT-with-Wonderful-Platform's-Seniorcare-robot-"Avadin.

Burns, D., K. Hamblin, D. U. Fisher, and C. Goodlad (2023), Is it time for job quality? Conceptualising temporal arrangements in new models of homecare. *Sociology of Health & Illness*, **45** (7), 1541–1559.

Byrne, T. (2000), *Local Government in Britain*. London: Penguin.

Carefull, S. (2021), Wellbeing automated call service. Presentation at Technology Enabled Care Services Association (TSA) ITEC Conference, 22 March.

Chamberlain, G. (2019), Schoolchildren in China work overnight to produce Amazon Alexa devices. *The Guardian*, accessed at https://www.theguardian.com/global-development/2019/aug/08/schoolchildren-in-china-work-overnight-to-produce-amazon-alexa-devices.

Committee on Standards in Public Life (2020), Artificial intelligence and public standards, accessed at https://assets.publishing.service.gov.uk/media/5e553b3486650c10ec300a0c/Web_Version_AI_and_Public_Standards.PDF.

Community Integrated Care (2022), Unfair to care 2022–23, accessed at https://www.unfairtocare.co.uk/wp-content/uploads/2022/12/Unfair-To-Care-22-23-Full-Report.pdf.

Connolly, J. and A. Van der Zwet (eds) (2021). *Public Value Management, Governance and Reform in Britain*. Cham, Switzerland: Palgrave Macmillan.

Consilium Research & Consultancy for Skills for Care (2018), *Scoping Study on the Emerging Use of Artificial Intelligence (AI) and Robotics in Social Care*, London: Skills for Care.

Crawford, K. (2021), *The Atlas of AI: Power, Politics, and the Planetary Costs of Artificial Intelligence*. New Haven, CT: Yale University Press.

DBEIS (2019), Ageing society grand challenge, accessed at https://www.businessandindustry.co.uk/industrial-strategy/ageing-society-grand-challenge/.

DHSC (2021), People at the heart of care: Adult social care reform. White Paper. London: HMSO.

DIISC (2022), A plan for digital health and social care. Policy Paper, accessed at https://www.gov.uk/government/publications/a-plan-for-digital-health-and-social-care/a-plan-for-digital-health-and-social-care.

Digital Social Care (2022), Digitising social care fund, accessed at https://www.digitalsocialcare.co.uk/digitising-social-care-fund/ (accessed 5 January 2023).

Dowling, E. and D. Harvie (2014), Harnessing the social: State, crisis and (big) society. *Sociology* **48** (5), 869–886.

Eccles, A. (2021), Remote care technologies, older people and the social care crisis in the United Kingdom: A Multiple Streams Approach to understanding the 'silver bullet' of telecare policy. *Ageing & Society*, **41** (8), 1726–1747.

Engelsen, P., M. Ferguson, R. Charlesworth, and S. Atkinson (2020), How AI meets social care: Trust. SOCITM, accessed at https://socitm.net/resource-hub/socitm-research/how-ai-meets-socialcare-trust/
.

European Commission (2018), Communication on enabling the digital transformation of health and care in the Digital Single Market; empowering citizens and building a healthier society, COM(2018) 233 final, Brussels.

European Parliament (2021), Artificial intelligence and public services, accessed at https://www.europarl.europa.eu/RegData/etudes/BRIE/2021/662936/IPOL_BRI(2021)662936_EN.pdf.

Eurostat (2022), Need for help with personal care or household activities by sex, age and level of difficulty experienced in those activities, accessed at https://ec.europa.eu/eurostat/databrowser/view/HLTH_EHIS_TADLH__custom_4942048/default/table?lang=en&page=time:2019.

Florek, K. (2021), Resilience of the long-term care sector. *EPSU*, accessed at https://www.epsu.org/sites/default/files/article/files/Resilience_report_V6_web.pdf.

Glasby, J., I. Litchfield, S. Parkinson, L. Hocking, and D. Tanner (2022a), If I knew then what I know now … A short guide to introducing new technology in adult social care, accessed at https://preview

-uob.cloud.contensis.com/documents/college-social-sciences/social-policy/brace/ai-and-social-care
-booklet-final-digital-accessible.pdf.

Glasby, J., I. Litchfield, S. Parkinson, L. Hocking, and D. Tanner (2022b), New and emerging technology for adult social care – the example of home sensors with artificial intelligence (AI) technology. Southampton: NIHR Health and Social Care Delivery Research Topic Report; 2022. DOI: https://doi .org/10.3310/hsdr-tr-134314.

Hamblin, K. A. (2020), Technology and social care in a digital world: Challenges and opportunities in the UK. *Journal of Enabling Technologies*, **14** (2), 115–125.

Hamblin, K. A. (2022a), Technology in care systems: Displacing, reshaping, reinstating or degrading roles? *New Technology, Work and Employment*, **37** (1), 41–58.

Hamblin, K. A. (2022b), Sustainable social care: The potential of mainstream 'smart' technologies. *Sustainability*, **14** (5), 2754.

Hamblin, K. A., D. Burns, and C. Goodlad (2023), Technology and homecare in the UK: Policy, storylines and practice. *Journal of Social Policy*, First View, 1–17.

Harvey, D. (2017), *Marx, Capital, and the Madness of Economic Reason*. Oxford: Oxford University Press.

Hayes, L. J. B. (2018), Work-time technology and unpaid labour in paid care work: A socio-legal analysis of employment contracts and electronic monitoring. In: S. Beynon-Jones and Grabham, E. (eds), *Law and Time*. Abingdon, UK and New York: Routledge, pp. 170–185.

Hayes, L. J. B. and S. Moore (2017), Care in a time of austerity: The electronic monitoring of homecare workers' time. *Gender, Work & Organization*, **24** (4), 329–344.

Hornborg, A. (2001), Symbolic technologies: Machines and the Marxian notion of fetishism. *Anthropological Theory*, **1** (4), 473–496.

Hudson, B. (2021). *Clients, Consumers or Citizens? The Privatisation of Adult Social Care in England*. Bristol: Policy Press.

Johnson, B. (2019), Boris Johnson's first speech as Prime Minister: 24 July 2019, accessed at https:// www.gov.uk/government/speeches/boris-johnsons-first-speech-as-prime-minister-24-july-2019.

Jones, P. (2021), *Work without the Worker: Labour in the Age of Platform Capitalism*. London and New York: Verso Books.

LGA (2020), 'Using predictive analytics in local public services', accessed at https://www.local.gov.uk/ publications/using-predictive-analytics-local-public-services.

Lipp, B. (2019), Interfacing RobotCare: On the techno-politics of RobotCare. PhD dissertation, Technical University of Munich.

MacLeavy, J. (2021), Care work, gender inequality and technological advancement in the age of COVID-19. *Gender, Work & Organization*, **28** (1), 138–154.

Maguire, D., M. Honeyman, D. Fenney, and J. Jabbal (2021), Shaping the future of digital technology in health and social care. The Kings Fund.

Manasi, A., S. Panchanadeswaran, E. Sours, and S. J. Lee (2022), Mirroring the bias: gender and artificial intelligence. *Gender, Technology and Development*, **26** (3), 295–305.

Molinari, F., C. Van Noordt, L. Vaccari, F. Pignatelli, and L. Tangi (2021), AI Watch. Beyond pilots: sustainable implementation of AI in public services, EUR 30868 EN, Publications Office of the European Union, Luxembourg, accessed at https://publications.jrc.ec.europa.eu/repository/handle/ JRC126665.

Munn, L. (2022), The uselessness of AI ethics. *AI and Ethics*, **3**, 869–877. https://doi.org/10.1007/ s43681-022-00209-w.

NHS AI Lab (2020), AI in adult social care, accessed at https://transform.england.nhs.uk/ai-lab/explore -all-resources/understand-ai/ai-adult-social-care/ (accessed 5 January 2023).

NHS Digital (2022), Using predictive analytics and machine learning models to inform future demand on care packages, accessed at https://digital.nhs.uk/services/social-care-programme/demonstrators- programme-2019-21-case-studies/using-predictive-analytics-and-machine-learning-models-to-inform -future-demand-on-care-packages#download-the-case-study.

Norman-Major, K. (2011), Balancing the four Es; or can we achieve equity for social equity in public administration? *Journal of Public Affairs Education*, **17** (2), 233–252.

PA Consulting (2019), 'Alexa can you support people with care needs?' Trialling consumer devices in adult social care, accessed at https://www2.paconsulting.com/rs/526-HZE-833/images/Trialling %20Consumer%20Devices%20report%20-%20PA%20Consulting.pdf.

Papadopoulos, C., T. Hill, and L. Battistuzzi (2020), The CARESSES study protocol: Testing and evaluating culturally competent socially assistive robots among older adults residing in long term care homes through a controlled experimental trial. *Archives of Public Health* **78**, 26. https://doi.org/10 .1186/s13690-020-00409-y.

Privacy International (2022), Buddi Limited – Immigration Enforcement's favourite tracking buddy, accessed at https://privacyinternational.org/long-read/4991/buddi-limited-immigration-enforcements -favourite-tracking-buddy.

Power, M. (1999), *The Audit Society: Rituals of Verification*. Oxford: Oxford University Press.

Rahman, M. M., M. Rosenberg, G. Flores, N. Parsell, S. Akter, M. A. Alam, and T. Edejer (2022), A systematic review and meta-analysis of unmet needs for healthcare and long-term care among older people. *Health Economics Review*, **12** (1), 60.

Sadowski, J. (2018). Potemkin AI, accessed at https://reallifemag.com/potemkin-ai/.

Say, M. (2022), NHS Digital chief calls for stronger emphasis on social care. *UK Authority*, accessed at https://www.ukauthority.com/articles/nhs-digital-chief-calls-for-stronger-emphasis-on-social-care/.

Schlogl, L., E. Weiss, and B. Prainsack (2021), Constructing the 'future of work': An analysis of the policy discourse, *New Technology, Work and Employment*, **36** (3), 307–326.

Skills for Care (2022), The size and structure of the adult social care sector and workforce in England, London: Skills for Care, accessed at https://www.skillsforcare.org.uk/adult-social-care-workforce -data/Workforce-intelligence/publications/national-information/The-size-and-structure-of-the-adult -social-care-sector-and-workforce-in-England.aspx.

Taylor, A. (2018), The automation charade, accessed at https://logicmag.io/failure/the-automation -charade/.

The King's Fund (2021), Shaping the future of digital technology in health and social care, accessed at https://assets.kingsfund.org.uk/f/256914/x/f6444844fd/shaping_future_digital_technology_health _social_care_2021.pdf.

TSA (2021), *From Stabilisation to Innovation: The Response and Redesign of TEC Services during COVID-19*, Wilmslow: TSA.

Turnpenny, A. and S. Hussein (2021), Recruitment and retention of the social care workforce: Longstanding and emerging challenges during the COVID-19 pandemic, accessed at https://www .pssru.ac.uk/resscw/files/2021/04/RESSCW%20Policy%20Brief_revised_final2.pdf.

UK Government (2023), Pro-innovation Regulation of Technologies Review Digital Technologies, accessed at https://assets.publishing.service.gov.uk/government/uploads/system/uploads/attachment _data/file/1142883/Pro-innovation_Regulation_of_Technologies_Review_-_Digital_Technologies_ report.pdf.

United Nations (2018), 'Global care crisis' set to affect 2.3 billion people warns UN labour agency, accessed at https://news.un.org/en/story/2018/06/1013372.

UniqueIQ (n.d.), Case study: Home Instead Sutton Coldfield, accessed at https://www.uniqueiq.co.uk/ case-study/home-instead-sutton-coldfield/.

Wade-Gery, L. (2021), Putting data, digital and tech at the heart of transforming the NHS, accessed at: https://www.gov.uk/government/publications/putting-data-digital-and-tech-at-the-heart-of-trans forming-the-nhs/putting-data-digital-and-tech-at-the-heart-of-transforming-the-nhs.

Walker, A. (2019), NHS gives Amazon free use of health data under Alexa advice deal. *The Guardian*, accessed at https://www.theguardian.com/society/2019/dec/08/nhs-gives-amazon-free-use-of-health -data-under-alexa-advice-deal?CMP=share_btn_tw.

Whitfield, G. J. and K. A. Hamblin (2022), Technology in social care: Spotlight on the English policy landscape 2019–2022. *Centre for Care*, accessed at https://centreforcare.ac.uk/wp-content/uploads/ 2022/12/Technology-in-social-care-report-Dec-2022_FINAL.pdf.

Wright, J. (2019), Robots vs migrants? Reconfiguring the future of Japanese institutional eldercare. *Critical Asian Studies*, **51** (3), 331–354.

Wright, J. (2021a), Comparing the development and commercialization of care robots in the European Union and Japan. *Innovation: The European Journal of Social Science Research*, DOI: 10.1080/13511610.2021.1909460.

Wright, J. (2021b), The Alexafication of adult social care: Virtual assistants and the changing role of local government in England. *International Journal of Environmental Research and Public Health*, **18** (2), 812.

Wright, J. (2023), *Robots Won't Save Japan: An Ethnography of Eldercare Automation*. Ithaca, NY: Cornell University Press.

Wright, J. and G. De Togni (forthcoming), Robots and artificial intelligence for healthcare in Japan and South Korea. *East Asian Science, Technology and Society*.

29. AI in child protection

Jenny Krutzinna

INTRODUCTION

In child protection, one crucial question regarding the use of AI is whether it is, or can be, ethical to use machine-learning approaches in children's social care systems (Leslie et al. 2020). In this policy domain, ethical concerns weigh heavily, as protecting children against abuse, neglect and maltreatment is legally and socially deemed a delicate issue, more so than other areas of administrative decision-making. The critique in this chapter will thus adopt the distinct lens of ethics of child protection, as this reflects prevailing discussions in both research and practice.

Child protection is a function and system that in its very essence involves risk assessment, with its key task being the timely and accurate identification of children at risk of harm. This necessarily requires making predictions, because decision-making is based not only on past events but also on the likelihood of future risks and the probability of those risks materialising, resulting in harm to a child or children. This duty is enshrined in law, meaning that child protection agencies and professionals always have to anticipate a child's longer-term care prospects (Henden 2022: 2). The complexity and challenges of "getting it right" are exposed in media coverage reporting extensively on cases where intervention came too late – or, less often, too early. This "doomed if you do, doomed if you don't" dilemma looms large over child protection workers having to make decisions under difficult circumstances (Munro 2019). These include the balancing act of reliance on evidence-based risk factors to identify children (and families) "at risk" on the one hand, and alertness regarding potential discrimination of marginalised groups who through their very position in society display some of the most common risk factors, on the other hand. This task requires significant professional reflexivity and the careful exercise of discretion (cf. Busch and Henriksen, Chapter 6 in this volume) for decision-making to remain sufficiently flexible to consider individual factors and specific context.

Here, the intrinsic tension between different decision-making approaches becomes apparent. Due to its reliance on risk assessment and prediction, child protection almost begs for the application of advanced algorithm- and machine learning-driven technologies and predictive analytics (*short*: AITs), as these promise greater accuracy and precision in risk identification. At the same time, this kind of decision-making contradicts the very approach of social work, which is guided by relational considerations, ethical principles and – not least – human rights. While this tension is not new but merely a new version of a long-standing debate, it has risen to new levels with the introduction of AITs in social care in general, and child protection specifically.

In this chapter, I provide an overview of the current child protection policy landscape in the era of the increasing popularity of AITs. Specific policy at the national level remains scarce, despite several countries having implemented machine-learning and predictive analytics within their child protection systems. Instead, supranational guidance such as from UNICEF and the EU is relied upon to varying degrees. This is unsurprising, given that child protection is traditionally an area of policy that is heavily informed by states' legal obligations. At the same time, the lack of explicit engagement and interpretation within a specific nation's economic, social and cultural context may compromise children's rights protection. Children's rights are afforded the strongest human rights protection via the United Nations (UN) Convention on the Rights of the Child (CRC 1989). The CRC sets out states' duties towards children but goes beyond defining specific rights by establishing a set of fundamental principles to inform all state actions affecting children. As this provides the frame for all child-related policies, it also has critical implications for AIT-related policies in child protection. I therefore begin this chapter by situating the topic within the broader context of children's rights.

In the second part, I outline the fundamental challenge of child protection as the accurate assessment and prediction of risk. The debate on how and on what basis decisions in child protection should be made has gained new traction through the arrival of novel AITs, as I describe in part three. Much of this debate revolves around the binary described earlier in this *Handbook* (Paul, Carmel and Cobbe, Chapter 1 in this volume), of techno-functionalist and socio-technical conceptions of AITs, and beliefs in techno-solutionism versus systems of oppression narratives. Marginalisation plays a critical role, because it is one of child protection's peculiarities that it (thankfully) affects only a very small proportion of the population directly; with most citizens never encountering this branch of government. This, and the fact that it often concerns some of the most despicable human acts, makes it a highly stigmatised context, with the risk of value-laden or prejudiced policies "sneaking in". Drawing on examples from current child protection practice, I explore the extent to which this is an actual rather than merely "academic" risk and discuss how this fits with the UN policy recommendations. Finally, in the conclusion to the chapter, I summarise the reviewed work and its limits and discuss what this means for critically minded research on public policy and AI.

CHILDREN'S RIGHTS AS FRAMEWORK FOR AI POLICY IN CHILD PROTECTION

All child protection policy may be said to be rights-based, rooted in well-established, international children's rights. The UN CRC (CRC 1989) is the most significant international legal instrument and secures near universal children's rights protection, with only the US yet to ratify the Convention. Its four fundamental principles concern non-discrimination (Article 2), the best interests of the child (Article 3), the right to life, survival and development (Article 6) and the views of the child (Article 12) and are determinative of the legality of all state actions concerning or affecting children. Consequently, child protection policy must respect these principles in their full scope, including in the governance of AIT use for the purposes of protecting children. States' responsibility to protect children may be broken into the broad duty to secure and protect the full set of children's rights across a range of dimensions (including development, education, play, health), and a narrower duty to protect children from harm in the form of abuse, neglect and maltreatment. The latter is this chapter's focus, while other policy areas affecting children are covered elsewhere in this volume (see e.g., on welfare benefits, Sleep and Redden, Chapter 27 in this volume; on healthcare, Pot and Prainsack, Chapter 30 in this volume).

Child protection as a public function is described in Article 10 CRC, which requires states to take "all appropriate legislative, administrative, social and educational measures to protect children" from all types of violence, abuse, neglect and maltreatment. Specifically, "[s]uch protective measures should, as appropriate, include effective procedures for […] prevention and for identification, reporting, referral, investigation, treatment and follow-up of instances of child maltreatment […]" (Art. 10(2)).

States' responses to this legal obligation differ, but typically include the establishment of some form of child protection *system*. This may include a dedicated agency but can also involve broader social welfare services or specialist law enforcement units that perform child protective functions. A novel global typology divides countries into institutionalised, emerging and nascent child protection systems (Berrick et al. 2023), which differ vastly in their level of sophistication concerning child (rights) protection. Consequently, the introduction and use of AITs in child protection has not yet made it onto the policy agenda in all countries, despite the explicit requirement to implement "effective procedures for […] identification […] of child maltreatment" in Art. 10(2). Discussions thus often take place in cross-national fora, typically led by the UN/UNICEF, as international organisations leading global child protection efforts. A key document is the recent UN policy guidance on AI for children, with the potential to influence policy development worldwide.

AI for Children: The UN Policy Recommendations

UNICEF recently published its updated "Policy guidance on AI for children" (UNICEF 2021) the aim of which is "to promote children's rights in government and private sector AI policies and practices, and to raise awareness of how AI systems can uphold or undermine these rights". Drawing on the CRC, the guidance offers nine requirements for child-centred AI (see Box 29.1) and provides guidance to support implementation. The road map for policymakers includes a cyclical process of "understand – adapt – design – implement – evaluate", and a development canvas for software teams. UNICEF's objective was to fill the gap left by existing AI policies, strategies and guidelines which "make only cursory mention of children" (Penagos et al. 2020). Although the policy guidance does not address specific public sectors, it aims at protecting and upholding child rights across sectors "in an evolving AI World" (UNICEF 2021).

BOX 29.1 FOUNDATIONAL REQUIREMENTS OF UNICEF'S "POLICY GUIDANCE ON AI FOR CHILDREN"

1. Support children's development and well-being.
2. Ensure inclusion of and for children.
3. Prioritise fairness and non-discrimination for children.
4. Protect children's data and privacy.
5. Ensure safety for children.
6. Provide transparency, explainability, and accountability for children.
7. Empower governments and businesses with knowledge of AI and children's rights.
8. Prepare children for present and future developments in AI.
9. Create an enabling environment.

The UNICEF policy guidance notes the potential of AI systems to support child development, to help achieve the Sustainable Development Goals (SDGs), especially those relating to education, health and poverty (2021: 20–22). On the other hand, it recognises risks for children's privacy, safety and security, and the threat to children's dignity and agency by algorithms that may manipulate choices, conceal the workings of public administrations and reduce children's democratic participation; while current policy and implementation fails to reflect on the disruptive effects of AIT on children's lives (2021: 7). The key risks identified in the guidance concern the systematic and automated discrimination and exclusion through bias; limitations of children's opportunities and development from AI-based predictive analytics and profiling; infringement on data protection and privacy rights; and exacerbation of the digital divide (2021: 22–3). Discrimination/exclusion and opportunity limitations are the most relevant in the present policy context, as the guidance specifically refers to the risks from unrepresentative and flawed data being used to make predictions that become the basis for public decision-making concerning children.

UNICEF's is the first explicit policy guidance concerning AI for children, yet its impact on national policies remains to be seen. Current policy developments in Europe – a region with some of the most sophisticated child protection systems – are cause for concern and serve as a reminder to critically review children's position within AIT policymaking globally, as will be explained in the following section.

AI Policy in Europe: The EU's Proposed Artificial Intelligence Act

The "proposal for a regulation of the European Parliament and of the Council laying down harmonised rules on Artificial Intelligence (Artificial Intelligence Act)" (2021), a response to the evolving landscape of AI in the EU, fails to adequately address the protection of children. While it recognises potential adverse impacts on fundamental rights and mentions specific rights, including those related to private and family life and non-discrimination, it only briefly acknowledges children's specific rights enshrined in the EU Charter and the CRC (Artificial Intelligence Act 2021: 28).

Despite highlighting the importance of considering rights in the context of high-risk AI systems, the Act's Annex III, which lists high-risk AI applications, completely overlooks children. This omission is concerning, and contradicts the Act's own reference to the CRC Committee's General Comment No. 25 (CRC Committee 2021), which emphasises preventing discrimination against children in automated decision-making processes. It appears that concern for children is exclusively with technology companies' potential manipulation of children in pursuit of their commercial interests, and not with states' public actions potentially endangering children's rights. The lack of consideration of child protection under Annex III's high-risk systems is symptomatic for the failure to critically analyse wider political factors influencing child protection policy (see next section).

Two key points emerge from this. First, the reference to children in vulnerable situations highlights the child protection system's unique responsibilities. Since children in this system are inherently vulnerable (see CRC Committee 2013), implementing AITs in child protection must adhere to strict standards to prevent discrimination and safeguard children's rights. Second, the risk factors currently used in child protection overlap with those considered for AITs. Correctly identifying children "in need" of state intervention is the holy grail of child protection, both from a human rights-perspective (avoiding unjustified intrusions into private and family life) and from a political viewpoint (avoiding reputational damage and disrupted public trust due to "wrong" decisions being exposed in the media). AITs are touted as a solution for improving risk assessment and prediction in child protection, but their speed, complexity and lack of transparency exacerbate existing risk assessment challenges (see next section).

Given child protection's embeddedness in the broader welfare system, it is vital to critically assess the political factors influencing the adoption of AITs and question their ethical appropriateness in this domain.

RISK ASSESSMENT AND PREDICTION AS ESSENCE IN CHILD PROTECTION SYSTEMS

Henden describes the core challenge of child protection as a prediction problem: knowing which children are at high risk of experiencing neglect and therefore needing early intervention to protect them from this (2022: 5). Thus, the ability to give the most correct answers to this question becomes critical, and explains the "surge of interest in using predictive analytics", while previously professionals used either actuarial instruments or guided professional judgement to make child protection decisions (Munro 2019: 3). This development is "part of the continuum of the history of the computerization, automation, and rationalization of social work" (Redden 2020: 103), which has included the introduction of various risk-assessment tools and computerised systems (Gillingham and Graham 2017). Even though risk assessment in child protection decision-making is a unifying feature of systems, why and how it is done depends on the specific policy orientation and wider welfare state system in which it takes place. Practice examples come mostly from systems where risk assessments are core to the child protection system (e.g., the US, England), set in in a managerialist context and reflecting specific political values (see also Sleep and Redden, Chapter 27 in this volume). Accordingly, AIT implementation follows the pattern of familiar categorisations of both welfare states (Esping-Andersen 1990, 1999), and child protection systems (Gilbert et al. 2011): liberal/residual welfare states with risk-oriented child protection systems such as the US, UK and New Zealand were quick to develop and introduce AITs, while social democratic/universalist welfare states with child rights-oriented systems have so far mostly refrained. Denmark's shift towards increasing managerialism (Andersen 2019) has made it the first Nordic country to trial predictive analytics in child protection. Local Danish governments are using predictive algorithms to screen incoming child maltreatment referrals, predicting risk of harm, likelihood of criminal behaviour, additional referrals, medical diagnoses and illegal school absenteeism (Jørgensen et al. 2022). This may be seen as the result of two intersecting political discourses: digitalisation as freeing resources and as opportunity for delivering and improving welfare services on the one hand, and social policy development moving towards more evidence-based social work practice, on the other. The latter is based on the optimistic view that "messy social problems" can be approached with the certainty of natural sciences through technocratic solutions (Jørgensen et al. 2022). Ethical and legal concerns appear to have had limited effect so far, with many local governments foreseeing predictive algorithms becoming common practice in Danish child protection (Jørgensen et al. 2022).

Prior to the availability of AITs, risk assessment was based on much simpler predictive tools and professional judgement. The popularity of actuarial approaches originated in the

Anglo-American child protection systems, where numerous frameworks and tools have been developed. A prominent example is the Common Assessment Framework (CAF), used to safeguard children and young people in the UK by guiding identification of risk-increasing and risk-reducing factors to facilitate child protection decision-making. But even these more basic tools have been criticised for their failure to embrace uncertainty in practice (Featherstone et al. 2010), basing risk assessment strictly on probabilities and thereby overlooking severe outliers, such as mothers (rather than fathers) abusing their children physically/sexually. Instead, such tools enforce reliance on typical risk factors, including gender, socioeconomic status and mental health, without sufficient room for factual uncertainty.

While risk assessment traditionally covers cases where a child is already known to child protection agencies, AITs facilitate population-wide screening. The availability of large-scale public sector datasets and advanced data mining technologies reinforces belief in the techno-solutionist promise of AITs as the key to better risk assessment (see Heidelberg, Chapter 4 in this volume). This matches the growing political interest in broader identification of potential "at risk" children, not least to keep public spending under control, as in England, where implementation of AITs has coincided with severe cuts in local child protection services and general austerity measures. The concept of a "troubled family" has been used to frame certain families "as risks not only to their children but to national fiscal stability and the perceived sustainability of public services for the wider deserving public" (Jørgensen et al. 2022: 384). Prediction, so it is claimed, allows early intervention and reduces the financial burden these families place on the state; it is, however, also an expression of political power and ideology (see Redden et al. 2020), typically targeting already marginalised groups (see, e.g., Horsley et al. 2020). Importantly, where such early intervention does not result in meaningful preventive measures, it is hard to see how such profiling could be deemed ethical.

AITs can be used to create risk profiles for individuals in a population with the help of algorithms developed based on large datasets and determine the probability that a child will experience a particular outcome (Cuccaro-Alamin et al. 2017). As essentially a form of statistical modelling, debate around their introduction into social care including child protection fits into the long-standing discussion regarding the use of clinical versus actuarial methods in professional practice (Henden 2022: 4). This is reflected in the classic arguments on either side: citing better reliability, higher predictive validity, increased efficiency as some of the advantages of actuarial methods, and greater flexibility and ability to detect individual- and context-specific factors as advantages of clinical approaches. Clearly, AI-driven tools are much more powerful and accurate than traditional actuarial ones, but they have yet to mitigate some of their disadvantages vis-à-vis clinical methods. Some argue that they do not have to, because expecting AITs to "take over" decision-making is greatly overestimating their role in child protection, and instead emphasising the importance of strengthening human–AI partnerships (Kawakami et al. 2022) to improve decision-making by exploiting the technology's strengths. This position exemplifies the techno-functional conceptualisation of AITs problematised in this *Handbook* (Paul, Carmel and Cobbe, Chapter 1 in this volume), whereby these are seen as neutral and independent systems, with an "ability to interpret external data correctly, to learn from such data, and to use those learnings to achieve specific goals and tasks through flexible adaptation" (Kaplan and Haenlein 2019: 15). Critics argue that AITs can never be neutral due to their embeddedness in society and the political system, as highlighted by many contributions in this volume. The socio-political conceptualisation of AITs proposed in this volume thus recognises AITs as potential systems of oppression (see e.g., O'Neil 2016;

Kerr 2021), and their application in child protection to the detriment of marginalised groups has been described (Eubanks 2018a; Keddell 2019).

The debate between these two contrasting positions also reveals deeper disagreement regarding the proper approach to child protection decision-making. This has implications for policymaking, because how one conceptualises the purpose of social work decision-making determines the priorities set in choosing the most appropriate approach. I explore this in more detail in the following section.

CHILD PROTECTION DECISION-MAKING: CURRENT DEBATES AND POLICY IMPLICATIONS

Child protection falls under the remit of social work more broadly, meaning that the use of AITs, and their framing within the child protection system, necessarily interacts with existing professional purposes and values. This is reflected in the main debates in the field, which although predating the emergence of AITs, gain new momentum in light of these "enhanced" decision-facilitating and decision-making technologies.

Child protection decision-making is both empirically and normatively complex (Henden 2022: 2). Taking place in a unique context of values and factual uncertainties, professional discretion in decision-making is essential. The social worker's expertise in assessing complex situations is also indispensable for ensuring the participation of those affected most by the decision, children and their families. Interventions in this policy field are exceptional: they are highly intrusive in the otherwise private sphere of family life, which explains the high expectations for always getting it right, often punished by public opprobrium if they are not met (e.g., Whewell 2018). In response, some argue for increased collaboration, training and staffing, while others call for the implementation of better risk assessment tools. While this may be a simplified description of the tension in the field, this dichotomy serves as useful heuristic for disentangling the many debates and arguments surrounding the advent of AITs in child protection.

Norms and Values: Constraint of Professional Discretion, Increased Ethical Tensions and Ethics Imperialism

Social work has been described as "among the most value based of all professions" (Reamer 2006; Landau 2008). Its fundamental values of respect for dignity and worth of all human beings, the promotion of wellbeing and of social and environmental justice (Banks 2020: 65) are however not easily integrated into everyday practice. The embeddedness of social workers within a wider welfare system has been described as leading to incongruities between individual/professional values, and those of the "system" (McCarthy et al. 2020). Institutional and societal structures may prevent social workers from acting as they would deem right, a position that requires a "broadening of the lens" to address resulting ethical tensions (Weinberg 2010). For instance, a social worker's conviction may be that parenting support would be most effective in averting risk of harm to a child. However, limitations in service availability or restrictive criteria may render such measures formally or practically unavailable – a situation not uncommon in times of budget cuts, which often affect child and family spending first. In practice, a social worker will attempt to avoid the much harsher alternative intervention of child removal, unless they are convinced this is in the child's and not merely the system's best interests. The social worker could, for instance, grant access to parenting support even where parents do not formally qualify, or take the decision that risk factors present do not currently warrant intrusive intervention. In both cases, the ethical tension is resolved by the child protection worker's resort to their own norms and values and deriving the most ethically justifiable decision from this contextualised position.

The introduction of AITs could potentially worsen this tension, as deliberately going against a decision of a sophisticated system aligned with administrative "values" requires much more audacity than departing from risk assessment based on observation of and conversations with the parties involved. The social worker may feel their professional discretion being restricted to the extent that professional norms and values are threatened, individually as well as collectively (cf. Busch and Henriksen, Chapter 6 in this volume). For example, the use of AITs could limit the inclusion of non-Western perspectives in social work practice, contradicting the profession's own agenda of working towards more inclusive social work values. The International Federation of Social Workers (IFSW) has chosen *Ubuntu* as its theme for the Global Agenda for Social Work and Development 2020–30 (IFSW 2020), a philosophy that

> emphasises that people's identities are continuously developing in the context of their reciprocal relationships with others, and thereby, through supporting and nurturing others, one's own identity and life quality are enhanced […] When an Ubuntu practising social worker is confronted with a problem, she does not seek to analyse it into components or parts, but rather she will ask in what larger context the problem resides. Individual identity and contributions are not denied but are seen as part of the whole. A successful individual is defined as someone that is committed to supporting others with integrity. (Mayaka and Truell 2021)

Ubuntu's inclusion in the Global Agenda marks an important recognition, globally, of the need to embrace a broader range of values, including those centred on interconnection and reciprocity found in Indigenous cultures (Mayaka and Truell 2021) in social work practice. Yet, this approach seems entirely incompatible with the rationalistic and probabilistic risk assessment intrinsic to AIT-based decision-making. AITs would thus appear to reinforce Western dominance by focusing on negative factors and individual responsibility, leaving little room for relational considerations prevalent in the Global South (on a similar comparative discussion of non-Western approaches value systems see Omotubora and Basu, Chapter 17 in this volume; Sleep and Redden, Chapter 27 in this volume).

The holistic and relational approach that underlies social work practice is widely seen as critical for safeguarding children's and families' right to self-determination and respect for private and family life (Gillingham 2011; Munro et al. 2013), which is undermined by AIT decision-making (Henden 2022). For example, child protection workers in the US have shown limited enthusiasm for decision-support tools, as statistical models were felt to overestimate risk in ways that disproportionately affected some groups, e.g., by "punishing" families based on demographic factors such as having more than three children or having children born close in time (Bosk 2018), potentially leading to unjustified interventions that violate privacy and self-determination rights (Leslie et al. 2020). Public approval is also crucial for the legitimacy of child protection decisions, with research indicating a preference for human discretion over algorithms (Jauernig et al. 2022). Mere improvements in accuracy or fairness are insufficient because the very artificiality of algorithms can evoke aversion in morally charged decisions (Jauernig et al. 2022). In New Zealand, public reactions have led to the abandonment of predictive tools in child protection, highlighting the importance of public sentiment (Jørgensen et al. 2022: 387–88).

Decision-makers' flexibility to account for individual and contextual factors, however, also comes with challenges. For instance, evidence has shown child protection workers to place excessive emphasis on memorable data, such as vivid, concrete or emotion-arousing data, to be focused on the narrow range of evidence available to them and overlooking significant data known to other professionals, and to struggle with correcting their judgements in light of new evidence (Munro 1999). Consequently, AIT proponents claim superiority of the technology-driven approach to decision-making, which avoids these human biases (cf. critical discussion of narratives around bias: Hong, Chapter 8 in this volume).

Facts and Data: Empirical Evidence, Improved Risk Assessment and Neutrality of Technology

Child protection decision-making in Western countries typically relies on comprehensive risk assessments that consider various factors to predict potential harm to a child. For instance, England's CAF evaluates child (developmental) needs, parenting capacity and family/social factors. Based on extensive research, this and similar frameworks include both risk-increasing and risk-mitigating factors (Ward et al. 2012). Negative factors such as poor parenting competency, and positive factors such as empathy for the child, strong social support networks and willingness to accept help are balanced to create a holistic risk profile guiding decision-making on the likelihood of harm to the child. In practice, such balancing may however be insufficiently thorough (e.g., Krutzinna and Skivenes 2020).

To enhance objectivity and reduce human bias, increasingly complex risk-assessment tools link evidence-based risk factors and "neutral" data from public agencies. These actuarial methods aim to improve decision-making efficiency and are popular with public administrations. Nevertheless, within the high-pressure domain of child protection, such promises often prove futile. Professionals and their "clients" express concern about the inadequate consideration of protective/risk-mitigating factors. The introduction of AITs into decision-making processes is feared to exacerbate this issue by over-emphasising risk-increasing factors, as administrative datasets seldom systematically include protective factors.

AITs and their models predict neglect or maltreatment risks solely based on statistical risk factors, disregarding the child and family's broader social context (Vaithianathan et al. 2017). Positive factors are ignored (Keddell 2019; Spratt and Callan 2004), despite evidence that they reduce risk and improve child care prospects (Ward et al. 2012). Critics argue that AITs may result in a one-sided focus on risk at the expense of a holistic assessment that considers all relevant circumstances (Henden 2022: 7). Furthermore, these systems often use extreme outcomes, such as child death, for risk modelling (Vaithianathan et al. 2021), although such events are rare in practice.

One of the first tools implemented was the Allegheny Family Screening Tool (FST), a supervised learning algorithm supposedly using over 100 factors about a child from a broad range of public databases. Developed in conjunction with academics, such as Emily Putnam-Hornstein, a prominent advocate for risk stratification tools, the FST has been famously criticised by Victoria Eubanks for systematically discriminating against marginalised people. Some of the key concerns have since been addressed by the tool's developers. The FST is closely observed and has served both as inspiration and a cautionary tale for administrations worldwide. The comprehensive practice experiences have shown risk-based decision-making in child protection to face the full array of challenges, including problems based on incomplete/selective data, inadequate weighing of information and personal biases, which depending on viewpoint, may provide an opportunity or a cause for concern for algorithmic intervention (Leslie et al. 2020: 14).

This once again leads to the fundamental ethical issue: Given that child protection decision-making necessarily entails an element of risk assessment, what approach is ethically justifiable? The answer carries important policy implications.

Policy Implications

As the previous sections have demonstrated, disagreement stems largely from vastly differing beliefs in humans and technology, their respective abilities and proper role within child protection. While many criticisms concerning decision-making apply also to human decision-makers, "the reification of these processes within algorithms render their articulation even more difficult, and can diminish other important relational and ethical aims of social work practice" (Keddell 2019: 281). This captures well the fundamental challenge in child protection policymaking concerning AI: intrinsic value differences make consensus difficult, leaving policymakers to decide which side to err on.

Concerns that children and their families will be negatively impacted (Church and Fairchild 2017; Eubanks 2018a, 2018b; Keddell 2015) weigh heavily. Techno-solutionists are, however, optimistic that current problems can be addressed by creating better models, or by improving the underlying data to include a wider selection of factors (Cuccaro-Alamin et al. 2017; Schwartz et al., 2017). In practice, this possibility seems limited, given the incompleteness of available data (Munro 2019) and the status quo of child welfare data as "administrative recording of factors – such as reports to child protection services or legal orders" (Keddell 2018) rather than "a record of truth" (Redden 2020). Thus, the biases of those reporting and investigating child neglect/abuse risk being reproduced in the reporting, the data and the outputs of any predictive system.

Value differences aside, three essential policy considerations emerge. These concern data quality, children's participation and accountability. First, a fundamental concern relates to data quality (requirement 2, UNICEF guidance). The UN regularly reminds states to collect better data, including disaggregated data that allows for meaningful analysis of the state of children's (rights) protection. Yet, even the most sophisticated public administrations fail in their data collection duties, especially regarding marginalised groups of children. If such public data is used as a basis for AI-based decision-making, it is inevitable that discrimination will be cemented into the child protection system (breaching requirement 3, UNICEF guidance).

Second, the CRC states unequivocally children's right to be heard and to have their views considered in all matters affecting them (Art. 12; requirement 1, UNICEF guidance). Consequently, policymakers must involve children both in the policymaking process and in the individual child protection decisions affecting them – a possibility not envisaged by AITs, with none of the predictive systems currently used providing a possibility for children to review and correct the data used.

Finally, requirement 5 of the UNICEF guidelines calls for transparency, explainability and accountability for children. This has found its way into data protection legislation, for instance, in Europe. However, such protections have limited practical value for those in a vulnerable situation, including children, who lack the resources to request insight, oversight or redress in relation to AI-based decision-making, which may also be a question of racial and class privilege (Benjamin 2019). Furthermore, the near omission of children in even the most recent legislation, the European AI Act, indicates limited focus on the importance of protecting children from *state* actions.

CONCLUSION

Child protection is a uniquely challenging policy domain, with stark power differentials in decision-making. Human rights violations occur when decisions exclude affected individuals from participation and understanding: "As the child protection system is a law-like process with implications for people's lives, people should instead have the right to be treated as an individual and have decisions made about their lives that they are able to participate in and understand" (Keddell 2019). This lack of human accountability is troubling, especially when dealing with society's most vulnerable. The tendency to label families as "troubled" and reduce welfare spending raises doubts about implementing AITs in child protection. For instance, while accurate predictive risk modelling could be invaluable for providing targeted preventative services (Gillingham 2017), the ethical issue turns on whether states will provide (= finance) such services.

A critical examination of AI policy in child protection must consider the power relations between children, families, professionals and the state (as well its managerial agenda in many contexts) in this domain. AITs should not be isolated but viewed as tools used by people with human abilities and limitations in a specific context (Munro 2019: 8). The acceptability of AITs in child protection hinges on values, trust in the political system, and acceptance by professionals and the public.

Overall, the challenges and power imbalances in child protection, coupled with the need for cooperation between parents and the state, raise acute questions about AIT implementation. Ethical considerations, including the potential for human rights violations by the state and reduced democratic participation, need close attention. Whether algorithms have a place in this policy area remains an open question when solutions are elusive (Edwards et al. 2022: 280). It will be crucial for policymakers to ensure AITs in child protection are used with a genuine focus on safeguarding children, rather than solely as tools for a managerial agenda. In the meantime, the absence of clear policies regarding AITs in child protection is worrisome. The rapid development and deployment of these tools across various public decision-making areas may result in an unwarranted "AI creep" into child protection. This risk is particularly imminent in countries like England, where services are increasingly outsourced to unregulated, unregistered and uninspected organisations (Jones 2015: 463). Without well-defined stances and dedicated policies to govern the use of AITs in child protection, the protection of children and their rights becomes vulnerable to unethical compromises.

REFERENCES

Andersen, J. (2019), 'Denmark: The Welfare State as a Victim of Neoliberal Economic Failure?', in S. Ólafsson, M. Daly, O. Kangas, and J. Palme (eds), *Welfare and the Great Recession: A Comparative Study*, Oxford: Oxford University Press, pp. 192–209.

Artificial Intelligence Act (2021), accessed 9 June 2023 at https://eur-lex.europa.eu/legal-content/EN/TXT/?uri=celex%3A52021PC0206.

Banks, S. (2020), *Ethics and Values in Social Work*, London: Bloomsbury.

Benjamin, R. (2019), *Race after Technology: Abolitionist Tools for the New Jim Code*, Medford, MA: Polity.

Berrick, J. D., N. Gilbert and M. Skivenes (2023), 'Child protection systems across the globe – an introduction', in J. D. Berrick, N. Gilbert, and M. Skivenes (eds), *Oxford Handbook of Child Protection Systems*, New York: Oxford University Press, pp. 1–22.

Bosk, E. A. (2018), 'What Counts? Wuantification, Worker Judgment, and Divergence in Child Welfare Decision Making', *Human Service Organizations: Management, Leadership & Governance*, **42** (2), 205–24.

Church, C. E. and A. J. Fairchild (2017), 'In Search of a Silver Bullet: Child Welfare's Embrace of Predictive Analytics', *Juvenile and Family Court Journal*, **68** (1), 67–81.

CRC (1989), 'Convention on the Rights of the Child'.

CRC Committee (2013), *General Comment No. 14 on the Right of the Child to Have His or Her Best Interests Taken as a Primary Consideration (Art. 3, Para. 1)*.

CRC Committee (2021), *General Comment No. 25 on Children's Rights in Relation to the Digital Environment*.

Cuccaro-Alamin, S., R. Foust, R. Vaithianathan and E. Putnam-Hornstein (2017), 'Risk Assessment and Decision Making in Child Protective Services: Predictive Risk Modeling in Context', *Children and Youth Services Review*, **79**, 291–98.

Edwards, R., V. Gillies and S. Gorin (2022), 'Problem-solving for Problem-solving: Data Analytics to Identify Families for Service Intervention', *Critical Social Policy*, **42** (2), 265–84.

Esping-Andersen, G. (1990), *The Three Worlds of Welfare Capitalism*, Oxford: Polity Press.

Esping-Andersen, G. (1999), *Social Foundations of Postindustrial Economies*, Oxford: Oxford University Press.

Eubanks, V. (2018a), 'A Child Abuse Prediction Model Fails Poor Families', *Wired*, 15 January, accessed 23 November 2020 at https://www.wired.com/story/excerpt-from-automating-inequality/.

Eubanks, V. (2018b), *Automating Inequality: How High-tech Tools Profile, Police, and Punish the Poor*, New York: St. Martin's Press.

Featherstone, B., C.-A. Hooper, J. Scourfield and J. S. Taylor (eds) (2010), *Gender and Child Welfare in Society*, Chichester, UK and Malden, MA: Wiley-Blackwell.

Gilbert, N., N. Parton and M. Skivenes (eds) (2011), *Child Protection Systems: International Trends and Orientations*, New York: Oxford University Press.

Gillingham, P. (2011), 'Decision-making Tools and the Development of Expertise in Child Protection Practitioners: Are We "Just Breeding Workers Who Are Good at Ticking Boxes"?', *Child & Family Social Work*, **16** (4), 412–21.

Gillingham, P. (2017), 'Predictive Risk Modelling to Prevent Child Maltreatment: Insights and Implications from Aotearoa/New Zealand', *Journal of Public Child Welfare*, **11** (2), 150–65.

Gillingham, P. and T. Graham (2017), 'Big Data in Social Welfare: The Development of a Critical Perspective on Social Work's Latest "Electronic Turn"', *Australian Social Work*, **70** (2), 135–47.

Henden, E. (2022), 'Algoritmer til barnets beste?', *Tidsskrift for Velferdsforskning*, **25** (3), 1–15.

Horsley, N., V. Gillies and R. Edwards (2020), '"We've Got a File on You": Problematising Families in Poverty in Four Periods of Austerity', *Journal of Poverty and Social Justice*, **28** (2), 227–44.

IFSW (2020), *2020 to 2030 Global Agenda for Social Work and Social Development Framework: 'Co-building Inclusive Social Transformation' – International Federation of Social Workers*, accessed 1 August 2022 at https://www.ifsw.org/2020-to-2030-global-agenda-for-social-work-and-social-development-framework-co-building-inclusive-social-transformation/.

Jauernig, J., M. Uhl and G. Walkowitz (2022), 'People Prefer Moral Discretion to Algorithms: Algorithm Aversion beyond Intransparency', *Philosophy & Technology*, **35** (1), 2.

Jones, R. (2015), 'The End Game: The Marketisation and Privatisation of Children's Social Work and Child Protection', *Critical Social Policy*, **35** (4), 447–69.

Jørgensen, A. M., C. Webb, E. Keddell and N. Ballantyne (2022), 'Three Roads to Rome? Comparative Policy Analysis of Predictive Tools in Child Protection Services in Aotearoa New Zealand, England, & Denmark', *Nordic Social Work Research*, **12** (3), 379–91.

Kaplan, A. and M. Haenlein (2019), 'Siri, Siri, in my Hand: Who's the Fairest in the Land? On the Interpretations, Illustrations, and Implications of Artificial Intelligence', *Business Horizons*, accessed at https://doi.org/10.1016/J.BUSHOR.2018.08.004.

Kawakami, A., V. Sivaraman, H.-F. Cheng, L. Stapleton, Y. Cheng, D. Qing, A. Perer, Z. S. Wu, H. Zhu and K. Holstein (2022), 'Improving Human-AI Partnerships in Child Welfare: Understanding Worker Practices, Challenges, and Desires for Algorithmic Decision Support', in *CHI Conference on Human Factors in Computing Systems*, New Orleans, LA: ACM, pp. 1–18.

Keddell, E. (2015), 'The Ethics of Predictive Risk Modelling in the Aotearoa/New Zealand Child Welfare Context: Child Abuse Prevention or Neo-liberal Tool?', *Critical Social Policy*, **35** (1), 69–88.

Keddell, E. (2018), *Risk Prediction Tools in Child Welfare Contexts: The Devil in the Detail*, accessed 14 June 2023 at http://www.husita.org/risk-prediction-tools-in-child-welfare-contexts-the-devil-in -the-detail/.

Keddell, E. (2019), 'Algorithmic Justice in Child Protection: Statistical Fairness, Social Justice and the Implications for Practice', *Social Sciences*, **8** (10), 281.

Kerr, A. D. (2021), 'Artificial Intelligence, Gender, and Oppression', in W. Leal Filho, A. Marisa Azul, L. Brandli, A. Lange Salvia, and T. Wall (eds), *Gender Equality*, Cham, Switzerland: Springer International Publishing, pp. 54–64.

Krutzinna, J. and M. Skivenes (2020), 'Judging Parental Competence: A Cross-country Analysis of Judicial Decision Makers' Written Assessment of Mothers' Parenting Capacities in Newborn Removal Cases', *Child & Family Social Work*, **26** (1), 50–60.

Landau, R. (2008), 'Social Work Research Ethics: Dual Roles and Boundary Issues', *Families in Society*, **89** (4), 571–77.

Leslie, D., L. Holmes, C. Hitrova and E. Ott (2020), *Ethics Review of Machine Learning in Children's Social Care*, What Works Centre for Children's Social Care, January, accessed 2 October 2022 at https://www.turing.ac.uk/sites/default/files/2020-02/wwcsc_ethics_of_machine_learning_in_csc_ jan2020.pdf.

Mayaka, B. and R. Truell (2021), 'Ubuntu and its Potential Impact on the International Social Work Profession', *International Social Work*, **64** (5), 649–62.

McCarthy, L. P., R. Imboden, C. S. Shdaimah and P. Forrester (2020), '"Ethics Are Messy": Supervision as a Tool to Help Social Workers Manage Ethical Challenges', *Ethics and Social Welfare*, **14** (1), 118–34.

Munro, E. (1999), 'Common Errors of Reasoning in Child Protection Work', *Child Abuse & Neglect*, **23** (8), 745–58.

Munro, E. (2019), 'Predictive Analytics in Child Protection', CHESS Working Paper No. 2019-03, Durham University.

Munro, E., J. S. Taylor and C. Bradbury-Jones (2013), 'Understanding the Causal Pathways to Child Maltreatment: Implications for Health and Social Care Policy and Practice', *Child Abuse Review*, **23** (1), 61–74.

O'Neil, C. (2016), *Weapons of Math Destruction: How Big Data Increases Inequality and Threatens Democracy*, New York: Crown.

Penagos, M., S. Kassir and S. Vosloo (2020), *National AI Strategies and Children*, UNICEF Office of Global Insight and Policy.

Reamer, F. G. (2006), 'Social Work Values and Ethics', in *Social Work Values and Ethics*, New York: Columbia University Press, Chapter 1.

Redden, J. (2020), 'Predictive Analytics and Child Welfare: Toward Data Justice', *Canadian Journal of Communication*, **45** (1), 101–11.

Redden, J., L. Dencik and H. Warne (2020), 'Datafied Child Welfare Services: Unpacking Politics, Economics and Power', *Policy Studies*, **41** (5), 507–26.

Schwartz, I. M., P. York, E. Nowakowski-Sims and A. Ramos-Hernandez (2017), 'Predictive and Prescriptive Analytics, Machine Learning and Child Welfare Risk Assessment: The Broward County Experience', *Children and Youth Services Review*, **81**, 309–20.

Spratt, T. and J. Callan (2004), 'Parents' Views on Social Work Interventions in Child Welfare Cases', *The British Journal of Social Work*, **34** (2), 199–224.

UNICEF (2021), 'Policy Guidance on AI for Children', accessed 1 October 2022 at https://www.unicef .org/globalinsight/media/2356/file/UNICEF-Global-Insight-policy-guidance-AI-children-2.0-2021 .pdf.

Vaithianathan, R., D. Benavides-Prado, E. Dalton, A. Chouldechova and E. Putnam-Hornstein (2021), 'Using a Machine Learning Tool to Support High-stakes Decisions in Child Protection', *AI Magazine*, **42** (1), 53–60.

Vaithianathan, R., E. Putnam-Hornstein, N. Jiang, P. Nand and T. Maloney (2017), *Developing Predictive Models to Support Child Maltreatment Hotline Screening Decisions: Allegheny County Methodology and Implementation*, available at https://www.alleghenycountyanalytics.us/wp-content/uploads/2019/ 05/Methodology-V1-from-16-ACDHS-26_PredictiveRisk_Package_050119_FINAL.pdf.

Ward, H., R. Brown and D. Westlake (2012), *Safeguarding Babies and Very Young Children from Abuse and Neglect*, London and Philadelphia: Jessica Kingsley Publishers.

Weinberg, M. (2010), 'The Social Construction of Social Work Ethics: Politicizing and Broadening the Lens', *Journal of Progressive Human Services*, **21** (1), 32–44.

Whewell, T. (2018), 'Norway's hidden scandal', *BBC News*, accessed 9 June 2023 at https://www.bbc.co .uk/news/resources/idt-sh/norways_hidden_scandal.

30. Governing AI technologies in healthcare: beyond the 'ethics bubble'

Mirjam Pot and Barbara Prainsack

INTRODUCTION

Important aspects of medicine and healthcare are becoming digitised – ranging from electronic patient records and online consultations to the widespread use of health apps. This opens up manifold questions for critical social science and policy research (Lupton 2017; Petersen 2018), e.g. about the politics underlying the promises about the digitisation of healthcare, new actor constellations, and the redistribution of responsibilities and power shifts to which these changes give rise. Moreover, digitisation affects how we define and come to know health and disease, as well as when and how they should be acted upon.

In this chapter, we focus on a particular set of digital health technologies, namely those supported by what we subsume under the broad label of artificial intelligence (AI). AI is an umbrella term for technologies that try to emulate human intelligence and, as such, their application in medicine and healthcare is not a new development. As Yu et al. (2018, p. 719) point out, 'the successes of AI from the 1970s through the 1990s that were once heralded as breakthroughs in medicine, such as the automated interpretation of electrocardiograms (ECGs), are now regarded as useful but are hardly considered to be examples of true AI'. What characterised such technologies in the past is that they were based on the curation of knowledge and the formulation of decision rules by experts. Such 'old' AI technologies (AIT) are increasingly replaced by so-called 'true AI' applications that are based on different kinds of machine learning methods and can identify patterns in data 'independently'. The latter are the main subject of our chapter.

We start with a short overview of some of the (potential) uses of AIT in healthcare as well as related expectations and problems as commonly discussed in the literature (section 1). We then discuss the role of 'ethics' in the governance of AIT (section 2) and, although they have entered the policy agenda only recently, current approaches and discussions regarding the regulation of AIT in healthcare (section 3). We subsequently identify some issues and caveats, such as the narrow focus on safety, or the assumption that some kinds of AIT are less in need of regulation than others (section 4). Furthermore, we highlight the usefulness of a political economy perspective in this process. Such a perspective seems to be particularly needed at a moment in time when major technology companies expand their engagement in healthcare.

THE PROMISES OF APPLYING AI IN HEALTHCARE

How are AIT in healthcare discussed and envisioned in the (mainly medical and technical) academic literature? The first insight that a structured review of this literature reveals is that discussions are mostly placeless in the sense that they refer to AIT in the abstract, without consideration of regional and national differences. The perspective taken is typically that of a rich country in the Global North. Within this context, at the core of clinical healthcare provision, AIT are expected to improve diagnosis and treatment. For example, in specialties such as radiology, dermatology and pathology, which rely heavily on image-based diagnosis, AIT are already used to analyse medical images. More broadly, AIT can also provide clinicians with treatment recommendations – e.g. when they are integrated into electronic health records. In addition, AIT are used for the monitoring of patients through the interpretation of vital signs, for example, in intensive care units and in surgical robots (Yu et al. 2018). In the clinical domain, AIT are seen to enable earlier and better detection of disease, more precise and effective treatment decisions, and the 'personalisation' of medicine. Particularly regarding diagnosis and treatment recommendations, however, many existing AIT have been developed for very specific tasks and it remains unclear whether they can be applied in more generic settings, and also how other types of 'contextual' information such as about patients' values or social support systems are to be integrated.

Supporters in the medical (and related technological) literature also expect that AIT will free administrative and clinical staff from routine tasks such as documentation, the management of electronic health records, the processing of insurance claims and billing. Other potential usages of AIT in the administrative domain are the scheduling of follow-up appointments or the filling of prescriptions. Advocates envision that these technologies will save time and cost. For healthcare workers specifically, proponents hope that AIT will allow them to spend more time with their patients (Topol 2019). At the same time, it has been shown that the implementation of AIT in healthcare can also come with 'various forms of "repair work" needed to enable algorithmic systems to work in practice' (Schwennesen 2019, p. 176). This means that rather than reducing workloads, AIT can also lead to an increase in clinical and administrative work (see also Bainbridge 1983). In administration, beyond the automation of some routine tasks, AIT are also expected to contribute to better resource allocation and planning of healthcare such as through predictions about lengths of hospital stays and readmissions (Reddy et al. 2019).

There are also expectations that AIT will enhance people's everyday healthcare practices. As part of wearable devices and smartphone applications, AIT enable inferences about patients' health status by measuring biomedical signals (such as heart rate or temperature) and analysing other automatically captured information (such as steps or sleep patterns). The expectation is that AIT will contribute towards a positive behaviour change in individual patients based on alerts and personalised recommendations (Martin 2012). At the same time, AIT are supposed to increase patients' compliance with therapies and treatment plans set up by healthcare professionals and thereby increase the efficient use of resources such as drugs. 'Patient engagement and adherence has long been seen as the "last mile" problem of healthcare – the final barrier between ineffective and good health outcomes' (Davenport and Kalakota 2019, p. 96), and the hope among advocates is that AIT will help to tackle it.

Whereas discussions of the expected benefits of AIT, as noted, typically take place without particular considerations of different spaces and places, in recent years, AIT have also entered the policy agenda on global health. In this context, AIT are expected to help address unmet basic health needs and severe resource limitations in terms of infrastructures, personnel (in particular specialists), and medical technologies. Hosny and Aerts (2019), for example, differentiate between three areas in which AIT could be applied in low- and middle-income countries: first, as part of low-cost tools such as portable devices and smartphones, AIT could be used – by patients as well as by non-specialised professionals (also off-site) – to identify common diseases, for the provision of health advice and triage. Second, AIT could support clinical decision-making and allow primary care doctors to perform specialised tasks such as the reading of radiology images – or help specialists with performing tasks that cut across several specialities. Third, in public health and health planning, AIT could contribute to earlier identification of disease outbreaks and a better allocation of scarce resources, but also, for example, to maintain cancer registries through the automated extraction of standardised data in pathology reports.

Noticeably, especially for AIT that could contribute to global health, ethical, regulatory or practical questions are often not adequately addressed (Schwalbe and Wahl 2020). For example, AIT for diagnosis and treatment recommendations need to be trained on data representing local populations and their disease profiles and cannot just be transferred from other contexts. Furthermore, in the case of treatment recommendations, these would need to be adapted to available and affordable options and, more generally, the availability of infrastructures such as stable electricity and internet connectivity has to be considered. More fundamentally, the introduction of AIT developed by multinational tech companies and with international funding could be seen as an instantiation of coloniality (Prainsack 2023; Gray, Chapter 15 in this volume). This concerns not only the question of who owns and is able to operate AIT as part of the healthcare infrastructure, but also what happens to and who will benefit from the healthcare data collected in the Global South (Ferryman 2021).

Overall, the proponents of AIT in the medical literature expect them to contribute to better healthcare but also to alleviate some of the structural problems that healthcare systems around the world are facing. These include the changing demographic composition of the population and respective changes in diseases, as well as shortages in the healthcare workforce and other resource constraints. AIT are also often associated with more far-reaching normative promises such as 'patient empowerment' or 'democratising healthcare' (Rubeis et al. 2022). In this sense, the overall discussion about the potential of AIT in healthcare is not only characterised by 'an exceptional amount of inflation about the abilities of AI' (Reddy et al. 2019, p. 22), but also a considerable techno-solutionism (cf. Paul, Carmel and Cobbe, Chapter 1 in this volume; Paul 2022).

GOVERNING AIT IN HEALTHCARE: FROM ETHICS TO REGULATION

There is also a growing literature addressing ethical questions pertaining to AIT in healthcare. Morley et al. (2020) differentiate three categories of ethical issues: the first group pertains to the *epistemic features* of AIT and includes questions regarding the status of AI-generated evidence. The evidence presented by AIT can be inconclusive (as it is often not sufficient to determine causal relationships), inscrutable (people working with AI-based recommendations rarely know on which data the AIT have been trained or the specific data underlying a particular decision) or misguided (outcomes are only as reliable as the data they are based on). Second, *normative concerns* include the potential problem of unfair and biased outcomes of AI-based analyses and recommendations, in the sense that AIT can lead to the unfair advantage or disadvantage of certain patient groups. Third, another frequently addressed ethical concern is the *problem of traceability* in the sense that harm caused by AIT can be difficult to detect, and accountability is often not clear (cf. Cobbe and Singh, Chapter 7 in this volume).

The discussion of ethical issues of AIT in healthcare (and beyond) has led to the development of a plethora of AI ethics guidelines by different stakeholders. European Union institutions, in particular, seek to position themselves as 'a global player in AI ethics' (Gerke et al. 2020). But the strong focus of academia, industry and policymakers on AI ethics has also been criticised (see also below). Munn (2022), for example, argues that most AI ethics guidelines are 'useless': they are often incoherent, not fully acted upon or only partially implemented, and their non-compliance remains without consequences. Munn concludes that too strong a focus on ethics at the cost of regulation is 'a dangerous distraction' that channels attention and resources away from more effective approaches of addressing issues of AI justice and the governance of AIT more generally (also see discussion on ethics by Rönnblom, Carlsson and Padden, Chapter 9 in this volume).

This observation is also in line with research on regulatory questions pertaining to AIT in healthcare. A review by Čartolovni et al. (2022) shows that the topic that has received the most attention in the discussion on the regulation of AIT in healthcare is the lack thereof. Beyond healthcare, also other authors concur that the 'governance of AI is a significantly underdeveloped area' (Taeihagh 2021). In this context, STS scholarship, in particular, is attentive to how the governance and regulation of AIT are intrinsically intertwined with imaginaries about these technologies and the futures they might bring about. Mager and Katzenbach (2021), for example, observe that the private sector plays a particularly prominent role in this context. For Nordic European countries, it has been shown that this has also led to changes in how the purpose and value of health data are understood. Health data are increasingly imagined as a source of economic growth, which stands in stark contrast with the initial focus on improving population health that underpinned the systematic, large-scale collection of population data in these countries (Tupasela et al. 2020; Hoeyer 2022).

In this sense, imaginaries about the economic potential of data and AIT also characterise many national AI strategies, with healthcare often being one of the central application areas. For example, comparing the strategies of China, the United States (US), France and Germany, Bareis and Katzenbach (2022) show striking similarities in their overall narratives as 'they all establish AI as an inevitable and massively disrupting technological development by building on rhetorical devices such as a grand legacy and international competition' (p. 855). Similarly, Radu (2021) shows that many national AI strategies are characterised by hybridity in the sense that 'market and state actions can no longer be disentangled, as there is a sharing of goals and a growing mutuality and reliance on one another', which 'may go as far as moving closer to a private sector logic' (p. 189) (also see Coglianese, Chapter 18 in this volume, on procurement and Paul, Chapter 20 in this volume on AI competition states).

However, even though economic rationales characterise many national AI strategies, some also problematise the oligarchic structure of the tech industry and the political clout that comes with it and include suggestions to counterbalance it by assigning a more active role to the state and to citizens. In this manner, the state is assigned the double role of 'promoting and facilitating AI development while at the same time being a guarantor of risk mitigation and enabler of societal engagement' (Ulnicane et al. 2021, p. 158). Against this backdrop, the *regulation* of AIT in healthcare has started to receive more attention recently (e.g. Reddy et al. 2020).

CURRENT REGULATORY APPROACHES AND DISCUSSIONS

Regulation of AIT in healthcare has, so far, focused predominantly on ensuring their safety and effectiveness. The core regulatory question in this regard is whether AIT fall within the definition of medical devices. If they do, they are subject to regulatory approval, such as by the European Medicines Agency (EMA) or the Food and Drug Administration (FDA) in the US. Medical device regulations in both the European Union and the US have recently seen changes and specifications (Gerke et al. 2020; Pesapane et al. 2018; Vokinger and Gasser 2021). While these regulations address similar challenges pertaining to medical AIT, it has been argued that 'overall, Europe takes a more heavy-handed approach to the regulation of AIM [medical AI], while the US approach emphasizes innovation and is more principle- and less detail-oriented' (Volking and Gasser 2021, p. 739).

In the European Union, two new Regulations have been introduced, namely the Medical Device Regulation (MDR, in force since 2020), and the In Vitro Diagnostic Medical Devices Regulation (IVDR, in force since 2022). Regarding the definition of medical devices, changes to the European Union regulatory framework imply that AIT for prediction and prognosis are now also included in that definition. General software used in healthcare settings (i.e. non-medical software, such as tools for administrative purposes, communication or the storing and transferring of data) or software relating to lifestyle and well-being, in contrast, do not fall within the remit of medical devices (Gerke et al. 2020). In the US, the regulations defining medical devices are the Federal Food, Drug and Cosmetic Act and the 21st Century Cures Act from 2016. As in the European Union, general software and lifestyle-related applications do not fall within the definition of medical devices. However, FDA regulations also exempt some AI-based software that functions as clinical decision support from the definition if the software does not analyse patterns, displays information 'normally communicated between healthcare professionals', provides recommendations rather than making decisions and allows clinicians to review how it has arrived at these recommendations (Gerke et al. 2020). These definitional questions are important in that they establish boundaries between technologies that are considered in need of safety regulation and scrutiny and others that are not.

A challenge that features prominently in discussions on how to regulate AIT in healthcare is how agencies can effectively regulate software that is constantly developing. An example would be AIT that adapt continuously on the basis of real-world data. Some authors have referred to the approach that regulatory bodies have adopted in this context as 'tentative governance' (Kuhlmann et al. 2019). Assessing the FDA's approach towards medical AIT in this regard, Boubker (2021, p. 453) writes that the current framework 'might not be well-suited for continuously learning algorithms' and stresses that a more proactive approach is necessary: 'The FDA cannot let Silicon Valley engage in their usual practice of "do first, ask for forgiveness later" when it comes to healthcare products that directly impact patient safety and privacy.'

Another unsolved regulatory issue related to AIT in healthcare is liability (Gerke et al. 2020). Current discussions focus on how existing liability systems, in which both individual persons and institutions (such as physicians and hospitals) can be held liable for their actions, can be adapted to a situation in which AIT are part of clinical decision-making processes. Existing proposals include the introduction of product liability, which would hold the company that developed the AIT responsible, or the extension of institutional responsibility (e.g. of the hospital) for not only reviewing the credentials and practices of healthcare professionals they employ but also for the software they purchase. Other suggestions include the introduction of *ex post* regulations such as setting up appropriate compensatory mechanisms (see also McMahon et al. 2020). Further regulatory questions that AIT in healthcare prompts pertain to data protection and privacy, potential biases, transparency, cybersecurity and intellectual property law (Gerke et al. 2020).

We have noted that regulatory frameworks are also politically relevant. However, there is also a larger politics at play in current regulations of medical AIT. Based on their study of how digital health technologies have been turned into regulatory objects, Lievevrouw et al. (2022) point to several aspects that are important for the critical study of the regulation of AIT in healthcare of which we wish to highlight two. First, the authors show how the adoption of a particular regulatory approach (e.g. a rather permissive vs. a rather strict approach) is not only shaping substantial policy but also (re-)shaping these very regulatory institutions and ultimately the state itself. Second, these authors contend that 'the making of quality and safety standards by regulatory agencies has been a crucial constitutive element for the shaping of the innovation pathways of digital health' (Lievevrouw et al. 2022, p. 570), which means that the state – also in performing the role of an active regulator – is enabling (rather than impeding) the development and proliferation of AIT in healthcare.

CHALLENGING DOMINANT POLICIES ON AIT IN HEALTHCARE

After having addressed some of the central features in current regulatory frameworks and debates, we challenge a few of their underlying assumptions that we believe should be reconsidered. These are (1) the idea that AIT that 'only' make recommendations are less in need of regulation than fully automated systems; (2) the regulatory focus on safety at the cost of aspects such as health equity as well as the idea that non-medical AIT used in healthcare – such as for communication – warrants less regulatory attention than medical AIT; (3) we argue that policy on AIT in healthcare should pay more explicit attention to the political economy within which digital practices are embedded.

The Inseparability of 'Thinking' and 'Acting AI'

Within discussions on the governance of AIT, an important difference used to revolve around AIT that take over entire tasks from humans ('acting AI'; see Prainsack and Steindl 2022), and AIT that are supposed to support human decision-making ('thinking AI'). Ethical problems and the need for regulation are generally seen as more pressing regarding the former than regarding the latter. In the case of acting AI, human beings would hand over decision-making to machines – which is seen to raise a number of questions regarding safety, accountability and also liability (cf. Cobbe and Singh, Chapter 7 in this volume). With regard to thinking AI, in contrast, human beings would be in a position to overrule the suggestions made by the machine, and thus would remain the ultimate decision-maker. We argue that the distinction between thinking AI and acting AI (irrespective of the labels that are used) cannot and should not be upheld. As early as in the 1980s, the psychologist Lisanne Bainbridge had already identified two misconceptions that are often made in the context of automated systems (e.g. Bainbridge 1983): the first is the assumption that humans, not machines, are the main source of errors. The irony, according to Bainbridge, is that humans are essential to correct the design mistakes made in automation processes (see also Schwennesen 2019). The second misconception is that complex processes can be fully automated. Therefore, human intelligence and experience are again needed to do those things that cannot be automated. Given that AIT are always, as all machines, 'technologies in practice' (Timmermans and Berg 2003), this is not surprising but unfortunately still not widely accepted.

Against this backdrop, it is a positive development that even the mainstream discussion of AIT in healthcare has moved away from the dichotomy between humans vs. machines and now focuses on complementarity. The humans-in-the-loop literature is an example of this (e.g. Fügener et al. 2021). Such systems combine human and machine intelligence, whereby humans train, test and improve AIT, and also action their 'recommendations'. It is important to note, however, that this has not reduced the need for ethical scrutiny and regulation. Just because a machine does not 'make a decision' – in the sense that its output is one precise answer or one pathway, this does not mean that decision-making rests solely and independently with humans. One reason for this is that the humans involved in decision-making may trust the machine more than they trust their own judgement (a phenomenon that has been referred to as automation bias; see Strauß 2021). Another is that it may be safer or easier for humans to go with a suggestion made by a machine than justifying an alternative stance – in particular in contexts that are stressful and when time is scarce, as is often the case in healthcare settings. A junior doctor, for example, may find it the safer option to follow the recommendation of the machine than deviate from it and have to explain themselves (if only in the case that something goes wrong). In terms of regulation, this means that high safety standards should not only apply to so-called acting AI, but also to thinking AI, which provides healthcare professionals with recommendations. Furthermore, liability regulations have to account for the fact that humans and machines often interact in unintended ways, with humans intervening in AI decision-making and the other way around.

Health Disparities and the Challenge of the Mundane

Besides challenging the differentiation between acting and thinking AI when it comes to ethics and regulation, we call for an expansion of the predominant focus of regulatory and approval processes beyond a narrow understanding of safety. While safety considerations remain crucial, AIT regulations in healthcare should also address questions of disparities and equity much more explicitly and systematically. The attempt to mitigate biases has been included in several regulatory frameworks for medical devices – but considerations about equity often only feature as an 'afterthought' (e.g. Gichoya et al. 2021). Addressing issues of disparities and equity both as part of premarket approval and postmarket assessments could contribute to the anticipation and mitigation of group harm (e.g. Ferryman 2020).

Solely focusing on medical device approval processes, however, ignores the fact that most AIT do not meet the definition of medical devices. Therefore, addressing health disparities also works towards extending the focus to more 'mundane' ancillary technologies such as those used for the scheduling of appointments, video consultations or monitoring of treatment adherence, which often are AI-enabled (for an overview of AI in telemedicine see Pacis et al. 2018). In this context, it is both relevant how these technologies are designed (e.g. which languages a chatbot is able to correctly process), as well as who has access to them. Regarding telemedicine applications specifically, the COVID-19 pandemic has been a catalyst both in terms of technology development and policy. For example, in some countries where the reimbursement of healthcare services depended on face-to-face contact, this was changed very rapidly during the pandemic (Ortega et al. 2020). This had clear advantages for many people, but it can also increase disparities. Ortega and colleagues see unequal access to broadband technologies, problems with the reimbursement of telemedicine (making it affordable only for the wealthy where basic insurance does not cover it) and a lack of awareness within institutions of the uneven distribution of the benefits of telemedicine, as reasons for increasing inequities. According to the authors, 'disparities in access to broadband connectivity and mobile technologies represent a social determinant of health now to an even greater extent than before the COVID-19 pandemic' (Ortega et al. 2020: 369; see also Webster 2020).

Another example for the nuanced effects in terms of empowerment and disempowerment are smartphone apps that provide AI-supported prediction of disease risks and other health-related information. They bridge lifestyle and healthcare (Lucivero and Prainsack 2015). Unless they meet the criteria of a medical device, such apps are currently largely unregulated (Crico et al. 2018; Kasperbauer and Wright 2020), despite the health-related consequences that their use can have. For example, it has been shown that pregnancy-related smartphone apps often provide inaccurate information, and they are also less likely to report on conditions that disproportionately affect women of colour (Tucker et al. 2021). This has led Grundy (2022, p. 124) to conclude that 'mobile health apps may risk widening health disparities through lack of inclusivity and the provision of health information and digital interventions that disproportionately address the health needs of already advantaged groups'. This example also speaks to more general observations about how digital technologies reproduce and reinforce inequalities along the lines of social categories such as race, gender and class (Benjamin 2019; Eubanks 2018).

While such 'mundane' non-clinical uses of AIT do not feature prominently in ethics and regulatory discourses, they should. The effects of discrimination within mundane uses of AIT in healthcare may not be as immediately visible as with AIT employed for diagnosis and treatment decisions that discriminate racially or according to other protected criteria – e.g. a skin cancer detector that does not work on dark skin. The effects of discrimination of mundane AI in healthcare, however, can be just as serious and damaging, and with these mundane AIT being exempted from regulations and scrutiny, biases, which can reinforce existing disparities, might become even harder to detect.

Considering the Political Economy of AIT in Health

Finally, we would like to point out that the governance of AIT in health should pay more attention to the political economy within which technological practices are embedded. The global healthcare landscape has seen a structural shift in the last two decades: with the increasing digitisation of healthcare, technology companies have joined the ranks of healthcare providers, pharmaceutical companies, manufacturers and regulators and become important players in the healthcare system. Amazon, for example, is heavily invested in healthcare. While its employee primary care service, Amazon Care, ceased operating at the end of 2022, Amazon has, for example, recently rolled out a subscription service for pharmaceuticals (RxPass) and established a telehealth service called Amazon Clinic (for examples of Amazon technology used in social care, see Whitfield, Wright and Hamblin, Chapter 28 in this volume). At the same time, technology companies have also become important players in health research: via their philanthropies, technology corporations run research institutes and provide funding for universities and other research outfits in areas that they consider worthy of investing in, thus taking over the role of publicly accountable, traditional research funders (e.g. McGoey 2015). They no longer merely collaborate on projects and public–private partnerships that are shaped by public funders; they now determine what is researched and how, and what gets published (Bero 2019).

Technology corporations have also been channelling significant amounts of funding into research on the ethics of AI (e.g. Ochigame 2019; Moss and Metcalf 2019). This is not a trivial development: while it is true that corporations have collaborated with academia for a long time, the focus of corporate interest and funding of research on *ethics and regulation* is relatively recent. Technology companies are not only funding research into ethics and governance of AI, but have endowed chairs and entire departments at universities – which goes beyond even the most notorious cases of ethics washing or greenwashing by big tobacco or the carbon industry in the past. The fact that there has been a rapid growth of interest in the ethics of AIT in the last decade – which has led some scholars to diagnose an 'AI ethics bubble' (for an overview, see Prainsack and Steindl 2022) – has to be understood in this context. These developments are taking place against the backdrop of tech corporations pushing further into areas of public expertise and service provision, inside and outside of healthcare. This manifests itself not only in generous deals made between public healthcare systems and private sector companies, but also in public institutions increasingly relying on technological solutions by big tech to provide their services. Examples include the use of technologies by Apple and Google in the context of the COVID-19 pandemic (Sharon 2021).

Technology companies, it could be argued, have a particularly great need to ensure that their development and use of AIT complies with ethical standards. But there is also a less sanguine explanation for the current AI ethics bubble. The corporations that are invested in making profits based on AIT have an interest in a seat at the table of regulation. While it is clearly in their interest to have a clear set of rules and not operate in a legal limbo, they also want regulation not to be too restrictive. It is for this reason that many companies – but also policymakers – are so supportive of 'ethics', or play it out against 'regulation' (High-level Expert Group on Artificial Intelligence 2019). If we have good ethics, so the argument goes, we do not need so much regulation – which is claimed to stifle innovation and put those places that have more 'red tape' at a disadvantage compared to others that do not. In the European Union, the notion of 'trustworthy AI' has been tainted by quite conspicuous attempts of corporations to keep regulation at bay by using ethics to make AIT 'trustworthy' (Yeung et al. 2020; Hagendorff 2020). It is also problematic in the sense that it suggests that the two are not only clearly separable but also mutually exclusive, denying that ethics needs regulation to be effective and enforceable, and regulation, in turn, needs ethics for its normative content (Mittelstadt 2019).

CONCLUSION

In this chapter, we have presented current discussions and practices regarding the governance of AIT in healthcare. While this domain has long been characterised by a strong focus on ethics, questions pertaining to regulation are gaining more importance. Regulatory efforts and discussions have been focusing, in particular, on AIT that are classified as medical devices, and on ensuring their safety. We argue that this focus is unduly narrow and misses, for example, how 'mundane' AIT in healthcare can cause both benefits and harm. Moreover, questions of health equity should more explicitly guide debates and regulatory efforts. We have also pointed to how the economy around AIT in healthcare influences regulation, and the important role big tech companies play in this context.

From a critical policy studies perspective, we argue that policymaking on AIT in healthcare should do three main things: first, it should address problems pertaining to the political economy of health data, including the grave power asymmetries between data subjects and data users, but also powerful corporations and other entities (such as non-profits or small and medium-sized enterprises). This opens up questions such as who has a say when it comes to the formulation of visions about the future of healthcare and the (potential) use of AIT in this field, but also questions regarding the distribution of benefits and harms that come with it. Second, regulations on AIT in healthcare should better accommodate the relational nature of data, both in the sense that the needs and interests of all people, not only primary data subjects (i.e. the individuals from whom the data come that are used for analyses), should be considered in regulation, but also in the sense that data are always made and never merely given (e.g. Leonelli 2016). This means that human agency is always part of AIT, starting with decisions on what will be datafied, other aspects of data curation, as well as developing, testing and using 'automated' systems. Third, rather than looking at the glitzy high-tech aspect of AIT, policy should also attend to more mundane uses and the 'basic' factors that shape benefits and harms of AIT in healthcare. For example, as the cases of telemedicine and health apps have shown, some of the biggest drivers of health inequities are related to technology access and the reinforcement of existing disparities through mundane AI-enabled technologies such as apps. The related policy challenges are often more similar to other fields of healthcare than to other instances of AIT use.

REFERENCES

Bainbridge, L. (1983), 'Ironies of Automation', *Automatica*, **19** (6), 775–779.
Bareis, J. and C. Katzenbach (2022), 'Talking AI into Being: The Narratives and Imaginaries of National AI Strategies and their Performative Politics', *Science, Technology, & Human Values*, **47** (5), 855–881.
Benjamin, R. (2019), *Race After Technology: Abolitionist Tools for the New Jim Code*, Cambridge: Polity.
Bero, L. (2019), 'When Big Companies Fund Academic Research, the Truth Often Comes Last', accessed 1 October 2022 at https://theconversation.com/when-big-companies-fund-academic-research-the-truth-often-comes-last-119164.
Boubker, J. (2021), 'When Medical Devices Have a Mind of their Own: The Challenges of Regulating Artificial Intelligence', *American Journal of Law & Medicine*, **47** (4), 427–454.
Čartolovni, A., A. Tomičić and E. L. Mosler (2022), 'Ethical, Legal, and Social Considerations of AI-based Medical Decision-support Tools: A Scoping Review', *International Journal of Medical Informatics*, **161**, 104738.
Crico, C., C. Renzi, N. Graf, A. Buyx, H. Kondylakis, L. Koumakis and G. Pravettoni (2018), 'mHealth and Telemedicine Apps: In Search of a Common Regulation', *Ecancermedicalscience*, **12**, 853.
Davenport, T. and R. Kalakota (2019), 'The Potential for Artificial Intelligence in Healthcare', *Future Healthcare Journal*, **6** (2), 94–98.
Eubanks, V. (2018), *Automating Inequality: How High-tech Tools Profile, Police, and Punish the Poor*, New York: St. Martin's Press.
Ferryman, K. (2021), 'The Dangers of Data Colonialism in Precision Public Health', *Global Policy*, **12**, 90–92.

Ferryman, K. (2020), 'Addressing Health Disparities in the Food and Drug Administration's Artificial Intelligence and Machine Learning Regulatory Framework', *Journal of the American Medical Informatics Association*, **27** (12), 2016–2019.

Fügener, A., J. Grahl, A. Gupta and W. Ketter (2021), 'Will Humans-in-the-loop Become Borgs? Merits and Pitfalls of Working with AI', *Management Information Systems Quarterly*, **45** (3), 1527–1556.

Gerke, S., T. Minssen and G. Cohen (2020), 'Ethical and Legal Challenges of Artificial Intelligence-driven Healthcare', in A. Bohr and K. Memarzadeh (eds), *Artificial Intelligence in Healthcare*, London: Academic Press, pp. 295–336.

Gichoya, J. W., L. G. McCoy, L. A. Celi and M. Ghassemi (2021), 'Equity in Essence: A Call for Operationalising Fairness in Machine Learning for Healthcare', *BMJ Health & Care Informatics*, **28** (1), e100289.

Grundy, Q. (2022), 'A Review of the Quality and Impact of Mobile Health Apps', *Annual Review of Public Health*, **43**, 117–134.

Hagendorff, T. (2020), 'The Ethics of AI Ethics: An Evaluation of Guidelines', *Minds & Machines*, **30**, 99–120.

High-level Expert Group on Artificial Intelligence (2019), *Ethics Guidelines for Trustworthy AI*, European Commission, Brussels.

Hoeyer, K. (2022), *Data Paradoxes: The Politics of Intensified Data Sourcing in Contemporary Healthcare*, Cambridge, MA: MIT Press.

Hosny, A. and H. J. Aerts (2019), 'Artificial Intelligence for Global Health', *Science*, **366** (6468), 955–956.

Kasperbauer, T. J. and D. E. Wright (2020), 'Expanded FDA Regulation of Health and Wellness Apps', *Bioethics*, **34** (3), 235–241.

Kuhlmann, S., Stegmaier, P. and Konrad, K. (2019), 'The Tentative Governance of Emerging Science and Technology: A Conceptual Introduction', *Research Policy*, **48** (5), 1091–1097.

Leonelli, S. (2016), *Data-centric Biology*, Chicago: University of Chicago Press.

Lievevrouw, E., L. Marelli and I. Van Hoyweghen (2022), 'The FDA's Standard-making Process for Medical Digital Health Technologies: Co-producing Technological and Organizational Innovation', *BioSocieties*, **17** (3), 549–576.

Lucivero, F. and B. Prainsack (2015), 'The Lifestylisation of Healthcare? "Consumer Genomics" and Mobile Health as Technologies for Healthy Lifestyle', *Applied & Translational Genomics*, **4**, 44–49.

Lupton, D. (2017), *Digital Health: Critical and Cross-disciplinary Perspectives*, London: Routledge.

Mager, A. and C. Katzenbach (2021), 'Future Imaginaries in the Making and Governing of Digital Technology: Multiple, Contested, Commodified', *New Media & Society*, **23** (2), 223–236.

Martin, T. (2012), 'Assessing mHealth: Opportunities and Barriers to Patient Engagement', *Journal of Health Care for the Poor and Underserved*, **23** (3), 935–941.

McGoey, L. (2015), *No Such Thing as a Free Gift: The Gates Foundation and the Price of Philanthropy*, London: Verso.

McMahon, A., A. Buyx and B. Prainsack (2020), 'Big Data Governance Needs More Collective Responsibility: The Role of Harm Mitigation in the Governance of Data Use in Medicine and Beyond', *Medical Law Review*, **28** (1), 155–182.

Mittelstadt, B. (2019), 'Principles Alone Cannot Guarantee Ethical AI', *Nature Machine Intelligence*, **1** (11), 501–507.

Morley, J., C. C. Machado, C. Burr, J. Cowls, I. Joshi, M. Taddeo and L. Floridi (2020), 'The Ethics of AI in Health Care: A Mapping Review', *Social Science & Medicine*, **260**, 113172.

Moss, E. and J. Metcalf (2019), 'The Ethical Dilemma at the Heart of Big Tech Companies', accessed 1 October 2022 at https://hbr.org/2019/11/the-ethical-dilemma-at-the-heart-of-big-tech-companies.

Munn, L. (2022), 'The Uselessness of AI Ethics', *AI and Ethics*, doi.org/10.1007/s43681-022-00209-w.

Ochigame, R. (2019), 'The Invention of "Ethical AI"', accessed 1 October 2022 at https://theintercept.com/2019/12/20/mit-ethical-ai-artificial-intelligence/?comments=1.

Ortega, G., J. A. Rodriguez, L. R. Maurer, E. E. Witt, N. Perez, A. Reich and D. W. Bates (2020), 'Telemedicine, COVID-19, and Disparities: Policy Implications', *Health Policy and Technology*, **9** (3), 368–371.

Pacis, D. M. M., E. D. Subido Jr. and N. T. Bugtai (2018), 'Trends in Telemedicine Utilizing Artificial Intelligence', *AIP Conference Proceedings*, **1933** (1), 040009.

Paul, R. (2022), 'Can *Critical Policy Studies* Outsmart AI? Research Agenda on Artificial Intelligence Technologies and Public Policy', *Critical Policy Studies*, **16** (4), 497–509. https://doi.org/10.1080/19460171.2022.2123018.

Pesapane, F., C. Volonté, M. Codari and F. Sardanelli (2018), 'Artificial Intelligence as a Medical Device in Radiology: Ethical and Regulatory Issues in Europe and the United States. *Insights into Imaging*, **9** (5), 745–753.

Petersen, A. (2018), *Digital Health and Technological Promise: A Sociological Inquiry*, London: Routledge.

Prainsack, B. (2023), 'Sociologies of precision medicine', in A. Petersen (ed.), *Handbook on the Sociology of Health and Medicine*, Cheltenham, UK and Northampton, MA, USA: Edward Elgar Publishing, pp. 439–454.

Prainsack, B. and E. Steindl (2022), 'Legal and Ethical Aspects of Machine Learning: Who Owns the Data?', in P. Veit-Hainbach and K. Herrmann (eds), *Artificial Intelligence/Machine Learning in Nuclear Medicine and Hybrid Imaging*, Cham, Switzerland: Springer, pp. 191–201.

Radu, R. (2021), 'Steering the Governance of Artificial Intelligence: National Strategies in Perspective', *Policy and Society*, **40** (2), 178–193.

Reddy, S., S. Allan, S. Coghlan and P. Cooper (2020), 'A Governance Model for the Application of AI in Health Care', *Journal of the American Medical Informatics Association*, **27** (3), 491–497.

Reddy, S., J. Fox and M. P. Purohit (2019), 'Artificial Intelligence-enabled Healthcare Delivery', *Journal of the Royal Society of Medicine*, **112** (1), 22–28.

Rubeis, G., K. Dubbala and I. Metzler (2022), '"Democratization" in the Context of Artificial Intelligence and Healthcare: Mapping an Elusive Term', *Frontiers in Genetics*, **13**, 902542.

Schwalbe, N. and B. Wahl (2020), 'Artificial Intelligence and the Future of Global Health', *The Lancet*, **395** (10236), 1579–1586.

Schwennesen, N. (2019), 'Algorithmic Assemblages of Care: Imaginaries, Epistemologies and Repair Work', *Sociology of Health & Illness*, **41**, 176–192.

Sharon, T. (2021), 'Blind-sided by Privacy? Digital Contact Tracing, the Apple/Google API and Big Tech's Newfound Role as Global Health Policy Makers', *Ethics and Information Technology*, **23** (Suppl. 1), 45–57.

Strauß, S. (2021), 'Deep Automation Bias: How to Tackle a Wicked Problem of AI?', *Big Data and Cognitive Computing*, **5** (2), 18.

Taeihagh, A. (2021), 'Governance of Artificial Intelligence', *Policy and Society*, **40** (2), 137–157.

Timmermans, S. and M. Berg (2003), 'The Practice of Medical Technology', *Sociology of Health & Illness*, **25** (3), 97–114.

Topol, E. (2019), *Deep Medicine: How Artificial Intelligence Can Make Healthcare Human Again*, New York: Basic Books.

Tucker, L., A. C. Villagomez and T. Krishnamurti (2021), 'Comprehensively Addressing Postpartum Maternal Health: A Content and Image Review of Commercially Available Mobile Health Apps', *BMC Pregnancy and Childbirth*, **21**, 311.

Tupasela, A., K. Snell and H. Tarkkala (2020), 'The Nordic Data Imaginary', *Big Data & Society*, doi.org/10.1177/2053951720907107.

Ulnicane, I., W. Knight, T. Leach, B. C. Stahl and W. G. Wanjiku (2021), 'Framing Governance for a Contested Emerging Technology: Insights from AI Policy', *Policy and Society*, **40** (2), 158–177.

Vokinger, K. N. and U. Gasser (2021), 'Regulating AI in Medicine in the United States and Europe', *Nature Machine Intelligence*, **3** (9), 738–739.

Webster, P. (2020), 'Virtual Health Care in the Era of COVID-19', *The Lancet*, **395** (10231), 1180–1181.

Yeung K., A. Howes and G. Pogrebna (2020), 'AI Governance by Human-rights Centred Design, Deliberation and Oversight: An End to Ethics Washing', in M. Dubber and F. Pasquale (eds), *The Oxford Handbook of AI Ethics*, Oxford: Oxford University Press, pp. 76–106.

Yu, K. H., A. L. Beam and I. S. Kohane (2018), 'Artificial Intelligence in Healthcare', *Nature Biomedical Engineering*, **2** (10), 719–731.

31. AI and urban governance: from the perils of smart cities to Amazon Inc. urbanism

Ilia Antenucci and Fran Meissner

INTRODUCTION

Urban territories offer fertile ground for analysing the entanglements of artificial intelligence technologies (AITs), policy and governance. In cities, we find both a high population density and a profusion of sensors collecting and storing data (Enlund et al. 2022). As urban residents go about their day-to-day activities an abundance of data is produced. Such "urban" data, in turn, is used to feed simple and more advanced machine learning (ML) applications that are increasingly shaping how we experience urban life and how cities are planned (Duarte and Álvarez 2019). To name but a few mundane examples, think about traffic lights, bus scheduling or rubbish collection. Despite this omnipresence, best practice frameworks for governing AITs in cities are few and far between (Koseki et al. 2022).

Against this backdrop, this chapter traces how the growing infiltration of AITs in urban processes is changing cities and how we live in cities. In recent years, debates around urban AITs have primarily focused on "smart city" projects. Scholars have offered a wealth of critical insights on how implementing AITs for urban management and governance in the name of efficiency transforms urban politics. They often point to problems associated with technocracy and corporatisation. In this chapter, we move beyond the smart city framework and propose an additional angle for exploring the urban impact of AITs. We argue that the extensive deployment of commercial AITs – proprietary technologies developed by private companies for profit – is increasingly shaping urban environments and what was previously the realm of public urban planning and governance. Two key factors concur with this process. First, AITs rely on ML systems, which automate the production of knowledge and decisions about the city. Second, technology companies developing those AITs are increasingly leading the implementation and management of critical urban infrastructures and services. Thus, private corporations effectively take charge of tasks which were previously controlled by democratic institutions, and commercial strategies seem to move faster and more effectively than public policy. In other words, AITs operate as technopolitical forces, which reconfigure not only the actors and forms of urban governance but its very political premises. This raises concerns about accountability and democratic oversight, especially when giant transnational corporations are involved.

We start this chapter by reviewing the rise and (relative) fall of the smart city as a major framework for the urban deployment of AIT. We situate the emergence of the smart city as the result of market opportunities, then outline some of the key arguments scholars have proposed about the relationship between city politics and AITs. We particularly emphasise how focusing on the urban shows the spatial implications of AI applications. In the second part of the chapter, we turn our attention to how Amazon is changing cities in ways that should be the object of public conversations and more democratic deliberation. We draw on Amazon as a case study to illustrate how powerful commercial AITs are ever more frequently controlling operations crucial to urban life. We focus on logistics and security. While Amazon is a long way from being the only important technology player, it is a major one, unique in its financial strength and the pervasiveness of its AITs in cities where it operates, and is continuously expanding across multiple market segments. With our case study we can thus examine the unfolding of Amazon's proprietary AITs in the urban space. In doing this, we dislocate the analysis of urban planning and policies from the traditional venues and institutions, such as city managers and city government alone (Tseng 2022). To conclude the chapter, we summarise and sketch out where we see an urgent need for additional research.

In highlighting the importance of cities as testing grounds for proprietary and commercial AITs, as well as the socio-political implications of such processes, we point to the tension between the flattening, calculative gaze of the software and the infrastructures within which it operates, and the multiple, irreducible realities of the city. While AITs seek to quantify and predict, to streamline and formalise, urban worlds remain too complex and intractable for even the sharpest algorithm. Importantly, while we stress the influence and pervasiveness of Amazon's technologies, we do not grant them any deterministic power over urban life. Rather, we chart how Amazon's AITs strive to tame urban unruliness or turn out to produce something unplanned. In this open dialectic between software control and living contingency, we see space for more proactively claiming back urban politics and planning.

HOW AITS BECAME CENTRAL TO PLANNING AND GOVERNING CITIES: FROM SMART CITIES TO REGULATING URBAN AI

AITs have become central to urban operations as a part of calls and initiatives to implement more smart technology in urban areas. The *smart city* is a buzz word, ubiquitous, elusive and loosely based on the idea that extensive automation of infrastructures and services makes cities safer, more efficient and sustainable. It is now well known that IBM was the first to recognise the marketability of data-informed urban planning (Alizadeh 2017; Söderström et al. 2014), and that most major technology players quickly followed suit. Smart city projects emerged as a major framework for AI experiments in urban environments, often exacerbating urban social divisions (Taylor 2021).

Implicit in the notion of the smart city is the assumption that urban politics, resulting from democratic contestations and negotiations, is a major disease of cities, generating inefficiency, delays and chaos. In framing politics in this way, autonomous technologies and data-driven decisions can be marketed as delivering what is "objectively" needed for the optimal functioning of urban systems, thus making politics and democratic processes redundant. For about a decade, this kind of technological solutionism (Paul, Carmel and Cobbe, Chapter 1 in this volume) hegemonised urban planning and development debates and seemed to define the inevitable destiny of cities worldwide, with little concern for local contexts (Ferreira et al. 2022).

Predating the current AI hype and focusing on smart city politics more generally, Wiig and Wyly (2015) collated work highlighting that the "right to the smart city" is a contested realm. They emphasise that smart technologies will not resolve basic questions over how to govern cities. In their systematic review of academic research on smart cities, Zhao et al. (2021) found that this scholarship often lacks theoretical grounding, is technology driven and prone to highlighting the benefits of smart cities over their failures. Relatedly, Kitchin (2019) notes that one of the most pressing issues with working towards more equitable smart cities is recognising the complex entanglements of interests behind the incorporation of AITs into urban planning. Looking at the case of New Town Kolkata in India, and contrary to the narratives about smart cities, Ghosh and Arora (2022, p. 333) show that the political processes of implementing smart city objectives are just as messy as other political processes and far from neutral, whereby "participatory democratic exercises [are] put at the service of technocracy and control". Albeit promising inclusiveness, smart city projects in fact systematically exclude, or further marginalise, lower-income and vulnerable citizens. As Datta and Odendaal (2019) note, the ubiquity of AITs in smart cities entails a *banality of power* that is reconfiguring how planning, citizenship and norms operate.

Criticism of smart urban governance has become more vocal. Scholars, journalists and professionals point more frequently to the many dark sides of the smart city. A recent UN-Habitat report focusing specifically on the risks cities take in adopting AITs highlights, amongst other things, possible misalignment between AIT and human values, unaudited algorithm deployment or inadequate demographic representations (Koseki et al. 2022). These and many other risks are linked to more general concerns about smart cities, such as extensive surveillance and privacy violations, private companies controlling public services and infrastructure, a lack of transparency and accountability, and enhanced inequality and discrimination.

Such concerns are not only evident in the literature that engages with urban governance in times of AITs but increasingly enter the field of practice. Yigitcanlar et al. (2023) show that city administrators are no longer just dazzled by the allure of smart city techno-fixes. Using interviews with city officials who understand themselves as champions of AITs, they show that narratives increasingly reflect a wariness about the potential negative effects of such technologies. However, they also conclude that this does not lead to a complete abandonment of hopes to adopt AITs but to a more piecemeal trial-and-error implementation. We might argue that such responses are entangled with what León and Rosen (2020, p. 503) have described as an "ideology of technology operating to restructure cities and their governance processes, priorities, and outcomes". In framing developments in terms of an ideology, these authors highlight that the narratives around urban growth have increasingly become bound up with cities facilitating the growth of the technology sector. Their observations ask us to heed further caution and more directly engage with how AITs transform cities. Authors like Hoop et al. (2022) focus on how to make the smart city more democratic – a city where marginalised voices can have a say. Yet despite those ambitions it seems that democratic processes are too often obscured, and problems with the experimental implementation of AITs in cities abound (Taylor 2021). As Shelton et al. (2015, p. 13) noted almost a decade ago, a crucial difference exists between the AI-enhanced city imaginaries and the "actually existing smart city".

Regardless, investments in urban digital infrastructures keep growing. Cities critically embracing AITs, however, are still few and far between (Baykurt 2022). It is increasingly clear that technologies alone will not automatically create better cities. Koseki et al. (2022) thus propose that cities must more proactively identify AI risks as part of the entire AI life cycle – including the design, implementation, deployment and maintenance of AI systems. In trying to systematically recognise the risks posed by specific AI systems, some cities, like Amsterdam and Helsinki, have started to take action to make AI used by city administrations more transparent. Both cities have introduced AI registers that make it easier – at least in theory – to recognise and contest AITs (Floridi 2020). Amsterdam and Helsinki are therefore amongst the many cities that initially embraced smart city solutions but have identified several issues, from obstacles to interoperability to failures in data-driven processes and, importantly, upholding democratic processes. It is important to be clear that when we mention AI, we generally refer to more or less limited applications of ML, that usually automate very specific functions or processes.

Technology companies keep promoting the idea that future cities will be fully automated, self-regulating systems. The idea of the self-driving cars is but one enigma that has kept captive almost a generation of technologists and urban planners with little evidence that these will truly improve (public) transit (Marx 2022; Wilt 2020). Still, the "robot city" is far from reality. With a few notable exceptions of spectacular greenfield projects, such as Songdo or Masdar, in which AITs are being built into the city fabric from scratch, the vast majority of urban experiments with AITs are taking place in very limited applications as well as in fragmented, seemingly mundane, and rarely contested, ways. As Murakami Wood (2023) notes, "platform city people" are expected to be many things like safe, entrepreneurial and sustainable – those imaginations, however, hardly align with experiences on the ground and are often exclusionary.

While we should be wary of rhetoric magnifying the impact of AI and automation, we should, at the same time, be careful not to underestimate the power of "narrow" ML applications. ML might be limited in its scope and capabilities and far from being able to imitate human intelligence, but that does not mean it is harmless. On the contrary, plenty of studies have shown how these applications can be harmful by the nature of their design. Time and again, research and many of the chapters in this *Handbook* point to issues with racial, gender and class bias in algorithmic code and training data (Benjamin 2019; Gebru 2021; O'Neil 2016). What might be even more concerning, and remains largely unquestioned, is how such systems generate "new norms and thresholds of what 'good', 'normal' and 'stable' look like in the world" (Amoore 2023, p. 21).

As Tseng (2022) notes, talking about the entanglements of urban governance and planning requires not only thinking about how to make urban AI more transparent and accountable but to recognise how these technologies are getting embedded in complex urban assemblages. These include the uneven spatial distribution of the material infrastructures upon which AITs depend, such as energy-intensive data centres and low-paid data workers. For each neighbourhood where smart technologies run smoothly and efficiently, there are several urban fringes where labour and resources are severely exploited. Such elements of spatial and environmental injustice concur to forming power differentials that, as Tseng observes, obscure and impede the democratic potential of AITs. Tseng does see the possibility of more effectively recognising the democratic potential by paying attention to the complexities of AI governance systems within their respective context. Such complexities, we argue below, include the growing use of commercial AITs in urban environments and their spatial and societal implications. As commercial AITs become more and more essential urban infrastructures, they produce specific configurations of what urban futures can and cannot be, effectively operating as city planners and policymakers. In the following section, we focus on these aspects of commercial AITs by examining examples of Amazon experimenting with logistics and security AITs.

AMAZON AND THE CITY: FROM OPTIMISATION TO CREEPING AUTOMATION OF URBAN PLANNING AND POLITICS

So far, we have outlined the complex relationships between urban politics and AITs that mark smart city projects. We now explore how proprietary AITs increasingly impact urban organisation and governance as part of commercial operations. To do this, we take a closer look at the experimentation of Amazon's commercial AITs in two key urban domains: logistics and security. In doing so, we trace how a single company – Amazon – operates more and more in ways that displace the conventional actors of urban planning and politics in those two policy domains. The analysis is based on a literature review and desk-based research conducted by one of the authors as part of a larger research project on Amazon and the city.[1] We here build on that research to emphasise the company's key role in determining how and who gets to imagine urban futures and the kinds of cities we live in. As a major player in global logistics, Amazon is running a tentacular apparatus of e-commerce and delivery.

For example, Amazon used selected US cities to test and launch its Prime services, which provide deliveries within 48 hours, often in less than a working day. Following the first experimentation phase, Prime has been extended to cover virtually all metropolitan areas in the US, many major cities in Europe, and a few in Africa, Asia, and South America. To achieve high-speed deliveries, Prime relies not only on a network of logistics facilities, vehicles and workers but also on a complex and extensive AIT architecture, which connects personal devices, such as smartphones, laptops and Echo products, to the algorithms that sort parcels, assign them to certain warehouses, trucks and vans, and calculate the fastest route for delivery.

Prime is an example of how AITs – developed for commercial purposes – increasingly organise key components of urban life, from restaurant reservations to dating apps, transport to home surveillance, and much more. Amazon has now also entered the security market by acquiring Ring, a company which produces smart cameras and other digital devices for home surveillance. By investigating Amazon's urban operations across logistics and security, we chart how AITs are deployed to tame the complexities and unruliness of urban life, from traffic issues to safety concerns. We also specifically highlight how AITs are changing urban rhythms and modes of policing cities and how these changes are moved out of reach for democratic engagement.

City Rhythms

Amazon's logistics is a global machinery made of vehicles, workers, buildings, infrastructures, computing hardware and software. Those entangled components continuously rework the urban space to optimise operations according to parameters of company profit and consumer convenience (Lyster 2016; Neves and Steinberg 2023; West 2022). Amazon's operations involve a wide range of ML technologies supporting activities, from shopping in Amazon GoStores to Echo's attentive services to sorting and picking up all manner of things in warehouses. Automatic speech recognition, natural language understanding and text-to-speech synthesis are only some ML techniques used.[2] They connect the (presumed) intimacy of someone's house, where Alexa chooses a playlist and recommends what to buy, with the fulfilment centres, where computer vision and depth sensing track the location of items across the shelves,[3] with the trucks and vans, which are provided with route optimisation models for last-mile delivery.[4]

As Lyster (2016, pp. 125–6) notes, logistics turn the city into a "multi-layered organism of exchange – a service platform" where traditional notions of urbanity and urban public space as the arenas for the provision of goods and services are eclipsed by a direct relationship between production and consumption. Altenried (2019) argues that, if seen from the perspective of delivery workers, logistical operations reshape the urban space through the entangled activities of human workers and software, which affect several urban components such as traffic, pollution and infrastructural development.

ML continuously ingests urban data from various sources – including GPS and GIS, weather forecasts, traffic information, the company historical data, etc. – to generate models of the fastest routes, optimal delivery times, number of vehicles and drivers required, etc. In sorting the city for the sake of logistical optimisation, ML generates normative knowledge and decisions. For example, in 2016, a Bloomberg study revealed that the debut of the Amazon Prime free same-day delivery service deliberately excluded minority (mostly black) neighbourhoods in several US cities, such as the Bronx in New York or South Side Chicago, thus enforcing the old racist practice of redlining in a new algorithmic form (Ingold and Soper 2016). Of course, Amazon's engineers were quick to claim that race did not play any part in their decision, which was based on a mere economic calculation: those ZIP codes were not profitable enough to justify the costs of same-day delivery, for reasons such as distance from the company's warehouses or low concentration of Prime subscribers. However, in US cities, ZIP codes are often a proxy for race and class (O'Neil 2016). In other words, socio-spatial racism, already built into the city fabric, is once again embedded in the calculation of logistical convenience and optimisation – a theme that is cross-cutting in the analysis that tries to make sense of the social impacts of AIT in our day-to-day lives (also see: Molnar, Chapter 23; Pot and Prainsack, Chapter 30; Sleep and Redden, Chapter 27; Whitfield, Wright, and Hamblin, Chapter 28, all in this volume).

At the same time, ML-based models for faster and cost-effective delivery generate metrics of efficiency and labour surveillance that intensify the exploitation of workers. For example, Amazon Flex drivers are formally employed as independent contractors. Regardless, they are subject to the strict discipline administered by the company's app, which sets tasks, goals and key performance indicators (Altenried 2019). If those "KPIs" are not met by the driver – i.e. if a parcel is delivered with some delay – the task is not remunerated. In the incessant effort to improve last-mile delivery, Amazon's researchers are now developing ML techniques that incorporate the "know-how" of drivers (i.e. historical data of drivers deviating from recommended routes based on experience or contingent decisions).[5] The goal is to generate more accurate predictive models to direct and control workers' performances by encoding drivers' lived experience and agency into the company's software. In so doing, the company tries to capture workers' practices that are not yet fully under the platform's control and to turn acts of independence from the platform into even more fine-grained tools of exploitation, surveillance and discipline.

These examples suggest that, as new-generation ML techniques, such as deep learning, are increasingly deployed in AITs to orchestrate and optimise logistical operations across urban spaces – from port terminals to last-mile delivery – they are producing new ontologies of the city and urban life that are dense with political effects. Deep learning methods render the city into abstract parameters – Prime subscriptions, GPS information, traffic estimates – which incorporate and reproduce existing spatial inequalities and labour exploitation patterns. Even more importantly, those are also actively recombined into sets of norms and parameters, which determine access to, or exclusion from, specific services, working experiences and remuneration, and overall, engineer new rhythms of space, time and agency in the city.

Security

In February 2018, Amazon acquired Ring, a company producing camera-enabled doorbells and other devices for home security, for approximately one billion US dollars. The purpose of buying Ring was to enlarge the range of Echo-compatible products and to achieve a leading market position in home surveillance and security (Kelly 2020). Since then, Ring's products have been aggressively marketed in the US, not only to private customers but also to law enforcement agencies. Ring devices use computer vision to detect motion within a set perimeter, such as a front porch or doorway, and send alerts to homeowners, allowing customers to monitor their properties, interact with visitors and open the door remotely (e.g. for Amazon couriers).

Through ML, Ring devices are developing ever more refined functions, from geofencing properties to detecting when a package is delivered to customising detectors for any object of interest (e.g. if a specific door is open or closed).[6] On the one hand, Ring contributes to the incessant optimisation of Amazon's urban logistical networks, as it makes home deliveries smoother and safer by allowing customers to open the door remotely, talk to the couriers and monitor their parcels. It also allows customers to share their footage and signal suspicious activities on the Neighbors app, a social network featuring posts from Ring users who live in the same area (up to 8km away). On the other hand, Ring partners with local law enforcement by allowing them to access footage – without a warrant – from private users who consent to that use. Participating police departments encourage residents to buy Ring devices to receive discounts on the products based on the number of local downloads of the Neighbors app. In recent years, several police departments have used their official social media profiles to promote Ring devices and signed agreements granting Amazon oversight over their public communications about such products (Frascella 2021).

Ring captures footage of people in public spaces, such as sidewalks, roads and parks, which can be shared on the Neighbors app without consent and accessed by local police departments with just a click. Ring thus enacts a systematic violation of privacy, which is nevertheless legal in the US in the absence of comprehensive federal laws (Frascella 2021). Amazon accumulates an immense amount of data, including sensitive data, with no clear policy in place to limit how the company can use this data to bolster its business.[7] For Bridges (2021, p. 838), Ring's "benign" interface of home security and neighbourhood social media is expanding a carceral logic, enhancing "the policing of race and class in residential spaces, (...) and blurring the boundaries between police work and civilian surveillance and between public and private space". By making it inviting and desirable for users to produce surveillance content and to share it on the Neighbors app, Amazon is actively cultivating a "symbiotic relationship" (Selinger and Durant 2022, p. 95) between citizens and law enforcement. It is also crafting a distinct neighbourhood ethos defined by racialised vigilantism and security anxiety. The Neighbors app regularly features discriminatory content, such as disproportionately signalling Afro-American individuals as suspicious or addressing Black Lives Matter protesters with racist language. A comprehensive map and analysis of Ring's and Neighbors's usage across the US (Calacci et al. 2022) demonstrates that white "enclaves" purchase Ring devices and post content on the Neighbors app more than others. The authors also observe that the *framing* of video subjects as criminals or suspects is a key feature of the platform, whereby footage of innocuous activities, such as someone walking on the street or knocking on a door, are arbitrarily described as suspicious or dangerous and often on a racial basis, i.e. mostly when the footage features people of colour. In this sense, the Ring Neighbors technologies operate as tools for racial gatekeeping, with white residents using the platform to reiterate the idea that people of colour do not belong and pose a threat to their neighbourhoods. The Neighbors app reproduces and magnifies racialised paranoia among urban dwellers in ways that result in more police calls and more Ring purchases.

So far, Ring has been almost exclusively a US phenomenon. Although it is also commercialised in other countries, its use for policing outside the US is for now much more limited, if existent at all. Yet, the police in the UK, for example, have been reported as promoting the use of Ring cameras.[8] The *Handbook*'s contribution on social care governance and AITs (Whitfield, Wright and Hamblin, Chapter 28 in this volume) clearly illustrates how this and similar technology is shaping the day-to-day access to social services in the UK with clear socio-spatial implications. The way we have portrayed its impact on urban governance through policing is, however, still unique to the US, where Ring devices and social media platforms like the Neighbors app have spread so pervasively as to produce societal effects. We should be wary of generalising evidence from the US, especially as some devices and functions could be illegal in other countries or much less compatible with spatial and cultural forms. Nevertheless, the case study illustrates the potential of such technologies, namely how the conflation of commercial interests, technological dispositions, and racial and class prejudice might generate new epistemologies of urban safety and security and new hybrids of public/private policing.

Amazon's Extrastatecraft?

In the preceding two sections of this chapter, we have traced what the growing apparatus of Amazon's AITs in logistics and security is doing *in* and *to* cities – focusing on two policy areas only: traffic flows and policing. We know that more empirical studies, especially beyond the US and Europe, are necessary to document and assess the impact of Amazon's AIT operations in different contexts. At this stage, however, we aim not to provide conclusions but to open up relevant questions. We focus on the dispositions of Amazon's technologies – what kind of knowledges and actions these technologies make happen and how they shape urban spaces. Dispositions that need to be considered in light of the company's pervasiveness and immense financial power. In other words, the urban epistemologies and "fields of action" (Neff et al. 2012) that emerge from Amazon's AITs are inextricably linked to the company's commercial interests. As this powerful techno-commercial assemblage performs its daily operations and expands, it also reworks the urban fabric.

Thus, the analysis shows how Amazon, through ML applications and AITs, increasingly exercises what Keller Easterling (2014) describes as infrastructural power over the urban space. AI has become an important building block of urban infrastructures that organise and dictate the city's rules. As such, it makes different forms of urbanity possible or impossible. Importantly, the *de facto forms of polity* (Easterling 2012) AITs contribute to are being generated much faster than any legislative process. As was shown, through its apparatus of AITs, Amazon is shaping crucial urban components such as circulation and distribution as well as security and law enforcement. These processes thus constitute a form of extrastatecraft

(Easterling 2012), effectively transforming how cities develop, are lived in and are governed beyond institutional paths of urban planning and policymaking.

What is particularly relevant for our analysis is not merely the pervasiveness of Amazon's urban infrastructures and their commercial purpose but also these technologies' unfolding potential and inherent agency. This means we need to consider not only what Amazon's infrastructures are doing in the present but, perhaps more importantly, what they can do in perspective and beyond their declared applications, i.e. the possibilities and socio-spatial effects that these technologies can generate or foreclose in time. Such inquiries are also relevant, of course, to a wide range of technologies that are being developed by other technology players, in different forms and at different scales: think of the like of social media platforms like Meta and Tencent, software producers like Google and Microsoft, and many more. Yet in terms of urban impact, as explained in the introduction to this chapter, its financial power and cross-industry ramifications so far make Amazon an unmatched player.

How can logistical optimisation affect pollution levels, consumption habits and working conditions in the urban environment? What patterns of community interactions and discrimination might emerge from the diffusion of Ring devices? These questions broadly define only some of the challenges Amazon's ever-expanding AITs pose to urban planners and policymakers. As the experiments and implementation of commercial AITs keep growing at speed, it is imperative to rethink strategies of urban policymaking that come to terms with the actual power of these technologies and bring them back to democratic scrutiny.

CONCLUSION

This chapter has shed light on the role of commercial AITs in transforming urban environments and governance. To trace back how AITs become part of urban planning and policies, we reviewed how smart city narratives turned out to be less miraculous than promised in delivering better governance and much more controversial regarding their socio-political effects. These include a lack of transparency and democratic oversight, technocratic solutionism, and the encoding of racial, gender and class discrimination in algorithmic systems. We showed how AITs are increasingly becoming crucial for urban organisation and governance not as part of institutional programmes but through commercial initiatives. Drawing on Amazon's experiments with AITs in logistics and security as a case study, we have pivoted attention to how proprietary, profit-driven ML systems are increasingly reconfiguring how urban spaces are known, sorted and experienced. Simultaneously, new practices and norms for urban communities are set. We have also observed how these new ML urban orders are infused with long-standing patterns of inequality and discrimination.

Based on these insights, the chapter emphasised AITs spatial impacts and the encroachment of AI into local political decision-making processes. The interplay between various technological applications and policy fields indicates that AI-driven changes are not isolated within a separate urban governance concern, but are increasingly permeating various policy domains. Thus, rather than viewing AI governance as an isolated area of concern, we argue that it needs to be integrated into, or "mainstreamed", across urban governance discussions. This raises questions about how urban governance, in collaboration with AITs, can be reconceptualised. In recent years, several scholars (Couldry and Powell 2014; Leszczynski 2020; Powell 2021; Rosol and Blue 2022) have highlighted the importance of exploring alternative urban imaginations and technologies and empowering those often marginalised by the pervasive influence of commercial and governance-driven AITs in cities. This call to action urges us to consider new avenues for urban AI that prioritise agency, not only of machines, reflexivity and inclusivity. In this context, achieving accountability and transparency alone – the current approach to governing urban AITs – is insufficient for fostering democratic AIT politics. Novel approaches to algorithms are required – approaches that reimagine the relationships between humans and ML systems.

ACKNOWLEDGEMENTS

Ilia Antenucci's contribution to this chapter was supported by the project "Automating the Logistical City", funded by Lower Saxony DIGITAL CREATIVITY175 Ministry of Science and Culture and the Niedersächsisches Vorab's call for proposals on "DigitalSociety" (Grant ID ZN 3752).

NOTES

1. See https://logistical.city.
2. See https://www.aboutamazon.eu/news/innovation/how-our-scientists-are-making-alexa-smarter (accessed: 12 October 2023).
3. See https:// feedvisor .com/ resources/ amazon -shipping -fba/ how -amazon -leverages -artificial -intelligence-to-optimize-delivery/ (accessed: 12 October 2023).
4. See https://www.amazon.science/blog/amazon-mit-team-up-to-add-driver-know-how-to-delivery -routing-models (accessed: 12 October 2023).
5. See https://www.amazon.science/blog/amazon-mit-team-up-to-add-driver-know-how-to-delivery -routing-models (accessed: 12 October 2023).
6. See https://ring.com/security-cameras (accessed: 12 October 2023).
7. See https://www.fightforthefuture.org/news/2019-10-07-open-letter-calling-on-elected-officials-to -stop/ (accessed: 12 October 2023).
8. See https://www.thetimes.co.uk/article/police-and-amazon-build-surveillance-state-with-free-all -seeing-doorbells-dwdt3t6q0 (accessed: 12 October 2023).

REFERENCES

Alizadeh, T. (2017), 'An investigation of IBM's Smarter Cities Challenge: What do participating cities want?', *Cities*, **63** (2), 70–80.
Altenried, M. (2019), 'On the last mile: Logistical urbanism and the transformation of labour', *Work Organisation, Labour & Globalisation*, **13** (1), 114–29.
Amoore, L. (2023), 'Machine learning political orders', *Review of International Studies*, **49** (1), 20–36.
Baykurt, B. (2022), 'Algorithmic accountability in US cities: Transparency, impact, and political economy', *Big Data & Society*, **9** (2), 205395172211154.
Benjamin, R. (2019), *Race After Technology: Abolitionist Tools for the New Jim Code*. Medford, MA: Polity.
Bridges, L. (2021), 'Infrastructural obfuscation: Unpacking the carceral logics of the Ring surveillant assemblage', *Information, Communication & Society*, **24** (6), 830–49.
Calacci, D., J. J. Shen and A. Pentland (2022), 'The cop in your neighbor's doorbell: Amazon Ring and the spread of participatory mass surveillance', *Proceedings of the ACM on Human-Computer Interaction*, **6** (CSCW2), 1–47.

Couldry, N. and A. B. Powell (2014), 'Big data from the bottom up', *Big Data & Society*, **1** (2), 205395171453927.

Datta, A. and N. Odendaal (2019), 'Smart cities and the banality of power', *Environment and Planning D: Society and Space*, **37** (3), 387–92.

Duarte, F. and R. Álvarez (2019), 'The data politics of the urban age', *Palgrave Communications*, **5** (1), 2.

Easterling, K. (2012), 'Zone: The spatial softwares of extrastatecraft', *Places Journal*, June, https://doi.org/10.22269/120610.

Easterling, K. (2014), *Extrastatecraft: The Power of Infrastructure Space/Keller Easterling*, London and New York: Verso.

Enlund, D., K. Harrison, R. Ringdahl, A. Börütecene, J. Löwgren and V. Angelakis (2022), 'The role of sensors in the production of smart city spaces', *Big Data & Society*, **9** (2), 205395172211102.

Ferreira, A., F. P. Oliveira and K. C. von Schönfeld (2022), 'Planning cities beyond digital colonization: Insights from the periphery', *Land Use Policy*, **114** (e20190061), 105988.

Floridi, L. (2020), 'Artificial intelligence as a public service: Learning from Amsterdam and Helsinki', *Philosophy & Technology*, **33** (4), 541–46.

Frascella, C. (2021), 'Amazon Ring master of the surveillance circus', *Federal Communications Law Journal*, **73** (3), 393–422.

Gebru, T. (2021), 'Race and gender', in M. D. Dubber, F. Pasquale and S. Das (eds), *The Oxford Handbook of Ethics of AI*, Oxford: Oxford University Press, pp. 253–69.

Ghosh, B. and S. Arora (2022), 'Smart as (un)democratic: The making of a smart city imaginary in Kolkata, India', *Environment and Planning C: Politics and Space*, **40** (1), 318–39.

Hoop, E. de, W. Boon, L. van Oers, A. Smith, P. Späth and R. Raven (2022), 'Deliberating the knowledge politics of smart urbanism', *Urban Transformations*, **4** (1), 449.

Ingold, D. and S. Soper (2016), 'Amazon doesn't consider the race of its customers: Should it?', accessed 28 July 2023, at www.bloomberg.com/graphics/2016-amazon-same-day/.

Kelly, M. (2020), 'Amazon bought Ring for market position, not technology, emails suggest', accessed 31 July 2023, at www.theverge.com/2020/7/30/21348483/amazon-jeff-bezos-alexa-ring-market-dominance-antitrust-hearing-congress.

Kitchin, R. (2019), 'Reframing, reimagining and remaking smart cities', in C. Coletta, L. Evans, L. Heaphy and R. Kitchin (eds), *Creating Smart Cities*, Abingdon, UK and New York: Routledge, pp. 219–30.

Koseki, S., S. Jameson, G. Franadi, D. Rolnick, C. Régis and J.-L. Denis (2022), 'AI and cities: Risks, applications and governance', UN-Habitat.

León, L. F. A. and J. Rosen (2020), 'Technology as ideology in urban governance', *Annals of the American Association of Geographers*, **110** (2), 497–506.

Leszczynski, A. (2020), 'Glitchy vignettes of platform urbanism', *Environment and Planning D: Society and Space*, **38** (2), 189–208.

Lyster, C. (2016), *Learning from Logistics: How Networks Change our Cities*, Basel and Berlin: Birkhäuser.

Marx, P. (2022), *Road to Nowhere*. London: Verso Books.

Murakami Wood, D. (2023), 'Platform city people: Social relations of AI-driven urbanism in an age of planetary crisis', Public Lecture, University of Twente, 15 June.

Neff, G., T. Jordan, J. McVeigh-Schultz and T. Gillespie (2012), 'Affordances, technical agency, and the politics of technologies of cultural production', *Journal of Broadcasting & Electronic Media*, **56** (2), 299–313.

Neves, J. and M. Steinberg (2023), 'The cultural politics of in/convenience', accessed 28 July 2023, at www.globalemergentmedia.com/in-progress/the-cultural-politics-of-in/convenience.

O'Neil, C. (2016), *Weapons of Math Destruction: How Big Data Increases Inequality and Threatens Democracy*. London: Penguin Books.

Powell, A. B. (2021), *Undoing Optimization*, Yale, CT: Yale University Press.

Rosol, M. and G. Blue (2022), 'From the smart city to urban justice in a digital age', *City*, **26** (4), 684–705.

Selinger, E. and D. Durant (2022), 'Amazon's Ring: Surveillance as a slippery slope service', *Science as Culture*, **31** (1), 92–106.

Shelton, T., M. Zook and A. Wiig (2015), 'The "actually existing smart city"', *Cambridge Journal of Regions, Economy and Society*, **8** (1), 13–25.

Söderström, O., T. Paasche and F. Klauser (2014), 'Smart cities as corporate storytelling', *City*, **18** (3), 307–20.

Taylor, L. (2021), 'Exploitation as innovation: Research ethics and the governance of experimentation in the urban living lab', *Regional Studies*, **55** (12), 1902–12.

Tseng, Y.-S. (2022), 'Assemblage thinking as a methodology for studying urban AI phenomena', *AI & Society*, **20** (3), 973.

West, E. (2022), *Buy Now: How Amazon Branded Convenience and Normalized Monopoly*, Cambridge, MA: MIT Press.

Wiig, A. and E. Wyly (2015), 'Introduction: Thinking through the politics of the smart city', *Urban Geography*, **37** (4), 485–93.

Wilt, J. (2020), *Do Androids Dream of Electric Cars?* Toronto, ON, Canada: Between the Lines.

Yigitcanlar, T., D. Agdas and K. Degirmenci (2023), 'Artificial intelligence in local governments: Perceptions of city managers on prospects, constraints and choices', *AI & Society*, **38**, 1135–50. https://doi.org/10.1007/s00146-022-01450-x.

Zhao, F., O.I. Fashola, T.I. Olarewaju and I. Onwumere (2021), 'Smart city research: A holistic and state-of-the-art literature review', *Cities*, **119** (5), 103406.

Index

accountability 94–108, 297
  account-giving 101, 102
  algorithmic *see* algorithmic accountability
  child protection 406–7
  contextual 95, 102–4, 105
  judicial decision-making 344–5, 347
  participatory 99–100, 103, 104
  point-oriented system-level 97
  process-oriented system-level 97
  street-level bureaucracy 82, 85–6, 87–8
  and transparency 100, 101–2, 170, 171–2, 185
  and trust 185
accumulation 32
Acheson, R. 284, 285
Achiume, E.T. 200, 308, 315
Ackroyd, S. 297
action
  political 9–13
  symbolic 72–3
actuarial methods 402
Adam, P. 150
Adams, R. 198
Administrative Conference of the United States (ACUS) 240
administrative law 98
administrative literacy 85
administrative tasks 412
adult social care *see* care
AeroSpace and Defence Industries Association of Europe (ASD) 311–12
Aerts, H.J. 412–13
Afghanistan 311
Africa 210, 212, 225–6
  see also under individual countries
African Commission on Human and Peoples' Rights 225
African Union 44
Agamben, G. 314
agile policymaking 2
agricultural platforms 212–13
AI and Ethics 125
AI fallacy 84
AI safety 114–15
Akkerman, M. 313
Alexa 391, 427
algorithm aversion 183, 187
algorithmic accountability 94–108
  contextual accountability 95, 102–4, 105

  model-focused 95–6
  supply chain 98–9, 103–4
  system-level 97–8, 102–3
  two concepts of 101–2
  two waves of 100–101
algorithmic audits 112, 174
"algorithmic bill of rights" 138
algorithmic coloniality 223
algorithms 7, 31, 58, 133–45
  code and the complexity of automated systems 134–5
  differentiation from heuristics 55
  explainability 135–42
  machine-learning algorithms 237–8
  mature 299
  predictive policing 297–302, 303
    life cycle of an algorithm in 298–300
    life cycle of an algorithm in DNA analysis 300–302
Alignment Problem in AI 58, 61, 63
Allegheny Family Screening Tool (FST) 405–6
Alliance for a Green Revolution in Africa (AGRA) 213
AlphaGo 110
Alston, P. 366–7, 369, 375
alternative utopias 47–8
Altman, S. 60, 61, 62, 249
Amazon 140, 389–90
  Alexa 391, 427
  Echo 390
  Flex drivers 428
  healthcare 418
  and home surveillance 429–30
  Prime 427, 428
    logistics 428
  urban governance 423–4, 427–31
    extrastatecraft 430–31
    logistics 427–9
    security 427, 429–30
  warehouses 353
American Civil Liberties Union (ACLU) 112
Amicelle, A. 35
Amoore, L. 36, 173–4
Amsterdam 176, 425–6
Anthropos 390
Aoki, N. 188
Apple 140
applied ethics 261, 262–3
Arendt, H. 314